MW00389312

MATHEMATICAL METHODS FOR NEURAL NETWORK ANALYSIS AND DESIGN

MATHEMATICAL METHODS FOR NEURAL NETWORK ANALYSIS AND DESIGN

Richard M. Golden

A Bradford Book
The MIT Press
Cambridge, Massachusetts
London, England

This book was set in Times Roman by Omegatype Typography, Inc., Champaign, Illinois.

Printed and bound in the United States of America

Library of Congress Cataloging-in-Publication Data

Golden, Richard M.
    Mathematical methods for neural network analysis and design /
Richard M. Golden.
      p.   cm.
    Includes bibliographical references and index.
    ISBN 0-262-07174-6 (hc : alk. paper)
    1. Neural networks (Computer science)—Mathematical models.
  I. Title.
  QA76.87.G64   1996
  006.3—dc20   96-25116
                                                         CIP

Contents

Preface

This book on mathematical methods for artificial neural network (ANN) analysis and design is one I wish had been available when I was a graduate student. Its goal is to teach readers how to analyze and design highly nonlinear ANN systems within a classical mathematics and electrical engineering framework.

Who Will Find This Book Valuable

Students unfamiliar with the classical mathematical methods introduced in this textbook will acquire a powerful set of tools for analyzing and designing many complex information-processing systems, which include ANN information-processing systems as an important special case. Researchers familiar with the specific areas of mathematics mentioned will learn how their expertise can be immediately applied to ongoing problems in ANN system analysis and design. The book is relatively self-contained and was intentionally written for a mathematically sophisticated, multidisciplinary audience consisting of advanced undergraduate students, graduate students, consultants, and researchers in the fields of cognitive science, computer science, econometrics, engineering, mathematics, mathematical biology, mathematical psychology, mathematical sociology, neural networks, and physics.

Basic Approach

This book explores mathematical methodologies found to be most important for ANN system analysis and design, emphasizing in particular (1) nonlinear deterministic and stochastic dynamical systems theory, (2) nonlinear optimization theory, and (3) parametric statistical inference theory. Other branches of mathematics have been deliberately omitted to force the reader to focus upon fundamental issues.

The methods of nonlinear analysis described here are directly applicable to large-scale complex systems. The guiding philosophy is to make weak statements about complex systems, as opposed to strong statements about simplified systems. An original contribution is the presentation of ANN algorithms as special cases of the classical engineering and mathematics literature to teach and develop intuitions about ANN system analysis and design. Although the textbook presents well-established theorems in mathematics and engineering relevant to ANN system analysis and design, the theorems and their proofs have been considerably rewritten to (1) develop a uniformity of notation and (2) simplify the mathematical presentation.

Furthermore, unlike other books on neural network analysis and design, the details of specific neural network architectures are considered primarily in the problems and examples rather than in the main text. The reason for this unique approach is to examine various methods of neural network analysis and design within a unified framework based firmly in traditional engineering design. And unlike most other books in the field of ANN systems, this one is not organized by algorithms. The number of published articles in the neural network field continues to grow rapidly as does the variety of algorithms introduced every year. By presenting fundamental mathematical tools that can be applied to large classes of high-dimensional nonlinear information-processing systems, this book should prove useful to researchers wishing to analyze most novel linear and nonlinear ANN systems already developed and yet to come.

Organization

Overall Organization

Because the analysis and design of neural networks is a relatively new field that requires technical tools from a wide variety of disciplines, very advanced topics and very elementary topics have been mixed together in sometimes unusual ways. In introducing the fundamental mathematical tools for the analysis and design of neural networks, I have decided what is relevant and what is not relevant on the basis of my experience with neural networks. I apologize if I have omitted relevant topics or "superficially" presented a particular branch of mathematical analysis in order to achieve the specific goals of a particular chapter. This textbook is not supposed to be the "end of the road" but rather a bridge to its "beginning." While some readers will undoubtedly possess expertise in neural networks, dynamical systems theory, optimization theory, or statistical inference, this book is designed to introduce them to the fundamentals of all four of these fields for the purposes of ANN system analysis and design.

A modular definition/theorem/algorithm format was chosen for two reasons. First, from a teaching perspective, such a format more explicitly identifies the unique and shared assumptions of particular analyses. An unfortunate consequence, however, is that the presentation is sometimes rather compact and difficult to follow. I have tried to address this problem by providing commentary on the main concepts of a particular definition, theorem, or algorithm immediately after its formal statement. Second, from a research perspective, the modular definition/theorem/algorithm format serves a valuable reference function. A researcher interested in the conditions required for establishing convergence of an algorithm or estimating the asymptotic variance of a set of parameters has a self-contained reference manual readily available.

Chapter Organization

Each chapter first introduces a new set of mathematical tools and then applies those tools to specific ANN system analysis and design problems (except chapters 1, 2, and 6). ANN researchers less interested in the theory may choose to focus on the applications discussed in the latter part of each chapter; those more interested in analysis and design of complex information-processing systems can focus upon the basic mathematical tools introduced at the beginning.

Each chapter concludes with a summary of that chapter's most important points followed by two groups of homework problems (except in chapters 1, 2, and 6). The first group, "Elementary Problems," reviews basic mathematical concepts and tests readers' understanding of specific points made within the chapter. The second, more difficult group, "Problems," is designed to (1) show readers how the mathematics in the chapter can be applied to practical ANN system analysis and design problems, (2) introduce readers to important ANN system architectures not discussed in the main text, and (3) help readers develop their problem-solving skills in ANN system analysis and design. The hints and solutions to odd-numbered problems (located in the back of the book) should provide readers valuable assistance in integrating the complex theoretical subject matter with specific ANN system applications.

Prerequisites

This textbook is specifically designed to be self-contained. Considering the advanced nature of the topics discussed, it requires only a minimal number of mathematical prerequisites: (1) linear algebra at the lower-division level, (2) multivariable or vector calculus at the lower-division level, (3) calculus-based probability theory and statistics at the upper-division level, and (4) a relatively high level of mathematical sophistication commensurate with a student pursuing doctoral work in mathematics, engineering, computer science, mathematical psychology, mathematical biology, or mathematical sociology. Some prior familiarity with artificial neural networks will also prove helpful.

Notes for the Student

Recommended Study Strategy

The student may find it helpful to study each chapter according to the following strategy. First, read the main text of the chapter once and attempt to summarize its essential ideas section by section. Skip over the proofs of theorems and perhaps also the formal statement of many of the theorems, definitions, and algorithms but carefully read the brief commentary on main concepts that follows most of these formal statements.

Second, read the chapter summary and actively compare it with the main text of that chapter. Third, carefully reread the chapter, pausing to think about each definition and theorem. Fourth, reread the "ANN Applications" section and try to relate the solutions presented in that section to the main text as well as to the chapter summary. And fifth, the solve some of the odd-numbered problems, checking your answers against the partial solutions at the end of the book.

Background Readings

Students who have never taken an introductory undergraduate course in real analysis will find the highly readable text by Rosenlicht (1968) to be a helpful reference. Students with exposure to linear algebra and vector calculus at only the lower-division level will find the texts by Marlow (1978) and by Marsden and Tromba (1976) to be helpful references. Students with exposure to calculus-based statistics at only the upper-division level will find the volume by Manoukian (1986) to be a concise and self-contained introduction to current topics in mathematical statistics. Students with a minimal background in artificial neural networks will find the collection of papers in Anderson and Rosenfeld 1988 to be extremely helpful. The review problems at the end of chapter 1 should also help students pinpoint weak spots in their mathematical preparation. Appendix A ("Mathematical Review") of Luenberger 1984 provides an excellent six-page summary of much of the mathematics used in the chapters that follow.

Notes for the Instructor

For students with a solid mathematics background (e.g., doctoral students in statistics), the material presented here can form the basis of an intensive one-semester course in ANN system analysis and design. It is recommended that the instructor in such a course skip over the proofs of many of the key theorems, focusing instead on the statements of those theorems and how the theorems apply to the ANN analysis and design problems at the end of each chapter. In addition, the instructor may wish to move quickly through chapters 1, 2, and 6.

Students who have only the minimal mathematical prerequisites listed above will probably require two semesters to effectively comprehend all of the material. The additional course time may be used to provide them with more experience solving ANN analysis and design problems as well as to strengthen their intuitions with supplemental computer simulation laboratory exercises, supplemental readings, and classroom proofs of key theorems.

Although difficult to read because of the intrinsic generality of the material, the book requires little in the way of mathematical preparation. However, because each chapter builds upon the concepts introduced in the previous chapter, for many students chapter $(N - 1)$ will be a prerequisite for reading chapter N $(N = 2 \ldots 8)$.

Note that key concepts and notation are introduced in section 1.5 (see also "Mathematical Notation" below). Chapter 1 is not a prerequisite for chapter 2 but is designed to facilitate understanding of chapter 2 and motivate the algorithms presented there. Although chapter 3 and chapter 4 are relatively independent, reading chapter 3 first will facilitate understanding of the concepts in chapter 4. Chapter 5 may be read without reading chapters 1–4; chapter 6 may be read without reading chapters 1–5. Section 1.4 is a prerequisite for the material in chapter 7. Some of the material in chapter 6 is a prerequisite for chapter 7 and chapter 8. Both section 4.1 and all of chapter 7 are prerequisites for the material in chapter 8.

Acknowledgments

This book represents the product of over ten years of interactions with members of the artificial neural network, cognitive science, engineering, mathematics, and psychology communities, for which I am quite grateful.

First, I must thank my thesis advisor, Professor Jim Anderson (Cognitive and Linguistic Science Department, Brown University) for his patience, support, and advanced training in ANN systems. My statistical pattern recognition approach to ANN system information processing originated from my interactions with Professor David Cooper (Engineering Department, Brown University), who profoundly influenced me when I was a graduate student in electrical engineering at Brown University.

During my studies as an Andrew Mellon Fellow at the University of Pittsburgh, Professor Walter Schneider (Psychology Department, University of Pittsburgh), Professor James McClelland (Psychology and Computer Science Department, Carnegie-Mellon University), and Professor Geoffrey Hinton (Computer Science Department, Carnegie-Mellon University) also helped shape my understanding of ANN systems. Professor Dean Mumme (a graduate student in mathematics who was supervised by Professor Schneider when I met him) introduced me to basic concepts of mathematical notation.

My three-year NIH postdoctoral fellowship with Professor David Rumelhart (Psychology Department, Stanford University) served as an invaluable introduction to advanced ANN system architectures; I am grateful to Dr. Rumelhart for his support, patience, and training. While at Stanford, I spent a considerable amount of time discussing ANN systems with my friend and colleague Dr. Yves Chauvin (Stanford University and Net-ID, Inc.), who increased my familiarity with the range of possible backpropagation network architectures. It was also at Stanford that I taught a short course in 1988, whose lecture notes gradually evolved over the years into this textbook.

Although I did not have an opportunity to directly study under the guidance of Professor Halbert White (Economics Department, University of California at San Diego) and Professor David Luenberger (Engineering Department, Stanford University), their articles and books (Luenberger 1979, 1984; White

1982, 1989a,b, 1994) have also profoundly shaped my thinking and thus the approach to ANN system analysis and design presented here.

I thank Betty Stanton at MIT Press for her assistance in obtaining excellent expert reviewers for this textbook. Professor Jerry Busemeyer (Purdue University) and Professor A. A. J. Marley (McGill University) carefully read an earlier draft and provided a number of helpful comments. I am grateful for the feedback I received from the six anonymous expert reviewers for chapters 3 through 6 and 8, and from Professor Michael Jordan (MIT), who provided feedback on chapter 7. I am especially grateful to Dr. Bob Dawes (QED Corporation, Parker, Texas, and Martingale Research Corporation, Allen, Texas) and Professor Janos Turi (University of Texas at Dallas) for discussions regarding specific topics in dynamical systems theory. I would also like to thank Professor Robert Serfling (University of Texas at Dallas) for discussions regarding specific topics in mathematical statistics.

I thank my students and colleagues at the University of Texas at Dallas for patiently helping me to improve the clarity, readability, and accuracy of this textbook; in particular, Professor Hervé Abdi, Greg Barton, Ted Cisek, Emmanuel Drege, Don Eager, Stephen Hayes, James Patterson, Kush Paul, Frederic Piat, Tim Schramm, Jeff Sprenger, Michael Thayer, and Jiangdong Yang. Jiangdong Yang assisted me in the proof of stochastic approximation lemma (SAL) 1 in chapter 4 and the proof of the Fundamental Probabilistic Belief Theorem in chapter 6. Stephen Hayes, my student almost since the beginning of this project, has been a constant source of helpful comments and criticisms.

My thanks also to Professor Alice O'Toole for permission to use her research equipment to prepare some of the figures for this book, and to Candice Walker, a graduate student working with Professor O'Toole, for her assistance in preparing those figures.

Finally, I thank my parents, Ralph and Sandy Golden for their encouragement and support throughout my academic career, and my wife, Karen, for her patience and support in this endeavor.

Comments and Questions

Comments and questions regarding this textbook are encouraged. Please use the email address GOLDEN@UTDALLAS.EDU or RMGCONSULT@AOL.COM to contact the author.

Mathematical Notation

Variables, Vectors, Sets, Functions

Notation	Signifies
x or X	scalar x or scalar X
$\mathbf{x}$	column vector $\mathbf{x}$
$\mathbf{0}_d$	d-dimensional column vector of zeros
$\mathbf{1}_d$	d-dimensional column vector of ones
$\mathbf{W}$	matrix $\mathbf{W}$
$\mathbf{I}$	identity matrix
$\{a_1, a_2,\ldots\} \times \{b_1, b_2,\ldots\}$	$\{(a_1, b_1), (a_1, b_2),\ldots, (a_i, b_j),\ldots\}$
$S^n, n = 2, 3,\ldots$	$S^2 = S \times S, S^3 = S \times S \times S,\ldots$
$\mathcal{R}^d$	vector space whose elements are d-dimensional real vectors
$\mathcal{R}^{d \times u}$	vector space whose elements are $d \times u$ real matrices
$A \subset B$	A is a proper subset of B
$A \subseteq B$	A is a subset of B
$\neg A$	complement of the set A
$f: D \to R$	function f with domain D and range R
$f(\cdot): D \to R$	function f with domain D and range R
$\mathbf{f}: D \to R$	vector-valued function $\mathbf{f}$ with domain D and range R
$f: A \times B \to C$	function f with domain $A \times B$ and range C
$\{\mathbf{x}(k)\}$	sequence (ordered set): $\{\mathbf{x}(1), \mathbf{x}(2),\ldots\}$
$\{\mathbf{x}(k)\}_{k=1}^n$	sequence (ordered set): $\{\mathbf{x}(1),\ldots, \mathbf{x}(n)\}$
$\mathbf{x}(k)$	kth element in sequence $\{\mathbf{x}(k)\}$
x_i	ith element of the vector $\mathbf{x}$
$x_i(k)$	ith element of the vector $\mathbf{x}(k)$
w_{ij}	real number in ith row, jth column of matrix $\mathbf{W}$
$\mathbf{x}^T$	transpose of column vector $\mathbf{x}$
$\lvert \mathbf{x} \rvert$	$(\mathbf{x}^T\mathbf{x})^{1/2}$, where $\mathbf{x}$ is a real column vector

Vector Calculus, Random Vectors

Notation	Signifies
dx/dt	derivative of function $x: \mathcal{R} \to \mathcal{R}$
$\partial x/\partial t$	partial derivative of function x with respect to t
$d\mathbf{x}/dt$	column vector with ith element dx_i/dt
$d\mathbf{W}/dt$	matrix with ijth (ith row, jth column) element dw_{ij}/dt
$d\mathbf{x}/d\mathbf{y}$	matrix with ijth (ith row, jth column) element $\partial x_i/\partial y_j$
$\nabla_{\mathbf{w}} f$	column vector (gradient) with ith element $\partial f/\partial w_i$
$df/d\mathbf{w}$	column vector (gradient) with ith element $\partial f/\partial w_i$
$\nabla_{\mathbf{w}}^2 f$	matrix with ijth (ith row, jth column) element $\partial^2 f/\partial w_i \partial w_j$
$\tilde{x}$	random variable $\tilde{x}$
$\tilde{\mathbf{x}}$	random vector $\tilde{\mathbf{x}}$
$\tilde{\mathbf{X}}$	random matrix $\tilde{\mathbf{X}}$
$\hat{x}$	observed value of $\tilde{x}$
$\hat{\mathbf{x}}$	observed value of $\tilde{\mathbf{x}}$
$\hat{\mathbf{X}}$	observed value of $\tilde{\mathbf{X}}$
$p(x)$ or $p_{\tilde{x}}(x)$	probability mass (or density) function for $\tilde{x}$
$p(\mathbf{x})$ or $p_{\tilde{\mathbf{x}}}(\mathbf{x})$	probability mass (or density) function for $\tilde{\mathbf{x}}$
$E[\tilde{x}]$ or $E_{\tilde{x}}[\tilde{x}]$	expectation of $\tilde{x}$ with respect to $p(x)$
$E[\tilde{x} \mid y]$ or $E_{\tilde{x}}[\tilde{x} \mid y]$	expectation of $\tilde{x}$ with respect to $p(x \mid y)$

1 Introduction

1.1 The General Theoretical Framework

An artificial neural network (ANN) system is an abstract mathematical model inspired by brain structures, mechanisms, and functions. An important hope of many researchers is that ANN systems may be used as a universal language by cognitive scientists, engineers, computer scientists, psychologists, biologists, neuroscientists, physicists, and mathematicians for specifying and testing theories of neural information processing. Researchers in the field of ANN systems tend to assume that the brain is best understood in terms of multiple levels of description. Any ANN system is an abstraction of selected aspects of brain processes that emphasizes some properties of brains while deliberately ignoring others. One goal of ANN system research is to develop a variety of models that provide complementary insights into the problem of understanding the brain/mind system.

This textbook is about methods for mathematically analyzing and designing the large class of algorithms called "artificial neural networks" in the psychology, computer science, engineering, cognitive science, and (sometimes) neuroscience literature. The following quote from the excellent introduction to ANN systems by J. A. Anderson (1995) provides a useful warning to readers interested in the mathematical analysis of *real* neural networks:

Mathematical analysis of the familiar kind is an indispensible tool; unfortunately, however, it is not entirely clear if it is completely suited to neurocomputing. To analyze a system, we have to have a clear idea about what the system is going to do and the problems we want to solve with it. We have not properly formulated the problems yet for neurocomputing. In fact, we often do not even know what the problems are. Therefore, careful mathematical analysis of simple neural networks—the kind found in [texts for engineers and physicists]—is useful, but may be providing definitive answers to questions that no one is really interested in asking. (p. viii)

Because it is likely that many ANN algorithms will become rapidly outdated or modified beyond recognition, it is important to equip researchers with *general mathematical tools* that can be applied to the analysis and design of extremely large classes of ANN systems. By providing the needed mathematical tools to obtain "definitive answers to questions" it is hoped that when good questions are formally proposed, this textbook will be helpful for obtaining "definitive answers" to aspects of such questions. In addition, this textbook should be helpful in formulating new questions about ANN dynamical systems that do have definitive answers.

1.1.1 ANN Analysis and Design Using Marr's Theory

Marr's theory (1982; see Simon 1969, chapter 5, for a related discussion) may be used as an organizational tool for ANN system analysis and design by helping the engineer select the appropriate branch of mathematics for a given analysis and design problem. Marr proposed that any complex information-processing system can be studied with respect to three distinct levels of description. The *computational level* of description specifies the goal of the computation and attempts to explain why that goal is appropriate. The *algorithmic level* of description specifies the algorithm used to compute the goal specified at the computational level. In particular, an *algorithm* is defined as a system of mathematical formulas that can be instantiated as an executable computer program. The *implementational level* of description specifies the details regarding how the algorithm is implemented. For example, an algorithm may be implemented by specific programming code (e.g., FORTRAN, PASCAL, or MATLAB), specific electronic hardware (e.g., a specialized integrated circuit), or by actual living brain tissue. In general, researchers in the field of ANN system analysis and design believe that knowledge regarding any one of the three levels of description provides important constraints upon the remaining levels.

Figure 1.1 illustrates how Marr's theory (1982) will be used to provide a balanced approach to the problem of ANN system analysis and design (also see Golden 1988b; Rumelhart and McClelland 1986). By viewing an ANN information-processing system using Marr's theoretical framework, the researcher interested in the analysis and design of ANN systems is less likely to omit asking critical questions about a given ANN system. The computational goal of an ANN system is formulated as the solution to an optimization problem where the ANN system seeks to minimize some objective function. That is, the ANN system selects the most preferable course of action, where *preferability* is directly indicated by the value of the objective function. The computational level of description for an ANN system must therefore explicitly specify this opti-

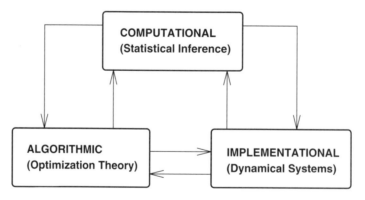

Figure 1.1
Proposed approach to ANN system analysis and design. ANN systems in this textbook are studied from the perspectives of nonlinear dynamical systems theory, optimization theory, and statistical inference, which correspond, respectively, to Marr's implementational, algorithmic, and computational levels of understanding (1982). The arrows represent the mutual interdependencies among the three major levels of understanding.

mization problem and clearly explain the motivation for selecting the objective function. Statistical inference, rational decision making, and the mathematical theory of evidence are branches of mathematics that can provide important insights into answering questions about the computational goal of an ANN system. Questions about how the ANN's computational goal is achieved are naturally formulated and answered at the algorithmic level of description. Specifically, nonlinear optimization theory can provide important insights regarding the effectiveness of an algorithm for achieving its computational goal. And finally, questions about specific detailed implementations of a given algorithm are naturally formulated and addressed at Marr's implementational level of description. Nonlinear dynamical systems theory is a useful branch of mathematics for characterizing the behavior of ANN systems at the implementational level and *defining* the concept of an ANN system.

1.1.2   Overview of Book

An ANN system model is (by the definition of the concept of "model") inspired by implementational level (i.e., neurophysiological) descriptions. Thus, ANN system modeling is fundamentally a "bottom-up" approach. In accordance with this consideration, first ANN implementational level, then ANN algorithmic level, and finally ANN computational level mathematical analysis and design problems are considered.

Implementational Level (Chapters 2, 3, 4)

Part I is concerned with issues of ANN system analysis and design at the implementational level. Section 1.4 provides a mathematical framework for naturally viewing all ANN systems as dynamical systems. Thus, by definition, mathematical dynamical systems theory becomes the language for defining the implementational level of description for an ANN system. A few specific ANN system algorithms are introduced in chapter 2. Chapter 3 provides an introduction to those aspects of high-dimensional nonlinear dynamical systems theory especially relevant to ANN system analysis and design. In particular, a powerful analytical method (LaSalle's invariant set theorem) for characterizing the long-term behavior of an ANN dynamical system is introduced. Chapter 4 extends the results of chapter 3 to high-dimensional nonlinear probabilistic dynamical systems by introducing the fundamental mathematical tool of stochastic approximation. Thus chapters 2, 3, and 4 are concerned with describing the behavior of an ANN system without reference to the ANN system's computational goals.

Algorithmic Level (Chapter 5)

Part II is concerned with issues of ANN system analysis and design at the algorithmic level of description. It is possible to view many ANN systems as nonlinear optimization algorithms that seek a minimum of some objective function. Chapter 5 provides an introduction to aspects of high-dimensional nonlinear optimization theory that are particularly relevant to ANN system analysis and design. Fundamental mathematical tools are introduced for indicating when the sequence of states generated by a large class of both deterministic and stochastic high-dimensional nonlinear dynamical systems will eventually converge to the minimum value of an implicit objective function. Additional tools for investigating the rate of convergence are also introduced. These mathematical tools are then shown to be directly applicable to the analysis and design of both classical nonlinear optimization algorithms and modern ANN systems.

Computational Level (Chapters 6, 7, 8)

Part III is concerned with issues of ANN system analysis and design at the computational level. As previously noted, the computational level of description is concerned with understanding the computational goals of an ANN system independent of the algorithm used to implement that system. Chapter 6 discusses theorems of rational decision making that describe conditions for the representation of preference by real-valued objective functions. Thus chapter 6 provides a sound theoretical foundation for the viewpoint that the computational goal of an intelligent rational ANN system should be to minimize the value of some real-valued objective function. Chapter 6 also introduces the concept of a Markov random field (a generalization of the Markov chain), and shows how this idea is relevant for constructing mathematically tractable probability distributions for high-dimensional sample spaces. Such high-dimensional sample spaces arise frequently in ANN system analysis and design problems. In addition, a classical statistical formulation of the "generalization problem" is reviewed in chapter 6. Chapter 7 shows how both the classification dynamics and learning dynamics of many ANN system architectures can be provided with meaningful and useful probabilistic interpretations. Chapter 8 uses the probabilistic interpretation of ANN systems provided in chapter 7 in order to show how asymptotic statistical theory can be used to refine the design of an ANN system and derive bounds on the prediction error of an ANN system.

1.2   Introduction to ANN Systems

Artificial neural networks are sometimes referred to as "neural networks," "connectionist systems," "neurocomputers," or "parallel distributed processing (PDP) models." Because the above terms can mean quite different things to different groups of people, the generic term ANN system (artificial neural network system) will be used to refer to any type of artificial neural network.

1.2.1   General Definitions

An ANN system consists of a collection of units where each unit has a scalar real-valued state, which is called the unit's "activation level." The activation levels of all units in the ANN system may also be arranged as elements of a vector, referred to as an "activation pattern." A parameter of the ANN system that can be interpreted as describing the degree to which the activation level of one unit in the system influences the activation level of another unit is often referred to as a "connection weight" or "connection strength." A parameter of the ANN system that can be interpreted as indicating the "baseline" activation level of a unit is often referred to as a "bias." Figure 1.2 illustrates a typical ANN system consisting of three units with activation levels, $x_1(t)$, $x_2(t)$, and $x_3(t)$. The ANN system in figure 1.2 consists of two connection weights, w_{13} and w_{23}, and a bias parameter, b_2, for unit 2.

The first major component of most ANN systems is an *environment*, which specifies what types of activation patterns are experienced or observed by the ANN dynamical system during classification and learning processes.

The second major component of most ANN systems is an *activation updating rule,* a large system of nonlinear differential or difference equations that describes how the activations of the units in the network becomes updated at each moment in time. The nonstandard term *classification dynamical system* will be used to refer to the activation updating rule to emphasize its functional goal of mapping a given input activation pattern into some category.

The third major component of most ANN systems is a *learning rule* or, equivalently, a *learning dynamical system.* The learning rule is always defined with respect to a particular activation updating rule because a theory of learning necessarily requires a theory of retrieval. The learning rule is a dynamical system that indicates how the parameters (e.g., connection strengths and biases) of the ANN system are updated as a function of the ANN system's current and past experiences (i.e., the sequence of activation patterns observed by the learning rule).

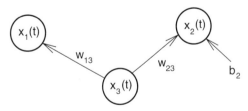

Figure 1.2
Generic ANN system. The activation levels of this ANN system at time t are $x_1(t)$ for unit 1, $x_2(t)$ for unit 2, and $x_3(t)$ for unit 3. The connection weights w_{13}, w_{23}, b_2 (which implicitly specify the ANN system's knowledge) are assumed to be fixed in this example. Connection weight w_{ij} indicates the degree to which unit i will be activated when unit j is activated. Bias weight b_i indicates the tendency for unit i to be activated regardless of the activation of the other units in the network.

The fourth major component of most ANN systems is an *interpretation function* for interpreting activation patterns. In ANN systems a given activation pattern is assigned a semantic interpretation; such assignments are referred to as "distributed representations." An important special case of a distributed representation occurs when the activity level of a single unit is assigned a semantic interpretation. This latter special case of a distributed representation is usually referred to as a "local representation."

The above informal definition of an ANN system will be adequate for now; a formal definition of an ANN system is provided in section 1.4.

1.2.2   Characteristics of ANN Systems

The form of an ANN system as defined in the previous section (and in section 1.4) is quite general. This generality will allow us to consider very large classes of ANN systems within a common theoretical framework. Nevertheless, there are some more specific characteristics of ANN systems that can be mentioned. Although neither necessary nor sufficient to define an ANN system, these characteristics are believed by many neuroscientists to be reasonable, and they have been incorporated into the design of many ANN system models. The purpose of this section is to propose an explicit set of criteria for identifying the degree to which a given algorithm may be interpreted as an ANN system.

Before considering ten basic characteristics of ANN systems, however, it is necessary to briefly review some neurophysiological facts. Figure 1.3 shows the smallest complete functional information-processing unit in the nervous system: the *neuron*. A neuron consists of thin, fiberlike *dendrites,* which carry incoming information into the cell's body. This information is transformed by chemical and electrical mechanisms that individually affect the voltage potential across the cell's outer membrane in a quasi-linear manner. When a critical membrane potential is reached, this potential is discharged by the neuron through the generation of an *action potential*. The action potential propagates information out of the cell body along the neuron's *axon,* which in turn connects, via a *synaptic junction,* to the dendritic inputs of other neurons in the system.

The characteristics of artificial and real neural systems described in this section are based upon the insightful discussion in Rumelhart and McClelland 1986 (see especially pp. 129–136) and upon selected papers from the excellent collections of articles in Kandel and Schwartz 1981, Anderson and Rosenfeld 1988, and Anderson, Pellionisz, and Rosenfeld 1990.

Characteristic 1: Informational activation patterns.   From an information-processing perspective, the rate at which action potentials are generated by a neuron is an important physical representation of information in the nervous system. Increased sensory stimulation directly corresponds to an increase in sensory neuron firing frequencies as well as an increase in the ability to psy-

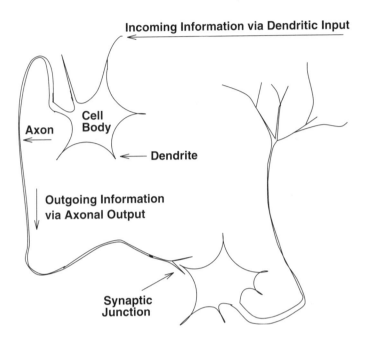

Incoming Information via Dendritic Input

Cell Body

Axon

Dendrite

Outgoing Information via Axonal Output

Synaptic Junction

Figure 1.3
Information transmission between neurons. Information corresponding to the firing rate of one neuron is transmitted along the neuron's axon toward the dendritic inputs of a second neuron, and transferred from the first neuron to the second neuron at the *synaptic junction*. In ANN system modeling the *activation level* of a unit corresponds roughly to the firing rate of a neuron, while the *connection strength* between two neurons indicates the efficiency of information transmission at the synaptic junction.

chologically detect the physical stimulus (Kandel 1981b,c,d; Kelly 1981a,b,c; Martin 1981a,b). Moreover, increased firing frequencies in specific motor neuron systems have been shown to evoke muscle responses (Ghez 1981a,b; Carew 1981a,b,c; Rowland 1981; Ghez and Fahn, 1981; Côté 1981). Another strategy used by the nervous system for representing information is *population coding* (e.g., Carew 1981a; Martin 1981a), which refers to the idea that information in the nervous system is represented as a spatially distributed pattern of neural activation. For example, increasing the magnitude of sensory stimulation sometimes results in an increase in the number of activated neurons rather than an increase in the firing rate of a single neuron (Martin 1981a).

Suppose that an activation pattern is represented as a vector such that each element of the vector corresponds to the activation level of a single unit. The magnitude of this vector can substantially increase in either one of two ways. First, a few elements in the vector might become very large in magnitude. Second, many additional elements in the vector might become just slightly larger in magnitude. Neurophysiological evidence supports the existence of increased neural activity in small numbers of neurons as well as population coding response properties when familiar stimuli are presented. Thus a common assumption in the ANN literature is that the magnitude of an ANN activation pattern vector is a direct measure of the *signal strength* of the stimulus activation pattern. The *identity* of the stimulus activation pattern is usually assumed to correspond to the direction of the ANN activation pattern vector.

Characteristic 2: Associative learning. A number of neurophysiological studies have demonstrated that the efficiency of information transmission at the synaptic junction linking a pair of neurons may be modified when both neurons are simultaneously activated (for reviews see Brown, Kairiss, and Keenan 1990; Brown et al. 1988). It is widely believed that such neuronal changes are the basis of learning in the brain, and that knowledge is stored in the connections among neuronal units (Brown, Kairiss, and Keenan 1990).

Characteristic 3: High-dimensional state spaces. There exist more than 10^{12} neurons in the human brain; each neuron has as many as 1,000 synaptic junctions, suggesting there are approximately 10^{15} potentially modifiable connection strengths in the human brain (Kandel 1981b, 14). These facts indicate that a realistic ANN system would have an approximately 10^{12}-dimensional activation pattern vector and approximately 10^{15} free parameters. Given these observations, it seems reasonable to note that tools developed for ANN system analysis and design must be applicable to high-dimensional state spaces.

Characteristic 4: Local interactions. The primary site of the higher cognitive functions and processes is located in the outer layer of the brain, which is called the "cerebral cortex" (Kandel 1981a). The wiring pattern of the cerebral cortex is fundamentally two-dimensional rather than three-dimensional (Crick and Asanuma 1986). Thus there exist severe restrictions upon the patterns of neuronal connectivity. Such restrictions suggest that the firing frequency of a neuron at any given moment in time is only functionally dependent upon a small subset of other neurons in the system. In addition, current theoretical and experimental work on the nature of learning in the nervous system (Brown, Kairiss, and Keenan 1990) also suggests that the learning process is based upon local interactions. Thus both the classification and learning equations of many ANN systems are also usually assumed to have local interaction properties.

Characteristic 5: Fast computations with slow computing units. Neurons operate on timescales of tens of milliseconds (Kandel 1981b). Feldman and Ballard (1982; also see Simon 1969, 67) have argued that because human perceptual and cognitive processes operate on timescales of tenths of seconds, the human brain must rely on massively parallel processing in order to effectively solve complex information processing problems on the order of seconds. This constraint suggests that the states of many neuronal units simultaneously change at each iteration of an ANN classification dynamical system in order to move the system state quickly from some initial state to a desired final state or trajectory. This constraint also suggests that the number of iterations required to accomplish this goal should have an order of magnitude of about 100.

Characteristic 6: Distributed processing and control.   Neuropsychological studies of people with lesions in specific regions suggest that many higher-level behaviors are not tied to particular brain regions but result from the interactions of many regions (Kandel 1981a). For example, Lashley (1950) trained rats to find their way through a maze, then surgically removed different regions of the brains of his rats in a systematic manner in order to find the origins of the rats' memory for the solution to the maze. Despite numerous experiments of this type, he was unable to identify where knowledge of the maze's solution resided in the rat's brain. Lashley concluded that memory for the maze's solution was apparently distributed throughout the brain. He also noted that although the location of the brain lesion was apparently behaviorally irrelevant, the magnitude of the brain lesion was roughly proportional to the magnitude of the behavioral deficit. These observations are supportive of the now well-accepted idea that complex behavioral procedures involve principles of distributed processing and control. Similarly, most ANN systems exhibit robust performance in the presence of extensive system damage.

Characteristic 7: Quasi-linear activation updating rule.   Neurons integrate incoming firing frequency information over both space and time, and the result of this integration process affects the firing frequency of the neuron (Kandel 1981b). Rashevsky (1960), Wilson and Cowan (1972, 1973), Anderson (1972), Grossberg (1973), and many other neural modelers have modeled the integration process for a particular unit as a quasi-linear *sigmoidal* (i.e., monotonically nondecreasing) function of a weighted sum of the firing frequencies of the units that are locally connected to the dendritic inputs of that unit. Grossberg (1973) has emphasized the importance of specific nonlinear components, while Anderson (1972) has emphasized the importance of the linear components. Undoubtedly, both linear and nonlinear factors can be either more or less relevant depending on the goals of the neural modeler.

Characteristic 8: Homogeneity of processing.   Although a large variety of distinct neural mechanisms are undoubtedly involved in physical learning and activation-updating processes, a common assumption of neural modelers is that the informationally relevant neural processes are effectively spatially homogeneous. That is, essentially the same mechanisms used for learning in one small region of the brain are invoked during the learning process in any other small region of the brain. Similarly, the general characteristics of the rule for modeling how a unit updates its activation level as a function of its neighboring units is also spatially invariant. From a computational perspective, this type of homogeneity assumption could be valuable for allowing extremely large numbers of processing units to effectively communicate in a parallel processing environment.

Characteristic 9: Tolerance of local imprecision. Von Neumann (1958) suggested that another important feature of the nervous system is its tolerance of local imprecision. In a digital computer, each individual (i.e., local) computation is done with considerable accuracy. The human brain, however, is a biological system where local computations are not likely to be accurate to more than a few decimal places. This does not mean that the human brain is not capable of precise computations. For example, people can accurately throw and catch footballs from a considerable distance even though their nervous systems are comprised of computational elements with very poor local precision. Brains and most ANN systems are able to perform precise computations using poor local precision because computations are spatially distributed.

Characteristic 10: Presence of analog processing. Finally, it should be emphasized that ANN systems (like real neural networks) are fundamentally analog machines (Anderson et al. 1977; Grossberg 1973; Rashevsky 1960; Sivilotti, Mahowald, and Mead 1987; von Neumann 1958). True, an analog machine can sometimes function as a digital or logical machine, but analog machines can only be simulated on digital machines at great costs of computational inefficiency. For example, Carver Mead and his colleagues (Sivilotti, Mahowald, and Mead 1987) have been successful in developing new types of image-processing circuitry inspired directly by biological neural networks. Rather than using digital computer logic gates to compute spatial-temporal derivatives for image processing applications indirectly, Mead's group directly designs analog circuitry to compute the necessary derivatives in a direct and application-specific fashion.

1.3   ANN System Applications

Most ANN systems are designed to: (1) construct a biologically plausible model of the nervous system, (2) construct a model of animal or human behavior, or (3) solve an engineering problem. Thus the success of a given ANN system application should be defined as some measure of how effectively the ANN system solves one or more of the above three modeling problems.

   To be sure, an exciting aspect of ANN model research involves developing both biologically and behaviorally feasible models that are capable of successfully solving real-world engineering tasks. However, ANN models that are purely biological, behavioral, or computational in nature are also of great interest. For example, a realistic model of some specific neural circuitry that exhibits realistic biological response properties yet whose functional goal is unknown would certainly still be interesting to the neuroscientist. On the other hand, many engineers would not find such a model very useful for solving practical engineering problems. Alternatively, a biologically unrealistic ANN model that processes images more efficiently than existing algorithms would probably be more interesting to engineers than to neuroscientists.

The goal of this section is to provide a few selected explicit examples of how ANN systems have been applied in the areas of (1) biology, (2) psychology, and (3) computing. A secondary goal of this section is to provide explicit examples of three major categories of ANN systems. *Classification dynamical systems* model how the activation levels of the units in the ANN system evolve in time. *Supervised learning systems* model how ANN systems can learn about their environments when feedback about the ANN system's performance is provided. *Unsupervised learning systems* model how ANN systems can learn about their environments without explicit feedback. The remainder of this section is divided into three parts corresponding to biological, behavioral, and computing applications. Each part, in turn, is divided into three subparts providing examples of classification dynamics systems, supervised learning systems, and unsupervised learning systems.

Figure 1.4 illustrates the organization of this section in order to allow the researcher concerned with a particular application area to "focus in" upon specific areas of interest. Figure 1.4 also illustrates how classification dynamical systems, supervised learning systems, and unsupervised learning systems all play important roles in biological, behavioral, and engineering applications.

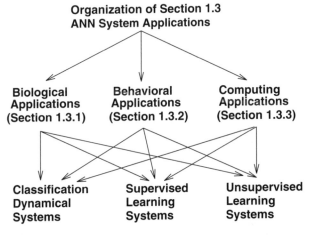

Figure 1.4
Organization of section 1.3: ANN system applications. ANN system applications are divided into three major parts: biological, behavioral, and computing; applications of classification dynamical systems, supervised learning systems, and unsupervised learning systems are then provided within each of the three parts.

1.3.1   Biological Applications: Implementational Level

Neuroscientists, interested in comparing the dynamical behavior of computer
simulation models to real neural systems, are concerned with how effectively a
given ANN system model can make predictions about a given set of neurophysiological data or provide insights into understanding neurophysiological
mechanisms. They are less concerned with modeling behavioral data unless
neurophysiological correlates can be clearly established, and because our current
understanding of the neurophysiological basis of many information-processing
tasks is still relatively undeveloped, they are also less concerned with the computational (i.e., functional) goals of an ANN system.

Biological Applications of ANN Classification Dynamical Systems

Recurrent lateral inhibition networks.   Figure 1.5 shows a standard ANN
system architecture that is sometimes referred to as a "recurrent lateral inhibition ANN." Such architectures have also been referred to as "winner-take-all
networks" (Feldman and Ballard 1982); if the inputs to the ith neuron in the architecture are strongly stimulated, then the ith neuron becomes strongly activated and tends to inhibit its neighboring units. Neural network architectures
consistent with the abstract ANN system depicted in Figure 1.5 have been
found in a variety of brain regions including cerebral cortex (Szentagothai
1967), hippocampus (Andersen et al. 1969), and the cerebellum (Eccles, Ito,
and Szentagothai 1967). Levine 1991, chapter 4, provides a good historical discussion of lateral inhibition ANN systems.

One early influential recurrent lateral inhibition ANN model, proposed by
Hartline and Ratliff (1957; see Hartline and Ratliff 1972 for a review), served

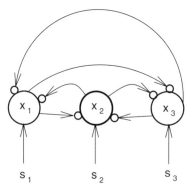

Figure 1.5
Recurrent lateral inhibition ANN system. Each of the three units (large circles) in a recurrent lateral inhibition ANN system inhibits the activation of its neighboring units. Note that an arrow
whose tail is attached to neuronal unit 1 and whose head is attached to a small circle which in turn
is attached to neuronal unit 2 represents the wiring assumption that when neuronal unit 1 is active,
the activation level of neuronal unit 2 should be decreased.

as a good quantitative model of two neural receptor units processing visual information from the compound eye of the *Limulus* horseshoe crab. In particular, Hartline and Ratliff experimentally demonstrated that the firing frequency of one receptor unit decreased as a linear function of a neighboring receptor unit, provided that the neighboring unit was firing above a certain threshold frequency. They also found that a mathematical recurrent lateral inhibition ANN model of the type depicted in Figure 1.5 provided an excellent quantitative fit to the neural response data collected in their laboratory.

Another early influential recurrent lateral inhibition ANN model was proposed by Wilson and Cowan (1972), whose system modeled the responses of *populations* of neurons in neural tissue. Let x_1 be the activation level of neuron 1, and x_2 be the activation level of neuron 2 in a neural network consisting of just two neurons. Let τ, r, w_{11}, w_{12}, w_{21}, and w_{22} be positive scalar parameters associated with the two neuron neural network. The constant w_{ij} is the connection strength from unit j to unit i. That is, w_{ij} indicates the degree to which the activation of unit j will influence the activation level of unit i. Wilson and Cowan also introduced the concept of a *sigmoidal function*, which is generally a monotonically increasing function with a finite lower and finite upper bound on the real numbers. In this textbook, a sigmoidal function will typically be denoted using the symbol $\mathcal{S}$. A typical functional form for a sigmoidal function (also discussed by Wilson and Cowan 1972) is given by the expression

$$\mathcal{S}_i(x) = \frac{1}{1 + \exp\left[-a_i(x - \theta)\right]},$$

where the strictly positive real number a_i and real number θ_i are free parameters of $\mathcal{S}_i$. And finally, define the constants b_1 and b_2 as *biases* such that b_i is large when a large external stimulus input is applied to neuron i. In general, the biases are time-varying, but it will be convenient in the following discussion to treat them as constant real numbers because their values in the situations of interest in the following discussion are slowly varying over time.

Given these definitions, Wilson and Cowan developed a two-neuron model of the lateral inhibition process that is formally defined by the following system of differential equations:

$$\tau\frac{dx_1}{dt} = -x_1 + (1 - rx_1)\mathcal{S}_1[w_{11}x_1 - w_{12}x_2 + b_1]$$

and

$$\tau\frac{dx_2}{dt} = -x_2 + (1 - rx_2)\mathcal{S}_2[w_{22}x_2 - w_{21}x_1 + b_2].$$

To understand the dynamics of the Wilson and Cowan (1972) equations, note that τ is a time-constant parameter which governs how rapidly the activation level of unit i changes as a function of time. Similarly, the nonnegative term $(1 - rx_i)$ tends to decrease the rate of change of the ith unit's activation level as x_i approaches its maximum value. The "lateral inhibition" property of the network arises primarily from the term $w_{ii} x_i - w_{ij} x_j$ $(i \neq j)$ because this term tends to increase the activation of units that are already activated and decrease the activation of units whose "neighbors" have large activation levels.

Wilson and Cowan (1972) found, through a combination of theoretical analyses and numerical solutions, that different choices for the external stimulus bias vector $\mathbf{b} = [b_1, b_2]$ caused the ANN system to converge to qualitatively different oscillatory modes. Thus different stimulus bias vectors were "classified" as different oscillatory patterns of neural activity. Second, they found that increasing b_1 with $b_2 = 0$ resulted in a systematic increase in limit cycle frequency as a function of b_1, which they suggested is consistent with the findings of Poggio and Viernstein (1964), who found that the frequency of oscillatory behavior of thalamic somatosensory neurons in monkeys increased as a function of stimulus intensity.

Research by Grossberg (1973, 1980; also see Cohen and Grossberg 1983) and his colleagues has provided important insights into classifying and understanding a variety of important recurrent lateral inhibition ANN systems. In particular, Grossberg (1973) considered the following family of recurrent lateral inhibition neural networks:

$$dx_i/dt = -Ax_i + (B - x_i)\mathcal{S}(x_i) - x_i\sum_{k \neq i} \mathcal{S}(x_k), \tag{1.1}$$

where x_i is a measure of the activity level of the ith neuron (or ith neuron population), and $\mathcal{S}$ is a continuous sigmoidal (i.e., monotonically increasing) function. Grossberg (1973) investigated how different forms of $\mathcal{S}$ in (1.1) resulted in different modes of behavior. In particular, he formally identified explicit conditions under which the activation level of a unit would become suppressed and when the activation level of a unit would be amplified to its maximum value. Grossberg also formally identified explicit conditions indicating when the initial activation pattern (i.e., the real vector whose ith element is the activation level of the ith unit in the network) in (1.1) would grow in magnitude with constant direction.

A biologically realistic ANN of *Tritonia* swimming response. Oscillatory neural networks play an important role in real neural systems. One reason such networks are important is that they can autonomously generate periodic signals for walking, swimming, eating, breathing, and other such repetitive behaviors. Oscillatory neural networks whose primary role is the generation of such periodic signals are known as "central pattern generators" (CPGs; Selverston and Mazzoni 1989; Selverston and Moulins 1985). For example, one type of central pattern generator consists of collections of individual neuron oscillators such as the heartbeat generator CPG in the lobster (Tazaki and Cooke 1983).

Some central pattern generators, however, do not contain any individual cells that are autonomous neural oscillators. One good example is the CPG neural network found in the sea mollusk *Tritonia,* which generates motor control signals for a complex escape swimming response when a specific brain cell is stimulated with a transient impulse (Willows 1967).

Getting (1983) developed a detailed mathematical model of the neural circuitry of a pure network central pattern generator responsible for generating the escape swimming response in *Tritonia.* In particular, he used a compartmental neural modeling computer program developed by Perkel, Mulloney, and Budelli (1981) to construct a biologically realistic neural network simulation model. First, he individually modeled the passive membrane properties of the three major types of swim interneurons: the "cerebral cell 2" (C2) interneuron, the "dorsal swim interneuron" (DSI), and the "ventral swim interneuron" (VSI). Second, he applied an isolated transient input signal to actual *Tritonia* swim interneurons submerged in a seawater preparation and measured the temporal response characteristics of the firing frequencies of these interneurons. He then used the resulting characteristic curves to set the parameters of physically isolated individual simulated swim interneurons so that they would reproduce the desired temporal response behaviors. Third, he recorded the time course of the postsynaptic potential (PSP) voltage generated at the output of each individual swim interneuron. Because the temporal characteristics of the PSP vary systematically as a function of the synaptic connections of a given swim interneuron's output to the other interneurons in the system, Getting found that several distinct PSPs had to be identified (the temporal characteristics of the six major types of interneuron connections observed in Getting 1983 are diagrammed in figure 1.6). And fourth, he exploited previous work (see Getting, Lennard, and Hume 1980) which identified critical characteristics of the functional interactions among the three types of swim interneurons by stimulating one interneuron while recording from another interneuron (see figure 1.7, which summarizes the results of this previous research).

Figure 1.8 shows how the network in figure 1.7 responds when C2 is stimulated by a transient impulse signal. The swim episode depicted in figure 1.8 represents approximately three cycles; during the course of each cycle first the dorsal swim interneurons (DSIs) fire, and then the ventral swim premotor interneurons (VSIs) fire corresponding to an oscillatory swimming pattern of dorsal and then ventral motor activity.

Getting (1983) reviews the sequence of events in a particular cycle as follows. First, the DSI begins to fire. The C2 begins firing rapidly just after the DSI begins to fire and stops firing after the VSI begins to fire. The DSI stops firing just after the VSI begins to fire. The cycle ends when the VSI stops firing. A similar pattern of qualitative results was obtained from simulation studies based upon the neural network described in figure 1.7. Thus a key result of the simulation studies was that the selected neurophysiological characteristics actually

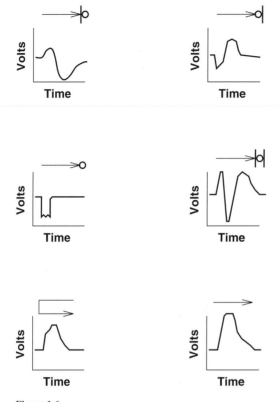

Figure 1.6
Interneuron connection types in *Tritonia*. Six alternative types of connections among interneurons are shown with their postsynaptic potentials (PSPs) plotted as a function of time. (From Getting 1983, figure 8; copyright 1983 by the American Physiological Society; adapted with permission.)

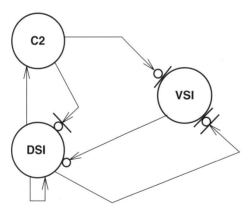

Figure 1.7
Neural model of central pattern generator in *Tritonia*. The six connection types depicted among the cerebral cell 2 interneuron (C2), dorsal swim interneuron (DSI), and ventral swim interneuron (VSI) represented in this figure are described in greater detail in figure 1.6. (From Getting 1983, figure 1; copyright 1983 by the American Physiological Society; adapted with permission.)

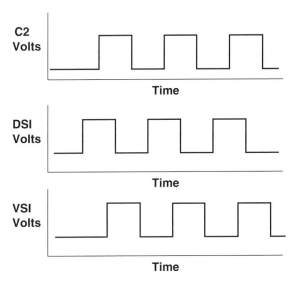

Figure 1.8
Tritonia central pattern generator response characteristics. For a particular "swim cycle" in *Tritonia*, the typical sequence of events is as follows. First, the DSI begins to fire. The C2 then begins firing rapidly just after the DSI begins to fire and stops firing after the VSI begins to fire. The DSI stops firing just after the VSI begins to fire. The cycle ends when the VSI stops firing. A similar pattern of qualitative results was obtained from simulation studies based upon the neural network described in figure 1.7. (From Getting 1983, figure 9; copyright 1983 by the American Physiological Society; adapted with permission.)

incorporated into the neural network model apparently provided a reasonably complete explanation of the operation of the swimming escape response CPG mechanism in *Tritonia*.

An abstract ANN of *Tritonia* swimming response. Kleinfeld and Sompolinsky (1988) have proposed a highly abstract neural network model using neurons that are much less biologically realistic than Getting's biologically plausible neural network model (1983). The Kleinfeld and Sompolinsky (1988) model consists of models of four interneurons: C2, DSI, and two types of VSIs. Let t_s and t_f be the time delays associated with slow and fast synaptic weight components. The actual magnitudes of t_s and t_f were based upon known qualitative characteristics of the desired output response characteristics of the neural network. The activation of the ith unit in the system at iteration t of the algorithm is computed using the formula

$$x_i(t) = \mathcal{S}\left[\sum_{j=1}^{4} \left[w_{ij}^s x_j(t - t_s) + w_{ij}^f x_j(t - t_f) \right] \right],$$

where w_{ij}^s and w_{ij}^f are the "weights" or equivalently the network parameters indicating how activity in one unit affects the activity level in another unit in the system. The sigmoidal function, $\mathcal{S}$, is defined such that $\mathcal{S}(x) = 0$ if $x \le 0.5$ and $\mathcal{S}(x) = 1$ if $x > 0.5$. The values of the weights w_{ij}^s and w_{ij}^f were chosen to be equal to either 0, 1, or -1 based upon qualitative consideration of the experimental data. Like Getting (1983), Kleinfeld and Sompolinsky were able to demonstrate that this minimal neural network was also adequate for modeling the aspects of the CPG response characteristics in the *Tritonia* escape swimming response shown in figure 1.8.

At first glance, one might question the usefulness of the Kleinfeld and Sompolinsky (1988) neural network model, which is quite abstract and, unlike the Getting (1983) model, is not as closely tied to the neurophysiological data. On the other hand, models such as those proposed by Kleinfeld and Sompolinsky (1988) provide an important complementary description of a given neural network that increases the value of much more complex and biologically realistic models such as the Getting (1983) compartmental neural model. In particular, the simpler, abstract Kleinfeld and Sompolinsky model has the following advantages. First, it is easier to understand and thus may provide insights into the essential basic principles of the more biologically realistic model. Second, to the extent that it captures the functionally relevant ideas of the more biologically realistic model, the simpler, abstract model provides a useful mechanism for accurately and efficiently communicating complex scientific ideas. Third, the simpler, abstract model may be easier to mathematically analyze and simulate thus permitting the analysis of much more complex neural networks whose fundamental principles are based upon the original biologically realistic neural network model.

Biological Applications of ANN Supervised Learning Systems

Simplified neurally plausible associative memory models. From the late 1950s to the early 1970s, a number of researchers began to investigate neurally plausible *ANN supervised learning systems* in order to explore their computational power and limitations. Some of the more influential papers published during this time period included articles by Amari (1967, 1972), Anderson (1968, 1972), Caianiello (1961), Grossberg (1972, 1973, 1974), Kohonen (1972), Minsky and Papert (1969), Nakano (1972), Rosenblatt (1962), Selfridge (1958), and Steinbuch and Schmitt (1967).

Anderson (1972) proposed a highly simplified associative neural network model where one group of neurons projected to another group of neurons. He suggested examples of such situations might include the projections from the thalamic nuclei to cortex as well as the various projection systems within cortex. Anderson also assumed as a first-order approximation that the activity level, r_i, of the ith neuron in the output layer was simply a weighted sum of the activity levels of the neurons in the input layer. That is,

$$r_i = \sum_{j=1}^{d} w_{ij} s_j, \tag{1.2}$$

where s_j is the activity level of the jth neuron in the input layer and w_{ij} is a coefficient corresponding to the synaptic weight transmission coefficient from neuron j in the input layer to neuron i in the output layer.

In addition, Anderson assumed that the synaptic weight transmission coefficient (i.e., the synaptic weight) was modified according to the following learning rule, commonly known as the "Hebbian learning rule": the change in the synaptic weight w_{ij} is proportional to the product of the activity level of the postsynaptic neuron, o_i, and the activity level of the presynaptic neuron, s_j. The Hebbian learning rule may be formally expressed as the difference equation

$$w_{ij}(t + 1) = w_{ij}(t) + \gamma o_i(t)s_j(t), \tag{1.3}$$

where $w_{ij}(t)$ is the synaptic weight strength at time t that measures the influence of the activity level of neuron j upon the activity level of neuron i, γ is a strictly positive number called the "stepsize" or "learning rate," $o_i(t)$ is the activation level of the ith postsynaptic neuron at time t, and $s_j(t)$ is the activation level of the jth presynaptic neuron at time t.

The learning rule in (1.3) is referred to as the "Hebbian learning rule" because it is a specific quantitative model of a general qualitative hypothesis proposed by Hebb (1949), although William James proposed essentially the same hypothesis in 1892 (James 1948, chap. 16). According to Hebb, when two neurons are simultaneously activated, a change occurs in the nervous system such that their activations become more highly correlated (or uncorrelated) in the future. Current evidence from the neurophysiological literature has been steadily accumulating in support of the Hebbian learning rule (see Brown et al. 1988 for a review).

The above network architectural assumptions and Hebbian learning rule, although fairly simple, are quite consistent with a very wide range of neural architectures. A key contribution of this research was the demonstration of the surprising fact that relatively simple neurally plausible network architectures were capable of learning and retrieving information under specific conditions.

Using backpropagation to discover optimal architectures.   The backpropagation ANN architecture (Rumelhart, Hinton, and Williams 1986; also see Chauvin and Rumelhart 1995; Le Cun 1985; Parker 1985; Werbos 1974) may be used as a *supervised learning algorithm* for multilayer neural networks. Typically, a backpropagation network consists of three sets of units connected by two layers of weights. The stimulus activation pattern is a list of the activation levels of one set of units, called the "input units." The response activation pattern is a list of the activation levels of another group of units, called the "output units." The remaining units in the network, called the "hidden units," integrate incoming information provided by the input units, while the output units integrate incoming information provided by the hidden units. A unit integrates information by computing a nonlinear sigmoidal transformation of a weighted sum of incoming signal magnitudes.

Initially, the connections among all of the units in the backpropagation network have randomly chosen values. An initial stimulus activation pattern over the input units is then presented to the network, which in turn generates an activation pattern over the hidden units of the network. The activation pattern over the hidden units then generates an activation pattern over the output units. An error signal between the generated activation pattern over the output units and the desired (also known as the "target") activation pattern is then computed. This error signal is then "backpropagated" through the network in order to generate an error signal for all connection strengths in the network. Finally, each connection strength weight is modified by an amount proportional to the product of the error signal for that weight and the magnitude of the incoming signal to that weight. Note that because the initial weights of the backpropagation network were randomly chosen, different hidden units will have different preferences for responding to particular patterns of incoming information. The specific details of the backpropagation algorithm are provided in chapter 2.

Although the backpropagation learning algorithm is not viewed as a biologically plausible learning mechanism (Stork 1989; Zipser and Andersen 1988), it is an algorithm that seeks a set of hidden units or interneurons which optimally perform a given task (e.g., Golden 1988a,b,c; Rumelhart, Hinton, and Williams 1986; Rumelhart et al. 1995; White 1989a,b). Thus, in applications of backpropagation learning to biological modeling, the backpropagation learning algorithm is typically not viewed as a theory of *how* interneurons acquire their functional behavior. But rather, given the hypothesis that interneuron functions are presumably optimal in some sense, the backpropagation learning algorithm is viewed as a mechanism for generating testable hypotheses regarding optimal interneuron functioning. Several researchers have begun to explore this particular approach to neural modeling (Kristan et al. 1989; Zipser and Andersen 1988).

For example, Zipser and Andersen (1988) were interested in how brains solve the following visual coordinate transformation problem. Imagine a person watching a pencil fall off a table. During the fall of the pencil, the person is constantly gathering visual information about the motion of the pencil by moving her eyes. The brain, however, must in some sense "subtract out" the eye motion from eye-image-invoked retina responses in order to deduce the motion of the pencil in a "head-centered" (i.e., person-centered) coordinate system.

One region of the brain known as "posterior parietal cortex" has been shown to participate in solving the visual coordinate transformation problem. Lesions in posterior parietal cortex of both monkeys and humans can result in the inability to transform "retina-centered" information from the visual field and current eye position into "head-centered" information. Moreover, posterior parietal cortex in monkeys contains neurons which respond to both visual information and eye position.

Andersen, Essick, and Siegel (1985) presented brief (500-millisecond) point flashes in the periphery of a monkey's visual field while recording neural activity in the monkey's cortex. The monkey's head was fixed so that it could not move, and the position of the monkey's eyes was monitored on-line with special apparatus. A typical experimental trial consisted of the following sequence of events. First, the monkey's eyes were fixated upon a fixation point directly ahead of the monkey. Second, a flash of light in one of eight locations surrounding the fixation point or at the fixation point itself was then displayed to the monkey. For each of the nine locations: (1) the eye position of the monkey was recorded, and (2) the activity level of a neuron in posterior parietal cortex was recorded both before and during the light flash.

Zipser and Andersen (1988) used the data collected in the Andersen, Essick, and Siegel (1985) experiment to train a backpropagation ANN to map eye position information and retinal location target information into a retina-independent (i.e., head-centered) coordinate system. The backpropagation ANN consisted of a set of input units, a set of hidden units, and a set of output units. The input units were divided into two groups. The activation level of a unit in the first group of input units indicated the intensity of the light flash at a particular point on the monkey's retinas. The activation pattern over the second group of input units indicated the current position of the monkey's eyes. The input units were then randomly connected to the hidden units which were randomly connected to the output units. The activation pattern over the output units represented information about the location of the light flash in a head-centered coordinate system (i.e., the effect of eye position is "subtracted out" of the information in the retinal image).

A classical backpropagation ANN was then trained by strengthening and weakening the connections among the units in the system depending upon the pattern of activations imposed over the network's output and input units. The network was trained with training stimuli derived from the actual data collected by Andersen, Essick, and Siegel (1985). The goal of the simulation exercise was to see if the hidden units in the backpropagation ANN would develop response characteristics similar to those of cortical neurons in monkey posterior parietal cortex.

Zipser and Andersen (1988) found that the hidden units in the backpropagation network acquired response properties qualitatively similar to those of real interneurons in monkey posterior parietal cortex. That any qualitative similarities in response properties were obtained was an important result because the backpropagation network was such a highly abstract model of the real neural system. The simulation results were interpreted as consistent with the hypothesis that the few biologically plausible assumptions embodied in the backpropagation network were sufficient to explain the observed similarities between hidden unit and biological neuronal unit response properties.

Biological Applications of ANN Unsupervised Learning Systems

Neural modeling of the development of topographic cortical maps is an important biological application of *ANN unsupervised learning systems*. A *topographic cortical map* is a region of cortex where neurons located in physical close proximity either (1) respond strongly to sensory stimuli with similar attributes, or (2) control neural motor systems with similar attributes. One important example of a topographic map occurs in visual cortex where flashes of light in neighboring regions of visual space evoke neural responses that are physically close together in visual cortex (Kandel 1981d). Topographic maps are found in other regions of the cortex besides visual cortex. Researchers have found that receptive fields in auditory cortex respond strongly to similar auditory signals (Kelly 1981c), that neighboring receptive fields in somatosensory cortical regions respond strongly to neighboring pressure receptors on the skin surface of the animal (Kandel 1981c), and that neighboring motor cortical regions control neural motor systems also in close physical proximity (Ghez 1981b).

Figure 1.9 illustrates some of the various types of topographic maps found in the brain. For example, the motor and tactile/sensory regions of cortex consist

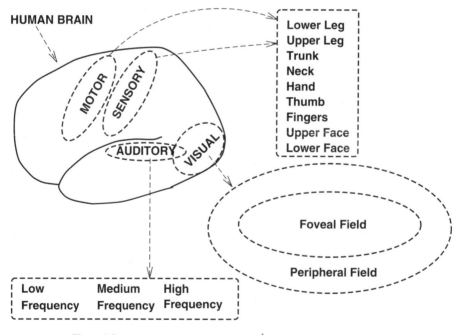

Figure 1.9
Examples of types of topographic maps in the brain. In this sideways schematic view of a human brain (anterior regions to the left and posterior regions to the right), various cortical regions concerned with specific functions such as motor control, tactile/sensory processing, auditory processing, and visual processing have been identified. Within each of these regions, as well as throughout the brain, one finds the presence of multiple overlapping topographic maps. Such maps have the property that neurons with similar response properties tend to be physically located next to one another.

of topographic maps where neurons receiving/sending signals to body parts close to one another tend to be physically close to one another in cortex. Thus the neural motor control system for the fingers is physically close to the neural motor control system for the thumb, and neurons controlling these two subsystems are located in close proximity in motor cortex. Similarly, in auditory cortex there are multiple overlapping tonotopic maps where neurons responding to similar auditory frequencies tend to be located physically next to one another. And in visual cortex there are retinotopic maps where visual stimuli presented close to one another in the visual field tend to activate neurons in visual cortex that are close to one another as well.

One predominant characteristic of topographic maps is the *cortical magnification factor*. Cortical regions responsible for more sophisticated information processing tasks are disproportionately larger than other cortical regions (see figure 1.9). Thus the region of motor cortex devoted to controlling the thumb is much larger than the region of motor cortex devoted to controlling the little finger (Ghez 1981b). Another important example is the retinotopic mapping in visual cortex. Although the fovea processes only a small fraction of the incoming visual information to the retina, the majority of visual cortex is devoted to processing foveal information (Kandel 1981d).

Experimental evidence indicates that the boundaries of the topographic maps in the cortex are not rigidly genetically specified but can be altered by manipulating an animal's sensory environment (Hirsch and Spinelli 1970; Blakemore and Cooper 1970; Blakemore and Mitchell 1973). Von der Malsburg (1973) suggested two possible computational reasons for animal brains to have this adaptive property. First, this adaptive property drastically reduces the amount of information that would have to be encoded into an animal's DNA in order to specify in detail the organization of a topographic map. Second, the ability to learn appropriate partitionings of cortical space (i.e., learn topographic map boundaries) as a function of experience is a useful evolutionary strategy given the hypothesis that such boundaries define how brain processing resources are allocated.

Using a simplified neural network model of cortical neuron processing, von der Malsburg (1973) demonstrated how topographic mappings could be acquired through experience. The von der Malsburg (1973) model consisted of an array of artificial neurons. Each model neuron updated its current activation level by an amount proportional to a weighted sum of the input signals impinging upon that neuron. The weights in that weighted sum will be referred to as the "connection strengths" of the neuron. When a neuron in the array became activated, that neuron would partially activate the neurons which were physically close to the activated unit. In addition, the von der Malsburg (1973) model involved a Hebbian-like learning rule (e.g., Anderson 1972; Grossberg 1972, 1974; Hebb 1949; Kohonen 1972; Rosenblatt 1962), which stated that if an incoming signal to a model neuron's connection weight was active and the model neuron's response was active, then that connection weight should be increased by some fixed amount. To prevent the connection weights in the system from growing without bound, von der Malsburg (1973) renormalized the connection weights to each model neuron in order to keep the sum of the connection weights to each neuron equal to a constant. The two critical assumptions of the von der Malsburg (1973) neural model were (1) an activated unit should activate its physically close neighboring units, and (2) connection strengths should be modified as a result of a Hebbian-like learning rule. These assumptions were chosen by von der Malsburg because of their biological plausibility.

A feature detection neuron's magnitude of response to some novel stimulus U is proportional to the similarity between U and familiar stimulus S. Thus feature detection neurons are characterized by a *unimodal* response property, like the complex orientation column feature detectors of Hubel and Wiesel (1963, 1968). A neuron that responds strongly to several distinct classes of stimuli is defined as having a *multimodal* response property. Von der Malsburg's ANN model (1973) tended to self-organize into a network of clusters of feature detection neurons with unimodal response properties (see table 1.1). Moreover, von der Malsburg found that clusters of feature detection neurons with similar response properties tended to be physically located close together on the artificial cortical surface, much like the complex orientation column cells in visual cortex (Hubel and Wiesel, 1968).

Kohonen (1982, 1984, 1989, 1990) has also extensively investigated the properties of self-organizing ANN systems using mathematical analyses and computer simulation work. Kohonen (1982) demonstrated that a simplified version of the more biologically realistic von der Malsburg (1973) neural network model was sufficient to account for some of the major qualitative phenomena associated with the development of topographic cortical maps in real brains.

In one such simulation, Kohonen (1982) described a fairly simple ANN system where an initially randomly connected group of model neurons learned to

Table 1.1
Response properties of von der Malsburg (1973) model neurons. As the learning process progresses, an individual model neuron gradually becomes committed to responding to a particular input stimulus.

	No response	Unimodal	Multimodal
Before learning	12	87	70
20 steps of learning	43	118	8
100 steps of learning	21	147	1

Adapted from Table 4 of Malsburg (1973), *Kybernetik, 14,* 85–100. © 1973 Springer-Verlag. Adapted with permission.

respond strongly to specific frequency components of a given set of acoustic signals. He found that if two model neurons learned to respond to approximately the same frequency component, then the two model neurons tended to be located physically close to one another in the neural network model. Moreover, a magnification factor property was also observed; frequency components that were dominant in the set of acoustic training stimuli were learned by more model neurons than less dominant frequency components. These qualitative features of the von der Malsburg (1973) and Kohonen (1982) models are characteristic properties that are consistently present in human cortex as well. The Kohonen learning algorithm reviewed in chapter 2 is closely related to the topographic map learning algorithm used by Kohonen (1982) in his early computer simulations.

More recently, Grajski and Merzenich (1990) have described a self-organizing ANN network for modeling the development of somatosensory topographic cortical maps in the adult monkey. Jenkins et al. (1990) found that when only relatively restricted skin surfaces of adult monkeys were permitted to receive sensory stimulation, the cortical magnification factor tended to increase. They also found that sensory experiences of this type also tended to decrease the size of skin sensor receptive fields, implying an increase in skin sensor response sensitivity. Conversely, Jenkins and Merzenich (1987) found that if a cortical lesion was made in order to disrupt a particular topographic representation of a digit in an adult monkey's finger, then the topographic map of neighboring regions would reorganize to reinstate the lesioned portion of the original topographic representation. Grajski and Merzenich (1990) showed that a Hebbian-type learning dynamics and a simplified network architecture consisting of a "skin layer," a "subcortical layer," and a "cortical layer" was sufficient to qualitatively explain how the cortical magnification factor could be altered by restricting external stimulation of the artificial skin layer or by making appropriate "lesions" in the cortical layer of the ANN system.

1.3.2   Behavioral Applications: Algorithmic Level

Experimental psychologists are interested in comparing the behavior of an ANN system to human performance in specific information-processing tasks. They are less concerned with neurophysiological interpretations of an ANN system and, like neuroscientists, are usually not interested in whether a given ANN system can solve computationally difficult problems.

Behavioral Applications of ANN Classification Dynamical Systems

In order to illustrate how ANN *classification dynamical systems* can be applied to investigate behavioral phenomena, consider the perceptual problem of perceiving a letter in the context of a word. In order to investigate this problem, psychologists have presented words to subjects and recorded (1) the response time required to identify a letter in a word (Mason 1975; Pollatsek, Well, and

Schindler 1975; Taylor, Miller, and Juola 1977), or (2) the accuracy of identifying a letter embedded in a word (Adams 1979; McClelland 1976; Reicher
1969). Psychologists have discovered that letters in words tend to be perceived
more efficiently than letters not embedded within words. This phenomenon is
referred to as the "word superiority effect" (WSE).

The WSE is interesting because it suggests that the human perceptual processing system is not organized in a strictly hierarchical manner. That is, letters
are not first perceived as distinct perceptual units, and then used to identify
words. Rather, the WSE suggests that the human perceptual system exploits the
contextual information in a letter string to help identify its component letters.

Given this is so, how might one pinpoint the origin of the contextual effects
of letter-within-word perception? In particular, is the contextual advantage of a
letter embedded within a letter string due to the fact that the letter string forms
a meaningful word? Or is perhaps this contextual advantage due to perceptual
regularities within the letter string that are exploited independently of the fact
that the letter string forms a recognizable word?

To evaluate these hypotheses, researchers (e.g., Adams 1979; McClelland
1976) compared letter recognition efficiency of letters embedded within nonsense letter strings that looked like words (pseudowords) to letter recognition
efficiency of letters embedded within nonsense letter strings that did not look
like words (nonwords). Again a WSE was observed, supporting the hypothesis that the WSE is not solely a function of the meaning of a letter string but is
derived in part from perceptual regularities in the letter string. Moreover,
these perceptual regularities are (surprisingly) not strongly dependent upon
the sequential order of the letters in the letter strings (McClelland and Johnston 1977; Johnston 1978). In particular, McClelland and Johnston (1977)
demonstrated that letters in high-bigram-frequency letter strings are *not* perceived more efficiently than letters in low-bigram-frequency letter strings.
Thus, for example, the letter *T* is *not* perceived more efficiently in the first letter position of the high-bigram-frequency letter string *THON* (note high-
bigram-frequency of letter cluster *TH*) relative to the first letter position of the
low-bigram-frequency letter string *TQHN* (note low-bigram-frequency of letter cluster *TQ*).

To account for these types of experimental phenomena, McClelland and
Rumelhart (1981; also see Rumelhart and McClelland 1982; Golden 1986b;
and Grossberg and Stone 1986) proposed an ANN model of letter-within-word
perception that provided considerable insights into the nature of the word superiority effect. In addition to having a tremendous impact upon researchers
who were studying the word superiority effect, the McClelland and Rumelhart
model sparked a substantial amount of interest among behavioral researchers
because it explained a significant amount of behavioral data in both an intuitive
and detailed manner.

The McClelland and Rumelhart (1981; also see Rumelhart and McClelland 1982) interactive activation (IA) model is shown in figure 1.10. The IA model consists of a set of position-specific letter feature detection nodes and a set of word nodes. A *position-specific* letter feature detection node is a unit that responds strongly (i.e., has a high activity level) when a particular letter in a particular letter position of a letter string stimulus is presented. For example, if the letter string *TRAP* is presented to the IA model, then the position-specific letter feature detection node associated with the letter *T* in the first letter position of the letter string would become strongly active. On the other hand, the letter feature detection node associated with the letter *T* in the second letter position of the letter string would not become active. All of the position-specific letter feature detection nodes within a letter position are wired up according to the rules of recurrent lateral inhibition so that only one letter can be assigned to a particular letter position in the letter string. Similarly, all of the word feature detection nodes in the network are wired up according to the rules of recurrent lateral inhibition so that only one word can be assigned to a particular letter string. Finally, the connections from each position-specific letter feature detector node to the word nodes are also wired up according to the rules of recurrent lateral inhibition in a special way. A given position-specific letter feature detector

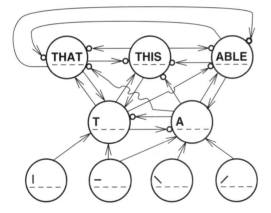

Figure 1.10
Interactive activation (IA) model of letter-in-word perception. Position-specific letter feature detection units gradually accumulate evidence over time supporting hypotheses about the presence or absence of particular letter feature fragments. The outputs of the feature detection units are available as inputs to the position-specific letter detection units, whose outputs are then fed into the word detection units, which in turn provide feedback down to the letter detection unit level. Thus both bottom-up information from the letter feature detection units and top-down information from the word detection units simultaneously influence the activation level of a letter feature detection unit. Additional constraints are present in the model to inhibit multiple words from being activated and to prevent two or more letter feature detection units assigned to a single letter position from becoming simultaneously activated. Adapted from Figure 1 of McClelland and Rumelhart (1981), *Psychological Review*, 88, 375–407. © 1981 by the American Psychological Association. Adapted with permission.

node (e.g., the node *T in letter position 1*) excites all word nodes that contain the designated letter in the appropriate letter position (e.g., the word nodes *TRAP, TRIP, TAKE, TIME*), and inhibits all word nodes that do not contain the designated letter in the appropriate letter position (e.g., the word nodes *ABLE* and *CART*). There is also top-down feedback where a given word node excites the relevant position-specific letter nodes.

Also note that although each node in the system processes information in a "neuronlike" manner by computing weighted sums of the activations of the other nodes in the network, the IA model is merely viewed as an interesting cognitive processing model that can be evaluated on the basis of *behavioral* as opposed to neurophysiological data. Indeed, it is highly unlikely a network architecture as depicted in figure 1.10 would be instantiated in real human brains, in the sense that each node would correspond to exactly one brain cell.

Table 1.2 shows actual and simulated results of the McClelland and Johnston (1977) experiments. The IA model correctly predicts letters in both words and pseudowords are more efficiently processed than letters by themselves. The IA model also correctly predicts that this advantage is due to perceptual regularities in the letter string as opposed to the presence or absence of a word in the model's lexicon: letters in pseudowords are perceived more efficiently than single letters. The model also correctly predicts that letters in high-bigram letter strings are perceived as efficiently as letters in low-bigram letter strings. Finally, note that the quantitative fit of the model to the human data (although obtained through manipulation of the free parameters of the IA ANN model) is nevertheless quite impressive.

Golden (1986b) discussed how a brain-state-in-a-box model (Anderson et al. 1977; Golden 1986a, 1993) version of the IA model could be developed in order to provide insights into how experience with the statistical structure of wordlike letter strings could lead to the acquisition of the word superiority

Table 1.2
Actual and simulated results of McClelland and Johnston 1977. Dependent variable is proportion of letters correctly identified.

	Word	Pseudoword	Single letter
Human data			
High BF	0.81	0.79	0.67
Low BF	0.78	0.77	0.64
Average	0.80	0.78	0.66
Simulation			
High BF	0.81	0.79	0.67
Low BF	0.79	0.77	0.67
Average	0.80	0.78	0.67

Note: BF = bigram frequency.
Adapted from Table 1 of McClelland and Rumelhart (1981), *Psychological Review, 88,* 375–407. © 1981 by the American Psychological Association. Adapted with permission.

effect. Briefly, the Golden (1986b) letter-in-word (LW) model consisted of a collection of position-specific feature detection units. By presenting the model with letters by themselves, *within-letter* feature correlations (i.e., connection strengths) were acquired by the model. These within-letter feature correlations were then used by the model as a guide for acquiring appropriate *between-letter* feature correlations.

The LW model was also a recurrent ANN model and made explicit qualitative response time predictions as well as qualitative predictions about letter recognition accuracy for WSE experiments. In particular, at each processing cycle (iteration) of the LW model, all units in the network compute a weighted sum of the activity levels of the other units in the network. It can be shown that under fairly general conditions (Golden 1986a, 1993) as the number of processing cycles increases, the change in activity levels of the units in the system will converge to zero. When the activity levels of the network converged to their final values, the number of cycles of the algorithm required for the network to converge was taken as a qualitative indicator of the neural network's letter identification response time.

Using the number of cycles of the LW model as a qualitative indicator of response time, Golden (1986b) qualitatively replicated a number of key findings in the literature, for example, that letters in words were classified more rapidly than letters in pseudowords and that letters in pseudowords were classified more rapidly than letters in nonwords. A similar pattern of results using response time as a dependent measure has been observed in adult subjects (Mason 1975; Taylor, Miller, and Juola 1977). Furthermore, the LW model classified letters in high-bigram-frequency letter strings as efficiently as letters in low-bigram-frequency letter strings. This latter finding is consistent with the experimental finding that humans do not exploit perceptual regularities involving the order of letters in the letter string in the WSE (McClelland and Johnston 1977; Johnston 1978).

Behavioral Applications of ANN Supervised Learning Systems

ANN supervised learning theories of animal and human behavior have provided important insights into the development of theoretical learning models based upon the classical conditioning literature. The standard classical conditioning paradigm is most naturally introduced through the well-known experiment of Pavlov (1927; see Hilgard and Bower 1966 and Hillner 1979 for reviews of the classical conditioning literature). Briefly, when meat powder is placed in the mouth of a dog, this *unconditioned stimulus* (UCS) causes the dog to salivate, that is, an *unconditioned response* (UR). Now, suppose that some arbitrary stimulus such as a light is flashed just prior to the presentation of the UCS. Also suppose that the flashing of the light in conjunction with the UCS is repeated a considerable number of times. Eventually, given certain conditions, presenting the light stimulus without the UCS will cause the dog to salivate. The light stimulus has become a *conditioned stimulus* (CS) and the dog's salivation response to the CS, a *conditioned response* (CR).

Rescorla and Wagner (1972) proposed a simple mathematical model for accounting for some of the major phenomena in classical conditioning theory. Sutton and Barto (1981) emphasized that the Rescorla-Wagner ANN model could be viewed as an important special case of the Widrow-Hoff (1960) learning rule. This is actually quite remarkable because the Widrow-Hoff learning rule was originally proposed, not to explain behavioral phenomena associated with classical conditioning paradigms, but rather as a mechanism for on-line learning of adaptive switching circuits! For purposes of continuity, the Rescorla-Wagner learning rule will be presented in the standard ANN notation used throughout this textbook.

The Rescorla-Wagner (1972) model consists of a group of input units and a single output unit. The activity level of the output unit is interpreted as a measure of the presence of the UCR/CR, so that larger activity levels correspond to a stronger UCR/CR. For simplicity, assume that the model consists of only two input units. Let the activity level of *stimulus* input unit 1, $s_1(t) \in \{0, 1\}$, be a measure of the presence of CS1 (e.g., the light flash in dog's eyes) and let the activity level of stimulus input unit 2, $s_2(t) \in \{0, 1\}$, be a measure of the presence of CS2 (e.g., a bell ring in the dog's presence) at time t. Let the *desired* or *target feedback response signal*, $o_i(t) \in \{0, 1\}$, of the ith output unit be a measure of the presence of the UCS (e.g., presence of meat powder in the dog's mouth) at time t.

The activity level of the *response* of the ith output unit at time t, $r_i(t)$, is assumed to be a weighted sum of $s_1(t)$ and $s_2(t)$ (the activation levels of stimulus units 1 and 2, respectively, at time t), so that

$$r_i(t) = \sum_{j=1}^{2} w_{ij}(t)s_j(t),$$

where $w_{ij}(t)$ is the value of the connection strength connecting input unit j to the ith output unit at time t. The Rescorla-Wagner (1972) learning rule (a special case of the Widrow-Hoff rule) is defined by the connection strength update equation

$$w_{ij}(t + 1) = w_{ij}(t) + \gamma[o_i(t) - r_i(t)]s_j(t), \tag{1.4}$$

where the learning rate γ is a small positive number.

Note the similarities and differences between the Rescorla-Wagner learning rule in (1.4) and the Hebbian learning rule in (1.3). Like the Hebbian learning rule, the weight update involves incrementing the weight by a product of a measure of the postsynaptic and presynaptic activity. Unlike the Hebbian learning rule, however, the postsynaptic activity measure is an error signal $o_i(t) - r_i(t)$ that is functionally dependent upon the unit's response $r_i(t)$.

The Rescorla-Wagner (1972) rule can also account for a number of important classical conditional phenomena such as blocking and deblocking (Hillner 1979). The standard *blocking* paradigm involves first repeatedly presenting the UCS and a potential CS together (e.g., $s_1(t) = 1$, $s_2(t) = 0$, $o_i(t) = 1$ for $t = 0, 1, 2,...$) to (1.4) until the appropriate weight in the model converges to the correct solution (i.e., $w_{i1}(t) \rightarrow 1$ as $t \rightarrow \infty$) while the other weight in the model remains at its initial value (i.e., $w_{i2}(t) = 0$ as $t \rightarrow \infty$). Suppose that at some time T: $w_{i1}(T) = 1$ and $w_{i2}(T) = 0$.

Now, given $w_{i1}(T) = 1$ and $w_{i2}(T) = 0$, it should be clear that repeatedly presenting the UCS, the first CS, and a *second* potential CS together (e.g., $s_1(t) = 1$, $s_2(t) = 1$, $o_i(t) = 1$ for $t = T + 1, T + 2, T + 3,...$) to (1.4) will not result in the growth of $w_{i2}(t)$ (i.e., $w_{i2}(t) = 0$ as $t \rightarrow \infty$). The error signal $o_i(t) - r_i(t)$ is equal to zero because

$$r_i(t) = w_{i1}(t)s_1(t) + w_{i2}(t)s_2(t) = (1)(1) + (0)(1) = 1$$

and $o_i(t) = 1$. This type of learning phenomenon has been observed in animals and humans as well (Kamin 1969).

Now suppose, for example, that the intensity of the UCS (e.g., double the amount of meat powder in the dog's mouth) is increased so that $o_i(t) = 2$ instead of $o_i(t) = 1$ and $s_1(t) = 1$ and $s_2(t) = 1$. In this case, the activity level of the output unit is still one (i.e., $r_i(t) = 1$) but since $o_i(t) = 2$, the error signal $o_i(t) - r_i(t)$ is now equal to $2 - 1 = 1$. The learning rule in (1.4) will permit learning in this case, and both $w_{i1}(t)$ (associated with the original CS) and $w_{i2}(t)$ (associated with the potential second CS) will be modified. Again this type of phenomena has been observed in animals and humans and is known as "deblocking" (Kamin 1969).

The Rescorla-Wagner (1972) model has also been successfully applied to a number of other behavioral phenomena such as overshadowing (a variant of blocking), conditioned inhibition, and the intertrial interval effect (see Hillner 1979, 148–151, for further discussion). On the other hand, the Rescorla-Wagner model has difficulty accounting for a number of other phenomena in the classical conditioning literature as noted by Sutton and Barto (1981). A number of interesting ANN models have been developed to address some of these problems (e.g., Blazis et al. 1986; Grossberg and Levine 1987).

Behavioral Applications of ANN Unsupervised Learning Systems

Knapp and Anderson (1984) have proposed an elegant ANN *unsupervised learning* model of human memory that provides an insightful account of some key phenomena in the human memory experimental literature, although their model has not been experimentally evaluated to the extent of other mathematical models of human memory in the literature. For example, more comprehensive ANN models of human memory have been proposed by a number of researchers (e.g., Estes 1972; Gillund and Shiffrin 1984; Lewandowsky and Murdock 1989; Murdock 1982, 1983), but a detailed review of those models and the relevant experimental data is not within the scope of this introductory review. Still, because many of its principles are common to many ANN unsupervised learning systems, this section will focus upon behavioral applications of the Knapp and Anderson (1984) model.

One classic model of human memory is the *prototype* model, which assumes that associated with the ith category is a d-dimensional prototype vector, $\mathbf{y}_i$. The prototype model also assumes that some bowl-shaped unimodal (convex) distance measure $V(\cdot, \mathbf{y}_i): S \rightarrow \mathscr{R}$ exists that obtains its minimum value at $\mathbf{y}_i$. The domain, S, of the function V is some subset of $\mathscr{R}^d$. The prototype model assumes that a stimulus vector $\mathbf{s}$ is classified as belonging to category $\mathbf{y}_i$ if $V(\mathbf{s}, \mathbf{y}_i) \leq V(\mathbf{s}, \mathbf{y}_j)$ for $j = 1 \ldots M$, where M is the number of categories. The function V can be assigned the psychological interpretation of a *similarity measure*. In particular, if $\mathbf{s}$ is more *similar* to $\mathbf{y}_i$ than $\mathbf{x}$, then $V(\mathbf{s}, \mathbf{y}_i) < V(\mathbf{x}, \mathbf{y}_i)$.

Posner and Keele (1968) generated a set of prototype vectors representing different visual displays of dot patterns. Next, they generated distortions of the original set of prototype dot patterns. Subjects were then presented the distortions of the original dot patterns and asked to classify the dot patterns into one of several categories. After each dot pattern was classified, feedback was provided to each subject indicating whether the subject's response was correct. In the second phase of the experiment, subjects were asked to classify the dot patterns in the first part of the experiment as well as novel dot patterns they had never seen before. Posner and Keele found that dot patterns more similar in structure to the original prototype dot patterns were classified more efficiently than highly distorted dot patterns. In fact, they found that prototype dot patterns were classified as efficiently as previously seen dot patterns even though the prototype dot patterns had never been presented in the first phase of the experiment. These findings provide evidence supporting the prototype theory of category classification.

An alternative model of human memory is the *exemplar* model, which states that a category in human memory is represented, not by a typical category member, but rather by a very large number of specific exemplars of that category. The definition of an exemplar model can be defined in terms of a similarity measure in a manner analogous to the definition of the prototype model. Let the exemplars of the ith category be defined by the set of n_i d-dimensional vectors: $E^i = \{\mathbf{e}^i_1, \mathbf{e}^i_2, \ldots, \mathbf{e}^i_{n_i}\}$. The exemplar model assumes that some similarity measure

$$V\left(\cdot, \mathbf{e}^i_1, \mathbf{e}^i_2, \ldots, \mathbf{e}^i_{n_i}\right): S \rightarrow \mathscr{R}$$

exists that obtains its minimum value for *any* member of the set E^i. As before S is a subset of $\mathscr{R}^d$. The exemplar model assumes that a stimulus vector $\mathbf{s}$ is classified as belonging to category i if

$$V\left(\mathbf{s}, \mathbf{e}_1^i, \mathbf{e}_2^i, \ldots, \mathbf{e}_{n_i}^i\right) \leq V\left(\mathbf{s}, \mathbf{e}_1^j, \mathbf{e}_2^j, \ldots, \mathbf{e}_{n_j}^j\right)$$

for $j = 1 \ldots M$, where M is the number of categories.

The exemplar model is more general than the prototype model in the sense that if the exemplars for each category are tightly clustered about each category prototype, then the exemplar model may make essentially the same predictions as the prototype model. Medin and Schaffer (1978) devised stimulus sets where the exemplars for each category were not tightly clustered about each category prototype. Then, using a memory retrieval task, they found that the predictions made by the exemplar theory were more consistent with the human subject data than predictions made by the prototype theory.

In an attempt to obtain additional insights into the relationships between the prototype and exemplar models in the context of learning, Knapp and Anderson (1984) proposed a simple extension of the Anderson (1972) model as a possible explanation. In the Knapp and Anderson (1984) model, each dot pattern stimulus categorized by the subjects was modeled as a two-dimensional activation pattern. In particular, each dot in a dot pattern stimulus resulted in a "bump" in the stimulus activation pattern as shown in figure 1.11. The shape of the bump generated by a dot pattern stimulus with M dots was determined by the formula

$$x_{ij} = \sum_{k=1}^{M} \exp[-r_k(x_{ij})/\lambda],$$

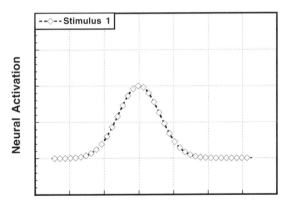

Neuron Unit Location on "Visual Cortex"

Figure 1.11
Neural activation "bump" in visual cortex. Example is due to the presence of a point light stimulus, as proposed by Knapp and Anderson (1984). In their original model, the "bump" is actually three-dimensional rather than two-dimensional because neuron location is specified by a two-dimensional vector. Adapted from Figure 3 of Knapp and Anderson (1984), *Journal of Experimental Psychology : Learning, Memory, and Cognition, 10,* 616–637. © 1984 by the American Psychological Association. Adapted with permission.

where x_{ij} is the activation level of a particular point in the two-dimensional activation pattern, and $r_k(x_{ij})$ is the distance of x_{ij} from the origin of the kth dot in the dot pattern stimulus. The strictly positive real number λ is a free parameter, called the "length constant" (small λ results in highly focused neural activity, while large λ causes a single dot to evoke a wide spatial distribution of neural activity).

Each two-dimensional stimulus activation pattern associated with a particular category was then "stored in memory" by adding all such stimulus patterns together in order to construct a composite memory trace. Thus a composite memory trace was formed for each category. New stimuli were categorized by computing a special *stimulus familiarity dot product* (actually a type of integral in this continuous case) between the composite two-dimensional memory trace and the novel two-dimensional stimulus activation pattern. The category associated with the composite memory trace whose dot product with the stimulus was maximal is then identified as the category used by the model to classify the stimulus.

Note that the addition of stimulus patterns in memory can be viewed as resulting from a simple learning rule where a connection strength weight is strengthened or weakened entirely on the basis of presynaptic activity. Thus no "teacher error signal" associated with a postsynaptic activity level is required. Also note that the integral dot product operation is equivalent to the response of a type of linear model neuron that computes a weighted sum (integral) of incoming input signals, where the weights correspond to elements in the composite memory trace and the input signals correspond to elements in the stimulus activation pattern.

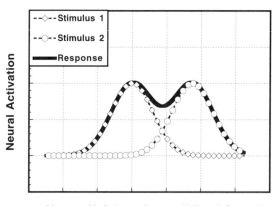

Neuron Unit Location on "Visual Cortex"

Figure 1.12
Two separated activation "bumps" in visual cortex. Because the two bumps of activation are widely separated, each can be stored and retrieved without interference. This illustrates the property of the Knapp and Anderson (1984) model that a few visually dissimilar stimuli will provide the model with "exemplar" model response properties. Adapted from Figure 5 of Knapp and Anderson (1984), *Journal of Experimental Psychology : Learning, Memory, and Cognition*, *10*, 616–637. © 1984 by the American Psychological Association. Adapted with permission.

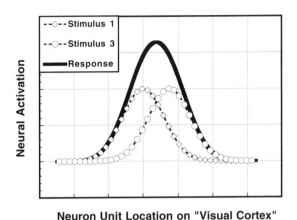

Neuron Unit Location on "Visual Cortex"

Figure 1.13
Two neighboring activation "bumps" in visual cortex. Because the two bumps of activation are close together, there is considerable interference. The model stores the resulting activation pattern, which is a "prototype" (dashed line) formed from adding the original two activation bumps together. This illustrates the property of the Knapp and Anderson (1984) model that many visually similar stimuli will provide the model with prototype response properties. Adapted from Figure 5 of Knapp and Anderson (1984), *Journal of Experimental Psychology : Learning, Memory, and Cognition, 10,* 616–637. © 1984 by the American Psychological Association. Adapted with permission.

Knapp and Anderson (1984) noted that the additive composite memory trace model of human classification and learning has characteristics of an exemplar model when the category contains a small number of dissimilar exemplars. Because in this case the cortical activation bumps will tend to be spread relatively far apart, the composite additive stored memory trace will tend to respond strongly to activity located at the locations of the original exemplar-generated memory trace bumps (figure 1.12). In addition, the composite memory trace model has characteristics of a prototype model when the category contains a large number of similar exemplars. In this case, the cortical activation bumps will tend to be located close to one another, and thus the composite additive stored memory trace will tend to respond strongly to activity located in a cortical area which is equally distant from the locations of the original activation bumps (figure 1.13).

Knapp and Anderson then compared the performance of their ANN model with human performance in a series of dot pattern classification experiments. In their experiment, subjects were presented with a series of dot patterns and asked to assign each dot pattern to one of three categories. After each classification subjects were provided feedback about their decision. After this "learning" phase of the experiment, subjects were asked to classify an additional set of dot patterns but were not provided feedback during this latter "testing" phase. Figure 1.14 shows experimental data collected from human subjects during the testing phase. In figure 1.14 the proportion of correctly classified dot patterns for each type of stimulus, prototype (P), old exemplar seen in both

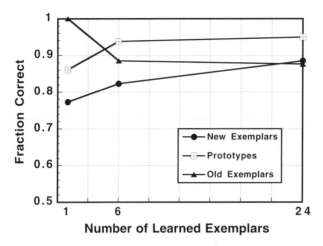

Figure 1.14
Fraction of items recalled as function of stimulus condition for human subjects. Adapted from Figure 8 of Knapp and Anderson (1984), *Journal of Experimental Psychology : Learning, Memory, and Cognition, 10*, 616–637. © 1984 by the American Psychological Association. Adapted with permission.

phases of the experiment (O), and new exemplar seen only in the second phase of the experiment (N), is plotted as a function of the number of exemplars in each category.

Figure 1.15 shows simulation data obtained from the Knapp and Anderson (1984) model using the best-fitting length constant ($\lambda = 11.3$). The integral dot product measure of familiarity between a given stimulus vector and the composite memory trace was assumed to be related through some monotonic transformation to human subject percentage correct responses. Note the qualitative similarities between figure 1.14 and figure 1.15. In both the human data and the simulation model data, the familiarity of the prototype dot pattern (relative to other category members) tends to increase as the number of category members increases. In addition, the familiarity advantage of previously seen exemplars relative to novel category exemplars tends to decrease as the number of category members increases. Such findings are consistent with the hypothesis that, like human memory, the Knapp and Anderson (1984) ANN memory system has exemplar model characteristics for categories with few exemplars and prototype model characteristics for categories with many exemplars.

1.3.3   Computing Applications: Computational Level

Computer scientists and engineers use ANN systems to develop new algorithms for attacking difficult computational problems. Engineers are happy to consider algorithms with either neurophysiological or behavioral motivations, but their ultimate criterion for evaluation is performance. An engineer would be quite interested in a nonbiologically or nonbehaviorally plausible ANN system capable of

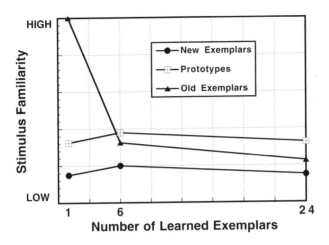

Figure 1.15
Stimulus familiarity as function of stimulus condition for simulation model. The stimulus familiarity measure in the Knapp-Anderson (1984) model is a special dot product measure for measuring the similarity between two neural activation patterns, and is assumed to be related via some monotonic transformation to the fraction of items recalled by human subjects. The simulation results in this figure should be compared with the human data shown in figure 1.14. Adapted from Figure 10 of Knapp and Anderson (1984), *Journal of Experimental Psychology : Learning, Memory, and Cognition, 10*, 616–637. © 1984 by the American Psychological Association. Adapted with permission.

solving difficult engineering problems. An important theme of this textbook is that many ANN systems can be naturally viewed as specific special cases of traditional areas of engineering system analysis and design. In fact, many algorithms have been proposed and developed within the engineering literature that could quite appropriately be classified as ANN systems according to the criteria previously proposed in this chapter. A short, illustrative, but certainly not comprehensive, list of such examples includes both past and present research in the areas of Markov random fields (Chellappa and Jain 1993; Cohen and Cooper 1987; Geman and Geman 1984; Marroquin 1985), linear and nonlinear adaptive filtering (Sibul 1987; Widrow and Hoff 1960; Widrow and Stearns 1985), optimal filtering (Anderson and Moore 1979), linear systems theory (Luenberger 1979), control theory (Bellman 1971), nonlinear optimization theory (Kushner and Clark 1978; Luenberger 1984), linear and nonlinear dynamical systems theory (Vidyasagar 1978; LaSalle 1976; Luenberger 1979), statistical pattern recognition (Duda and Hart 1973; Patrick 1972), and linear (Montgomery and Peck 1982) and nonlinear regression analysis (Bates and Watts 1988). Even though some algorithms in these areas *are* ANN systems according to the criteria presented earlier in this chapter, engineers and computer scientists do not (and should not) feel obligated to refer to such algorithms as ANN systems. Nevertheless, it is crucial that the relationship between known ANN systems and the existing engineering literature be recognized so that ANN systems can be evaluated and compared to known algorithms in a rational and systematic manner.

Finally, it should be emphasized that many of the algorithms in the ANN field are unique and have not been previously proposed by researchers in other fields. For the most part, the reason for this unique perspective is that ANN system algorithms tend to be motivated from either behavioral or neural modeling considerations, with little or no concern for mathematical tractability. Still, a wide variety of ANN system algorithms have proven to be useful in solving a range of interesting and practical engineering problems. To illustrate the success of ANN system algorithms in addressing engineering problems, some representative applications of ANN systems are briefly discussed.

Computing Applications of ANN Classification Dynamical Systems

Geman and Geman (1984) proposed and investigated the convergence properties of a class of stochastic optimization algorithms they refer to as "Gibbs sampler algorithms." The Gibbs sampler algorithm can be viewed as a good example of a stochastic ANN classification dynamical system as follows. Consider a group of d units where the activity level of each unit is constrained to take on exactly one of M distinct values. For the case of image processing, each unit typically corresponds to a pixel in the image and the activity level of a unit is the value of that pixel. To introduce the Gibbs sampler algorithm, let us review an important special case of the Gibbs sampler algorithm known as the "Boltzmann machine neural network model" (Ackley, Hinton, and Sejnowski 1985; also see Smolensky's 1986 "harmony theory," which is an important special case of the Boltzmann machine neural network).

Let $x_1(t), \ldots, x_d(t)$ be the activation levels of a set of d units at time t, where $x_i(t) \in \{0, 1\}$ for $i = 1 \ldots d$. Let $\mathcal{S}: \mathfrak{R} \rightarrow (0, 1)$ be a sigmoidal function defined such that

$$\mathcal{S}(\varphi) = 1/(1 + \exp[-\varphi])$$

for all $\varphi \in \mathfrak{R}$. Let the conditional probability that the activation level of unit i takes on the value of one at algorithm iteration t, given the activation levels of the other $(d-1)$ units in the network,

$$p_{i,t} = \mathcal{S}\left[\frac{\sum_{j=1}^{d} w_{ij} x_j(t)}{\tau_t}\right],$$

where w_{ij} is the ijth element of a d-dimensional real symmetric matrix, $\mathbf{W}$, whose on-diagonal elements are equal to zero. Note that the conditional probability that the activation level of unit i takes on the value of zero at algorithm iteration t, given the activation levels of the other $(d-1)$ units in the network, is $(1 - p_{i,t})$.

The particular parametric form of each unit's conditional probability distribution (indexed by the value of the connection strength matrix $\mathbf{W}$) is chosen in advance based upon prior knowledge of the local structural relations in the image. The Gibbs sampler algorithm works by picking a unit in the network at random. Suppose the ith unit is chosen. The activation level of the ith unit at iteration t of the algorithm is then chosen to be equal to one with probability $p_{i,t}$, and to be equal to 0 with probability $(1 - p_{i,t})$. The strictly positive *temperature parameter*, τ_t, is then decreased according to the annealing schedule, and then another unit is chosen at random to be updated.

The sequence of positive real numbers $\tau_1, \tau_2, \tau_3, \ldots$ is called the "annealing schedule" for the Boltzmann machine. The annealing schedule for the Boltzmann machine (and Gibbs sampler) is usually chosen such that for $t = 1, 2, \ldots,$

$$\tau_t = \frac{C}{1 + \log [t]},$$

where C is some very large positive real number (see discussions in chapter 2 and chapter 5 for a more detailed discussion of the annealing schedule for Gibbs sampler algorithms). It is important to note that if t is small (i.e., τ_t is large), then $p_{i,t} \approx 0.5$ and $1 - p_{i,t} \approx 0.5$ regardless of the activation levels of the other units in the network. On the other hand, if t is large (i.e., τ_t is small), then the Boltzmann machine's behavior is approximately equivalent to the behavior of a special type of *deterministic* ANN classification dynamical system, the Hopfield (1982) model (see chapter 2 and chapter 5 for further discussion).

Some very important special cases of the Gibbs sampler algorithm in the ANN system literature include the Boltzmann machine (Ackley, Hinton, and Sejnowski 1985) and harmony theory (Smolensky 1986). The performance of the Gibbs sampler is illustrated in figure 1.16, figure 1.17, and figure 1.18. Figure 1.16 shows the original image and figure 1.17 shows the image corrupted with noise. After 1,000 iterations, the algorithm manages to successfully "clean up" the corrupted image as shown in figure 1.18.

A deterministic version of the Gibbs Sampler algorithm known as the "iterated conditional modes" (ICM) algorithm was proposed by Besag (1986). The ICM algorithm is a generalization of the Hopfield (1982) algorithm (see chapter 2 for a detailed description of the Hopfield 1982 algorithm) where the units in the network can take on more than two activation levels and the activation updating rule does not have to be quasi-linear. The ICM algorithm is also closely related to the Hopfield (1984), Cohen-Grossberg (1983) ANN system algorithm, and the brain-state-in-a-box algorithm (Anderson et al. 1977; Golden 1986a). Although such deterministic classification dynamical ANN systems will converge much more rapidly, the quality of the solutions obtained using deterministic algorithms is usually (but not always) inferior to their stochastic counterparts.

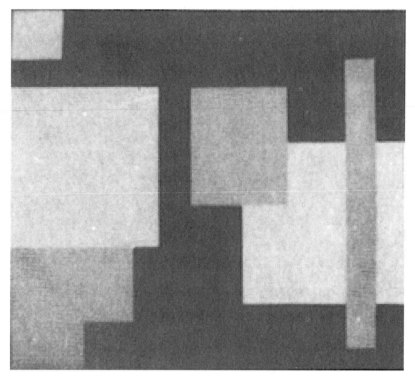

Figure 1.16
"Hand-drawn" image before processing by Gibbs sampler algorithm. A large array of pixels where each pixel is identified by a specific gray level. The image depicted in the pixel array was "hand-drawn." Adapted from Figure 6(a) of Geman and Geman (1984), Stochastic relaxation, Gibbs distributions, and the Bayesian restoration of images, *IEEE Transactions on Pattern Analysis and Machine Intelligence*, PAMI-6: 721–741. © 1984 IEEE. Adapted with permission.

ANN classification dynamical systems such as the stochastic Gibbs sampler algorithm, the ICM algorithm, and the Hopfield (1984) algorithm have been applied to solving local depth reconstruction problems in image processing (Clifford and Nasrabadi 1988), image segmentation (Chou et al. 1993; Cohen and Cooper 1987; Hainsworth and Mardia 1993; Jain and Nadabar 1993; Menon and Wells 1990), image labeling (Chou et al. 1993; Jamison and Schalkoff 1988), image estimation (Rangarajan and Chellappa 1993), as well as scheduling tasks (Poliac et al. 1987), and optimizing electronic wiring layout schemes (Kirkpatrick, Gelatt, and Vecchi 1983; Lu and Thomborson 1991).

Computing Applications of ANN Supervised Learning Systems

There are many types of ANN supervised learning systems (e.g., the Carpenter, Grossberg, and Reynolds, 1991 ARTMAP learning system) besides the Widrow-Hoff (1960) learning rule and the backpropagation learning rule. In this brief

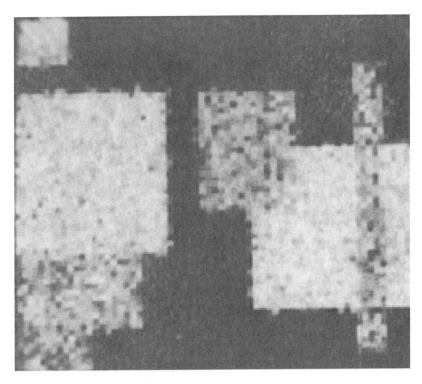

Figure 1.17
"Hand-drawn" image corrupted with noise before processing by Gibbs sampler algorithm. Obtained by corrupting with noise the image in figure 1.16. Adapted from Figure 6(b) of Geman and Geman (1984), Stochastic relaxation, Gibbs distributions, and the Bayesian restoration of images, *IEEE Transactions on Pattern Analysis and Machine Intelligence*, PAMI-6: 721–741. © 1984 IEEE. Adapted with permission.

review, however, only the Widrow-Hoff learning rule and the backpropagation learning rule are discussed because these two learning algorithms are already widely used in the engineering literature.

Widrow-Hoff learning rule.   The classical Widrow-Hoff learning rule expressed in (1.4) (Bitmead 1983; Daniell 1970; Macchi and Eweda 1983; Widrow and Hoff 1960; Widrow et al. 1975; Widrow and Stearns 1985) was one of the earliest ANN *supervised learning* systems proposed for solving linear adaptive prediction and control problems. Widrow and Stearns 1985 (also see Sibul 1987; Alexander 1986; Widrow et al. 1975) reviews many of the most important engineering applications of this learning rule. The Widrow-Hoff learning rule has been applied to engineering problems such as canceling periodic interference of broadband signals (e.g., "hum" cancellation on telephone lines), identifying the characteristics of multipath communication channels, eliminating sidelobe antenna interference, developing notch filters, and echo cancellation.

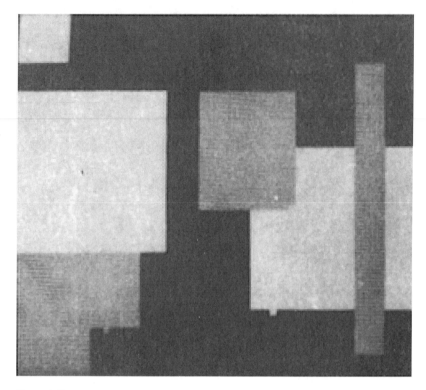

Figure 1.18
Reconstruction of "hand-drawn" image corrupted with noise by Gibbs sampler algorithm. Obtained through application of 1,000 iterations of the Gibbs sampler algorithm to the image in figure 1.17. Compare Figure 1.16 with the image in this figure. Adapted from Figure 6(c) of Geman and Geman (1984), Stochastic relaxation, Gibbs distributions, and the Bayesian restoration of images, *IEEE Transactions on Pattern Analysis and Machine Intelligence*, PAMI-6: 721–741. © 1984 IEEE. Adapted with permission.

Backpropagation learning rule.   The backpropagation learning rule described in section 1.3.1 (Chauvin and Rumelhart 1995; Rumelhart, Hinton, and Williams 1986) is another very popular ANN supervised learning algorithm. Like the Widrow-Hoff learning rule, the backpropagation learning rule may be used in a supervised learning mode. As previously noted in section 1.3.1, the backpropagation learning rule allows for the supervised learning of multilayered ANN systems. If the hidden nodes (intermediate level nodes) are nonlinear and a sufficient number of such nodes are present in the network, arbitrary nonlinear input to output mappings can be represented and thus potentially learned (Cybenko 1989; Funahashi 1989; Hecht-Nielsen 1989; Hornik, Stinchcombe, and White 1989; Stinchcombe and White 1989).

The backpropagation learning algorithm has been applied to problems in the areas of speech perception (Waibel 1989; Waibel et al. 1989; Waibel, Sawai, and Shikano 1989; Yuhas et al. 1990), image processing (Hwang and Tseng

1993; LeCun et al. 1990a,b; Lisa et al. 1993), signal processing and communication systems (Bas and Marks 1991; Lo and Hafez 1992; Mitra and Poor 1993), financial prediction (Refenes, Azema-Barac, and Zapranis 1993), medical prediction and diagnosis (Hu, Tompkins, and Xue 1992; Niederberger, Pursell, and Golden 1996), control theory applications (Elsley 1990; Jordan 1992; Plumer 1993; Schley et al. 1991; Tesauro 1990), predicting and classifying biological structures (Errington and Graham 1993; Qian and Sejnowski 1988), and predicting impact damage to automotive paint finishes (Ramamurthy and Uriquidi-Macdonald 1993).

Computing Applications of ANN Unsupervised Learning Systems

Biological applications of ANN unsupervised learning systems designed to model the development and organization of topographic maps in cortex were discussed in section 1.3.1. From a computational perspective, such unsupervised learning systems (1) learn to detect familiar activation patterns in the presence of noise (usually by preserving the direction of the activation pattern vector and increasing the magnitude), (2) acquire new feature detection units whose activity levels increase when a familiar pattern is presented (the acquisition of such units can be viewed as equivalent to acquiring an orthonormal set of basis functions for representing a given stimulus), and (3) learn to reconstruct *any* missing region of some novel stimulus activation pattern corrupted by noise. Various types of ANN self-organizing learning systems and ANN unsupervised learning systems have been applied to problems in the areas of image processing (Ahalt, Chen, and Krishnamurthy 1989; Dhawan and Arata 1993; O'Toole et al. 1993; Manikopoulos, Anoniou, and Metzelopoulo 1990; Thacore et al. 1991), speech processing (Kohonen 1990) and classification of phonocardiograms (Tansel et al. 1991). Unsupervised learning algorithms are especially well suited for estimating parameters (i.e., learning connection strengths) of ANN classification dynamical systems such as the Hopfield (1984) model or the Gibbs sampler (Geman and Geman 1984).

1.4   Formal Definition of ANN Systems

In this section the concept of an artificial neural network (ANN) will be formally defined. Such a definition of an ANN system will provide an explicit language and theoretical framework for discussing extremely large classes of ANN systems. The strategy for developing a formal general definition of an ANN system is as follows.

First, a theoretical model of a physical environment, an *event environment,* will be defined. Second, a theoretical model of a physical system operating in an event environment, a *dynamical system,* will be defined. The first two definitions are derived from research in the field of dynamical systems theory. In particular, the definitions of an event environment and a dynamical system are based upon the approach of Kalman, Falb, and Arbib (1969, 3–13). An artificial neural network (ANN) is then formally defined as a theoretical model of a physical system existing in some physical environment (i.e., an ANN is defined as a type of dynamical system).

The following presentation of ANN systems is relatively abstract. Readers desiring a more concrete introduction to ANN systems may choose to read chapter 2 before reading this section. The function notation $G: A \times B \rightarrow C$ used in this section and throughout is a standard mathematical notation (Rosenlicht 1968, 8). In particular, $G: A \times B \rightarrow C$ refers to a function called G with two arguments. The first argument of G is an element of the set A, while the second argument of G is an element of the set B. The range of the function G is the set C.

1.4.1   Models of Physical Environments

An event environment is a theoretical model of an environment. Particular sequences and subsequences of events are formally represented as event history functions that map a given time index into a specific event object. The concept of an event environment is now formally defined.

Definition: Event history function.   Let $T \subseteq \Re$ be a set of *time indices* and let Ω_E be a set of *events*. Let $[t_0, t_f) \subseteq T$ where the *initial time*, t_0, and the *final time*, t_f, are related such that $t_0 < t_f$. Then $u: [t_0, t_f) \rightarrow \Omega_E$ is an *event history function* with respect to T and Ω_E.

Note that if T is the set of positive integers, then an event history function maps the set T into an ordered sequence of events. The more general concept of an event history function permits the consideration of models of physical environments where time is a continuous as opposed to a discrete quantity.

Definition: Event environment.   Let $T \subseteq \Re$ be a set of *time indices*. Let Ω_E be a set of *events*. An *event environment generated from T and Ω_E* is a subset, E, of the set of all event history functions that map subsets of T to Ω_E.

1.4.2   Models of Physical Systems

A *dynamical system* is a theoretical model of a physical system where the current *system state* and environmental inputs determine successive states of the physical system. The system state of a dynamical system is a list of *state variables*, which may or may not be directly observable. The concept of a dynamical system is now formally defined.

Definition: Dynamical system.   Let $T \subseteq \Re$ be a set of *time indices*. Let $\Omega \subseteq \Re^d$ be a set of *system states*. Let E be an event environment generated from T and Ω_E, where Ω_E is a set of *stimulus events*. A *dynamical system* is a function

$$\Psi: \Omega \times T \times T \times E \rightarrow \Omega$$

such that the *final state* $\mathbf{x}_f = \Psi(\mathbf{x}_0, t_0, t_f, \eta)$ observed at some *final time, t_f*, is determined by an *initial state*, $\mathbf{x}_0$, which occurs at some *initial time*, t_0, and a particular history of events defined by the event history function

$$(\eta: [t_0, t_f) \rightarrow \Omega_E) \in E$$

and where Ψ has, in addition, the following two properties.

- *Property 1:* Consistent assignment of system states to time indices. For all $t_0 \in T$, for all $\mathbf{x}_0 \in \Omega$, and for all $\eta \in E$:

$$\Psi(\mathbf{x}_0, t_0, t_0, \eta) = \mathbf{x}_0.$$

- *Property 2:* Consistent composition of dynamics. For all $\mathbf{x}_a \in \Omega$, and $t_a, t_b, t_c \in T$ such that $t_a < t_b < t_c$:

$$\Psi(\Psi(\mathbf{x}_a, t_a, t_b, \eta_a), t_b, t_c, \eta_b) = \Psi(\mathbf{x}_a, t_a, t_c, \eta_c),$$

where $(\eta_a: [t_a, t_b) \rightarrow \Omega_E) \in E$, $(\eta_b: [t_b, t_c) \rightarrow \Omega_E) \in E$, and where $\eta_c(\cdot) = \eta_a(\cdot)$ on $[t_a, t_b)$ and $\eta_c(\cdot) = \eta_b(\cdot)$ on $[t_b, t_c)$.

Note that property 1 of a dynamical system Ψ constrains the dynamical system to map the current system state into itself when the initial time and final time are identical. Property 2 of a dynamical system Ψ states that the current system state uniquely determines the future behavior of the dynamical system.

The next definition introduces the concept that a dynamical system must have some type of semantic representation which assigns meaning to sequences of system states.

Definition: Interpretation function.   Let $T \subseteq \mathcal{R}$ be a set of *time indices*. Let Ω_I be a set of *interpretations*. Let Ω be a set of system states. The domain of an interpretation function, D_I, is a set of event history functions defined such that

$$D_I = \{(u: [t_0, t_f) \rightarrow \Omega): t_0, t_f \in T\}.$$

An *interpretation function*, $\mathcal{I}$, is a function defined with respect to T and Ω such that $\mathcal{I}: D_I \rightarrow \Omega_I$.

Definition: Interpretable dynamical system.   An *interpretable dynamical system* is an ordered pair $(\Psi, \mathcal{I})$, where

$$\Psi: \Omega \times T \times T \times E \rightarrow \Omega$$

is a dynamical system, and $\mathcal{I}: D_I \rightarrow \Omega_I$ is an interpretation function whose domain, D_I, is defined with respect to T and Ω.

Thus the interpretation function is used to map sequences and subsequences of system states generated by the dynamical system into a set of *interpretations*. For example, some ANN systems can be viewed as physical systems that map their inputs into specific types of oscillatory cycles. Different oscillatory cycles (sequences of system states), in turn, might correspond to different neural or cognitive categories (elements of the set of interpretations). It is important to realize that the interpretation function is simply a convenient device for classifying the system's behaviors. The interpretation function is not necessarily a component of the physical system.

A dynamical system that is not part of an interpretable dynamical system is simply a function $\Psi: \Omega \times T \times T \times E \rightarrow \Omega$ and therefore not a model of a physical system. The mathematics of dynamical systems theory is concerned with understanding characteristics of Ψ. The mathematical modeler must always construct an interpretation function for a given dynamical system in order for that dynamical system to be a mathematical model of some aspect of the physical world.

1.4.3   ANN Dynamical Systems

The concept of an ANN dynamical system is defined for the purposes of formally discussing a very large class of algorithms commonly referred to as "artificial neural networks." Provided with a formal definition of an ANN dynamical system, the ANN engineer will more readily appreciate the wide range of options currently available for analyzing and designing ANN systems and will be able to more effectively select the appropriate ANN system architecture for a given task domain.

An ANN dynamical system is a special case of a dynamical system. The system state of an ANN dynamical system is partitioned into three subsets: (1) the *hidden memory state activation pattern*, (2) the *output response activation pattern*, (3) and the *connection strength parameter vector*. The hidden memory state activation pattern is a representation of the *recent past history* of the ANN dynamical system. The connection strength parameter vector is a set of parameters that in conjunction with the ANN system architecture specify the knowledge base (i.e., long-term memory) of the ANN system. Learning is thus the process in which the connection strength parameter vector is updated.

The environment of an ANN dynamical system is also partitioned into two event environments. The first event environment, E_s, is used to specify the sequence of inputs to the ANN system. The second event environment, E_o, is used to specify a sequence of feedback signals provided by the environment to the ANN which influence the behavior of the ANN's learning dynamics. Figure 1.19 illustrates the concept of an ANN dynamical system which is formalized in the following definition (the student may find it helpful to refer to figure 1.19).

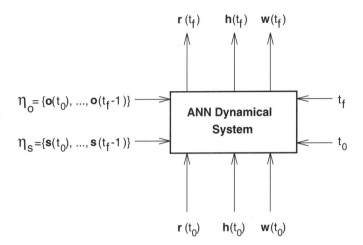

Figure 1.19
Discrete-time ANN dynamical system. The set of time indices, T, is the set of nonnegative integers; the behavior of the system is shown for initial time, $t_0 = 0$, and final time, $t_f \in T$. The ANN dynamical system takes as input (1) a sequence of input stimulus events $\eta_s = \{\mathbf{s}(t_0),\ldots, \mathbf{s}(t_f - 1)\} \in E$ on $[t_0, t_f)$; (2) a sequence of response feedback activation patterns $\eta_0 = \{\mathbf{o}(t_0),\ldots, \mathbf{o}(t_f - 1)\} \in E$ on $[t_0, t_f)$ (e.g., a sequence of desired response vectors in certain types of learning algorithms); (3) the current response activation pattern $\mathbf{r}(t_0) \in \Omega_R$; (4) the current hidden memory state $\mathbf{h}(t_0) \in \Omega_H$; and (5) current connection strength parameter vector $\mathbf{w}(t_0) \in W$. The ANN dynamical system updates its response to obtain $\mathbf{r}(t_f) \in \Omega_R$, updates its hidden memory units to obtain $\mathbf{h}(t_f) \in \Omega_H$, and updates its connection strength parameter vector to obtain $\mathbf{w}(t_f) \in W$. Note that the process of constructing $\mathbf{w}(t_f)$ is typically defined as the *learning process*.

Definition: ANN dynamical system.   Let

- $\Omega_S \subseteq \mathcal{R}^k$ be a set of *input stimulus activation patterns*,

- $\Omega_H \subseteq \mathcal{R}^m$ be a set of *hidden memory state activation patterns*,

- $\Omega_R \subseteq \mathcal{R}^n$ be a set of *output response activation patterns*,

- $\Omega_O \subseteq \mathcal{R}^l$ be a set of *response feedback activation patterns*,

- $W \subseteq \mathcal{R}^q$ be a set of *connection strength parameter vectors*,

- $T \subseteq \mathcal{R}$ be a set of *time indices*,

- E_S be an event environment generated from Ω_S and T,

- and E_O be an event environment generated from Ω_O and T.

An *ANN dynamical system* is a dynamical system

$$\Psi: \Omega \times T \times T \times E \to \Omega,$$

where the set of *system states* $\Omega = \Omega_H \times \Omega_R \times W$ and the *environment* $E = E_S \times E_O$.

In all ANN applications, it is necessary to formally define an interpretable ANN dynamical system, which is simply an ANN dynamical system with an interpretation function. The interpretation function might be used to interpret the behavior of the ANN dynamical system as a particular set of oscillations of neural activity in a particular region of the brain. Or alternatively, the interpretation function might assign a semantic code such as visual color = red or sensation = warm to a particular sequence of system states.

Also note that the purpose of the hidden memory state activation pattern $\mathbf{h} \in \Omega_H$ is an additional memory containing information about the past sequence of system states that is not available in the connection strength parameter vector. The Jordan sequential network and Elman-style networks reviewed in chapter 2 are examples of ANN architectures where Ω_H is not empty. The following definition will help to further clarify the role of the hidden memory state activation pattern $\mathbf{h}$.

Definition: ANN temporal memory dynamical system.   Let $\Omega_H \subseteq \mathcal{R}^m$ be a set of hidden memory state unit activation patterns. Let $\Omega_R \subseteq \mathcal{R}^n$ be a set of output response unit activation patterns. Let $W \subseteq \mathcal{R}^q$ be a set of connection strength parameter vectors. Let

$$\Psi: \Omega \times T \times T \times E \to \Omega$$

be an ANN dynamical system, where $\Omega = \Omega_H \times \Omega_R \times W$. If the set Ω_H is not empty, then Ψ is an *ANN temporal memory dynamical system*.

Because the hidden memory state vector $\mathbf{h}$ is a set of state variables providing information about the past history of the ANN's environment that are independent of the connection strength parameter state vector, a temporal memory ANN dynamical system must thus be functionally dependent on $\mathbf{h}$.

Notice that the above definitions of an ANN dynamical system include ANN dynamical systems that are permitted to learn (i.e., update $\mathbf{w} \in W$) while the ANN dynamical system is classifying stimuli (i.e., generating $\mathbf{r} \in \Omega_R$). In most practical applications of ANN dynamical systems, it is assumed that the connection strength parameter vector $\mathbf{w}$ is constant while stimuli are classified. Almost all ANN dynamical systems considered in this textbook (and in the literature) satisfy this assumption in practice. The assumption that the classification dynamics and learning dynamics of an ANN dynamical system may be *uncoupled* is formally presented in the following definition.

Definition: Uncoupled ANN dynamical system.   Let $T_C \subseteq T_L \subseteq T$, where $T \subseteq \mathcal{R}$ is a set of time indices. Let $W \subseteq \mathcal{R}^q$. Let the set of *system states* $\Omega = \Omega_H \times \Omega_R \times W$ and the *environment* $E = E_S \times E_O$. Let the set of *classification dynamical system states* $\Omega_C = \Omega_H \times \Omega_R$. Let the set of *learning dynamical system states* $\Omega_L = \Omega_H \times W$, and the *learning environment* $E_L = E_S \times E_O$. An *uncoupled ANN dynamical system* on $\tau = [t_0, t_f) \subseteq T_c$ (where $t_f > t_0$) is an ANN dynamical system

$$\Psi: \Omega \times T \times T \times E \rightarrow \Omega,$$

which may be represented as a pair of dynamical systems (Ψ_C, Ψ_L) consisting of an *ANN classification dynamical system*

$$\Psi_C: \Omega_C \times T_C \times T_C \times E_S \times W \rightarrow \Omega_C$$

and an *ANN learning dynamical system*

$$\Psi_L: \Omega_L \times T_L \times T_L \times E_L \rightarrow \Omega_L,$$

such that for every $t \in \tau$:

$$\mathbf{w}_0 = \Psi_L(\mathbf{w}_0, t_0, t, (\eta_s, \eta_o))$$

for all ($\eta_o: [t_0, t) \rightarrow \Omega_O) \in E_O$ and for all ($\eta_s: [t_0, t) \rightarrow \Omega_S) \in E_S$.

Figure 1.20 and figure 1.21 illustrate the concept of an uncoupled ANN dynamical system. Almost all ANN systems in this textbook will be analyzed as uncoupled ANN dynamical systems (but see problem 3-10 for an example of an ANN dynamical system which is not uncoupled). In the special case where an ANN dynamical system's classification and learning dynamics are uncoupled, it is possible to analyze the classification dynamical system and ignore the learning dynamical system.

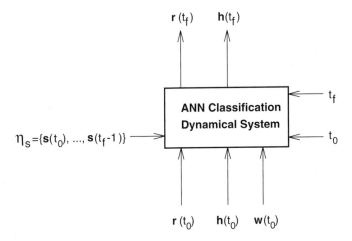

Figure 1.20
Discrete-time ANN classification dynamical system. The system is assumed to be defined on some closed interval, $\tau \subseteq T_C \subseteq T$, where the set of time indices, T, is the set of nonnegative integers and T_C is the set of time indices for the classification dynamical system; the behavior of the system is shown for initial time, $t_0 \in T$, and final time, $t_f \in T$, such that $t_0, t_f \in \tau$. The response of the ANN classification dynamical system, $\mathbf{r}(t_f) \in \Omega_R$, and hidden memory state, $\mathbf{h}(t_f) \in \Omega_H$, are functionally dependent upon the initial connection strength parameter (i.e., weight) vector $\mathbf{w}(t_0) \in W$, the input sequence of stimuli $\{\mathbf{s}(0),..., \mathbf{s}(t_f - 1)\} \in E_s$, and the hidden memory state $\mathbf{h}(t_0) \in \Omega_H$.

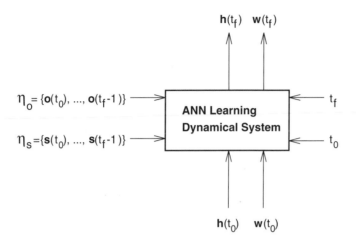

Figure 1.21
Discrete-time ANN learning dynamical system. The system is assumed to be defined on some
closed interval, $\tau \subseteq T_C \subseteq T$, where the set of time indices, T, is the set of nonnegative integers and
T_C is the set of time indices for the classification dynamical system illustrated in figure 1.20; the
behavior of the ANN learning dynamical system is shown for initial time, $t_0 \in T$, and final time,
$t_f \in T$, such that $t_0, t_f \in \tau$. The connection strength parameter (i.e., weight) vector, $\mathbf{w}(t_f) \in W$, and
hidden memory state, $\mathbf{h}(t_f) \in \Omega_H$, are functionally dependent upon the initial connection strength
parameter vector $\mathbf{w}(t_0) \in W$, the input sequence of stimuli $\{\mathbf{s}(0),...,\mathbf{s}(t_f-1)\} \in E_s$, the input sequence of response feedback stimuli $\{\mathbf{o}(0),...,\mathbf{o}(t_f-1)\} \in E_o$, and the hidden memory state
$\mathbf{h}(t_0) \in \Omega_H$.

The concepts of an ANN dynamical system and an uncoupled ANN dynamical system will now be used to formally characterize several important classes
of ANN dynamical systems.

Definition: ANN feedforward classification dynamical system.   Let Ω_H be
a set of hidden memory state activation patterns. Let Ω_R be a set of output response activation patterns. Let $\Omega_C = \Omega_H \times \Omega_R$ be a set of classification dynamical system states. An *ANN feedforward classification dynamical system* is
an ANN classification dynamical system

$$\Psi_C: \Omega_C \times T \times T \times E_S \times W \to \Omega_C,$$

which has the property that there exists a function $\Psi_C^*: T \times T \times E_S \times W \to \Omega_C$
such that

$$\Psi_C([\mathbf{h}, \mathbf{r}], t_0, t_f, \eta, \mathbf{w}) = \Psi_C^*(t_0, t_f, \eta, \mathbf{w})$$

for all $\mathbf{h} \in \Omega_H$, for all $\mathbf{r} \in \Omega_R$, for all $\mathbf{w} \in W$, for all $t_0, t_f \in T$, and for all
$\eta \in E_S$.

Thus a feedforward ANN classification dynamical system is an ANN classification dynamical system that is not functionally dependent upon the previous
hidden memory state, $\mathbf{h}(t_0)$, or the previous response state, $\mathbf{r}(t_0)$.

Definition: ANN supervised learning dynamical system.   Let (Ψ_C, Ψ_L) be an uncoupled ANN dynamical system defined with respect to a set of output response activation patterns, Ω_R, a set of response feedback activation patterns, Ω_O, and set of time indices, T. Let E_O be an event environment generated from Ω_O and T. Let $E_L = E_S \times E_O$ be a learning environment. The learning dynamical system

$$\Psi_L: \Omega_L \times T \times T \times E_L \rightarrow \Omega_L$$

is an *ANN supervised learning dynamical system* if $\Omega_O = \Omega_R$.

Thus an ANN supervised learning dynamical system is an ANN learning dynamical system where the response feedback sequence is a sequence of output response activation patterns that are elements of the set of states of the ANN classification dynamical system.

Definition: ANN unsupervised learning dynamical system.   Let E_S be an event environment generated from a set of input stimulus activation patterns, Ω_S, and a set of time indices, T. Let E_O be an event environment generated from a set of response feedback activation patterns Ω_R and T. Let $E_L = E_S \times E_O$ be a learning environment. A learning dynamical system

$$\Psi_L: \Omega_L \times T \times T \times E_L \rightarrow \Omega_L$$

is an *ANN unsupervised learning dynamical system* if there exists a function

$$\Psi_L^*: \Omega_L \times T \times T \times E_S \rightarrow \Omega_L$$

such that

$$\Psi_L(\cdot, \ \cdot, \ \cdot, \ (\eta_s, \eta_o)) = \Psi_L^*(\cdot, \ \cdot, \ \cdot, \ \eta_s)$$

for all $(\eta_s, \eta_o) \in E_L$.

Note that the key property of the definition of an ANN unsupervised learning dynamical system is that such a dynamical system is not functionally dependent upon feedback signals from the environment.

Definition: ANN reinforcement learning dynamical system.   Let (Ψ_C, Ψ_L) be an uncoupled ANN dynamical system defined with respect to a set of output response activation patterns $\Omega_R \subseteq \mathcal{R}^n$ and set of time indices, T. Let E_S be an event environment generated from a set of input stimulus activation patterns, Ω_S and T. Let E_R be an event environment generated from Ω_R and T. Let $E_L = E_S \times E_O$ be a learning environment, where E_O is generated from a set of response feedback activation patterns $\Omega_O \subseteq \mathcal{R}^l$ and T. The learning dynamical system

$$\Psi_L: \Omega_L \times T \times T \times E_L \rightarrow \Omega_L$$

is an *ANN reinforcement learning dynamical system* if

$$n > l > 0,$$

where n is the dimensionality of $\Omega_R \subseteq \mathcal{R}^n$ and l is the dimensionality of $\Omega_O \subseteq \mathcal{R}^l$. Moreover, if $l = 1$, $\mathbf{\Psi}_L$ is a *scalar reinforcement learning dynamical system.*

The reinforcement learning dynamical system definition captures the intuition that an ANN learning dynamical system that receives some indirect information about the desired response should be called a "reinforcement learning dynamical system."

1.5   Relevant Mathematical Concepts

This section reviews background mathematical concepts that will be used throughout this textbook. The reader may also want to refer to the "Mathematical Notation" tables located just before chapter 1.

1.5.1   Vector Magnitude: The Notation $|\mathbf{x}|$

Definition: Vector magnitude.   Let $\mathbf{x}$ be a real d-dimensional vector. The *magnitude* of the vector $\mathbf{x}$ is defined as $\sqrt{\mathbf{x}^T \mathbf{x}}$.

The notation $|\mathbf{x}|$ will always refer to the vector magnitude of a real d-dimensional vector $\mathbf{x}$ throughout this textbook.

1.5.2   Special Sets and Set Properties

Definition: Bounded set.   Let $\Omega \subseteq \mathcal{R}^d$. The set Ω is a *bounded set* if there exists a finite positive real number K such that $|\mathbf{x}| \leq K$ for all $\mathbf{x} \in \Omega$.

Geometrically, a bounded set in $\mathcal{R}^d$ is a set that is contained in some ball of finite radius.

Definition: Lower bound for a set.   Let $\Omega \subseteq \mathcal{R}$. Assume there exists a finite positive real number K such that $x \geq K$ for all $x \in \Omega$. The real number K is a *lower bound* for the set Ω. If Ω has a lower bound, then Ω is *bounded from below*.

The notation $a = \inf S$ means that a is the greatest lower bound for the set S. For example, if S has a smallest element, then $a = \inf S$ is the smallest element of S. The notation

$$\inf_{\mathbf{y} \in \mathcal{H}} |\mathbf{y}|$$

means $\inf \{ |\mathbf{y}| \in \mathcal{R} : \mathbf{y} \in \mathcal{H} \}$. Similarly, the concept of an *upper bound* for a set may be defined. The notation $a = \sup S$ means that a is the least upper bound of the set S.

Definition: δ-neighborhood.   Let $\mathcal{H} \subseteq \mathcal{R}^d$. *The δ-neighborhood, $N_{\mathcal{H}}$, of the set $\mathcal{H}$* is defined as

$$N_{\mathcal{H}} = \left\{ \mathbf{x} \in \mathcal{R}^d \colon \inf_{\mathbf{y} \in \mathcal{H}} \left| \mathbf{x} - \mathbf{y} \right| < \delta \right\},$$

where the strictly positive real number δ is the *size* of the δ-neighborhood. The *δ-neighborhood, $N_{\mathbf{x}}$, of a point* $\mathbf{x} \in \mathcal{H}$ is the δ-neighborhood of the set $\{\mathbf{x}\}$.

Figure 1.22 shows a geometric interpretation of the concept of the δ-neighborhood of a set.

Definition: Open set.   Let $\Omega \subseteq \mathcal{R}^d$. The set Ω is an *open set* in $\mathcal{R}^d$ if for every $\mathbf{x} \in \Omega$ there exists a δ-neighborhood of $\mathbf{x}$ that contains only elements of Ω.

For example, the set $(0, 1)$ is an example of an open set in $\mathcal{R}$, while $\mathcal{R}^d$ is an open set in $\mathcal{R}^d$. The set $[0, 1)$, however, is not an open set because a δ-neighborhood of 0 cannot be constructed which contains only elements of $[0, 1)$.

Definition: Closed set.   Let $\Omega \subseteq \mathcal{R}^d$. The set Ω is a *closed set* in $\mathcal{R}^d$ if the set of all points in $\mathcal{R}^d$ that are not in Ω is an open set.

The set $[0, 1]$ is an example of a closed set in $\mathcal{R}$. Also note that $\mathcal{R}^d$ is a closed set in $\mathcal{R}^d$. It is important to note that some sets are simultaneously neither open or closed. Thus the set $[0, 1)$ is not an open set in $\mathcal{R}$, and the set $[0, 1)$ is not a closed set in $\mathcal{R}$. Similarly, some sets may be simultaneously open and closed such as the set $\mathcal{R}^d$ in $\mathcal{R}^d$.

Definition: The closure of a set.   Let $\Omega \subseteq \mathcal{R}^d$. The *closure of the set Ω, $\overline{\Omega}$,* is a subset of $\mathcal{R}^d$ such that $\overline{\Omega}$ is the smallest closed set containing Ω.

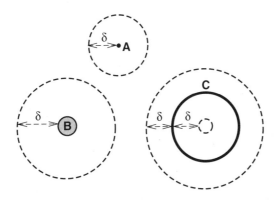

Figure 1.22
Illustrating concept of δ-neighborhood of set. Example A illustrates a δ-neighborhood of a point; example B illustrates a δ-neighborhood of a set of all points contained in some ball; and example C illustrates another type of δ-neighborhood of a set defined as the boundary of some ball.

Note that Ω is a closed set if and only if $\Omega = \overline{\Omega}$. Thus, if $\Omega = [0, 1)$, then the closure of Ω, $\overline{\Omega}$, would be given by the formula $\overline{\Omega} = [0, 1]$.

Definition: The boundary of a set.   Let $\Omega \subseteq \mathcal{R}^d$. The *boundary* of the set Ω is the intersection of the closure of Ω and the closure of the complement of Ω.

Thus the boundary for the set $[0, 3)$ would be $\{0, 3\}$. Geometrically, a closed set in $\mathcal{R}^d$ is a set which contains its boundary.

Definition: The interior of a set.   Let $\Omega \subseteq \mathcal{R}^d$. The *interior* of the set Ω is the intersection of the complement of the boundary of Ω and the closure of Ω.

Definition: Convex set.   Let $\Omega \subseteq \mathcal{R}^d$. If for every $\mathbf{x}, \mathbf{y} \in \Omega$ and for every $a \in (0, 1)$:

$$\mathbf{x}a + (1 - a)\mathbf{y} \in \Omega,$$

then Ω is a *convex set*.

Geometrically, a convex region is a subset, Ω, of $\mathcal{R}^d$ such that a line segment connecting any two points within Ω always remains entirely within Ω. Thus the δ-neighborhood of a point in $\mathcal{R}^d$ is always a convex set.

The concept of a subsequence is now introduced.

Definition: Subsequence.   If $a_1, a_2, a_3,\ldots$ is a sequence of real numbers (or random variables) and if $n_1, n_2, n_3,\ldots$ is a sequence of any positive integers such that $n_1 < n_2 < n_3 < \ldots$ then the sequence $a_{n_1}, a_{n_2}, a_{n_3},\ldots$ is a *subsequence* of $a_1, a_2, a_3,\ldots$.

Thus, given a sequence $1, 2, 4, 8, 16, 32, 64$ one of many possible subsequences of that sequence is $1, 4, 16, 32$.

1.5.3   Special Types of Functions

Definition: Bounded function.   Let $\Omega \subseteq \mathcal{R}^d$. A function $f: \Omega \to \mathcal{R}$ is *bounded* on Ω if there exists a finite positive real number K such that for all $\mathbf{x} \in \Omega$: $|f(\mathbf{x})| \leq K$.

A vector-valued function such as $\mathbf{f}: \mathcal{R}^d \to \mathcal{R}^c$ is a bounded function on Ω where $\Omega \subseteq \mathcal{R}^d$ if there exists a finite positive real number K such that for all $\mathbf{x} \in \Omega$: $|\mathbf{f}(\mathbf{x})| \leq K$.

Definition: Lower bound for a function.   Let $\Omega \subseteq \mathcal{R}^d$ and $f: \Omega \to \mathcal{R}$. Assume there exists a finite real number K such that $f(\mathbf{x}) \geq K$ for all $\mathbf{x} \in \Omega$. The real number K is a *lower bound* for f on Ω.

Definition: Continuous function.   Let $\Omega \subseteq \mathcal{R}^d$ and $f: \Omega \to \mathcal{R}$. The function f is *continuous at* $\mathbf{x} \in \Omega$ if given every strictly positive real number ε and an $\mathbf{x}$

in Ω, there exists a positive real number $\delta(\varepsilon, \mathbf{x})$ (possibly functionally dependent upon ε and $\mathbf{x}$) such that

$$\left| f(\mathbf{x}) - f(\mathbf{y}) \right| < \varepsilon$$

for all $\mathbf{y}$ in a $\delta(\varepsilon, \mathbf{x})$-neighborhood of $\mathbf{x}$. The function f is *continuous on* Ω if f is continuous at $\mathbf{x}$ for all $\mathbf{x} \in \Omega$.

A vector-valued function such as $\mathbf{f}: \mathcal{R}^d \to \mathcal{R}^c$ or a matrix-valued function such as $\mathbf{F}: \mathcal{R}^d \to \mathcal{R}^{d \times d}$ is continuous on some subset Ω where $\Omega \subseteq \mathcal{R}^d$ if the components of such functions (which are real-valued functions) are continuous on Ω.

Definition: Gradient. Let $\Omega \subseteq \mathcal{R}^d$ and $f: \Omega \to \mathcal{R}$. The *gradient of f on* Ω is a function $\mathbf{g}: \Omega \to \Omega$ (also denoted as $\nabla f: \Omega \to \Omega$) defined such that the ith element of $\mathbf{g}(\mathbf{x})$ is $\partial f / \partial x_i$ for all $\mathbf{x} = [x_1, \ldots, x_d] \in \Omega$ ($i = 1 \ldots d$). The *gradient of f evaluated at* $\mathbf{x}$ is the vector $\mathbf{g}(\mathbf{x})$ (also denoted as $\nabla_{\mathbf{x}} f$) where $\mathbf{x} \in \Omega$.

Definition: Hessian. Let $\Omega \subseteq \mathcal{R}^d$ and $f: \Omega \to \mathcal{R}$. The *Hessian of f on* Ω is a function $\mathbf{H}: \Omega \to \mathcal{R}^{d \times d}$ (also denoted as $\nabla^2 f: \Omega \to \mathcal{R}^{d \times d}$) defined such that the ijth element of $\mathbf{H}(\mathbf{x})$ is $\partial^2 f / \partial x_i \partial x_j$ for all $\mathbf{x} = [x_1, \ldots, x_d] \in \Omega$ ($i, j = 1 \ldots d$). The *Hessian of f evaluated at* $\mathbf{x}$ is the matrix $\mathbf{H}(\mathbf{x})$ (also denoted as $\nabla_{\mathbf{x}}^2 f$) where $\mathbf{x} \in \Omega$.

1.5.4   The Concept of "Approaching a Set"

The key concept of *approaching a set* is now introduced.

Definition: Approaching a set. Let $\Omega \subseteq \mathcal{R}^d$. Let $\mathcal{H}$ be a subset of Ω. Let $\mathbf{x}(\cdot): \mathcal{R} \to \Omega$. Then $\mathbf{x}(t)$ *approaches the set* $\mathcal{H}$ (i.e., $\mathbf{x}(t) \to \mathcal{H}$) as $t \to \infty$ if

$$\inf_{\mathbf{y} \in \mathcal{H}} \left| \mathbf{x}(t) - \mathbf{y} \right| \to 0$$

as $t \to \infty$.

For example, let $\mathcal{H} = \{-1, 1, 14\}$. If $x(t) \to 14$ as $t \to \infty$, then $x(t) \to \mathcal{H} = \{-1, 1, 14\}$ as $t \to \infty$. If $x(t) = [1 - (0.5)^t](-1)^t$ for $t = 0, 1, 2, \ldots$, then $x(t) \to \mathcal{H} = \{-1, 1, 14\}$ as $t \to \infty$. If $x(t) \to \{2, 14\}$ as $t \to \infty$, then $x(t)$ may or may not approach $\mathcal{H} = \{-1, 1, 14\}$ as $t \to \infty$. The terms *converges to the set* and *approaches the set* mean exactly the same thing.

1.5.5   Multivariable Taylor's Theorem

A particular multivariable version of Taylor's theorem that is also referred to as the "mean value theorem" is now introduced (for a review of this important theorem see, among other sources, Marlow 1978; Rosenlicht 1968; and Marsden and Tromba 1981).

Theorem: Multivariable Taylor's Theorem.   Let Ω be a convex open subset of $\mathscr{R}^d$. Let $\mathbf{x}^*$ be in the interior of Ω. Assume $V: \Omega \rightarrow \mathscr{R}$ is a function whose gradient and Hessian exist and are continuous on Ω. Let $\mathbf{g}: \Omega \rightarrow \mathscr{R}^d$ denote the gradient of V and $\mathbf{H}: \Omega \rightarrow \mathscr{R}^{d \times d}$ denote the Hessian of V. There exists a real number $\theta \in (0, 1)$ such that for all $\mathbf{x} \in \Omega$:

$$V(\mathbf{x}) = V(\mathbf{x}^*) + R_1, \tag{1.5}$$

where $R_1 = \mathbf{g}(\mathbf{c})^T [\mathbf{x} - \mathbf{x}^*]$ and $\mathbf{c} = \mathbf{x}^* + \theta(\mathbf{x} - \mathbf{x}^*)$.
In addition, there exists a real number $\theta \in (0, 1)$ such that for all $\mathbf{x} \in \Omega$:

$$V(\mathbf{x}) = V(\mathbf{x}^*) + \mathbf{g}(\mathbf{x}^*)^T [\mathbf{x} - \mathbf{x}^*] + R_2, \tag{1.6}$$

where

$$R_2 = (1/2)[\mathbf{x} - \mathbf{x}^*]^T \mathbf{H}(\mathbf{c})[\mathbf{x} - \mathbf{x}^*]$$

and

$$\mathbf{c} = \mathbf{x}^* + \theta(\mathbf{x} - \mathbf{x}^*).$$

In addition, suppose the third partial derivative of V exists and is continuous on Ω. Let

$$\frac{\partial^3 V}{\partial x_i \partial x_j \partial x_k}(\mathbf{q})$$

denote the third partial derivative of V with respect to x_i, x_j, and x_k, and then evaluated at $\mathbf{q} \in \Omega$. Let $\mathbf{x} = [x_1, \ldots, x_d]$ and $\mathbf{x}^* = [x_1^*, \ldots, x_d^*]$. There exists a real number $\theta \in (0, 1)$ such that for all $\mathbf{x} \in \Omega$:

$$V(\mathbf{x}) = V(\mathbf{x}^*) + \mathbf{g}(\mathbf{x}^*)^T [\mathbf{x} - \mathbf{x}^*] + \frac{[\mathbf{x} - \mathbf{x}^*]^T \mathbf{H}(\mathbf{x}^*)[\mathbf{x} - \mathbf{x}^*]}{2} + R_3, \tag{1.7}$$

where

$$R_3 = (1/6)\sum_{i=1}^{d}\sum_{j=1}^{d}\sum_{k=1}^{d} \frac{\partial^3 V}{\partial x_i \partial x_j \partial x_k}(\mathbf{c})(x_i - x_i^*)(x_j - x_j^*)(x_k - x_k^*)$$

and

$$\mathbf{c} = \mathbf{x}^* + \theta(\mathbf{x} - \mathbf{x}^*).$$

Proof.   See Rosenlicht (1968, 204).   ■

Equation (1.5) is the *zero-order* Taylor expansion of V with remainder term R_1; equation (1.6) is the *first-order* Taylor expansion of V with remainder term R_2; equation (1.7) is the *second-order* Taylor expansion of V with remainder term R_3. Finally note that the statement

$$\mathbf{c} = \mathbf{x}^* + \theta(\mathbf{x} - \mathbf{x}^*)$$

for some real number $\theta \in (0, 1)$ may be interpreted geometrically to mean that $\mathbf{c}$ is a point located on the line segment connecting the point $\mathbf{x}$ and the point $\mathbf{x}^*$.

Although higher-order Taylor expansions can be constructed in a similar manner, the first-order and second-order expansions will be adequate for covering most topics in this textbook. The following notation is helpful for characterizing the magnitude of the remainder term in the Taylor expansion.

Definition: (Big) O notation.   Suppose that $h: \mathfrak{R} \to \mathfrak{R}$. The notation $h(x) = O(x)$ means that there exists a finite nonnegative real number K such that

$$\frac{|h(x)|}{|x|} \leq K \quad \text{as} \quad x \to 0.$$

Thus $R_2 = O(|\mathbf{x} - \mathbf{x}^*|^2)$ in (1.6) if the second derivative of V is bounded. Similarly, $R_3 = O(|\mathbf{x} - \mathbf{x}^*|^3)$ in (1.7) if the third derivative of V is bounded.

1.6   Chapter Summary

Marr's theory of understanding complex information-processing systems (1982) was reviewed in order to approach the analysis and design of ANN systems in a systematic and complete manner. The plan of this book was also discussed: the same group of ANN systems will be analyzed from the perspective of different branches of mathematics. Such an approach is designed to emphasize the similarities between ANN systems and well-studied algorithms in engineering science (specifically dynamical systems theory, nonlinear optimization theory, and statistical inference) as well as emphasize the unique and important distinctive features of ANN systems.

Typical characteristics of ANN system algorithms were listed to aid in the identification of ANN-like algorithms. Illustrative applications of classification dynamics, supervised and unsupervised learning ANN systems in the fields of neuroscience, behavioral psychology, and engineering were also presented.

A formal mathematical definition of the concept of an ANN system was proposed. A distinguishing feature of this definition was that ANN systems were defined as special cases of dynamical systems, rather than as nonlinear optimization algorithms or statistical pattern recognition algorithms. Additional key concepts, definitions, and notations to be used throughout this textbook were also introduced.

1.7   Additional Reading

The volumes edited by Anderson and Rosenfeld (1988) and by Anderson, Pellionisz, and Rosenfeld (1990) are excellent collections of classic articles in the field of ANN systems with applications from the areas of neuroscience, psychology, and engineering. Arranged in chronological order, the articles in these volumes also provide a good historical perspective on the development of the field of neurocomputing. The textbooks by Levine (1991), McClelland, Rumelhart, and the PDP Group (1986), Quinlan (1991), Rumelhart, McClelland, and the PDP Group (1986), and especially Anderson (1995) provide useful organized introductions to the ANN modeling field with applications from the fields of psychology and neuroscience. The textbooks by Gallant (1994), Hassoun (1995), Haykin (1994), Hertz, Krogh, and Palmer (1991), Kosko (1992), and Kung (1993) present a wide variety of ANN systems from an engineering perspective.

1.8   Elementary Problems

1.1-1. A telephone can be viewed as a complex information-processing system. Describe a telephone at (a) the implementational level, (b) the algorithmic level, and (c) the computational level.

1.1-2. Comment briefly upon possible difficulties associated with using Marr's approach (1982) to obtain a *unique* description of an ANN system at the implementational, algorithmic, or computational level.

1.1-3. Discuss some of the relationships between neuroscience, dynamical systems theory, and Marr's implementational level (1982).

1.1-4. Discuss some of the relationships between psychology, optimization theory, and Marr's algorithmic level (1982).

1.1-5. Discuss some of the relationships between engineering, statistics, and Marr's computational level (1982).

1.2-1. An engineer designs an algorithm that computes the quantity $\mathbf{r} = \mathbf{Wf}$, where $\mathbf{W}$ is a d-dimensional matrix and $\mathbf{f}$ is a d-dimensional column state vector indicating the status of a particular robot. The d-dimensional column vector $\mathbf{r}$ is a control signal used to send signals to a robot arm. (a) Propose an implementation of the engineer's algorithm that could probably be called an ANN system. Explain your proposed implementation. (b) Now propose an implementation of the engineer's algorithm that would probably not be called an ANN system. Explain your proposed implementation.

1.2-2. The engineer in problem 1.2-1 designs an algorithm that can update the parameter matrix $\mathbf{W}$ based upon observing ordered pairs of the form $(\mathbf{x}(t), \mathbf{f}(t))$, which correspond to correct robot arm position $\mathbf{x}(t)$ for a given robot system state $\mathbf{f}(t)$. In particular, the matrix $\mathbf{W}$ is updated according to the rule

$$\mathbf{W}(t+1) = \mathbf{W}(t) + \gamma[\mathbf{x}(t) - \mathbf{r}(t)]\mathbf{f}(t)^T,$$

where $\mathbf{r}(t) = \mathbf{W}(t)\mathbf{f}(t)$ and the positive stepsize γ satisfies $1 > \gamma > 0$. (a) Propose an implementation of the engineer's algorithm which would likely be called an ANN system. Explain your proposed implementation. (b) Now propose an implementation of the engineer's algorithm which would probably not be called an ANN system. Explain your proposed implementation.

1.3-1. A new ANN algorithm is proposed that has the following two properties: (1) the algorithm is not biologically plausible, and (2) the algorithm's performance is substantially and consistently worse than existing algorithms. Nevertheless, a group of respected scientists (who are not ANN researchers) are quite excited about the new ANN algorithm and believe the algorithm constitutes a significant scientific advance. How could this situation arise?

1.3-2. Give an example of an ANN classification dynamical system (a) modeling an actual biological system, (b) modeling actual behavioral phenomena, and (c) solving an actual engineering problem.

1.3-3. Give an example of an ANN supervised learning dynamical system (a) modeling an actual biological system, (b) modeling actual behavioral phenomena, and (c) solving an actual engineering problem.

1.3-4. Give an example of an ANN unsupervised learning dynamical system (a) modeling an actual biological system, (b) modeling actual behavioral phenomena, and (c) solving an actual engineering problem.

1.3-5. Define the Rescorla-Wagner (1972) model of animal conditioning, and then define the Widrow-Hoff (1960) learning rule. Discuss the relationships between these two learning rules.

1.3-6. Explain how the backpropagation learning algorithm could be used for the purposes of system identification. Discuss the relationship of the system identification problem to the Zipser-Andersen (1988) ANN model.

1.3-7. Consider an ANN system consisting of eight nodes. The activity level of each node is constrained to take on a value between -1 (feature absent) and 1 (feature present). The activity level, $x_i(t)$, of the ith node ($i = 1 \ldots 8$) in the network at time t is given by the formula

$$x_i(t+1) = \mathcal{S}\left[\sum_{j=1}^{8} w_{ij} x_j(t) + b_i \right],$$

where $\mathcal{S}: \mathfrak{R} \to [-1, 1]$ is a function defined such that $\mathcal{S}(x) = 1$ for $x > 1$, $\mathcal{S}(x) = x$ for $|x| \leq 1$, and $\mathcal{S}(x) = -1$ for $x < -1$. At time $t = 0$, $x_i(0) = 0$ for $i = 1 \ldots 8$. Also $w_{ij} = w_{ji}$ for $i, j = 1 \ldots 8$. Finally, b_i (the ith element of the 8-dimensional vector **b**) represents an external forcing stimulus to the ith node ($i = 1 \ldots d$). Explain how to select w_{ij} so that the resulting ANN system implements a recurrent lateral inhibition system. Speculate on the expected behavior of this recurrent lateral inhibition network when: (1) **b** = [0 0 0 0 1 0 0 0], (2) **b** = [0.001 0.007 0.1 0.7 0 0 0 0.1], and (3) **b** = [0 0 0 1 0 0 1 0.1].

1.3-8. A weatherman is interested in predicting the amount of rainfall (measured in inches with two-digit accuracy) for the next day given (1) the past history of rainfall for the last twenty days, and (2) the current month of the year. Suggest two schemes for representing this information in a backpropagation network so that the backpropagation ANN could learn to predict the amount of rainfall for the next day. The first scheme should involve a *local* representation scheme where activation levels must be chosen with two-digit accuracy. The second scheme should involve a *distributed* representation scheme where the activation level of each unit is either *active* or *inactive* yet the overall precision of the computations with respect to the system is not sacrificed.

1.3-9. Suppose that a particular biologically plausible neural network model is proposed. Now suppose that a simplified, less biologically realistic version of the original model is proposed. Provide three reasons why the less biologically realistic model might still be quite useful and interesting to a neuroscientist.

1.3-10. Explain the differences between a classification dynamics ANN, a supervised learning ANN, and an unsupervised learning ANN.

1.3-11. Design a cognitive psychology experiment using stimuli such as *ROAD* and *RODE* to test the hypothesis that the visual structure of the letter string stimulus influences the magnitude of the word superiority effect when the phonetic structure of the letter string stimulus is held constant. Explain how such an experiment can further our understanding of the human information-processing system.

1.3-12. Design a version of the McClelland and Rumelhart (1981), Rumelhart and McClelland (1982) interactive activation (IA) model for perceiving objects in the context of rooms. Present your design by drawing a figure such as shown in figure 1.10.

1.3-13. Explain how the backpropagation learning algorithm could be used as an adaptive learning system to cancel out interference from an incoming signal. In particular, assume that the incoming signal is known to be corrupted with *additive noise* so that the receiver observes a d-dimensional random vector at time t: $\tilde{\mathbf{x}}(t)$, which may be expressed as $\tilde{\mathbf{x}}(t) = \mathbf{s}(t) + \tilde{\mathbf{n}}(t)$. Assume also that $\tilde{\mathbf{n}}(t-1)$ provides useful information about the probability distribution of $\tilde{\mathbf{n}}(t)$.

1.3-14. Define the term *cortical magnification factor*.

1.9   Math Review Problems

Calculus Review Problems

1-1. Compute the derivative of $f(x) = e^{(x+10)^2}$.

1-2. Plot the function $\mathcal{S}: \mathcal{R} \to (0, 1)$ where $\mathcal{S}(x) = 1/(1 + \exp[-x])$ for all $x \in \mathcal{R}$. Compute the derivative of $\mathcal{S}$. Show that the derivative of $\mathcal{S}$ is strictly positive on $\mathcal{R}$. Show that the derivative of $\mathcal{S}$ may be expressed using the formula

$$\frac{d\mathcal{S}}{dx} = \mathcal{S}(x)[1 - \mathcal{S}(x)]$$

for all $x \in \mathcal{R}$.

1-3. Consider a function $f: \mathcal{R} \to \mathcal{R}$ defined such that $f(x) = (x+3)^2 + \sin(x)$. Expand the function f in a second-order Taylor expansion about the point $x = 7$. HINT: Let df/dx_0 be the first derivative of f evaluated at x_0 and d^2f/dx_0^2 be the second derivative of f evaluated at x_0. Then

$$f(x) \approx f(x_0) + (df/dx_0)(x - x_0) + (1/2)(x - x_0)(d^2f/dx_0^2)(x - x_0)$$

(when x is sufficiently close to x_0 and the third derivative of f is continuous).

1-4. Consider a function $f: \mathcal{R} \to \mathcal{R}$ defined such that $f(x) = \sin(x^3) + \exp(x)$. Expand the function f in a second-order Taylor expansion about the point $x = 7$.

1-5. Give the formal definition (using the standard ε argument) of the concept that a sequence $x_1, x_2, x_3, \ldots, x_n, \ldots$ converges to the constant a as $n \to \infty$.

1-6. Explain what the notation

$\mathbf{f}: \mathcal{R}^q \to \mathcal{R}^d$

means in precise English.

1-7. Compute the gradient and the Hessian of the function $f(x, y) = x^2 + y^2 + 2x$, where f maps the vector $\mathbf{u} = [x, y]$ into $x^2 + y^2 + 2x$.
    HINT: Let f be a function of some vector $\mathbf{u}$. If $\mathbf{g}$ is the gradient of function f with respect to vector $\mathbf{u}$, then the ith element of $\mathbf{g}$ is the partial derivative of f with respect to the ith element of the vector $\mathbf{u}$. Also if $\mathbf{H}$ is the Hessian of f, then the ijth element of the matrix $\mathbf{H}$ (ith row, jth column) is the second partial derivative of f with respect to the ith and jth elements of $\mathbf{u}$.

1-8. Compute the gradient and the Hessian of the function $f(x, y, z) = (x^3 + y^2)z$, where f maps the vector $\mathbf{u} = [x, y, z]$ into $(x^3 + y^2)z$.

1-9. Explain what the notation

$\mathbf{G}: \mathcal{R}^q \times \mathcal{R} \times Q \to \mathcal{R}^{d \times l}$

means in precise English.

Linear Algebra

1-10. Prove that the vectors [0   0   1], [1   0   0] and [0   9   0] are linearly independent.

1-11. Prove that the vectors [1   0   1], [0   0   1] and [1   0   2] are linearly dependent.

1-12. Let $\mathbf{x}$ be a d-dimensional column vector and $\mathbf{A}$ be a d-dimensional matrix. Show that the matrix expression $\mathbf{x}^T \mathbf{A} \mathbf{x}$ is a scalar H that can be expressed by the formula

$$H = \sum_{i=1}^{d} \sum_{j=1}^{d} a_{ij} x_i x_j,$$

where a_{ij} is the ijth element of $\mathbf{A}$ and x_i is the ith element of $\mathbf{x}$.

1-13. Suppose a d-dimensional matrix $\mathbf{M}$ has strictly positive real eigenvalues. What is the rank of the matrix $\mathbf{M}$?

Calculus-Based Probability and Statistics

1-14. Let $m \in \mathcal{R}$. Let σ^2 be a strictly positive finite real number. A univariate Gaussian probability density function with mean m and variance σ^2 is a function $p: \mathcal{R} \rightarrow (0, \infty)$ such that, for all $x \in \mathcal{R}$,

$$p(x) = [\sigma \sqrt{2\pi}]^{-1} \exp \left[-\frac{(x-m)^2}{2\sigma^2} \right].$$

Consider a univariate Gaussian probability density function, p, with mean $m = 1$ and variance $\sigma^2 = 1$. Show that the formula for $E[x^3]$ (the expected value of x^3 with respect to p) is given by the expression

$$E[x^3] = K \int_{-\infty}^{+\infty} x^3 \exp \left[-(1/2)(x-1)^2 \right] dx,$$

where K is a constant and then given an explicit formula for K. HINT: See solution to problem 1-15.

1-15. Consider a uniform probability density function for a random variable $\tilde{x}$ on the interval 2 to 5. That is, $p(x) = 1/3$ if $2 \leq x \leq 5$ and $p(x) = 0$ if $x < 2$ or $x > 5$. Explicitly construct an integral whose value is the expected value of $\tilde{x}$, and then evaluate that integral. Explicitly construct an integral whose value is the variance of $\tilde{x}$, and then evaluate that integral.

1-16. Box 1 contains 3 red balls and 3 white balls. Box 2 contains 2 red balls and 1 white ball. Box 3 contains 1 red ball and 1 white ball. A box is chosen at random, and then a ball is chosen at random from that box. The ball is observed to be red. What is the probability that box 2 is chosen? Show all of your intermediate reasoning steps using a clear, unambiguous notation.

   HINT: This is an easy problem if you develop a good notation. Use the definition of a conditional probability, $p(a|b) = p(a \cap b)/p(b)$, to help you solve this problem. See solution to problem 1-17 for additional help.

1-17. Box 1 contains 2 red balls and 3 white balls. Box 2 contains 1 red ball and 1 white ball. Box 3 contains 3 red balls. A box is chosen at random, and then a ball is chosen at random from that box. The ball is observed to be red. What is the probability that box 3 is chosen? Show all of your intermediate reasoning steps using a clear, unambiguous notation.

I   IMPLEMENTATIONAL LEVEL

The mathematical methods introduced in chapters 2, 3, and 4 are relevant for asking and answering questions that correspond to Marr's implementational level of understanding (1982), which is concerned with understanding *all* aspects of the *behavior* of a given complex information-processing system. Chapter 2 provides an explicit summary of a variety of specific ANN system architectures that will be mathematically analyzed and discussed in the other chapters. Chapter 3 shows how deterministic dynamical systems theory may be used to investigate the long-term behavior of a given ANN system. Chapter 4 shows how stochastic dynamical systems theory may be used to analyze (1) stochastic ANN systems whose behaviors are not deterministic and therefore not completely predictable, and (2) both deterministic and stochastic ANN learning systems which learn in environments characterized by uncertainty.

Thus chapters 2, 3, and 4 are concerned with characterizing the behavior of a given ANN system. Issues concerned with improving or evaluating the efficiency, or evaluating the rationality of computations for an ANN system are either ignored or not emphasized.

2

ANN Dynamical Systems

Some computationally simple representative ANN systems are now formally presented and briefly discussed. By presenting a few of the best-known and most fundamental architectures in the ANN system modeling field, it is hoped that a good appreciation for the range of research in this area will be obtained.

An additional goal of this chapter is to introduce the various ANN systems within a functional taxonomy in order to facilitate the selection of an appropriate class (or conjunction of classes) for a particular problem. It is important to understand that although for expository reasons the various functional categories are treated as mutually exclusive, in fact ANN systems that are members of several of the proposed functional categories are quite common.

In order to formally state the functional categories of the following ANN systems, the computational goal of an ANN dynamical system must be formally defined. The computational goal of an ANN system will be defined as the solution to a particular type of nonlinear optimization problem.

Definition: Objective function. Let $S \subseteq \mathcal{R}^d$. An *objective function* $V: S \to \mathcal{R}$ defined with respect to some agent A has the property for all $\mathbf{x}, \mathbf{y} \in S$ that

$$V(\mathbf{x}) \leq V(\mathbf{y})$$

if the agent A believes that the system state $\mathbf{x}$ is at least as preferable as the system state $\mathbf{y}$.

The two major types of objective functions used throughout this textbook are the *classification objective function,* which maps a system state of an ANN classification dynamical system (i.e., an activation pattern) into a real number, and the *learning objective function,* which maps a system state of the ANN learning dynamical system (i.e., a connection strength parameter vector for nontemporal learning dynamical systems) into a real number.

Note that the agent A in the definition of an objective function could be either the engineer designing the ANN system or, alternatively, the ANN system itself. The identity of the agent A will depend upon whether the ANN system is a model of a real brain process or a device designed to compute some function. (The concept of representing systems of preferences as objective functions will be developed more completely in chapter 6, where it will be noted that not all such systems can be so represented.)

Now suppose that an objective function $V: \mathcal{R}^d \to \mathcal{R}$ is a continuous function on $\mathcal{R}^d$. In this special case, system states that are very similar to one another will tend to be assigned approximately the same degree of preference by the objective function V. The objective functions for almost all ANN dynamical systems are continuous implying that the *principle of similarity,*

Similar system states (in an Euclidean distance sense) should be assigned approximately equal preferences,

is common to almost all ANN dynamical system architectures.

To illustrate the principle of similarity, consider an ANN dynamical system that has acquired a continuous classification objective function as the by-product of some learning process. The ANN classification dynamical system can use the classification objective function to make decisions about activation patterns that were never previously observed during the learning process because of the principle of similarity. That is, if **x** is a novel stimulus and **x** is similar to some previously observed stimulus **y**, then the ANN classification dynamical system's dynamics will process stimulus **x** in a manner which is appropriate for processing stimulus **y**.

2.1   ANN Classification Dynamical Systems

A *classification objective function* maps a system state of an ANN classification dynamical system into a real number. The classification objective function will usually be denoted by the function $V: S \rightarrow \mathfrak{R}$, where $S \subseteq \mathfrak{R}^d$ is a set of activation patterns. Thus, if $V(\mathbf{x}) \leq V(\mathbf{y})$, then, with respect to the classification objective function V, activation pattern **x** is at least as preferable as activation pattern **y**.

To illustrate the concept of a classification objective function, consider the following image-processing problem. Suppose that each activation pattern in the domain of $V: S \rightarrow \mathfrak{R}$ corresponds to a particular assignment of pixel values to locations in some image. An ANN classification dynamical system has been proven to be an optimization algorithm searching for the activation pattern $\mathbf{x}^*$ such that $V(\mathbf{x}^*) \leq V(\mathbf{x})$ for all $\mathbf{x} \in S$. In this case, the ANN classification dynamical system is searching for the *most preferred* activation pattern $\mathbf{x}^*$, where the system of preference is implicitly specified by the classification objective function V. Researchers in the field of ANN systems sometimes refer to the classification objective function V as an *energy* or *potential* function for the activation updating rule of the ANN dynamical system.

2.1.1   Feedforward Networks of McCulloch-Pitts Neurons

The McCulloch and Pitts (1943) formal neuron (also known as a "logical threshold unit") is defined as follows (see Minsky 1967 for a good review). Let $s_j(t)$ be the activation value of the jth input unit at time t that is constrained to take on the values of either 0 or 1. Let $r_i(t)$ be the activation value of the ith output unit. Let w_{ij} be the ijth element of the d-dimensional matrix of parameters **W**. Then

$$r_i(t + 1) = \mathscr{S}\left(\left(\sum_{j=1}^{d} w_{ij}s_j(t)\right) + b_i\right), \tag{2.1}$$

where

$\mathcal{S}(x) = 1$ if $x > 0$ and $\mathcal{S}(x) = 0$ if $x \leq 0$.

Figure 2.1 illustrates some of the important features of a McCulloch-Pitts (1943) model neuron.

For $i = 1 \dots d$: let $w_{ij} = 1$ for $j = 1 \dots d$ and $b_i = 0.5 - d$. In this case (2.1) implements a logical AND operator (i.e., it is an AND logic gate) because $r_i(t + 1) = 1$ if and only if $s_j(t) = 1$ for $j = 1 \dots d$.

On the other hand, for $i = 1 \dots d$: let $w_{ij} = 1$ for $j = 1 \dots d$ and choose $b_i = -0.5$. In this case, (2.1) implements a logical OR operator (i.e., it is an OR logic gate) because $r_i(t + 1) = 0$ if and only if $s_j(t) = 0$ for $j = 1 \dots d$.

Finally, consider a McCulloch-Pitts formal neuron with only a single input so that $r_i(t + 1) = \mathcal{S}(w_{i1}s_1(t) + b_i)$. Let $w_{i1} = -1$ and let $b_i = 0.5$. In this case, (2.1) implements a logical NOT operator (i.e., it is a NOT logic gate).

Note that the McCulloch-Pitts network of formal neurons as described here is a *feedforward network*. A feedforward classification dynamical system is an ANN classification dynamical system where the response vector **r** is some function of the input vector **s** and a connection strength parameter vector **w**.

The classical paper "A Logical Calculus of Ideas Immanent in Nervous Activity" by McCulloch and Pitts (1943) noted that (1) any logical expression could be represented using AND, OR, and NOT operators, and (2) a network of logical threshold units could be designed to compute such logical expressions. For example, consider the two-layer network of logical threshold units in figure 2.2. An array of *input units* is first activated by some external stimulus.

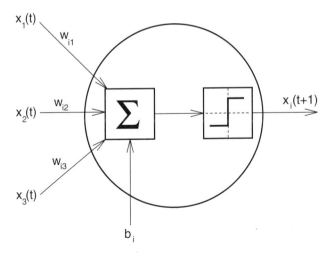

Figure 2.1
McCulloch-Pitts model neuron with three inputs. The notation $x_i(t)$ indicates the activation level of neuron i at time t. Model neuron i first computes a weighted sum of its inputs $x_1(t)$, $x_2(t)$, $x_3(t)$, where the weights are determined by the connection strengths w_{i1}, w_{i2}, and w_{i3}, and bias b_i; the weighted sum is then passed through a discontinuous threshold sigmoidal nonlinearity to obtain the new activation level of the ith neuron, denoted as $x_i(t + 1)$.

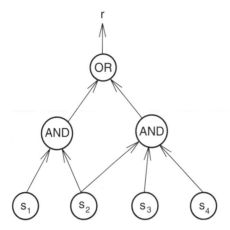

Figure 2.2
Network of McCulloch-Pitts formal neurons. A McCulloch-Pitts feedforward network of formal
neurons is connected to realize an arbitrary logical function; the activation levels of the input units,
s_1, s_2, s_3, s_4, are assumed to have the values of only zero or one. Neurons that can implement AND,
OR, and NOT operations are constructed; the response of the network, r, is an activation level restricted to the values of zero and one.

Each input unit is associated with some unique *assertion*. If the activation level
of an input unit is equal to one, then the assertion for that input unit is *true*. If
the activation level of an input unit is equal to zero, then the assertion for that
input unit is *false*. Similarly, each output unit is associated with some unique
assertion. The activation level of an output unit has the value of one if the output unit's assertion is *true* and has the value of zero otherwise. The intermediate layer of units are called "hidden units" because the units in this layer are
neither input units nor output units. Each hidden unit computes a logical AND
function in terms of the activation levels of the input units. The output unit then
computes a logical OR function on the activation levels of the hidden units. Because any arbitrary logical expression may be represented as a disjunction of
conjunctions (e.g., McCulloch-Pitts 1943; Mano 1986, chap. 2) it follows that
any arbitrary logical expression can be represented by a McCulloch-Pitts
neural network which has only two layers of weights.

   A (nonunique) classification objective function for a McCulloch-Pitts feedforward network of formal neurons can be easily constructed. Let $\Phi: \mathcal{R}^d \rightarrow \{0, 1\}$
define a particular McCulloch-Pitts feedforward network that maps an input
vector $\mathbf{s} \in \mathcal{R}^d$ into either a zero or a one. Thus the response of the McCulloch-
Pitts feedforward network given input stimulus $\mathbf{s}$ is defined as $r = \Phi(\mathbf{s})$. Let V:
$\mathcal{R}^d \times \{0, 1\} \rightarrow \mathcal{R}$ define the classification objective function $V(\mathbf{s}, \cdot): \{0, 1\} \rightarrow \mathcal{R}$
for each $\mathbf{s} \in \mathcal{R}^d$. In particular, for all $\mathbf{s} \in \mathcal{R}^d$ and all $r \in \{0, 1\}$ define V such that

$$V(\mathbf{s}, r) = \big| r - \Phi(\mathbf{s}) \big|.$$

For a given $\mathbf{s} \in \mathcal{R}^d$, the $r*$ for which $V(\mathbf{s}, \cdot)$ obtains its minimum value is given by the formula: $r* = \Phi(\mathbf{s})$.

2.1.2   Nonfeedforward Classification Dynamical Systems

Hopfield (1982) Model

The Hopfield (1982) model consists of a set of symmetrically connected McCulloch and Pitts (1943) formal neurons. The updating dynamics of a Hopfield (1982) ANN system is closely related to ANN systems proposed earlier by McCulloch and Pitts (1943), Caianiello (1961), Little (1974), and Amari (1977). The big difference is that Hopfield (1982) focused upon symmetrically connected networks of McCulloch and Pitts (1943) neurons and emphasized how such symmetric networks could be analyzed using a Lyapunov function analysis (see chapter 3 for a review of such analyses). The Hopfield (1982) model is also a special case of the iterated conditional modes (ICM) algorithm of Besag (1986). Briefly, the ICM algorithm corresponds to the Gibbs sampler algorithm (Geman and Geman 1984) in the limit where the temperature parameter is sufficiently close to zero. At this limit, the Gibbs sampler algorithm becomes a deterministic updating rule.

A typical application of a Hopfield (1982) ANN classification dynamical system is to reconstruct or estimate an unobservable portion of a given activation pattern given the values of the remaining portions of the activation pattern are known (i.e., observable). For example, let $\mathbf{x}$ be an activation pattern which is the initial system state for a Hopfield (1982) ANN classification dynamical system. In addition, assume that $\mathbf{x} \in \mathcal{R}^d$ is a digitized image, with some image regions having known values and the remaining image regions having unknown values, then $\mathbf{x}^u \in \mathcal{R}^u$ would represent that portion of the image associated with the unknown values while $\mathbf{x}^k \in \mathcal{R}^{d-u}$ would represent the remaining known portion of the image. The goal of the ANN classification dynamical system is to estimate $\mathbf{x}^u$, given $\mathbf{x}^k$. As a second example, $\mathbf{x} \in \mathcal{R}^d$ might be the concatenation of a known analog acoustic signal represented by $\mathbf{x}^k$ and an unknown classification label, $\mathbf{x}^u \in \mathcal{R}^u$. As a third example, $\mathcal{R}^{d-u}$ might be an empty set so that $\mathbf{x}^u = \mathbf{x} \in \mathcal{R}^u = \mathcal{R}^d$ is a particular electronic wiring scheme which satisfies a highly restrictive set of constraints. Finding a value $\mathbf{x}^u* \in \mathcal{R}^d$ such that $V(\mathbf{x}^u*) \leq V(\mathbf{x}^u)$ for all $\mathbf{x}^u \in \mathcal{R}^d$ would then be interpreted as a permissible wiring scheme.

Hopfield (1982) showed that if the matrix of connection strengths $\mathbf{W} \in \mathcal{R}^{d \times d}$ is symmetric and $\mathbf{b} \in \mathcal{R}^d$ is a vector of connection strength biases, then each iteration of the Hopfield (1982) model decreases the objective function $V: \mathcal{R}^d \to \mathcal{R}$, where for all $\mathbf{x} \in \mathcal{R}^d$:

$$V(\dot{\mathbf{x}}) = -\mathbf{x}^T[(1/2)\mathbf{W}\mathbf{x} + \mathbf{b}].$$

Thus the Hopfield (1982) model may be viewed as a heuristic search procedure that attempts to compute a minimum value of the classification objective function V.

Before explicitly presenting the Hopfield (1982) model in algorithmic form, it will first be useful to introduce some notation for representing sequences of random numbers. Note that, an *observation* is defined as a value of some random variable, while a sequence of observations is referred to as a "sample path."

Definition: RAND[t] Stochastic process.   The sequence of numbers

$RAND[1], RAND[2], RAND[3]\ldots,$

is a sample path of a sequence of independent and identically distributed random variables where the probability density function of each random variable is a uniform probability density function on the open interval $(0, 1)$.

Definition: IRAND[t,b,e] Stochastic process.   Let b and e be finite positive integers such that $b < e$. The sequence

$IRAND[1, b, e], \quad IRAND[2, b, e], \quad IRAND[3, b, e]\ldots,$

is a sample path of a sequence of independent and identically distributed random variables where the probability mass function of each random variable is a uniform probability mass function on the integers in the closed interval $[b, e]$.

Algorithm: Hopfield (1982).   Consider an ANN system with d units where the activation of the ith unit at time t is $x_i(t)$ and the connection strength from unit j to unit i is w_{ij}. Let the bias connection strength for unit i be b_i. Let $\mathbf{W}$ be a d-dimensional real symmetric matrix whose ijth element is w_{ij} and $\mathbf{b}$ be a d-dimensional real vector with ith element b_i. Let $x_i(t)$ be the ith element of

$$\mathbf{x}(t) = [\mathbf{x}^k(t), \mathbf{x}^u(t)] \in \{0, 1\}^d,$$

where

$$\mathbf{x}^k(t) = [x_1(t),\ldots, x_k(t)] \quad \text{and} \quad \mathbf{x}^u(t) = [x_{k+1}(t),\ldots, x_d(t)].$$

Let *logical threshold function* $\mathcal{S}: \mathcal{R} \to \{0, 1\}$ be defined as

$\mathcal{S}(x) = 1 \quad \text{if} \quad x > 0, \qquad \mathcal{S}(x) = 0 \quad \text{if} \quad x < 0.$

• Step 1: Choose initial guess for $\mathbf{x}(0) \in \{0, 1\}^d$. Set $t = 0$.

• Step 2: Update activation level of unit m at iteration t. For $m = IRAND[t, k + 1, d]$: Let

$$\varphi_m(t) = \sum_{j=1}^{d} w_{mj} x_j(t) + b_m.$$

Let $x_m(t + 1) = \mathcal{S}(\varphi_m(t))$ if $\varphi_m(t) \neq 0$, and $x_m(t + 1) = x_m(t)$ if $\varphi_m(t) = 0$. Let $t = t + 1$.

- Step 3: Terminate algorithm after a fixed number of iterations. If

$t < t_{max}$,

then return to step 2, otherwise continue to step 4.

- Step 4: Report final value of activation pattern. Report $\mathbf{x}(0) = \left[\mathbf{x}^k(0), \mathbf{x}^u(0)\right]$ was classified as

$$\mathbf{x}(t) = \left[\mathbf{x}^k(0), \mathbf{x}^u(t)\right]$$

in t iterations of the algorithm.

Cohen-Grossberg (1983) and Hopfield (1984) Networks

Another closely related ANN system is the Hopfield (1984) model, which is a continuous-time and continuous-state-space version of the Hopfield (1982) model. Again, although closely related ANN systems similar to the Hopfield (1984) model had been previously proposed (Grossberg 1973; Wilson and Cowan 1972), Hopfield (1984) showed how a classification objective function viewpoint was useful for analyzing such ANN classification dynamical systems. Cohen and Grossberg (1983) described how classification objective functions could be constructed for a much wider class of ANN systems, which included the Hopfield (1984) ANN system as a special case. (See section 3.4.2 and problem 3-2 for additional details.)

Gibbs Sampler, Boltzmann Machine, and Harmony Theory

The stochastic version of the Hopfield (1982) model called the "Boltzmann machine" (Ackley, Hinton, and Sejnowski 1985), first introduced in chapter 1, is now formally presented. The Boltzmann machine is identical to the Hopfield (1982) model, with the important exception that the weighted sum to the ith unit in the ANN system is used to compute the probability that the ith unit will move to either an *on* state ($x_i(t) = 1$) or an *off* state ($x_i(t) = 0$). The ith unit then moves into either an *on* or *off* state based upon the computed probability distribution. This probability distribution is also functionally dependent upon a special strictly positive parameter, referred to as the "temperature." If the temperature parameter, τ, is very large, then each unit has approximately a probability of one-half of entering into an *on* or *off* state. That is, the probability that a unit will enter into a particular state tends to be functionally independent of the activation of the neighboring units in the large-temperature case. Alternatively, if the temperature parameter, τ, is very small, then each unit will turn *on* only if the weighted sum of the activations of the neighboring units exceeds a threshold value. Thus the Boltzmann machine looks like a deterministic network of

McCulloch-Pitts neurons, that is, a Hopfield (1982) network, in the low-temperature case. An *annealing schedule* is a function that indicates the value of the Boltzmann machine's temperature as a function of the current iteration number. Thus the sequence $\tau_1, \tau_2, \tau_3,\ldots$ indicates that the temperature parameter $\tau = \tau_k$ at the kth iteration of the algorithm. Moreover, Geman and Geman (1984) showed that there exists a finite positive real number C such that if

$$\tau_k = C/(1 + \log(k)), \quad k = 1, 2,\ldots$$

then convergence to the minimum value of the Hopfield (1982) classification objective function is guaranteed with a high probability (see chapter 5 for more details).

Finally, it is important to note that Smolensky's (1986) harmony theory may be viewed as an important special case of the Boltzmann machine, while the Boltzmann machine may be viewed as an important special case of Geman and Geman's (1984) Gibbs sampler algorithm (also discussed in greater detail in chapter 5).

Algorithm: Boltzmann machine.   Consider an ANN system with d units where the activation level of the ith unit at time t is denoted by $x_i(t)$, the connection strength from unit j to unit i is denoted by w_{ij}, and the connection strength bias for unit i is denoted by b_i. Let $\mathbf{W}$ be a d-dimensional real symmetric weight matrix with ijth element w_{ij}, and $\mathbf{b}$ be a d-dimensional real bias vector with ith element b_i. Let $x_i(t)$ be the ith element of

$$\mathbf{x}(t) = [\mathbf{x}^k(t), \mathbf{x}^u(t)] \in \{0, 1\}^d,$$

where

$$\mathbf{x}^k(t) = [x_1(t),\ldots, x_k(t)] \quad \text{and} \quad \mathbf{x}^u(t) = [x_{k+1}(t),\ldots, x_d(t)].$$

Let $\tau_1, \tau_2,\ldots$ be an *annealing schedule* defined such that as $t \to \infty$, $\tau_t \to 0$. Let the *logistic sigmoidal function* $\mathcal{S}: \mathcal{R} \to (0, 1)$ be defined for all $x \in \mathcal{R}$ by

$$\mathcal{S}(x) = 1/[1 + \exp(-x)].$$

• Step 1: Pick an initial activation pattern. Choose initial guess for $\mathbf{x}(0) \in \{0, 1\}^d$. Let $\tau_0 > 0$. Set $t = 0$.

• Step 2: Select a unit at random. Let the selected unit be active with probability equal to the predicted probability that the unit will be active. For $i = IRAND(t, k + 1, d)$: Compute

$$p_{i,t} = \mathcal{S}\left[\frac{\left[\sum_{j=1}^d w_{ij} x_j(t)\right] + b_i}{\tau_t}\right].$$

If $RAND(t) \le p_{i,t}$, THEN $x_i(t + 1) = 1$ ELSE $x_i(t + 1) = 0$. Let $t = t + 1$.

- Step 3: Terminate algorithm after a fixed number of iterations. If

$t < t_{max}$,

then return to step 2. Otherwise, continue to step 4.

- Step 4: Report resulting activation pattern as answer. Report $\mathbf{x}(0) = [\mathbf{x}^k(0), \mathbf{x}^u(0)]$ was classified as

$$\mathbf{x}(t) = [\mathbf{x}^k(0), \mathbf{x}^u(t)]$$

in t iterations of algorithm.

Brain-State-in-a-Box (BSB) Model

The "brain-state-in-a-box" (BSB) model (Anderson et al. 1977; Golden 1986a, 1993; Hui and Zak 1992) is a continuous-state discrete-time ANN system that also attempts to minimize the quadratic Hopfield (1982) classification objective function. Figure 2.3 shows the ANN interpretation of a BSB model unit. Each unit computes a weighted sum of its inputs, which is added to its current state to obtain the *net input* to the BSB model unit. The net input to the unit is then truncated using a piecewise linear sigmoidal nonlinearity. Figure 2.4 shows how BSB model units operate in parallel in a continuous state space with a discrete-time update rule to update the pattern of activation over the units. The final activation pattern over the units is interpreted as the BSB model's

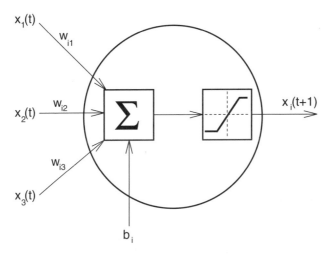

Figure 2.3
BSB model neuron with three inputs. The notation $x_i(t)$ indicates the activation level of unit i at time t. Model neuron i first computes a weighted sum of its inputs $x_1(t)$, $x_2(t)$, $x_3(t)$, where the weights are determined by the connection strengths w_{i1}, w_{i2}, and w_{i3}, and bias b_i; the weighted sum is then passed through a piecewise linear sigmoidal nonlinearity to obtain the new activation level of the ith unit, denoted as $x_i(t+1)$.

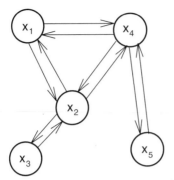

Figure 2.4
Set of BSB model neurons. Note that all connections among the units are symmetrical. The notation x_i indicates the activation level of unit i.

choice for an activation pattern $\mathbf{x}^u$. The formal algorithm for the BSB model is
now presented.

Algorithm: Brain-state-in-a-box (BSB). Consider a BSB ANN system
with d units where the activation level of the ith unit is $x_i(t)$ and the connection
strength from unit j to unit i is w_{ij}. The bias connection strength for the ith unit
is b_i. Let $\mathbf{W}$ be a d-dimensional real symmetric weight matrix with ijth element
w_{ij} and $\mathbf{b}$ be a d-dimensional real bias vector with ith element b_i. Let $x_i(t)$ be the
ith element of $\mathbf{x}(t) = [\mathbf{x}^k(t), \mathbf{x}^u(t)] \in [-1, 1]^d$, where

$$\mathbf{x}^k(t) = \left[\mathbf{x}_1(t),\ldots, \mathbf{x}_k(t)\right] \quad \text{and} \quad \mathbf{x}^u(t) = \left[\mathbf{x}_{k+1}(t),\ldots, \mathbf{x}_d(t)\right].$$

Let $\mathscr{S}: \mathscr{R} \to [-1, 1]$ be the piecewise linear sigmoidal function

$\mathscr{S}(x) = 1$ if $x > 1$, $\mathscr{S}(x) = -1$ if $x < -1$, $\mathscr{S}(x) = x$ if $|x| \leq 1$.

• Step 1: Choose an initial activation pattern. Choose initial guess for $\mathbf{x}(0) \in$
$[-1, 1]^d$. Set $t = 0$.

• Step 2: Simultaneously update units in the network. For $i = k + 1 \ldots d$:
Compute

$$x_i(t + 1) = \mathscr{S}\left[x_i(t) + \gamma\left(\left(\sum_{j=1}^{d} w_{ij} x_j(t)\right) + b_i\right)\right],$$

where γ is a strictly positive stepsize. Let $t = t + 1$.

• Step 3: Check if activation pattern has substantially changed its value. Let
$\varepsilon > 0$. If $|\mathbf{x}(t) - \mathbf{x}(t - 1)| < \varepsilon$, then go to step 4. Otherwise, return to step 2.

• Step 4: Report final activation pattern as a classification of initial activation
pattern. Report $\mathbf{x}(0) = \left[\mathbf{x}^k(0), \mathbf{x}^u(0)\right]$ was classified as

$$\mathbf{x}(t) = \left[\mathbf{x}^k(0), \mathbf{x}^u(t)\right]$$

in t algorithm iterations.

Golden (1986a, 1993) proved the following useful result about the classification dynamics behavior of the BSB model. Let $\mathbf{W}$ be a real symmetric matrix whose ijth element is the connection strength from unit j to unit i. Let $\mathbf{b}$ be a real vector whose ith element is the bias connection strength for unit i. Let $\gamma \in (0, \infty)$ be the stepsize of the BSB model as defined in the above BSB model algorithm. Let the scalar index t denote the tth iteration of the BSB model algorithm. Let $\lambda_{\min}$ be the smallest eigenvalue of $\mathbf{W}$. If either $\lambda_{\min} > 0$, or $0 < \gamma < 2/\left|\lambda_{\min}\right|$, then, for all positive integer t,

$$V([\mathbf{x}^k, \mathbf{x}^u(t+1)]) \leq V([\mathbf{x}^k, \mathbf{x}^u(t)]), \quad \text{where} \quad V(\mathbf{x}) = -\mathbf{x}^T[(1/2)\mathbf{W}\mathbf{x} + \mathbf{b}].$$

Thus the BSB model is seeking a minimum value of the Hopfield (1982) classification objective function.

Golden's analysis (1986a, 1993) also investigated the long-term behavior (i.e., asymptotic stability) of the BSB dynamical system. Grossberg (1988) has showed how the Cohen-Grossberg (1983) theorem could be used to prove a result similar to that of Golden (1986a, 1993) for a continuous-time approximation to the discrete-time BSB model. Hui and Zak (1992) investigated the stability properties of the BSB model for a restricted class of nonsymmetric, diagonally dominant matrices. Marcus and Westervelt (1989) analyzed the stability of a large class of discrete-time continuous-state dynamical systems that correspond essentially to the discrete-time version of the continuous-time, continuous-state Hopfield (1984) ANN classification dynamical systems.

2.2   ANN Learning Dynamical Systems

A *learning objective function* maps the system state of an ANN learning dynamical system into a real number. The learning objective function will usually be denoted by the function $l: W \rightarrow \mathcal{R}$, where $W \subseteq \mathcal{R}^q$ is a set of connection strength parameter vectors. Like the classification objective function, the learning objective function embodies an implicit system of preference, which is formally defined by the function l.

For example, suppose that each connection strength parameter vector in the domain of $l: W \rightarrow \mathcal{R}$ corresponds to a particular wiring scheme in an ANN learning dynamical system. An ANN learning dynamical system has been proven to be an optimization algorithm that is searching for the connection strength parameter vector $\mathbf{w}^*$ such that $l(\mathbf{w}^*) \leq l(\mathbf{w})$ for all $\mathbf{w} \in W$. In this case, the ANN learning dynamical system is searching for the *most preferred* wiring scheme (i.e., connection strength parameter vector) $\mathbf{w}^*$, where the system of preference is implicitly specified by the learning objective function l. Researchers in the field of ANN systems sometimes refer to the learning objective function l as the "error function" for an ANN learning algorithm.

Typically, an *experience* or *training stimulus* for an ANN is an ordered pair of the form $\mathbf{x}^k = (\mathbf{s}^k, \mathbf{o}^k)$, where $\mathbf{s}^k$ is the kth *stimulus* activation pattern over the *input units* and $\mathbf{o}^k$ is the kth desired *output* response feedback activation pattern over the *output units* that is externally imposed upon the ANN by the ANN system's environment. The set of all such experiences for a given ANN at a particular moment in time can thus be represented as a set of n activation patterns,

$$\mathbf{X}_n = \{\mathbf{x}^1, \mathbf{x}^2, \ldots, \mathbf{x}^n\},$$

where $\mathbf{x}^k = (\mathbf{s}^k, \mathbf{o}^k)$ for $k = 1 \ldots n$. The computational goal for an ANN learning dynamical system is to find a connection strength parameter vector, $\mathbf{w}$, that is most preferable with respect to the learning objective function l, where the functional form of l is determined in part by the training data set $\mathbf{X}_n$.

Several distinct categories of learning problems can be defined. These categories are not mutually exclusive and can almost always be viewed as special cases of the learning problem. These six major categories of learning problems are: (1) supervised learning problems, (2) unsupervised learning problems, (3) reinforcement learning problems, (4) temporal learning problems, (5) prior knowledge problems, and (6) topographic map learning problems.

2.2.1   Supervised Learning

Typically, supervised learning assumes that the statistical environment of the ANN generates a specific desired output feedback response, $\mathbf{o}$, and stimulus $\mathbf{s}$ with some probability. The ANN system must attempt to learn this probability distribution. Note that the kth *training stimulus*, $\mathbf{x}^k$, for the supervised learning problem may be expressed as the vector $\mathbf{x}^k = (\mathbf{s}^k, \mathbf{o}^k)$, where $\mathbf{s}^k$ is called the "input vector" and the response feedback signal $\mathbf{o}^k$ is usually called the "target vector" or "desired response" feedback vector. Section 1.4 provides a formal definition of the supervised learning problem for ANN dynamical systems.

Perceptrons

Rosenblatt (1958, 1962) was one of the first researchers in the field to devise networks of McCulloch-Pitts (1943) neurons that could learn from experience; he referred to such neural networks as "perceptrons." Rosenblatt's 1962 book *Principles of Neurodynamics* summarizes his original simulation experiments with perceptrons.

The most representative ANN system perceptron architecture considered by Rosenblatt consisted of a set of input units (*s*-units), a set of hidden units

(a-units), and a single output unit (r-unit). Rosenblatt's basic idea was that the connection strengths from the input unit layer to the hidden unit layer should be randomly chosen according to some probability law and their values fixed for the entire learning process. A learning rule could then be developed based upon the perceptron's responses to adjust the weights from the hidden units to the single output unit of the perceptron. It seems plausible that Rosenblatt reasoned that if enough different types of hidden units representing different logical conjunctions of input unit assertions could be generated, then the learning process from the hidden units to the output response unit might be able to exploit the high-order logical conjunctions at the hidden layer to represent complex logical expressions. Rosenblatt proposed and explored a number of different learning rules for the hidden mapping to output layer mapping as well as a variety of rules for randomly selecting the input to hidden layer mapping. The following generic perceptron learning procedure is representative of the many types of ANN systems explored by Rosenblatt (1958, 1962).

Algorithm: Perceptron learning.   Consider an ANN system with d input units, v hidden units, and one output unit. The mapping from the input units to the hidden units is fixed and defined by a particular randomly chosen function $\mathbf{q} \colon \mathfrak{R}^d \to \{0,\ 1\}^v$. The mapping from the hidden units to the output unit is modifiable and its value at an iteration of the learning algorithm is defined by a v-dimensional weight (connection strength parameter) vector.

- Step 0: Initialization. Let $t = 0$. Let $\mathbf{w}(t) \in \mathfrak{R}^v$ be an arbitrary initial weight vector that defines the initial mapping from the hidden units to the output unit.

- Step 1: Choose a stimulus from training set at random. Choose stimulus

$$\mathbf{x}^k(t) = (\mathbf{s}^k(t),\ o^k(t)) \in \{0,\ 1\}^{d+1},$$

where $k = IRAND(t,\ 1,\ n)$ and n is the number of training stimuli. Note that input stimulus $\mathbf{s}^k(t) \in \{0,\ 1\}^d$ and response feedback signal $o^k(t) \in \{0,\ 1\}$.

- Step 2: Compute hidden unit activations from input unit activations. Compute

$$\mathbf{h}^k(t) = \mathbf{q}(\mathbf{s}^k(t)).$$

- Step 3: Compute output unit activation from hidden unit activations. Compute

$$\mathbf{r}^k(t) = \mathscr{S}(\mathbf{w}(t)^T \mathbf{h}^k(t)),$$

where $\mathscr{S} \colon \mathfrak{R} \to \{0,\ 1\}$ is defined such that for all $x \in \mathfrak{R}$:

$$\mathscr{S}(x) = 1 \text{ if } x \geq 0 \quad \text{and} \quad \mathscr{S}(x) = 0 \text{ if } x < 0.$$

- Step 4: Change connections from hidden units to output unit.

$$\mathbf{w}(t+1) = \mathbf{w}(t) + \left[o^k(t) - r^k(t)\right]\mathbf{h}^k(t).$$

• Step 5: Check stopping criterion. If $t > t_{\max}$ or $o^k(t) = r^k(t)$ for $k = 1\dots n$, then stop. Otherwise, let $t = t + 1$ and go to step 1.

Duda and Hart (1973) proposed an analysis of the perceptron learning rule based upon the work of Ridgway (1962), which investigated the perceptron learning problem (also see Block 1962; Minsky and Papert 1969; and Nilsson 1965 for related analyses). The following discussion of the perceptron learning rule is based upon the approach of Duda and Hart (1973). Consider the learning problem associated with learning the mapping from the hidden unit layer to the output unit in a given perceptron. It can be shown that the perceptron learning rule will always converge in a finite number of iterations to a correct classification of all members in the training set provided that such a classification exists for a given input to hidden unit mapping. It can also be shown that the perceptron learning rule seeks a minimum value of the learning objective function $l: \mathcal{R}^q \rightarrow [0, \infty)$, where l is defined such that

$$l(\mathbf{w}) = \left|\mathbf{w} - k\mathbf{w}^*\right|^2$$

and where k is a specific positive number and $\mathbf{w}^* \in \mathcal{R}^q$ is a weight vector that correctly classifies all members of the training stimulus set (if $\mathbf{w}^*$ exists).

Widrow-Hoff Learning Rule

The Widrow-Hoff learning rule was originally proposed as a discrete-time adaptive algorithm for constantly updating the parameters of a linear filter in real-time engineering applications (Widrow and Hoff 1960; Widrow and Stearns 1985; see Widrow and Lehr 1990 for a review). The Widrow-Hoff learning rule was informally discussed in chapter 1, and one version of this learning rule is now explicitly described (see figure 2.5).

Algorithm: Widrow-Hoff learning.   Consider an ANN system with d input units and one output unit. Let the connection strength parameter vector for the ANN system have dimension d.

• Step 0: Initialization. Let $t = 0$. Let $\mathbf{w}(t) \in \mathcal{R}^d$ be an arbitrary initial weight vector.

• Step 1: Choose stimulus from training set at random. Choose input stimulus $\mathbf{s}(t)$ and target response feedback signal $\mathbf{o}(t)$ such that

$$(\mathbf{s}(t), \mathbf{o}(t)) = (\mathbf{s}^k, \mathbf{o}^k),$$

where $(\mathbf{s}^k, \mathbf{o}^k) \in \mathcal{R}^{d+1}$ and $k = IRAND(t, 1, n)$ and where n is the number of training stimuli.

• Step 2: Compute output unit activation for current stimulus. Compute

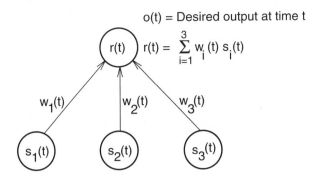

o(t) = Desired output at time t

$$r(t) = \sum_{i=1}^{3} w_i(t)\, s_i(t)$$

Widrow-Hoff Learning Rule

$$w_i(t+1) = w_i(t) + \gamma\,[o(t) - r(t)]\, s_i(t)$$

Figure 2.5
Learning using the Widrow-Hoff rule. The typical setup for the Widrow-Hoff learning rule involves several input units and several output units; in this example, there is a single output unit
whose activation level at time t is denoted by $r(t)$. The activation level of the output unit is a
weighted sum of the activation levels of the three input units at time t, denoted by $s_1(t)$, $s_2(t)$, and
$s_3(t)$. The input stimulus at time t is represented as a vector, $[s_1(t), s_2(t), s_3(t)]$, and the *desired output* of the network by the scalar $o(t)$. At each time interval indexed by t, the three weights $w_1(t)$,
$w_2(t)$, and $w_3(t)$ are updated using the formula shown in the figure. The constant γ is always positive and can be interpreted as the stepsize or learning rate of the algorithm.

$r(t) = \mathbf{w}(t)^T \mathbf{s}(t)$.

- Step 3: Update weights. For $j = 1 \ldots d$:

$w_j(t + 1) = w_j(t) + \gamma[o(t) - r(t)]s_j(t),$

where $w_j(t)$ is the jth element of $\mathbf{w}(t)$ and $s_j(t)$ is the jth element of $\mathbf{s}(t)$.

- Step 4: Let $t = t + 1$ and go to step 1.

Widrow and Hoff (1960) noted that the Widrow-Hoff learning rule is a
heuristic procedure for searching for a set of weights, $\mathbf{w}^*$, that minimize the
learning objective function

$$l(\mathbf{w}) = \sum_{k=1}^{n} \mid o^k - \mathbf{w}^T \mathbf{s}^k \mid^2,$$

where $(\mathbf{s}^k, o^k)$ is the kth training stimulus, $k = 1 \ldots n$. For this reason, the
Widrow-Hoff learning rule is sometimes referred to as the Least Mean Square
(LMS) learning rule.

It is well known that if the stepsize γ is decreased toward zero in an appropriate manner, then the Widrow-Hoff learning rule, under fairly general conditions, will converge to the set of weights which minimize the expected squared
error learning objective function l (e.g., Blum 1954; Duda and Hart 1973;

White 1989a,b; also see chapter 4). However, if γ approaches zero as time increases, then the Widrow-Hoff learning rule ceases to be adaptive as time increases. To address this problem, Macchi and Eweda (1983; also see Bitmead 1983; Daniell 1970) showed that a *fixed* stepsize γ could always be chosen such that the sequence of weight vectors generated by the Widrow-Hoff learning rule would converge to a set of weights where the expected squared error between the asymptotic weight vector and the optimal weight vector was as small as desired.

Backpropagation Learning

Overview. A backpropagation ANN system with one layer of hidden units (Rumelhart, Hinton, and Williams 1986) has a structure similar to Rosenblatt's multilayer perceptron (1958, 1962) in figure 2.2. One important difference between the backpropagation network and Rosenblatt's perceptron is that the weights between the input units and hidden units in the backpropagation algorithm are modified by the network's experiences. The input unit to hidden unit mapping in the original perceptron was initially randomly chosen and not modifiable through learning. In order to develop the backpropagation algorithm, Rumelhart, Hinton, and Williams (1986) replaced the "hard" logical threshold unit sigmoidal nonlinearity with a "soft" differentiable sigmoidal nonlinearity, as shown in figure 2.6. After making this substitution, they found that learning rules for the resulting network architecture could be derived in a straightforward manner using classical techniques from optimization theory. Note that if the magnitude of the weights in the backpropagation network is large, then the backpropagation network is a close approximation to a network of logical threshold units.

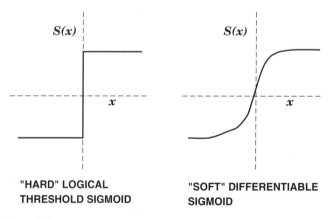

"HARD" LOGICAL THRESHOLD SIGMOID   **"SOFT" DIFFERENTIABLE SIGMOID**

Figure 2.6
Comparison of McCulloch-Pitts sigmoid and backpropagation sigmoid. The McCulloch-Pitts formal neuron sigmoidal function is a "hard" logical threshold sigmoid, while the backpropagation sigmoidal function is a "soft" differentiable sigmoidal function. The backpropagation soft differentiable sigmoidal function shown in this figure is the function $\mathcal{S}: \mathcal{R} \to (0, 1)$, defined such that $\mathcal{S}(x) = 1/(1 + \exp[-x])$ for all $x \in \mathcal{R}$.

In the Rumelhart, Hinton, and Williams (1986) backpropagation algorithm, the weights from the input to the hidden unit layer as well as the weights from the hidden to output unit layer are initially set to very small random values. During the learning process, some nodes have an initial disposition (because of the initial random weights) to detect some critical features while other nodes have an initial disposition to detect other critical features. Note that a "critical feature" is a statistical regularity in the ANN system's environment which can be exploited by the ANN to help solve the desired prediction problem. Because the goal of the learning process is to minimize the expected value of an error signal at the output units of the network, the limited number of units in the hidden layer are forced to compete to select the most relevant critical features for achieving the desired input unit to output unit mapping. Such a mapping can be shown to exist whenever at least one layer of sufficiently many hidden units is present (Cybenko 1989; Funahashi 1989; Hecht-Nielsen 1989; Hornik, Stinchcombe, and White 1989; Stinchcombe and White 1989). Figure 2.7 provides an illustration of a typical backpropagation network with three input units, two hidden units, and two output units. For presentation purposes, only a subset of the connections is labeled; the notation used in figure 2.7 is consistent with the notation used in the classical on-line backpropagation network learning algorithm described below.

A key characteristic of the backpropagation learning algorithm is that hidden units actively compete among themselves to extract the most relevant critical

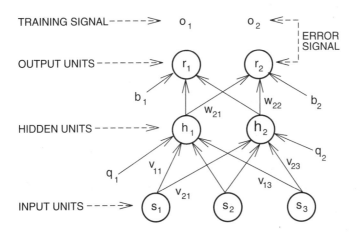

Figure 2.7
Classical backpropagation network. The network consists of three input units, two hidden units, and two output units. The activations of the input units are denoted by s_1, s_2, s_3, those of the hidden units by h_1 and h_2, and those of the output units by r_1 and r_2. The *desired response* of the network for a given input stimulus is denoted by the target activations o_1 and o_2. The input unit to hidden unit connection strength parameters are defined by a matrix **V** whose ijth element is v_{ij}, which indicates the connection strength from input unit j to hidden unit i. The hidden unit biases are q_1 and q_2. The matrix **W** defines the connection strengths from the hidden units to the output units, where the kith element of **W** is w_{ki}, which indicates the connection strength from hidden unit i to output unit k. The output unit biases are b_1 and b_2.

features from the training set. For this reason, choosing the correct number of hidden units in a backpropagation network is an important issue. Too few hidden units (e.g., zero units) and the network cannot learn. Too many hidden units (e.g., billions of units) and the network will memorize its training set. What is required is just the right number of hidden units so that the network is constrained to learn *only* the essential discriminating regularities in the training set. One heuristic method for choosing an appropriate number of hidden units is to assume that each hidden unit is merely a logical threshold unit, capable of only a single binary discrimination. Then, if each possible pattern of activity over the hidden units corresponds to a different training stimulus, a training set with M stimuli will require $\log_2 M$ hidden units. For example, if there are 8 distinct fifty-dimensional input patterns, then 3 (i.e., $\log_2 8$) binary-valued hidden units can recode these 8 fifty-dimensional input patterns as 8 three-dimensional activation patterns over 3 hidden units. Typically, more hidden units are required, but this heuristic is still helpful for selecting the appropriate order of magnitude for the number of hidden units.

Classical on-line backpropagation algorithm.   Many different versions of the backpropagation learning algorithm have been developed. The following version was originally proposed by Rumelhart, Hinton, and Williams (1986).

Algorithm: Classical on-line backpropagation.   Consider an ANN system with c input units, d hidden units, and p output units where the input units are connected to the hidden units and the hidden units are connected to the output units.

• Step 0: Initialize weights to small values. Let $t = 0$. Choose the following matrices and vectors such that their elements are observed values of a set of random variables that are independent and identically distributed according to either a Gaussian or uniform probability density with zero mean and strictly positive variance σ^2:

$\mathbf{V} = d \times c$-dimensional input unit to hidden unit weight matrix;

$\mathbf{W} = p \times d$-dimensional hidden unit to output unit weight matrix;

$\mathbf{b} = p$-dimensional output unit weight bias vector;

$\mathbf{q} = d$-dimensional hidden unit weight bias vector.

• Step 1: Pick training stimulus from stimulus set at random. Let $\mathbf{x}(t)$ be the training stimulus selected at the tth iteration of the learning algorithm. Define

$\mathbf{x}(t) = [\mathbf{s}(t), \mathbf{o}(t)]$,

where input stimulus $\mathbf{s}(t) \in \mathscr{R}^c$ and response feedback signal $\mathbf{o}(t) \in \mathscr{R}^p$. Let $\mathbf{x}(t)$ be selected such that

$\mathbf{x}(t) = [\mathbf{s}(t), \mathbf{o}(t)] = [\mathbf{s}^k, \mathbf{o}^k],$

where $k = IRAND(t, 1, N)$ and $(\mathbf{s}^k, \mathbf{o}^k)$ is an element of the training set

$\{(\mathbf{s}^1, \mathbf{o}^1),\ldots, (\mathbf{s}^n, \mathbf{o}^n)\}.$

- Step 2: Compute hidden unit response of network

$\mathbf{h}(t) = \mathscr{S}(\mathbf{V}\mathbf{s}(t) + \mathbf{q}),$

where $\mathscr{S}: \mathscr{R}^d \to (0, 1)^d$ is defined such that the ith element of $\mathscr{S}$, $\mathscr{S}_i: \mathscr{R} \to (0, 1)$, is defined such that for all $x \in \mathscr{R}$:

$\mathscr{S}_i(x) = 1/[1 + \exp(-x)].$

- Step 3: Compute output unit response of network

$\mathbf{r}(t) = \mathscr{S}(\mathbf{W}\mathbf{h}(t) + \mathbf{b}).$

- Step 4: Compute error signal for output units. Let the real p-dimensional column vector $\boldsymbol{\delta}_r(t)$ be defined such that

$\boldsymbol{\delta}_r(t) = \mathbf{o}(t) - \mathbf{r}(t).$

- Step 5: "Backpropagate" error signal from output units to hidden units. Let $\mathbf{D_r}(\mathbf{r}(t))$ be a p-dimensional matrix whose ith on-diagonal element is $r_i(t)$ $(1 - r_i(t))$, where r_i is the ith element of $\mathbf{r}(t)$ and the off-diagonal elements are equal to zero. Then

$\boldsymbol{\delta}_h(t) = \mathbf{W}^T \mathbf{D_r}(\mathbf{r}(t))\boldsymbol{\delta}_r(t).$

- Step 6: Change weights. Let $\mathbf{D_h}(\mathbf{h}(t))$ be a d-dimensional matrix whose ith on-diagonal element is $h_i(t)(1 - h_i(t))$, where $h_i(t)$ is the ith element of $\mathbf{h}(t)$ and the off-diagonal elements are equal to zero.

$\mathbf{W}(t + 1) = \mathbf{W}(t) + \gamma \mathbf{D_r}(\mathbf{r}(t))\boldsymbol{\delta}_r(t)\mathbf{h}(t)^T;$

$\mathbf{V}(t + 1) = \mathbf{V}(t) + \gamma \mathbf{D_h}(\mathbf{h}(t))\boldsymbol{\delta}_h(t)\mathbf{s}(t)^T;$

$\mathbf{b}(t + 1) = \mathbf{b}(t) + \gamma \mathbf{D_r}(\mathbf{r}(t))\boldsymbol{\delta}_r(t);$

$\mathbf{q}(t + 1) = \mathbf{q}(t) + \gamma \mathbf{D_h}(\mathbf{h}(t))\boldsymbol{\delta}_h(t).$

- Step 7: If algorithm has not converged, continue learning. Let $t = t + 1$. If $t > t_{\max}$ OR $(1/t)\sum_{k=1}^{t} |\mathbf{o}(k) - \mathbf{r}(k)|^2 < \varepsilon$, then stop. Otherwise, return to step 1.

Notice that the backpropagation algorithm gets its name from step 5, where the error at the output units $\boldsymbol{\delta}_r(t)$ is "backpropagated" to the hidden unit layer in order to compute error signals $\boldsymbol{\delta}_h(t)$ for the hidden units. Rumelhart, Hinton, and Williams (1986) showed that the classical backpropagation algorithm could be viewed as a heuristic procedure for searching for the minimum of a squared error objective function. They also mentioned a more general form of the backpropagation algorithm that can be viewed as a heuristic procedure for searching for the minimum of the expected value of some error function, l. The error function l is thus a learning objective function for the more general version of the backpropagation algorithm.

The initial variance, σ^2, of the probability distribution that generates the connection strength parameter vector for the backpropagation algorithm is an important parameter. If σ^2 is chosen to be too large, then the backpropagation learning algorithm (which is highly sensitive to initial conditions) may converge to an undesirable solution. Choosing σ^2 to be too small is usually not too serious a problem, but the learning speed of the backpropagation algorithm will tend to be slightly reduced. Some initial experimentation with the algorithm is usually desirable in order to select an appropriate value of σ^2.

On-line backpropagation algorithm.   The following algorithm will be referred to as "on-line backpropagation." The on-line backpropagation algorithm is a straightforward generalization of the classical on-line backpropagation algorithm.

Algorithm: On-line backpropagation.   Consider an ANN system with d input units and p output units. Let the connection strength parameter vector for the ANN system have dimension q.

• Step 0: Initialize weights to small values. Let $t = 0$. Assume elements of $\mathbf{w}(t) \in \mathcal{R}^q$ are the observed values of a set of independent and identically distributed random variables where each random variable has a mean of zero and strictly positive variance σ^2.

• Step 1: Pick a training stimulus at random. Let input stimulus $\mathbf{s}(t) = \mathbf{s}^k \in \mathcal{R}^d$ and response feedback signal $\mathbf{o}(t) = \mathbf{o}^k \in \mathcal{R}^p$, where $k = IRAND(t, 1, n)$ and $\mathbf{x}^k = (\mathbf{s}^k, \mathbf{o}^k)$ is an element of the training set

$$\{(\mathbf{s}^1, \mathbf{o}^1),\ldots, (\mathbf{s}^n, \mathbf{o}^n)\}.$$

• Step 2: Compute output unit response of network

$$\mathbf{r}(t) = \mathbf{f}(\mathbf{s}(t), \mathbf{w}(t)),$$

where the differentiable function $\mathbf{f}: \mathcal{R}^d \times \mathcal{R}^q \to \mathcal{R}^p$ defines the *architecture* of the backpropagation network.

• Step 3: Change weights. Let the differentiable function $c: \mathcal{R}^p \times \mathcal{R}^p \to \mathcal{R}$ define the *error function* for the backpropagation network. Then

$$\mathbf{w}(t + 1) = \mathbf{w}(t) - \gamma \mathbf{g}(\mathbf{w}(t)),$$

where the notation $\mathbf{g}(\mathbf{w}(t))$ indicates the gradient of $c(\mathbf{o}(t), \mathbf{f}(\mathbf{s}(t), \cdot))$ evaluated at $\mathbf{w}(t)$.

- Step 4: If algorithm has not converged, continue learning. Let $t = t + 1$. If $t > t_{max}$ OR $(1/t)\sum_{k=1}^{t} c([\mathbf{o}(k), \mathbf{f}(\mathbf{s}(k))], \mathbf{w}(t)) < \varepsilon$, then stop. Otherwise, return to step 1.

Batch or off-line backpropagation learning algorithm. Another important variation of the backpropagation learning algorithm also described by Rumelhart, Hinton, and Williams (1986), is the *batch* or *off-line learning algorithm.*

Algorithm: Batch backpropagation learning. Consider an ANN system with d input units and p output units. Let the connection strength parameter vector for the ANN system have dimension q.

- Step 0: Initialize weights to small values. Let $t = 0$. Assume the elements of $\mathbf{w}(t) \in \mathfrak{R}^q$ are observed values of a set of random variables that are independent and identically distributed with zero mean and strictly positive variance σ^2.

- Step 1: Change weights. Let the differentiable function $c: \mathfrak{R}^p \times \mathfrak{R}^p \to \mathfrak{R}$ define the *pattern error function* for the backpropagation network. Define the training set as the set of training stimuli

$$\{(\mathbf{s}^1, \mathbf{o}^1),\ldots, (\mathbf{s}^n, \mathbf{o}^n)\},$$

where input stimulus $\mathbf{s}^k \in \mathfrak{R}^d$ and response feedback signal $\mathbf{o}^k \in \mathfrak{R}^p$. Let $\mathbf{f}: \mathfrak{R}^d \times \mathfrak{R}^q \to \mathfrak{R}^p$ be differentiable in its second argument. Then

$$\mathbf{w}(t + 1) = \mathbf{w}(t) - \gamma(1/n)\sum_{k=1}^{n} \mathbf{g}^k(\mathbf{w}(t)),$$

where the notation $\mathbf{g}^k(\mathbf{w}(t))$ indicates the gradient of $c(\mathbf{o}^k, \mathbf{f}(\mathbf{s}^k, \cdot))$ evaluated at $\mathbf{w}(t)$.

- Step 2: If algorithm has not converged, continue learning. Let $t = t + 1$. If $t > t_{max}$ OR

$$(1/n)\sum_{k=1}^{n} c([\mathbf{o}^k, \mathbf{f}(\mathbf{s}^k, \mathbf{w}(t))]) < \varepsilon,$$

then stop. Otherwise, return to step 1.

Historical origins of the backpropagation learning algorithm. From a historical perspective, Amari (1967) was one of the earliest researchers to recognize that stochastic gradient descent algorithms (see chapter 4 for additional details) could be viewed as implementations of ANN system learning algorithms. Such learning algorithms are essentially equivalent to the on-line backpropagation learning algorithm. Werbos (1974) identified and provided an excellent description of a general class of multilayer network architectures with essentially the same structure as the class of classical on-line backpropagation learning algorithms. He also derived the general form of the computationally efficient backpropagation algorithm for such multilayer network architectures. The Werbos (1974) analysis may be viewed as an important special case of both on-line and off-line backpropagation that incorporates the multilayer hierarchical network features of the classical backpropagation algorithm, although he did not emphasize or discuss the importance of hidden units with differentiable sigmoidal functions. Rumelhart, Hinton, and Williams (1986; also see Le Cun 1985; and Parker 1985 for related work) introduced the classical backpropagation network architecture, which incorporated differentiable sigmoidal hidden units. In many respects, the success and power of classical backpropagation arises from these three distinct factors: (1) the realization that many ANN algorithms may be viewed as nonlinear optimization algorithms that seek a minimum of some learning objective function (Amari 1967; Rumelhart, Hinton, and Williams 1986; Werbos 1974), (2) the realization of the power of a multilayer hierarchical structure (Rumelhart, Hinton, and Williams 1986; Werbos 1974), and (3) the importance of differentiable sigmoidal hidden units (Rumelhart, Hinton, and Williams 1986) that implement "soft" logical mappings.

2.2.2   Unsupervised Learning

Typically in unsupervised learning, the statistical environment is assumed to generate some target vector, $\mathbf{x}$, with a particular probability. No other information is known. The ANN system must attempt to learn this probability distribution. The unsupervised learning problem may be informally defined by letting a training stimulus, $\mathbf{x}^k$, have the form $\mathbf{x}^k = \mathbf{s}^k$, where $\mathbf{s}^k$ is the stimulus input vector. Several example applications of unsupervised learning ANN systems were discussed in chapter 1. Section 1.4 provides a formal definition of unsupervised learning for ANN learning dynamical systems.

Hebbian Learning

One important ANN learning algorithm is the *Hebbian learning rule* (Anderson 1972; Grossberg 1972, 1974; Hebb 1949; James 1948), which states that the connection strength weight between two units in the ANN should be increased by an amount proportional to the product of the activations of the two units.

Algorithm: Autoassociative Hebbian learning.   Consider an ANN system with d units that are interconnected. A square d-dimensional connection strength parameter matrix defines the connections among the d units.

• Step 0: Initialization. Let $t = 0$. Let $\mathbf{W}(0) \in \mathfrak{R}^{d \times d}$ be a weight matrix of zeros. Let $\{\mathbf{s}^1, \ldots, \mathbf{s}^n\}$ be a set of n training stimuli such that $\mathbf{s}^k \in \mathfrak{R}^d$ for $k = 1 \ldots n$.

- Step 1: Pick training stimulus at random. Let $\mathbf{s}(t) = \mathbf{s}^k$, where $k = IRAND$ $(t, 1, n)$, and $\mathbf{s}^k \in \{\mathbf{s}^1, \ldots, \mathbf{s}^n\}$.
- Step 2: Compute output unit activations for current stimulus. Compute the pattern of activation over the output units, $\mathbf{r}(t)$, given pattern of activation over the input units, $\mathbf{s}(t)$, using

$\mathbf{r}(t) = \mathbf{W}(t)^T \mathbf{s}(t)$.

- Step 3: Update weights. Update the connection strength $w_{ij}(t)$ between the ith and jth unit in the network using

$w_{ij}(t + 1) = w_{ij}(t) + \gamma s_i(t) s_j(t)$,

where $w_{ij}(t)$ is the ijth element of $\mathbf{W}(t)$, $s_i(t)$ is the ith element of $\mathbf{s}(t)$, and γ is a positive stepsize for $i, j = 1 \ldots d$.
- Step 4: Let $t = t + 1$ and go to step 1.

Note that step 3 of the autoassociative Hebbian learning rule may be equivalently expressed in vector notation as

$\mathbf{W}(t + 1) = \mathbf{W}(t) + \gamma \mathbf{s}(t) \mathbf{s}(t)^T$.

The autoassociative Hebbian learning rule can be shown to minimize the learning objective function, $l: \mathcal{R}^{d \times d} \rightarrow \mathcal{R}$, defined such that

$$l(\mathbf{W}) = -(1/M) \sum_{k=1}^{M} p_k [\mathbf{s}^k]^T \mathbf{W} \mathbf{s}^k, \tag{2.2}$$

where $\mathbf{s}^k$ is the kth training stimulus ($k = 1 \ldots M$), assumed to occur with probability p_k in the statistical environment. The autoassociative Hebbian learning rule is an unstable learning rule because the connection strength magnitudes tend to grow without bound toward infinity. Section 4.3.2 shows how adjustment of the learning rate γ and the introduction of a weight decay mechanism can stabilize this learning rule and develop a version of the autoassociative Hebbian learning rule that minimizes the learning objective function in (2.2).

It can be shown, under fairly general conditions, that the matrix of weights, $\mathbf{W}$, formed by the autoassociative Hebbian learning rule essentially learns a useful linear subspace within which the training sequence can be represented (Anderson et al. 1977; Anderson and Mozer 1981). To see this, note that $\mathbf{W}$ must always be symmetric because of the manner in which the autoassociative Hebbian learning rule forms connections. Let λ_i be the ith eigenvalue associated with eigenvector $\mathbf{e}_i$ for matrix $\mathbf{W}$. The eigenvectors are orthogonal because $\mathbf{W}$ is real and symmetric. Thus

$$l(\mathbf{W}) = -(1/M) \sum_{k=1}^{M} p_k [\mathbf{s}^k]^T \mathbf{W} \mathbf{s}^k$$

$$l(\mathbf{W}) = -(1/M) \sum_{k=1}^{M} p_k [\mathbf{s}^k]^T \left[\sum_{i=1}^{d} \lambda_i \mathbf{e}_i \mathbf{e}_i^T \right] \mathbf{s}^k$$

$$l(\mathbf{W}) = -(1/M) \sum_{k=1}^{M} p_k \lambda_k ([\mathbf{s}^k]^T \mathbf{e}_k)^2 \tag{2.3}$$

since $[\mathbf{s}^k]^T \mathbf{e}_i = 0$ if $k \neq i$. Thus inspection of (2.3) shows that the learning objective function l becomes smaller if the linear subspace spanned by the eigenvectors of $\mathbf{W}$ is also spanned by the stimulus vectors in the training set. Because of this analysis, the magnitude of the response vector $\mathbf{r}(t)$ is usually interpreted as the psychological *familiarity* of the input $\mathbf{s}(t)$, while the direction of the response vector $\mathbf{r}(t)$ is usually interpreted as the *identity* of the input pattern $\mathbf{s}(t)$.

Autoassociative Widrow-Hoff Learning

Consider the *autoassociative Widrow-Hoff learning rule* (Anderson 1995, 502–504) where the target vector, $\mathbf{o}(t)$, is always set equal to the stimulus vector, $\mathbf{s}(t)$. This manipulation transforms the supervised learning version of the Widrow-Hoff rule into an unsupervised learning rule. In particular, we have

$$w_{ij}(t+1) = w_{ij}(t) + \gamma [s_i(t) - \mathbf{w}_i^T \mathbf{s}(t)] s_j(t),$$

where $\mathbf{w}_i^T$ is the ith row of the matrix $\mathbf{W}$ whose ijth element is w_{ij}. The learning rule in this case will behave similarly to the autoassociative Hebbian learning rule although (1) it will be much more stable because of the error correction learning property, and (2) forces the eigenvalues of the basis vectors spanning the linear subspace spanned by the stimulus vectors to approach unity (see problem 3-1). The autoassociative Widrow-Hoff learning rule seeks a weight matrix $\mathbf{W}$ that obtains a minimum value of the function l, where l is defined such that

$$l(\mathbf{W}) = (1/n) \sum_{k=1}^{n} | \mathbf{s}^k - \mathbf{W} \mathbf{s}^k |^2.$$

The Nonlinear Autoencoder

As with the Widrow-Hoff learning rule, an autoassociative version of a backpropagation learning rule can be developed from the associative version. Such autoassociative backpropagation networks, or *autoencoders* (Ackley, Hinton, and Sejnowski 1985; Cottrell, Munro, and Zipser 1987), minimize a sum-squared error function (i.e., learning objective function) as in backpropagation, but the target vector, **o**, is always the same as the input vector, **s**. Autoencoders are designed to "compress" the information in a given stimulus vector so that it can be compactly represented over a small number of hidden units. In order to prevent the autoencoder network from memorizing the set of training stimuli, the number of hidden units must be chosen to be smaller than the number of training stimuli. This constraint tends to force the learning rule to learn the distinctive features of the stimulus set without memorization. Bourlard and Kamp (1988) showed that if the output units of an autoencoder are linear, then a minimum mean square error solution obtained using nonlinear hidden units is the same as a minimum mean square error solution obtained using linear hidden units. Baldi and Hornik (1989) showed that when both the hidden and output units are linear, the network learns a useful linear subspace for representing the stimulus set whose dimension is equal to the number of hidden units.

Adaptive Resonance Theory

Carpenter, Grossberg, and Rosen (1991) and Carpenter et al. (1992) have been investigating a particular class of unsupervised learning algorithms that they refer to as "adaptive resonance theory" (ART) learning algorithms. Unlike most ANN learning algorithms where the stepsize of the algorithm must be decreased to guarantee convergence (e.g., see the algorithms analyzed in chapter 4), the ART algorithm's stability is guaranteed in a relatively large class of environments for a fixed stepsize. Although highly successful supervised learning versions of ART have been recently developed (Carpenter et al. 1992), for expository reasons the simpler unsupervised, "fuzzy" ART system will be described.

Briefly, fuzzy ART consists of two layers of units. The first layer of units (referred to as the "F_1 layer") are "input units." The second layer of units (referred to as the "F_2 layer") are "hidden units." As each input pattern of activation is presented to the ART system, the input units in the F_1 layer become active. These units, in turn, activate units in the F_2 layer. The units in the F_2 layer then compete with one another via some implicit lateral inhibition process until the unit that is maximally active inhibits the activation levels of the remaining units. Thus the learning process is only enabled for the winning unit at the hidden unit F_2 layer. The winning unit at the F_2 layer then generates a feedback signal to the F_1 layer that is primarily dependent upon how the input units in the F_1 layer are connected to the winning unit. If there is agreement between the input signal and the generated feedback signal, then *resonance* occurs and the connections from the F_1 layer to the winning unit are changed by an amount proportional to the "agreement" between input signal and feedback signal.

If agreement between the input signal and the generated feedback signal is not present, then a *reset operation* occurs and the winning unit is temporarily *disabled.* The units in the F_2 layer then compete with one another to decide which of the remaining units is the winning unit. If the "second-place" winning unit is also disabled, then a "third-place" winning unit is selected. This process continues until a winning unit is found that "resonates" with the incoming activation pattern. Learning occurs at this point and the connections from the F_1 layer to the winning unit are modified. Carpenter, Grossberg, and Rosen (1991) have identified explicit conditions guaranteeing the stability of learning in the ART system for a relatively large class of statistical (including certain types of nonstationary statistical) environments.

Note that the decision rule for deciding if a given hidden unit resonates with a given input activation pattern at layer F_1 can be viewed as a test to decide if the input activation pattern is sufficiently similar to the category prototype weight vector associated with the hidden unit. Also note that the criteria for deciding how much agreement between input signal and feedback signal is necessary for declaring a resonant state is determined by the *vigilance parameter ρ*. The vigilance parameter ρ is a constant that determines the size of the categories learned by the ART system. If ρ is large, then the ART system tends to group input patterns into a relatively small number of clusters. If ρ is small, then the ART system tends to group input patterns into a relatively large number of clusters.

Finally, it is important to note that adaptive resonance theory (like other unsupervised learning algorithms) may be viewed as a type of clustering algorithm. Baruah and Holden (1991) have pointed out how some versions of adaptive resonance theory are closely related to specific types of classical clustering algorithms.

Before presenting the fuzzy ART unsupervised learning algorithm, it will be necessary to introduce some special notation. Let the notation $\mid \mathbf{x} \mid_1$ be defined as

$$\mid \mathbf{x} \mid_1 = \sum_{i=1}^{M} \mid x_i \mid,$$

where x_i is the ith element of the M-dimensional vector $\mathbf{x}$. Now let $\mathbf{x}$ and $\mathbf{y}$ be two vectors such that the ith elements of $\mathbf{x}$ and $\mathbf{y}$ are the scalars x_i and y_i respectively. Define the fuzzy AND operator (Zadeh 1965) $\tilde{\cap}$ such that if $\mathbf{z} = \mathbf{x} \tilde{\cap} \mathbf{y}$, then the ith element of $\mathbf{z}$, z_i, is equal to the smallest member of the set $\{x_i, y_i\}$.

The following description of fuzzy ART unsupervised learning is based upon the discussion in Carpenter et al. (1992, 700–701). Another good discussion of a close relative of this algorithm may also be found in Hertz, Krogh, and Palmer (1991, 229–230).

Algorithm: Fuzzy ART unsupervised learning

• Step 0: Initialization. Let the *choice parameter ε* be a small positive number. Let $\gamma \in (0, 1]$ be the *learning rate parameter* ($\gamma = 1$ for *fast learning mode*). Let ρ be the positive *vigilance* parameter. Let $\mathbf{s}^1, \ldots, \mathbf{s}^n$ be a set of n d-dimensional training vectors that satisfy the following two normalization conditions for $i = 1\ldots n$: (i) there exists some strictly positive constant h such that $|\mathbf{s}^i| = h$, and (ii) $\mathbf{s}^i \in [0, 1]^d$. Also set $\mathbf{w}_i(0) = \mathbf{1}_d$ for $i = 1\ldots n$. Let $t = 0$.

• Step 1: Pick training stimulus at random and enable all hidden units. Let the training stimulus at iteration t of the algorithm, $\mathbf{s}(t)$, be defined such that

$$\mathbf{s}(t) = \mathbf{s}^i,$$

where $i = IRAND(t, 1, n)$ and $\mathbf{s}^i$ is the ith element of the training set $\{\mathbf{s}^1,\ldots, \mathbf{s}^n\}$. Let $\mu_i = 1$ for $i = 1\ldots n$.

• Step 2: Decide which enabled hidden unit is responding maximally. Let the activation level, $r_i(\mathbf{s}(t))$, of the ith hidden unit ($i = 1\ldots n$) in response to input activation pattern $\mathbf{s}(t)$ be defined as

$$r_i(\mathbf{s}(t)) = \frac{\left|\mathbf{s}(t) \tilde{\cap} \mathbf{w}_j(t)\right|_1}{\varepsilon + \left|\mathbf{w}_j(t)\right|_1}.$$

Let $i*$ be defined as the smallest positive integer that satisfies the condition $\mu_{i*} = 1$ and in addition satisfies

$$r_{i*}(\mathbf{s}(t)) \geq r_i(\mathbf{s}(t)),$$

for all $i \in \{j \in \{1, 2,\ldots, n\}: \mu_j = 1\}$.

• Step 3: Check if the input activation pattern, $\mathbf{s}(t)$, is similar enough to the chosen category $\mathbf{w}_{i*}(t)$ (i.e., decide if resonance mode or reset mode should be selected). If the input activation pattern is sufficiently similar to the chosen category (i.e., resonance mode), then update weight vector with a fuzzy conjunction of the input vector and the current value of the weight vector. If the input activation pattern $\mathbf{s}(t)$ is not sufficiently similar to the chosen category $\mathbf{w}_{i*}(t)$ (i.e., reset mode), then temporarily disable the chosen category (i.e., set $\mu_{i*}(t) = 0$). In particular, this step of the algorithm is completely specified by the following decision rule. If

$$\frac{\left|\mathbf{s}(t) \tilde{\cap} \mathbf{w}_{i*}(t)\right|_1}{\left|\mathbf{s}(t)\right|_1} \geq \rho,$$

then

$$\mathbf{w}_{i*}(t + 1) = \gamma\left[\mathbf{s}(t) \tilde{\cap} \mathbf{w}_{i*}(t)\right] + (1 - \gamma)\mathbf{w}_{i*}(t)$$

and let $t = t + 1$ and go to step 1. If

$$\frac{\left|\mathbf{s}(t) \tilde{\cap} \mathbf{w}_{i*}(t)\right|_1}{\left|\mathbf{s}(t)\right|_1} < \rho,$$

then set $\mu_{i*} = 0$ and go to step 2.

2.2.3   Reinforcement Learning

Consider the problem of learning to drive a car. In a supervised learning paradigm, an instructor is constantly providing specific feedback such as "Please apply the car brakes immediately" to the student driver. In an unsupervised learning paradigm, the student driver learns by simply watching other people drive. In a *reinforcement learning* paradigm, the student tries driving the car and receives partial feedback (e.g., honking horns from other drivers or shouts from angry pedestrians) from the environment. Thus the student driver is forced to solve the *credit assignment* problem that asks what associative mappings must be learned in order to prevent or facilitate different types of partial feedback from the environment.

More formally, in supervised learning, the ANN system is provided with a training stimulus, $\mathbf{x} = (\mathbf{s}, \mathbf{o_r})$, consisting of both a stimulus vector, $\mathbf{s}$, and a desired response vector, $\mathbf{o_r}$. In unsupervised learning, the ANN system is provided with a training stimulus, $\mathbf{x}$, which consists of just a stimulus vector $\mathbf{s}$. Reinforcement learning represents a compromise between supervised and unsupervised learning, where indirect information about $\mathbf{o_r}$ is provided in the training stimulus. In particular, for reinforcement learning, $\mathbf{x} = (\mathbf{s}, \mathbf{o_c})$, where $\mathbf{s}$ is the stimulus vector and $\mathbf{o_c}$ is a reinforcement signal that provides only certain clues about the nature of the desired response, $\mathbf{o_r}$.

One powerful solution to this problem based upon classical nonlinear optimal control theory (Bellman 1971; Bellman and Kalaba 1965; Luenberger 1979) has recently been explored in the context of ANN systems (Barto, 1990; Jordan and Rumelhart 1992; Munro 1987; Rumelhart et al. 1986; Werbos 1990; R. J. Williams 1988, 1992). Using the terminology provided in the definition of backpropagation learning, let the architecture of an ANN system that is a function mapping an input vector, $\mathbf{s}$, into an output vector, $\mathbf{r}$, using a set of weights, $\mathbf{w}$, be represented as $\mathbf{r} = \mathbf{f}(\mathbf{s}, \mathbf{w})$. Because the target, $\mathbf{o_r}$, for the network's response, $\mathbf{r}$, is not directly provided to the network, it is not possible to generate an error signal, such as $\delta = \mathbf{o_r} - \mathbf{r}$, in the usual manner.

On the other hand, suppose that the ANN is designed to have prior knowledge of how the reinforcement signal $\mathbf{o_c}$ is related to the unobservable desired network response $\mathbf{o_r}$. This internalized theory can be represented as a (usually differentiable and noninvertible) function, $\mathbf{c}$, which maps $\mathbf{o_r}$ into $\mathbf{o_c}$. The function $\mathbf{c}$ represents the network's theory about the relationship between its responses and observable environmental events. Then, if $\mathbf{f}$ specifies a backpropagation network architecture with one layer of hidden units, the learning problem can be solved using a two-layer backpropagation network architecture that maps $\mathbf{s}$ into a prediction of the reinforcement signal, $\mathbf{r_c}$ using the formula

$$\mathbf{r_c} = \mathbf{c}(\mathbf{f}(\mathbf{s}, \mathbf{w})).$$

As shown in figure 2.8, the error signal

$$\delta_c = \mathbf{o}_c - \mathbf{r_c}$$

is computed at the output of the backpropagation network and then backpropagated to update the network's weights in the usual manner. Note that the last layer of connections represented by the prior knowledge function **c** is not modified during the learning process.

One might argue that the above process is overly complex. Why not simply directly learn the desired mapping from **s** to the observed reinforcement signal $\mathbf{o}_c$? The answer to this question is that although a backpropagation network can *represent* such a mapping with a sufficient number of hidden units (Cybenko 1989; Funahashi 1989; Hecht-Nielsen 1989; Hornik, Stinchcombe, and White 1989), this learning problem is a very difficult one. The reinforcement learning network is designed to simplify this problem by dividing the problem up into two learning subproblems. First, learn how responses affect the occurrence of observable environmental events. And second, learn to map stimuli into responses by backpropagating the reinforcement signal between the model's

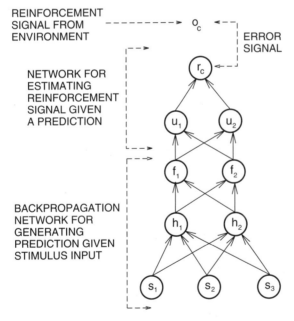

Figure 2.8
One approach to solving the reinforcement learning problem. A backpropagation network maps stimulus activation pattern (s_1, s_2, s_3) into an output unit activation pattern (f_1, f_2). Although a training signal is not available to train the network, the environment does provide a less specific reinforcement signal, o_c, which may be used by the learning machine. To solve this problem, a second backpropagation network for mapping the output unit activation pattern of the original network (f_1, f_2) into a prediction of the environmental reinforcement signal, r_c, is required. The error signal $(o_c - r_c)$ can then be computed and exploited by the learning machine.

expectations of which events will occur in the environment and the actual environmental events.

It should be noted that many of these concepts are well known and form the basis of modern optimal control theory (e.g., Bellman 1971; Bellman and Kalaba 1965; Luenberger 1979). In control theory, the transfer function **c** is often referred to as the "plant model" (i.e., the system to be controlled). The transfer function **f** can be viewed as a parameterized control law that is estimated from the data. This type of learning process is also consistent with theories proposed by psychologists (e.g., Piaget 1954; Rumelhart et al. 1986) who have suggested that human learning is characterized by first learning a mental model of reality, and then exploiting that mental model to learn how to control one's environment.

Now consider the case where **c** is essentially unknown. In this case, **c** might be represented as a parametric function of some weight vector **v** as well as response vector $\mathbf{r} = \mathbf{f}(\mathbf{s}, \mathbf{w})$. The learning process then proceeds in two stages. In stage one, the ANN system might generate random output activation patterns and use the resulting reinforcement signals from its environment to "learn" the function $\mathbf{c}(\cdot; \mathbf{v})$ by estimating the parameter vector **v**. Thus the ANN system would first learn an internalized causal mental model of the world, $\mathbf{c}(\cdot, \mathbf{v})$. In stage two, the ANN system would then use its constructed internal model of the world, **c**, in order to learn how to control its environment. (Jordan 1992, Jordan and Rumelhart 1992; Munro 1987; and Rumelhart et al. 1986 discuss such a two-stage learning process in further detail.)

2.2.4   Temporal Learning

Let $p_1, \ldots, p_M$ be a sequence of positive real numbers such that $0 < p_l \le 1$ and $\sum_{l=1}^{M} p_l = 1$, where M is a finite positive integer. It will usually be assumed in this textbook that the statistical environment of an ANN temporal learning system generates a *trajectory* of the form

$$[\mathbf{s}_l(0), \mathbf{o}_l(0)], [\mathbf{s}_l(1), \mathbf{o}_l(1)], [\mathbf{s}_l(2), \mathbf{o}_l(2)], \ldots, [\mathbf{s}_l(T_l), \mathbf{o}_l(T_l)] \qquad (2.4)$$

with probability p_l ($l = 1 \ldots M$), where $\mathbf{o}_l(t)$ is the tth desired output or target response feedback signal of the network to the tth stimulus $\mathbf{s}_l(t)$ in the lth sequence of training stimuli learned by the ANN learning system.

The goal of an ANN system *temporal learning* algorithm is to minimize a learning objective function that measures the distance between the observed relative frequency of particular trajectories in its environment and the ANN system's predictions of those relative frequencies. Good reviews of recent developments in the ANN literature concerned with temporal learning are available (Barto 1990; Chauvin and Rumelhart 1995; Hertz, Krogh, and Palmer 1991; Mozer 1993). In this section only the most classical network architectures are considered for expository reasons.

Finally, the representational scheme in (2.4) is appropriate in many situations and will be exploited in this textbook. However this type of representational scheme is limited in the sense that it is not designed to model statistical environments where a learning machine observes a single long sequence of training stimuli and attempts to identify temporal regularities. There are certainly mathematical techniques one may use to analyze this latter case (e.g., Kuan, Hornik, and White 1994) but such techniques will not be discussed because of their additional complexity.

Jordan Sequential Network

Jordan (1992) has proposed a backpropagation type ANN architecture for learning and generating sequences of items that can be viewed as a backpropagation implementation of the temporal associative memory system proposed by Kohonen (1984, 16–20), which, in turn, was based upon the even more general notation of a finite state machine (Minsky 1967).

A representative Jordan (1992) sequential network is shown in figure 2.9. Like the standard backpropagation network architecture, the Jordan sequential network consists of a set of input units, a set of hidden units, and a set of output units. Unlike the standard backpropagation network algorithm, some of the input units in figure 2.9 function as a kind of memory buffer with an exponentially decaying memory.

Let $[\mathbf{s}_l(0), \mathbf{o}_l(0)]\dots[\mathbf{s}_l(T_l), \mathbf{o}_l(T_l)]$ be the lth trajectory of n trajectories, where

$$\mathbf{s}_l(t) = [\mathbf{c}_l, \mathbf{y}_l(t)].$$

Let c_i^l denote the activation of the ith *plan* input unit for trajectory l. Let $o_i^l(t)$ denote the ith element of $\mathbf{o}_l(t)$. Let $y_j^l(t)$ (jth element of $\mathbf{y}_l(t)$) denote the activation of the jth *state* input unit for the tth element of trajectory l. Finally, $y_j^l(t)$ is computed using the formula

$$y_j^l(t) = o_j^l(t-1) + \mu y_j^l(t-1), \tag{2.5}$$

where the memory decay rate parameter μ ($0 < \mu < 1$) specifies the degree to which the past history of desired target outputs influences the next prediction of the network.

Another popular variant of the Jordan sequential network is to have inputs that compute an exponentially weighted sum of the network's *actual* responses rather than its *desired* responses. This latter variant is much more complicated to analyze because the network desired response, $\mathbf{o}(t)$, is functionally dependent upon the network's previous pattern of responses $\mathbf{r}(t-1),\dots, \mathbf{r}(0)$, where $\mathbf{r}(t)$ is the response of the network at time t. In the version of the Jordan (1986, 1992) network presented in figure 2.9, the desired response $\mathbf{o}(t)$ is *not* functionally dependent upon the past history of responses

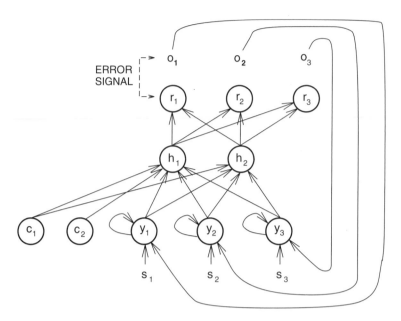

Figure 2.9
Jordan sequential network. A Jordan sequential network maps an exponentially weighted average of its past target output (i.e., activation pattern o_1, o_2, o_3) and the activation pattern representing the plan (i.e., c_1, c_2) into an output activation pattern (i.e., r_1, r_2, r_3). The error signal is used to update the weights, as in the standard backpropagation algorithm.

by the network, $\mathbf{r}(t-1),\ldots,\mathbf{r}(0)$. Or in other words, $\mathbf{o}(t)$ is *not* functionally dependent upon the network's previous set of connection strengths.

Elman Sequential Network

Elman (1990) has proposed an interesting approach to learning temporal sequences that is best illustrated by referring to figure 2.10. Let $\mathbf{s}(t)$ refer to the activation pattern over the input units. Let $\mathbf{h}(t)$ refer to the activation pattern over the hidden units. Let $\mathbf{r}(t)$ refer to the activation pattern over the output units which is a differentiable function of $\mathbf{h}(t)$. In the *Elman sequential network,* the hidden unit activation pattern $\mathbf{h}(t)$ is a differentiable function of $\mathbf{h}(t-1)$ as well as $\mathbf{s}(t)$. The implication of this functional relationship is that the Elman network is performing an integration of information over the past history of stimuli like the Jordan network but that the integration process for the Elman network takes place in the hidden unit activation space. The Elman network therefore can sometimes pick up more subtle temporal regularities relative to the Jordan network because only the important features of the past stimulus history are fed back through the network. Another way to think about the Elman network is that if the network can learn a temporal sequence with a relatively small number of hidden units, then it has "compressed" information about the entire past history of the sequence into the activation pattern over the hidden units.

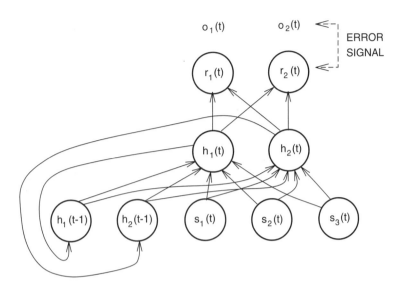

Figure 2.10
Elman sequential network. An Elman sequential network maps a compressed representation of the past sequence of inputs. That is, the activation pattern $[h_1(t-1), h_2(t-1)]$ and the incoming signal activation pattern $\mathbf{s}(t) = [s_1(t), s_2(t), s_3(t)]$ are mapped into an output activation pattern, $[r_1(t), r_2(t)]$, resulting in a new compressed representation, $[h_1(t), h_2(t)]$, of the past sequence $\mathbf{s}(t), \mathbf{s}(t-1), \ldots, \mathbf{s}(0)$.

Two basic variations of the Elman sequential network learning algorithm should be mentioned. The first version is based upon "unfolding the network" in time (Minsky and Papert 1969; Rumelhart, Hinton, and Williams 1986). Figure 2.11 shows how an Elman sequential network can be unfolded in time, and then be trained using standard backpropagation methods. Note that when a network is unfolded in time the learning procedure must be constrained so that all "copies" of the network are updated in the same way. Thus, after computing the weight changes for each copy of the original network, the average weight change is applied to the system. Such a procedure may be considered to be a "batch" version of Elman sequential network learning. The second, "on-line" version of the algorithm known as "real-time recurrent learning" (RTRL; Williams and Zipser 1989a,b) simply updates the weights of the network each time a training stimulus is presented.

As previously noted, one important property of the Jordan network is that the Jordan network integrates information in the "target response" space by simply computing a weighted average of the past history of target response measurements with more recent measurements being weighted as more important. The Elman sequential network, on the other hand, integrates information in the "hidden unit" space, so that a more sophisticated integration of information can take place; in particular, it does not necessarily weight recent

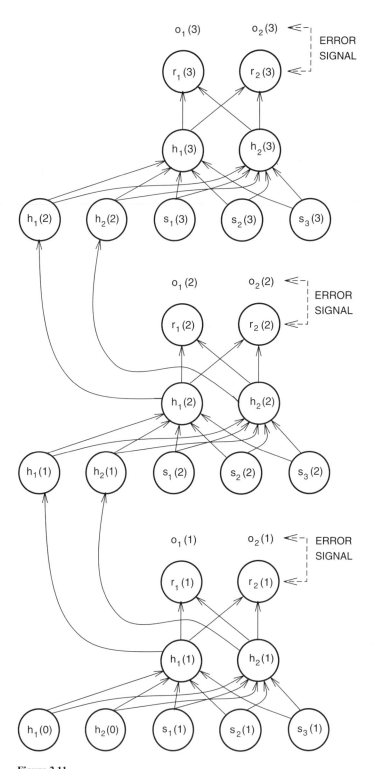

Figure 2.11
Elman sequential network unfolded in time. The Elman sequential network depicted in figure 2.10 is unfolded in time so that it appears to be a multilayer backpropagation network, with one stage for each item in the sequence. In this example, the sequence consists of only three items. Note that the learning process is constrained so that all three stages always have *exactly* the same weights.

sensor measurements (e.g., $\mathbf{s}(t-1)$, $\mathbf{s}(t-2)$) as more important than tempo-rally distant sensor measurements (e.g., $\mathbf{s}(t-10)$, $\mathbf{s}(t-11)$). The basic prob-lem with the Elman sequential network is that it is more difficult to analyze and to effectively use.

Mental Model (Unsupervised Temporal) Learning

In this section the concept of *mental model learning* is introduced. An ANN mental model learning dynamical system is formally defined as a special type of unsupervised ANN temporal learning dynamical system (see section 1.4 for additional details). The ANN learning system is provided information regard-ing temporal sequences of events in its environment but is not provided any di-rect information regarding a desired sequence of responses. Knowledge of the nature of the responses that must be generated by the ANN classification dy-namical system as a function of the entire ANN system's connection strength parameter vector is assumed to be "prewired" or implicitly incorporated into the ANN system's architecture. The essential idea behind mental model learn-ing is exactly the same as ideas that have been introduced into the classical mathematical theory of optimal control (Barto 1990; Jordan 1992; Jordan and Rumelhart 1992; Kalman, Falb, and Arbib 1969; Munro 1987; Rumelhart et al. 1986; Werbos 1990; R. J. Williams 1988).

A generic optimal control problem consists of three elements. The first two elements are illustrated in figure 2.12 using a backpropagation implementation. First, a plant (i.e., system) to be controlled is formally represented as a func-tion, $\mathbf{c}$, that maps the current system state,

$$\mathbf{s}(t) = (s_1(t), s_2(t),\ldots, s_d(t)),$$

and control signal,

$$\mathbf{f}(t) = (f_1(t), f_2(t),\ldots, f_m(t)),$$

into an estimate of the next system state,

$$\hat{\mathbf{s}}(t+1) = (\hat{s}_1(t+1), \hat{s}_2(t+1),\ldots, \hat{s}_d(t+1)).$$

Second, a control law that maps the current system state, $\mathbf{s}(t)$, and control law pa-rameters, $\mathbf{w}$, into the control signal $\mathbf{f}(t)$. The third required element of an optimal control theory problem is an objective function, l, that maps a plant trajectory

$$\mathbf{s}(0), \mathbf{s}(1), \mathbf{s}(2),\ldots,$$

into a number indicating the quality (i.e., goodness) of the trajectory. That is, the third element indicates how the error signal for the system will be com-puted. The goal of the generic optimal control problem is to select a set of con-trol law parameters, $\mathbf{w}$, such that the value of the objective function l is minimized across all possible trajectories of the plant.

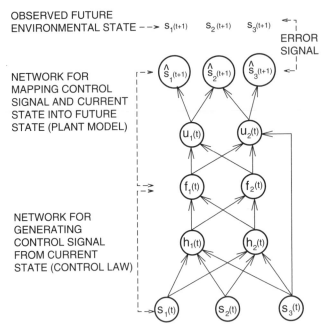

OBSERVED FUTURE
ENVIRONMENTAL STATE $--\rightarrow$ $s_1(t+1)$ $s_2(t+1)$ $s_3(t+1)$

ERROR
SIGNAL

NETWORK FOR
MAPPING CONTROL
SIGNAL AND CURRENT
STATE INTO FUTURE
STATE (PLANT MODEL)

NETWORK FOR
GENERATING
CONTROL SIGNAL
FROM CURRENT
STATE (CONTROL LAW)

Figure 2.12
Optimal control theory and backpropagation. Backpropagation can be applied to solving certain types of nonlinear optimal control problems. The current state $s_1(t)$, $s_2(t)$, $s_3(t)$ in conjunction with network parameters are used to generate control signal $f_1(t), f_2(t)$, which is then used in conjunction with the current state $s_3(t)$ to predict the future environmental state $\hat{s}_1(t+1)$, $\hat{s}_2(t+1)$, $\hat{s}_3(t+1)$. This latter mapping (known as the "plant model") is assumed to be previously learned using a system identification paradigm. The error signal between the observed future environmental state $s_1(t+1), s_2(t+1), s_3(t+1)$ and the estimated future environmental state $\hat{s}_1(t+1)$, $\hat{s}_2(t+1), \hat{s}_3(t+1)$ is then propagated backward through the plant model in order to adjust the control law parameters.

For example, consider the problem of designing a control law which learns to assist in the management of the control of an airplane during landing. The quality of a landing is based upon the learning objective function l that assigns a number to a given landing trajectory. Some trajectories will be assigned low numbers, indicating good landings, while other trajectories will be assigned large numbers, indicating poor landings (or crashes). The control signals to the aircraft at time t are the elements of the vector $\mathbf{f}(t)$. The current state of the airplane is the vector $\mathbf{s}(t)$. In addition, the airplane contains an internal theoretical model of its behavior, which is the plant model function $\mathbf{c}$.

An ANN system version of the optimal control problem based upon the classical backpropagation network architecture is depicted in figure 2.12, which shows how the plant model mapping and control law mapping are modeled as backpropagation networks. It is important to note that either Jordan-style or Elman-style backpropagation architectures may be incorporated into the design of a mental model learning ANN system.

Temporal Reinforcement Learning

Unlike supervised temporal learning or unsupervised (mental model) temporal learning, the desired response or target vector for the learning machine may not always be available during the course of learning. A classical example of a *temporal reinforcement learning* problem is game playing where the desired response of the learning machine is only available at certain points in time during the course of the game (possibly only at the end of the game) and then the obtained information must be used to revise the performance of the game playing algorithm. Another example might involve learning to control an aircraft during landing under adverse conditions where the feedback signals to the aircraft designed to improve learning performance are frequently corrupted and thus not accessible to the aircraft. Problem 4-7 (also see problems 4-9, 5-7, and 7-3) illustrate some important principles of temporal reinforcement learning ANN systems (for further discussion see Jaakkola, Jordan, and, Singh 1994; Sutton 1988; R. J. Williams and Zipser 1995).

2.2.5 Prior Knowledge Learning Strategies

It should be noted that specific network architectures such as those in classical backpropagation and optimal control theory are excellent examples of introducing constraints upon the learning process of an ANN system. Such constraints can be viewed as providing the ANN with *prior knowledge* about its environment. If exploited properly by the ANN, such knowledge can vastly simplify the learning problem faced by the ANN system and result in increased learning efficiency. In this section, several other important strategies for introducing constraints into ANN system learning algorithms are described.

Initial Conditions for Learning

For a very large class of important ANN learning dynamical systems, the initial conditions of such learning systems (even for nontemporal learning dynamical systems) can considerably influence the outcome of the learning process. For example, consider the classical backpropagation ANN learning algorithm (also see self-organizing ANN learning systems such as von der Malsburg 1973). Two researchers can train two identical batch backpropagation learning algorithms with respect to exactly the same network architecture and exactly the same set of training data, yet can obtain quite different solutions that differ substantially in quality. The differences in the two outcomes of the learning process are due to the initial conditions of the learning algorithm, that is, the initial connection strength parameter vector, $\mathbf{w}(t_0)$. Different initial conditions will "bias" the learning algorithm to develop some types of feature detection units at the hidden unit layer, but not others.

Error Functions

The objective function used by an ANN system for classification and learning, as previously noted, plays a crucial role in specifying how the ANN system will generalize. For example, let

$$\mathbf{x}^j = (\mathbf{s}^j, \mathbf{o}^j)$$

be the jth training stimulus presented to a classical backpropagation learning network, where $\mathbf{s}^j \in \mathcal{R}^d$ and $\mathbf{o}^j \in \mathcal{R}^p$. The network architecture can be summarized as a single function $\mathbf{f}$ that maps $\mathbf{s}^j$ and the weights of the network, $\mathbf{w}$, into the network's response, $\mathbf{r}^j$, which is a p-dimensional vector. In particular,

$$\mathbf{r}^j = \mathbf{f}(\mathbf{s}^j, \mathbf{w}),$$

where each element of $\mathbf{r}^j$ is constrained to lie in the open interval $(0, 1)$ due to the sigmoidal nonlinearity at the output layer. The classical backpropagation also uses the sum-squared error function (i.e., learning objective function), l_n, which is defined as

$$l_n(\mathbf{w}) = (1/n)\sum_{j=1}^{n} \left| \mathbf{o}^j - \mathbf{r}^j \right|^2. \tag{2.6}$$

The error function in (2.6) imposes a very specific set of assumptions about which weight vectors in the weight space are likely to be learned by the learning algorithm.

Alternatively, consider the cross-entropy error function (Baum and Wilczek 1988; Hinton 1989)

$$l_n(\mathbf{w}) = -(1/n)\sum_{j=1}^{n}\sum_{i=1}^{p} \left[o_i^j \log\left(r_i^j\right) + \left(1 - o_i^j\right) \log\left(1 - r_i^j\right) \right], \tag{2.7}$$

where r_j^i is the ith element of $\mathbf{r}^j$ and o_j^i is the ith element of $\mathbf{o}^j$ for $i = 1 \ldots p$. Golden (1988c; also see section 7.3) shows that the cross-entropy error function in (2.7) is preferable when the target activation pattern, $\mathbf{o}^j$, consists of zeros and ones while the sum-squared error function in (2.6) is preferable when the target activation pattern, $\mathbf{o}^j$, is real-valued.

Weight Sharing

Another commonly used approach for introducing constraints into the learning process in ANN systems is *weight sharing*. Consider the ANN system in figure 2.13. Although at first glance such an ANN system seems to be equivalent to a classical backpropagation architecture, the additional constraint that all hidden units have identical weight vectors has been introduced. Such a constraint is useful for using backpropagation to discover a sophisticated feature

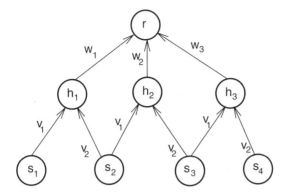

Figure 2.13
Weight-sharing concept in backpropagation context. A simple backpropagation network with one output unit, three hidden units, and four input units illustrates the weight-sharing concept. Each of the three hidden units is constrained to have exactly the same set of weights, (v_1, v_2). Such networks are useful for solving certain types of orientation- and translation-invariant feature detection problems.

detector subject to the assumption that the features such a detector would want to classify could be located any place in the input field. This approach has been successfully used by a number of researchers in the ANN field (Fukishima 1980; Le Cun et al. 1990a,b; Rumelhart, Hinton, and Williams 1986).

Learning Minimal Network Solutions

A *minimal network solution* to a learning problem is a solution to the learning problem that involves a minimal number of free parameters. Such solutions usually tend to reduce the effects of "overfitting" (i.e., memorizing statistical flukes in the data), and thus result in improved generalization performance. The previously discussed method of weight sharing is one method for reducing the dimensionality of the ANN learning parameter space.

A second method for parameter dimensionality reduction may be implemented by combining the sum-squared error function for classical backpropagation given by

$$l_n(\mathbf{w}) = (1/n)\sum_{i=1}^{n} \mid \mathbf{o}^i - \mathbf{r}^i \mid^2, \tag{2.8}$$

with the *weight decay* penalty term $(1/2)\lambda \mid \mathbf{w} \mid^2$ to obtain a new error function, $l'_n(\mathbf{w})$, given by

$$l'_n(\mathbf{w}) = l_n(\mathbf{w}) + (1/2)\lambda \mid \mathbf{w} \mid^2 = (1/n)\sum_{i=1}^{n} \mid \mathbf{o}^i - \mathbf{r}^i \mid^2 + (1/2)\lambda \mid \mathbf{w} \mid^2.$$

Note that if the positive constant λ is small, then the influence of the weight decay term on the learning process is minimal and the ANN learning process is biased to simply minimize $l_n(\mathbf{w})$ with respect to $\mathbf{w}$, as in classical backpropagation. If the positive constant λ is very large, then the network will learn to set all weights equal to zero (in order to minimize the weight decay term), and the resulting network will not be able to learn the training stimulus set. Thus the constant λ must be set in an appropriate manner somewhere between these two extremes. In practice, λ should initially be set equal to zero. After the network is trained to some solution that minimizes $l_n(\mathbf{w})$, the magnitude of λ should gradually be increased to some constant level, λ_0, during the remainder of the learning process so that a solution minimizing $l'_n(\mathbf{w})$ for $\lambda = \lambda_0$ is obtained. The constant λ_0 represents the "trade-off" between the error performance measure and the constraint measure. Large values of λ_0 bias the system to satisfy the constraints, while small values of λ_0 bias the system to improve its performance. Some insights into how to pick the value of λ_0 will be discussed in chapter 7. If λ_0 is unknown, then it can be shown that gradually increasing the value of λ during the learning process is still a good idea. Platt and Barr (1987) provide formal specific conditions for the stability of the learning process in this latter case; briefly, they showed when the sequence of states generated by the learning algorithm will eventually converge to a set of weights where the constraints are completely satisfied. (Other methods of weight decay are reviewed by Hanson and Pratt 1989; Hergert, Finnoff, and Zimmerman 1992; and Weigend, Rumelhart, and Huberman 1991.)

A third method of constraining the learning algorithm of a backpropagation ANN system to learn a parsimonious solution may be obtained by minimizing the number of hidden units in the network. Define the *active hidden unit* penalty term, $q_n(\mathbf{w})$, as

$$q_n(\mathbf{w}) = (1/2)\sum_{i=1}^{n} |\,\mathbf{h}^i\,|^2,$$

where $\mathbf{h}^i$ is the ith activation pattern over the hidden units, and $\mathbf{r}^i$ is functionally dependent on $\mathbf{h}^i$ as in classical backpropagation. Now combining (2.8) with the active hidden unit penalty term (Chauvin 1989), the following new error function for the learning process is obtained:

$$l'_n(\mathbf{w}) = l_n(\mathbf{w}) + \lambda q_n(\mathbf{w}) = (1/n)\sum_{i=1}^{n} |\,\mathbf{o}^i - \mathbf{r}^i\,|^2 + (\lambda/2)\sum_{i=1}^{n} |\,\mathbf{h}^i\,|^2.$$

As before, if λ is appropriately chosen, the $\mathbf{w}^*$ that minimizes $l'_n(\mathbf{w})$ will be a good solution because $l_n(\mathbf{w})$ is minimized, but the solution will also tend to be parsimonious because $q_n(\mathbf{w})$ is also minimized.

Biased Feature Detector Development

A less commonly used approach is the construction of learning objective functions in order to appropriately constrain what types of feature detection hidden units will evolve from the learning process (Krogh, Thorbergsson, and Hertz 1990). Combining (2.8) with the *orthogonal feature detection* penalty term

$$q_n(\mathbf{w}) = (1/n) \sum_{i=1}^{n} \sum_{j=2}^{d} \sum_{k=1}^{j-1} h_j^i h_k^i,$$

where h_j^i is the activation of the jth hidden unit for training stimulus i, yields the new objective function for learning:

$$l_n'(\mathbf{w}) = l_n(\mathbf{w}) + \lambda q_n(\mathbf{w}) = (1/n) \sum_{i=1}^{n} |\mathbf{o}^i - \mathbf{r}^i|^2 + (\lambda/n) \sum_{i=1}^{n} \sum_{j=2}^{d} \sum_{k=1}^{j-1} h_j^i h_k^i.$$

Weight vectors that minimize l_n' will tend to find architectures where the hidden units are biased to have orthogonal response properties.

2.2.6   Topographic Map Learning Algorithms

Topographic map learning models are unsupervised learning algorithms that create new feature units during the learning process such that physically neighboring feature units learn to recognize similar features. This end product results in topographic maps in the ANN analogous to those found in the cerebral cortex (Cowey 1981; Ghez 1981b; Kandel 1981c,d; Kelly 1981c). In addition, some topographic map learning models may dedicate more feature units to detecting subpatterns of activation that occur more frequently, a type of neural organization similar to the "magnification factor" found in animal cortical representations (Cowey 1981; Kandel 1981d). From an engineering perspective, topographic map learning models may be useful for creating networks that learn to wire themselves up according to an efficient two-dimensional wiring scheme (Cowey 1981).

Kohonen Learning Algorithm

The basic concepts behind many topographic map learning models (e.g., Grajski and Merzenich 1990; Grossberg 1976; von der Malsburg 1973; Willshaw and von der Malsburg 1976) can be viewed as variations of the classical Kohonen (1984, 1990) competitive learning model shown in figure 2.14. The Kohonen (1990) model consists of two groups of units: input units and hidden units. Initially, the connections from the input units to the hidden units are random. When an incoming activation pattern is presented to the system, the hidden unit responding most strongly to the input pattern has its weights modified so as to match the incoming activation pattern. The critical distinguishing feature of the topographic map learning model, however, is that hidden units *physically close* to the hidden unit with maximal response also have their weights adjusted (but to a lesser extent than the hidden unit with maximal response) so as to match the incoming activation pattern. This latter property of

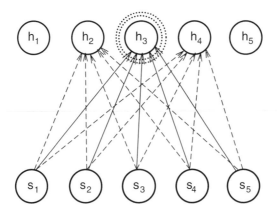

Figure 2.14
Kohonen topographic map learning network. The Kohonen topographic map learning network in this example consists of five input units that are completely connected to five hidden units. Initially, input units and hidden units are randomly connected; upon presentation of a stimulus, the hidden unit that responds most strongly to the stimulus (in this example hidden unit 3, which is surrounded by dots) is then trained to respond even more strongly to the stimulus in the future (solid arrows indicate substantial learning). The units *physically close* to the maximally responding units (units 2 and 4 in this example) are also trained at weaker learning levels (dashed arrows indicate small learning increments) to respond strongly to the stimulus that the maximally responding unit (unit 3) has detected.

the learning rule tends to result in ANN systems that can learn topographic maps of the input pattern distribution over the hidden units that are qualitatively similar to cortical topographic maps. The *Kohonen topographic learning* model is now formally presented.

Algorithm: Kohonen topographic learning model.   Consider an ANN system with m hidden units and p input units.

• Step 0: Initialize weights to small values. Let $t = 0$. Assume the elements of $\mathbf{w}(0) \in \mathfrak{R}^p$ are observed values of a set of independent and identically distributed random variables with mean zero and strictly positive variance σ^2.

• Step 1: Pick training stimulus at random. Let the training stimulus at iteration t of the algorithm, $\mathbf{x}(t)$, be defined such that

$$\mathbf{x}(t) = \mathbf{x}^k,$$

where $k = IRAND(t, 1\ N)$ and $\mathbf{x}^k \in \mathfrak{R}^p$ is the kth element of the training set $\{\mathbf{x}^1,\ldots, \mathbf{x}^n\}$.

• Step 2: Decide which hidden unit is responding maximally. For the current value of t, let i^* identify the i^*th hidden unit such that

$$\left| \mathbf{w}_{i^*}(t) - \mathbf{x}(t) \right| \leq \left| \mathbf{w}_j(t) - \mathbf{x}(t) \right|$$

for $j = 1\ldots m$.

- Step 3: Update weights. Let $\mathbf{d}_j$ be a two-dimensional position vector indicating the *physical location* of hidden unit j on some physical surface. For $j = 1 \ldots m$, let the physical neighborhood function

$$N_{i*}(\mathbf{d}_j, \mathbf{d}_{i*}, t): \mathcal{R}^2 \times \mathcal{R}^2 \times \mathcal{R} \to \mathcal{R}$$

be associated with the $i*$th hidden unit. For $j = 1 \ldots m$:

$$\mathbf{w}_j(t+1) = \mathbf{w}_j(t) + \gamma_t N_{i*}(\mathbf{d}_j, \mathbf{d}_{i*}, t)(\mathbf{x}(t) - \mathbf{w}_j(t)),$$

where $\gamma_t > 0$ and $i*$ is the $i*$th hidden unit selected in step 2.
- Step 4: Check if algorithm has converged. If $t > t_{\max}$ or

$$\sum_{j=1}^{m} \left| \mathbf{w}_j(t) - \mathbf{w}_j(t-1) \right|^2 < \varepsilon$$

for some $\varepsilon > 0$, then stop. Otherwise, let $t = t + 1$ and return to step 1.

The neighborhood function N_{i*} is always nonnegative. In addition, as $\left| \mathbf{d}_j - \mathbf{d}_{i*} \right|$ becomes large, the value of N_{i*} tends to decrease. This property of N_{i*} may be interpreted as a quantitative instantiation of the idea that units physically close together should acquire similar response properties. The neighborhood function N_{i*} also tends to decrease as the number of iterations, t, of the algorithm become large. This latter property of N_{i*} may be interpreted as a quantitative instantiation of the idea that as various groups of neurons learn to recognize specific environmental features, they are forced to commit themselves to recognizing only those features. One reasonable choice of neighborhood function with the above properties is to choose a Gaussian-like neighborhood function N_{i*} so that

$$N_{i*}(\mathbf{d}_j, \mathbf{d}_{i*}, t) = [2\pi t]^{-1/2} \exp\left[-\left| \mathbf{d}_j - \mathbf{d}_{i*} \right|^2 / 2t \right].$$

Elastic Net Algorithm

Durbin and Willshaw (1987; also see Burr 1988, and Durbin, Szeliski, and Yuille 1989) have proposed a variation of the Kohonen topographic map learning algorithm that is much easier to analyze yet exhibits many of the same key qualitative features. They present their algorithm as a solution to the traveling salesman problem, but for purposes of continuity, the elastic net algorithm is presented with an ANN interpretation.

Algorithm: Elastic net algorithm.   Consider an ANN system with d hidden units and q input units.

- Step 0: Initialize weights to small values. Let $t = 0$. Let the elements of the real q-dimensional connection weight parameter vectors $\mathbf{w}_1(0), \ldots, \mathbf{w}_d(0)$ for the d hidden units be observed values of a set of independent and identically distributed random variables with common mean zero and strictly positive variance σ^2.

- Step 1: Compute response of each hidden unit. The response of hidden unit i ($i = 1 \ldots d$) to the jth stimulus pattern $\mathbf{x}^j$ over the input units at iteration t is denoted as $r_{ij}(t)$, which is computed using the formula

$$r_{ij}(t) = \frac{\exp\left(-|\mathbf{x}^j - \mathbf{w}_i(t)|^2/2\sigma_t^2\right)}{\sum_{k=1}^{d} \exp\left(-|\mathbf{x}^j - \mathbf{w}_k(t)|^2/2\sigma_t^2\right)}. \tag{2.9}$$

- Step 2: Update weights. Let $\mathbf{x}^j$ be the jth element of the training set $\{\mathbf{x}^1, \ldots, \mathbf{x}^n\}$. For $i = 1 \ldots d$:

$$\mathbf{w}_i(t+1) = \mathbf{w}_i(t) + (\gamma_t/n)\sum_{j=1}^{n} r_{ij}(t)[\mathbf{x}^j - \mathbf{w}_i(t)]$$

$$+ \gamma_t 2\lambda\left[\left(\frac{\mathbf{w}_{i+1}(t) + \mathbf{w}_{i-1}(t)}{2}\right) - \mathbf{w}_i(t)\right], \tag{2.10}$$

where $\gamma_t > 0$ and $\lambda > 0$, and where $\mathbf{w}_{d+1}$ is defined as $\mathbf{w}_1$.

- Step 3: Check if algorithm has converged. If $|\mathbf{w}_i(t) - \mathbf{w}_i(t-1)|$ is sufficiently small for all $i = 1 \ldots d$, then stop. Otherwise, let $t = t + 1$ and return to step 1.

The weight update rule in the elastic net algorithm possesses many of the same qualitative features as the original Kohonen learning rule. First, hidden units compete among themselves to select the hidden unit that is maximally responding. This competition is quantitatively instantiated by the denominator in (2.9). Second, units which are responding most strongly are trained with the stimulus pattern at a higher learning rate. This assumption is quantitatively instantiated by the $r_{ij}(t)[\mathbf{x}^j - \mathbf{w}_i(t)]$ term in the weight update rule in (2.10). Third, assuming that the hidden units are labeled such that hidden units i and $i + 1$ are located physically next to one another, the second term of the weight update rule tends to make the average value of the weight vectors of the neighboring units $i - 1$ and $i + 1$ closer to the weight vector for unit i.

The main advantage, however, of the elastic net algorithm is that a learning objective function for the elastic net algorithm can be constructed. Durbin, Szeliski, and Yuille (1989) have shown that each iteration of the elastic net algorithm tends to decrease the value of the following learning objective function:

$$l_n(\{\mathbf{w}_i\}) = -(\sigma_t^2/n)\sum_{j=1}^{n} \log\left[\sum_{i=1}^{d} \exp\left(-|\mathbf{x}^j - \mathbf{w}_i|^2/2\sigma_t^2\right)\right]$$

$$+ \frac{\lambda}{2}\sum_{i=1}^{d} |\mathbf{w}_{i+1} - \mathbf{w}_i|^2. \tag{2.11}$$

2.3   Chapter Summary

A small but representative group of ANN system architectures was reviewed at the computational and functional level to aid the engineer interested in selecting an appropriate algorithm for a given application. Two major computational goals of ANN systems were formally defined.

The first major computational goal of an ANN system involves computing the minimum value of a classification objective function $V: S \to \mathcal{R}$ (section 2.1), where the ANN classification dynamical system seeks an activation pattern $\mathbf{x}^* \in S \subseteq \mathcal{R}^d$ such that $V(\mathbf{x}^*) \le V(\mathbf{x})$ for all $\mathbf{x} \in S \subseteq \mathcal{R}^d$. Examples of ANN system architectures of this type were reviewed: the BSB model (Anderson et al. 1977; Golden 1986a, 1993), the Hopfield (1982) model, Smolensky's harmony theory (1986), the Boltzmann machine, and the Gibbs sampler (Geman and Geman 1984).

The second major computational goal of an ANN system involves computing the minimum value of a learning objective function $l: \mathcal{R}^q \to \mathcal{R}$ (section 2.2), where the ANN learning dynamical system seeks a connection strength parameter vector $\mathbf{w}^* \in \mathcal{R}^q$ (for nontemporal learning dynamical systems) such that $l(\mathbf{w}^*) \le l(\mathbf{w})$ for all $\mathbf{w} \in \mathcal{R}^q$.

Six not necessarily mutually exclusive classes of learning algorithms were described: (1) supervised learning, (2) unsupervised learning, (3) reinforcement learning, (4) temporal learning, (5) prior knowledge learning, and (6) topographic map learning. Examples of ANN system architectures from each of these six categories were also discussed in detail, including Rosenblatt's perceptron (1958, 1962), Hebbian (1949; Anderson 1972) and Widrow-Hoff (1960) learning architectures, supervised, unsupervised, partially supervised (reinforcement), and temporal sequence backpropagation algorithms, adaptive resonance theory (ART; Carpenter, Grossberg, and Rosen 1991; Carpenter et al. 1992), and finally the Kohonen (1984, 1990) and elastic net (Durbin and Willshaw 1987) topographic map learning algorithms. Table 2.1 provides a summary of the types of computational functions that can be solved by ANN systems.

Table 2.1
Functional summary of chapter 2 algorithms. Note that the algorithms described in chapter 2 are a small, biased sample of ANN system algorithms selected primarily for historical and expository reasons.

Computation	Section
Reconstructing patterns	2.1
Supervised learning	2.2.1
Unsupervised learning	2.2.2
Reinforcement learning	2.2.3
Learning sequences of patterns	2.2.4
Prior knowledge learning	2.2.5
Learning topographic maps	2.2.6

2.4   Problems

2-1. Write a computer program which has options for simulating the brain-state-in-a-box (BSB), Hopfield (1982), or Boltzmann machine algorithm. The program should print out the value of the classification objective function at each iteration of the algorithm. Discuss how you would evaluate the performance of the system.

2-2. Consider the problem of simulating a reinforcement learning ANN system as described in section 2.2.3. The simulated ANN system is designed to model a small organism that can smell quite well in its environment but whose sense of sight is quite poor. The learning problem is to teach the organism to intelligently search for a piece of cheese. The current stimulus state, $\mathbf{s}$, is a vector indicating the current sensory state of the organism. Describe a method for representing smell and sight information in $\mathbf{s}$. The motor response of the organism at a given instant in time is represented by the vector $\mathbf{r}$. Describe a method for representing motor control information in $\mathbf{r}$. Assume that the organism obtains feedback from its environment in the form of a scalar reinforcement signal, a, that indicates the strength of the smell of the cheese. If a is very large, then the organism is close to the cheese. If a is close to its lower limit of zero, then the organism is far away from the cheese. The organism will use a to attempt to find the cheese. Assume that the function $\mathbf{f}$ which maps the stimulus state $\mathbf{s}$ into the ANN system's response $\mathbf{r}$ may be modeled as a classical backpropagation network. Assume the ANN system's internal model of the world, $\mathbf{c}$, which maps $\mathbf{r}$ into a *prediction* of reinforcement signal a is not completely known but may be modeled as another classical backpropagation network. Describe in detail how to train this reinforcement learning ANN system to (a) obtain an internal model of its environment, and then (b) exploit that internal model to control its behavior. Discuss how you would evaluate the performance of the system.

2-3. Discuss the degree to which the (a) brain-state-in-a-box model, (b) Boltzmann machine, (c) Widrow-Hoff learning rule, (d) backpropagation, and (e) Hebbian learning algorithm are ANN systems with respect to the ten characteristics of ANN systems proposed in section 1.2.2.

2-4. Design an ANN system that can learn to respond to an object in one section of its visual field, and then will respond strongly to that object when it is presented for the first time in a different section of its visual field. Show how to solve the problem using a weight-sharing strategy.

2-5. Design an ANN system that can learn to respond to an object in one section of its visual field, and then will respond strongly to that object when it is presented for the first time in a different section of its visual field. Solve the problem using a linear ANN that combines Widrow-Hoff learning and a special input stimulus representation scheme.

2-6. Let a feedforward ANN classification dynamical system be defined as a function $\varphi: \mathcal{R}^2 \rightarrow \mathcal{R}$ such that the ANN system's scalar response $r = \varphi(\mathbf{s})$ is determined by the input stimulus $\mathbf{s} \in \mathcal{R}^2$. Let $(\mathbf{s}^i, o^i)$ be the ith training stimulus, which is interpreted as indicating that when input stimulus $\mathbf{s}^i$ is presented, then the scalar response o^i is desired $(i = 1 \ldots M)$. Now consider the following set of four training stimuli:

$([0, 0], 0), ([0, 1], 1), ([1, 0], 1), ([1, 1], 0).$

The problem of learning this set of four training stimuli is known as the "exclusive-or problem" in the ANN system literature (Rumelhart, Hinton, and Williams 1986). Prove that any learning rule (such as the Widrow-Hoff learning rule) that models the mapping from $\mathbf{s}$ to $\mathbf{r}$ as a linear mapping (such that $r = \varphi(\mathbf{s}) = \mathbf{Ws}$, where $\mathbf{W}$ is a 1×2 dimensional matrix) will be unsuccessful at solving the exclusive-or problem. Then prove that any learning rule which models the mapping from $\mathbf{s}$ to a layer of *linear* hidden units, $\mathbf{h}$, as one linear mapping and the mapping from $\mathbf{h}$ to $\mathbf{r}$ as another linear mapping will be unsuccessful at solving the exclusive-or problem.

2-7. Suppose a classical backpropagation network was used to learn the four training stimuli in problem 2-6. (a) Prove that there exists a classical backpropagation network with four hidden units that can solve the exclusive-or problem described in problem 2-6. Then (b) prove that there exists a classical backpropagation network with two sigmoidal hidden units that can solve the exclusive-or problem. Assume that if the output response of the network is within some small number, ε, of the desired response, the learning procedure is successful.

2-8. Suppose a classical backpropagation network has initial weights chosen from a distribution with mean zero and standard deviation σ. Provide a short heuristic (*not* mathematically rigorous) argument that shows that the learning algorithm will converge very slowly if σ multiplied by the number of inputs to each hidden unit is greater than about 3. Assume the activation of any input unit in the network has a magnitude about equal to 1.

2-9. Write a description of the Elman temporal learning algorithm in algorithmic form similar to the form in which classical backpropagation was presented in chapter 2.

2-10. Consider the problem of designing an optimal wiring scheme for an integrated circuit chip on which there are three types of devices: A, B, and C. The integrated circuit consists of 100 type-A devices, 100 type-B devices, and 100 type-C devices. Assume the existence of at least three constraints: (1) the total length of wire should be minimized, (2) the distance between devices A and B should always be maximized to avoid interference, and (3) the distance from device A to device C should always be minimized because those two devices are frequently connected to one another. Devise a method for representing a particular wiring scheme as a high-dimensional vector. Construct a quadratic Hopfield (1982) objective function that maps a given wiring scheme into a real number. Design the objective function so that "poor" wiring schemes are assigned larger numbers, while "better" wiring schemes are assigned smaller numbers. Explain how algorithms such as the brain-state-in-a-box (BSB) model, Hopfield (1982) model, or Boltzmann machine could then be used to solve the problem of selecting an appropriate wiring scheme.

2-11. Consider an optimal control problem where only a subset of the elements of the environmental state, $s(t)$, is observable, while the remaining element values are not observable. Explain how one could combine the concepts behind an Elman-style backpropagation network and the generic backpropagation optimal control theory network to construct a backpropagation network to solve this problem. Explain how to unfold the network in time so that a learning algorithm for the network can be developed.

2-12. Rewrite the classical backpropagation algorithm using scalar notation as opposed to vector-matrix notation.

2-13. Explain how an unsupervised autoassociative Hebbian learning rule where the stepsize γ is strictly negative and the initial weight matrix **W** is the identity matrix can learn to be a *novelty detector*. (Such a network is described in Kohonen 1984.)

2-14. Write a computer program to simulate the classical backpropagation learning algorithm. Then use the computer program to empirically investigate the issues raised in problems 2-4, 2-5, 2-6, 2-7, or 2-8.

3 Deterministic Nonlinear Dynamical Systems Analysis

The theory of dynamical systems is especially applicable to understanding issues at Marr's implementational level of analysis (1982). The dynamical system theorist is interested, not in the computational goal of an ANN system or determining a method for efficiently achieving that goal, but rather in understanding the *behavior* of a given ANN dynamical system.

Consider an ANN classification discrete-time dynamical system consisting of a large number of units, where each unit has a real-valued activation state. The list of the activations of all units in the system is called the system "state vector" and may be represented as a single point in a high-dimensional state space. As the units in the ANN system update their activation values, the system state changes. Geometrically, the evolution of the system state over time may be visualized as a *trajectory* (i.e., an ordered sequence of system state vectors) in a high-dimensional *activation state space*. Note that each point in the activation state space corresponds to a unique activation pattern.

Now imagine plotting several possible permissible trajectories of a classification dynamical system for a two-dimensional state space (see figure 3.1). A plot as shown in figure 3.1 is referred to as a "phase plane." In the phase plane, some trajectories may merge together and approach "vortices" in the system state space, while other trajectories might emanate outward from such vortices. Hopfield (1982) suggested that a vortex in the phase plane that attracted

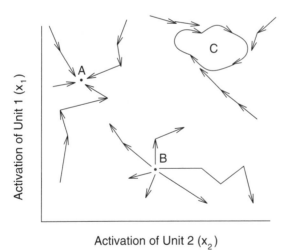

Activation of Unit 1 (x_1)

Activation of Unit 2 (x_2)

Figure 3.1
Long-term asymptotic behaviors in activation state space. Each point on the graph corresponds to a possible activation pattern, (x_1, x_2), in a two model neuron system. The arrows diagram alternative trajectory paths traced out by a particular ANN discrete-time *classification* dynamical system whose initial conditions are systematically varied. Although the dynamical behavior of the system may be quite complex, the system may be analyzed qualitatively by investigating the location and nature of particular types of "vortices," technically referred to as "invariant sets." The figure illustrates a few types of invariant sets that will be discussed in greater detail later in the chapter: stable equilibrium point (A); unstable equilibrium point (B); and orbitally stable periodic invariant set (i.e., limit cycle) (C).

trajectories could be defined as a perceptual or cognitive category. For example, a perceptual input could be considered to be an initial condition for an ANN classification dynamical system. Using the classification dynamics (activation updating) rule of the ANN system, the perceptual input is mapped into some perceptual category that would correspond to a vortex in the phase plane.

The learning dynamics of an ANN system can be represented in a similar manner. In this case, the system state vector is a particular pattern of connection strengths that represents a specific knowledge state of the ANN system. The learning rule of the ANN system is then viewed as a dynamical system that generates trajectories in a high-dimensional *weight state space*. The initial condition for the ANN learning dynamics represents an initial prior knowledge state. Using the learning rule, this prior knowledge state is mapped into some knowledge state vortex (figure 3.2).

The detailed mathematical analysis of high-dimensional nonlinear dynamical systems is very difficult. On the other hand, it is usually not difficult to make a number of specific qualitative statements about a large variety of a special class of high-dimensional nonlinear ANN systems using a version of LaSalle's Invariant Set Theorem (1960).

LaSalle's Invariant Set Theorem is a natural extension of the classical Lyapunov function method of analysis proposed by A. M. Lyapunov in 1893 (LaSalle, 1960; Liapunov, 1907). The basic idea behind such analyses is that the

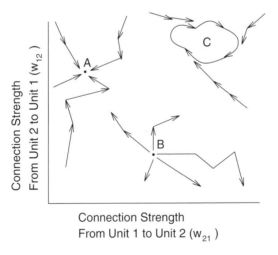

Connection Strength
From Unit 2 to Unit 1 (w_{12})

Connection Strength
From Unit 1 to Unit 2 (w_{21})

Figure 3.2
Long-term asymptotic behaviors in weight state space. Each point on the graph corresponds to a possible pattern of connection strengths in an ANN system with only two weights, (w_{12}, w_{21}). As in activation state space (see figure 3.1), complex learning dynamics may be investigated by characterizing the learning dynamical system's behavior in terms of invariant sets (i.e., "vortices"). The figure illustrates a few types of invariant sets which will be discussed in greater detail later in this chapter: stable equilibrium point (A); unstable equilibrium point (B); and orbitally stable periodic invariant set (i.e., limit cycle) (C).

qualitative behavior of a high-dimensional nonlinear dynamical system can be at least partially understood if the vortices in the phase plane can be characterized and identified. In particular, such an analysis could be useful for at least two important reasons: (1) different dynamical systems with similar placements of vortices might be considered to have equivalent dynamics in a certain sense, and (2) various possible long term behaviors of the system can be identified.

This chapter will formally introduce the concept of an *invariant set* and discuss the various types. An invariant set is a region of the state space such that all trajectories initiated in the region remain there for all time. An example invariant set is a "vortex" in the phase plane that "attracts" trajectories.

Next, it will introduce a version of LaSalle's powerful Invariant Set Theorem (1960) as an important tool for studying the conditions under which a trajectory generated by a dynamical system converges to a particular invariant set. It will then discuss applications of these ideas to the classification dynamics of the Hopfield (1982) ANN and Hopfield (1984) ANN systems, as well as a continuous-time version of the backpropagation learning algorithm, and conclude with a formal proof of the Invariant Set Theorem.

3.1   Autonomous Dynamical Systems

This chapter describes mathematical tools for analyzing a special class of linear and nonlinear dynamical systems known as *autonomous dynamical systems* or *time-invariant dynamical systems*. An autonomous dynamical system takes as input some initial state $\mathbf{x}_0 \in \mathcal{R}^d$ at some initial time $t_0 \in \mathcal{R}$ and returns some final state $\mathbf{x}_f \in \mathcal{R}^d$ at final time t_f $(t_f \geq t_0)$. The reader should compare the following formal definition of an autonomous dynamical system with the more general formal definition of a dynamical system provided in section 1.4.

In addition, because this textbook will discuss only continuous-time dynamical systems where the set of time indices $T = [0, \infty)$ and only discrete-time dynamical systems where the set of time indices $T = \{0, 1, 2, ...\}$, it will be convenient at this point to appropriately restrict the set T in the following definition.

Definition: Autonomous dynamical system.   Let $T = \{0, 1, 2, ...\}$ or $T = [0, \infty)$. Let $\Omega \subseteq \mathcal{R}^d$. Let

$$\Psi^*: \Omega \times T \times T \times E \to \Omega$$

be a dynamical system. An *autonomous dynamical system* is a function $\Psi: \Omega \times T \to \Omega$ with the property that

$$\Psi(\mathbf{x}_0, t_f - t_0) = \Psi^*(\mathbf{x}_0, t_0, t_f, \eta)$$

for all $\eta \in E$, for all $\mathbf{x}_0 \in \Omega$, and for all $t_0, t_f \in T$ such that $t_0 \leq t_f$.

Notice that an autonomous dynamical system is a dynamical system that has the following two properties: (1) the state generated by a dynamical system is not functionally dependent upon an event history function (i.e., an environmental sequence of events), and (2) the state generated by a dynamical system is not functionally dependent upon the current time index, but only upon the *time difference* between the initial time index and the final time index.

Because only autonomous dynamical systems will be analyzed in this chapter, the term *dynamical system* will be used to refer to autonomous (discrete-time or continuous-time) dynamical systems.

Definition: Trajectory of a dynamical system.   Let $T = \{0, 1, 2,...\}$ or $T = [0, \infty)$. Let $\Omega \subseteq \mathcal{R}^d$. Let

$$\Psi: \Omega \times T \rightarrow \Omega$$

be a dynamical system. A *trajectory* with respect to Ψ and initiated at $\mathbf{x}_0 \in \Omega$ is a function, $\mathbf{x}(\cdot; \mathbf{x}_0): T \rightarrow \Omega$, such that for all $\mathbf{x}_0 \in \mathcal{R}^d$:

$$\mathbf{x}(t; \mathbf{x}_0) = \Psi(\mathbf{x}_0, t)$$

for $t \in T$.

Note that in cases where the initial state, $\mathbf{x}_0$, is irrelevant, the trajectory function evaluated at time t, $\mathbf{x}(t, \mathbf{x}_0)$, will sometimes be referred to as $\mathbf{x}(t)$, where the parameter $\mathbf{x}_0$ indicates the point in state space where the trajectory was originally initiated will be suppressed.

3.1.1   Discrete-Time Dynamical Systems

The important special case where the set of time indices, T, of an autonomous dynamical system is the set of nonnegative integers is now considered.

Definition of a Discrete-Time Dynamical System Generator

Definition: Discrete-time dynamical system generator.   Let $T = \{0, 1, 2,...\}$. Let $\Omega \subseteq \mathcal{R}^d$. Let $\mathbf{f}: \Omega \rightarrow \Omega$. Construct a dynamical system $\Psi: \Omega \times T \rightarrow \Omega$ such that

(i) $\Psi(\mathbf{x}_0, 0) = \mathbf{x}_0$,

and

(ii) $\Psi(\mathbf{x}_0, t) = \mathbf{f}(\Psi(\mathbf{x}_0, t - 1))$

for $t = 1, 2, 3,...$.

The function $\mathbf{f}$ is the *discrete-time dynamical system generator* for Ψ.

Note that a discrete-time dynamical system generator allows one to compute trajectories of a given discrete-time dynamical system using an iterative algorithm. Given an initial system state $\mathbf{x}_0 \in \mathcal{R}^d$, one uses the formula

$$\mathbf{x}(1) = \mathbf{\Psi}(\mathbf{x}_0, 1) = \mathbf{f}(\mathbf{x}_0)$$

to compute $\mathbf{x}(1)$ and then uses the formula

$$\mathbf{x}(2) = \mathbf{\Psi}(\mathbf{x}_0, 2) = \mathbf{f}(\mathbf{x}(1))$$

to compute $\mathbf{x}(2)$. Continuing in this manner, for any $t = 1, 2, 3,...$, one may compute $\mathbf{x}(t)$ from $\mathbf{x}(t-1)$ using the formula

$$\mathbf{x}(t) = \mathbf{\Psi}(\mathbf{x}_0, t) = \mathbf{f}(\mathbf{x}(t-1)). \tag{3.1}$$

Thus the trajectory, $\mathbf{x}: \{0, 1, 2,...\} \rightarrow \mathcal{R}^d$, of a discrete-time dynamical system traces a path initiated at $\mathbf{x}_0$ through the state space. The dynamical system $\mathbf{\Psi}: \Omega \times T \rightarrow \Omega$ will sometimes be referred to as the "solution" to the d difference equations in (3.1).

The EUC Theorem for Discrete-Time Dynamical Systems

The following "existence, uniqueness, and continuous dependence on initial conditions" (EUC) theorem establishes conditions such that any continuous function $\mathbf{f}: \Omega \rightarrow \Omega$ on Ω may be interpreted as the discrete-time dynamical system generator for exactly one discrete-time dynamical system. In addition, the theorem establishes conditions on the generator function $\mathbf{f}$ for a dynamical system $\mathbf{\Psi}: \Omega \times \{0, 1, 2,...\} \rightarrow \Omega$ such that $\mathbf{\Psi}(\cdot, t)$ is continuous on Ω for all $t = 0, 1, 2,...$. This latter condition is usually referred to as a "continuous dependence on initial state" condition. The above EUC conditions are important because they are required for LaSalle's Invariant Set Theorem (reviewed in the following sections) to be applicable.

Theorem: EUC Theorem for Discrete-Time Systems.   Let $T = \{0, 1, 2,...\}$. Let $\Omega \subseteq \mathcal{R}^d$. If $\mathbf{f}: \Omega \rightarrow \Omega$ is a continuous function on Ω, then there exists a unique discrete-time dynamical system $\mathbf{\Psi}: \Omega \times T \rightarrow \Omega$ such that (i) $\mathbf{f}$ is a discrete-time dynamical system generator for $\mathbf{\Psi}$, and (ii) $\mathbf{\Psi}(\cdot, t)$ is continuous on Ω for all $t \in T$.

Proof.   First, the existence and uniqueness properties of $\mathbf{\Psi}$ are established from the construction of $\mathbf{\Psi}$ from $\mathbf{f}$.

Second, the assertion that $\mathbf{\Psi}(\cdot, t)$ is continuous on Ω follows directly from (i) the assumption that $\mathbf{f}$ is continuous on Ω, and (ii) the construction of $\mathbf{\Psi}$ given $\mathbf{f}$.

Third, note that $\mathbf{\Psi}(\mathbf{x}_0, 0) = \mathbf{x}_0$ by the construction of $\mathbf{\Psi}$ such that $\mathbf{\Psi}$ satisfies property 1 in the definition of a dynamical system (see section 1.4).

Fourth, note that the construction of $\mathbf{\Psi}$ given $\mathbf{f}$ implies that

$$\mathbf{\Psi}(\mathbf{\Psi}(\mathbf{x}_0, t_1), t_2) = \mathbf{\Psi}(\mathbf{x}_0, t_1 + t_2)$$

for all $\mathbf{x}_0 \in \Omega$ and for all $t_1, t_2 \in T$. Thus $\mathbf{\Psi}$ satisfies property 2 in the definition of a dynamical system (see section 1.4). ∎

This textbook will sometimes refer to a discrete-time dynamical system generator as a "discrete-time dynamical system" because any discrete-time dynamical system generator uniquely determines a discrete-time dynamical system.

3.1.2   Continuous-Time Dynamical Systems

The case of nonlinear, autonomous continuous-time dynamical systems is now considered.

Definition of a Continuous-Time Dynamical System Generator

Definition: Continuous-time dynamical system generator.   Let $T = [0, \infty)$. Let $\Omega \subseteq \mathcal{R}^d$. Let $\mathbf{f}: \Omega \to \Omega$ be a continuous function on Ω. Construct a dynamical system $\boldsymbol{\Psi}: \Omega \times T \to \Omega$ differentiable in its second argument on T such that for all $\mathbf{x}_0 \in \Omega$:

(i) $\boldsymbol{\Psi}(\mathbf{x}_0, 0) = \mathbf{x}_0$

and

(ii) $\dfrac{d\boldsymbol{\Psi}(\mathbf{x}_0, t)}{dt} = \mathbf{f}(\boldsymbol{\Psi}(\mathbf{x}_0, t))$

for all $t \in T$.

The function $\mathbf{f}$ is the *continuous-time dynamical system generator* for $\boldsymbol{\Psi}$.

The concept of a continuous-time dynamical system generator provides a mechanism for interpreting

$$\frac{d\mathbf{x}}{dt} = \mathbf{f}(\mathbf{x})$$

in conjunction with some known initial condition $\mathbf{x}(0) = \mathbf{x}_0 \in \mathcal{R}^d$ as the definition of a continous-time dynamical system where the trajectory $\mathbf{x} = \mathbf{x}(\cdot\,; \mathbf{x}_0)$: $T \to \Omega$ is defined such that $\mathbf{x}(\cdot\,; \mathbf{x}_0) = \boldsymbol{\Psi}(\mathbf{x}_0, \cdot)$ on T for all $\mathbf{x}_0 \in \Omega$.

As in the previous discrete-time case, a continuous-time dynamical system generator will usually be referred to as simply a "continuous-time dynamical system." In addition, the continuous-time dynamical system is said to be a "continuous-time solution" to the system of differential equations associated with the dynamical system's continuous-time dynamical system generator.

The EUC Theorem for Continuous-Time Dynamical Systems

An EUC theorem for continuous-time dynamical systems analogous to the EUC theorem for discrete-time dynamical systems is now desired. In order to state this theorem, it is appropriate to introduce the concept of a *Lipschitz condition*.

Definition: Lipschitz condition. Let $\Omega \subseteq \mathcal{R}^d$. A continuous function $\mathbf{f}: \Omega \to \Omega$ satisfies a *Lipschitz condition* on Ω if there exists a finite real number K such that for all $\mathbf{x}, \mathbf{y} \in \Omega$:

$$|\mathbf{f}(\mathbf{x}) - \mathbf{f}(\mathbf{y})| \leq K |\mathbf{x} - \mathbf{y}|.$$

The following proposition is helpful for deciding if a given function satisfies a Lipschitz condition on some $\Omega \subseteq \mathcal{R}^d$.

Proposition: Lipschitz Condition for Differentiable Functions. Let Ω be a convex subset of $\mathcal{R}^d$. A continuous function $\mathbf{f}: \Omega \to \Omega$ satisfies a Lipschitz condition on Ω if the gradient of $\mathbf{f}$ is bounded on Ω.

Proof. Using the mean value (Multivariable Taylor's) theorem, there exists a real number $\theta \in (0, 1)$ such that

$$\mathbf{f}(\mathbf{x}) - \mathbf{f}(\mathbf{y}) = \nabla \mathbf{f}(\mathbf{c})^T (\mathbf{x} - \mathbf{y}),$$

where $\mathbf{c} = \mathbf{y} + \theta(\mathbf{x} - \mathbf{y})$. Using the Cauchy-Schwarz inequality (i.e., $\mathbf{a}^T \mathbf{b} \leq |\mathbf{a}| |\mathbf{b}|$) and the assumption that the gradient of $\mathbf{f}$ is bounded on Ω, it follows that a finite real number K exists such that

$$\mathbf{f}(\mathbf{x}) - \mathbf{f}(\mathbf{y}) = \nabla \mathbf{f}(\mathbf{c})^T (\mathbf{x} - \mathbf{y}) \leq |\nabla \mathbf{f}(\mathbf{c})| |\mathbf{x} - \mathbf{y}| \leq K |\mathbf{x} - \mathbf{y}|. \quad \blacksquare$$

Theorem: EUC Theorem for Continuous-Time Systems. Let $\mathbf{f}: \mathcal{R}^d \to \mathcal{R}^d$ be a continuous function on $\mathcal{R}^d$ and assume that $\mathbf{f}$ satisfies a Lipschitz condition on $\mathcal{R}^d$. Then for every $T_{\max} \in [0, \infty)$ there exists a unique continuous-time dynamical system $\mathbf{\Psi}: \mathcal{R}^d \times [0, T_{\max}] \to \mathcal{R}^d$ generated by $\mathbf{f}$ which has the property that for all $t \in [0, T_{\max}]$: $\mathbf{\Psi}(\cdot, t)$ is continuous on $\mathcal{R}^d$.

Proof. Given $\mathbf{f}: \mathcal{R}^d \to \mathcal{R}^d$ is a continuous function on $\mathcal{R}^d$ and satisfies a Lipschitz condition on ("is Lipschitz on") $\mathcal{R}^d$, Vidyasagar (1978, Theorem 25, 82) has shown that, for every $T_{\max} \in [0, \infty)$ and for every $\mathbf{x}_0 \in \mathcal{R}^d$, a unique function $\mathbf{x}(\cdot; \mathbf{x}_0): [0, T_{\max}] \to \mathcal{R}^d$ exists such that

(i) $\mathbf{x}(0; \mathbf{x}_0) = \mathbf{x}_0,$ (3.2)

and

(ii) $\dfrac{d\mathbf{x}(\cdot; \mathbf{x}_0)}{dt} = \mathbf{f}(\mathbf{x}(\cdot; \mathbf{x}_0))$ (3.3)

on $[0, T_{\max}]$. Vidyasagar (1978, Theorem 58, 86) has also shown that $\mathbf{x}(t, \cdot)$ is continuous on $\mathcal{R}^d$ for all $t \in [0, T_{\max}]$. Using (3.2) and (3.3), define a dynamical system $\mathbf{\Psi}: \mathcal{R}^d \times [0, T_{\max}] \to \mathcal{R}^d$ such that $\mathbf{\Psi}(\mathbf{x}_0, \cdot) = \mathbf{x}(\cdot; \mathbf{x}_0)$ on $[0, T_{\max}]$ for all $\mathbf{x}_0 \in \mathcal{R}^d$ and for all $T_{\max} \in [0, \infty)$.

The two properties of a dynamical system introduced in section 1.4 must now be verified. Property 1 has already been verified by construction of $\mathbf{\Psi}$ using the constraint in (3.2). Property 2 will now be verified. Let $T_{\max} \in [0, \infty)$. Because Ψ is unique, the solution Ψ may be explicitly expressed in terms of the generator function $\mathbf{f}$ by the formula for all $t_1 \in [0, T_{\max}]$:

$$\Psi(\mathbf{x}_0, t_1) = \mathbf{x}_0 + \int_0^{t_1} \mathbf{f}(\Psi(\mathbf{x}_0, s))ds. \tag{3.4}$$

Let $\mathbf{x}_1 = \Psi(\mathbf{x}_0, t_1)$ so that for all $t_2 \in [0, T_{\max}]$:

$$\Psi(\mathbf{x}_0, t_1 + t_2) = \mathbf{x}_1 + \int_{t_1}^{t_1+t_2} \mathbf{f}(\Psi(\mathbf{x}_0, s))ds. \tag{3.5}$$

Inspection of (3.4) and (3.5) shows that for every $t_1 \in [0, T_{\max}]$, for every $t_2 \in [0, T_{\max}]$, and for every $\mathbf{x}_0 \in \mathcal{R}^d$:

$$\Psi(\mathbf{x}_0, t_1 + t_2) = \Psi(\Psi(\mathbf{x}_0, t_1), t_2). \quad \blacksquare \tag{3.6}$$

In order to keep discussions simple, generator functions for continuous-time dynamical systems that satisfy a Lipschitz condition on $\mathcal{R}^d$ will be considered. Such Lipschitz conditions are usually referred to as "global Lipschitz conditions." It is also important to emphasize that a global Lipschitz condition is a *sufficient* but not necessary condition for the solution of a given continuous-time dynamical system to exist, be unique, and continuously dependent upon its initial state. The following examples will provide some insights into the relationship between the Lipschitz condition and ANN dynamical system models.

Example 1: Variant of continuous-time Hopfield (1984) ANN system. Let $\mathbf{f}: \mathcal{R}^d \to \mathcal{R}^d$. Consider a variant of the continuous-time Hopfield (1984) neural network where the activation x_i of the ith neuron in the network ($i = 1 \dots d$) is given by

$$dx_i/dt = f_i(x_1, \ldots, x_d), \tag{3.7}$$

where

$$f_i(x_1, \ldots, x_d) = \mathcal{S}\left(\sum_{j=1}^d w_{ij} x_j \right)$$

and where

$$\mathcal{S}(x) = 1/(1 + \exp[-x])$$

for every $x \in \mathcal{R}$. The parameters w_{ij} for $i = 1 \dots d$ and $j = 1 \dots d$ are assumed to be known, real numbers. Because

$$\partial f_i / \partial x_j = f_i(1 - f_i) w_{ij}$$

is a continuous and bounded function on $\mathcal{R}^d$, $\mathbf{f}$ is Lipschitz on $\mathcal{R}^d$. Thus the EUC Theorem for Continuous-Time dynamical systems implies that a unique dynamical system $\mathbf{\Psi} \colon \mathcal{R}^d \times T \to \mathcal{R}^d$ can be constructed for the generator function

$$\mathbf{f}(\cdot) = [f_1(\cdot), f_2(\cdot), \ldots, f_d(\cdot)],$$

where f_i is defined as in (3.7) such that $\mathbf{\Psi}(\cdot, t)$ is continuous on $\mathcal{R}^d$ in its first argument for every $t \in [0, \infty)$.

Example 2: Continuous-time BSB ANN dynamical system. Problem 3-8 considers a type of continuous-time brain-state-in-a-box ANN system model where the generator function is: (1) continuous, (2) not differentiable everywhere, but (3) satisfies a Lipschitz condition on a closed and bounded subset of $\mathcal{R}^d$.

Example 3: Continuous-time Hopfield (1982) dynamical system. Now suppose a researcher proposes a continuous-time version of the Hopfield (1982) neural network by defining a dynamical system of the form of (3.7), where $\mathcal{S}$ is a McCulloch-Pitts formal neuron sigmoidal function such that

$$\mathcal{S}(x) = 1 \text{ if } x > 0 \text{ and } \mathcal{S}(x) = 0 \text{ if } x \le 0.$$

Because $\mathcal{S}$ is not continuous at 0, the right-hand side of (3.7) is a generator function that is not continuous on $\mathcal{R}^d$. Thus the EUC Theorem for Continuous-Time Systems is not applicable. For this case, a dynamical system

$$\mathbf{\Psi} \colon \mathcal{R}^d \times [0, \infty) \to \mathcal{R}^d$$

generated by $\mathbf{f}$ with continuous first partial derivatives with respect to its second argument cannot be constructed because $\mathbf{f}$ is not continuous on $\mathcal{R}^d$.

Example 4: Lipschitz condition sufficient but not necessary for existence of solutions. Consider the scalar differential equation

$$\frac{dx(t)}{dt} = -x(t)^2, \tag{3.8}$$

where $x \colon [0, \infty) \to \mathcal{R}$ and $t \in [0, \infty)$. The generator function for (3.8) is $-x^2$, which satisfies the Lipschitz condition on any closed and bounded interval in $\mathcal{R}$ but does *not* satisfy the *global* Lipschitz condition on $\mathcal{R}$. Thus the EUC Theorem is not applicable. Nevertheless, $-x^2$ is a generator function for the continuous-time dynamical system

$$x(t) = \psi(x(0), t) = x(0)/(1 + t)$$

for all $t \in [0, \infty)$ and for $x(0) = -1$.

3.1.3   Discrete-Time or Continuous-Time System Models?

Both discrete-time and continuous-time systems have their advantages and disadvantages for system-modeling problems. First, some systems are simply naturally modeled as either discrete-time or continuous-time systems; for example, a theory about how continuous physical changes in the firing rates of biologically plausible units evolve in an ANN network is sometimes best represented as a continuous-time system. In addition, one could argue that continuous-time systems are more general because the physical world on a neural timescale (we are not concerned with building models at the quantum timescale) is essentially continuous, and a discrete-time system must make assumptions about how time should be partitioned. On the other hand, some ANN networks sequentially processing a sequence of activation patterns that represent symbolic information are most naturally represented as discrete-time systems. A discrete-time formulation of a continuous-time system is also usually of practical interest since most continuous-time systems are formulated as discrete-time systems for simulation purposes and the stability properties of the simulation model may then be investigated using the discrete-time model. Finally, some methods of analysis of ANN systems are vastly simplified by modeling a fundamentally continuous-time problem as a discrete-time problem, and vice-versa.

An important warning must be provided at this point. The results obtained for a discrete-time formulation of a continuous-time dynamical system are usually irrelevant for understanding the behavior of the original continuous-time dynamical system and vice versa. (Specific examples illustrating these issues may be found in section 3.4.3 and problem 3-8.)

3.2   Invariant Sets

The analysis of a nonlinear dynamical system involves identifying the behavioral vortices of the dynamical system. In order to classify such vortices, the concept of an *invariant set* is now introduced. An invariant set is a region of the state space of a particular dynamical system such that any trajectory initiated in the invariant set will remain there forever.

Definition: Invariant set.   Let $T = \{0, 1, 2,...\}$ or $T = [0, \infty)$. Let $\Omega \subseteq \mathcal{R}^d$. Let $\Psi: \Omega \times T \rightarrow \Omega$ be a dynamical system. Let $\mathcal{H}$ be a subset of Ω. Then $\mathcal{H}$ is an *invariant set* with respect to Ψ if for every $\mathbf{x}_0 \in \mathcal{H}$: $\Psi(\mathbf{x}_0, t) \in \mathcal{H}$ for all $t \in T$.

Note that although the entire state space of any dynamical system is an invariant set, the concept of an invariant set is particularly useful when one can demonstrate that specific regions of a dynamical system's state space are invariant sets.

3.2.1   Types of Invariant Sets

Several important types of invariant sets that frequently arise in the analysis of nonlinear dynamical systems will now be described.

Equilibrium Points

The first major type of invariant set contains a single element.

Definition: Equilibrium point. Let $T = \{0, 1, 2,...\}$ or $T = [0, \infty)$. Let $\Omega \subseteq \mathcal{R}^d$. Let $\Psi: \Omega \times T \rightarrow \Omega$ be a dynamical system. If there exists an invariant set, $\mathcal{H}$, with respect to Ψ consisting of exactly one point $\mathbf{x}^*$ ($\mathbf{x}^* \in \Omega$) such that $\mathcal{H} = \{\mathbf{x}^*\}$, then $\mathbf{x}^*$ is an *equilibrium point*.

Thus, if the trajectory of a dynamical system is initiated at an equilibrium point, then the system state does not change as a function of time. For a discrete-time dynamical system of the form

$$\mathbf{x}(t + 1) = \mathbf{f}(\mathbf{x}(t)),$$

where $\mathbf{f}: \mathcal{R}^d \rightarrow \mathcal{R}^d$ is the dynamical system's generator, an equilibrium point $\mathbf{x}^*$ would have the property that

$$\mathbf{x}^* = \mathbf{f}(\mathbf{x}^*). \tag{3.9}$$

The system of d equations in (3.9) can thus be solved to find the equilibrium points associated with the dynamical system $\mathbf{x}(t + 1) = \mathbf{f}(\mathbf{x}(t))$.

Now consider a continuous-time dynamical system of the form

$$d\mathbf{x}/dt = \mathbf{f}(\mathbf{x}),$$

with dynamical system generator $\mathbf{f}: \mathcal{R}^d \rightarrow \mathcal{R}^d$. An equilibrium point $\mathbf{x}^*$ for this dynamical system would have the property that

$$d\mathbf{x}^*/dt = \mathbf{0}_d,$$

where the notation $d\mathbf{x}^*/dt$ indicates $d\mathbf{x}/dt$ evaluated at the point $\mathbf{x}^*$ and $\mathbf{0}_d$ is a d-dimensional vector of zeros. The system of d equations

$$d\mathbf{x}^*/dt = \mathbf{f}(\mathbf{x}^*) = \mathbf{0}_d$$

can then be solved to find the equilibrium points of the continuous-time dynamical system associated with $d\mathbf{x}/dt = \mathbf{f}(\mathbf{x})$. Note that any subset of equilibrium points is also an invariant set.

Periodic Invariant Sets

The second major type of invariant set is the *periodic invariant set*. The system state in this case changes its values as a function of time in a periodic or oscillatory manner. For example, it is easy to imagine neural systems that attempt to converge to certain types of oscillatory behaviors.

Definition: Periodic invariant set.   Let $T = \{0, 1, 2,...\}$ or $T = [0, \infty)$. Let $\Omega \subseteq \mathcal{R}^d$. Let $\Psi: \Omega \times T \rightarrow \Omega$ be a dynamical system. Let $\mathcal{H} \subseteq \Omega$ be a nonempty invariant set with respect to Ψ which does not contain any equilibrium points. Then $\mathcal{H}$ is a *periodic invariant set* if there exists a finite number $\tau \in T$ such that, for every $x_0 \in \mathcal{H}$, $x_0 = \Psi(x_0, \tau)$.

Note that the union of any set of equilibrium points and periodic invariant sets with respect to some dynamical system is also an invariant set. A *limit cycle* is a special type of isolated periodic invariant set.

Other Types of Invariant Sets

There are other types of invariant sets that cannot be defined in terms of sets of equilibrium points and periodic invariant sets. For example, a *chaotic invariant set* has been defined as an invariant set that does not contain an equilibrium point element and that does not contain a periodic invariant set (M. W. Hirsch 1989). Devaney (1992) provides another definition of a chaotic invariant set that captures such intuitions about chaos such as (1) sensitivity to initial conditions, (2) randomness, and (3) regularity.

The important point is that a taxonomy of invariant sets can be defined in terms of particular desirable (or undesirable) properties. Explicitly defining a class of invariant sets with characteristics of interest is an important first step toward understanding whether a given dynamical system will exhibit behavior patterns with those characteristics as well.

3.2.2   Stability of Invariant Sets

Each of the three major types of invariant sets may be further classified as (1) orbitally stable, (2) asymptotically orbitally stable, (3) marginally orbitally stable, (4) orbitally unstable, or (5) globally asymptotically orbitally stable. An invariant set is *orbitally stable* if all trajectories initiated sufficiently close to the invariant set remain in some desired neighborhood of the invariant set as time increases. An invariant set is *orbitally unstable* if the invariant set is not orbitally stable. An invariant set is *marginally orbitally stable* if all trajectories initiated sufficiently close to the invariant set remain in the neighborhood of the invariant set but do not approach the invariant set as time increases. An invariant set is *asymptotically orbitally stable* if all trajectories initiated sufficiently close to the invariant set remain in some desired neighborhood of the invariant set and approach the invariant set as time increases. Finally, an invariant set is *globally asymptotically orbitally stable* with respect to some set Ω if the invariant set is orbitally stable and all trajectories initiated in Ω approach the invariant set as time increases.

Now consider the special case where an invariant set $\mathcal{H}$ consists of a single point $\mathbf{x}^*$, so that $\mathbf{x}^*$ is an equilibrium point. The equilibrium point $\mathbf{x}^*$ is said to be "stable," "asymptotically stable," "marginally stable," or "unstable" if $\mathcal{H}$ is orbitally stable, asymptotically orbitally stable, marginally orbitally stable, or orbitally unstable, respectively.

Figure 3.3 illustrates the intuitive ideas behind the three basic categories of stability with respect to an invariant set consisting of an equilibrium point. Consider a nonlinear dynamical system that describes the behavior of a marble rolling upon a frictionless surface in a uniform gravitational field. Each three-dimensional state of the dynamical system indicates the current position of the marble in a three-dimensional space.

Consider the example of an asymptotically stable equilibrium point as shown in case (a) of figure 3.3. As before, if the marble is placed directly on the bottom of the valley-shaped bowl, then the marble will remain in that position for all time. Thus, the bottom of the valley-shaped bowl is an equilibrium point; moreover, if the marble is placed very close to the bottom of the valley-shaped bowl, the marble will approach the same position. Therefore, the equilibrium point in this case is asymptotically stable.

Case (b) of figure 3.3 illustrates the situation of an unstable equilibrium point where the marble is balanced on the top of a hill-shaped bowl. If the marble is placed directly on the top of the hill-shaped bowl, the marble remains in the same position for all time. Thus the top of the hill-shaped bowl is an equilibrium point. On the other hand, if the marble is placed very close to the top of the hill, then the marble will move away from the equilibrium point. Therefore, the equilibrium point is unstable.

An example of a marginally stable equilibrium point is shown in case (c) of figure 3.3. Every marble position in the interior of the bottom of the bowl is a marginally stable equilibrium point because a marble placed anywhere in the interior of the bowl's bottom will remain in that position for all time. Case (c)

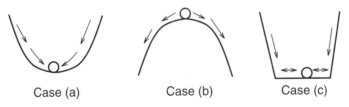

Case (a)   Case (b)   Case (c)

Figure 3.3
Three basic stability classifications of invariant sets. Consider a state space whose points indicate specific ball positions and three dynamical systems which describe the motion of a ball on three different types of bowls. Case (a): The single point at the bottom of bowl is an equilibrium point that is asymptotically stable. Case (b): The single point at the top of the bowl is an equilibrium point that is unstable. Case (c): The entire bottom of the flat bowl is an invariant set that is asymptotically stable. Note that the interior of the entire bottom of the flat bowl consists of marginally stable equilibrium points.

of figure 3.3 also may be interpreted as an example of an asymptotically orbitally stable invariant set, where the invariant set is defined to be the entire set
of points in the bottom of the bowl. Figure 3.4 summarizes some of the relationships among these basic categories of stability.

Before introducing methods for deciding when the trajectory of a given
nonlinear dynamical system will converge to an invariant set, it is necessary to
provide some formal definitions of the basic stability categories. As the formal
definitions are read, readers should attempt to see how the formal definitions
explicitly capture the intuitive notions of the stability categories just discussed.

Definition: Orbitally stable invariant set.   Let $T = \{0, 1, 2,...\}$ or $T = [0, \infty)$.
Let $\Omega \subseteq \mathcal{R}^d$. Let $\Psi\colon \Omega \times T \to \Omega$ be a dynamical system. Let $\mathcal{H}$ be a nonempty
invariant set with respect to Ψ. Let Q be an open set such that $\mathcal{H} \subset Q$. The set
$\mathcal{H}$ is an *orbitally stable invariant set* if for every ε-neighborhood U of $\mathcal{H}$ contained in Q, there exists a δ-neighborhood W of $\mathcal{H}$ such that $\Psi(\mathbf{x}_0, \cdot) \in U$ on T
for all $\mathbf{x}_0 \in W$.

Figure 3.5 illustrates the situation described in the formal definition of an orbitally stable invariant set. An invariant set $\mathcal{H}$ is orbitally stable with respect to
some region Q that contains $\mathcal{H}$ if a neighborhood W of $\mathcal{H}$ exists such that a trajectory initiated in W will remain in any desired neighborhood, U, of $\mathcal{H}$ for all
time where U is a subset of Q.

In order to understand why the open set Q is important in the definition of an
orbitally stable invariant set, consider the following situation. Suppose that a
dynamical system is associated with only a single invariant set consisting of a
single equilibrium point. In this case, let $\mathcal{H}$ be the set containing the single
equilibrium point and let Q be $\mathcal{R}^d$. Given this setup, the definition of an orbitally stable invariant set may be applied. However, most ANN dynamical
systems have multiple equilibrium points and may have many periodic and
other types of invariant sets as well.

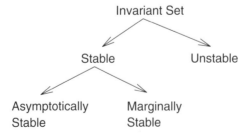

Figure 3.4
Stability hierarchy for three basic stability classifications. An invariant set can be classified as either *orbitally stable* or *orbitally unstable*; an *orbitally stable* invariant set can then be classified as
either *asymptotically orbitally stable* or *marginally orbitally stable*.

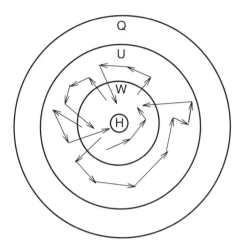

Figure 3.5
Graphical representation of orbitally stable invariant set definition. Note that all trajectories initiated in the neighborhood W of the invariant set H remain in the desired neighborhood U of H if H is orbitally stable.

Consider a dynamical system with just two isolated stable equilibrium points separated by some positive distance. To prove that the *set* of the two equilibrium points is stable, $\mathcal{H}$ must be defined as the set consisting of the two equilibrium points and Q must be chosen to contain $\mathcal{H}$. On the other hand, to prove that an *individual* equilibrium point (for this dynamical system with two equilibrium points) is stable, $\mathcal{H}$ must be defined as the set that contains only the equilibrium point of interest and Q must be chosen to contain $\mathcal{H}$ and exclude the other equilibrium point. Thus the introduction of the set Q provides a useful tool for discussing local stability properties of selected regions of the state space.

Definition: Orbitally unstable invariant set. Let $T = \{0, 1, 2,...\}$ or $T = [0, \infty)$. Let $\Omega \subseteq \mathcal{R}^d$. An invariant set $\mathcal{H} \subseteq \mathcal{R}^d$ is *orbitally unstable* with respect to a dynamical system, $\Psi: \Omega \times T \to \Omega$, if it is not stable.

Definition: Attractor. Let $T = \{0, 1, 2,...\}$ or $T = [0, \infty)$. Let $\Omega \subseteq \mathcal{R}^d$. Let $\Psi: \Omega \times T \to \Omega$ be a dynamical system. An invariant set $\mathcal{H} \subset \Omega$ is an *attractor* with respect to Ψ if for every $\mathbf{x}_0 \in W$ (where W is some δ-neighborhood of $\mathcal{H}$): As $t \to \infty$, $\Psi(\mathbf{x}_0, t) \to \mathcal{H}$.

An example of a dynamical system that approaches a set is illustrated in case (c) of figure 3.3, where the set $\mathcal{H}$ (i.e., the bottom of the flat bowl) is an attractor.

Definition: Asymptotically orbitally stable invariant set. Let $T = \{0, 1, 2,...\}$ or $T = [0, \infty)$. Let $\Omega \subseteq \mathcal{R}^d$. Let $\Psi: \Omega \times T \to \Omega$ be a dynamical system. An invariant set $\mathcal{H} \subseteq \Omega$ is *asymptotically orbitally stable* with respect to

Ψ if (i) $\mathcal{H}$ is orbitally stable with respect to Ψ, and (ii) $\mathcal{H}$ is an attractor with respect to Ψ.

The condition that $\mathcal{H}$ is orbitally stable is required to prevent a given trajectory initiated in some neighborhood of the invariant set from leaving a desired neighborhood of the invariant set.

Definition: Marginally orbitally stable invariant set.   Let $T = \{0, 1, 2,...\}$ or $T = [0, \infty)$. Let $\Omega \subseteq \mathcal{R}^d$. Let $\Psi: \Omega \times T \to \Omega$ be a dynamical system. An invariant set $\mathcal{H} \subseteq \Omega$ is *marginally orbitally stable* with respect to Ψ if (i) $\mathcal{H}$ is orbitally stable with respect to Ψ, and (ii) $\mathcal{H}$ is not asymptotically orbitally stable with respect to Ψ.

Definition: Globally asymptotically orbitally stable invariant set.   Let $T = \{0, 1, 2,...\}$ or $T = [0, \infty)$. Let $W \subseteq \Omega \subseteq \mathcal{R}^d$. Let $\Psi: \Omega \times T \to \Omega$ be a dynamical system. An invariant set $\mathcal{H} \subseteq W$ is *globally asymptotically orbitally stable* with respect to W if (i) $\mathcal{H}$ is orbitally stable with respect to Ψ, and (ii) for all $\mathbf{x}_0 \in W$, as $t \to \infty$, $\Psi(\mathbf{x}_0, t) \to \mathcal{H}$.

3.3   Invariant Set Theorem

An important tool for classifying and identifying the invariant sets of a given dynamical system is the *Invariant Set Theorem*. Before stating the theorem, however, the concept of a *Lyapunov function* (also referred to as a "Liapunov function") will be introduced.

3.3.1   Lyapunov Functions

A Lyapunov function for a dynamical system is a special function (1) that maps any state of a particular dynamical system into a real number, and (2) whose value, as the dynamical system evolves in time, is nonincreasing on the dynamical system's trajectories. Lyapunov functions are used for studying the stability properties of dynamical systems and are especially useful for the analysis of high-dimensional nonlinear dynamical systems. In particular, if a Lyapunov function for an autonomous dynamical system exists and the trajectories of the dynamical system are bounded in an appropriate way, then the long-term behavior of the dynamical system can usually be characterized in an insightful, qualitative way. The concept of a Lyapunov function for a discrete-time dynamical system is now formally defined.

Definition: Lyapunov function for discrete-time systems.   Let $T = \{0, 1, 2,...\}$. Let Ω be a nonempty subset of $\mathcal{R}^d$. Let $\overline{\Omega}$ be the closure of Ω. Let $V: \overline{\Omega} \to \mathcal{R}$ be a continuous function on $\overline{\Omega}$. Let the dynamical system $\Psi: \Omega \times T \to \Omega$ be generated by $\mathbf{f}: \Omega \to \Omega$. Let the function $\dot{V}: \overline{\Omega} \to \mathcal{R}$ be continuous on $\overline{\Omega}$ and defined such that, for all $\mathbf{x} \in \Omega$,

$\dot{V}(\mathbf{x}) = V(\mathbf{f}(\mathbf{x})) - V(\mathbf{x})$.

If $\dot{V}(\mathbf{x}) \le 0$ for all $\mathbf{x} \in \overline{\Omega}$, then V is a *discrete-time Lyapunov function* on $\overline{\Omega}$ with respect to $\mathbf{\Psi}$.

The assumption that $\dot{V}(\mathbf{x}) \le 0$ for all $\mathbf{x} \in \overline{\Omega}$ for the discrete-time dynamical system corresponding to the system of difference equations

$\mathbf{x}(t+1) = \mathbf{f}(\mathbf{x}(t))$

implies that

$V(\mathbf{x}(t+1)) \le V(\mathbf{x}(t))$

for $t = 0, 1, 2, \dots$. The concept of a Lyapunov function for a continuous-time dynamical system is now introduced.

Definition: Lyapunov function for continuous-time systems. Let $T = [0, \infty)$. Let Ω be a nonempty subset of $\mathcal{R}^d$. Let $\overline{\Omega}$ be the closure of Ω. Let $V: \overline{\Omega} \to \mathcal{R}$ be a continuous function on $\overline{\Omega}$ such that ∇V exists on Ω. Let the dynamical system $\mathbf{\Psi}: \Omega \times T \to \Omega$ be generated by $\mathbf{f}: \Omega \to \Omega$. Let the function $\dot{V}: \overline{\Omega} \to \mathcal{R}$ be continuous on $\overline{\Omega}$ and defined such that, for all $\mathbf{x} \in \Omega$,

$\dot{V}(\mathbf{x}) = [\nabla_{\mathbf{x}} V(\mathbf{x})]^T \mathbf{f}(\mathbf{x})$.

If $\dot{V}(\mathbf{x}) \le 0$ for all $\mathbf{x} \in \overline{\Omega}$, then V is a *continuous-time Lyapunov function* on $\overline{\Omega}$ with respect to $\mathbf{\Psi}$.

Let the continuous function $\mathbf{f}: \mathcal{R}^d \to \mathcal{R}^d$ that is the continuous-time dynamical system generator for $\mathbf{\Psi}: \mathcal{R}^d \times T \to \mathcal{R}^d$ be Lipschitz on $\mathcal{R}^d$. Then the existence, uniqueness, and continuous dependence on initial conditions properties of $\mathbf{\Psi}$ are guaranteed by the EUC Theorem for Continuous-Time Dynamical Systems. It is then helpful to note that $\dot{V} \le 0$ on $\overline{\Omega}$ for the continuous-time dynamical system implicitly specified by $d\mathbf{x}/dt = \mathbf{f}(\mathbf{x})$ may be expressed as

$\dot{V} = [\nabla_{\mathbf{x}} V(\mathbf{x})]^T \mathbf{f}(\mathbf{x}) = [\nabla_{\mathbf{x}} V(\mathbf{x})]^T [d\mathbf{x}/dt] = dV/dt \le 0$.

3.3.2 Discussion of the Invariant Set Theorem

This section introduces the key mathematical tool for nonlinear dynamical system analysis: the *Invariant Set Theorem*. (Discussions related to the statement and proof of the theorem presented here may be found in LaSalle 1960, Theorem 1, 522, and 1976, Theorem 6.3, 6; Leighton 1976, chap. 9; Luenberger 1979, 345–346, and Vidyasagar 1978, Lemma 81, 157.)

Theorem: Invariant Set Theorem. Let $T = \{0, 1, 2, \dots\}$ or $T = [0, \infty)$. Let Ω be a nonempty bounded subset of $\mathcal{R}^d$. Let $\overline{\Omega}$ be the closure of Ω. Let $\mathbf{f}: \Omega \to \Omega$. Let $\mathbf{f}$ be the generator function for exactly one dynamical system $\mathbf{\Psi}: \Omega \times T \to \Omega$. Let $\mathbf{\Psi}(\cdot, t)$ be continuous on Ω for all $t \in T$. Let $V: \overline{\Omega} \to \mathcal{R}$ be a Lyapunov function on $\overline{\Omega}$ with respect to Ψ. Let S denote the subset of $\overline{\Omega}$ defined such that

$$S = \{\mathbf{x} \in \overline{\Omega}: \dot{V}(\mathbf{x}) = 0\}.$$

Let $\mathcal{H}$ denote the largest invariant set contained in S with respect to Ψ. Then $\mathcal{H}$ is nonempty and for every $\mathbf{x}_0 \in \Omega$: as $t \to \infty$, $\Psi(\mathbf{x}_0, t) \to \mathcal{H}$.

Proof.   See section 3.5.   ■

First, note that Ω is an invariant set with respect to Ψ. Second, note that the EUC conditions for the discrete-time dynamical system case of the Invariant Set Theorem are satisfied if $\mathbf{f}: \Omega \to \Omega$ is continuous on Ω by the EUC Theorem for Discrete-Time Systems. The EUC conditions for the continuous-time dynamical system case of the Invariant Set Theorem are satisfied if a function $\mathbf{f}^*: \mathcal{R}^d \to \mathcal{R}^d$ can be constructed such that (1) $\mathbf{f}^* = \mathbf{f}$ on Ω, (2) $\mathbf{f}^*$ is continuous on $\mathcal{R}^d$, and (3) $\mathbf{f}^*$ is Lipschitz on $\mathcal{R}^d$. Given such a function $\mathbf{f}^*$, the EUC Theorem for Continuous-Time Systems is applicable.

The important main conclusion of the Invariant Set Theorem is that, for every $\mathbf{x}_0 \in \Omega$, the trajectory $\mathbf{x}(\cdot, \mathbf{x}_0) = \Psi(\mathbf{x}_0, \cdot)$ has the property $\mathbf{x}(t, \mathbf{x}_0) \to \mathcal{H}$ as $t \to \infty$, where $\mathcal{H}$ is the largest invariant set in

$$S = \{\mathbf{x} \in \overline{\Omega}: \dot{V}(\mathbf{x}) = 0\}.$$

Although the conclusion of the theorem seems rather weak, it is possible in many ANN applications to characterize the nature of the invariant set $\mathcal{H}$. If this can be done, then the Invariant Set Theorem is a powerful tool for ANN deterministic autonomous dynamical system analysis and design.

Typically, the Invariant Set Theorem is applied by constructing (1) a closed, bounded, and invariant set $\overline{\Omega}$ and (2) a Lyapunov function V on $\overline{\Omega}$. The Lyapunov function assumption has already been discussed; the assumption that $\overline{\Omega}$ is a closed, bounded, invariant set is usually satisfied in two distinct ways. First, if the system state space is an activation state space, then the activations of the units usually have minimum and maximum firing rates. Thus $\overline{\Omega}$ is by definition a closed, bounded, invariant set. A second common approach for constructing a set $\overline{\Omega}$ that is a closed, bounded, and invariant set is now described.

Proposition: Closed, Bounded, Invariant Set.   Let $T = \{0, 1, 2,...\}$ or $T = [0, \infty)$. Let $V: \mathcal{R}^d \to \mathcal{R}$. Let

$$\Omega_s = \{\mathbf{x} \in \mathcal{R}^d: V(\mathbf{x}) \le s\} \tag{3.10}$$

be a nonempty set where s is a finite real number. Let $\mathbf{f}: \Omega_s \to \Omega_s$ be the generator function for exactly one dynamical system $\Psi: \Omega_s \times T \to \Omega_s$ such that $\Psi(\cdot, t)$ is continuous on Ω_s for all $t \in T$. Let V be a Lyapunov function for Ψ on

Ω_s. If V has the property that $V(\mathbf{x}) \to +\infty$ as $|\mathbf{x}| \to \infty$, then Ω_s is a *closed, bounded, and invariant set* with respect to $\mathbf{\Psi}$.

Proof. The set Ω_s is a closed set by construction because V is continuous (Rosenlicht 1968, 91). And if V is a Lyapunov function, then Ω_s is also an invariant set because, if a trajectory was initiated in Ω_s and left Ω_s, the condition that V is nonincreasing along all trajectories would be violated.

Now, using a proof by contradiction, assume that Ω_s is *not* a bounded set. Then for every $\mathbf{x}_t \in \Omega_s$, there exists an $\mathbf{x}_{t+1} \in \Omega_s$ such that $|\mathbf{x}_t| < |\mathbf{x}_{t+1}|$. Thus, a sequence $\mathbf{x}_1, \mathbf{x}_2,\ldots$ in Ω_s exists such that $|\mathbf{x}_t| \to \infty$ as $t \to \infty$, and $V(\mathbf{x}_t) \to +\infty$ as $t \to \infty$ by the assumed property of V. But the condition that $V(\mathbf{x}) \le s$, where s is a finite positive real number must be violated for some $\mathbf{x} \in \Omega_s$. Therefore, Ω_s must be a bounded set. ∎

When applying this proposition, it is important to realize that the Lyapunov function V must have the property that for all $\mathbf{x} \in \mathcal{R}^d$: if $|\mathbf{x}| \to \infty$, then $V(\mathbf{x}) \to +\infty$ (*not* $V(\mathbf{x}) \to -\infty$). For example, let $V: \mathcal{R} \to \mathcal{R}$ be defined such that for all $x \in \mathcal{R}$: $V(x) = x$. Assume V is the Lyapunov function for some dynamical system $\mathbf{\Psi}: \mathcal{R} \times T \to \mathcal{R}$. Now construct a set Ω_s such that

$$\Omega_s = \{x \in \mathcal{R}: V(x) \le s\} = \{x \in \mathcal{R}: x \le s\}.$$

The Closed, Bounded, and Invariant Set Proposition does *not* apply because, as $|x| \to \infty$, $V(x) \to +\infty$ or $V(x) \to -\infty$. Direct inspection of Ω_s indicates that Ω_s is a closed set (because V is continuous) and an invariant set (because V is a Lyapunov function) but is not a bounded set.

3.4 ANN Applications

3.4.1 Hopfield (1982) Neural Network

Problem. Consider a Hopfield (1982) network (as described in chapter 2) a discrete-time classification dynamical system of symmetrically connected threshold units that describes how the activations of the units become updated as a function of time. Let $x_i(t)$ be the activation of the ith unit at iteration t in a network consisting of d units. Let $\{w_{ij}\}$ and $\{b_i\}$ be the weights and biases of the network respectively. The activation updating rule is given by picking some unit at each iteration of the algorithm using a deterministic or stochastic procedure and updating its state as required by the following rule. Assume the ith unit in a d-unit system has been chosen for updating at ANN classification dynamical system algorithm iteration t. Let

$$x_i(t+1) = \mathcal{S}[\varphi_i(t)] \text{ where } \varphi_i(t) = \left[\sum_{j=1, j \neq i}^{d} w_{ij} x_j(t) + b_i \right] \tag{3.11}$$

and where $\mathscr{S}[\varphi_i(t)] = 1$ if $\varphi_i(t) > 0$, $\mathscr{S}[\varphi_i(t)] = 0$ if $\varphi_i(t) < 0$, and $x_i(t + 1) = x_i(t)$ if $\varphi_i(t) = 0$. Let the initial state of the Hopfield (1982) network be a vector $\mathbf{x}(0) \in \{0, 1\}^d$, then prove that all trajectories of the network approach the largest set of system equilibrium points.

Solution.   Because the activation updating rule is quasi-linear, consider the quadratic function

$$V(x_1, \ldots, x_d) = -(1/2)\sum_{i=1}^{d} \sum_{j=1, j\neq i}^{d} w_{ij} x_i x_j - \sum_{i=1}^{d} b_i x_i$$

as a candidate Lyapunov function because the derivative of the quadratic polynomial V with respect to $\mathbf{x}$ is a linear function and (3.11) defines a quasi-linear dynamical system.

Note that the discrete-time version of the Invariant Set Theorem does *not* apply because the $\mathscr{S}$ function in the right side of the activation updating rule in (3.11) is not a continuous function of the system state. Still, as we will see, the basic approach used to prove the Invariant Set Theorem (see section 3.5) is still relevant because the state space is finite.

Let $\dot{V} = V(\mathbf{x}(t + 1)) - V(\mathbf{x}(t))$ so that:

$$\dot{V} = \left[-(1/2)\sum_{k=1}^{d} \sum_{j=1}^{d} w_{kj} x_k(t + 1)x_j(t + 1) - \sum_{k=1}^{d} b_k x_k(t + 1) \right]$$

$$- \left[-(1/2)\sum_{k=1}^{d} \sum_{j=1}^{d} w_{kj} x_k(t)x_j(t) - \sum_{k=1}^{d} b_k x_k(t) \right].$$

Assume that at iteration t the activation level of unit i is only updated. This implies that $x_j(t + 1) = x_j(t)$ for $j \neq i$. Thus, after cancellation of common terms,

$$\dot{V} = -(1/2)x_i(t + 1)\sum_{j=1}^{d} w_{ij} x_j(t) - (1/2)x_i(t + 1)\sum_{j=1}^{d} w_{ji} x_j(t)$$

$$- \left[-(1/2)x_i(t)\sum_{j=1}^{d} w_{ij} x_j(t) - (1/2)x_i(t)\sum_{j=1}^{d} w_{ji} x_j(t) \right] - (x_i(t + 1) - x_i(t))b_i,$$

and since $w_{ji} = w_{ij}$ for $i, j = 1 \ldots d$ by definition:

$$\dot{V} = -[x_i(t + 1) - x_i(t)]\varphi_i(t).$$

Note that if $\varphi_i(t) > 0$, then $x_i(t + 1) = 1$. Assume $x_i(t + 1) \neq x_i(t)$ and $\varphi_i(t) > 0$ so that $x_i(t + 1) = 1$ and $x_i(t) = 0$ which implies $\dot{V} < 0$. Now note that if $\varphi_i(t) < 0$, then $x_i(t + 1) = 0$. Assume $x_i(t + 1) \neq x_i(t)$ and $\varphi_i(t) < 0$ so that $x_i(t + 1) = 0$ and $x_i(t) = 1$ which again implies $\dot{V} < 0$. Thus, if $x_i(t + 1)$

$\neq x_i(t)$, then $\dot{V} < 0$. Also note V has a lower bound in the state space because V is a continuous function on a d-dimensional hypercube that is a closed and bounded set.

Suppose the lower bound of V was never reached. Because the state space is finite and $\dot{V} < 0$, after a finite number of iterations where the system visited all 2^d possible system states, the system would have to move into an additional system state such that $\dot{V} < 0$. This contradiction thus leads to the conclusion that the lower bound of V is eventually reached. But if we assume the lower bound of V is reached and $x_i(t + 1) \neq x_i(t)$, this also leads to a contradiction since $\dot{V} < 0$. Thus, if the lower bound of V is reached,

$$x_i(t + 1) = x_i(t).$$

Therefore, all trajectories approach the largest set of system equilibrium points.

3.4.2 Analysis of a Hopfield (1984) Logistic ANN

Problem. Consider the following special case of a Hopfield (1984; also see Cohen and Grossberg 1983) ANN. Define the sigmoidal logistic function, $\mathcal{S}: \mathcal{R} \rightarrow (0, 1)$, such that for all $u_i \in \mathcal{R}$:

$$\mathcal{S}(u_i) = \frac{1}{1 + \exp(-u_i)}.$$

Note that a unique inverse $\mathcal{S}^{-1}: (0, 1) \rightarrow \mathcal{R}$ exists and is defined such that for all $x_i \in (0, 1)$:

$$\mathcal{S}^{-1}(x_i) = \log[x_i/(1 - x_i)].$$

Let x_i be the *activation level* of the ith unit in a network consisting of d units, where the *net input* to the ith unit is defined by the formula

$$u_i = \mathcal{S}^{-1}(x_i).$$

A popular special case of the Hopfield (1984) ANN has activation updating dynamics specified by the following continuous-time dynamical system:

$$du_i/dt = (1/C_i)\sum_j w_{ij} x_j - (u_i/[C_i R_i]) + I_i/C_i, \qquad (3.12)$$

where I_i is the constant external input or "bias" of the ith unit, and w_{ij} is the connection strength indicating the effect of activating unit j upon the activation value of unit i for $i = 1 \ldots d$. The constant coefficients w_{ij} form a symmetric matrix, that is $w_{ij} = w_{ji}$ for $i, j = 1 \ldots d$. The constants C_i and R_i are positive real numbers that roughly correspond to the respective capacitance and resistance across the neuron's membrane when the ith unit is interpreted as the ith neuron in a set of d neurons. Investigate the long-term behavior of (3.12).

HINT: Let V: $(0, 1)^d \to \mathcal{R}$ be defined such that for all $\mathbf{x} \in (0, 1)^d$:

$$V(\mathbf{x}) = -(1/2)\sum_{i=1}^{d}\sum_{j=1}^{d} w_{ij}\, x_i x_j$$

$$+ \sum_{i=1}^{d}(1/R_i)[x_i \log x_i + (1 - x_i)\log(1 - x_i)] - \sum_{i=1}^{d} I_i x_i. \qquad (3.13)$$

The function V has been proposed as a candidate Lyapunov function for this ANN dynamical system.

Solution. The first step of the analysis is to construct an appropriate generator function. Implicitly define a continuous-time dynamical system $\mathbf{\Psi}_x$: $(0, 1)^d \times [0, \infty) \to (0, 1)^d$ by the differential equation $d\mathbf{x}/dt = \mathbf{f}(\mathbf{x})$, where the generator function $\mathbf{f}_x$: $(0, 1)^d \to (0, 1)^d$ is defined such that for all $\mathbf{x} \in (0, 1)^d$: the ith element of $\mathbf{f}_x$ is given by

$$f_i^x(\mathbf{x}) = (1/C_i)x_i(1 - x_i)\left[\sum_{j=1}^{d} w_{ij}\, x_j - u_i/R_i + I_i\right]$$

for $i = 1 \dots d$. Note that the ith element of $d\mathbf{x}/dt$, dx_i/dt, is therefore

$$dx_i/dt = [dx_i/du_i][du_i/dt] = f_i^x(\mathbf{x})$$

for $i = 1 \dots d$.

Unfortunately, a function $\mathbf{f}^*$: $\mathcal{R}^d \times [0, \infty) \to \mathcal{R}^d$ cannot be constructed such that $\mathbf{f}_x^*(\mathbf{x}) = \mathbf{f}_x(\mathbf{x})$ for all $\mathbf{x} \in (0, 1)^d$, $\mathbf{f}_x^*$ is continuous on $\mathcal{R}^d$, and $\mathbf{f}_x^*$ is Lipschitz on $\mathcal{R}^d$. Thus $\mathbf{f}_x$ is not Lipschitz on $\mathcal{R}^d$. This means that another approach must be used to establish the required EUC conditions.

To establish the required EUC conditions for $\mathbf{\Psi}_x$, a generator function, $\mathbf{f}_u$: $\mathcal{R}^d \to \mathcal{R}^d$, for a different dynamical system $\mathbf{\Psi}_u$: $\mathcal{R}^d \to \mathcal{R}^d$ will be constructed and a relationship between $\mathbf{\Psi}_u$ and the original dynamical system $\mathbf{\Psi}_x$ then exploited.

Define $\underline{\mathcal{S}}(\mathbf{u})$ as a vector of the same dimension as the vector $\mathbf{u}$ and define the ith element of $\underline{\mathcal{S}}(\mathbf{u})$ such that

$$\mathcal{S}(u_i) = 1/(1 + \exp(-u_i))$$

for all $u_i \in \mathcal{R}$ and $i = 1 \dots d$. Similarly, define $\underline{\mathcal{S}}^{-1}$ such that

$$\underline{\mathcal{S}}^{-1}(\underline{\mathcal{S}}(\mathbf{u})) = \mathbf{u}$$

for all $\mathbf{u} \in \mathcal{R}^d$.

Now define $\mathbf{\Psi}_u$ such that for all $\mathbf{u} \in \mathcal{R}^d$:

$$\mathbf{\Psi}_u(\mathbf{u}, \cdot) = \underline{\mathcal{S}}^{-1}[\mathbf{\Psi}_x(\underline{\mathcal{S}}(\mathbf{u}), \cdot)] \qquad (3.14)$$

on $[0, \infty)$. And because $\underline{\mathcal{S}}$ is invertible,

$$\Psi_x(\mathbf{x}, \cdot) = \underline{\mathscr{S}}[\Psi_u(\underline{\mathscr{S}}^{-1}(\mathbf{x}), \cdot)] \tag{3.15}$$

on $[0, \infty)$ for all $\mathbf{x} \in (0, 1)^d$.

The generator function $\mathbf{f}_u$ is now defined. Because $\mathbf{f}_x$ is a generator function for Ψ_x,

$$\frac{d\Psi_x(\mathbf{x}, t)}{dt} = \mathbf{f}_x(\Psi_x(\mathbf{x}, t)) \tag{3.16}$$

for all $\mathbf{x} \in (0, 1)^d$ and for all $t \in [0, \infty)$.

Let $d\mathbf{x}/d\mathbf{u}$ be a d-dimensional square diagonal matrix whose ith on-diagonal element is $\mathscr{S}(u_i)[1 - \mathscr{S}(u_i)]$ for $u_i \in \mathscr{R}$ $(i = 1 \dots d)$. Substituting (3.15) into (3.16) gives

$$\frac{d\Psi_u(\underline{\mathscr{S}}^{-1}(\mathbf{x}), t)}{dt} = [d\mathbf{x}/d\mathbf{u}]^{-1}\mathbf{f}_x(\Psi_x(\mathbf{x}, t)) \tag{3.17}$$

for all $\mathbf{x} \in (0, 1)^d$ and for all $t \in [0, \infty)$.

Now define $\mathbf{f}_u: \mathscr{R}^d \to \mathscr{R}^d$ such that

$$\mathbf{f}_u(\mathbf{u}) = [d\mathbf{x}/d\mathbf{u}]^{-1}\mathbf{f}_x(\underline{\mathscr{S}}(\mathbf{u}))$$

for all $\mathbf{u} \in \mathscr{R}^d$. Substituting the expression for $\mathbf{f}_u$ into (3.17) and using (3.14), (3.17) becomes:

$$\frac{d\Psi_u(\mathbf{u}, t)}{dt} = \mathbf{f}_u(\underline{\mathscr{S}}^{-1}(\Psi_x(\underline{\mathscr{S}}(\mathbf{u}), t))) = \mathbf{f}_u(\Psi_u(\mathbf{u}, t)) \tag{3.18}$$

for all $\mathbf{u} \in \mathscr{R}^d$ and for all $t \in [0, \infty)$. Thus Ψ_u is generated by $\mathbf{f}_u$.

Let $f_i^u: \mathscr{R}^d \times T \to \mathscr{R}$ be the ith element of $\mathbf{f}_u$. Note that

$$\frac{\partial f_i^u}{\partial u_i} = (1/C_i)w_{ii}x_i(1 - x_i) - (1/[C_iR_i])$$

and

$$\frac{\partial f_i^u}{\partial u_j} = (1/C_i)w_{ij}x_j(1 - x_j)$$

are bounded on $\mathscr{R}^d$ since $x_i = \mathscr{S}(u_i) \in (0, 1)$ for all $u_i \in \mathscr{R}$. Thus the $\mathbf{f}_u$ satisfies a Lipschitz condition on $\mathscr{R}^d$. Thus, by the relation in (3.15), satisfaction of the EUC conditions for Ψ_u implies satisfaction of the EUC conditions for Ψ_x.

The Invariant Set Theorem will now be used. Let $\overline{\Omega} = [0, 1]^d$, so that $\overline{\Omega}$ is a closed, bounded, and invariant set with respect to Ψ_x. Note that V is not continuous everywhere on $\overline{\Omega}$ because of terms in the definition of V, such as $x_i \log x_i$, that are not defined at $x_i = 0$. However, a new function $V_x: \overline{\Omega} \to \mathscr{R}$ can be constructed such that V_x is continuous on $[0, 1]^d$. In order to do this, it is necessary to note that $x_i(1 - x_i)u_i$ is not defined for $x_i \in \{0, 1\}$ and that

$$x_i(1 - x_i)u_i = x_i(1 - x_i) \log\left[\frac{x_i}{1 - x_i}\right] \to 0$$

as $x_i \to 0$ or $x_i \to 1$. Because V_x must be defined such that V_x is continuous on $[0, 1]^d$, it is appropriate to define $x_i(1 - x_i)u_i = 0$ if $x_i = 0$ or if $x_i = 1$.

Given that V_x is now defined on $[0, 1]^d$ such that V_x is continuous on $[0, 1]^d$, it will now be shown that V_x is a Lyapunov function on $\overline{\Omega} = [0, 1]^d$ with respect to Ψ_x. First, note that

$$\frac{\partial V_x}{\partial x_i} = -\left[\sum_{i=1}^{d} w_{ij}x_j - u_i/R_i + I_i\right],$$

where we have used the constraint $w_{ij} = w_{ji}$ for $i, j = 1 \dots d$ to compute the first term. Second, note that inspection of $\partial V_x/\partial x_i$ shows that

$$\frac{\partial V_x}{\partial x_i} = -C_i f_i^x(\mathbf{x})/[x_i(1 - x_i)], \tag{3.19}$$

where $f_i^x: (0, 1)^d \to \mathcal{R}$ is the ith element of the generator function $\mathbf{f}_x$. Thus

$$\dot{V}_x = \sum_{i=1}^{d} (\partial V_x/\partial x_i) f_i^x(\mathbf{x})$$

for all $x_i \in (0, 1)$, $i = 1 \dots d$. Substituting the formula for f_i^x, it then follows that

$$\dot{V}_x = -\sum_{i=1}^{d} (1/C_i) x_i(1 - x_i)\left[\sum_{j=1}^{d} w_{ij}x_j - (u_i/R_i) + I_i\right]^2 \le 0$$

for all $x_i \in (0, 1)$, $i = 1 \dots d$.

In order for the Invariant Set Theorem to be applicable, $\dot{V}$ must be continuous on the closure of Ω which is $\overline{\Omega}$. In order to achieve this goal, we can try to define $\dot{V}_x$ in an appropriate way on the boundary of the set $\overline{\Omega} = [0, 1]^d$. By L'Hospital's rule (Rosenlicht 1968, 109–110; Goldberg, 1964, 229) it follows that

$$x_i(1 - x_i)u_i^2 = x_i(1 - x_i)[\log [x_i/(1 - x_i)]]^2 \to 0$$

as $x_i \to 0$ or as $x_i \to 1$, provided that $x_i \in (0, 1)$. Thus $\dot{V}_x$ may be defined on the boundary of $\overline{\Omega}$ such that $\dot{V}_x$ is continuous on $\overline{\Omega}$ if $x_i(1 - x_i)u_i^2$ is defined as zero for $x_i = 0$ or $x_i = 1$. As before, it will be also necessary to define $x_i(1 - x_i)u_i = 0$ for $x_i = 0$ or $x_i = 1$. Fortunately, this definition of $\dot{V}_x$ on the boundary of $[0, 1]^d$ does not violate the Lyapunov function condition that $\dot{V}_x$ is nonpositive. Given these definitions, $\dot{V}_x$ has been defined such that $\dot{V}_x$ is a continuous function on $[0, 1]^d$.

By direct application of the Invariant Set Theorem, all trajectories initiated in Ω approach the largest invariant set in $\overline{\Omega}$, where

$$\dot{V}_x = -\sum_{i=1}^{d} (1/C_i)x_i(1 - x_i)\left[\sum_{j=1}^{d} w_{ij}x_j - (u_i/R_i) + I_i\right]^2 = 0.$$

Thus all trajectories initiated in Ω approach $\mathcal{H}$, where $\mathcal{H}$ contains the largest set of system equilibrium points which includes the vertices of a unit hypercube located at the origin and specific points on the boundary of the unit hypercube.

3.4.3   Analysis of Backpropagation Learning

Problem.   Let $l: \mathcal{R}^q \to \mathcal{R}$ be a function with continuous first partial derivatives on $\mathcal{R}^q$. In the *batch version* of the backpropagation learning algorithm, the M training stimuli are used to update the current set of weights, $\mathbf{w}(t)$, of the backpropagation network using the rule

$$\mathbf{w}(t + 1) = \mathbf{w}(t) - \gamma\nabla_{\mathbf{w}(t)}l(\mathbf{w}(t)), \tag{3.20}$$

where the stepsize γ is a positive real number and $\nabla_{\mathbf{w}(t)}l(\mathbf{w}(t))$ is the gradient of the learning objective function l evaluated at $\mathbf{w}(t)$. Also make the unlikely assumption that l has the property that, if $|\mathbf{w}| \to \infty$, then $l(\mathbf{w}) \to +\infty$. Explain why the stability of the nonlinear discrete-time system in (3.20) cannot be investigated using the function l as a candidate Lyapunov function.

Propose a continuous-time version of the backpropagation learning algorithm that can be analyzed using l as a Lyapunov function. You may assume that the generator function for the continuous-time version of the backpropagation learning algorithm satisfies a global Lipschitz condition on $\mathcal{R}^q$ even though some continuous-time ANN backpropagation learning dynamical systems do not satisfy such a condition (see problem 3.1-4).

To investigate the long-term behavior of the continuous-time dynamical system you constructed, define a set Ω_s such that

$$\Omega_s = \{\mathbf{w} \in \mathcal{R}^q: l(\mathbf{w}) \leq s\},$$

where s is some finite positive real number. Then prove that all trajectories initiated in Ω_s converge to the largest set of system equilibrium points in Ω_s. Describe that set of system equilibrium points in Ω_s.

Solution.   The discrete-time Invariant Set Theorem does not apply because $l(\mathbf{w}(t + 1))$ is not necessarily less than or equal to $l(\mathbf{w}(t))$ for each $t > 0$. A continuous-time approximation to (3.20) is given by

$$d\mathbf{w}/dt = -\gamma\nabla_{\mathbf{w}(t)}l(\mathbf{w}(t)), \tag{3.21}$$

which exploits the assumption that $d\mathbf{w}/dt$ is approximately $[\mathbf{w}(t + \delta) - \mathbf{w}(t)]/\delta$ when δ is sufficiently small. The problem then asks us to analyze the continuous-time system in (3.21). It is important to realize that the conclusions we obtain from this analysis do not directly apply to (3.20). Nevertheless, some insights into (3.20) may be obtained from analysis of the approximation of (3.20) provided in (3.21).

Because it is unlikely that l will have bounded second partial derivatives, it is also unlikely that the right-hand side of (3.21) satisfies a global Lipschitz condition (see problem 3.1-4).

Let $\mathbf{f}: \mathcal{R}^q \to \mathcal{R}^q$ be the generator function for (3.21) such that for all $\mathbf{w} \in \mathcal{R}^q$: $\mathbf{f}(\mathbf{w}) = -\gamma \nabla_{\mathbf{w}} l$. Inspection of (3.21) shows that

$$\dot{l}(\mathbf{w}) = [\nabla_{\mathbf{w}} l(\mathbf{w})]^T \mathbf{f}(\mathbf{w}) = -\gamma \left| \nabla_{\mathbf{w}} l(\mathbf{w}) \right|^2 \tag{3.22}$$

for all $\mathbf{w} \in \mathcal{R}^q$. Thus l is a Lyapunov function for (3.21).

Note that Ω_s is a closed, bounded, and invariant set by the Closed, Bounded, and Invariant Set Proposition. It then immediately follows that the largest invariant set where $\dot{l} = 0$ is the set of equilibrium points, $\mathcal{H} \subseteq \Omega_s$, which is defined as

$$\mathcal{H} = \{\mathbf{w} \in \Omega_s: \nabla_{\mathbf{w}} l = \mathbf{0}_q\}.$$

3.5   Proof of the Invariant Set Theorem

The version of the Invariant Set Theorem proved in this section differs from the one originally formulated and proved by LaSalle (1960) in three minor respects. First, it does not assume that the main problem is the analysis of a single equilibrium point at the origin; multiple types of invariant sets can be handled. Second, it requires only that $\dot{V}$ be continuous on $\overline{\Omega}$ rather than that the gradient of V be continuous on $\overline{\Omega}$. And finally, it applies to discrete-time dynamical systems rather than merely to continuous-time dynamical systems. (Vidyasagar 1978, 156–157, provides a good discussion of the continuous-time dynamical system version of the theorem provided here, while LaSalle 1976, 1–6, provides a nice discussion of the discrete-time case.)

Definition: Positive limit set.   Let $T = \{0, 1, 2,...\}$ or $T = [0, \infty)$. Let $\Omega \subseteq \mathcal{R}^d$. Let $\mathbf{\Psi}: \Omega \times T \to \Omega$ be a dynamical system. Let $\mathbf{x}_0 \in \Omega$. A set $L \subseteq \Omega$ is a *positive limit set* with respect to the trajectory $\mathbf{\Psi}(\mathbf{x}_0, \cdot)$ if an ordered sequence of elements in T ($t_1, t_2,...$ where $t_1 < t_2 < t_3 < ...$) exists such that, as $n \to \infty$, $\mathbf{\Psi}(\mathbf{x}_0, t_n) \to \mathbf{y}$, where the *limit point* $\mathbf{y} \in L$.

Definition: Bounded trajectory.   Let $T = \{0, 1, 2,...\}$ or $T = [0, \infty)$. Let $\Omega \subseteq \mathcal{R}^d$. Let $\mathbf{\Psi}: \Omega \times T \to \Omega$ be a dynamical system. Let $\mathbf{x}_0 \in \Omega$. If there exists a finite positive real number C such that $\left| \Psi(\mathbf{x}_0, t) \right| < C$ for all $t \in T$, then $\Psi(\mathbf{x}_0, \cdot)$ is a *bounded trajectory* initiated at $\mathbf{x}_0$.

Lemma: Positive limit set lemma.   Let $T = \{0, 1, 2,...\}$ or $T = [0, \infty)$. Let $\Omega \subseteq \mathcal{R}^d$. Assume $\mathbf{f}: \Omega \to \Omega$ is a dynamical system generator function for exactly one dynamical system $\Psi: \Omega \times T \to \Omega$ such that $\Psi(\cdot, t)$ is continuous on Ω for all $t \in T$. Let $\mathbf{x}_0 \in \Omega$. If $\Psi(\mathbf{x}_0, \cdot)$ is a bounded trajectory initiated at $\mathbf{x}_0$, then the positive limit set, L, of $\Psi(\mathbf{x}_0, \cdot)$ is nonempty and invariant. In addition, $\Psi(\mathbf{x}_0, t) \to L$ as $t \to \infty$.

Proof.   Let $\mathbf{x}_0 \in \Omega$. First, note that the limit set L for the bounded trajectory $\Psi(\mathbf{x}_0, \cdot)$ initiated in Ω at $\mathbf{x}_0$ is nonempty by the Bolzano-Weierstrass Theorem (Knopp 1956, 15), which states that every bounded infinite set contains at least one limit point.

Now show that as $t \to \infty$, $\Psi(\mathbf{x}_0, t) \to L$, where L is the positive limit set for the trajectory $\Psi(\mathbf{x}_0, \cdot)$. A proof by contradiction will be used. Assume there exists a strictly positive real number ε such that for all $t^* \in T$ there is a $t > t^*$ such that

$$\left| \Psi(\mathbf{x}_0, t) - \mathbf{y} \right| \geq \varepsilon$$

for all $\mathbf{y} \in L$. Thus a sequence $t_1, t_2, t_3,\dots$ (where $t_1 < t_2 < t_3 < \dots$) can be constructed such that as $n \to \infty$:

$$\left| \Psi(\mathbf{x}_0, t_n) - \mathbf{y} \right| \geq \varepsilon$$

for all $\mathbf{y} \in L$. But because $\Psi(\mathbf{x}_0, \cdot)$ is a bounded trajectory, the Bolzano-Weierstrass Theorem and the definition of L imply that the sequence $\Psi(\mathbf{x}_0, t_1)$, $\Psi(\mathbf{x}_0, t_2),\dots$ must have a limit point in L, which is a contradiction.

Third, it will now be shown that the positive limit set, L, for the bounded trajectory $\Psi(\mathbf{x}_0, \cdot)$ is an invariant set. Assume $\mathbf{y} \in L$. Let $t^* \in T$. Let $t_1, t_2,\dots$, where $t_1 < t_2 < \dots$, have the property that $\Psi(\mathbf{x}_0, t_n) \to \mathbf{y}$ as $n \to \infty$. Because $\Psi(\cdot, t^*)$ is continuous on Ω,

$$\Psi(\Psi(\mathbf{x}_0, t_n), t^*) \to \Psi(\mathbf{y}, t^*)$$

as $n \to \infty$. Now by property 2 of the definition of a dynamical system (see section 1.4),

$$\Psi(\Psi(\mathbf{x}_0, t_n), t^*) = \Psi(\mathbf{x}_0, t^* + t_n) \to \Psi(\mathbf{y}, t^*) \in L$$

as $n \to \infty$. Therefore, for every $t^* \in T$, if $\mathbf{y} \in L$, then $\Psi(\mathbf{y}, t^*) \in L$, which implies that the positive limit set L is an invariant set.   ∎

Proof of the Invariant Set Theorem.   Because Ω is bounded and invariant, all trajectories initiated in Ω are bounded trajectories. Let $\mathbf{x}_0 \in \Omega$. Let the closure of Ω be denoted as $\overline{\Omega}$.

Because $\overline{\Omega}$ is closed and bounded and V is continuous on $\overline{\Omega}$, V has a finite lower bound on $\overline{\Omega}$. And because V is a Lyapunov function on $\overline{\Omega}$ and V has a finite lower bound on $\overline{\Omega}$: as $t \to \infty$, $V(\Psi(\mathbf{x}_0, t)) \to V^*$, where V^* is a finite real number.

By the Positive Limit Set Lemma, the bounded trajectory $\Psi(\mathbf{x}_0, t) \to L$ as $t \to \infty$, where the positive limit set L is nonempty and invariant. Because V is continuous on $\overline{\Omega}$: if $\mathbf{y} \in L$, then $V(\mathbf{y}) = V^*$. Because L is an invariant set, $V(\Psi(\mathbf{y}, t)) = V^*$ for all $t \in T$ and for all $\mathbf{y} \in L$. Because, in addition, $\dot{V}(\cdot)$ exists on $\overline{\Omega}$, $\dot{V}(\mathbf{y}) = 0$ for all $\mathbf{y} \in L$. This implies that $L \subseteq S$ and that $\dot{V}(\Psi(\mathbf{x}_0, t)) \to 0$ as $t \to \infty$.

Using a proof by contradiction, assume that $\Psi(\mathbf{x}_0, t) \nrightarrow S$ as $t \to \infty$. Thus there exists a $\mathbf{x}^* \in \overline{\Omega}$ where $\dot{V}(\mathbf{x}^*) \neq 0$ and a sequence $t_1, t_2, \ldots$ where $(t_1 < t_2 < \ldots)$ such that as $n \to \infty$: $\Psi(\mathbf{x}_0, t_n) \to \mathbf{x}^*$ because L is nonempty and $L \subseteq \overline{\Omega}$. Then because $\dot{V}$ is continuous on $\overline{\Omega}$, $\dot{V}(\Psi(\mathbf{x}_0, t_n)) \to \dot{V}(\mathbf{x}^*) \neq 0$ as $n \to \infty$. But this contradicts the previous conclusion, that $\dot{V}(\Psi(\mathbf{x}_0, t)) \to 0$ as $t \to \infty$. Therefore, the trajectory $\Psi(\mathbf{x}_0, t) \to S$ as $t \to \infty$.

Let $\mathcal{H}$ be the largest invariant set in S so that the nonempty and invariant set L in S is also contained in $\mathcal{H}$. Therefore, $\Psi(\mathbf{x}_0, t) \to \mathcal{H}$ as $t \to \infty$. ∎

3.6   Chapter Summary

The important concept of an invariant set was defined as a region of the state space such that any trajectory initiated in the region will remain there for all time. The Invariant Set Theorem was introduced as a powerful tool for investigating the stability properties of ANN systems. The basic idea of the theorem is to construct a continuous scalar-valued Lyapunov function whose value is nonincreasing on a given dynamical system's trajectory and to show that the dynamical system's trajectories are bounded in some way. Given these conditions, it is sometimes possible to investigate the asymptotic (long-term) behavior of the nonlinear dynamical system; in particular, one may be able to conclude that all trajectories converge to the largest invariant set where the change in the Lyapunov function's value is zero. The theorem and closely related analysis techniques were then used to investigate the asymptotic long-term behavior of the Hopfield (1982), Hopfield (1984), and continuous-time backpropagation ANN systems; the theorem was formally proved. The following procedure may be followed when applying the Invariant Set Theorem to the analysis of a nonlinear autonomous dynamical system.

• Step 1: Put dynamical system into canonical form. That is, into the form of a discrete-time dynamical system,

$$\mathbf{x}(t + 1) = \mathbf{f}(\mathbf{x}(t)),$$

or a continuous-time dynamical system,

$$dx/dt = f(x).$$

- Step 2: Check conditions of relevant EUC Theorem. If the dynamical system is a continuous-time dynamical system of the form $dx/dt = f(x)$, then check to see if $f: \mathcal{R}^d \rightarrow \mathcal{R}^d$ is continuous and if f satisfies a Lipschitz condition on $\mathcal{R}^d$. If the dynamical system is a discrete-time dynamical system of the form $x(t+1) = f(x(t))$, then check to see if $f: \Omega \rightarrow \Omega$ is continuous on $\Omega \subseteq \mathcal{R}^d$.

- Step 3: Check if $\overline{\Omega}$ is closed, bounded, and invariant set. It may be helpful to consider constructing $\overline{\Omega}$ such that

$$\overline{\Omega} = \{x \in \mathcal{R}^d : V(x) \leq s\},$$

provided that (1) V is a Lyapunov function (see step 4 below) on $\overline{\Omega}$, and (2) V has the property that $V(x) \rightarrow +\infty$ if $|x| \rightarrow \infty$.

- Step 4: Find a Lyapunov function V. Let $\overline{\Omega}$ be the closure of Ω. The candidate Lyapunov function $V: \overline{\Omega} \rightarrow \mathcal{R}$ must be continuous on $\overline{\Omega}$. In addition, the function V must have the following properties. If the dynamical system is a discrete-time dynamical system, then

$$\dot{V}(x) = V(f(x)) - V(x) \leq 0$$

for all $x \in \Omega$. If the dynamical system is a continuous-time dynamical system, then

$$\dot{V}(x) = [\nabla_x V]^T f(x) \leq 0$$

for all $x \in \Omega$. In addition, function $\dot{V}$ must be continuous on $\overline{\Omega}$.

- Step 5: Conclude $x(t) \rightarrow \mathcal{H}$ as $t \rightarrow \infty$. Let

$$S = \{x \in \overline{\Omega} : \dot{V}(x) = 0\}.$$

If the conditions of the Invariant Set Theorem are satisfied, conclude that all trajectories initiated in Ω converge to the largest invariant set, $\mathcal{H}$, where $\mathcal{H}$ is a subset of S. Try to explicitly identify the contents of $\mathcal{H}$.

3.7   Elementary Problems

3.1-1. Consider the following list of five functions.

1. $V(x) = 1/x$
2. $V(x) = x^2$
3. $V(x) = \log(x)$
4. $V(x) = \exp(x)$
5. $V(x) = x$

For each of the five functions, answer the following four questions. First, is the function continuous (i.e., continuous everywhere)? Second, at what specific points (if any) is the function not continuous? Third, is the first derivative of the function continuous (i.e., continuous everywhere)? And fourth, does V satisfy the Lipschitz condition on $\mathcal{R}$?

3.1-2. Let $x(t)$ be a scalar-valued function of a scalar time variable t and let a be a real number. Write the solution to

$$dx/dt = ax(t)$$

using Ψ function notation. Show that the solution $\Psi(\cdot, t)$ is a continuous function of $\mathbf{x}(0)$ for all $t \in (0, \infty)$.

3.1-3. Explain why the function $f: \mathcal{R} \to \mathcal{R}$ which is defined such that for all $x \in \mathcal{R}: f(x) = \sin(x)$ satisfies the Lipschitz condition on $\mathcal{R}$. Discuss the implications of this observation with respect to the solution of the differential equation: $dx/dt = \sin(x)$.

3.1-4. Show that the learning objective function $l: \mathcal{R}^q \to \mathcal{R}$ for a classical backpropagation ANN system does not have bounded second partial derivatives on $\mathcal{R}^q$.

HINT: Consider a simple backpropagation ANN system with just one weight from one input unit to one hidden unit and another weight from the only hidden unit to the only output unit. Let Ω^* be a closed and bounded subset of $\mathcal{R}^q$. Suppose the stability analysis is limited to deciding if an equilibrium point $\mathbf{x}^*$ in the interior of Ω^* is asymptotically stable. For such analyses, it is usually sufficient simply to show that the generator function is Lipschitz on Ω^*. Such a *local* Lipschitz condition is guaranteed, for example, if the generator function has continuous partial derivatives on Ω^*. Local Lipschitz conditions of this type are satisfied by almost all continuous-time backpropagation ANN learning dynamical systems of interest. (Both Vidyasagar 1978 and Grimshaw 1990 provide good introductions to EUC Theorems that require the generator function to only satisfy a local Lipschitz condition.

3.1-5. Let $\mathbf{A}$ be a d-dimensional real symmetric square matrix. Consider the discrete-time, linear, dynamical system

$$\mathbf{x}(t+1) = \mathbf{A}x(t).$$

Using Ψ function notation, write down the solution to this discrete-time linear dynamical system. Show that the solution is a continuous function of $\mathbf{x}(0)$.

3.1-6. Consider the following ANN system. Let $\mathbf{x}(t) = [x_1(t),\ldots, x_d(t)]$, where $x_i(t)$ is a scalar-valued function of a scalar time variable t for $i = 1\ldots d$. Let w_{ij} be the ijth element of d-dimensional matrix $\mathbf{W}$. Let $\mathcal{S}: \mathcal{R} \to [0, 1]$ be such that $\mathcal{S}(x) = 1$ if $x > 1$, $\mathcal{S}(x) = x$ if $0 \le x \le 1$, and $\mathcal{S}(x) = 0$ if $x < 0$. Show that the right-hand side of

$$dx_i/dt = \mathcal{S}\left[\sum_{j=1}^{d} w_{ij}x_j(t)\right]$$

satisfies the Lipschitz condition on $[0, 1]^d$.

3.1-7. Which of the following three sets are closed?

1. $G = \{\{x_1, x_2\} \in \mathcal{R}^2: x_i \in [0, 1], i = 1,\ldots 2\}$
2. $G = \{\mathbf{x} \in \mathcal{R}^d: |\mathbf{x}|^2 < 16\}$
3. $G = \{x \in \mathcal{R}: 1/x \le 16\}$

3.1-8. Which of the following three sets are bounded?

1. $G = \{\{x_1, x_2\} \in \mathcal{R}^2: x_i \in [0, 1], i = 1,\ldots 2\}$
2. $G = \{\mathbf{x} \in \mathcal{R}^d: |\mathbf{x}|^2 < 16\}$
3. $G = \{x \in \mathcal{R}: 1/x \le 16\}$

3.2-1. Find all 2^d equilibrium points of the system of d differential equations

$$dx_i/dt = x_i(1 - x_i)$$

where $x_i(t) = 1/(1 + \exp[-t])$ for $t \in [0, \infty]$ and for $i = 1\ldots d$.

3.2-2. Show that the point $(0, 0)$ and the set of points (x, y) that satisfy $x^2 + y^2 = 1$ are invariant sets associated with the system of differential equations

$$dx/dt = y + x(1 - x^2 - y^2)$$

$$dy/dt = -x + y(1 - x^2 - y^2).$$

HINT: If the initial condition of the dynamical system $dx/dt = y$ and $dy/dt = -x$ is the point $(x(0), y(0))$, which satisfies $x(0)^2 + y(0)^2 = 1$, then the resulting trajectory will be a function $(x(t), y(t))$, which satisfies $x(t)^2 + y(t)^2 = 1$ for all nonnegative t.

3.2-3. Find all equilibrium points of the linear discrete-time dynamical system in problem 3.1-5 and explicitly identify any constraints on **A** that are necessary for such equilibrium points to be (a) unstable, (b) stable but not asymptotically stable, and (c) asymptotically stable.

3.3-1. Consider the following continuous-time ANN learning dynamical system that continually updates the connection strength parameter vector $\mathbf{w} \in \mathcal{R}^q$ using only one training stimulus $(o, \mathbf{s})$ where $o \in \{0, 1\}$ and $\mathbf{s} \in \mathcal{R}^q$:

$$\frac{d\mathbf{w}}{dt} = -\gamma(o - r)\mathbf{s}, \tag{3.23}$$

where the response of the ANN classification dynamical system is r such that $r = \mathbf{w}^T\mathbf{s}$ and the learning rate parameter γ is a strictly positive real number.

Use the EUC Theorem for Continuous-Time Systems to show that this ANN learning dynamical system has a unique solution that is continuously dependent on the initial state $\mathbf{w}(0)$. Find a Lyapunov function for this differential equation by constructing a learning objective function $l: \mathcal{R}^q \to \mathcal{R}$ such that the gradient of l is negative one multiplied by the right-hand side of (3.23). Using the Invariant Set Theorem, prove that all trajectories approach the largest invariant set where $dV/dt = 0$. Describe the contents of that invariant set. HINT: Consider a squared error function for l.

3.3-2. Repeat problem 3.3-1 but replace equation (3.23) with the following ANN learning dynamical system:

$$\frac{d\mathbf{w}}{dt} = -\gamma_1(o - r)\mathbf{s} \tag{3.24}$$

and

$$\frac{db}{dt} = -\gamma_2(o - r),$$

where the response of the ANN classification dynamical system is r such that $r = \mathbf{w}^T\mathbf{s} + b$ and the learning rate parameters γ_1 and γ_2 are strictly positive real numbers.

3.3-3. Show that

$$V(x, y) = (1 - x^2 - y^2)^2$$

is a Lyapunov function for the system of differential equations in problem 3.2-2.

3.3-4. Find a Lyapunov function for the system of differential equations in problem 3.2-1.

3.3-5. Investigate the global asymptotic stability of the system in problem 3.2-2 using the Invariant Set Theorem. Assume the system has a unique solution that is continuously dependent upon every initial state. (Such a unique solution with the continuous dependence property does in fact exist, as shown in Vidyasagar 1978, 30–31.)

3.3-6. Investigate the global asymptotic stability of the system in problem 3.2-1 using the Invariant Set Theorem.

3.4-1. In the backpropagation learning example in section 3.4.3, the claim is made that "the discrete-time Invariant Set Theorem does not apply because $l(\mathbf{w}(t + 1))$ is not necessarily less than or equal to $l(\mathbf{w}(t))$ for each $t > 0$." Justify this claim by constructing an appropriate example where $l(\mathbf{w}(t+1)) > l((\mathbf{w}(t))$.

3.8   Problems

3-1. Let $\mathbf{s}_k$ be the kth d-dimensional stimulus vector ($k = 1 \ldots n$) learned by the autoassociative Widrow-Hoff learning rule. Assume $n < d$. This learning rule can be expressed by the weight update rule

$$\mathbf{W}(t+1) = \mathbf{W}(t) + (\gamma/n) \sum_{k=1}^{n} [\mathbf{s}_k - \mathbf{W}(t)\mathbf{s}_k]\mathbf{s}_k^T,$$

where γ is a positive real number and $\mathbf{W}(0)$ is a d-dimensional matrix of zeros. Write the scalar form of this equation and discuss how the scalar version of the equation can be viewed as an ANN system. Let $a(i, t) = \mathbf{e}_i^T \mathbf{W}(t) \mathbf{e}_i$, where $\mathbf{e}_i$ is the ith eigenvector of the matrix

$$\mathbf{C} = (1/n) \sum_{j=1}^{n} \mathbf{s}_j \mathbf{s}_j^T.$$

Write a difference equation showing how $a(i, t)$ changes as a function of time t. Now consider the classification (activation updating) rule

$$\mathbf{g} = \mathbf{W}(t)\mathbf{s},$$

where $\mathbf{s}$ is a d-dimensional input vector and $\mathbf{g}$ is a d-dimensional output vector. Provide an ANN system interpretation of this classification rule by inspecting its scalar form. Then discuss in a few sentences how the classification performance of this classification rule evolves as a function of the learning process.

3-2. The Cohen-Grossberg class of continuous-time networks includes the continuous-time Hopfield (1984) network as an important special case. In this problem, a version of the Cohen-Grossberg Theorem is proved (see the original Cohen and Grossberg 1983 paper for a more general statement and proof of the theorem). For $i = 1 \ldots d$: Let $F_{min}^i, F_{max}^i \in \mathfrak{R}$ such that $F_{min}^i < F_{max}^i$. Let $x_i \in [F_{min}^i, F_{max}^i]$ be the activation of the ith unit in a d-neuron system that is defined by $x_i = \mathscr{S}_i(u_i)$, where $\mathscr{S}_i : \mathfrak{R} \rightarrow [F_{min}^i, F_{max}^i]$ has continuous first derivatives that are strictly positive. Thus $\mathscr{S}_i$ is an invertible and monotonically increasing function such that the inverse of $\mathscr{S}_i$, $\mathscr{S}_i^{-1} : [F_{min}^i, F_{max}^i] \rightarrow \mathfrak{R}$, is defined. Let $\mathbf{W}$ be a d-dimensional symmetric matrix whose ijth element indicates the degree of influence of the activation of the jth unit in the network upon the activation level of the ith unit. The equation for one version of a Cohen-Grossberg network is

$$du_i/dt = z_i(u_i)\left[b_i(u_i) - \sum_{k=1}^{d} w_{ik}\mathscr{S}_k(u_k) \right],$$

where $b_i : \mathfrak{R} \rightarrow \mathfrak{R}$ has bounded first partial derivatives on $\mathfrak{R}$; $z_i : \mathfrak{R} \rightarrow (0, \infty)$ has bounded first partial derivatives on $\mathfrak{R}$; and $x_i = \mathscr{S}_i(u_i)$ is the activation level for the ith unit in the system for $i = 1 \ldots d$. Note that $u_i = \mathscr{S}_i^{-1}[x_i]$ is the *net input* to the ith unit. Let $\mathbf{x} = [x_1, \ldots, x_d]$. Consider the Lyapunov function

$$V(\mathbf{x}) = -\sum_{i=1}^{d} \int_0^{u_i} b_i(v_i)\mathscr{S}_i{}'(v_i)dv_i + (1/2)\sum_{j=1}^{d}\sum_{k=1}^{d} w_{jk}x_jx_k,$$

where the notation $\mathscr{S}_i{}'(u_i)$ indicates the derivative of $\mathscr{S}_i$ evaluated at u_i. Show that the Hopfield (1984) network is a special case of the Cohen-Grossberg (1983) network. Show that V is a Lyapunov function for a Cohen-Grossberg network. (HINT: Use the fundamental theorem of calculus.) Apply the Invariant Set Theorem to investigate the long-term asymptotic behavior of this continuous-time dynamical system, introducing additional restrictions upon the class of continuous-time dynamical systems under consideration if necessary.

3-3. Consider a Kosko (1988) bidirectional associative memory (BAM) ANN consisting of one layer of p A-units with activation values $a_1(t), \ldots, a_p(t)$ and one layer of d B-units with activation values $b_1(t), \ldots, b_d(t)$ at time t. The activation value of a unit in either the A-layer or the B-layer can only take on the values of 1 or -1. Let $\mathscr{S}: \mathscr{R} \rightarrow \{-1, 1\}$ so that for all $\varphi \in \mathscr{R}$: $\mathscr{S}(\varphi) = 1$ if $\varphi > 0$ and $\mathscr{S}(\varphi) = -1$ if $\varphi < 0$. The classification dynamical system for the BAM network is given by

$$a_i(t+1) = \mathscr{S}[\varphi_i(t)] \text{ where } \varphi_i(t) = \sum_{j=1}^{d} u_{ij} b_j(t) \tag{3.25}$$

if $\varphi_i(t) \neq 0$ and $a_i(t+1) = a_i(t)$ if $\varphi_i(t) = 0$, and

$$b_i(t+1) = \mathscr{S}[\psi_i(t)] \text{ where } \psi_i(t) = \sum_{i=1}^{p} w_{ji} b_i(t) \tag{3.26}$$

if $\psi_i(t) \neq 0$ and $b_i(t+1) = b_i(t)$ if $\psi_i(t) = 0$.
    The classification dynamics of this model can now be specified.

• Step 1: Update the activations of a group of randomly chosen units in the A-layer according to (3.25).

• Step 2: Update the activations of a group of randomly chosen units in the B-layer according to (3.26).

• Go to step 1 until activation pattern stabilizes.

Figure 3.6 illustrates the network architecture of a BAM ANN.
    Suppose that you are given a "learning algorithm" which someone says will store a pattern of information

$$\mathbf{x}^* = \left(a_1^*, \ldots, a_p^*, b_1^*, \ldots b_d^* \right)$$

such that $\mathbf{x}^*$ will be an asymptotically stable equilibrium point of the BAM ANN algorithm. Explain how learning a pattern of information, $\mathbf{x}^*$, can be viewed as forcing $\mathbf{x}^*$ to be an equilibrium point. Let the ijth element of $\mathbf{W}$ be w_{ij} and the ijth element of $\mathbf{U}$ be u_{ij}. What conditions on $\mathbf{W}$ and $\mathbf{U}$ will guarantee that $\mathbf{x}^*$ is an equilibrium point? Now prove that all trajectories of the BAM ANN system converge to the largest set of system equilibrium points using the following "candidate" Lyapunov function:

$$V(a_1, \ldots, a_p, b_1, \ldots, b_d) = -\sum_{i=1}^{p} \sum_{j=1}^{d} a_i b_j (w_{ji} + u_{ij}).$$

Note that the Invariant Set Theorem does *not* apply to the stability analysis of the BAM ANN system.

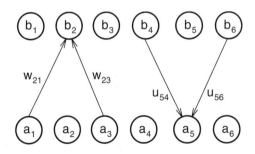

Figure 3.6
BAM ANN system. For presentation reasons, only a subset of the connections is shown and labeled.

3-4. Prove the perceptron convergence theorem, using Ridgway's learning objective function (see Duda and Hart 1973 on Ridgway's 1962 proof; discussion in chapter 2) as a candidate Lyapunov function and then applying the Invariant Set Theorem. Assume that the number and magnitude of training vectors are finite.

HINT: Because an assumption of the perceptron convergence theorem is that a solution $\mathbf{w}^*$ exists, the candidate Lyapunov function may include $\mathbf{w}^*$ in its description. Consider using a Lyapunov function $V: \mathcal{R}^d \to \mathcal{R}$ defined such that for all $\mathbf{w} \in \mathcal{R}^d$: $V(\mathbf{w}) = |\mathbf{w} - C\mathbf{w}^*|^2$, where $\mathbf{w}^*$ is the set of weights that correctly classifies all training vectors and C is a finite positive real number. Show that because the set of training vectors is finite, a strictly positive number ε exists that satisfies $\mathbf{x}_k^T \mathbf{w}^* C > \varepsilon$ for all M training stimuli $\mathbf{x}_1, \ldots, \mathbf{x}_M$. Also show that a positive number β exists such that for $k = 1 \ldots M$: $|\mathbf{x}_k| < \beta$.

3-5. Let $\mathcal{S}: \mathcal{R} \to [-1, 1]$ be defined such that $\mathcal{S}(x) = x$ for all $|x| \le 1$, $\mathcal{S}(x) = 1$ for all $x > 1$, and $\mathcal{S}(x) = -1$ for all $x < -1$. Let $\mathbf{A}$ be a d-dimensional real square matrix whose ijth element is a_{ij}. It is assumed that $\mathbf{A}$ is symmetric and positive semidefinite. The brain-state-in-a-box (BSB) neural network model is defined by the classification dynamical system

$$x_{k+1}(i) = \mathcal{S}\left[x_k(i) + \gamma \sum_{j=1}^{d} a_{ij} x_k(j) \right],$$

where $x_k(i)$ is the activation of the ith unit in the d-unit system at iteration k of the algorithm, γ is a positive stepsize that is not a function of k, and a_{ij} is a real-valued number indicating the connection strength between unit j and unit i. Prove, for any positive γ, that every trajectory of the BSB dynamical system as defined in this problem converges to the set of system equilibrium points as time increases. (Golden 1986a, 1993 prove the more general result, which does not require that $\mathbf{A}$ be positive semidefinite, provided $\gamma < 2/|\lambda_{\min}|$, where $\lambda_{\min}$ is the smallest eigenvalue of the matrix $\mathbf{A}$.)

HINT: Show that for $i = 1 \ldots d$ and every positive integer k:

$$x_{k+1}(i) = x_k(i) + \gamma a(i,k) \sum_{j=1}^{d} a_{ij} x_k(j),$$

where $a(i,k) \ge 0$. Also use $V(\mathbf{x}) = -(1/2)\sum_{i=1}^{d}\sum_{j=1}^{d} a_{ij} x(i) x(j)$ as a Lyapunov function for the proposed BSB dynamical system, where $\mathbf{x}_k = [x_k(1), \ldots, x_k(d)]$ is the system state vector at iteration k of the algorithm.

3-6. Consider a neural network with the following activation updating dynamics. Let $[a_1(t), \ldots, a_d(t)]$ be the d-dimensional activation pattern at iteration t over the network's units.

$$a_i(t+1) = \mathcal{S}[\varphi_i(t)],$$

if $\varphi_i(t) \neq 0$, and $a_i(t+1) = a_i(t)$ if $\varphi_i(t) = 0$ where

$$\varphi_i(t) = \sum_{j=1}^{d} w_{ij} a_j(t) - \mu \sum_{k=1}^{d}\sum_{l=1}^{d} a_k(t) a_l(t),$$

where $\mathcal{S}(x)$ is equal to 1 if $x > 0$ and $\mathcal{S}(x)$ is equal to -1 if $x < 0$, $w_{ij} = w_{ji}$ for $i, j = 1 \ldots d$, and where μ is a small positive real number. Thus $a_i(t)$ is either equal to $+1$ or -1. Prove that all trajectories of this nonlinear dynamical system converge to the largest set of system equilibrium points. Specify explicit conditions for a given pattern of activation to be an equilibrium point. (For additional discussions of higher-order ANN systems, see Giles and Maxwell 1987.) HINT: Compare this problem to the analysis of the Hopfield (1982) network in section 3.4.1.

3-7. Consider the BSB dynamical system defined in problem 3-5. Consider a matrix $\mathbf{A}$ and a hypercube vertex $\mathbf{c}$ (that is, a vector $\mathbf{c}$ whose elements are either 1 or -1) such that the vector $\mathbf{h} = \mathbf{Ac}$ remains in the hypercube quadrant associated with $\mathbf{c}$. That is, the ith element of $\mathbf{h}$, $h(i)$, has the same sign as the ith element of $\mathbf{c}$. Prove that $\mathbf{c}$ is an asymptotically stable equilibrium point of the BSB dynamical system. Indicate why this result is relevant for "teaching" the BSB dynamical system to correctly classify stimuli.

3-8. Explain why the Cohen-Grossberg Theorem is *not* applicable to analyzing the discrete-time BSB model. Then explain the motivation behind the following continuous-time approximation of the discrete-time BSB model dynamical system:

$$dx_i/dt = -x_i + \mathcal{S}\left[\sum_{j=1}^{d} w_{ij}x_j\right],$$

where $\mathcal{S}: \mathcal{R} \rightarrow [-1, 1]$ is defined such that $\mathcal{S}(x) = x$ for $|x| \leq 1$, $\mathcal{S}(x) = 1$ for $x > 1$, and $\mathcal{S}(x) = -1$ for $x < -1$.

Now show how a variant of the Cohen-Grossberg Theorem (see problem 3-2) can be used to analyze your continuous-time approximation to the discrete-time BSB model following Grossberg (1988) by showing how the variable transformation

$$y_i = \sum_{j=1}^{d} w_{ij}x_j$$

yields the equivalent continuous-time BSB model dynamical system

$$dy_i/dt = -y_i + \sum_{j=1}^{d} w_{ij}\mathcal{S}(y_j).$$

3-9. Consider a linear discrete-time ANN system of the form

$$\mathbf{x}(t+1) = \mathbf{W}\mathbf{x}(t),$$

where $\mathbf{W}$ is a d-dimensional real symmetric square matrix of constant parameters (connection strength weights). Assume the rank of $\mathbf{W}$ is equal to d. Use the EUC Theorem to establish existence, uniqueness, and continuous dependence of solutions. Show that $V(\mathbf{x}) = |\mathbf{x}|^2$ for all $\mathbf{x} \in \mathcal{R}^d$ defines a Lyapunov function for this linear system. Prove that this linear system has a unique equilibrium point at $\mathbf{x} = \mathbf{0}_d$. Show that if all eigenvalues of $\mathbf{W}$ have magnitudes that are strictly less than one, then this equilibrium point is an asymptotically stable equilibrium point. Show that all trajectories initiated with finite initial conditions will converge to this equilibrium point if all eigenvalues of $\mathbf{W}$ have magnitudes that are strictly less than one.

3-10. Kosko (1988) proposed an extension of the Cohen-Grossberg Theorem (see problem 3-2) that allows for Hebbian learning to occur concurrently with the activation updating dynamics. Consider the following special case of the Cohen-Grossberg-Kosko Theorem. Let the sigmoidal function $\mathcal{S}_i: \mathcal{R} \rightarrow [F_{min}^i, F_{max}^i]$ be a monotonically increasing function with a continuous first derivative. Let x_i be the activation of the ith unit in a d-neuron system. Let $\mathbf{W}$ be a d-dimensional real symmetric connection strength matrix. Let w_{ij} be the ijth element of $\mathbf{W}$. The system of equations for a Cohen-Grossberg-Kosko network are

$$du_i/dt = z_i(u_i)\left[-b_i(u_i) + \sum_{k=1}^{d} w_{ik}x_k\right]$$

and

$$dw_{ij}/dt = -w_{ij} + x_ix_j$$

where $x_i = \mathcal{S}(u_i)$ is the activation level of the ith neuron in the d-neuron system, $b_i: \mathcal{R} \rightarrow \mathcal{R}$ is a function with bounded first partial derivatives that are continuous on $\mathcal{R}$, and $z_i: \mathcal{R} \rightarrow (0, \infty)$ is a function with bounded first partial derivatives that are continuous on $\mathcal{R}$ for $i = 1\ldots d$ and $j = 1\ldots d$. Let $\mathbf{u} = [u_1,\ldots, u_d]$. Consider also the following candidate Lyapunov function:

$$V(\mathbf{u}, \mathbf{W}) = \sum_{i=1}^{d}\int_0^{u_i} b_i(v_i)\mathcal{S}_i'(v_i)dv_i - (1/2)\sum_{j=1}^{d}\sum_{k=1}^{d} w_{jk}x_jx_k + (1/4)\sum_{i=1}^{d}\sum_{j=1}^{d} w_{ij}^2,$$

where $x_i = \mathcal{S}(u_i)$. The notation $\mathcal{S}_i'(u_i)$ indicates the derivative of $\mathcal{S}_i$ evaluated at u_i. First, show that the EUC Theorem for Continuous-Time Systems is not applicable because the Cohen-Grossberg-Kosko dynamical system generator does not satisfy a Lipschitz condition on $\mathcal{R}^d \times \mathcal{R}^{d \times d}$. Prove that if it could be shown that a solution to the Cohen-Grossberg-Kosko dynamical system does exist and is continuously dependent on the initial state, then all trajectories converge to a set containing the largest set of system equilibrium points. Describe in detail the set of system equilibrium points. Additional restrictions on the class of continuous-time dynamical systems under consideration may be introduced if desired.

HINT: The solution here is very similar to the Hopfield (1984) example in the text. Note that in this problem

$$\dot{V} = \sum_{i=1}^{d} \frac{\partial V}{\partial x_i}(dx_i/dt) + \sum_{i=1}^{d}\sum_{j=1}^{d} \frac{\partial V}{\partial w_{ij}}(dw_{ij}/dt).$$

3-11. Prove the following *Lyapunov Stability Theorem*.

Theorem: Lyapunov Stability Theorem. Let $T = \{0, 1, 2,...\}$ or $T = [0, \infty)$. Let $\Omega \subseteq \mathcal{R}^d$. Let $\overline{\Omega}$ be the closure of Ω. Let $\mathbf{x}^* \in \Omega$. Let $\mathbf{\Psi}: \Omega \times T \rightarrow \Omega$ be a dynamical system generated by a particular generator function $\mathbf{f}: \Omega \rightarrow \Omega$. Assume that $\mathbf{\Psi}(\cdot, t)$ is continuous on Ω for all $t \in T$. Let $V: \overline{\Omega} \rightarrow \mathcal{R}$ be a Lyapunov function on $\overline{\Omega}$. Assume there exists a finite number $\delta > 0$ such that

$$\Omega_\delta = \{\mathbf{x} \in \overline{\Omega}: |\mathbf{x} - \mathbf{x}^*| \leq \delta\}$$

is an invariant set. Assume the largest invariant set where $\dot{V} = 0$ in Ω_δ is the set $\{\mathbf{x}^*\}$. Then $\mathbf{x}^*$ is an asymptotically stable equilibrium point with respect to $\mathbf{\Psi}$.

Give an example of a situation where Ω_δ as defined in the above Lyapunov stability theorem is *not* an invariant set.

A stochastic dynamical system is a dynamical system whose behavior has an unpredictable component, such as an ANN system that updates its activation pattern according to a probabilistic rule, or an ANN system with a deterministic learning rule that updates its weights on-line in response to events generated by a stochastic environment. Even though the learning rule is deterministic in this second instance, the learning process must be modeled as a stochastic dynamical system because the model is constantly revising and updating its connection strengths based on a randomly presented sequence of training stimuli.

Stochastic dynamical systems may be viewed within the general dynamical system framework presented in section 1.4, with each sample path of a stochastic dynamical system seen as a trajectory generated by a particular deterministic dynamical system. Thus the description of a stochastic dynamical system is actually a set of weak constraints on an entire class of deterministic dynamical systems. The uncertainty in the stochastic dynamical system, a result of our uncertainty regarding which member of the large class of deterministic dynamical systems is generating the trajectory of interest.

This chapter will introduce the concept of stochastic convergence in order to describe a version of the Invariant Set Theorem called the "stochastic approximation theorem," suitable for the analysis of a large class of discrete-time stochastic dynamical systems. It will apply the stochastic approximation theorem to a variety of ANN system analysis and design problems, and conclude with a formal proof of the theorem.

4.1 Stochastic Convergence Concepts

We will begin this brief introduction by reviewing the concept of deterministic convergence. Let $\mathbf{x}(0)$, $\mathbf{x}(1)$, $\mathbf{x}(2)$,... (where $\mathbf{x}(t) \in \mathcal{R}^d$ for $t = 0, 1, 2,...$) be a sequence of d-dimensional real vectors that converge to some vector $\mathbf{x}^*$, where $\mathbf{x}^* \in \mathcal{R}^d$. This statement can be expressed using the notation $\mathbf{x}(t) \rightarrow \mathbf{x}^*$ as $t \rightarrow \infty$. Or equivalently, given a positive ε, a T_ε exists such that for every $t > T_\varepsilon$, the magnitude of the vector $\mathbf{x}(t) - \mathbf{x}^*$ is less than the strictly positive real number ε. Figure 4.1 illustrates the concept of deterministic convergence, which was frequently exploited in the previous discussion of the Invariant Set Theorem.

Analogous to a deterministic sequence, a *stochastic sequence* or *stochastic process* is an ordered sequence of random variables with a common sample space. A particular value of this ensemble of random variables is called a "sample path" or "sample trajectory." For example, consider the following stochastic process. A fair coin is flipped k times and the percentage

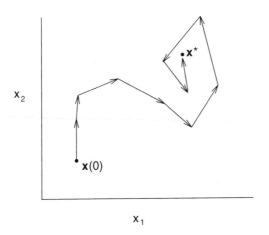

Figure 4.1
Deterministic convergence. Example of deterministic convergence in an activation state space to a
real vector **x***; a trajectory initiated at **x**(0) converges to the asymptotic state **x***.

of times the coin comes up heads, $x(k)$, is recorded. Thus the sequence of
events

heads, tails, heads, heads, tails, heads, heads, tails, tails, tails,...

corresponds to the sample path of scalars

$x(1), x(2), x(3), x(4), x(5),...,$

where $x(1) = 1$ (i.e., proportion of times the coin comes up heads after 1 coin
flip), $x(2) = \frac{1}{2}$ (i.e., proportion of times the coin comes up heads after 2 coin
flips), $x(3) = \frac{2}{3}$ (i.e., proportion of times the coin comes up heads after 3 coin
flips), and so on. Note that for this sample path as $k \to \infty$, $x(k) \to \frac{1}{2}$.

   At first glance, it might seem obvious that for all possible sample paths: as
$k \to \infty$, $x(k) \to \frac{1}{2}$, but such an observation would be wrong. The reason for this
mistake is that there exist some sample paths that do *not* converge to the real
number $\frac{1}{2}$. For example, suppose that a fair coin is flipped an infinite number of
times and each time the coin always comes up heads, which corresponds to the
highly improbable sequence of events

heads, heads, heads, heads, heads, heads,...,

and accordingly the proportion of coin flips which were heads for the first k
coin tosses, $x(k)$, would be equal to 1 for $k = 1, 2, 3,....$ Thus the limiting value
of the sequence $x(1), x(2), x(3),...$ would be 1 (in this improbable case) and
not $\frac{1}{2}$.

   In general, very few stochastic processes occur in practice where *all* sample
trajectories of such stochastic processes converge to the same value. Because
of these rare but nevertheless present situations, the standard deterministic no-

tation of convergence is essentially useless for the direct analysis of stochastic processes. In this section, several different definitions of convergence of stochastic processes will be introduced which have proved to be quite useful. The notions of stochastic convergence can be grouped into four major categories: (1) convergence with probability one, (2) convergence in mean square, (3) convergence in probability, and (4) convergence in distribution. Because these four concepts of stochastic convergence will frequently arise in future discussions, each of them will now be considered in detail.

Convergence with Probability One

The first major category of stochastic convergence is called "almost sure," "with probability one," or "almost everywhere" convergence. A stochastic process consisting of a sequence of real d-dimensional vectors is said to converge with probability one to a particular real d-dimensional vector $\mathbf{x}^*$ if the probability of selecting a sample path which deterministically converges to that real vector is equal to one. It is important that one not confuse the convergence of a stochastic process (which is a sequence of random vectors) with the convergence of a sample path of a stochastic process (which is a sequence of real vectors). Figure 4.2 illustrates the concept of convergence with probability one. In this situation, almost all sample paths of the stochastic dynamical system converge to the real vector $\mathbf{x}^*$. Some sample paths (not shown) will not converge to $\mathbf{x}^*$, but the probability of choosing any member of that set of sample paths is equal to zero. Note that figure 4.2 is misleading because it only shows a few trajectories after a few iterations of a stochastic dynamical system. Nevertheless, the trajectories shown in figure 4.2 are representative of the types of

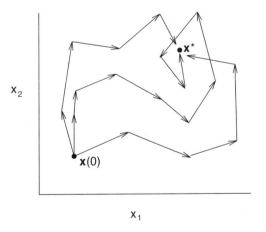

Figure 4.2
Convergence with probability one. Example of convergence with probability one in an activation state space to a real vector $\mathbf{x}^*$. Almost every trajectory (sample path) converges to the asymptotic state $\mathbf{x}^*$; some trajectories (not shown) will not converge to $\mathbf{x}^*$, but the probability of choosing any member of that set of trajectories is equal to zero.

trajectories which might arise from a stochastic process which converges with probability one to some real vector.

It is possible for $\tilde{\mathbf{x}}(t) \to \tilde{\mathbf{x}}^*$ with probability one as $t \to \infty$, where $\tilde{\mathbf{x}}^*$ is a random vector. For example, consider the following stochastic process suggested by Larson and Shubert (1979, 414). Let $\tilde{y}(0), \tilde{y}(1), \tilde{y}(2),\dots$ be a stochastic sequence such that the random variable $\tilde{y}(n)$ takes on the values of either zero or one. Let $\tilde{\mathbf{x}}$ be a random variable. Then the stochastic sequence $\tilde{\mathbf{x}}(0), \tilde{\mathbf{x}}(1), \tilde{\mathbf{x}}(2),\dots$ defined by

$$\tilde{\mathbf{x}}(n) = \tilde{\mathbf{x}}\big[1 - (1/n)\big]^{\tilde{y}(n)}$$

converges with probability one to the random variable $\tilde{\mathbf{x}}$ as $n \to \infty$. It is now appropriate to introduce the following definition.

Definition: Convergence with probability one.   A stochastic process, $\tilde{\mathbf{x}}(0)$, $\tilde{\mathbf{x}}(1), \tilde{\mathbf{x}}(2),\dots$, whose elements are d-dimensional random vectors defined with respect to some common sample space $S \subseteq \mathcal{R}^d$ *converges with probability one (w.p.1), almost surely (a.s.), or almost everywhere (a.e.)* to a random variable $\tilde{\mathbf{x}}^*$ (where $\tilde{\mathbf{x}}^*$ may be a constant real vector) if

$$p\Big(\lim_{t \to \infty} \tilde{\mathbf{x}}(t) = \tilde{\mathbf{x}}^*\Big) = 1.$$

A very important theorem that describes a key relationship between the probability of an event and the relative frequency of that event under certain conditions is known as the "strong law of large numbers." This theorem cannot be stated without using the concept of convergence with probability one. (For a review of this theorem, see Karr 1993 or D. Williams 1991.)

Theorem: Strong Law of Large Numbers (Kolmogorov).   Let $\tilde{x}(0), \tilde{x}(1),\dots$ be a sequence of independent and identically distributed random variables with the common probability mass (density) function $p_{\tilde{x}}: S \to [0, \infty)$, where $S \subseteq \mathcal{R}$. For $n = 0, 1, 2,\dots$, assume $E_{\tilde{x}}\big[\big|\tilde{x}(n)\big|\big] < \infty$, and define $\mu = E_{\tilde{x}}[\tilde{x}(n)]$. Then as $n \to \infty$:

$$(1/n)\sum_{k=1}^{n} \tilde{x}(k) \to \mu$$

with probability one.

Proof.   See Williams (1991, 119–120).   ∎

Convergence in Mean Square

Convergence with probability one places some relatively tough requirements on a stochastic process by placing specific constraints on the behavior of individual sample trajectories generated by that stochastic process. For this reason, alternative notions of stochastic convergence have been developed. One such alternative concept of stochastic convergence, which involves slightly different constraints, is *convergence in mean square.*

According to the standard notation of this textbook, $|\mathbf{x}|$ is defined such that $|\mathbf{x}| = \sqrt{\mathbf{x}^T\mathbf{x}}$, where $\mathbf{x}$ is a real vector.

Definition: Convergence in mean square.   A stochastic process, $\tilde{\mathbf{x}}(0)$, $\tilde{\mathbf{x}}(1)$, $\tilde{\mathbf{x}}(2),\ldots$, whose elements are random d-dimensional vectors with common sample space $S \subseteq \mathfrak{R}^d$ converges in mean square (m.s.) to a random variable $\tilde{\mathbf{x}}^*$ (or constant real vector $\mathbf{x}^*$) if (i) $E\big[|\tilde{\mathbf{x}}(n) - \tilde{\mathbf{x}}^*|^2\big]$ exists for $n = 0, 1, 2,\ldots$, and (ii) as $n \rightarrow \infty$:

$$E\big[|\tilde{\mathbf{x}}(n) - \tilde{\mathbf{x}}^*|^2\big] \rightarrow 0.$$

Let $|\tilde{\mathbf{d}}(t)| = |\tilde{\mathbf{x}}(t) - \tilde{\mathbf{x}}^*|$ be a measure of the distance between $\tilde{\mathbf{x}}(t)$ and $\mathbf{x}^*$. If the expected value of $|\tilde{\mathbf{d}}(t)|^2$ converges to zero, then the stochastic process $\tilde{\mathbf{x}}(0)$, $\tilde{\mathbf{x}}(1),\ldots$ converges in mean square to $\tilde{\mathbf{x}}^*$ (see figure 4.3).

A version of the law of large numbers based on mean square rather than with probability one convergence is easily proved using this new alternative notion of stochastic convergence.

Theorem: Law of Large Numbers (Mean Square Convergence).   Consider a stochastic process $\tilde{x}(0)$, $\tilde{x}(1)$, $\tilde{x}(2),\ldots$ of independent and identically distributed random variables with the common probability mass (density) function $p_{\tilde{x}} : S \rightarrow [0, \infty)$, where $S \subseteq \mathfrak{R}$. Assume there exists a finite real number C such that, for $t = 0, 1, 2,\ldots$,

$$E_{\tilde{x}}[\tilde{x}(t)] = \mu < C < \infty$$

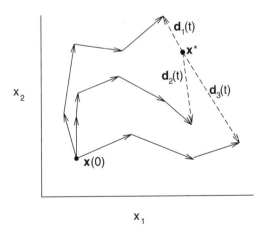

Figure 4.3
Mean square convergence. The distance $\tilde{\mathbf{d}}(t)$ is a random vector whose magnitude $|\tilde{\mathbf{d}}(t)| = |\tilde{\mathbf{x}}(t) - \mathbf{x}^*|$; the real vectors $\mathbf{d}_1(t)$, $\mathbf{d}_2(t)$, $\mathbf{d}_3(t)$ (indicated by the three dashed vectors) are representative values of the random vector $\tilde{\mathbf{d}}(t)$. Convergence in mean square implies that $E\big[|\tilde{\mathbf{d}}(t)|^2\big] \rightarrow 0$ as $t \rightarrow \infty$. Note that only a few representative sample paths are shown in this figure.

and

$$\sigma^2 = E_{\tilde{x}}\big[|\tilde{x}(t) - \mu|^2\big] < C < \infty.$$

Let

$$\tilde{y}(t) = (1/t)\sum_{i=1}^{t} \tilde{x}(i).$$

Then the stochastic process $\tilde{y}(0)$, $\tilde{y}(1)$, $\tilde{y}(2)$,... converges in mean square to μ as $t \to \infty$.

Proof.   To show that $\tilde{y}(0)$, $\tilde{y}(1)$, $\tilde{y}(2)$,... converges in mean square to μ, it is necessary to show that

$$E_{\tilde{y}}\big[|\tilde{y}(t) - \mu|^2\big] \to 0$$

as $t \to \infty$. Let $VAR[\tilde{y}]$ denote the variance of the random variable $\tilde{y}$. Then

$$VAR[\tilde{y}(t)] = (1/t)^2 \sum_{i=1}^{t} VAR[\tilde{x}(i)] = \sigma^2/t$$

since $E[\tilde{y}(t)] = E[\tilde{x}(t)] = \mu$ for $t = 0, 1, 2,....$ Therefore, because σ is a finite real number, $VAR[\tilde{y}(t)] \to 0$ as $t \to \infty$. ∎

Convergence in Probability

The third major category of stochastic convergence is called "convergence in probability."

Definition: Convergence in probability.   A stochastic process, $\tilde{\mathbf{x}}(0)$, $\tilde{\mathbf{x}}(1)$, $\tilde{\mathbf{x}}(2)$,..., whose elements are d-dimensional random vectors with common sample space $S \subseteq \mathfrak{R}^d$ *converges in probability* to a d-dimensional random vector (or constant real vector) $\tilde{\mathbf{x}}^*$ if, for every strictly positive real number ε, as $t \to \infty$:

$$p\big(|\tilde{\mathbf{x}}(t) - \tilde{\mathbf{x}}^*| < \varepsilon\big) \to 1.$$

Figure 4.4 illustrates the concept of convergence in probability.

The following two theorems are especially useful. The first theorem is known as the "Markov Inequality" (Karr, 1993; Manoukian, 1986) and will be used in a variety of applications throughout the book. The second theorem uses the Markov Inequality to show that mean square convergence implies convergence in probability.

Theorem: Markov Inequality.   If $\tilde{x}$ is a random variable such that

$$E\big[|\tilde{x}|^r\big] < \infty$$

for a positive real number r, then

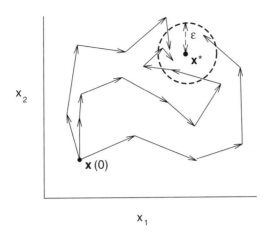

Figure 4.4
Convergence in probability. Example of convergence in probability in an activation state space to a constant real vector **x***. As time *t* increases, a greater percentage of the sample paths occupies the ball about **x*** whose radius is ε. Note that, unlike convergence with probability one, there is no strong requirement that a particular sample path which enters the ball must remain in that ball for all time.

$$p(|\tilde{x}| \geq \varepsilon) \leq \frac{E[|\tilde{x}|^r]}{\varepsilon^r}$$

for every positive real number ε.

Proof. Let $\varphi_\varepsilon : \mathfrak{R} \rightarrow \{0, 1\}$ be defined such that $\varphi_\varepsilon(a) = 1$ if $a \geq \varepsilon$ and $\varphi_\varepsilon(a) = 0$ if $a < \varepsilon$. Let $\tilde{y} = \varphi_\varepsilon(\tilde{x})$, where $\tilde{x}$ is a random variable such that $E[|\tilde{x}|^r] < \infty$. Also note that

$$|\tilde{x}|^r \geq |\tilde{x}|^r \tilde{y} \geq \varepsilon^r \tilde{y}.$$

Therefore, $E[|\tilde{x}|^r] \geq \varepsilon^r E[\tilde{y}]$. And since

$$E[\tilde{y}] = (1)p(|\tilde{x}| \geq \varepsilon) + (0)p(|\tilde{x}| < \varepsilon), \; p(|\tilde{x}| \geq \varepsilon) \leq \frac{E[|\tilde{x}|^r]}{\varepsilon^r}. \quad \blacksquare$$

Theorem: Mean Square Convergence Implies Convergence In Probability.
If a stochastic process $\tilde{\mathbf{x}}(0), \tilde{\mathbf{x}}(1), \tilde{\mathbf{x}}(2),\ldots$ converges in mean square to a random variable (or constant real vector) $\tilde{\mathbf{x}}^*$, then the stochastic process converges in probability to $\tilde{\mathbf{x}}^*$.

Proof. Direct application of the Markov Inequality gives the relationship

$$p(|\tilde{\mathbf{x}}(t) - \tilde{\mathbf{x}}^*| \geq \varepsilon) \leq E[|\tilde{\mathbf{x}}(t) - \tilde{\mathbf{x}}^*|^2]/\varepsilon^2.$$

Thus, if $E[|\tilde{\mathbf{x}}(t) - \tilde{\mathbf{x}}^*|^2] \rightarrow 0$ as $t \rightarrow \infty$, then as $t \rightarrow \infty$:

$$p(|\tilde{\mathbf{x}}(t) - \tilde{\mathbf{x}}^*| \geq \varepsilon) \rightarrow 0$$

for every positive ε. Therefore, convergence in mean square implies convergence in probability. ∎

It should also be noted that convergence with probability one also implies convergence in probability (Serfling 1980, 10), but the proof of this statement will be omitted.

Convergence in Distribution

The fourth major category of stochastic convergence is called "convergence in distribution."

Definition: Distribution function.   Let $\mathbf{a} = [a_1,\ldots, a_d] \in \mathcal{R}^d$. Let $\tilde{\mathbf{x}}$ be a d-dimensional random vector. The *distribution function* $F_{\tilde{\mathbf{x}}} \colon \mathcal{R}^d \to [0,\ 1]$ for $\tilde{\mathbf{x}}$ is defined such that $F_{\tilde{\mathbf{x}}}(\mathbf{a})$ is the probability that $\tilde{x}_i < a_i$ where $\tilde{x}_i$ is the ith element of $\tilde{\mathbf{x}}$ for $i = 1\ldots d$.

Definition: Convergence in distribution.   Consider a stochastic process $\tilde{\mathbf{x}}(0)$, $\tilde{\mathbf{x}}(1)$, $\tilde{\mathbf{x}}(2),\ldots$, where the tth d-dimensional random vector in the sequence, $\tilde{\mathbf{x}}(t)$, has the distribution function $F_{\tilde{\mathbf{x}}(t)} \colon \mathcal{R}^d \to [0,\ 1]$. If $F_{\tilde{\mathbf{x}}(t)}(\mathbf{a}) \to F_{\tilde{\mathbf{x}}*}(\mathbf{a})$ as $t \to \infty$ for all $\mathbf{a}$ such that $F_{\tilde{\mathbf{x}}*}$ is continuous at $\mathbf{a}$, then the stochastic sequence $\tilde{\mathbf{x}}(0)$, $\tilde{\mathbf{x}}(1)$, $\tilde{\mathbf{x}}(2),\ldots$ *converges in distribution* to $\tilde{\mathbf{x}}*$ as $t \to \infty$.

Figure 4.5 provides a graphical illustration of convergence in distribution for a distribution function defined with respect to a one-dimensional random vector. Convergence in distribution places even weaker restrictions on a stochastic process than (1) convergence in mean square, (2) convergence with probability one, or (3) convergence in probability.

It is convenient at this point to introduce and define the concept of a multivariate Gaussian density function.

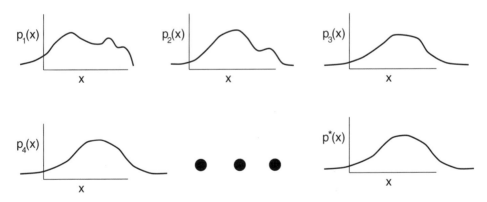

Figure 4.5
Convergence in distribution. A sequence of probability density functions, $p_1(\mathbf{x}), p_2(\mathbf{x}), p_3(\mathbf{x})$, $p_4(\mathbf{x}),\ldots$, converges to the probability density function $p*(\mathbf{x})$.

Definition: Multivariate Gaussian density function.   Let **m** be an arbitrary real d-dimensional vector, and let **C** be an arbitrary real d-dimensional square positive definite symmetric matrix. Let the real number $DET[\mathbf{C}]$ be the determinant of **C**. A *multivariate Gaussian density function* is a probability density function $p: \mathcal{R}^d \to (0, \infty)$ defined such that, for all $\mathbf{x} \in \mathcal{R}^d$,

$$p(\mathbf{x}) = \frac{\exp\left[-(1/2)(\mathbf{x} - \mathbf{m})^T \mathbf{C}^{-1}(\mathbf{x} - \mathbf{m})\right]}{(2\pi)^{d/2}[DET(\mathbf{C})]^{1/2}}.$$

A random vector $\tilde{\mathbf{x}}$ defined with respect to a multivariate Gaussian density function is a *Gaussian random vector*.

Assume that the Gaussian random vector, $\tilde{\mathbf{x}}$, has a multivariate Gaussian probability density function with parameters **m** and **C**. It can be shown that the mean $E[\tilde{\mathbf{x}}]$ of $\tilde{\mathbf{x}}$ is equal to **m** and the covariance matrix $E[(\tilde{\mathbf{x}} - \mathbf{m})(\tilde{\mathbf{x}} - \mathbf{m})^T]$ of $\tilde{\mathbf{x}}$ is equal to **C**. Thus **m** and **C** are typically referred to as the "mean vector" and "covariance matrix" of $\tilde{\mathbf{x}}$, respectively.

Also note that in the special case where **m** is a real number m and **C** is a positive real number σ^2, then the multivariate Gaussian density function reduces to the univariate Gaussian density function defined in math review problem 1-14.

A multivariate central limit theorem is now presented (following the presentation of Larson and Shubert 1979, 396–397). It should be noted that typically the term *central limit theorem* is reserved for a more general version of the following theorem. (Wilks 1962, 256–259, provides a useful introduction to the classical central limit theorem, while White 1994, appendix 3, reviews a number of useful central limit theorems that relax some of the restrictions of the classical multivariate central limit theorem.) The particular version of the central limit theorem presented here (which is essentially a multivariate version of the Lindeberg-Lévy central limit theorem) was chosen not because of its generality but because the verification of its assumptions are relatively straightforward.

The notation $\mathbf{C}^{-1/2}$ in the following theorem refers to a matrix $\mathbf{C}^{-1/2} \in \mathcal{R}^{d \times d}$ such that $[\mathbf{C}^{-1/2}][\mathbf{C}^{-1/2}] = \mathbf{C}^{-1} \in \mathcal{R}^{d \times d}$.

Theorem: Multivariate Central Limit Theorem.   Let the stochastic sequence $\tilde{\mathbf{x}}(0)$, $\tilde{\mathbf{x}}(1)$, $\tilde{\mathbf{x}}(2)$,... be a sequence of independent and identically distributed d-dimensional random vectors with the common probability mass (density) function $p_{\tilde{\mathbf{x}}}: S \to [0, \infty)$, where $S \subseteq \mathcal{R}^d$. Assume $\mathbf{m} = E_{\tilde{\mathbf{x}}}[\tilde{\mathbf{x}}(n)]$ is finite and assume $\mathbf{C} = E_{\tilde{\mathbf{x}}}[(\tilde{\mathbf{x}} - \mathbf{m})(\tilde{\mathbf{x}} - \mathbf{m})^T]$ is finite and nonsingular. For $n = 0, 1, 2,...$, let

$$\tilde{\mathbf{m}}_n = n^{-1}\sum_{j=1}^{n} \tilde{\mathbf{x}}(j).$$

Then as $n \to \infty$:

$$(\tilde{\mathbf{m}}_n - \mathbf{m})^T [\mathbf{C}/n]^{-1/2}$$

converges in distribution to a Gaussian random vector with mean vector $\mathbf{0}_d$ and covariance matrix equal to the identity matrix.

Proof.   See Larson and Shubert (1979, 396–397.)   ■

The Multivariate Central Limit Theorem states that given n independent and identically distributed random vectors with common finite mean $\mathbf{m}$ and common finite nonsingular covariance matrix $\mathbf{C}$, then the probability distribution of the average of the n random vectors is approximately Gaussian with mean $\mathbf{m}$ and covariance matrix $\mathbf{C}/n$ for n sufficiently large.

The following theorem discusses the relationships among the four types of stochastic convergence. (A more detailed discussion of the relationships among these four types of stochastic convergence and additional types of stochastic convergence may be found in Serfling 1980 and Larson and Shubert 1979.)

Theorem: Basic Stochastic Convergence Relationships.   Convergence with probability one implies convergence in probability, but the converse statement is not true. Convergence in mean square implies convergence in probability, but the converse statement is not true. Convergence in probability implies convergence in distribution, but the converse statement is not true.

Proof.   See Serfling (1980, 10–12) and Lukacs (1975, 33–37).   ■

Figure 4.6 summarizes the Basic Stochastic Convergence Relationships Theorem.

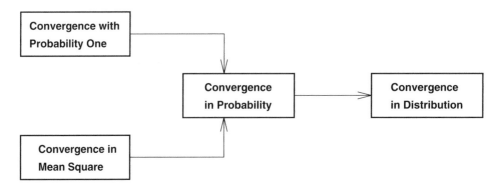

Figure 4.6
Relationships among basic types of stochastic convergence. Either convergence with probability one or convergence in mean square implies convergence in probability, which then implies convergence in distribution.

Operations on Stochastic Processes

The following theorems (see Serfling 1980 for further discussion and proofs; also see Karr 1993) are helpful when working with functions, sums, and products of random variables.

Theorem: Functions of Stochastic Processes. Let $\tilde{x}$ and the sequence of random variables $\tilde{x}(1), \tilde{x}(2),\ldots$ be defined with respect to common sample space $S \subseteq \mathcal{R}$. Let $g: S \rightarrow S$ be a continuous function on S.

1. If $\tilde{x}(t) \rightarrow \tilde{x}$ with probability one as $t \rightarrow \infty$, then $g(\tilde{x}(t)) \rightarrow g(\tilde{x})$ with probability one as $t \rightarrow \infty$.

2. If $\tilde{x}(t) \rightarrow \tilde{x}$ in probability as $t \rightarrow \infty$, then $g(\tilde{x}(t)) \rightarrow g(\tilde{x})$ in probability as $t \rightarrow \infty$.

3. If $\tilde{x}(t) \rightarrow \tilde{x}$ in distribution as $t \rightarrow \infty$, then $g(\tilde{x}(t)) \rightarrow g(\tilde{x})$ in distribution as $t \rightarrow \infty$.

Proof. See Serfling (1980, 24–25). ∎

Theorem: Addition and Multiplication of Stochastic Processes. Let the random variable $\tilde{x}$ and the sequence of random variables $\tilde{x}(1), \tilde{x}(2),\ldots$ be defined with respect to common sample space $S \subseteq \mathcal{R}$. Let the random variable $\tilde{y}$ and the sequence of random variables $\tilde{y}(1), \tilde{y}(2),\ldots$ be defined with respect to common sample space $S \subseteq \mathcal{R}$.

1. If $\tilde{x}(t) \rightarrow \tilde{x}$ in probability and $\tilde{y}(t) \rightarrow \tilde{y}$ in probability as $t \rightarrow \infty$, then $\tilde{x}(t) + \tilde{y}(t) \rightarrow \tilde{x} + \tilde{y}$ in probability and $\tilde{x}(t)\tilde{y}(t) \rightarrow \tilde{x}\tilde{y}$ in probability as $t \rightarrow \infty$.

2. If $\tilde{x}(t) \rightarrow \tilde{x}$ with probability one and $\tilde{y}(t) \rightarrow \tilde{y}$ with probability one as $t \rightarrow \infty$, then $\tilde{x}(t) + \tilde{y}(t) \rightarrow \tilde{x} + \tilde{y}$ with probability one and $\tilde{x}(t)\tilde{y}(t) \rightarrow \tilde{x}\tilde{y}$ with probability one as $t \rightarrow \infty$.

Proof. See Serfling (1980, 26). ∎

In general, however, if $\tilde{x}(t) \rightarrow \tilde{x}$ in distribution as $t \rightarrow \infty$ and $\tilde{y}(t) \rightarrow \tilde{y}$ in distribution as $t \rightarrow \infty$, then it is not necessarily true that either $\tilde{x}(t)\tilde{y}(t) \rightarrow \tilde{x}\tilde{y}$ in distribution as $t \rightarrow \infty$ or $\tilde{x}(t) + \tilde{y}(t) \rightarrow \tilde{x} + \tilde{y}$ in distribution as $t \rightarrow \infty$.

The following theorem, however, is a useful tool for dealing with sums and products of stochastic processes where one stochastic process converges in distribution to a random variable and the other stochastic process converges in probability (or in distribution) to a constant real number.

Theorem: Slutsky's Theorem. Let $\tilde{x}(1), \tilde{x}(2),\ldots$ be a stochastic process that converges in distribution to the random variable $\tilde{x}$. Let $\tilde{y}(1), \tilde{y}(2),\ldots$ be a stochastic process that converges in probability to the finite real number K. Then $\tilde{x}(t) + \tilde{y}(t) \rightarrow \tilde{x} + K$ in distribution as $t \rightarrow \infty$ and $\tilde{x}(t)\tilde{y}(t) \rightarrow \tilde{x}K$ in distribution as $t \rightarrow \infty$.

Proof.   See Serfling (1980, 19).   ■

The following theorem will be useful for investigating linear transformations of random vectors that have a multivariate Gaussian distribution.

Theorem: Gaussian Random Vector Linear Transformation.   Let **F** be an $m \times d$ real matrix which has rank m where $m \leq d$. Let **f** be a m-dimensional real vector. Assume $\tilde{\mathbf{z}}_n$ is a d-dimensional Gaussian random vector with d-dimensional real mean vector **m** and d-dimensional real covariance matrix **C**, then $\mathbf{F}\tilde{\mathbf{z}}_n + \mathbf{f}$ is a Gaussian random vector with mean vector $\mathbf{Fm} + \mathbf{f}$ and covariance matrix $\mathbf{FCF}^T$.

Proof.   Follows directly from Theorem 6.2.3 from Larson and Shubert (1979, 388–389).   ■

Another useful theorem, which will be exploited in chapter 8, involves the close relationship between sums of squares of Gaussian random variables and a special random variable known as a "chi-square random variable."

Definition: Chi-square Random Variable.   Let $v \in \{1, 2, 3,...\}$. A random variable, $\tilde{x}$, is a *chi-square random variable* with v degrees of freedom if $\tilde{x}$ has probability density function $p_{\tilde{x}}(\cdot; v)\colon \mathfrak{R} \to (0, \infty)$, where

$$p_{\tilde{x}}(x; v) = \frac{x^{(v-2)/2}\exp\left[-x/2\right]}{2^{v/2}\Gamma(v/2)}$$

and

$$\Gamma(x) = \int_0^\infty y^{x-1}\exp\left[-y\right] dy$$

for all $x > 0$, and $p_{\tilde{x}}(x) = 0$ for all $x \leq 0$.

The notation $\tilde{\chi}^2(v)$ will be used to indicate that $\tilde{\chi}^2(v)$ is a chi-square random variable with v degrees of freedom. A *critical value* at the a significance level of $\tilde{\chi}^2(v)$ is some positive number, $\chi_a^2(v)$, defined such that

$$1 - a = \int_0^{\chi_a^2(v)} p_{\tilde{x}}(x; v)\, dx,$$

where $p_{\tilde{x}}$ is the probability density function for the chi-square random variable $\tilde{\chi}^2(v)$.

Critical values at desired significance levels for the chi-square distribution can only be computed using numerical integration methods. Fortunately, computer programs which compute the chi-square distribution (or the gamma distribution, which includes the chi-square distribution as a special case) are readily available. For example, the GAMMAINC function in the MATLAB programming language may be used or the FORTRAN programming code (described by Press et al. 1986) may be used. Tables containing useful critical values at selected significance levels for the chi-square distribution are also readily available (e.g., DeGroot 1975; Mendenhall, Scheaffer, and Wackerly 1981; Walpole and Myers 1978).

Chi-square random variables have a number of important and interesting properties. The following property of a chi-square random variable will be especially useful in chapter 8.

Theorem: Chi-square/Normal Distribution.   The sum of the squares of r independent and identically distributed Gaussian random variables with common mean zero and common variance one is a chi-square random variable with r degrees of freedom.

Proof.   See Theorem 2 from DeGroot (1975, 323–324).   ■

4.2   Stochastic Approximation Theorem

This section presents an analogous version of the Invariant Set Theorem that can be applied to stochastic dynamical systems. This theorem, which will be referred to as the "stochastic approximation theorem," explicitly provides conditions for a class of stochastic discrete-time dynamical systems to converge with probability one to a subset of the state space. (The statement of the theorem is inspired by White 1989a,b, 1992; also see Fabian 1994. White 1989a,b proved his stochastic approximation theorem by showing that the conclusions of the theorem were obtained as a special case from the work of Ljung 1977.)

For expository reasons, an original proof of a weak version of White's stochastic approximation theorem is provided that is relatively easy to understand and that is based largely upon a straightforward extension of the work of Blum (1954). In presenting this version of the theorem, the concept of a stochastic Lyapunov function will be introduced and the relationship of such functions to supermartingale stochastic processes will be exploited. (This approach to investigating stochastic convergence was originally described by Bucy 1965 and Kushner 1965, 1966.)

Stochastic approximation methods originated with the work of Robbins and Monro (1951). These methods were then extended in a variety of different ways by later researchers. Wasan (1969) provides an excellent review of early work in the field of stochastic approximation. The stochastic approximation theorem provided in this chapter is by no means the most powerful or most general result available in the literature. (Students with advanced mathematics backgrounds may find Geman 1979, Kushner and Clark 1978, Kushner 1984, Ljung 1977, and Ljung, Pflug, and Walk 1992 to be helpful introductions to past and current research related to the analysis of stochastic difference and differential equations. A good review of the application of stochastic Lyapunov function methods to the analysis of stochastic *differential* equations may be found in Kushner 1967.)

Researchers in the field of ANN system analysis and design have also recognized the importance of stochastic approximation theory for analyzing and designing stochastic ANN classification and learning systems (e.g., Amari 1967, 1977; Finnoff 1994; Geman 1979; Haykin 1994, appendix B; Jaakkola, Jordan, and Singh 1994; Kohonen 1984; Kuan, Hornik, and White 1994; White 1989a,b).

The version of the stochastic approximation theorem developed here will be introduced in five stages. First, the class of stochastic discrete-time dynamical systems under consideration will be formally introduced. Second, the concept of an almost stochastic Lyapunov function will be defined. Third, a stochastic version of the Invariant Set Theorem will then be stated for this class of stochastic discrete-time dynamical systems. Fourth, applications of the theorem to ANN system analysis and design will be provided. And fifth, a version of the stochastic approximation theorem described by White (1989a,b, 1992; also see Fabian 1994 for a review) will be proved using a variant of the approach of Blum (1954).

Definition: Bounded stochastic sequence.   A stochastic sequence

$$\tilde{\mathbf{x}}(0), \tilde{\mathbf{x}}(1), \tilde{\mathbf{x}}(2),\ldots$$

is a *bounded stochastic sequence* if there exists a finite real number K such that $|\tilde{\mathbf{x}}(t)| < K$ with probability one (w.p.1) for $t = 0, 1, 2,\ldots$. A *bounded random vector (variable)* is a bounded stochastic sequence consisting of exactly one random vector (variable).

Note that if the sample space common to each element in the stochastic sequence is bounded, then the stochastic sequence will be bounded.

Definition: Bounded discrete-time stochastic dynamical system.   Let $\tilde{\mathbf{n}}(0)$, $\tilde{\mathbf{n}}(1)$, $\tilde{\mathbf{n}}(2),\ldots$ be a bounded stochastic sequence of independent and identically distributed q-dimensional random vectors with the common probability mass (density) function $p_{\tilde{\mathbf{n}}}: S \rightarrow [0, \infty)$, where $S \subseteq \mathscr{R}^q$. Assume the sequence of strictly positive real numbers $\eta_0, \eta_1, \eta_2,\ldots$ satisfies

$$\lim_{k \longrightarrow \infty} \left[\sum_{t=1}^{k} \eta_t \right] = \infty \tag{4.1}$$

and

$$\lim_{k \longrightarrow \infty} \left[\sum_{t=1}^{k} \eta_t^2 \right] < \infty. \tag{4.2}$$

Let $\mathbf{f}: \mathcal{R}^d \times \mathcal{R}^q \to \mathcal{R}^d$ be a continuous function in both arguments on $\mathcal{R}^d$ and $\mathcal{R}^q$. Assume the stochastic sequence of d-dimensional random vectors $\tilde{\mathbf{x}}(0)$, $\tilde{\mathbf{x}}(1),\dots$ is a bounded stochastic process such that for $t = 0, 1, 2,\dots$:

$$\tilde{\mathbf{x}}(t + 1) = \tilde{\mathbf{x}}(t) + \eta_t \mathbf{f}(\tilde{\mathbf{x}}(t), \tilde{\mathbf{n}}(t)). \qquad (4.3)$$

Then the stochastic sequence $\tilde{\mathbf{x}}(0)$, $\tilde{\mathbf{x}}(1)$, $\tilde{\mathbf{x}}(2),\dots$ is generated by a *bounded discrete-time stochastic dynamical system* with *generator function* $\mathbf{f}$ with respect to the stochastic sequence $\{\tilde{\mathbf{n}}(t)\}$ and $\{\eta_t\}$.

The notation

$$\lim_{k \to \infty} \left[\sum_{t=1}^{k} \eta_t \right] = \infty$$

is typically expressed using the more conventional notation

$$\sum_{t=1}^{\infty} \eta_t = \infty.$$

The "expanded" version is used in (4.1) and (4.2) for expository reasons. Both types of notation will be used interchangeably throughout this textbook.

Suppose the assumption that the stochastic sequence $\{\tilde{\mathbf{x}}(t)\}$ is bounded cannot be verified but the other assumptions of the definition of a bounded discrete-time stochastic dynamical system can be verified. In this case, one is permitted to assert that the stochastic sequence $\{\tilde{\mathbf{x}}(t)\}$ is either (1) generated by a bounded discrete-time stochastic dynamical system, or (2) $\{\tilde{\mathbf{x}}(t)\}$ is not a bounded stochastic sequence. This type of assertion is very useful for many important ANN system analysis and design problems where it is difficult to verify the assumption that the stochastic sequence $\{\tilde{\mathbf{x}}(t)\}$ is bounded. Examples illustrating this approach are provided in the applications section of this chapter.

The positive number η_t in (4.3) will be referred to as the "stepsize" at iteration t for the bounded discrete-time stochastic dynamical system defined by (4.3). Note that condition (4.1) prevents the sequence of stepsizes from decreasing too rapidly while condition (4.2) forces the sequence of stepsizes to decrease in value. For example, suppose that for $t > 0$: $\eta_t = 1/t$, then conditions (4.1) and (4.2) will be satisfied. On the other hand, if for $t > 0$: $\eta_t = 0.001$, then condition (4.1) will be satisfied but condition (4.2) will not be satisfied.

For deterministic discrete-time dynamical systems, the basic method for showing that a given trajectory defined by some sequence of d-dimensional real vectors

$$\mathbf{x}(0), \mathbf{x}(1),\dots$$

converges was based upon the idea that some Lyapunov function $V: \mathcal{R}^d \to \mathcal{R}$ could be found such that V had (1) a lower bound, and (2) $V(\mathbf{x}(t+1)) \leq V(\mathbf{x}(t))$ for $t = 0, 1, 2, \ldots$.

For stochastic discrete-time dynamical systems, the basic strategy for showing that the stochastic sequence of d-dimensional random vectors

$$\tilde{\mathbf{x}}(0), \tilde{\mathbf{x}}(1), \ldots$$

converges is to attempt to find some function $V: \mathcal{R}^d \to \mathcal{R}$ such that the stochastic sequence $V(\tilde{\mathbf{x}}(0)), V(\tilde{\mathbf{x}}(1)), \ldots$ has the properties (1) $E\big[\, |V(\tilde{\mathbf{x}}(t))| \,\big]$ is bounded for $t = 0, 1, 2, \ldots$, and (2) that w.p.1

$$E\big[V(\tilde{\mathbf{x}}(t+1)) \,|\, \tilde{\mathbf{x}}(t)\big] \leq V(\tilde{\mathbf{x}}(t))$$

for $t = 0, 1, 2, \ldots$. A stochastic process such as $V(\tilde{\mathbf{x}}(0)), V(\tilde{\mathbf{x}}(1)), V(\tilde{\mathbf{x}}(2)), \ldots$ that essentially has these two properties is referred to as a "supermartingale process."

The following formal definition of a supermartingale process is less general than the typical definition but will suffice for the purposes of the applications discussed in this book.

Definition: Supermartingale process.   Let $\tilde{V}(0), \tilde{V}(1), \tilde{V}(2), \ldots$ and $\tilde{\mathbf{x}}(0), \tilde{\mathbf{x}}(1), \tilde{\mathbf{x}}(2), \ldots$ be stochastic processes such that $\tilde{V}(t)$ is functionally dependent upon $\tilde{\mathbf{x}}(0), \ldots, \tilde{\mathbf{x}}(t)$ for $t = 0, 1, 2, \ldots$.

The stochastic process $\{\tilde{V}(t)\}$ is a *supermartingale* with respect to $\{\tilde{\mathbf{x}}(t)\}$ if, for $t = 0, 1, 2, \ldots$, (i) there exists a finite real number K such that:

$$E[\,|\tilde{V}(t)|\,] < K < \infty,$$

and, (ii) with probability one,

$$E\big[\tilde{V}(t+1) \,|\, \tilde{\mathbf{x}}(1), \ldots, \tilde{\mathbf{x}}(t)\big] \leq \tilde{V}(t).$$

The convergence properties of supermartingale processes are now reviewed. The key convergence theorem for supermartingales is the supermartingale convergence theorem.

Theorem: Supermartingale Convergence Theorem.   Let the stochastic process $\tilde{V}(0), \tilde{V}(1), \tilde{V}(2), \ldots$ be a supermartingale stochastic process with respect to $\tilde{\mathbf{x}}(0), \tilde{\mathbf{x}}(1), \tilde{\mathbf{x}}(2), \ldots$. Then as $t \to \infty$, $\tilde{V}(t)$ converges to some random variable $\tilde{V}$ with probability one.

Proof.   See Karlin and Taylor (1975, Theorem 5.1, 278).   ■

It will also be convenient to define a simple but important variation of the supermartingale sequence, an *almost supermartingale sequence*. This definition is considerably less general than the definition given by Walk (1992, 9) but will be adequate for the following discussion.

Definition: Almost supermartingale sequence.   Suppose that $\beta_1, \beta_2, \beta_3,\ldots$ is a sequence of positive real numbers and that there exists a finite real number C such that

$$\sum_{k=1}^{\infty} \beta_k < C < \infty.$$

The stochastic process $\tilde{U}(0), \tilde{U}(1), \tilde{U}(2),\ldots$ is an *almost supermartingale sequence* with respect to the stochastic process $\tilde{\mathbf{x}}(0), \tilde{\mathbf{x}}(1), \tilde{\mathbf{x}}(2),\ldots$ and $\{\beta_t\}$ if $\tilde{U}(t)$ is functionally dependent on $\tilde{\mathbf{x}}(0),\ldots, \tilde{\mathbf{x}}(t)$ for $t = 0, 1, 2,\ldots$, and provided there exists a finite real number C such that for $t = 0, 1, 2,\ldots$, (i) $E\big[\big|\tilde{U}(t)\big|\big] < C < \infty$, and (ii) with probability one,

$$E[\tilde{U}(t+1)\,|\,\tilde{\mathbf{x}}(t)] \le \tilde{U}(t) + \beta_t.$$

Theorem: Almost Supermartingale Convergence Theorem.   Let $\tilde{U}(0)$, $\tilde{U}(1), \tilde{U}(2),\ldots$ be an almost supermartingale stochastic process with respect to $\tilde{\mathbf{x}}(0), \tilde{\mathbf{x}}(1), \tilde{\mathbf{x}}(2),\ldots$ and $\{\beta_t\}$. Then, as $t \to \infty$, $\tilde{U}(t)$ converges to some random variable $\tilde{U}$ with probability one.

Proof.   For $t = 0, 1, 2,\ldots$, define the function $Z_t\colon \mathcal{R} \overset{.}{\to} \mathcal{R}$ such that

$$Z_t(u) = u - \sum_{k=1}^{t-1} \beta_k \tag{4.4}$$

for all $u \in \mathcal{R}$. Then

$$E[Z_{t+1}(\tilde{U}(t+1))\,|\,\tilde{\mathbf{x}}(t)] = E[\tilde{U}(t+1)\,|\,\tilde{\mathbf{x}}(t)] - \sum_{k=1}^{t} \beta_k.$$

Using the assumption that $\{\tilde{U}(t)\}$ is an almost supermartingale stochastic process,

$$E[\tilde{U}(t+1)\,|\,\tilde{\mathbf{x}}(t)] \le \tilde{U}(t) + \beta_t$$

with probability one. Thus we have with probability one

$$E[Z_{t+1}(\tilde{U}(t+1))\,|\,\tilde{\mathbf{x}}(t)] \le (\tilde{U}(t) + \beta_t) - \left(\beta_t + \sum_{k=1}^{t-1} \beta_k\right)$$

and, with probability one:

$$E[Z_{t+1}(\tilde{U}(t+1))\,|\,\tilde{\mathbf{x}}(t)] \le Z_t(\tilde{U}(t)).$$

Also, for all $t = 0, 1, 2,\ldots$, by the triangle inequality,

$$E\big[\,|\,Z_t(\tilde{U}(t))\,|\,\big] = E\left[\left|\,\tilde{U}(t) - \sum_{k=1}^{t-1} \beta_k\,\right|\right] \le E\big[\,|\,\tilde{U}(t)\,|\,\big] + \sum_{k=1}^{t-1} \beta_k$$

is finite because both terms on the right-hand side are finite by assumption.

Therefore, $\{Z_t(\tilde{U}(t))\}$ is a supermartingale process and converges with probability one to a random variable by the supermartingale convergence theorem. Now note that

$$\tilde{U}(t) = Z_t(\tilde{U}(t)) + \sum_{k=1}^{t-1} \beta_k. \tag{4.5}$$

Because the first term on the right-hand side of (4.5) converges with probability one to a random variable and the second term on the right-hand side of (4.5) converges to a finite real number by assumption, the left-hand side of (4.5) converges to a random variable with probability one. ∎

The concept of a stochastic version of the deterministic discrete-time version of a Lyapunov function is now introduced.

Definition: Almost stochastic Lyapunov function. Suppose that the stochastic sequence $\tilde{\mathbf{x}}(0), \tilde{\mathbf{x}}(1), \tilde{\mathbf{x}}(2),\dots$ is generated by a bounded discrete-time stochastic dynamical system as defined in (4.3). An *almost stochastic Lyapunov function* is a continuous function $V\colon \mathfrak{R}^d \to \mathfrak{R}$ with the property that for $t = 0, 1, 2,\dots$, a finite real number K exists such that with probability one

$$E\big[V(\tilde{\mathbf{x}}(t+1))\,|\,\tilde{\mathbf{x}}(t)\big] \le V(\tilde{\mathbf{x}}(t)) + K\eta_t^2,$$

where $\eta_1, \eta_2,\dots$ are defined as in (4.3).

Consider a bounded discrete-time stochastic dynamical system as in (4.3) with generator function $\mathbf{f}\colon \mathfrak{R}^d \times \mathfrak{R}^q \to \mathfrak{R}^d$ that generates the stochastic sequence $\tilde{\mathbf{x}}(0), \tilde{\mathbf{x}}(1), \tilde{\mathbf{x}}(2),\dots$ with respect to the stochastic sequence $\{\tilde{\mathbf{n}}(t)\}$.

It will be shown (see the Almost Stochastic Lyapunov Function Lemma in section 4.4) that, for $V\colon \mathfrak{R}^d \to \mathfrak{R}$ to be an almost stochastic Lyapunov function, it is necessary that (i) the Hessian of V is continuous on $\mathfrak{R}^d$, (ii) there exists an $\bar{\mathbf{f}}\colon \mathfrak{R}^d \to \mathfrak{R}^d$ such that for all $\mathbf{x} \in \mathfrak{R}^d$:

$$\bar{\mathbf{f}}(\mathbf{x}) = E_{\tilde{\mathbf{n}}}[\mathbf{f}(\mathbf{x}, \tilde{\mathbf{n}})],$$

and (iii) for all $\mathbf{x} \in \mathfrak{R}^d$:

$$\mathbf{g}(\mathbf{x})^T \bar{\mathbf{f}}(\mathbf{x}) \le 0, \tag{4.6}$$

where $\mathbf{g}\colon \mathfrak{R}^d \to \mathfrak{R}^d$ is the gradient of V. Note that the condition in (4.6) is similar to the condition required for a function to be a Lyapunov function for a continuous-time deterministic dynamical system. The key theorem of this chapter is now stated.

Theorem: Stochastic Approximation Theorem.   Suppose the stochastic process

$$\tilde{\mathbf{x}}(1),\ \tilde{\mathbf{x}}(2),\ldots \tag{4.7}$$

is generated by the bounded discrete-time stochastic dynamical system in (4.3) defined by the generator function $\mathbf{f}: \mathcal{R}^d \times \mathcal{R}^q \to \mathcal{R}^d$. Assume there exists an $\bar{\mathbf{f}}: \mathcal{R}^d \to \mathcal{R}^d$ such that for all $\mathbf{x} \in \mathcal{R}^d$:

$$\bar{\mathbf{f}}(\mathbf{x}) = E_{\tilde{\mathbf{n}}}[\mathbf{f}(\mathbf{x},\ \tilde{\mathbf{n}})] < \infty.$$

Let $V: \mathcal{R}^d \to \mathcal{R}$ be a continuous function on $\mathcal{R}^d$. Assume the gradient of V, $\mathbf{g}: \mathcal{R}^d \to \mathcal{R}^d$, and the Hessian of V, $\mathbf{H}: \mathcal{R}^d \to \mathcal{R}^{d \times d}$, exist and are continuous on $\mathcal{R}^d$. Assume that for all $\mathbf{x} \in \mathcal{R}^d$:

$$\mathbf{g}(\mathbf{x})^T \bar{\mathbf{f}}(\mathbf{x}) \leq 0. \tag{4.8}$$

Let $\mathcal{H} = \{\mathbf{x} \in \mathcal{R}^d : \mathbf{g}(\mathbf{x})^T \bar{\mathbf{f}}(\mathbf{x}) = 0\}$,
where $\mathbf{g}$ and $\bar{\mathbf{f}}$ are defined as in (4.8) with respect to (4.3). Then $\tilde{\mathbf{x}}(t) \to \mathcal{H}$ with probability one as $t \to \infty$.

Proof.   See section 4.4.   ∎

Several important points regarding this theorem should be noted. First, the Stochastic Approximation Theorem is applicable to a very large class of discrete-time stochastic dynamical systems. The state vector $\mathbf{x}$ can be identified as a pattern of connection strengths, and thus (4.3) becomes an on-line learning algorithm. Or alternatively, the state vector $\mathbf{x}$ can be identified as an activation pattern, and thus (4.3) becomes a classification dynamical system driven by noise. Specific examples illustrating such applications are described in section 4.3. Second, it should be emphasized that a stochastic process that converges with probability one to $\mathcal{H}$ may diverge to infinity with probability one (because $\mathcal{H}$ may contain points at infinity) or may converge to a random variable that takes on values within the set $\mathcal{H}$.

Third, suppose one has difficulty in verifying that $\{\tilde{\mathbf{x}}(t)\}$ is bounded.

Given that all of the assumptions of the Stochastic Approximation Theorem are verified for the stochastic sequence $\{\tilde{\mathbf{x}}(t)\}$ with the sole exception that it is unknown if the stochastic sequence $\{\tilde{\mathbf{x}}(t)\}$ is bounded, then either (i) $\tilde{\mathbf{x}}(t) \to \mathcal{H}$ with probability one as $t \to \infty$, or (ii) $\{\tilde{\mathbf{x}}(t)\}$ is not a bounded stochastic process. Fabian (1994) reviews methods for showing that $\{\tilde{\mathbf{x}}(t)\}$ is bounded.

Fourth, the similarities and differences between the Stochastic Approximation Theorem for bounded discrete-time stochastic dynamical systems and the Invariant Set Theorem for deterministic dynamical systems should be clearly understood by readers. If these similarities and differences have not yet been identified, then readers should compare these two key theorems at this point.

One final, inevitable question concerns the existence and construction of the almost stochastic Lyapunov function. Why should such a function exist? And if it does exist, how might one go about finding it? Although answers to these questions are not provided in this textbook, the following procedure can be applied to many popular ANN systems (see examples in next section of this chapter and the end of this chapter). First, construct the deterministic analogue to (4.3) by computing the expected value of $\mathbf{f}(\mathbf{x}(t), \tilde{\mathbf{n}}(t))$ with respect to $\tilde{\mathbf{n}}(t)$, given $\mathbf{x}(t)$, which is denoted by $\bar{\mathbf{f}}(\mathbf{x}(t))$. Thus the deterministic dynamical system

$$\mathbf{x}(t + 1) = \mathbf{x}(t) + \eta_t \bar{\mathbf{f}}(\mathbf{x}(t))$$

is obtained. Second, find some function V such that $\bar{\mathbf{f}} = -\nabla V$. Note this is an integration operation. Many stochastic ANN systems (see, for example, chapter 2 and the problems at the end of this chapter) can be analyzed using an approach of this type but of course this procedure is only a heuristic for constructing candidate almost Stochastic Lyapunov functions for the specific class of bounded discrete-time stochastic dynamical systems considered in this chapter.

4.3 ANN Applications

4.3.1 Backpropagation Learning

Problem.   The stochastic environment of an on-line backpropagation learning algorithm is defined as the stochastic process: $(\tilde{\mathbf{s}}(0), \tilde{\mathbf{o}}(0)), (\tilde{\mathbf{s}}(1), \tilde{\mathbf{o}}(1)),\ldots$ $(\tilde{\mathbf{s}}(t), \tilde{\mathbf{o}}(t)),\ldots$ where an observed value of the random vector $\tilde{\mathbf{s}}(t)$ is the activation pattern imposed over the input units at iteration t of the algorithm, and an observed value of the random vector $\tilde{\mathbf{o}}(t)$ is the desired response of the backpropagation ANN algorithm (i.e., the desired activation pattern over the output units) at iteration t of the learning algorithm. In this problem it will be assumed that the random vector $(\tilde{\mathbf{s}}(t), \tilde{\mathbf{o}}(t))$ has a probability distribution specified by the probability mass function

$$p_e: \{(\mathbf{s}^1, \mathbf{o}^1),\ldots, (\mathbf{s}^M, \mathbf{o}^M)\} \rightarrow [0, 1],$$

where M is a finite positive integer and $(\mathbf{s}^j, \mathbf{o}^j) \in \mathcal{R}^d$ for $j = 1\ldots M$.

The weights, $\mathbf{w}(t)$, of the backpropagation network map an input vector $\mathbf{s}(t)$ at time t into an output vector $\mathbf{r}(t)$ using the formula

$$\mathbf{r}(t) = \mathbf{\Phi}[\mathbf{s}(t), \mathbf{w}(t)],$$

where $\mathbf{\Phi}$ has continuous second partial derivatives. The function $\mathbf{\Phi}$ represents the architecture of the backpropagation neural network, which may have multiple layers of hidden units. Assume the backpropagation neural network seeks a minimum of l: $\mathcal{R}^q \rightarrow [0, \infty)$, where

$$l(\cdot) = E_{(\tilde{\mathbf{s}}, \tilde{\mathbf{o}})}\left[\left|\tilde{\mathbf{o}} - \boldsymbol{\Phi}(\tilde{\mathbf{s}}, \cdot)\right|^2\right].$$

Let $\mathbf{g}$: $\mathcal{R}^q \rightarrow \mathcal{R}^q$ be the gradient of l and let $\mathbf{g}(\mathbf{w}(t))$ be the gradient of l evaluated at $\mathbf{w}(t)$. Let $\mathbf{f}$: $\mathcal{R}^q \times \mathcal{R}^d \rightarrow \mathcal{R}^q$ be defined such that $\mathbf{f}(\cdot, [\mathbf{s}, \mathbf{o}])$ is the negative of the gradient of $\left|\mathbf{o} - \boldsymbol{\Phi}(\mathbf{s}, \cdot)\right|^2$ for a given training stimulus $[\mathbf{s}, \mathbf{o}]$.

The random weight vector $\tilde{\mathbf{w}}(t)$ is then updated using the learning rule

$$\tilde{\mathbf{w}}(t + 1) = \tilde{\mathbf{w}}(t) + \eta_t \mathbf{f}(\tilde{\mathbf{w}}(t), [\tilde{\mathbf{s}}(t), \tilde{\mathbf{o}}(t)]). \tag{4.9}$$

Assume the probability distribution of $\tilde{\mathbf{w}}(0)$ is a uniform distribution with respect to a bounded sample space. Note that (4.9) is of the form of (4.3). Assume the sequence of positive real numbers $\eta_0, \eta_1, \ldots$ satisfies (4.1) and (4.2).

Prove that (4.9) generates a stochastic process $\tilde{\mathbf{w}}(0)$, $\tilde{\mathbf{w}}(1), \ldots$ such that $\{\tilde{\mathbf{w}}(t)\}$ is not bounded or $\tilde{\mathbf{w}}(t) \rightarrow \mathcal{H}$ with probability one as $t \rightarrow \infty$, where

$$\mathcal{H} = \left\{\mathbf{w} \in \mathcal{R}^q: \left|\mathbf{g}(\mathbf{w})\right|^2 = 0\right\}.$$

Solution. The first step is to realize that (4.9) has the same form of (4.3) and thus could be a bounded discrete-time stochastic dynamical system. First, note that there exists a finite real number K such that $\left|(\tilde{\mathbf{s}}(t), \tilde{\mathbf{o}}(t))\right| < K$ for $t = 0, 1, 2, \ldots$ and that $(\tilde{\mathbf{s}}(t), \tilde{\mathbf{o}}(t))$ are independently and identically distributed for $t = 0, 1, 2, \ldots$. Second, note that (4.1) and (4.2) are satisfied by assumption. Third, note that $\mathbf{f}$ and the Hessian of l are continuous everywhere. Fourth, note that $\left|\tilde{\mathbf{w}}(0)\right| < K$ for some finite K, which is consistent with the assumption that the stochastic process $\{\tilde{\mathbf{w}}(t)\}$ is bounded.

To show that l is an almost stochastic Lyapunov function, it is necessary to show that $\bar{\mathbf{f}}$ exists and that

$$\mathbf{g}(\mathbf{w})^T \bar{\mathbf{f}}(\mathbf{w}) \leq 0$$

for all $\mathbf{w} \in \mathcal{R}^q$. This condition is satisfied because, for $t = 0, 1, 2, \ldots,$

$$\bar{\mathbf{f}}_t = E_{(\tilde{\mathbf{s}}(t), \tilde{\mathbf{o}}(t))}\left[\mathbf{f}(\mathbf{w}(t), [\tilde{\mathbf{s}}(t), \tilde{\mathbf{o}}(t)]) \mid \mathbf{w}(t)\right] = -\mathbf{g}(\mathbf{w}(t))$$

is finite. Thus

$$\mathbf{g}(\mathbf{w}(t))^T \bar{\mathbf{f}}_t = -\left|\mathbf{g}(\mathbf{w}(t))\right|^2 \leq 0.$$

Let $\mathcal{H}$ be defined such that

$$\mathcal{H} = \left\{\mathbf{w} \in \mathcal{R}^q: \left|\mathbf{g}(\mathbf{w})\right|^2 = 0\right\}.$$

Because the conditions of the Stochastic Approximation Theorem are satisfied given the assumption that the stochastic process $\{\tilde{\mathbf{w}}(t)\}$ is bounded, it is concluded that $\tilde{\mathbf{w}}(t) \rightarrow \mathcal{H}$ with probability one as $t \rightarrow \infty$ or the stochastic process $\{\tilde{\mathbf{w}}(t)\}$ is not bounded.

4.3.2   On-Line Hebbian Learning with Weight Decay

Problem.   Following Amari (1977), consider a simple Hebbian learning rule where in addition to incrementing the weight between two simultaneously active units, each weight in the neural network is decremented by a constant amount at each instant in time. Such a learning rule is sometimes referred to as "Hebbian learning with weight decay."

More formally, suppose that at time t, the activation of unit i is given by $x_i(t)$. Assume there are only M training vectors. The statistical environment generates a stochastic sequence of independent and identically distributed random vectors of the form $\tilde{\mathbf{x}}(1)$, $\tilde{\mathbf{x}}(2)$, $\tilde{\mathbf{x}}(3)$,..., where

$$\tilde{\mathbf{x}}(t) = \left[\tilde{x}_1(t),..., \tilde{x}_d(t)\right]$$

can take on the value $\left[x_1^k,..., x_d^k\right]$ with probability p_k, where $k \in \{1,..., M\}$. Now define the particular Hebbian learning rule with weight decay as

$$\tilde{w}_{ij}(t+1) = \tilde{w}_{ij}(t)\left(1 - \frac{\lambda}{100+t}\right) + \frac{\tilde{x}_i(t)\tilde{x}_j(t)}{100+t}, \tag{4.10}$$

where λ $(0 < \lambda < 100)$ is the *forgetting rate* of the neural network.

Assume the elements of $\mathbf{W}(0)$ are chosen according to a uniform probability distribution on the closed interval $[0, 1]$. Note that if $\lambda = 0$, the above learning rule reduces to simple Hebbian learning without weight decay.

Use the Stochastic Approximation Theorem to investigate the asymptotic behavior of this stochastic learning algorithm.

Solution.   Let the ijth element of the random matrix $\tilde{\mathbf{W}}(t)$ be defined as $\tilde{w}_{ij}(t)$. First note that (4.10) can be put into the form of (4.3) as follows:

$$\tilde{w}_{ij}(t+1) = \tilde{w}_{ij}(t) + \eta_t \tilde{f}_{ij}(\tilde{w}_{ij}(t), \tilde{x}_i(t)\tilde{x}_j(t))$$

where $\eta_t = 1/(100+t)$ and $f_{ij}: \mathcal{R} \times \mathcal{R} \rightarrow \mathcal{R}$ is defined such that

$$f_{ij}(\tilde{w}_{ij}(t), \tilde{x}_i(t)\tilde{x}_j(t)) = -[\lambda\tilde{w}_{ij}(t) - \tilde{x}_i(t)\tilde{x}_j(t)].$$

Second, construct a stochastic Lyapunov function. Note that $\bar{f}_{ij}: \mathcal{R} \rightarrow \mathcal{R}$ exists and can be expressed as

$$\bar{f}_{ij}(w_{ij}) = -[\lambda w_{ij} - c_{ij}], \tag{4.11}$$

where

$$c_{ij} = \sum_{k=1}^{M} p_k x_i^k x_j^k$$

because $x_i^k x_j^k$ occurs with probability p_k in the environment. Integrating (4.11) with respect to w_{ij} suggests the following stochastic Lyapunov function l given by:

$$l(\mathbf{W}) = \sum_{i=1}^{d} \sum_{j=1}^{d} l_{ij}(w_{ij}),$$

where

$$l_{ij}(w_{ij}) = (1/2)\lambda w_{ij}^2 - c_{ij} w_{ij}.$$

This implies that

$$\frac{\partial l}{\partial w_{ij}} = \lambda w_{ij} - c_{ij}.$$

Thus

$$U(\mathbf{W}) = \sum_{i=1}^{d} \sum_{j=1}^{d} [\partial l_{ij}/\partial w_{ij}]\bar{f}_{ij}(w_{ij}) \leq 0$$

for $t = 0, 1, 2,\ldots$.

Third, note the random vectors $\tilde{\mathbf{x}}(0)$, $\tilde{\mathbf{x}}(1)$, $\tilde{\mathbf{x}}(2)$,... are bounded and independently and identically distributed. Fourth, note that $|\tilde{\mathbf{W}}(0)| < K$ for some finite K which is consistent with the assumption that $\{\tilde{\mathbf{W}}(t)\}$ is bounded. Fifth, note that the Hessian of l with respect to $\mathbf{W}$ is $\lambda\mathbf{I}$, where $\mathbf{I}$ is a d^2-dimensional identity matrix, thus l has continuous second partial derivatives with respect to $\mathbf{W}$. Sixth, note that choosing $\eta_t = 1/(100 + t)$ satisfies both (4.1) and (4.2) and yields (4.10).

Now consider the case where λ is strictly positive:

$$l_{ij}(w_{ij}) = \frac{\lambda}{2}\left(w_{ij} - \frac{c_{ij}}{\lambda}\right)^2 - \frac{c_{ij}^2}{2\lambda}$$

which shows that $w_{ij} = (c_{ij}/\lambda)$ is a strict global minimum. Because the gradient vanishes at the unique critical point $c_{ij} = \lambda w_{ij}$, the contents of $\mathcal{H}$ consist of the single strict global minimum $w_{ij} = c_{ij}/\lambda$. Let $\mathbf{C}$ be a d-dimensional real square matrix such that the ijth element of $\mathbf{C}$ is c_{ij}. Thus $\tilde{\mathbf{W}}(t)$ converges with probability one to the matrix $\mathbf{C}/\lambda$ as $t \to \infty$ or $\{\tilde{\mathbf{W}}(t)\}$ is not bounded. Note that if $\lambda = 0$, then $\mathcal{H}$ contains a point at ∞.

4.3.3 Stochastic Hopfield (1984) Neural Network

Problem. Let $\tilde{\mathbf{u}}(0)$ be a bounded d-dimensional random vector. Let $\mathcal{S}: \mathcal{R} \to (0, 1)$ be defined such that

$$\mathcal{S}(x) = 1/(1 + \exp[-x])$$

for all $x \in \mathcal{R}$. Consider the following discrete-time version of the stochastic Hopfield (1984) neural network whose activation updating dynamics are specified by

$$\tilde{u}_i(t + 1) = \tilde{u}_i(t) + \eta_t \left[\left(\frac{1}{C_i} \right) \sum_{j=1}^{d} w_{ij} \tilde{x}_j(t) - \frac{\tilde{u}_i(t)}{R_i C_i} + \frac{I_i}{C_i} \right] + \eta_t \tilde{n}(t), \qquad (4.12)$$

where w_{ij}, I_i, C_i, and R_i are as specified in (3.12), and where the stochastic process $\{\tilde{n}(t)\}$ is a bounded stochastic sequence of independent and identically distributed random variables such that $E[\tilde{n}(t)] = 0$ for $t = 0, 1, 2,...$, and $\tilde{x}_i(t) = \mathcal{S}(\tilde{u}_i(t))$ for $i = 1...d$ and $t = 0, 1, 2,....$

The additive noise process $\tilde{n}(t)$ is useful from a practical computational perspective as a heuristic to "escape" local minima and saddlepoints. The additive noise $\tilde{n}(t)$ is also useful as a "modeling tool" for representing the uncertainty or intrinsic error in the model.

Which conditions on $\{\eta_t\}$ will guarantee that either (1) $\tilde{\mathbf{u}}(0)$, $\tilde{\mathbf{u}}(1)$, $\tilde{\mathbf{u}}(2),...$ will converge with probability one to a set containing the set of system equilibrium points of a Hopfield (1984) net as $t \rightarrow \infty$ or (2) the stochastic sequence $\{\tilde{\mathbf{u}}(t)\}$ is not bounded?

Solution. The solution to this problem will exploit results obtained in section 3.4.2. Let $\mathcal{S}: \mathcal{R} \rightarrow (0, 1)$ be defined such that for all $x \in \mathcal{R}: \mathcal{S}(x) = 1/(1 + \exp[-x])$. Let the generator function $\mathbf{f}: \mathcal{R}^d \times \mathcal{R}^d \rightarrow \mathcal{R}^d$ be defined as a vector of d functions, where the ith function ($i = 1...d$), $f_i: \mathcal{R}^d \times \mathcal{R}^d \rightarrow \mathcal{R}$ is such that for all $\mathbf{u} = [u_1,..., u_d] \in \mathcal{R}^d$ and $\mathbf{n} = [n_1,... n_d] \in \mathcal{R}^d$:

$$f_i(\mathbf{u}, \mathbf{n}) = \left(\frac{1}{C_i} \right) \sum_{j=1}^{d} w_{ij} \mathcal{S}(u_j) - \frac{u_i}{R_i C_i} + \frac{I_i}{C_i} + n_i.$$

Note that $\mathbf{f}$ is continuous in both arguments on $\mathcal{R}^d$.

The candidate Lyapunov function $V: \mathcal{R}^d \rightarrow \mathcal{R}$ (inspired by the analysis of section 3.4.2) is defined such that for all $\mathbf{u} \in \mathcal{R}^d$

$$V(\mathbf{u}) = -(1/2) \sum_{i=1}^{d} \sum_{j=1}^{d} w_{ij} x_i x_j$$
$$+ \sum_{i=1}^{d} (1/R_i)[x_i \log x_i + (1 - x_i) \log (1 - x_i)] - \sum_{i=1}^{d} I_i x_i, \qquad (4.13)$$

where $\{w_{ij}\}$ are the elements of a d-dimensional real square symmetric matrix, $\{I_i\}$ is a set of d real numbers, $\{R_i\}$ is a set of d strictly positive real numbers, and $x_i = \mathcal{S}(u_i)$ for $i = 1...d$. First, note that V has continuous first and second partial derivatives on $\mathcal{R}^d$ (show this!).

Let $\bar{\mathbf{f}}(\cdot) = E[\mathbf{f}(\cdot, \tilde{\mathbf{n}})]$. The ith element, $\bar{f}_i$, of $\bar{\mathbf{f}}$ is defined for all $\mathbf{u} \in \mathcal{R}^d$ such that

$$\bar{f}_i(\mathbf{u}) = \left[\frac{1}{C_i}\right] \sum_{j=1}^{d} w_{ij} \mathcal{S}(u_j) - \frac{u_i}{R_i C_i} + \frac{I_i}{C_i},$$

and thus $\bar{\mathbf{f}}$ exists on $\mathcal{R}^d$.

Second, note that

$$\frac{\partial V}{\partial u_i} = -C_i \bar{f}_i(\mathbf{u}) x_i (1 - x_i),$$

where $x_i = \mathcal{S}(u_i)$.

$$\sum_{i=1}^{d} (\partial V / \partial u_i) \bar{f}_i(\mathbf{u}) = -\sum_{i=1}^{d} C_i x_i (1 - x_i)(\bar{f}_i(\mathbf{u}))^2 \le 0.$$

Thus, given that the sequence of stepsizes $\{\eta_t\}$ is decreased such that (4.1) and (4.2) are satisfied, either (1) $\tilde{\mathbf{u}}(t) \to \mathcal{H}$ with probability one as $t \to \infty$, where

$$\mathcal{H} = \{\mathbf{u} \in R^d : x_i(1 - x_i)(\bar{f}_i(\mathbf{u}))^2 = 0, i = 1 \ldots d\},$$

or (2) $\{\tilde{\mathbf{u}}(t)\}$ is not bounded. Note that, because the stochastic analysis took place in the "u-space," $\mathcal{H}$ also contains several points located at ∞. These points correspond to points on the boundary of a hypercube in "x-space."

4.4   Stochastic Approximation Theorem Proof

In this section the Stochastic Approximation Theorem presented in section 4.2 is proved. As previously noted, the statement of the specific theorem presented here was largely inspired by White (1989a,b, 1992; also see Fabian 1994), while the proof of the theorem is based largely upon the arguments of Blum (1954).

Lemma: Expectation Existence.   If the stochastic sequence $\tilde{\mathbf{x}}(0)$, $\tilde{\mathbf{x}}(1)$, $\tilde{\mathbf{x}}(2)$,... is generated by a bounded discrete-time stochastic system as defined in (4.3), then there exists some finite real number K such that, for $t = 0, 1, 2,\ldots$, $|E[\tilde{\mathbf{x}}(t)]| < K$.

Proof.   By assumption, $p(\mathbf{x}(0))$ exists. Also $p(\mathbf{x}(t) \mid \mathbf{x}(t - 1))$ exists for $t = 0, 1, 2,\ldots$ by assumption. Thus, because

$$p(\mathbf{x}(0),\ldots, \mathbf{x}(t)) = p(\mathbf{x}(0)) \prod_{i=1}^{t} p(\mathbf{x}(i) \mid \mathbf{x}(i - 1))$$

is a valid probability mass (density) function for $t = 0, 1, 2,\ldots$, it follows that $p(\mathbf{x}(t))$ exists for $t = 0, 1, 2,\ldots$ (show that $p(\mathbf{x}(t))$ exists by summing (integrating) over possible values of $\mathbf{x}(0),\ldots, \mathbf{x}(t - 1)$). And because $\{\tilde{\mathbf{x}}(t)\}$ is a bounded stochastic sequence by assumption, there exists a finite real number K such that

$\left|\tilde{\mathbf{x}}(t)\right| < K < \infty$ w.p.1 for $t = 0, 1, 2,\ldots$. Therefore, for $t = 0, 1, 2,\ldots$, there exists a finite real number K such that $\left|E[\tilde{\mathbf{x}}(t)]\right| < K < \infty$. ∎

Lemma: Almost Stochastic Lyapunov Function Lemma. Let $V: \mathcal{R}^d \to \mathcal{R}$. Assume the Hessian of V is continuous on $\mathcal{R}^d$. Let $\mathbf{g}(\mathbf{x})$ be the gradient of V evaluated at $\mathbf{x}$. Let the stochastic sequence $\tilde{\mathbf{x}}(0)$, $\tilde{\mathbf{x}}(1)$, $\tilde{\mathbf{x}}(2),\ldots$ be generated by the bounded stochastic discrete-time dynamical system with generator function $\mathbf{f}: \mathcal{R}^d \times \mathcal{R}^q \to \mathcal{R}^d$ as in (4.3) with respect to the bounded stochastic sequence $\tilde{\mathbf{n}}(0)$, $\tilde{\mathbf{n}}(1)$, $\tilde{\mathbf{n}}(2),\ldots$ and the sequence of positive stepsizes η_1, $\eta_2,\ldots$. Assume there exists an $\bar{\mathbf{f}}: \mathcal{R}^d \to \mathcal{R}^d$ such that, for all $\mathbf{x} \in \mathcal{R}^d$,

$$\bar{\mathbf{f}}(\mathbf{x}) = E_{\tilde{\mathbf{n}}}[\mathbf{f}(\mathbf{x}, \tilde{\mathbf{n}})] < \infty.$$

Also assume, for all $\mathbf{x} \in \mathcal{R}^d$,

$$\mathbf{g}(\mathbf{x})^T \bar{\mathbf{f}}(\mathbf{x}) \leq 0.$$

Then V is an almost stochastic Lyapunov function with respect to (4.3), and there exists a finite real number K such that w.p.1

$$\left| E\big[V(\tilde{\mathbf{x}}(t + 1)) \mid \tilde{\mathbf{x}}(t)\big] - V(\tilde{\mathbf{x}}(t)) - \eta_t \mathbf{g}(\tilde{\mathbf{x}}(t))^T \bar{\mathbf{f}}(\tilde{\mathbf{x}}(t)) \right| \leq \eta_t^2 K \qquad (4.14)$$

for $t = 0, 1, 2,\ldots$.

Proof. Let the notation $\mathbf{g}(\mathbf{x})$ and $\mathbf{H}(\mathbf{x})$ refer to the gradient and Hessian of V, respectively, evaluated at the point $\mathbf{x}$.

Expanding V in a first-order Taylor expansion about $\mathbf{x}(t)$, we obtain

$$V(\mathbf{x}(t + 1)) = V(\mathbf{x}(t)) + \mathbf{g}(\mathbf{x}(t))^T[\mathbf{x}(t + 1) - \mathbf{x}(t)] + R_2(t), \qquad (4.15)$$

where the scalar remainder term, $R_2(t)$, is given by

$$R_2(t) = (1/2)[\mathbf{x}(t + 1) - \mathbf{x}(t)]^T \mathbf{H}(\mathbf{c}(t))[\mathbf{x}(t + 1) - \mathbf{x}(t)] \qquad (4.16)$$

and

$$\mathbf{c}(t) = \mathbf{x}(t) + \mu[\mathbf{x}(t + 1) - \mathbf{x}(t)],$$

where $0 < \mu < 1$.

Define $\mathbf{f}_t$ such that $\mathbf{f}_t = \mathbf{f}(\mathbf{x}(t), \mathbf{n}(t))$, where $\mathbf{n}(t) \in \mathcal{R}^q$. Using (4.3),

$$\mathbf{x}(t + 1) = \mathbf{x}(t) + \eta_t \mathbf{f}_t$$

and thus

$$\mathbf{x}(t + 1) - \mathbf{x}(t) = \eta_t \mathbf{f}_t. \qquad (4.17)$$

Substituting (4.17) into (4.15) and (4.16),

$$V(\mathbf{x}(t + 1)) = V(\mathbf{x}(t)) + \eta_t \mathbf{g}(\mathbf{x}(t))^T \mathbf{f}_t + R_2(t), \qquad (4.18)$$

with the remainder term, $R_2(t)$, given by

$$R_2(t) = (1/2)\eta_t^2 \mathbf{f}_t^T \mathbf{H}(\mathbf{c}(t))\mathbf{f}_t, \tag{4.19}$$

where $\mathbf{c}(t) = \mathbf{x}(t) + \mu\eta_t \mathbf{f}_t$. Note that $R_2(t)$ is a continuous function of $\mathbf{x}(t)$, $\mathbf{n}(t)$, and $\mathbf{c}(t)$ because $\mathbf{f}$ and $\mathbf{H}$ are continuous.

Now define the random variable $\tilde{R}_2(t)$ for $t = 0, 1, 2,...$ and $\mu \in \mathcal{R}$ $(0 < \mu < 1)$ such that

$$\tilde{R}_2(t) = (1/2)\eta_t^2 \mathbf{f}(\tilde{\mathbf{x}}(t), \tilde{\mathbf{n}}(t))^T \mathbf{H}(\tilde{\mathbf{c}}(t))\mathbf{f}(\tilde{\mathbf{x}}(t), \tilde{\mathbf{n}}(t)),$$

where

$$\tilde{\mathbf{c}}(t) = \tilde{\mathbf{x}}(t) + \mu\eta_t \mathbf{f}(\tilde{\mathbf{x}}(t), \tilde{\mathbf{n}}(t)).$$

Note that $\{\tilde{\mathbf{c}}(t)\}$ is a bounded stochastic sequence because $\mathbf{f}$ is continuous, both $\{\tilde{\mathbf{n}}(t)\}$ and $\{\tilde{\mathbf{x}}(t)\}$ are bounded stochastic sequences, $\{\eta_t\}$ is a bounded sequence, and $0 < \mu < 1$.

Because $\{\tilde{\mathbf{n}}(t)\}$, $\{\tilde{\mathbf{c}}(t)\}$, and $\{\tilde{\mathbf{x}}(t)\}$ are bounded stochastic sequences and $R_2(t)$ is continuous with respect to $\mathbf{n}(t)$, $\mathbf{x}(t)$, and $\tilde{\mathbf{c}}(t)$, $\{\tilde{R}_2(t)\}$ is a bounded stochastic sequence as well. Thus a finite real number K exists such that, for all $t = 0, 1, 2,...$, $|\tilde{R}_2(t)| \leq K$ with probability one.

Using these observations and (4.18), it follows that there exists some positive finite real number K such that, for $t = 0, 1, 2,...$, (4.14) is satisfied. The expectations in (4.14) exist because V and $\mathbf{f}$ are continuous, $E[\tilde{\mathbf{x}}(t)]$ exists by the Expectation Existence Lemma, and $E[\tilde{\mathbf{n}}(t)]$ exists because $\{\tilde{\mathbf{n}}(t)\}$ is a bounded stochastic sequence of independent and identically distributed random variables with common probability mass (density) function $p_{\tilde{\mathbf{n}}}$. Therefore, w.p.1

$$E[V(\tilde{\mathbf{x}}(t+1)) \mid \tilde{\mathbf{x}}(t)] \leq V(\tilde{\mathbf{x}}(t)) + \eta_t^2 K \tag{4.20}$$

because $\mathbf{g}(\tilde{\mathbf{x}}(t))^T \bar{\mathbf{f}}(\tilde{\mathbf{x}}(t)) \leq 0$ by assumption. ∎

For expository reasons, the remaining proof of the Stochastic Approximation Theorem has been partitioned into three lemmas and a main proof. SAL will be used as an abbreviation for Stochastic Approximation Lemma.

The Almost Stochastic Lyapunov Function Lemma exploited the condition in (4.2) that

$$\sum_{t=1}^{\infty} \eta_t^2 < \infty.$$

The first lemma (SAL 1) exploits the condition in (4.1) that

$$\sum_{t=1}^{\infty} \eta_t = \infty.$$

Lemma: Stochastic Approximation Lemma 1.   Let η_1, η_2,... be a sequence of positive real numbers that satisfies (4.1). Assume a_1, a_2, a_3,... is a sequence of positive real numbers, and there exists a finite real number B such that

$$\lim_{n \to \infty} \sum_{t=1}^{n} \eta_t a_t < B < \infty. \tag{4.21}$$

Then there exists a subsequence of a_1, a_2, a_3,... that converges to zero.

Proof.   Assume the greatest lower bound of the set $A = \{a_1, a_2,....\}$ is some $\varepsilon > 0$. Then, using (4.1),

$$\lim_{n \to \infty} \sum_{t=1}^{n} \eta_t a_t \geq \lim_{n \to \infty} \sum_{t=1}^{n} \varepsilon \eta_t = \infty. \tag{4.22}$$

But (4.22) implies that (4.21) is false. This contradiction implies that A has a greatest lower bound of zero.

Define q_1 as a_1 and find the smallest value of i for $i > 1$ such that $q_1 > a_i > 0$. Such an a_i can always be found because the greatest lower bound of A is zero. Now define q_2 as a_i and find the smallest value of j for $j > i$ such that $q_2 > a_j > 0$. Continuing in this manner, the sequence q_1, q_2, q_3,... (which is a subsequence of a_1, a_2,...) is constructed. Because q_1, q_2, q_3,... is a strictly decreasing sequence of positive numbers with greatest lower bound of zero, the sequence q_1, q_2, q_3,... must converge to zero (Rosenlicht 1968, 50). ∎

Lemma: Stochastic Approximation Lemma 2.   Assume the stochastic sequence $\{\tilde{\mathbf{x}}(t)\}$ of d-dimensional random vectors is generated by a bounded discrete-time stochastic system with generator function $\mathbf{f}$: $\mathcal{R}^d \times \mathcal{R}^q \to \mathcal{R}^d$ with respect to $\{\tilde{\mathbf{n}}(t)\}$ and stepsize sequence $\{\eta_t\}$. Assume the gradient, $\mathbf{g}$: $\mathcal{R}^d \to \mathcal{R}^d$, and Hessian of V exist and are continuous on $\mathcal{R}^d$. Assume $\bar{\mathbf{f}}(\cdot) = E[\mathbf{f}(\cdot, \tilde{\mathbf{n}})]$ exists on $\mathcal{R}^d$. Assume $\mathbf{g}(\mathbf{x})^T \bar{\mathbf{f}}(\mathbf{x}) \leq 0$ for all $\mathbf{x} \in \mathcal{R}^d$. Let the sequence of nonpositive real numbers u_0, u_1, u_2,... be defined such that

$$u_t = E\left[\mathbf{g}(\tilde{\mathbf{x}}(t))^T \bar{\mathbf{f}}(\tilde{\mathbf{x}}(t))\right]$$

for $t = 0, 1, 2,...$. Then there exists a subsequence of u_0, u_1, u_2,... that converges to zero.

Proof.   Let U: $\mathcal{R}^d \to \mathcal{R}$ be defined such that

$$U(\tilde{\mathbf{x}}(t)) = \mathbf{g}(\tilde{\mathbf{x}}(t))^T \bar{\mathbf{f}}(\tilde{\mathbf{x}}(t)),$$

so that $u_t = E[U(\tilde{\mathbf{x}}(t))]$.

Take the expectation of the result in (4.14) obtained from the Almost Stochastic Lyapunov Function Lemma

$$\left| E[V(\tilde{\mathbf{x}}(t+1))] - E[V(\tilde{\mathbf{x}}(t))] - \eta_t E[U(\tilde{\mathbf{x}}(t))] \right| \leq \eta_t^2 K, \tag{4.23}$$

where K is some finite positive real number.

By the Expectation Existence Lemma, $E[\tilde{\mathbf{x}}(t)]$ exists for $t = 0, 1, 2,\ldots$ and because V, $\mathbf{g}$, and $\mathbf{f}$ are continuous by assumption, all expectations in (4.23) exist. Summing both sides of (4.23),

$$\left| \sum_{t=0}^{t=T-1} \left(E[V(\tilde{\mathbf{x}}(t+1))] - E[V(\tilde{\mathbf{x}}(t))] \right) - \sum_{t=0}^{t=T-1} \eta_t E[U(\tilde{\mathbf{x}}(t))] \right|$$
$$\leq \sum_{t=0}^{t=T-1} K\eta_t^2. \tag{4.24}$$

The terms on the left-hand side of (4.24) cancel, yielding

$$\left| E[V(\tilde{\mathbf{x}}(T))] - E[V(\tilde{\mathbf{x}}(0))] - \sum_{t=0}^{t=T-1} \eta_t E[U(\tilde{\mathbf{x}}(t))] \right| \leq \sum_{t=0}^{t=T-1} K\eta_t^2, \tag{4.25}$$

where $E[V(\tilde{\mathbf{x}}(T))]$ and $E[V(\tilde{\mathbf{x}}(0))]$ are finite real numbers for finite T by the Expectation Existence Lemma and the assumption that V is continuous.

Given $\{\tilde{\mathbf{x}}(t)\}$ is a bounded stochastic process, by the Expectation Existence Lemma, and the assumption that V is continuous, there exists a finite real number C such that

$$\left| E[V(\tilde{\mathbf{x}}(T))] - E[V(\tilde{\mathbf{x}}(0))] \right| < C. \tag{4.26}$$

Using (4.2), (4.26), and (4.25), it follows that there exists a finite real number B such that

$$\lim_{T\to\infty} - \sum_{t=0}^{t=T-1} \eta_t E[U(\tilde{\mathbf{x}}(t))] < B < \infty. \tag{4.27}$$

Therefore, by SAL 1, there exists a subsequence of $E[U(\tilde{\mathbf{x}}(1))]$, $E[U(\tilde{\mathbf{x}}(2))],\ldots$ that converges to zero. ∎

The following lemma is also used to prove the Stochastic Approximation Theorem.

Lemma: Stochastic Approximation Lemma 3.   Given a sequence S of random variables that converges in probability to some random variable (or real number) $\tilde{x}$, there exists a subsequence of S that converges with probability one to $\tilde{x}$.

Proof.   See Lukacs 1975, 48–49, Theorem 2.4.3. ∎

Main proof of the Stochastic Approximation Theorem.   Let $U: \mathcal{R}^d \to \mathcal{R}$ be defined for all $\mathbf{x} \in \mathcal{R}^d$ such that

$$U(\mathbf{x}) = \mathbf{g}(\mathbf{x})^T \bar{\mathbf{f}}(\mathbf{x}).$$

For $t = 0, 1, 2,\dots,$ let u_t be defined such that $u_t = E[U(\tilde{\mathbf{x}}(t))]$, where the expectation exists because U is continuous and by the Expectation Existence Lemma.

By SAL 2, there exists a subsequence of

$$u_1, u_2, u_3,\dots \tag{4.28}$$

that converges to zero. Thus (see elementary problem 4.4-1) there exists a subsequence of random variables in

$$U(\tilde{\mathbf{x}}(1)), U(\tilde{\mathbf{x}}(2)),\dots \tag{4.29}$$

that converges in probability to zero.

Because U is a continuous function on $\mathcal{R}^d$, there exists a subsequence of random variables $\tilde{\mathbf{x}}(1), \tilde{\mathbf{x}}(2),\dots$ generated by (4.3) that converges in probability to $\mathcal{H}$. To see this, assume such a sequence does not exist. This would imply that a subsequence of the sequence of random variables $\{U(\tilde{\mathbf{x}}(t))\}$ would not converge to zero in probability as $t \to \infty$, which would contradict the observation in (4.29).

Now because a subsequence of $\{\tilde{\mathbf{x}}(t)\}$ converges in probability to $\mathcal{H}$, it follows from SAL 3 that a subsequence of $\{\tilde{\mathbf{x}}(t)\}$ converges with probability one to $\mathcal{H}$. Because V is a continuous function, it follows that a subsequence of

$$V(\tilde{\mathbf{x}}(1)), V(\tilde{\mathbf{x}}(2)),\dots \tag{4.30}$$

converges to $\mathcal{G}$ with probability one, where

$$\mathcal{G} = \{g \in \mathcal{R}: g = V(\mathbf{x}), \mathbf{x} \in \mathcal{H}\}.$$

By the Almost Stochastic Lyapunov Function Lemma, there exists a finite real number K such that w.p.1

$$E[V(\tilde{\mathbf{x}}(t + 1)) \mid \tilde{\mathbf{x}}(t)] \leq V(\tilde{\mathbf{x}}(t)) + K\eta_t^2$$

for $t = 0, 1, 2,\dots.$ Thus the stochastic process $\{V(\tilde{\mathbf{x}}(t))\}$ is an almost supermartingale sequence because (i) there exists a finite real number C such that

$$\sum_{t=1}^{\infty} \eta_t^2 K < C < \infty,$$

using (4.2), and (ii) $E[|V(\tilde{\mathbf{x}}(t))|]$ is finite, by the Expectation Existence Lemma, the assumption that V is continuous, and the assumption that the stochastic sequence $\{\tilde{\mathbf{x}}(t)\}$ is bounded.

Thus, by the Almost Supermartingale Convergence Theorem, $V(\tilde{\mathbf{x}}(t))$ converges to some random variable with probability one as $t \to \infty$. That is, all subsequences of (4.30) converge to some random variable with probability one as $t \to \infty$.

Because a subsequence of (4.30) converges with probability one to the set $\mathcal{G}$ and (4.30) converges with probability one to a random variable, it follows that (4.30) converges with probability one to the set $\mathcal{G}$. Therefore,

$$\tilde{\mathbf{x}}(1), \tilde{\mathbf{x}}(2),\ldots \tag{4.31}$$

converges with probability one to the set $\mathcal{H}$ because V is continuous. ∎

4.5   Chapter Summary

The Stochastic Approximation Theorem was shown to be roughly analogous to the deterministic Invariant Set Theorem developed in chapter 3 for the analysis of nonlinear deterministic dynamical systems. The Stochastic Approximation Theorem exploits the concept of an almost stochastic Lyapunov function whose expected value of the system state is nonincreasing as the stochastic dynamical system evolves in time. The theorem states that under fairly general conditions if the stepsize of the algorithm is decreased at an appropriate rate, then convergence with probability one to a particular region of the state space can be guaranteed. The Stochastic Approximation Theorem was then used to investigate the asymptotic long-term behavior of on-line classical backpropagation learning, on-line Hebbian learning with weight decay, and a stochastic version of the Hopfield (1984) ANN system; the theorem was formally proved at the end of the chapter.

The following procedure for applying the Stochastic Approximation Theorem sets forth the key conditions that must be checked to investigate stochastic convergence.

- Step 1: Check if algorithm is bounded discrete-time stochastic system.

  a. Try to express the stochastic dynamical system in the form of equation (4.3).

  b. Check if $\tilde{\mathbf{n}}(0), \tilde{\mathbf{n}}(1),\ldots$ consists of independently and identically distributed random variables.

  c. Check if there exists a finite real number K such that, for $t = 0, 1, 2,\ldots$, $|\tilde{\mathbf{n}}(t)| < K$ with probability one.

  d. Check if $\mathbf{f}$ in (4.3) is continuous with respect to both of its arguments.

  e. Check to make sure that the sequence of stepsizes $\eta_1, \eta_2, \eta_3,\ldots$ satisfies (4.1) and (4.2).

f. Check to make sure that $\left| \tilde{\mathbf{x}}(0) \right| < K$ with probability one for some finite real number K (so that the assumption that $\{\tilde{\mathbf{x}}(t)\}$ is bounded is not immediately violated).

- Step 2: Find twice differentiable almost stochastic Lyapunov function V.

a. Show that $\bar{\mathbf{f}}$ exists by explicitly computing $\bar{\mathbf{f}}$.

b. Try integrating $\bar{\mathbf{f}}$ in order to obtain a function V such that $\nabla_{\mathbf{x}} V^T \bar{\mathbf{f}}(\mathbf{x})$ is less than or equal to zero for all $\mathbf{x} \in \mathfrak{R}^d$.

c. Check if the gradient of V and Hessian of V are continuous.

- Step 3: Check asymptotic behavior of dynamical system.

a. Investigate the contents of the set $\mathcal{H}$, defined such that

$$\mathcal{H} = \{\mathbf{x} \in \mathfrak{R}^d : \nabla_{\mathbf{x}} V^T \bar{\mathbf{f}}(\mathbf{x}) = 0\}.$$

b. If all assumptions of the Stochastic Approximation Theorem have been verified except for the assumption that $\{\tilde{\mathbf{x}}(t)\}$ is bounded, then conclude that $\tilde{\mathbf{x}}(t) \to \mathcal{H}$ with probability one as $t \to \infty$ or $\{\tilde{\mathbf{x}}(t)\}$ is not bounded.

4.6   Elementary Problems

4.1-1. Let $\tilde{\mathbf{x}}(1), \tilde{\mathbf{x}}(2),\ldots$ be a stochastic sequence of independent and identically distributed random d-dimensional vectors with common probability mass function p: $\{\mathbf{x}^1,\ldots,\mathbf{x}^M\} \to [0,1]$, where M is a finite positive integer and $\mathbf{x}^k \in \mathfrak{R}^d$ for $k = 1\ldots M$. Define for $t = 1, 2, 3,\ldots$:

$$\tilde{V}_t = (1/t)\sum_{i=1}^{t} V(\tilde{\mathbf{x}}(i)),$$

where $V: \mathfrak{R}^d \to \mathfrak{R}$ is continuous on $\mathfrak{R}^d$. Prove the stochastic sequence of random scalars $\tilde{V}_1, \tilde{V}_2, \tilde{V}_3,\ldots$ converges with probability one to some real number C. Give an explicit formula for the real number C. HINT: Use the Strong Law of Large numbers.

4.1-2. Show that the stochastic sequence of random scalars $\tilde{V}_1, \tilde{V}_2, \tilde{V}_3,\ldots$ defined in problem 4.1-1 converges in mean square to some real number C. Give an explicit formula for the real number C.

4.1-3. Use the result obtained in problem 4.1-2 and the Markov Inequality to prove that the stochastic sequence of random scalars $\tilde{V}_1, \tilde{V}_2, \tilde{V}_3,\ldots$ defined in problem 4.1-1 converges in probability to some real number C. Give an explicit formula for the real number C.

4.1-4. Let $\tilde{\mathbf{x}}(1), \tilde{\mathbf{x}}(2),\ldots$ be a stochastic sequence of independent and identically distributed random d-dimensional vectors with common probability mass function p: $\{\mathbf{x}^1,\ldots,\mathbf{x}^M\} \to [0,1]$, where M is a finite positive integer and $\mathbf{x}^k \in \mathfrak{R}^d$ for $k = 1\ldots M$. Let $\mathbf{w} \in W$ where W is a closed and bounded subset of $\mathfrak{R}^q$. Define

$$\tilde{V}_t(\mathbf{w}) = (1/t)\sum_{i=1}^{t} V(\tilde{\mathbf{x}}(i), \mathbf{w}),$$

where $V: \mathfrak{R}^d \times \mathfrak{R}^q \to \mathfrak{R}$ is continuous in both arguments. Show the stochastic sequence of functions $\tilde{V}_1, \tilde{V}_2, \tilde{V}_3,\ldots$ converges *uniformly* with probability one to some function $V^*: \mathfrak{R}^q \to \mathfrak{R}$. Give an explicit formula for the function V^*. HINT: Let E be a subset of $\mathfrak{R}^d$. Let $f_n: E \to \mathfrak{R}$ and $f: E \to \mathfrak{R}$. A deterministic sequence of functions $f_1, f_2,\ldots$ converges uniformly to f on E if given every $\varepsilon > 0$, there is a positive integer N such that $\left| f(p) - f_n(p) \right| < \varepsilon$ whenever $n > N$ for all p in E.

4.2-1. Let $\eta_1, \eta_2,\ldots$ be a sequence of positive real numbers. Suppose that $\eta_t = 1$ for $0 \le t \le 100$, $\eta_t = t/1000$ for $100 < t \le 500$, and $\eta_t = 1/(200 + t)$ for $t > 500$. Verify that as $t \to \infty$, the sequence of positive real numbers $\eta_1, \eta_2,\ldots$ satisfies (4.1) and (4.2).

4.2-2. Show that $\eta_t = 0.000001$ for $t = 0, 1, 2,\ldots$ satisfies (4.1) but not (4.2). Also show that $\eta_t = (0.25)^t$ for $t = 0, 1, 2,\ldots$ does not satisfy (4.1) but satisfies (4.2).

4.2-3. Darken and Moody (1990, 1991) have proposed the search and converge approach to generating a sequence of positive stepsizes for stochastic approximation algorithms. A researcher (inspired by the Darken and Moody approach) suggests the following formula for generating a sequence of positive stepsizes $\eta_1, \eta_2,\ldots$:

$$\eta_t = \eta_0 \frac{(t/\tau) + 1}{(t/\tau)^2 + 1} \tag{4.32}$$

for $t = 0, 1, 2, 3,\ldots$, where it is assumed that $0 < \eta_0 < 1$ and τ is a positive integer. Note that for $t \ll \tau$, η_t is approximately given by the formula $\eta_0(1 + (t/\tau))$; for $t \gg \tau$, η_t is approximately given by the formula $\eta_t = \eta_0/(t/\tau)$. Plot η_t as a function of t for $t = 0, 100, 200, 300,\ldots, 1,000$, with $\tau = 500$ and $\eta_0 = 0.1$. In many applications of backpropagation, it is appropriate to initially increase the stepsize of the algorithm gradually and then gradually decrease the stepsize. The formula in (4.32) has this qualitative feature. Now show that (4.32) satisfies (4.1) and (4.2) when η_0 and τ are positive real numbers. HINT: Use the comparison test.

4.3-1. Let a random vector $\tilde{\mathbf{n}}$ be called a *truncated Gaussian* random vector if it can be constructed by adding a finite number of random vectors each of which has common probability mass (density) function, so that the sample space of the probability mass (density) function is a bounded set whose elements have finite magnitudes. By the central limit theorem, the average of a large number of truncated Gaussian random vectors will have a probability distribution that is approximately Gaussian.

Now let $\tilde{x}(0) = x_0 \in \mathcal{R}$. Let the stochastic sequence $\tilde{x}(0), \tilde{x}(1),\ldots$ be defined such that for $t = 0, 1, 2,\ldots$:

$$\tilde{x}(t+1) = \tilde{x}(t) - \eta_t[(\tilde{x}(t) - 1)^3 + (\tilde{x}(t) - 14)^7] + \eta_t \tilde{n}(t),$$

where $\eta_t = 100/(100 + (t/5))$ and $\{\tilde{n}(t)\}$ is a sequence of independent and identically distributed zero-mean truncated Gaussian random vectors. Prove that $\tilde{x}(0), \tilde{x}(1),\ldots$ is not bounded or that $\tilde{x}(0), \tilde{x}(1),\ldots$ will converge with probability one to the roots of the equation

$$(x - 1)^3 + (x - 14)^7 = 0.$$

4.3-2. Consider the following stochastic dynamical system:

$$\tilde{x}(t+1) = \tilde{x}(t) - \eta_t(\tilde{x}(t) - 1/\lambda)^9 + \eta_t \tilde{n}(t),$$

where $\eta_t = 1/(1 + t)$ and $\{\tilde{n}(t)\}$ is a sequence of independent and identically distributed zero-mean truncated Gaussian random vectors (see problem 4.3-1 for the definition of a truncated Gaussian random vectors). Assume $\tilde{x}(0)$ is a bounded random variable. Prove that the stochastic process $\tilde{x}(0), \tilde{x}(1),\ldots$ is not bounded or $\tilde{x}(0), \tilde{x}(1),\ldots$ will converge with probability one to the point $1/\lambda$. What happens when $\lambda = 0$?

4.3-3. Higher-order forms of Hebbian learning are also plausible in the nervous system. Let $\mathbf{x}^1,\ldots, \mathbf{x}^M$ be a set of M d-dimensional real vectors where M is finite. Define the stochastic process $\tilde{\mathbf{x}}(0), \tilde{\mathbf{x}}(1), \tilde{\mathbf{x}}(2),\ldots$ whose elements are independently and identically distributed with probability mass function $p: \{\mathbf{x}^1,\ldots, \mathbf{x}^M\} \to [0, 1]$. Let $\tilde{x}_i(t)$ be the ith element ($i = 1\ldots d$) of the d-dimensional random vector $\tilde{\mathbf{x}}(t)$ for $t = 0, 1, 2,\ldots$.

Let $w_{ijk}(t)$ be an observed value of a triple connection strength at time t which may be interpreted to mean that when units j and k are active, then unit i will tend to be active as well. It is assumed that $w_{ijk}(t)$ is an observed value of the random variable $\tilde{w}_{ijk}(t)$, which is updated using a third-order Hebbian learning rule with weight decay defined by the ANN learning dynamical system

$$\tilde{w}_{ijk}(t+1) = \tilde{w}_{ijk}(t)\left[1 - \frac{\lambda}{1 + 4t}\right] + \left[\frac{1}{1 + 4t}\right]\tilde{x}_i(t)\tilde{x}_j(t)\tilde{x}_k(t),$$

where an observed value of $\tilde{x}_i(t)$ is the activation level of the ith unit at iteration t of the learning algorithm. Use the Stochastic Approximation Theorem to identify explicit conditions for the third-order Hebbian learning rule to converge to a solution. (See Giles and Maxwell 1987 for additional discussions of higher-order ANN systems.)

4.4-1. Why does (4.28) imply that (4.29) converges in probability to zero? HINT: Use the Markov Inequality in conjunction with the definition of the concept of convergence in probability.

4.7   Problems

4-1. Let $\eta_1, \eta_2,\dots$ be a sequence of real positive numbers such that $\eta_t = 1/t$ for $t = 1, 2,\dots$. Consider a statistical environment defined by the sequence of independent and identically distributed random vectors $(\tilde{\mathbf{s}}(0), \tilde{\mathbf{o}}(0)), (\tilde{\mathbf{s}}(1), \tilde{\mathbf{o}}(1)),\dots, (\tilde{\mathbf{s}}(t), \tilde{\mathbf{o}}(t))$. The probability distribution of the tth random vector in the environment is defined by a probability mass function that assigns a probability p_k to the ordered pair $(\mathbf{s}^k, \mathbf{o}^k) \in \mathscr{R}^s \times \mathscr{R}^o$, where $k = 1\dots M$ and M is finite. Assume $(\mathbf{s}^k, \mathbf{o}^k)$ is finite for $k = 1\dots M$ as well. Let $\tilde{\mathbf{W}}(0)$ be a bounded random matrix. A Widrow-Hoff on-line learning rule is defined as

$$\tilde{\mathbf{W}}(t+1) = \tilde{\mathbf{W}}(t) + \gamma_t[\tilde{\mathbf{o}}(t) - \tilde{\mathbf{r}}(t)]\tilde{\mathbf{s}}(t)^T,$$

where $\tilde{\mathbf{r}}(t) = \tilde{\mathbf{W}}(t)\tilde{\mathbf{s}}(t)$. Analyze the long-term behavior of this stochastic dynamical system. HINT: Use the function $l: \mathscr{R}^{o \times s} \longrightarrow [0, \infty)$ defined by

$$l(\mathbf{W}) = E\big[\,|\,\tilde{\mathbf{o}} - \mathbf{W}\tilde{\mathbf{s}}\,|^2\big]$$

as a candidate stochastic Lyapunov function.

4-2. Explicitly define an on-line Widrow-Hoff learning rule with weight decay. Now use the Stochastic Approximation Theorem to derive a set of sufficient conditions for a version of the Widrow-Hoff on-line learning rule with weight decay to converge with probability one to the solution of a sum-squared error minimization problem. HINT: See solution to problem 4-1.

4-3. Consider the following scalar formulation of the classical on-line backpropagation algorithm described in chapter 2. First, define the sequence of independent and identically distributed random vectors $(\tilde{\mathbf{s}}(0), \tilde{\mathbf{o}}(0)), (\tilde{\mathbf{s}}(1), \tilde{\mathbf{o}}(1)),\dots$, such that each element in the sequence has a probability distribution specified by a probability mass function that assigns probability mass p_n to $(\mathbf{s}^n, \mathbf{o}^n)$, where $n = 1\dots M$, M is finite, $(\mathbf{s}^n, \mathbf{o}^n)$ is finite, and $(\mathbf{s}^n, \mathbf{o}^n) \in \mathscr{R}^c \times \mathscr{R}^p$.

Note that a particular realization of $\tilde{\mathbf{s}}(t)$, $\mathbf{s}(t)$, is used to refer to the c-dimensional activation pattern over the input units at iteration t of the classical on-line backpropagation algorithm, while a particular realization of $\tilde{\mathbf{o}}(t)$, $\mathbf{o}(t)$, is used to refer to the desired p-dimensional activation pattern over the output units at iteration t. The jth element of $\mathbf{s}(t)$ is referred to as $s_j(t)$, and the kth element of $\mathbf{o}(t)$ is referred to as $o_k(t)$.

Let $\mathscr{S}: \mathscr{R} \longrightarrow (0, 1)$ be defined such that $\mathscr{S}(x) = 1/(1 + \exp[-x])$ for $x \in \mathscr{R}$.

A scalar version of on-line backpropagation may be defined by the following algorithm.

• Step 1: Define initial values of connection weight parameter vectors. Let $\tilde{v}_{ji}(0)$, $\tilde{w}_{kj}(0)$, $\tilde{b}_k(0)$, $\tilde{q}_j(0)$ for $i = 1\dots c$, $j = 1\dots d$, $k = 1\dots p$ be random variables with uniform probability density functions defined with respect to some closed and bounded sample space. A realization of this set of random variables is a particular connection strength parameter vector for the ANN learning dynamical system.

• Step 2: Define forward propagation equations from input to output units. The net input to the jth hidden unit at iteration t is defined by a realization of

$$\tilde{\psi}_j(t) = \sum_{i=1}^{c} \tilde{v}_{ji}(t)\tilde{s}_i(t) + \tilde{q}_j(t),$$

and the activation level of the jth hidden unit at iteration t is a realization of

$$\tilde{h}_j(t) = \mathscr{S}(\tilde{\psi}_j(t)).$$

The net input to the kth output unit at iteration t is given by a realization of:

$$\tilde{\varphi}_k(t) = \sum_{j=1}^{d} \tilde{w}_{kj}(t)\tilde{h}_j(t) + \tilde{b}_k(t),$$

and the activation level of the kth output unit at iteration t is given by

$$\tilde{r}_k(t) = \mathcal{S}(\tilde{\varphi}_k(t)).$$

• Step 3: Define backward error propagation equations. The error signal at the kth output unit at iteration t is a realization of

$$\tilde{\delta}_{r_k}(t) = \tilde{o}_k(t) - \tilde{r}_k(t),$$

and the error signal at the jth hidden unit at iteration t is computed by backward error propagation of the error signals at the output units using the formula

$$\tilde{\delta}_{h_j}(t) = \sum_{k=1}^{p} \tilde{w}_{kj}(t)\big[\tilde{r}_k(t)(1 - \tilde{r}_k(t))\big]\tilde{\delta}_{r_k}(t).$$

• Step 4: Update connection strength parameter vector elements. Let $\gamma_1, \gamma_2,...$ be a sequence of positive real numbers that satisfy (4.1) and (4.2). Update the connections from hidden units to output units:

$$\tilde{w}_{kj}(t+1) = \tilde{w}_{kj}(t) + \gamma_t \tilde{r}_k(t)\big(1 - \tilde{r}_k(t)\big)\tilde{\delta}_{r_k}(t)\tilde{h}_j(t).$$

Update the connections from input units to hidden units:

$$\tilde{v}_{ji}(t+1) = \tilde{v}_{ji}(t) + \gamma_t \tilde{h}_j(t)\big(1 - \tilde{h}_j(t)\big)\tilde{\delta}_{h_j}(t)\tilde{s}_i(t).$$

Update the bias parameters for the output units:

$$\tilde{b}_k(t+1) = \tilde{b}_k(t) + \gamma_t \tilde{r}_k(t)\big(1 - \tilde{r}_k(t)\big)\tilde{\delta}_{r_k}(t),$$

and the bias parameters for the hidden units:

$$\tilde{q}_j(t+1) = \tilde{q}_j(t) + \gamma_t \tilde{h}_j(t)\big(1 - \tilde{h}_j(t)\big)\tilde{\delta}_{h_j}(t).$$

Explicitly describe the relationship between the scalar version of the scalar on-line backpropagation algorithm presented in this problem and the matrix version presented in chapter 2. Show that the stochastic processes

$$\tilde{w}_{kj}(0), \tilde{w}_{kj}(1), \tilde{w}_{kj}(2),...,$$

$$\tilde{v}_{ji}(0), \tilde{v}_{ji}(1), \tilde{v}_{ji}(2),...,$$

$$\tilde{b}_k(0), \tilde{b}_k(1), \tilde{b}_k(2),...,$$

$$\tilde{q}_j(0), \tilde{q}_j(1), \tilde{q}_j(2),...,$$

converge with probability one to a set $\mathcal{H}$ or are not bounded with probability one. Describe the contents of the set $\mathcal{H}$. HINT: The following function has been proposed as a candidate stochastic Lyapunov function for the discrete-time stochastic dynamical system

$$l\big(\{w_{kj}\}, \{v_{ji}\}, \{b_k\}, \{q_j\}\big) = (1/2)\sum_{n=1}^{M} p_n \sum_{k=1}^{p} (o_k^n - r_k^n)^2.$$

4-4. Consider a classical on-line backpropagation algorithm as described in problem 4-3 but assume that the hidden units are *radial basis functions*, following Poggio and Girosi (1990). Radial basis functions are useful when the desired mapping from input units to output units is not well represented by a logical (i.e., Boolean) function. In particular, let $h_i(t)$ be the activation of the ith hidden unit, given input pattern $s(t)$. Assume that $h_i(t) = \exp\big[-|\mathbf{v}_i - \mathbf{s}(t)|^2\big]$, where $\mathbf{v}_i$ is the connection strength vector that identifies the mapping from $\mathbf{s}(t)$ to hidden unit activation $h_i(t)$. Let the response of the network $\mathbf{r}(t)$ be defined by the linear equation $\mathbf{r}(t) = \mathbf{W}\mathbf{h}(t)$, where $\mathbf{h}(t) = [h_1(t),..., h_d(t)]$. Derive a variation of the on-line backpropagation algorithm described in problem 4-3 that uses the radial basis function architecture. HINT: Use the expected sum-squared error risk function in problem 4-3 and compute its first derivative to derive the learning algorithm.

4-5. Let the stochastic sequence $\tilde{\mathbf{x}}(0), \tilde{\mathbf{x}}(1),\ldots$ consist of independent and identically distributed p-dimensional random vectors with the common probability mass function $p_{\tilde{\mathbf{x}}}: \{\mathbf{x}^1,\ldots, \mathbf{x}^M\} \rightarrow [0, 1]$, where M is a finite positive integer and $\mathbf{x}^k \in \mathcal{R}^p$ for $k = 1\ldots M$.

The on-line version of the elastic net algorithm described in chapter 2 is now defined as follows. Let the quantity $\tilde{\mathbf{w}}_i(t)$ denote a p-dimensional random vector for $i = 1\ldots d$ and $t = 0, 1, 2,\ldots$. Let $\tilde{\mathbf{w}}(0)$, $\tilde{\mathbf{w}}(1),\ldots$ be a stochastic process where the pd-dimensional random vector $\tilde{\mathbf{w}}(t) = [\tilde{\mathbf{w}}_1(t),\ldots, \tilde{\mathbf{w}}_d(t)]$ for $t = 0, 1,\ldots$. Let $\gamma_1, \gamma_2,\ldots$ be a sequence of positive real numbers defined such that

$$\gamma_t = 3t/(1 + 5t^2)$$

for $t = 0, 1, 2,\ldots$. Let λ be a positive real number. Let the stochastic dynamical system generator function $\mathbf{f}: \mathcal{R}^{pd} \times \mathcal{R}^p \rightarrow \mathcal{R}^{pd}$, where $\mathbf{f} = [\mathbf{f}_1,\ldots, \mathbf{f}_d]$ and the ith element of $\mathbf{f}$ is a function $\mathbf{f}_i: \mathcal{R}^{pd} \times \mathcal{R}^p \rightarrow \mathcal{R}^p$ $(i = 1\ldots d)$. Let $\mathbf{f}_i: \mathcal{R}^{pd} \times \mathcal{R}^p \rightarrow \mathcal{R}^p$ $(i = 1\ldots d)$ be defined such that for all

$$\mathbf{w} = [\mathbf{w}_1,\ldots, \mathbf{w}_d] \in \mathcal{R}^{pd}$$

and for all $\mathbf{x} \in \mathcal{R}^p$:

$$\mathbf{f}_i(\mathbf{w}, \mathbf{x}) = r_i(\mathbf{x}, \mathbf{w})(\mathbf{x} - \mathbf{w}_i) + 2\lambda \left[\frac{\mathbf{w}_{i+1} + \mathbf{w}_{i-1}}{2} - \mathbf{w}_i \right],$$

where $\mathbf{r}_i: \mathcal{R}^p \times \mathcal{R}^{pd} \rightarrow \mathcal{R}$ is such that for all $\mathbf{x} \in \mathcal{R}^p$ and for all $\mathbf{w} \in \mathcal{R}^{pd}$:

$$r_i(\mathbf{x}, \mathbf{w}) = \frac{\exp(-|\mathbf{x} - \mathbf{w}_i|^2/2\sigma_t^2)}{\sum\limits_{k=1}^{d} \exp(-|\mathbf{x} - \mathbf{w}_k|^2/2\sigma_t^2)}.$$

Note that $\mathbf{w}_{d+1}$ is defined as $\mathbf{w}_1$.

Assume $\{\tilde{\mathbf{w}}(t)\}$ is generated from the stochastic, discrete-time, dynamical system

$$\tilde{\mathbf{w}}_i(t+1) = \tilde{\mathbf{w}}_i(t) + \gamma_t \mathbf{f}_i(\tilde{\mathbf{w}}(t), \tilde{\mathbf{x}}(t))$$

Use the Stochastic Approximation Theorem to prove that the stochastic process $\tilde{\mathbf{w}}(0), \tilde{\mathbf{w}}(1),\ldots$ either (1) is not a bounded stochastic sequence, or (2) converges with probability one to some set $\mathcal{H}$. Explicitly define the contents of the set $\mathcal{H}$.

4-6. Consider the sequence of independent and identically distributed random variables $\tilde{\mathbf{x}}(0)$, $\tilde{\mathbf{x}}(1),\ldots$ where the probability distribution of the tth random variable in the sequence is specified by a probability mass function that assigns probability p_k to vector $\mathbf{x}^k$, where $k = 1\ldots M$, and where M is finite. Let $\tilde{M}_1, \tilde{M}_2,\ldots$ be a sequence of independent and identically distributed scalar random variables with the common probability mass function $p: \{1, 2, 3,\ldots, M_{max}\} \rightarrow [0, 1]$, where M_{max} is a finite positive integer. Suppose that for $k = 0, 1, 2,\ldots$, that

$$\tilde{\mathbf{x}}(k) = \{(\tilde{\mathbf{s}}^k(0), \tilde{\mathbf{o}}^k(0)), (\tilde{\mathbf{s}}^k(1), \tilde{\mathbf{o}}^k(1)),\ldots(\tilde{\mathbf{s}}^k(\tilde{M}_k), \tilde{\mathbf{o}}^k(\tilde{M}_k))\},$$

where $\mathbf{x}(k)$, a realization of $\tilde{\mathbf{x}}(k)$, is the kth sequence of training stimuli used to train a Jordan sequential network (as defined in Chapter 2). The training stimulus pair $(\tilde{\mathbf{s}}^k(t), \tilde{\mathbf{o}}^k(t))$ refers to the presentation of input stimulus $\tilde{\mathbf{s}}^k(t)$ and the desired target response $\tilde{\mathbf{o}}^k(t)$ as the tth pair of items in the kth sequence of training stimuli used to train the Jordan sequential network.

Propose a stochastic approximation algorithm for a Jordan sequential network that learns sequences of training stimuli by updating its weights after each sequence of training stimuli is presented to the network. Explicitly write down the stochastic Lyapunov function for the proposed algorithm. Explain why the stochastic approximation theory described in chapter 4 cannot be used to update the network's weights after each training stimulus has been presented (see Kuan, Hornik, and White 1994 for a stochastic approximation analysis that does allow the network's weights to be updated after each training stimulus is presented). HINT: See solution to problem 4-7.

4-7. Consider the problem of learning to drive a car where a female instructor (a thrill seeker) decides at random (at one-second intervals) to cover your eyes with her hands. This is an example of a learning problem where the training data is not always directly observable. In this problem, it is assumed that you periodically (once a week) take a drive with the thrill seeker instructor and that each such visit corresponds to a sequence of events where some events in the sequence are not observable.

Let $\tilde{M}^{(0)}, \tilde{M}^{(1)}, \ldots$ be a sequence of independent and identically distributed random variables with common probability mass function $p_M: \{1, 2, \ldots, M_{max}\} \to [0, 1]$, where M_{max} is a finite positive integer. Let M_k be an observed value of the random variable $\tilde{M}^{(k)}$. Semantically, M_k is the *length* of the kth event sequence (i.e., the number of events which occurred on your last visit with your driving instructor).

The *identity* of the kth event sequence is denoted by the vector $\mathbf{x}(k)$, which is an observed value of the random vector $\tilde{\mathbf{x}}(k)$. The stochastic sequence $\tilde{\mathbf{x}}(0), \tilde{\mathbf{x}}(1), \ldots$ consists of independent and identically distributed random vectors with common probability mass (density) function whose sample space is some closed and bounded set in $\mathcal{R}^d$. It is assumed that the vector $\mathbf{x}(k)$ may be partitioned such that $\mathbf{x}(k) = [\mathbf{x}^k(0), \ldots, \mathbf{x}^k(M_k)]$ and that for $t = 0 \ldots M_k$:

$$\mathbf{x}^k(t) = (\mathbf{s}^k(t), [\mathbf{o}^k(t), \mathbf{D}^k(t)]),$$

where $\mathbf{s}^k(t) \in \mathcal{R}^s$ is the tth input stimulus presented in the kth event sequence, $[\mathbf{o}^k(t), \mathbf{D}^k(t)]$ is the tth response feedback signal provided by the environment in the kth sequence. In particular, $\mathbf{o}^k(t) \in \mathcal{R}^m$ represents *potentially available desired response* feedback signal information whose accessibility is determined by the diagonal matrix $\mathbf{D}^k(t) \in \mathcal{R}^{m \times m}$.

Let $d_{k,i}(t)$ be the ith on-diagonal element of the diagonal matrix $\mathbf{D}^k(t)$ for the tth event in the kth sequence.

- If $d_{k,i}(t) = 1$, then the ith element of $\mathbf{o}^k(t)$ is *observable*.
- If $d_{k,i}(t) = 0$, then the ith element of $\mathbf{o}^k(t)$ is *not observable*.

Let the response of the ANN system, $\mathbf{r}^k(t)$, given the $(t-1)$th input stimulus $\mathbf{s}^k(t-1)$ in the kth sequence be defined as $\mathbf{r}^k(t) = \mathbf{W}\mathbf{s}^k(t-1)$, where $\mathbf{W}$ is the weight matrix whose parameters must be estimated. Let the learning objective function

$$\hat{l}_n = \frac{1}{n} \sum_{k=1}^{n} l^k$$

and

$$l^k = \sum_{t=0}^{M_k} [\mathbf{o}^k(t) - \mathbf{r}^k(t)]^T \mathbf{D}^k(t) [\mathbf{o}^k(t) - \mathbf{r}^k(t)] + \lambda \sum_{t=1}^{M_k} |\mathbf{r}^k(t) - \mathbf{r}^k(t-1)|^2.$$

What is the purpose of the matrix $\mathbf{D}^k(t)$? What is the purpose of the term $|\mathbf{r}^k(t) - \mathbf{r}^k(t-1)|^2$?

Design a stochastic approximation algorithm (assume the matrix $\mathbf{W}$ is updated each time a value of the random trajectory $\tilde{\mathbf{x}}$ is observed) that generates a stochastic process of random weight matrices $\tilde{\mathbf{W}}(0), \tilde{\mathbf{W}}(1), \ldots$ that either (1) converges to a critical point of l with probability one, or (2) is not bounded. Explain how the proposed stochastic approximation algorithm can be interpreted as a special type of backpropagation temporal memory learning system by explicitly deriving all formulas for the update rule in scalar form and drawing a network diagram. (For related discussions see Jaakkola, Jordan, and Singh 1994; Jordan 1992; Munro 1987; Sutton 1988; and R. J. Williams and Zipser 1995.)

4-8. In chapter 2, Chauvin's method (1989) for minimizing the number of hidden units in a classical on-line backpropagation algorithm was described. Explicitly write down the ANN learning objective function proposed by Chauvin for a classical on-line backpropagation network architecture. Explain in one or two sentences the basic principles behind its construction. Explicitly compute the gradient of the ANN learning objective function you have constructed. Use that gradient and constraints obtained from the Stochastic Approximation Theorem to design an on-line backpropagation learning algorithm that generates a stochastic sequence of random weight vectors that either (1) is not bounded, or (2) converges with probability one to a critical point of your ANN learning objective function.

4-9. Repeat problem 4-7 but let $\mathbf{r}^k(t)$ be the response of an Elman-style recurrent network (as described in chapter 2) with one hidden layer, so that $\mathbf{r}^k(t)$ is functionally dependent upon $\mathbf{s}^k(0), \ldots, \mathbf{s}^k(t-1)$.

II ALGORITHMIC LEVEL

Marr's algorithmic level of description (1982) is concerned with understanding the algorithms required to achieve a specific set of computational goals. The algorithmic level provides an important bridge between the implementational level and the computational level because all aspects of the behavior of a given ANN dynamical system may not be relevant to the ANN system's information-processing goals. Unlike the implementational level, the computational goals of an information-processing system must be defined in order to achieve an understanding of that system at the algorithmic level. The algorithmic level of description, however, is not concerned with the justification or description of the computational goals of the information-processing system.

Chapter 5 introduces selected mathematical tools from nonlinear optimization theory, a branch of mathematics concerned with searching for the minimum value of some function, and uses them to analyze and design a variety of ANN system architectures. Because most ANN systems can be viewed as non-linear optimization algorithms and a large class of important and relevant nonlinear optimization algorithms can be expressed as nonlinear dynamical systems, there is indeed a close relationship between nonlinear optimization theory and dynamical systems theory. On the other hand, unlike nonlinear optimization theory, dynamical systems theory (see chapters 3 and 4) does not require the specification of a computational goal (i.e., a function to be minimized), is not concerned with the speed and accuracy at which a given algorithm converges to a set of solutions, and does not require the concept of a "correct answer." (It is important to note that neither dynamical systems theory nor nonlinear optimization theory is relevant for evaluating the "intelligence" or "rationality" of an ANN system's computation, such issues are addressed by mathematical tools applicable to the computational level of analysis; see chapters 6, 7, 8.)

5   Nonlinear Optimization Theory

Nonlinear optimization theory, like dynamical system theory, is relevant for understanding both classification and learning processes of ANN information-processing systems. In chapter 2, the relevance of nonlinear optimization theory for ANN system analysis and design was indirectly introduced by showing how most ANN dynamical systems could be viewed as searching for the minimum value of some objective function.

The goal of an ANN classification dynamical system may usually be formulated as an optimization problem. Let $S \subseteq \mathcal{R}^d$ be a set of activation patterns, and let $V: S \rightarrow \mathcal{R}$ be a classification objective function (as defined in chapter 2). The goal of an ANN classification dynamical system may then be formulated as

Find the activation pattern $\mathbf{x}^*$ such that $V(\mathbf{x}^*) \leq V(\mathbf{x})$ for all $\mathbf{x} \in S$.

Similarly, the goal of an ANN learning dynamical system may also be formulated as an optimization problem in most cases. Let $W \subseteq \mathcal{R}^q$ be a set of connection strength parameter vectors, and let $l: W \rightarrow \mathcal{R}$ be a learning objective function (as defined in chapter 2). The goal of an ANN learning dynamical system may then be formulated as

Find the connection strength parameter vector $\mathbf{w}^*$ such that $l(\mathbf{w}^*) \leq l(\mathbf{w})$ for all $\mathbf{w} \in W$.

This chapter presents basic principles of nonlinear optimization theory that are especially relevant to ANN systems. First, it will introduce a series of definitions in order to explicitly define the goals of the nonlinear optimization problem. These definitions will be useful for determining more precisely the computational goals of an ANN system and when the ANN system has achieved those goals. Second, it will examine a broad class of deterministic nonlinear optimization algorithms that includes most popular nonlinear optimization algorithms as special cases. Third, it will develop a theory of stochastic nonlinear optimization algorithms. Fourth, it will discuss methods for defining and computing convergence rates. And fifth, it will apply nonlinear optimization theory to both classical optimization algorithms and ANN systems.

5.1   Optimization Goals

Typically, it is very difficult to prove that a practical nonlinear optimization algorithm will generate a sequence of system states that will converge to the minimum value of some nonlinear function. For this reason, it will be convenient to define some characteristics of nonlinear functions helpful in identifying necessary but not sufficient conditions for convergence to a function's minimum value. In particular, *critical point*, *local minimum*, and *global minimum* will be formally defined.

Definition: Critical point.   Let $\Omega \subseteq \mathcal{R}^d$. Let $V: \Omega \rightarrow \mathcal{R}$ be differentiable on Ω. If $\mathbf{x}^* \in \Omega$ is in the interior of Ω and $\nabla_{\mathbf{x}^*} V(\mathbf{x}^*) = \mathbf{0}_d$, then $\mathbf{x}^*$ is a *critical point* of V.

Definition: Local minimum.   Let Ω be a subset of $\mathcal{R}^d$ and let $\mathbf{x}^*$ be a point in the interior of Ω. Let V be a function such that $V: \Omega \rightarrow \mathcal{R}$. Let $N_{\mathbf{x}^*}$ be a δ-neighborhood of $\mathbf{x}^*$. If $V(\mathbf{y}) \geq V(\mathbf{x}^*)$ for all $\mathbf{y} \in N_{\mathbf{x}^*}$, then $\mathbf{x}^*$ is a *local minimum*. If $V(\mathbf{y}) > V(\mathbf{x}^*)$ for all $\mathbf{y} \in N_{\mathbf{x}^*}$ such that $\mathbf{y} \neq \mathbf{x}^*$, then $\mathbf{x}^*$ is a *strict local minimum*.

The following proposition provides a necessary but not sufficient condition for identifying local minima.

Proposition: Weak Local Minimum Test.   Let Ω be a subset of $\mathcal{R}^d$ and let $\mathbf{x}^*$ be a point in the interior of Ω. Let $V: \Omega \rightarrow \mathcal{R}$ have continuous second partial derivatives on Ω. If $\mathbf{x}^*$ is a local minimum, then $\mathbf{x}^*$ is a critical point.

Proof.   Let $\mathbf{g}(\mathbf{x}^*)$ be the gradient of V evaluated at $\mathbf{x}^*$. Expand V in a first-order Taylor expansion about $\mathbf{x}^*$ to obtain:

$$V(\mathbf{x}) = V(\mathbf{x}^*) + \mathbf{g}(\mathbf{x}^*)^T [\mathbf{x} - \mathbf{x}^*] + O(|\mathbf{x} - \mathbf{x}^*|^2) \tag{5.1}$$

because V has continuous second partial derivatives on Ω. Assume $\mathbf{x}^*$ is a local minimum and $\mathbf{g}(\mathbf{x}^*) \neq \mathbf{0}_d$. This implies that

$$V(\mathbf{x}) - V(\mathbf{x}^*) < 0$$

for at least one $\mathbf{x}$ sufficiently close to $\mathbf{x}^*$ which contradicts the definition of a local minimum. Therefore, if $\mathbf{x}^*$ is a local minimum, then $\mathbf{g}(\mathbf{x}^*)$ is a vector of zeros, implying $\mathbf{x}^*$ is a critical point.   ∎

The following proposition provides a set of necessary and sufficient conditions for identifying a point as a strict local minimum.

Proposition: Strict Local Minimum Test.   Let Ω be a subset of $\mathcal{R}^d$ and let $\mathbf{x}^*$ be a point in the interior of Ω. Let $V: \Omega \rightarrow \mathcal{R}$ have continuous third partial derivatives on Ω. The d-dimensional real vector $\mathbf{x}^*$ is a strict local minimum if and only if (i) $\mathbf{x}^* \in \mathcal{R}^d$ is a critical point of V, and (ii) the Hessian of V evaluated at $\mathbf{x}^*$ is positive definite.

Proof.   Let $\mathbf{g}(\mathbf{x}^*)$ be the gradient of V evaluated at $\mathbf{x}^*$. Assume that $\mathbf{g}(\mathbf{x}^*) = \mathbf{0}_d$ and let $\mathbf{H}(\mathbf{x}^*)$ be the Hessian of V evaluated at $\mathbf{x}^*$. Expand V (which has continuous third partial derivatives) in a Taylor expansion about $\mathbf{x}^*$ to obtain for some sufficiently small $\varepsilon = |\mathbf{x} - \mathbf{x}^*|$:

$$V(\mathbf{x}) = V(\mathbf{x}^*) + \mathbf{g}(\mathbf{x}^*)^T (\mathbf{x} - \mathbf{x}^*) \\ + (1/2)(\mathbf{x} - \mathbf{x}^*)^T \mathbf{H}(\mathbf{x}^*)(\mathbf{x} - \mathbf{x}^*) + O(\varepsilon^3). \tag{5.2}$$

If $\mathbf{x}^*$ is a strict local minimum, then some δ-neighborhood, $N_{\mathbf{x}^*}$, exists such that $V(\mathbf{x}) > V(\mathbf{x}^*)$ for all $\mathbf{x} \in N_{\mathbf{x}^*}$ such that $\mathbf{x} \neq \mathbf{x}^*$. Also by the Weak Local Minimum Test, it follows that $\mathbf{g}(\mathbf{x}^*) = \mathbf{0}_d$. From (5.2) it then immediately follows that the Hessian of V evaluated at $\mathbf{x}^*$ must be positive definite.

Now suppose that $\mathbf{g}(\mathbf{x}^*) = \mathbf{0}_d$ and that the Hessian of V evaluated at $\mathbf{x}^*$ is positive definite. Then, from (5.2), it immediately follows that $\mathbf{x}^*$ is a strict local minimum.   ∎

Definition: Global minimum.   Let $\Omega \subseteq \mathcal{R}^d$. Let $V: \Omega \rightarrow \mathcal{R}$. If for all $\mathbf{x} \in \Omega$: $V(\mathbf{x}^*) \leq V(\mathbf{x})$, then $\mathbf{x}^*$ is a *global minimum* on Ω. If for all $\mathbf{x} \in \Omega$ such that $\mathbf{x} \neq \mathbf{x}^*$: $V(\mathbf{x}^*) < V(\mathbf{x})$, then $\mathbf{x}^*$ is a *strict global minimum* on Ω.

Definition: Local and global maxima.   Let $\Omega \subseteq \mathcal{R}^d$. Let $V: \Omega \rightarrow \mathcal{R}$. If $\mathbf{x}^*$ is a (strict) local minimum of V on Ω, then $\mathbf{x}^*$ is a (strict) *local maximum* of $-V$ on Ω. If $\mathbf{x}^*$ is a (strict) global minimum of V on Ω, then $\mathbf{x}^*$ is a (strict) *global maximum* of $-V$ on Ω.

Examples of critical points, local minima and maxima, strict local minima and maxima, global minima and maxima, and strict global minima and maxima are shown in figure 5.1.

Some basic concepts of convex functions are now introduced. First, note that a *linear function* $V: \mathcal{R}^d \rightarrow \mathcal{R}$ is defined as a function with the properties that

1. $V(a\mathbf{x}) = aV(\mathbf{x})$ for all $\mathbf{x} \in \mathcal{R}^d$, and

2. $V(\mathbf{x}_1 + \mathbf{x}_2) = V(\mathbf{x}_1) + V(\mathbf{x}_2)$ for all $\mathbf{x}_1, \mathbf{x}_2 \in \mathcal{R}^d$.

Thus, if V is a linear function then for all $0 < a < 1$, and for all $\mathbf{x}_1, \mathbf{x}_2 \in \mathcal{R}^d$:

$$V(\mathbf{y}(a)) = aV(\mathbf{x}_1) + (1 - a)V(\mathbf{x}_2), \tag{5.3}$$

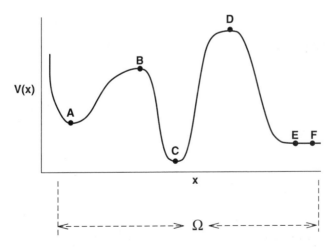

Figure 5.1
Local and global minima and maxima. The graph of the function V on Ω depicts local minima of V (points A, C, E, F), global minimum of V (point C) on Ω, local maxima of V (points B and D), global maximum of V on Ω (point D), and strict local minima (points A and C).

where

$$\mathbf{y}(a) = a\mathbf{x}_1 + (1 - a)\mathbf{x}_2.$$

Now a convex function, V, is defined as a function such that the value of V is less than or equal to a "linearized" version of V evaluated along *any* line segment in the function's domain. From this definition and (5.3), for all $0 < a < 1$:

$$V(\mathbf{y}(a)) \leq aV(\mathbf{x}_1) + (1 - a)V(\mathbf{x}_2), \tag{5.4}$$

where

$$\mathbf{y}(a) = a\mathbf{x}_1 + (1 - a)\mathbf{x}_2$$

for all $\mathbf{x}_1, \mathbf{x}_2 \in \mathcal{R}^d$. The concept of a convex function is illustrated in Figure 5.2.

Definition: Convex function on a convex region.   Let Ω be a convex region of $\mathcal{R}^d$. The function $V: \Omega \rightarrow \mathcal{R}$ is *convex* on Ω if for every $a \in (0, 1)$:

$$V(a\mathbf{x}_1 + (1 - a)\mathbf{x}_2) \leq aV(\mathbf{x}_1) + (1 - a)V(\mathbf{x}_2)$$

for all $\mathbf{x}_1, \mathbf{x}_2 \in \Omega$. The function V is *strictly convex* if for every $a \in (0, 1)$:

$$V(a\mathbf{x}_1 + (1 - a)\mathbf{x}_2) < aV(\mathbf{x}_1) + (1 - a)V(\mathbf{x}_2)$$

for all $\mathbf{x}_1, \mathbf{x}_2 \in \Omega$.

A "bowl-shaped" function is therefore an example of a *convex function*. Identifying convex functions is important because any critical point of a convex function is a global minimum of the function. Thus, if one can prove that an algorithm will generate a sequence of states which converge to a critical point of a convex function, then one has demonstrated that the trajectory of the algorithm will converge to a global minimum of the function.

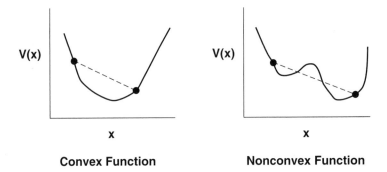

Figure 5.2
Convex and nonconvex functions. A convex function, V, is defined as a function such that the value of V is less than or equal to a "linearized" version of V evaluated along *any* line segment (e.g., dashed line in figure) connecting two points in the function's domain.

If the Hessian of a convex function exists on a convex region, then an alternative but equivalent definition of a convex function is useful. This equivalent definition is essentially the multivariate generalization of the observation in univariate calculus that a function $V: \mathcal{R} \rightarrow \mathcal{R}$ whose second derivative is positive everywhere is convex. For example, if $V(x) = x^2$, then the second derivative of V is the strictly positive number 2 regardless of x.

Theorem: Convex Function on a Convex Region.   Let Ω be a convex region of $\mathcal{R}^d$. Let $V: \Omega \rightarrow \mathcal{R}$ have continuous second partial derivatives on Ω. The function V is convex on Ω if and only if the Hessian of V is positive semidefinite everywhere on Ω. The function V is strictly convex on Ω if and only if the Hessian of V is positive definite everywhere on Ω.

Proof.   See Luenberger (1984, 180).   ■

Given the above definitions of a convex function and a convex region, the following theorem for identifying the unique strict global minimum of a convex function can be stated and proved.

Theorem: Strict Global Minimum Test.   Let $\Omega \subseteq \mathcal{R}^d$. Let $V: \Omega \rightarrow \mathcal{R}$ be a convex function on the convex region Ω. Let $\mathbf{x}^*$ be a point in the interior of Ω. If $\mathbf{x}^*$ is a strict local minimum of V, then $\mathbf{x}^*$ is the unique strict global minimum on Ω.

Proof.   Let $\mathbf{x}^*$ be a strict local minimum of some convex function V on Ω. Also suppose there exists a $\mathbf{y}$ such that $V(\mathbf{y}) \leq V(\mathbf{x}^*)$. Then because V is convex for every $a \in (0, 1)$,

$$V(a\mathbf{y} + (1 - a)\mathbf{x}^*) \leq aV(\mathbf{y}) + (1 - a)V(\mathbf{x}^*).$$

Since $V(\mathbf{y}) \leq V(\mathbf{x}^*)$,

$$aV(\mathbf{y}) + (1 - a)V(\mathbf{x}^*) \leq V(\mathbf{x}^*)$$

for every $a \in (0, 1)$. Thus, for every $a \in (0, 1)$:

$$V(a\mathbf{y} + (1 - a)\mathbf{x}^*) \leq V(\mathbf{x}^*),$$

which is equivalent to

$$V(\mathbf{x}^* + a(\mathbf{y} - \mathbf{x}^*)) \leq V(\mathbf{x}^*). \tag{5.5}$$

Because every $a \in (0, 1)$ satisfies it, equation (5.5) contradicts the assumption that $\mathbf{x}^*$ is a strict local minimum.   ■

One important application of the above definitions and theorems is that they provide important insights into the criteria for (1) stopping a search algorithm, and (2) interpreting the answer of a search algorithm. Most convergence theorems simply prove that a sequence of states $\mathbf{x}(1), \mathbf{x}(2), \mathbf{x}(3),\dots$ generated by a search algorithm will converge to a critical point, $\mathbf{x}^*$, of the objective function V. Such theorems do not prove that $\mathbf{x}(t)$ will actually *reach* that critical point. Thus the problem of deciding when a given estimate $\mathbf{x}(t)$ is sufficiently close to $\mathbf{x}^*$ must be considered. This practical problem can be addressed in several ways. If $\mathbf{x}(1)$, $\mathbf{x}(2)$, $\mathbf{x}(3)$,... is converging to an equilibrium point, then $|\mathbf{x}(t+1) - \mathbf{x}(t)|$ must converge to zero as $t \to \infty$. Thus a stopping criterion based upon the quantity $|\mathbf{x}(t+1) - \mathbf{x}(t)|$ can be developed. One problem with this type of stopping criterion, however, is that the condition for stopping is dependent upon the convergence properties of the algorithm. A better method for deciding when $\mathbf{x}(t)$ is sufficiently close to $\mathbf{x}^*$ is to compute the gradient of V. If some norm of the gradient evaluated at the point $\mathbf{x}(t)$ is sufficiently small, then one may conclude that $\mathbf{x}(t)$ is sufficiently close to $\mathbf{x}^*$. It is also useful to compute the eigenvalues of the Hessian of V evaluated at $\mathbf{x}(t)$. If these eigenvalues are also strictly positive, then the Hessian is positive definite. Thus, by the Strict Local Minimum Test, if the gradient of V evaluated at $\mathbf{x}(t)$ is close to zero and the Hessian of V evaluated at $\mathbf{x}(t)$ is positive definite, then this is a good indication that $\mathbf{x}(t)$ is close to a strict local minimum. Finally, if it is known that the function V is a convex function and $\mathbf{x}(t)$ is close to a strict local minimum, then this means that $\mathbf{x}(t)$ is close to the *unique* strict global minimum.

5.2   Deterministic Nonlinear Optimization

5.2.1   Descent Algorithms

Most deterministic nonlinear optimization algorithms which occur frequently in the classical nonlinear optimization literature and the ANN literature can be expressed formally as members of the following class of algorithms.

Definition: Descent algorithm.   Assume $V: \mathcal{R}^d \to \mathcal{R}$ has continuous second partial derivatives on $\mathcal{R}^d$. Let $\mathbf{g}: \mathcal{R}^d \to \mathcal{R}^d$ be the gradient of V. Assume there exists a sequence of d-dimensional real vectors $\mathbf{x}(0)$, $\mathbf{x}(1)$,... such that for $t = 0, 1, 2,...$:

$$\mathbf{x}(t+1) = \mathbf{x}(t) + \gamma_t \mathbf{f}(t), \tag{5.6}$$

where the *stepsize* $\gamma_t \in (0, \infty)$ and the *descent direction* $\mathbf{f}(t) \in \mathcal{R}^d$ satisfies either (i)

$$\mathbf{g}(\mathbf{x}(t))^T \mathbf{f}(t) < 0, \tag{5.7}$$

or (ii) $|\mathbf{g}(\mathbf{x}(t))| = |\mathbf{f}(t)| = 0$. The difference equation in (5.6) is a *descent algorithm* defined with respect to the *objective function V* generating the sequence $\mathbf{x}(0)$, $\mathbf{x}(1)$,....

Note that the algorithm in (5.6) cannot be analyzed using the techniques described in chapter 3 because it is *not* an autonomous (i.e., time-invariant) discrete-time dynamical system as defined in chapter 3. The reason why the algorithm in (5.6) is called a "descent algorithm" will be clear from the following proposition, which states (under general conditions) that at each iteration of the descent algorithm a stepsize γ_t can be found such that the value of V decreases or does not change.

Proposition: Descent Algorithm Proposition. Assume $V: \mathcal{R}^d \to \mathcal{R}$ has continuous second partial derivatives on $\mathcal{R}^d$. Let $\mathbf{g}: \mathcal{R}^d \to \mathcal{R}^d$ be the gradient of V. Assume there exists a sequence of d-dimensional real vectors $\mathbf{x}(0), \mathbf{x}(1),\ldots$ with the property that for $t = 0, 1, 2,\ldots$:

$$\mathbf{x}(t + 1) = \mathbf{x}(t) + \gamma_t \mathbf{f}(t),$$

where $\gamma_t \in (0, \infty)$, and $\mathbf{f}(t) \in \mathcal{R}^d$ are defined such that either: (i) $\mathbf{g}(\mathbf{x}(t))^T \mathbf{f}(t) < 0$, or (ii) $|\mathbf{g}(\mathbf{x}(t))| = |\mathbf{f}(t)| = 0$. Then for each $t = 0, 1, 2,\ldots$, there exists a γ_t such that if $\mathbf{x}(t + 1) \neq \mathbf{x}(t)$:

$$V(\mathbf{x}(t + 1)) < V(\mathbf{x}(t)).$$

Proof. Expand V in a Taylor expansion about the point $\mathbf{x}(t)$ and evaluate at $\mathbf{x}(t + 1)$ to obtain for some sufficiently small strictly positive real number γ_t:

$$V(\mathbf{x}(t + 1)) = V(\mathbf{x}(t)) + \mathbf{g}(\mathbf{x}(t))^T (\mathbf{x}(t + 1) - \mathbf{x}(t)) + O(\gamma_t^2),$$

where $\mathbf{g}(\mathbf{x}(t))$ is the gradient of V evaluated at $\mathbf{x}(t)$. For the case $\mathbf{x}(t + 1) \neq \mathbf{x}(t)$, it is possible to choose a γ_t such that:

$$V(\mathbf{x}(t + 1)) < V(\mathbf{x}(t))$$

since

$$\mathbf{g}(\mathbf{x}(t))^T (\mathbf{x}(t + 1) - \mathbf{x}(t)) = \gamma_t \mathbf{g}(\mathbf{x}(t))^T \mathbf{f}(t) < 0. \quad \blacksquare$$

5.2.2   Stepsize Selection Strategies

Equation (5.6) may be viewed as a heuristic search algorithm designed to update $\mathbf{x}(t)$ such that the revised estimate $\mathbf{x}(t + 1)$ is closer to the global minimum, where distance to the global minimum at point $\mathbf{x}$ is given by $V(\mathbf{x})$. There are some problems, however, with this heuristic search algorithm. These problems arise because the restrictions on the stepsize sequence $\gamma_0, \gamma_1,\ldots$ are relatively weak and must be at least slightly strengthened.

In particular, if γ_t is chosen to be too large for some iteration t, then V may increase in value as illustrated in figure 5.3. On the other hand, if the sequence $\gamma_1, \gamma_2,\ldots$ converges too rapidly, then the algorithm may take a long time to converge, and may not even converge to a critical point of the function V (figure 5.3). For example, suppose that $\gamma_t = 1/t^{10}$. Clearly in this case, the sequence

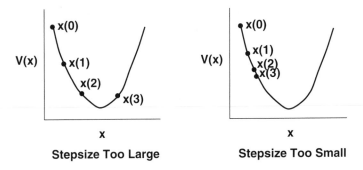

Figure 5.3
If stepsize is too small or too big. If the stepsize of the descent algorithm is chosen to be too large
(or constant), then the algorithm may be unable to converge to a strict local minimum. If the stepsize of the descent algorithm is chosen to decrease too rapidly, then the algorithm may not even
converge to a critical point!

$\{\gamma_t\}$ would most likely converge to zero before the sequence of states generated
by the algorithm in (5.6) converged to a critical point.

The "Properly Chosen" Stepsize Strategy

Fortunately, appropriate bounds upon γ_t can be computed using only informa-
tion about the value of V at $\mathbf{x}(t)$ and the first derivative of V at $\mathbf{x}(t)$. It will be
shown in section 5.2.3 that, if the stepsize is chosen at each iteration of a descent
algorithm to satisfy these bounds, then a result concerning the asymptotic behavior of the descent algorithm under consideration may be directly obtained.

The basic idea for this approach is based upon the work of Wolfe (1969,
1971) whose ideas were quite similar to those of Armijo (1966). Dennis and
Schnabel (1983) and Luenberger (1984) provide good accessible reviews of
this literature. Battiti (1989, 1992) provides a good review of these issues from
an ANN perspective. Using the approach of Wolfe (1969, 1971; as reviewed by
Dennis and Schnabel 1983), some weak constraints on the sequence of stepsizes are now introduced. It will be shown that, by choosing the stepsize of the
descent algorithm to satisfy these relatively weak constraints, convergence to a
critical point can be guaranteed.

The nonstandard terminology *properly chosen stepsize* is introduced for expository reasons. Wolfe (1969) has used the term *serious step,* which satisfies
even weaker constraints than the constraints presented here. In the nonlinear
optimization literature, selecting a good stepsize for a given iteration of a descent algorithm is usually referred to as a "line search procedure" because it involves searching for a particular point (i.e., the scalar stepsize) on some line or
line segment.

Definition: Properly chosen stepsize.   Assume $V: \mathfrak{R}^d \rightarrow \mathfrak{R}$ has continuous
second partial derivatives on $\mathfrak{R}^d$. Let $\mathbf{g}: \mathfrak{R}^d \rightarrow \mathfrak{R}^d$ be the gradient of V. Assume

there exists a sequence of d-dimensional real vectors $\mathbf{x}(0)$, $\mathbf{x}(1)$,... with the property that for $t = 0, 1, 2,...$:

$$\mathbf{x}(t + 1) = \mathbf{x}(t) + \gamma_t \mathbf{f}(t),$$

where $\gamma_t \in (0, \infty)$, and $\mathbf{f}(t) \in \mathcal{R}^d$ is defined such that $\mathbf{g}(\mathbf{x}(t))^T \mathbf{f}(t) \leq 0$. The step-size γ_t is *properly chosen* at iteration t for $t \in \{0, 1, 2,...\}$ if given $\mathbf{x}(t)$ and $\mathbf{f}(t)$:

$$V(\mathbf{x}(t) + \gamma_t \mathbf{f}(t)) \leq V(\mathbf{x}(t)) + a\gamma_t \mathbf{g}(\mathbf{x}(t))^T \mathbf{f}(t) \tag{5.8}$$

and

$$\mathbf{g}(\mathbf{x}(t) + \gamma_t \mathbf{f}(t))^T \mathbf{f}(t) \geq \beta\, \mathbf{g}(\mathbf{x}(t))^T \mathbf{f}(t) \tag{5.9}$$

are satisfied, where a and β are real numbers that satisfy

$$0 < a < \beta < 1.$$

A properly chosen stepsize γ_t satisfies both of the constraints in (5.8) and (5.9). It will be shown in section 5.2.3 that these constraints are sufficient to permit a fairly detailed convergence analysis of a very large class of descent algorithms. An important advantage of the concept of a properly chosen stepsize is that it gives the engineer considerable flexibility in the choice of the stepsize at each step of the algorithm.

One important question that needs to be addressed, however, is whether the constraints defined by (5.8) and (5.9) are really mutually consistent. That is, when does a γ_t exist such that γ_t is a properly chosen stepsize? Wolfe (1969, 1971) has explicitly identified the conditions for the existence of a properly chosen stepsize; the following theorem and proof is based upon the discussion of his research by Dennis and Schnabel (1983), although it should be emphasized that Wolfe's analysis is more general than the theorem stated and proved here.

Theorem: Properly Chosen Stepsize Existence.   Assume $V: \mathcal{R}^d \to \mathcal{R}$ has: (i) continuous second partial derivatives on $\mathcal{R}^d$, and (ii) a lower bound on $\mathcal{R}^d$. Let $\mathbf{g}: \mathcal{R}^d \to \mathcal{R}^d$ be the gradient of V. Let $t \in \{0, 1, 2,...\}$. Let $\mathbf{x}(t) \in \mathcal{R}^d$ and $\mathbf{x}(t + 1) \in \mathcal{R}^d$. Let

$$\mathbf{x}(t + 1) = \mathbf{x}(t) + \gamma_t \mathbf{f}(t),$$

where $\gamma_t \in (0, \infty)$, and $\mathbf{f}(t) \in \mathcal{R}^d$ is defined such that $\mathbf{g}(\mathbf{x}(t))^T \mathbf{f}(t) < 0$. Let a and β be positive real numbers defined as in (5.8) and (5.9) so that $0 < a < \beta < 1$. Then there exists strictly positive real numbers $\gamma_{\min}$ and $\gamma_{\max}$ ($\gamma_{\min} < \gamma_{\max}$) such that every $\gamma_t \in (\gamma_{\min}, \gamma_{\max})$ satisfies both (5.8) and (5.9).

Proof.   Let $\mathbf{x}(t + 1) = \mathbf{x}(t) + \gamma \mathbf{f}(t)$. Expand V in a Taylor Expansion about $\mathbf{x}(t)$ and use (5.8) to show that for all sufficiently small positive γ:

$$V(\mathbf{x}(t + 1)) \leq V(\mathbf{x}(t)) + a\gamma\, \mathbf{g}_t^T \mathbf{f}(t) \tag{5.10}$$

since $0 < a < 1$. Since V has a lower bound, and $a\mathbf{g}_t^T\mathbf{f}(t) < 0$, there exists a real positive number γ^* such that

$$V(\mathbf{x}^*) = V(\mathbf{x}(t)) + a\gamma^*\mathbf{g}_t^T\mathbf{f}(t) \tag{5.11}$$

where $\mathbf{x}^* = \mathbf{x}(t) + \gamma^*\mathbf{f}(t)$.

By the Taylor Expansion (Mean Value) Theorem, there exists a $\gamma_t \in (0, \gamma^*)$ such that:

$$V(\mathbf{x}^*) - V(\mathbf{x}(t)) = \mathbf{g}(\mathbf{x}(t) + \gamma_t\mathbf{f}(t))^T(\mathbf{x}^* - \mathbf{x}(t)),$$

$$V(\mathbf{x}^*) - V(\mathbf{x}(t)) = \mathbf{g}(\mathbf{x}(t) + \gamma_t\mathbf{f}(t))^T[\gamma^*\mathbf{f}(t)]. \tag{5.12}$$

Using (5.11), (5.12), and (5.9),

$$\mathbf{g}(\mathbf{x}(t) + \gamma_t\mathbf{f}(t))^T\mathbf{f}(t) = a\,\mathbf{g}_t^T\mathbf{f}(t) \geq \beta\,\mathbf{g}_t^T\mathbf{f}(t). \tag{5.13}$$

Note (5.13) is a consistent system of equations derived from both (5.8) and (5.9) since $\beta > a > 0$ and $\mathbf{g}_t^T\mathbf{f}(t) < 0$. Also note there exists an interval $(\gamma_{min}, \gamma_{max})$ where $\gamma_{max} < \gamma^*$ such that for all $\gamma_t \in (\gamma_{min}, \gamma_{max})$ (5.13) is satisfied because $\mathbf{g}$ is continuous. ∎

Equation (5.8) is essentially a check to see if the stepsize γ_t in (5.6) is too large. Equation (5.9) is essentially a check to see if the stepsize γ_t in (5.6) is too small. Let $\mathbf{x}(t + 1) = \mathbf{x}(t) + \gamma_t\mathbf{f}(t)$. Expand V in a Taylor Expansion about $\mathbf{x}(t + 1)$ and evaluate at $\mathbf{x}(t)$ to obtain:

$$V(\mathbf{x}(t)) - V(\mathbf{x}(t + 1)) = \mathbf{g}(\mathbf{x}(t + 1))^T[\mathbf{x}(t) - \mathbf{x}(t + 1)] + O(\gamma_t^2),$$

$$V(\mathbf{x}(t + 1)) - V(\mathbf{x}(t)) = \gamma_t\mathbf{g}(\mathbf{x}(t) + \gamma_t\mathbf{f}(t))^T\mathbf{f}(t) + O(\gamma_t^2). \tag{5.14}$$

Thus, (5.10), (5.13), and (5.14) imply that if γ_t is properly chosen and $\mathbf{g}_t^T\mathbf{f}(t) < 0$:

$$\gamma_t\beta\mathbf{g}_t^T\mathbf{f}(t) \leq V(\mathbf{x}(t + 1)) - V(\mathbf{x}(t)) \leq a\gamma_t\mathbf{g}_t^T\mathbf{f}(t). \tag{5.15}$$

Thus, (5.15) shows that (5.9) prevents the objective function value from decreasing too slowly while (5.8) prevents the objective function value from decreasing too rapidly.

It is also worth noting that (5.15) suggests that if the size of the interval $[a, \beta]$ is larger, then the choice of the stepsize γ_t at each iteration is less constrained. Dennis and Schnabel (1983) suggest a fairly small value for a such as $a = 10^{-4}$. A relatively large value of β (subject to the constraint that $\beta < 1$) may be chosen so that the choice of the stepsize γ_t is less constrained.

The "Optimal Stepsize" Search Strategy

Another important stepsize search strategy is now introduced, where one selects an "optimal stepsize" such that at each iteration of the descent algorithm, the stepsize is chosen to decrease the objective function's value as rapidly as possible.

Definition: Optimal stepsize.   Assume $V: \mathcal{R}^d \to \mathcal{R}$ has continuous second partial derivatives on $\mathcal{R}^d$. Let $\mathbf{g}: \mathcal{R}^d \to \mathcal{R}^d$ be the gradient of V. Assume there exists a sequence of d-dimensional real vectors $\mathbf{x}(0), \mathbf{x}(1),\ldots$ with the property that for $t = 0, 1, 2,\ldots$:

$$\mathbf{x}(t+1) = \mathbf{x}(t) + \gamma_t \mathbf{f}(t),$$

where $\gamma_t \in (0, \infty)$, and $\mathbf{f}(t) \in \mathcal{R}^d$ is defined such that $\mathbf{g}(\mathbf{x}(t))^T \mathbf{f}(t) \leq 0$. For all $t \in \{0, 1, 2,\ldots\}$: the stepsize γ_t is *optimal* on $(0, \Omega]$ if

$$V(\mathbf{x}(t) + \gamma \mathbf{f}(t)) \geq V(\mathbf{x}(t) + \gamma_t \mathbf{f}(t))$$

for all $\gamma \in (0, \Omega]$, where $\Omega \in (0, \infty)$.

A number of researchers have demonstrated the computational advantage of an optimal stepsize strategy for specific ANN algorithms such as backpropagation (Battiti 1989, 1992; Hagan and Menhaj 1994; Jones, Lustig, and Kornhauser 1990; Kramer and Sangiovanni-Vincentelli 1989; Møller 1990; Watrous 1987). Still, because an optimal stepsize search strategy tends to not be very exact in extremely high-dimensional state spaces (without additional computational costs), the properly chosen stepsize analysis is still relevant for investigating the behavior of descent algorithms that do not *exactly* compute the optimal stepsize at each algorithm iteration. The convergence theorem for descent algorithms with properly chosen stepsizes described in the next section thus provides a robust convergence analysis of inexact optimal stepsize search methods, as well as algorithms where the stepsize is *not* optimal at each algorithm iteration.

5.2.3   A Convergence Theorem for Descent Algorithms

This section introduces a convergence theorem for descent algorithms that exploits the concept of a properly chosen stepsize introduced in the previous section. The theorem identifies explicit conditions for the sequence of states generated by a descent algorithm to converge to a critical point of the objective function. Once a critical point has been identified, then tests such as the *strict local minimum test* and the *strict global minimum test* may be used to possibly identify the nature of the critical point.

Given this perspective on the nonlinear optimization problem, suppose that we are content to investigate the conditions under which the sequence of states generated by a descent algorithm with a properly chosen stepsize will always converge to a critical point. Is the discrete-time Invariant Set Theorem applicable? Why is another convergence theorem required to analyze the asymptotic behavior of a descent algorithm that is a discrete-time dynamical system?

The reason why a new convergence theorem is required is that the quantity $\gamma_t \mathbf{f}(t)$ is time-variant. In particular, $\gamma_t \mathbf{f}(t)$ is not necessarily (but certainly could be) a continuous function of the system state $\mathbf{x}(t)$. Fortunately, Wolfe (1969, 1971; also see Armijo 1966 and Goldstein 1966 for related work) has investigated the explicit conditions under which descent algorithms with properly chosen stepsizes will converge to the critical points of V.

The main theorem of this chapter, which will be referred to as the "Descent Algorithm Convergence Theorem," provides a set of explicit conditions for a sequence of vectors generated by a descent algorithm to converge to the critical point of a given objective function. Before presenting the theorem and its proof, which are based upon research by Wolfe (1969, 1971) as reviewed by Dennis and Schnabel (1983), two useful definitions are provided.

Definition: Row matrix norm.   If $\mathbf{H}$ is a d-dimensional matrix whose jth row is the row vector $\mathbf{h}_j^T$ $(j = 1 \ldots d)$, then the *row matrix norm* $|\mathbf{H}|_r$ is the least upper bound for the set: $\{|\mathbf{h}_1|, \ldots, |\mathbf{h}_d|\}$.

Definition: Function bounded on a sequence.   A matrix-valued function $\mathbf{H} \colon \mathcal{R}^d \to \mathcal{R}^{d \times d}$ is *bounded on the sequence* of d-dimensional vectors $\mathbf{x}(0)$, $\mathbf{x}(1), \ldots$ if there exists some finite positive constant K such that $|\mathbf{H}(\mathbf{x}(t))|_r < K$ for $t = 0, 1, 2, \ldots$.

Theorem: Descent Algorithm Convergence Theorem.   Assume $V \colon \mathcal{R}^d \to \mathcal{R}$ has (i) continuous second partial derivatives on $\mathcal{R}^d$, and (ii) a lower bound on $\mathcal{R}^d$. Let $\mathbf{g} \colon \mathcal{R}^d \to \mathcal{R}^d$ be the gradient of V. Assume there exists a sequence of d-dimensional real vectors $\mathbf{x}(0)$, $\mathbf{x}(1), \ldots$ such that for $t = 0, 1, 2, \ldots$:

$$\mathbf{x}(t + 1) = \mathbf{x}(t) + \gamma_t \mathbf{f}(t),$$

where γ_t is a properly chosen stepsize as defined by (5.8) and (5.9), with respect to V, and either (i) $\mathbf{g}(\mathbf{x}(t))^T \mathbf{f}(t) < 0$, or (ii) $|\mathbf{g}(\mathbf{x}(t))| = |\mathbf{f}(t)| = 0$. Let

$$\rho_t = \left[\frac{\mathbf{g}(\mathbf{x}(t))}{|\mathbf{g}(\mathbf{x}(t))|}\right]^T \left[\frac{\mathbf{f}(t)}{|\mathbf{f}(t)|}\right].$$

Then either: (i) $|\mathbf{g}(\mathbf{x}(t))| \to 0$ as $t \to \infty$, (ii) $\rho_t \to 0$ as $t \to \infty$, or (iii) the sequence $\mathbf{x}(0)$, $\mathbf{x}(1), \ldots$ is not bounded. Moreover, if the Hessian of V is bounded on the sequence $\mathbf{x}(0)$, $\mathbf{x}(1), \ldots$, then either: (i) $|\mathbf{g}(\mathbf{x}(t))| \to 0$ as $t \to \infty$, or (ii) $\rho_t \to 0$ as $t \to \infty$.

Proof.   Let $\mathbf{g}_t = |\mathbf{g}(\mathbf{x}(t))|$. By the Properly Chosen Stepsize Existence Theorem, a properly chosen stepsize γ_t exists regardless of how $\mathbf{f}(t)$ is chosen, so let $|\mathbf{f}(t)| = 1$ for all nonnegative t such that $\mathbf{x}(t + 1) \neq \mathbf{x}(t)$ without any loss in generality.

Using (5.8),

$$V(\mathbf{x}(n)) - V(\mathbf{x}(0)) = \sum_{t=0}^{n-1} [V(\mathbf{x}(t+1) - V(\mathbf{x}(t))] \leq \sum_{t=0}^{n-1} a\gamma_t \mathbf{g}_t^T \mathbf{f}(t).$$

Since V has a lower bound it follows that:

$$\lim_{n \to \infty} a \sum_{t=0}^{n-1} \gamma_t \mathbf{g}_t^T \mathbf{f}(t) \geq -C \tag{5.16}$$

where C is a strictly positive finite constant.

Since the sequence of summations in (5.16) converges (Rosenlicht 1968, 143), Corollary 1 of Rosenlicht (1968, 142) implies that as $t \to \infty$: $\gamma_t \mathbf{g}_t^T \mathbf{f}(t) \to 0$.

It is now necessary to show that as $t \to \infty$, $\mathbf{g}_t^T \mathbf{f}(t) \to 0$. From (5.9),

$$\mathbf{g}_{t+1}^T \mathbf{f}(t) \geq \beta \mathbf{g}_t^T \mathbf{f}(t) \tag{5.17}$$

and, therefore

$$[\mathbf{g}_{t+1} - \mathbf{g}_t]^T \mathbf{f}(t) \geq (\beta - 1)\mathbf{g}_t^T \mathbf{f}(t) > 0. \tag{5.18}$$

Now expand $\mathbf{g}$ in a multivariable Taylor expansion about $\mathbf{x}(t)$, and evaluate the resulting expression at $\mathbf{x}(t+1)$ to obtain

$$\mathbf{g}_{t+1} = \mathbf{g}_t + \mathbf{H}(\mathbf{c}_t)[\mathbf{x}(t+1) - \mathbf{x}(t)], \tag{5.19}$$

where $\mathbf{H}(\mathbf{c}_t)$ is the Hessian of V evaluated at some point $\mathbf{c}_t$ on the line segment, l_H, connecting $\mathbf{x}(t)$ and $\mathbf{x}(t+1)$.

Two cases are now considered. In the first case, suppose the Hessian of V, $\mathbf{H}$, is bounded on $\mathbf{x}(0)$, $\mathbf{x}(1),\dots$, so that a strictly positive finite constant $\mu > |\mathbf{H}(\mathbf{x}(t))|_r$ exists for $t = 0, 1, 2,\dots$. In the second case, suppose that the Hessian of V is not bounded. For this second case, if $\mathbf{x}(0)$, $\mathbf{x}(1),\dots$ is bounded, then the continuous Hessian of V is bounded on $\mathbf{x}(0)$, $\mathbf{x}(1),\dots$. Otherwise, the sequence $\mathbf{x}(0)$, $\mathbf{x}(1),\dots$ is not bounded and the theorem is proved. Thus, from the analysis of both the first and second cases, only the situation where the Hessian of V is bounded on the sequence $\{\mathbf{x}(t)\}$ needs to be considered.

Suppose the Hessian of V is bounded on the sequence $\{\mathbf{x}(t)\}$ with respect to the row matrix norm. Using the Cauchy-Schwarz inequality (i.e., $|\mathbf{a}||\mathbf{b}| \geq \mathbf{a}^T\mathbf{b}$), (5.19), and the assumption that the Hessian of V is bounded,

$$|\mathbf{g}_{t+1} - \mathbf{g}_t| \leq |\mathbf{H}(\mathbf{c}_t)|_r |\mathbf{x}(t+1) - \mathbf{x}(t)| \leq \mu |\mathbf{x}(t+1) - \mathbf{x}(t)|. \tag{5.20}$$

Now using the relation $\mathbf{x}(t+1) - \mathbf{x}(t) = \gamma_t \mathbf{f}(t)$ and the convenient assumption $|\mathbf{f}(t)| = 1$, (5.20) yields

$$\mu\gamma_t \geq |\mathbf{g}_{t+1} - \mathbf{g}_t|. \tag{5.21}$$

Using (5.18), (5.21), and the Cauchy-Schwarz inequality,

$$\mu\gamma_t \geq \left|\mathbf{g}_{t+1} - \mathbf{g}_t\right|\left|\mathbf{f}(t)\right| \geq [\mathbf{g}_{t+1} - \mathbf{g}_t]^T\mathbf{f}(t) \geq (\beta - 1)\mathbf{g}_t^T\mathbf{f}(t). \qquad (5.22)$$

Dividing both sides of (5.22) by μ gives

$$\gamma_t \geq \frac{(\beta - 1)\mathbf{g}_t^T\mathbf{f}(t)}{\mu}.$$

Multiplying both sides by the negative quantity $\mathbf{g}_t^T\mathbf{f}(t)$ gives

$$\mathbf{g}_t^T\mathbf{f}(t)\gamma_t \leq (\beta - 1)\frac{[\mathbf{g}_t^T\mathbf{f}(t)]^2}{\mu}.$$

Taking the limit as $t \rightarrow \infty$:

$$0 = \lim_{t \rightarrow \infty}\mathbf{g}_t^T\mathbf{f}(t)\gamma_t \leq \lim_{t \rightarrow \infty}(\beta - 1)\frac{[\mathbf{g}_t^T\mathbf{f}(t)]^2}{\mu} \leq 0.$$

Therefore, $[\mathbf{g}_t^T\mathbf{f}(t)]^2 \rightarrow 0$ as $t \rightarrow \infty$, which implies that $\mathbf{g}_t^T\mathbf{f}(t) \rightarrow 0$ as $t \rightarrow \infty$.   ■

5.3   Stochastic Nonlinear Optimization

The Stochastic Approximation Theorem is a powerful tool for the analysis and design of stochastic nonlinear optimization algorithms as well as stochastic nonlinear dynamical systems. An important advantage of stochastic nonlinear optimization methods is that they sometimes provide useful heuristic techniques for escaping local minima and converging to "deeper" local minima or even global minima. Indeed, stochastic optimization methods form the basis of a set of techniques designed to develop algorithms that can converge to the set of global minima for nonconvex functions. The proof of such methods is beyond the scope of this book but some illustrative theorems can be stated.

The intuitive idea behind these methods is that a stochastic nonlinear optimization algorithm will eventually wander away from critical points and even strict local minima until it eventually converges to a strict global minimum that has no "directions of escape." Figure 5.4 illustrates this concept. Because an important application of this type of analysis arises in the field of statistical physics, the algorithm for generating the stepsize sequence is sometimes called the "annealing schedule" for the algorithm.

One basic practical problem with stochastic optimization algorithms designed to converge to global minima is that usually the time for the algorithm to converge as prescribed by the annealing schedule is too long for most practical applications. Nevertheless, inspection of such global optimization algorithms can provide important insights into heuristic methods for seeking "deeper" local minima.

One important global stochastic optimization algorithm that plays an important role in ANN system analysis and design is the *Gibbs sampler* developed by

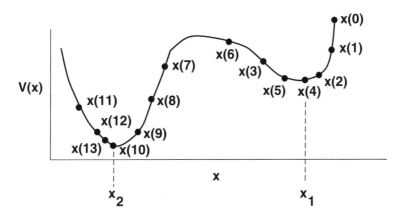

Figure 5.4
A stochastic algorithm wandering away from local minimum to global minimum. The stochastic search algorithm is initiated at the point $\mathbf{x}(0)$ and wanders toward the strict local minimum at point $\mathbf{x}_1$. After diverging briefly to point $\mathbf{x}(3)$, the algorithm returns to $\mathbf{x}(4)$ and still remains in some neighborhood of the strict local minimum $\mathbf{x}_1$ by iteration 5. At iteration 6, the algorithm wanders to the point $\mathbf{x}(6)$ and subsequently converges to the strict global minimum $\mathbf{x}(10)$. The algorithm tries to escape the strict global minimum, points $\mathbf{x}(11)$ and $\mathbf{x}(12)$, but eventually returns to the point $\mathbf{x}(13)$, close to the strict global minimum $\mathbf{x}_2$. It should be emphasized that this is a relatively naive example designed to emphasize how stochastic nonlinear optimization algorithms are *supposed* to work; in practice, such algorithms sometimes converge too slowly to the set of global minima. On the other hand, stochastic algorithms are usually more successful at seeking out "deeper" local minima than deterministic descent algorithms.

Geman and Geman (1984). This algorithm is relevant for analyzing an ANN system consisting of d units located at d "sites." Each unit at a site can take on only one of m possible activity levels. Each unit updates its activity level purely on the basis of the activity levels of the units in its neighborhood.

The activation updating dynamics of the Boltzmann machine ANN system and the harmony theory ANN systems may be viewed as important special cases of the Gibbs sampler algorithm. The following discussion will assume some familiarity with the Boltzmann machine ANN algorithm. If the reader is unfamiliar with this algorithm, then the material in chapter 2 describing the Boltzmann machine ANN algorithm should be reviewed at this point.

Consider a Boltzmann machine with d units where the activation level of the ith unit ($i = 1 \ldots d$) at iteration t is defined as the variable $x_i(t)$. The variable $x_i(t)$ is a binary-valued variable that can take on the value of zero or the value of one. The Boltzmann probability distribution assigns a probability mass to a particular activation pattern $\mathbf{x} = [x_1, \ldots, x_d]$ according to the formula

$$p_\tau(\mathbf{x}) = \left(1/Z_\tau\right) \exp\left[-\frac{V(\mathbf{x})}{\tau} \right], \tag{5.23}$$

where the positive number τ is referred to as the "temperature parameter,"

$$V(\mathbf{x}) = -\sum_{i=2}^{d}\sum_{j=1}^{i-1} x_i x_j w_{ij},$$

and

$$Z_\tau = \sum_{\mathbf{y}\in\{0,1\}^d} \exp\left[-\frac{V(\mathbf{y})}{\tau}\right].$$

The function $V: \mathfrak{R}^d \to \mathfrak{R}$ is called the "potential function" for the Boltzmann probability mass function $p_\tau(\mathbf{x})$. Define the $(d-1)$-dimensional vector

$$\mathbf{n}_i = [x_1,\ldots, x_{i-1}, x_{i+1},\ldots, x_d].$$

Now using the definition of a conditional probability, it follows that

$$p_\tau(x_i \mid \mathbf{n}_i) = \frac{p_\tau(\mathbf{x})}{p_{\mathbf{n}_i}(\mathbf{n}_i)}.$$

Let the real d-dimensional vector $\mathbf{q}_i(j)$ be defined such that

$$\mathbf{q}_i(j) = [x_1,\ldots, x_{i-1}, x_i = j, x_{i+1},\ldots, x_d].$$

Using this notation, note that $p_{\mathbf{n}_i}(\mathbf{n}_i)$ may be computed from $p_\tau(\mathbf{x})$ by the formula

$$p_{\mathbf{n}_i}(\mathbf{n}_i) = p_\tau(\mathbf{q}_i(1)) + p_\tau(\mathbf{q}_i(0)).$$

Thus

$$p_\tau(x_i = 1 \mid \mathbf{n}_i) = \frac{p_\tau(\mathbf{q}_i(1))}{p_\tau(\mathbf{q}_i(1)) + p_\tau(\mathbf{q}_i(0))}$$

reduces after some algebra (see problem 5-10) to the local conditional probability

$$p_\tau(x_i = 1 \mid \mathbf{n}_i) = \mathscr{S}\left[\frac{\sum_{j=1, j\neq i}^{d} w_{ij} x_j}{\tau}\right], \tag{5.24}$$

where $\mathscr{S}: \mathfrak{R} \to (0,1)$ is defined such that $\mathscr{S}(x) = 1/(1 + \exp[-x])$.

The Boltzmann machine algorithm works by first setting up the set of connection strengths $\{w_{ij}\}$ in order to model a desired set of constraints among the unit activation levels. The temperature parameter τ is then set to some large positive value, which will be called τ_0. At each iteration of the algorithm, one of the d units is chosen at random. Suppose unit number i ($i = 1\ldots d$) is chosen at iteration t of the algorithm. Let the activation level of unit i that was randomly chosen on the tth iteration of the algorithm be referred to as $x_i(t)$. Then $x_i(t) = 1$ with probability $p(x_i(t) = 1 \mid \mathbf{n}_i)$ and $x_i(t) = 0$ with probability $1 - p(x_i(t) = 1 \mid \mathbf{n}_i)$.

After updating the activation level of a unit, the temperature parameter τ is changed according to some annealing schedule so that τ is assigned some new value τ_t. Another unit is then chosen at random and this process is repeated an infinite number of times. Geman and Geman (1984) proved with an appropriate annealing schedule that this type of algorithm will generate a stochastic sequence $\tilde{\mathbf{x}}(0)$, $\tilde{\mathbf{x}}(1)$,..., which will converge in distribution to a random vector $\tilde{\mathbf{x}}^*$ whose values are elements of the set of global minima of V.

A version of the Geman and Geman (1984) Gibbs sampler algorithm is now formally presented, using a notation similar to the above description of the Boltzmann machine. Note that the Geman and Geman algorithm is much more general than the Boltzmann machine algorithm because the potential function V can be almost arbitrarily chosen.

Algorithm: Gibbs sampler.   Let m and d be positive finite integers. Let S be a set of m^d vectors such that each element of S is a d-dimensional state vector, $\mathbf{x} = [x_1,..., x_d] \in \{1, 2, 3,... m\}^d$. Assume the *potential function* $V: S \rightarrow \mathcal{R}$ has the property that

$$Z = \sum_{\mathbf{y} \in S} V(\mathbf{y})$$

exists. Let the *annealing schedule* τ_1, τ_2,... be a sequence of strictly positive real numbers. Define $p_{\tau_t}: \{1,..., m\}^d \rightarrow (0, \infty)$ such that for all $\mathbf{x} \in \{1,... m\}^d$:

$$p_{\tau_t}(\mathbf{x}) = (1/Z) \exp\left[-V(\mathbf{x})/\tau_t\right]. \tag{5.25}$$

- Step 0: Initialization. Let $t = 0$. Choose any value for $\mathbf{x}(0)$ such that $\mathbf{x}(0) \in \{1,... m\}^d$.
- Step 1: Pick unit at random. Let the unit i be chosen where $i = IRANDOM$ $(1, m, t)$.
- Step 2: Update activation level of selected unit. Let

$$\mathbf{n}_i(t) = \{x_1(t),..., x_{i-1}(t), x_{i+1}(t),..., x_d(t)\}.$$

Let

$$q_{it}(j) = V(x_1(t),..., x_{i-1}(t), x_i(t) = j, x_{i+1}(t),..., x_d(t)).$$

Compute

$$p_{\tau_t}(x_i = k \mid \mathbf{n}_i(t)) = \frac{\exp\left[-q_{it}(k)/\tau_t\right]}{\sum_{j=1}^{m} \exp\left[-q_{it}(j)/\tau_t\right]}$$

for $k = 1... m$. Let $x_i(t + 1) = k$ with probability $p_{\tau_t}(x_i = k \mid \mathbf{n}_i(t))$.
- Step 3: Let $t = t + 1$. Go to step 1.

Theorem: Gibbs Sampler Convergence Theorem. Let $S = \{1, 2,..., m\}^d$. Let $V: S \rightarrow \mathcal{R}$ be a potential function for a Gibbs sampler algorithm with annealing schedule $\tau_1, \tau_2,...$ that generates the stochastic sequence $\{\tilde{\mathbf{x}}(t)\}$. Let V_{max} and V_{min} be the respective maximum and minimum values of V on S. Assume that (i) as $t \rightarrow \infty$, $\tau_t \rightarrow 0$, and (ii) for $t = 2, 3, 4,...$:

$$\tau_t \geq \frac{|V_{max} - V_{min}|d}{\log[t]}.$$

Let $\mathcal{H}$ be the set of all G global minima of V on $\{1,..., m\}^d$. Let $\tilde{\mathbf{x}}^*$ be a random vector whose uniform probability mass function is $p_{\tilde{\mathbf{x}}^*} \colon \mathcal{H} \rightarrow \{1/G\}$. Then $\tilde{\mathbf{x}}(1), \tilde{\mathbf{x}}(2),...$ converges in distribution to $\tilde{\mathbf{x}}^*$.

Proof. See Geman and Geman (1984, Theorem B). ■

5.4   Convergence Rate Analysis

Consider a discrete-time dynamical system algorithm that generates a sequence of points $\mathbf{x}(1)$, $\mathbf{x}(2)$, $\mathbf{x}(3)$ converging to some point $\mathbf{x}^*$. How might one measure the speed or rate of convergence of a particular algorithm? Although this is a difficult question to answer directly, some insights into the speed of convergence of such algorithms can usually be obtained when the algorithm is initiated very close to its asymptotic state, that is, when $\mathbf{x}(1)$ is very close to $\mathbf{x}^*$. In particular, the asymptotic convergence rate of an algorithm is usually obtained using the following procedure (Luenberger 1984). First, construct some computationally convenient objective function that maps $\mathbf{x}(t)$ into some scalar $V(\mathbf{x}(t))$. The natural choice of such an objective function would be either the *classification objective function* if $\mathbf{x}$ is an activation pattern or the *learning objective function* if $\mathbf{x}$ is a pattern of connection strengths. Still, other choices of $V(\mathbf{x}(t))$ may be appropriate if they are still meaningful yet more computationally tractable. Second, study the speed at which $\mathbf{x}(t)$ approaches $\mathbf{x}^*$ using a measure such as $|V(\mathbf{x}(t)) - V(\mathbf{x}^*)|$. With this introduction, the formal definition of the convergence rate of an algorithm is now provided following the approach of Luenberger (1984, 190).

Definition: Convergence rate. Let $V: \mathcal{R}^d \rightarrow \mathcal{R}$. Let $\mathbf{x}^*$ be a strict local minimum of V. Suppose a descent algorithm with objective function V generates a sequence of real d-dimensional vectors $\mathbf{x}(1)$, $\mathbf{x}(2),...$, which converges to $\mathbf{x}^*$. Let ρ be a finite real number. Assume there exists a unique positive real number Q such that:

$$Q = \sup\left\{q \in (0, \infty): \lim_{t \rightarrow \infty} \frac{|V(\mathbf{x}(t + 1)) - V(\mathbf{x}^*)|}{|V(\mathbf{x}(t)) - V(\mathbf{x}^*)|^q} = \rho\right\}. \tag{5.26}$$

Then the descent algorithm which generates the sequence $\{\mathbf{x}(t)\}$ has a *convergence rate of order Q* with respect to V. Moreover, if $Q = 1$, then the algorithm *converges linearly* with *convergence ratio p*. Finally, if the algorithm converges linearly with convergence ratio $p = 0$, then the algorithm *converges superlinearly*.

To illustrate the concept of the convergence rate of an algorithm, consider a descent algorithm that generates a sequence of d-dimensional real vectors $\mathbf{x}(0)$, $\mathbf{x}(1)$, $\mathbf{x}(2)$,... that converges to some vector $\mathbf{x}^* \in \mathcal{R}^d$. Suppose one could prove that the objective function $V: \mathcal{R}^d \rightarrow \mathcal{R}$ has the property that in some δ-neighborhood of $\mathbf{x}^*$

$$[V(\mathbf{x}(t+1)) - V(\mathbf{x}^*)] = \rho[V(\mathbf{x}(t)) - V(\mathbf{x}^*)]^Q$$

for $0 \leq \rho < 1$ and $Q \geq 0$. If $Q = 2$, then the descent algorithm has a convergence rate of order two in some neighborhood of $\mathbf{x}^*$. If $Q = 1$, then the descent algorithm converges linearly in some neighborhood of $\mathbf{x}^*$ with convergence ratio ρ.

Note that this definition of convergence rate may be extended to the class of stochastic discrete-time nonlinear optimization algorithms. To see this, first rewrite the stochastic discrete-time dynamical system as a deterministic discrete-time dynamical system driven by noise. This can always be done for the set of stochastic discrete-time dynamical systems considered in this chapter. Then investigate the convergence rate of the deterministic component of the stochastic system by assuming the variance of the noise is zero. Although such a convergence analysis is purely heuristic, valuable insights into the convergence properties of the stochastic dynamical system can sometimes be obtained.

5.5 Classical and ANN Applications

5.5.1 Classical Optimization Algorithms

This section will analyze a very important special type of descent algorithm called the "modified Newton algorithm" (Luenberger 1984). Most classical nonlinear optimization algorithms relevant to ANN system analysis and design problems can be viewed as special cases of the modified Newton algorithm.

Definition: Modified Newton algorithm.   Assume $V: \mathcal{R}^d \rightarrow \mathcal{R}$ has continuous second partial derivatives. Let $\mathbf{g}: \mathcal{R}^d \rightarrow \mathcal{R}^d$ be the gradient of V. Let $\mathbf{Q}(0)$, $\mathbf{Q}(1)$, $\mathbf{Q}(2)$... be a sequence of real positive definite square d-dimensional matrices. Let $\mathbf{x}(0)$, $\mathbf{x}(1)$, $\mathbf{x}(2)$... be a sequence of real d-dimensional vectors. A *modified Newton algorithm* is a descent algorithm whose difference equation is defined for $t = 0, 1, 2,...$ by:

$$\mathbf{x}(t+1) = \mathbf{x}(t) + \gamma_t \mathbf{f}(t)$$

and where the positive real number γ_t is a properly chosen stepsize and the real d-dimensional descent direction vector

$$\mathbf{f}(t) = -\mathbf{Q}(t)\mathbf{g}(\mathbf{x}(t)).$$

Theorem: Modified Newton Convergence.   Let $\mathbf{Q}(1)$, $\mathbf{Q}(2)$,... be a sequence of real symmetric positive definite d-dimensional matrices with the property that there exist strictly positive finite real numbers μ_{min} and μ_{max} such that for $t = 0, 1, 2,...$: The minimum eigenvalue of $\mathbf{Q}(t)$ is greater than μ_{min} and the maximum eigenvalue of $\mathbf{Q}(t)$ is less than μ_{max}. Let $\gamma_1, \gamma_2,...$ be a sequence of properly chosen positive stepsizes as in (5.8) and (5.9). Let $V: \mathcal{R}^d \rightarrow \mathcal{R}$ have (i) continuous second partial derivatives, and (ii) a lower bound on $\mathcal{R}^d$. Let $\mathbf{g}: \mathcal{R}^d \rightarrow \mathcal{R}^d$ be the gradient of V. Let the sequence of real d-dimensional vectors $\mathbf{x}(0)$, $\mathbf{x}(1)$, $\mathbf{x}(2)$,... be defined such that for $t = 0, 1, 2,...$:

$$\mathbf{x}(t+1) = \mathbf{x}(t) - \gamma_t \mathbf{Q}(t)\mathbf{g}(\mathbf{x}(t)). \tag{5.27}$$

Let $\mathcal{H}$ be the set of critical points of V. Then either (i) $\{\mathbf{x}(t)\}$ is not bounded, or (ii) $\mathbf{x}(t) \rightarrow \mathcal{H}$ as $t \rightarrow \infty$. If, in addition, the Hessian of V is bounded on $\mathbf{x}(0)$, $\mathbf{x}(1)$,..., then $\mathbf{x}(t) \rightarrow \mathcal{H}$ as $t \rightarrow \infty$.

Proof.   Let $\mathbf{g}_t = \mathbf{g}(\mathbf{x}(t))$. Let $\mathbf{f}(t) = -\mathbf{Q}(t)\mathbf{g}_t$. The theorem follows immediately from the direct application of the Descent Algorithm Convergence Theorem if it can be shown that:

$$\rho_t = [\mathbf{g}_t/|\mathbf{g}_t|]^T[\mathbf{f}(t)/|\mathbf{f}(t)|]$$

does not approach zero as $t \rightarrow \infty$ if $|\mathbf{g}_t| > 0$. Since

$$\rho_t = \frac{|\mathbf{g}_t^T \mathbf{Q}(t)\mathbf{g}_t|}{|\mathbf{g}_t||\mathbf{Q}(t)\mathbf{g}_t|} \geq (\mu_{min}/\mu_{max}) > 0,$$

$\rho_t \nrightarrow 0$ as $t \rightarrow \infty$. ∎

Steepest Descent Algorithm

Let $\mathbf{x}(1)$, $\mathbf{x}(2)$,... be a sequence of d-dimensional real vectors generated by the *gradient descent algorithm*

$$\mathbf{x}(t+1) = \mathbf{x}(t) - \gamma_t \mathbf{g}_t, \tag{5.28}$$

where $\mathbf{g}_t$ is the gradient of the objective function $V: \mathcal{R}^d \rightarrow \mathcal{R}$ evaluated at $\mathbf{x}(t)$, and the stepsize sequence $\gamma_0, \gamma_1, \gamma_2,...$ is a sequence of strictly positive numbers. Thus the batch backpropagation ANN learning dynamical system defined in chapter 2 is an example of a gradient descent algorithm. The Modified Newton Convergence Theorem identifies conditions such that if γ_t is a properly chosen stepsize at each iteration t of the algorithm, any trajectory of the gradient descent algorithm will approach the set of critical points of the objective function V. A *steepest descent algorithm* is defined as a gradient descent algorithm where the sequence of stepsizes γ_0, γ_1, γ_2 is a sequence of optimally chosen stepsizes.

Now consider the rate of convergence of the steepest descent algorithm. Let $\mathbf{x}^*$ be a strict local minimum. Assume $\mathbf{x}(t) \to \mathbf{x}^*$ as $t \to \infty$. Also assume that γ_t is optimally chosen for every iteration $t \in \{0, 1, 2,...\}$. It can be shown that the convergence rate of the steepest descent algorithm is linear with a convergence ratio determined by the eigenvalues of the Hessian of V evaluated at $\mathbf{x}^*$. In particular, define the *condition number*, r^*, of the Hessian of V evaluated at $\mathbf{x}^*$ by the formula

$$r^* = \frac{\lambda_{\max}}{\lambda_{\min}},$$

where $\lambda_{\max}$ and $\lambda_{\min}$ are the largest and smallest eigenvalues of the real symmetric positive definite Hessian of V evaluated at $\mathbf{x}^*$. It can be shown (see Luenberger 1984 for a review) that the sequence of objective functions $V(\mathbf{x}(0))$, $V(\mathbf{x}(1))$,... converges to $V(\mathbf{x}^*)$ linearly with a convergence ratio no greater than

$$[(r^* - 1)/(r^* + 1)]^2,$$

where r^* is the condition number of the Hessian of V evaluated at $\mathbf{x}^*$.

A geometric interpretation of the behavior of the steepest descent algorithm may be obtained by expanding V in a first-order Taylor expansion about the point $\mathbf{x}(t)$ to obtain

$$V(\mathbf{x}(t + 1)) = V(\mathbf{x}(t)) + \mathbf{g}(\mathbf{x}(t))^T[\mathbf{x}(t + 1) - \mathbf{x}(t)] + O(\gamma_t^2),$$

where $\mathbf{g}(\mathbf{x}(t))$ is the gradient of V evaluated at $\mathbf{x}(t)$. Using the Cauchy-Schwarz inequality (i.e., $|\mathbf{a}||\mathbf{b}| \geq \mathbf{a}^T\mathbf{b}$), it follows that the function V will decrease most rapidly (i.e., $|V(\mathbf{x}(t + 1)) - V(\mathbf{x}(t))|$ obtains its maximum value) at each iteration of the steepest descent algorithm (for a given γ_t of fixed magnitude) if $\mathbf{x}(t + 1) - \mathbf{x}(t)$ is chosen according to (5.28). Hence the name "steepest descent algorithm".

Now expand V in a second-order Taylor expansion about the point $\mathbf{x}^*$ to obtain

$$V(\mathbf{x}) = V(\mathbf{x}^*) + \frac{1}{2}[\mathbf{x} - \mathbf{x}^*]^T\mathbf{H}[\mathbf{x} - \mathbf{x}^*] + O(|\mathbf{x} - \mathbf{x}^*|^3),$$

where $\mathbf{H}$ is the Hessian of V evaluated at $\mathbf{x}^*$. Figure 5.5 shows two contour plots of V as a function of $\mathbf{x}$ when the dimension of $\mathbf{x}$ is equal to two. If the condition number of $\mathbf{H}$ is close to one, then the objective function V does not possess any "narrow valleys" in the vicinity of $\mathbf{x}^*$, and so convergence is relatively rapid. If the condition number of $\mathbf{H}$ is large, then the objective function V does possess "narrow valleys," and convergence may be quite slow. Thus the convergence rate analysis of steepest descent has a geometric interpretation. Intuitively, these

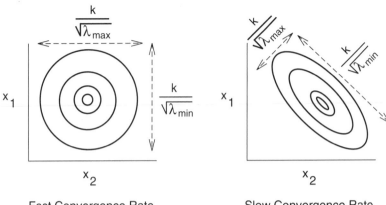

Fast Convergence Rate   Slow Convergence Rate

Figure 5.5
Comparison of fast and slow convergence rate cases. Each of the two contour plots in this figure
corresponds to a different strict local minimum. Each ellipsoid (and circle) corresponds to a set of
points that have the same value of the objective function. Innermost ellipsoids correspond to
smaller values of the objective function relative to outermost ellipsoids. The length of a principal
axis of an ellipsoid is proportional to the inverse of the square root of one of the eigenvalues of the
Hessian of the function evaluated at the strict local minimum. The fastest asymptotic rate of convergence occurs when all lengths of the principal axes for a given strict local minimum are approximately the same magnitude.

results make sense. The choice of a descent direction for a fixed stepsize is more
limited when more narrow valleys in the objective function surface are present.

Classical Newton Algorithm

The classical Newton algorithm is motivated by the following analysis. First,
consider a discrete-time dynamical system of the form

$$\mathbf{x}(t + 1) = \mathbf{x}(t) + \gamma_t \mathbf{f}(t).$$

Now expand the gradient of V in a first-order Taylor expansion about the point
$\mathbf{x}(t)$ to obtain, for some sufficiently small γ_t,

$$\mathbf{g}(\mathbf{x}(t + 1)) = \mathbf{g}(\mathbf{x}(t)) + \mathbf{H}(\mathbf{x}(t))[\mathbf{x}(t + 1) - \mathbf{x}(t)] + O(\gamma_t^2), \tag{5.29}$$

where $\mathbf{g}(\mathbf{x}(t))$ is the gradient of V evaluated at $\mathbf{x}(t)$ and $\mathbf{H}(\mathbf{x}(t))$ is the Hessian of
V evaluated at $\mathbf{x}(t)$. Now assume that $\mathbf{x}(t)$ is very close to a strict local minimum
$\mathbf{x}^*$. The basic idea of the classical Newton algorithm is to set

$$\mathbf{x}(t + 1) = \mathbf{x}^*$$

in (5.29), and then solve explicitly for the search direction $\gamma_t \mathbf{f}(t)$. Note that
$\mathbf{g}(\mathbf{x}(t + 1)) = \mathbf{0}_d$ because $\mathbf{x}^*$ is a critical point by the strict local minimum test.
Thus (5.29) becomes, for some sufficiently small γ_t,

$$\mathbf{0}_d = \mathbf{g}(\mathbf{x}(t)) + \mathbf{H}(\mathbf{x}(t))[\mathbf{x}(t + 1) - \mathbf{x}(t)] + O(\gamma_t^2),$$

which can be solved (since **H** is positive definite by the Strict Local Minimum Test) for the search direction $\gamma_t \mathbf{f}(t)$ to obtain, for some sufficiently small γ_t,

$$\gamma_t \mathbf{f}(t) = -\mathbf{H}^{-1}(\mathbf{x}(t))\mathbf{g}(\mathbf{x}(t)) + O(\gamma_t^2).$$

Thus, if $\mathbf{x}(t)$ is sufficiently close to a strict local minimum $\mathbf{x}^*$, then the *classical Newton algorithm,* given by the update equation

$$\mathbf{x}(t + 1) = \mathbf{x}(t) - \mathbf{H}^{-1}(\mathbf{x}(t))\mathbf{g}(\mathbf{x}(t)),$$

reaches the strict local minimum $\mathbf{x}^*$ in about one iteration. In practice, however, several iterations may be required when V is not a quadratic function because the terms of order γ_t^2 are neglected in the classical Newton algorithm.

Now if $\mathbf{x}(t)$ remains close to strict local minimum $\mathbf{x}^*$ as $t \rightarrow \infty$, then $\mathbf{H}^{-1}(\mathbf{x}(t))$ is positive definite. Thus the Modified Newton Convergence Theorem can be used to prove that $\mathbf{x}(t)$ will converge to the strict local minimum $\mathbf{x}^*$. Moreover, it can be shown that the convergence rate of the classical Newton algorithm is of *order two* (e.g., Luenberger 1984, 225).

Although the classical Newton algorithm sounds quite good, it possesses two very serious problems that limit its applicability to ANN analysis and design problems. First, considerable memory/computational requirements are required for storing, updating, and inverting an estimate of the Hessian of V at each step of the algorithm. In particular, the steepest descent algorithm only requires the storage and manipulation of roughly d free parameters at each algorithm iteration, while the classical Newton algorithm requires the storage and manipulation of roughly d^2 free parameters at each algorithm iteration. For this reason the respective memory/computational requirements for the steepest descent algorithm will be referred to as $O(d)$, while the memory/computational requirements for the classical Newton algorithm will be referred to as $O(d^2)$. Such order of magnitude computational requirements are very important for comparing and contrasting nonlinear optimization algorithms for ANN systems because for most ANN systems d is quite large (e.g., $d \approx 500$ is typical).

Second, if $\mathbf{x}(t)$ is sufficiently close to a critical point of V that is *not* a *strict local minimum*, the classical Newton algorithm will either fail because the inverse of the Hessian of V does not exist or converge at an order-two rate to a critical point which could be a local maximum. That is, when $\mathbf{x}(t)$ is not close to a strict local minimum, there is no guarantee that the inverse of the Hessian of V will be positive definite. Thus the classical Newton algorithm may go "uphill," as illustrated in figure 5.6.

Levenberg-Marquardt Descent Algorithm

A compromise between the classical Newton and steepest descent algorithm is the Levenberg-Marquardt descent algorithm, which has the form

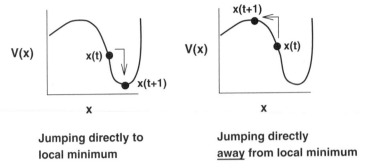

Jumping directly to   Jumping directly
local minimum   <u>away</u> from local minimum

Figure 5.6
Jumping the wrong way with classical Newton algorithm. The left-hand figure shows how the classical Newton algorithm is supposed to work; in the vicinity of a strict local minimum the algorithm is guaranteed to jump directly to that strict local minimum. The right-hand figure shows a problem associated with applying the classical Newton algorithm to multimodal functions; the algorithm will jump to the nearest critical point, which may even be a local *maximum*!

$$\mathbf{x}(t+1) = \mathbf{x}(t) - \gamma_t \mathbf{H}^{-1}(\mathbf{x}(t))\mathbf{g}_t - \gamma_t \varepsilon_t \mathbf{g}_t,$$

where $\mathbf{g}_t$ and $\mathbf{H}^{-1}(\mathbf{x}(t))$ are the gradient and inverse Hessian of V evaluated at $\mathbf{x}(t)$, respectively. The sequence of strictly positive numbers $\varepsilon_1, \varepsilon_2,\dots$ is chosen such that ε_1 is initially large and $\varepsilon_t \to 0$ as $t \to 0$. Thus the Levenberg-Marquardt algorithm has the characteristics of a steepest descent algorithm when $\mathbf{x}(t)$ is far away from a strict local minimum. When $\mathbf{x}(t)$ becomes close to a strict local minimum, then the inverse Hessian term should be dominant to increase the convergence rate.

A basic problem with the Levenberg-Marquardt descent algorithm is the storage, construction, and inversion of the d-dimensional Hessian matrix. Thus, like the classical Newton method, the Levenberg-Marquardt algorithm has $O(d^2)$ computation/memory requirements, where d is the number of free parameters (i.e., the dimensionality of the Hessian). The advantage of the Levenberg-Marquardt descent algorithm is that it provides a useful mechanism for avoiding the situation depicted in figure 5.6, where uphill rather than downhill steps are taken by the algorithm.

Another basic problem with the Levenberg-Marquardt descent algorithm is choosing ε_t at each iteration of the algorithm. If ε_t is chosen too small, then it is likely that $\mathbf{Q}(t) = \mathbf{H}^{-1}(\mathbf{x}(t)) + \varepsilon_t \mathbf{I}$, where $\mathbf{I}$ is the identity matrix, may not be strictly positive definite. If ε_t is chosen too large, then the desirable order two convergence property of the classical Newton algorithm may be lost. Many software packages exploit the Levenberg-Marquardt algorithm to solve nonlinear optimization problems by checking $\mathbf{Q}(t)$ for positive definiteness at each iteration and adjusting ε_t accordingly, but such methods may be quite computationally intensive for large-scale ANN problems. On the other hand, Hagen and Menhaj (1994) have reported that, for certain backpropagation learning problems where the number of weights is relatively small (i.e., about a few hundred weights), a version of the Levenberg-Marquardt algorithm can solve practical problems several orders of magnitude faster than classical back-propagation.

Shanno Algorithm

Shanno (1978) has proposed a type of modified Newton algorithm that implic-itly computes a positive definite approximation to the inverse of the Hessian of the objective function using computational/memory requirements which are roughly $O(d)$ as opposed to $O(d^2)$. Thus the Shanno algorithm (1) has the low computational/memory $O(d)$ requirements of the steepest descent algorithm, (2) tends to avoid the uphill jumping problem depicted in figure 5.6, like the steepest descent algorithm and Levenberg-Marquardt algorithm, and (3) tends to have the fast, order two convergence rate properties of the classical Newton algorithm. Shanno's algorithm may also be viewed as a generalization of the class of conjugate gradient algorithms that are popular in the literature (see dis-cussion in following section).

It should be noted that the Shanno (1978) algorithm is usually referred to as a "one-step (memoryless) Broyden-Fletcher-Goldfarb-Shanno (BFGS) algo-rithm," a "memoryless quasi-Newton conjugate gradient algorithm," or a "one-step secant (OSS) algorithm" in the literature. The nonstandard term *Shanno algorithm* is introduced in order to clearly distinguish this particular algorithm from the more general class of one-step (memoryless) BFGS algorithms and because this particular algorithm was proposed by Shanno (1978, 244–247).

The following introduction to the Shanno algorithm is based upon the dis-cussion of Luenberger (1984, 280). Battiti (1992) discusses this algorithm from an ANN system perspective.

Algorithm: Shanno algorithm.   Let $\mathbf{g}: \mathcal{R}^d \to \mathcal{R}^d$ be the gradient of the objec-tive function $V: \mathcal{R}^d \to \mathcal{R}$. Let the notation $\mathbf{g}_t$ be defined such that $\mathbf{g}_t = \mathbf{g}(\mathbf{x}(t))$.

- Step 0: Let $t = 0$. Let $\mathbf{x}(0) \in \mathcal{R}^d$.
- Step 1: Set $\mathbf{f}(t) = -\mathbf{g}_t$. Go to step 3.
- Step 2: If t is a multiple of M where $M \le d$, then go to step 1. Otherwise com-pute $\mathbf{u}_t = \mathbf{g}_t - \mathbf{g}_{t-1}$ and the scalars a_t, b_t, c_t, defined such that

$$a_t = \frac{\mathbf{f}(t-1)^T \mathbf{g}_t}{\mathbf{f}(t-1)^T \mathbf{u}_t},$$

$$b_t = \frac{\mathbf{u}_t^T \mathbf{g}_t}{\mathbf{f}(t-1)^T \mathbf{u}_t},$$

$$c_t = \gamma_{t-1} + \frac{|\mathbf{u}_t|^2}{\mathbf{f}(t-1)^T \mathbf{u}_t},$$

and descent vector

$$\mathbf{f}(t) = -\mathbf{g}_t + a_t \mathbf{u}_t + (b_t - c_t a_t)\mathbf{f}(t-1).$$

- Step 3: Compute

$$\mathbf{x}(t+1) = \mathbf{x}(t) + \gamma_t \mathbf{f}(t), \tag{5.30}$$

where γ_t is a properly chosen stepsize according to (5.8) and (5.9). Let $t = t + 1$. Go to step 2 until $|\mathbf{g}_t|$ is sufficiently small.

Notice that the Shanno algorithm does not involve the explicit computation, storage, or inversion of the Hessian of the objective function V. The analysis of the Shanno algorithm is based upon considering the following formally equivalent algorithm (see problem 5–12).

Algorithm: Shanno algorithm (inefficient form).   Let $\mathbf{g} \colon \mathcal{R}^d \to \mathcal{R}^d$ be the gradient of the objective function $V \colon \mathcal{R}^d \to \mathcal{R}$. Let the notation $\mathbf{g}_t$ be defined such that $\mathbf{g}_t = \mathbf{g}(\mathbf{x}(t))$.

- Step 0: Let $t = 0$. Let $\mathbf{x}(0) \in \mathcal{R}^d$.
- Step 1: Set $\mathbf{f}(t) = -\mathbf{g}_t$. Go to Step 3.
- Step 2: If t is a multiple of M, where $M \le d$, then go to step 1. Otherwise, compute $\mathbf{u}_t = \mathbf{g}_t - \mathbf{g}_{t-1}$,

$$c_t = \gamma_{t-1} + \frac{|\mathbf{u}_t|^2}{\mathbf{f}(t-1)^T \mathbf{u}_t},$$

and

$$\mathbf{H}_t = \mathbf{I} - \frac{\mathbf{u}_t \mathbf{f}(t-1)^T + \mathbf{f}(t-1)\mathbf{u}_t^T}{\mathbf{f}(t-1)^T \mathbf{u}_t} + c_t \frac{\mathbf{f}(t-1)\mathbf{f}(t-1)^T}{\mathbf{f}(t-1)^T \mathbf{u}_t}, \tag{5.31}$$

and

$$\mathbf{f}(t) = -\mathbf{H}_t \mathbf{g}_t.$$

- Step 3: Compute $\mathbf{x}(t+1) = \mathbf{x}(t) + \gamma_t \mathbf{f}(t)$ where γ_t is a properly chosen stepsize according to (5.8) and (5.9). Let $t = t + 1$. Go to step 2 until $|\mathbf{g}_t|$ is sufficiently small.

The inefficient form of the Shanno algorithm is useful for analysis because the Shanno algorithm can now be immediately recognized as a descent algorithm if it can be shown that $\mathbf{H}_t$ is positive definite for all nonnegative t. Thus the Descent Algorithm Convergence Theorem may then be used to investigate the global convergence properties of the Shanno (1978) algorithm.

Theorem: Shanno Algorithm Convergence Theorem.   Assume $V \colon \mathcal{R}^d \to \mathcal{R}$ has (i) continuous second partial derivatives, and (ii) a lower bound on $\mathcal{R}^d$. Let the sequence of d-dimensional real vectors $\mathbf{x}(0)$, $\mathbf{x}(1)$, $\mathbf{x}(2)$,... be defined such that, for $t = 0, 1, 2,...$,

$$\mathbf{x}(t + 1) = \mathbf{x}(t) + \gamma_t \mathbf{f}(t),$$

where γ_t is a properly chosen stepsize as in (5.8) and (5.9) and where the descent direction vector $\mathbf{f}(t)$ is defined as in (5.30) with respect to the objective function V. Let $\mathbf{g}_t$ be the gradient of V evaluated at $\mathbf{x}(t)$. Then either (i) $\mathbf{x}(t)$ approaches the set of critical points of V as $t \to \infty$, (ii) $[\mathbf{g}_t/|\mathbf{g}_t|]^T[\mathbf{f}(t)/|\mathbf{f}(t)|] \to 0$ as $t \to \infty$, or (iii) $\{\mathbf{x}(t)\}$ is not bounded.

Proof. Let $\mathbf{H}_t$ be defined as in (5.35). Let $\mathbf{g}_t$ be the gradient of V evaluated at the state $\mathbf{x}(t)$ generated by the Shanno algorithm.

Suppose that it could be proved that, given any nonnegative integer t, either (i) $\mathbf{g}_t = \mathbf{0}_d$, or (ii) $\mathbf{H}_t$ is positive definite. If there exists a t^* such that $\mathbf{g}_{t^*} = \mathbf{0}_d$, then the conclusion of the Shanno Algorithm Convergence Theorem is immediately obtained. To see this, note that if there exists a t^* such that $\mathbf{g}_{t^*} = \mathbf{0}_d$, then $\mathbf{f}(t^*) = \mathbf{0}_d$, and so $\mathbf{x}(t) = \mathbf{x}(t^*)$ for all $t > t^*$.

If $\mathbf{H}_t$ is positive definite and $|\mathbf{g}(t)| > 0$, then

$$\mathbf{g}_t^T \mathbf{f}(t) = -\mathbf{g}_t^T \mathbf{H}_t \mathbf{g}_t < 0.$$

Thus, because γ_t is a properly chosen stepsize, the conclusion of the Shanno Algorithm Convergence Theorem immediately follows from the Descent Algorithm Convergence Theorem.

The remainder of the proof will assume that there does not exist a t^* such that $\mathbf{g}_{t^*} = \mathbf{0}_d$, and granted this assumption, it will be shown that $\mathbf{H}_t$ is positive definite for all nonnegative integer t.

Define

$$\mathbf{A}_t = \mathbf{I} - \frac{\mathbf{u}_t \mathbf{u}_t^T}{|\mathbf{u}_t|^2}. \tag{5.32}$$

Now note that $\mathbf{H}_t$ can be rewritten as

$$\mathbf{H}_t = \mathbf{A}_t + \frac{\gamma_{t-1}\mathbf{f}(t-1)\mathbf{f}(t-1)^T}{\mathbf{f}(t-1)^T\mathbf{u}_t} + \mathbf{v}_t\mathbf{v}_t^T, \tag{5.33}$$

where

$$\mathbf{v}_t = |\mathbf{u}_t|\left[\frac{\mathbf{f}(t-1)}{\mathbf{f}(t-1)^T\mathbf{u}_t} - \frac{\mathbf{u}_t}{|\mathbf{u}_t|^2}\right].$$

To check the validity of the assertion that $\mathbf{H}_t$ may be rewritten as (5.33), simply expand (5.33) and show that the expression in (5.31) is obtained.

The matrix $\mathbf{v}_t\mathbf{v}_t^T$ in (5.33) is also positive semidefinite because, for any $\mathbf{x}$,

$$\mathbf{x}^T\mathbf{v}_t\mathbf{v}_t^T\mathbf{x} = (\mathbf{x}^T\mathbf{v}_t)^2 \geq 0.$$

also note that by (5.9)

$$\mathbf{f}(t-1)^T\mathbf{g}_t > \beta\mathbf{f}(t-1)^T\mathbf{g}_{t-1} \tag{5.34}$$

where $0 < \beta < 1$. From (5.34),

$$\mathbf{f}(t-1)^T\mathbf{g}_t - \mathbf{f}(t-1)^T\mathbf{g}_{t-1} + (1-\beta)\mathbf{f}(t-1)^T\mathbf{g}_{t-1} \geq 0. \tag{5.35}$$

Assume $\mathbf{f}(t-1)^T\mathbf{g}_{t-1} < 0$, then from (5.35) and from $0 < \beta < 1$,

$$\mathbf{f}(t-1)^T\mathbf{u}_t > 0. \tag{5.36}$$

Now note that each of the three terms on the right-hand side of (5.33) is a positive semidefinite matrix because $\mathbf{f}(t-1)^T\mathbf{u}_t$ is a strictly positive real number. It will now be shown that $\mathbf{H}_t$ is a positive definite matrix by considering the following two distinct cases.

Case 1. By examining (5.32), note that the quantity $\mathbf{x}^T\mathbf{A}_t\mathbf{x}$ in (5.33) is a strictly positive real number for all $\mathbf{x}$ where $|\mathbf{x}| > 0$ that satisfy $\mathbf{x} \neq \lambda\mathbf{u}_t$, where λ is an arbitrary real nonzero number. Referring to (5.33) and (5.36), this implies that $\mathbf{H}_t$ is a positive definite matrix for this case.

Case 2. By examining (5.32), note that the quantity $\mathbf{x}^T\mathbf{A}_t\mathbf{x}$ in (5.33) is equal to zero if $\mathbf{x} = \lambda\mathbf{u}_t$, where λ is an arbitrary real nonzero number. Referring to (5.33) and (5.36), this implies that $\mathbf{H}_t$ is a positive definite matrix for this case.

Thus $\mathbf{H}_t$ is positive definite if $\mathbf{f}(t-1)^T\mathbf{g}_{t-1} < 0$. Also if $\mathbf{H}_t$ is positive definite and $|\mathbf{g}_t|$ is strictly positive, then $\mathbf{f}(t)^T\mathbf{g}_t < 0$. Also note that $\mathbf{H}_0$ is positive definite by inspection of the initialization procedure of the algorithm. Therefore, by induction, the conclusion of the Shanno Algorithm Convergence Theorem is proved. ∎

The Shanno Algorithm Convergence Theorem shows that the trajectories generated by the Shanno algorithm may converge to critical points of the objective function V. Luenberger (1984) reviews previous research in the nonlinear optimization literature demonstrating that $\mathbf{H}_t$ in (5.35) can be viewed as a positive definite estimate of the inverse of the Hessian of V evaluated at $\mathbf{x}(t)$. The quality of the approximation is to some extent determined by the number of inner loops, M, in the Shanno algorithm. If $M = d$, where d is the dimension of $\mathbf{x}(t)$, then a fairly good approximation to the inverse of the Hessian of V is constructed. (A proof relating $\mathbf{H}_t$ to the inverse of the Hessian of V is beyond the scope of this introduction but interested readers are encouraged to consult chapters 8 and 9 of Luenberger 1984 for a review.)

Assume that $\mathbf{x}(t) \to \mathbf{x}^*$ as $t \to \infty$, where $\mathbf{x}^*$ is a strict local minimum of V. Because $\mathbf{H}_t$ in the Shanno algorithm is approximately equal to the inverse of the Hessian of V evaluated at $\mathbf{x}^*$, as in the classical Newton algorithm, the convergence rate of the Shanno algorithm is approximately order two. One potential practical problem is that the Shanno algorithm may converge very rapidly to a shallow local minimum because the algorithm tends to seek out the nearest local minimum. The solution to this problem is to begin the learning process with a gradient descent algorithm involving a properly chosen stepsize. Then, in the final stages of learning, the Shanno algorithm can be used to converge rapidly to a (hopefully deep) local minimum.

The Shanno algorithm thus has a number of important properties worth reviewing. First, the algorithm uses only gradient information and thus does not require intensive computational or memory requirements compared to the classical Newton method. Second, unlike classical Newton, every step of the algorithm is always in a descent direction. Third, the Shanno algorithm has approximately order two convergence properties in some sufficiently small neighborhood of a strict local minimum. And fourth, the Shanno algorithm does not require that the optimal stepsize γ_t be computed at each iteration of the algorithm. Instead, a very sloppy estimate of the optimal stepsize can be computed at each iteration of the algorithm that satisfies (5.8) and (5.9), and the Shanno algorithm will still be a descent algorithm.

It is also important to emphasize that Shanno's algorithm is a special case of an important class of nonlinear optimization algorithms known as "Broyden-Fletcher-Goldfarb-Shanno (BFGS) algorithms," which are closely related to the class of Davidon-Fletcher-Powell (DFP) algorithms (Chapters 8 and 9 of Luenberger 1984 provide a good introduction to these important techniques for solving high-dimensional nonlinear optimization problems, which frequently arise in the analysis and design of ANN systems.)

The Conjugate Gradient Algorithm is a Special Case of the Shanno Algorithm

A number of ANN researchers have used conjugate gradient algorithms for learning in backpropagation ANN learning dynamical systems, and demonstrated that such algorithms are superior to the backpropagation learning algorithm (Battiti 1992; Hagan and Menhaj 1994; Johansson, Dowla, and Goodman 1992; Kramer and Sangiovanni-Vincentelli 1989; Møller 1990). Shanno (1978) has noted that conjugate gradient algorithms can be viewed as approximations to the Shanno algorithm, where the quality of the approximation is good, provided that the stepsize is optimally chosen. It can be shown (see problem 5-14) that in this case the Shanno algorithm reduces to the following *generic conjugate gradient algorithm*.

Algorithm: Generic conjugate gradient algorithm. Let $\mathbf{g}: \mathcal{R}^d \to \mathcal{R}^d$ be the gradient of the objective function $V: \mathcal{R}^d \to \mathcal{R}$. Let the notation $\mathbf{g}_t = \mathbf{g}(\mathbf{x}(t))$. Let $\mathbf{u}_t = \mathbf{g}_t - \mathbf{g}_{t-1}$.

- Step 0: Let $t = 0$. Let $\mathbf{x}(0) \in \mathcal{R}^d$.
- Step 1: Set $\mathbf{f}(t) = -\mathbf{g}_t$. Go to step 3.

- Step 2: If t is a multiple of the number of free parameters, d, go to step 1. Otherwise, set

$$\mathbf{f}(t) = -\mathbf{g}_t + b_t \mathbf{f}(t - 1),$$

where b_t is defined by

$$b_t = \frac{\mathbf{u}_t^T \mathbf{g}_t}{\mathbf{u}_t^T \mathbf{f}(t - 1)}. \tag{5.37}$$

- Step 3: Compute $\mathbf{x}(t + 1) = \mathbf{x}(t) + \gamma_t \mathbf{f}(t)$ where γ_t is an optimal stepsize. Let $t = t + 1$. Go to step 2 until $|\mathbf{g}_t|$ is sufficiently small.

Problem 5-14 shows that the above generic conjugate gradient algorithm reduces to the well-known Polak-Ribière (1969) conjugate gradient algorithm when the stepsize is optimally chosen. For reference purposes, the two algorithms are identical except that the formula for b_t in (5.37) is given by the revised expression

$$b_t = \frac{\mathbf{u}_t^T \mathbf{g}_t}{|\mathbf{g}_{t-1}|^2}.$$

Shanno (1978) has also noted that the Fletcher-Reeves (1964) conjugate gradient algorithm is a special case of the Polak-Ribière (1969) algorithm if one makes the additional assumption that the objective function can be locally approximated as a quadratic objective function. Again, for reference purposes, the Fletcher-Reeves conjugate gradient algorithm can be obtained from (5.37) by replacing the formula for b_t in (5.37) with the expression

$$b_t = \frac{|\mathbf{g}_t|^2}{|\mathbf{g}_{t-1}|^2}.$$

Shanno (1978, 247; also see Luenberger 1984, 280; and McCormick and Ritter 1972) further notes that the generic conjugate gradient algorithm will not build an effective approximation to the inverse Hessian of the objective function as effectively as the Shanno algorithm for nonquadratic objective functions or when the stepsize is not optimally chosen at each iteration. And since exact objective function and gradient function evaluations are computationally expensive and tend to have poor payoffs in high-dimensional state space search problems, it is likely that the stepsize will not be optimal in most ANN applications.

Thus assuming that the computational complexity of an iteration of the generic conjugate gradient algorithm is roughly the same as an iteration of the Shanno algorithm, the Shanno algorithm is expected to converge more rapidly to a nearby strict local minimum, take fewer uphill steps, and have greater numerical robustness than the generic conjugate gradient algorithm. These points are particularly relevant to researchers in the field of ANN systems. The objective functions for many ANN learning systems are not quadratic (or even unimodal), and ANN learning systems operate in very high-dimensional state spaces.

An Empirical Backpropagation Learning Algorithm Study

Despite the importance of theoretical analyses, it should be remembered that one must be cautious about "rank-ordering" optimization algorithms with respect to arbitrary nonlinear objective functions. The ANN system engineer needs to understand, both theoretically and empirically, the strengths and weaknesses associated with a particular optimization algorithm. Ultimately, comparisons among algorithms should be done from both a theoretical and empirical perspective with respect to the specific objective function of interest.

An example of an empirical computer simulation study designed to compare various backpropagation learning algorithms is described by Johansson et al. (1992), who compared backpropagation learning algorithms using either: (1) a version of the on-line backpropagation learning algorithm, (2) the steepest descent algorithm, (3) the Fletcher-Reeves conjugate gradient algorithm, (4) the Polak-Ribière conjugate gradient algorithm, or (5) the Shanno algorithm.

Johansson et al. (1992) found that backpropagation learning using the Shanno algorithm was slightly slower in speed relative to the Polak-Ribière conjugate gradient algorithm. The Shanno algorithm, however, was the only learning algorithm that consistently converged to an appropriate solution; thus exhibiting greater numerical robustness relative to the other algorithms. The Shanno algorithm tended to converge to a solution slightly faster than the Fletcher-Reeves algorithm which, in turn, converged to a solution at a faster rate than the steepest descent algorithm. The speed of convergence for on-line backpropagation learning was consistently an order of magnitude slower than the speed of convergence of the other four learning algorithms. This empirically observed pattern of results is generally consistent with the theoretical analyses discussed here.

5.5.2 ANN Applications

Stepsize Selection for Batch Backpropagation

Problem. Let $\mathbf{r}(\mathbf{s}^k, \mathbf{w}(t)) \in \mathfrak{R}^m$ indicate the *response* of a feedforward ANN system (see chapter 2) to a given stimulus $\mathbf{s}^k$ for some weight vector $\mathbf{w}(t)$. Let the *desired response* of the ANN system for a given stimulus $\mathbf{s}^k$ be the vector $\mathbf{o}^k$. Let $c: \mathfrak{R}^m \times \mathfrak{R}^m \to \mathfrak{R}$ be some *pattern error function*. Let $l: \mathfrak{R}^q \to \mathfrak{R}$ evaluated at $\mathbf{w}(t)$ be defined as

$$l(\mathbf{w}(t)) = \left(1/n\right) \sum_{k=1}^{n} c(\mathbf{o}^k, \mathbf{r}(\mathbf{s}^k, \mathbf{w}(t))),$$

where $(\mathbf{s}^k, \mathbf{o}^k)$ is the kth training stimulus in the set of n training stimuli. Let $\mathbf{g}: \mathcal{R}^q \to \mathcal{R}^q$ be the gradient of l, so that $\mathbf{g}(\mathbf{w}(t))$ is the gradient of l evaluated at $\mathbf{w}(t)$.

Let the learning algorithm for the feed-forward ANN system be given by the formula

$$\mathbf{w}(t+1) = \mathbf{w}(t) + \gamma\, \mathbf{f}(t).$$

The vector $\mathbf{f}(t)$ is chosen so that for $t = 0, 1, 2,\ldots$: either: (i) $\mathbf{f}(t)^T \mathbf{g}(\mathbf{w}) < 0$, or (ii) $\left|\mathbf{f}(t)\right| = \left|\mathbf{g}(\mathbf{w}(t))\right| = 0$. Thus, if $\mathbf{f}(t) = -\mathbf{g}(\mathbf{w}(t))$, the learning rule becomes equivalent to a batch backpropagation learning algorithm.

Devise a simple procedure for monitoring the above learning algorithm in order to guarantee that the learning algorithm converges to the set of critical points of the learning objective function l.

Solution.   The conditions of the Descent Algorithm Convergence Theorem can be used to derive a set of error messages that can be printed out at various intervals during the learning process. These conditions are taken directly from the conditions of the Descent Algorithm Convergence Theorem. Note that the following computations are *not* computationally intensive and can be done at regular intervals during the learning process. For example, checking the conditions for the stepsize to be properly chosen at each iteration only requires computation of the gradient of l (which is automatically computed by backpropagation) and the evaluation of l at the current set of weights.

Let a and β be positive numbers such that $0 < a < \beta < 1$. In order to minimize the number of warning messages regarding the choice of γ_t at each algorithm iteration, choose a to be a small positive number close to zero, and choose β to be close to one. Let the positive number $w_{\max}$ be an upper bound on the magnitude of any individual weight in the backpropagation network. For backpropagation networks with sigmoidal logistic functions, choosing $w_{\max}$ to be about equal to 5 is probably a reasonable strategy. The following algorithm can then be used to closely monitor the learning behavior of a given backpropagation network. Let ε be some small positive number whose magnitude roughly corresponds to the desired precision of the solution. For example, $\varepsilon = 0.0001$ would suggest that a solution accurate to about four decimal places is acceptable. Let $\delta_{\max}$ be the smallest cosine of the angle permitted between the search direction $\mathbf{f}(t)$ and the gradient vector $\mathbf{g}(\mathbf{w}(t))$.

- Step 1: Check if stepsize is too large. If

$$l(\mathbf{w}(t) + \gamma_t \mathbf{f}(t)) > l(\mathbf{w}(t)) + a\gamma_t \mathbf{g}(\mathbf{w}(t))^T \mathbf{f}(t),$$

then print: "Stepsize γ_t is too large. Decrease γ_t."

- Step 2: Check if stepsize is too small. If

$$\mathbf{g}(\mathbf{w}(t) + \gamma_t \mathbf{f}(t))^T \mathbf{f}(t) < \beta \mathbf{g}(\mathbf{w}(t))^T \mathbf{f}(t),$$

then print: "Stepsize γ_t is too small. Increase γ_t."

• Step 3: Check if the magnitude of the weights is too large. If the absolute value of the largest element in $\mathbf{w}(t)$ is greater than w_{max}, then print: "Estimated weights are out of bounds. Restart algorithm."

• Step 4: Check that search direction $\mathbf{f}(t)$ is acceptable. If

$$\left[\frac{\mathbf{f}(t)}{|\mathbf{f}(t)|}\right]^T \left[\frac{\mathbf{g}(\mathbf{w}(t))}{|\mathbf{g}(\mathbf{w}(t))|}\right] < \delta_{max},$$

then print: "Search direction is almost orthogonal to gradient. Pick new $\mathbf{f}(t)$."

• Step 5: Check if a critical point has been reached. If $|\mathbf{g}(\mathbf{w}(t))| < \varepsilon$, then print: "Gradient is sufficiently small. A critical point has been reached."

Analysis of Batch Hebbian Learning

A "batch" Hebbian learning rule with "weight decay" suitable for learning a set of weights for a linear autoassociative memory system is specified by the ANN learning dynamical system

$$w_{ij}(t+1) = w_{ij}(t)(1 - \gamma_t \lambda) + \gamma_t (1/n) \sum_{m=1}^{n} x_i^m x_j^m, \qquad (5.38)$$

where x_i^m is the ith element of the mth member of the n training stimuli. Let

$$c_{ij} = (1/n) \sum_{m=1}^{n} x_i^m x_j^m,$$

and assume for convenience that matrix $\mathbf{C}$, whose ijth element is c_{ij}, has full rank. Then (5.38) becomes

$$w_{ij}(t+1) = w_{ij}(t)(1 - \gamma_t \lambda) + \gamma_t c_{ij}.$$

Thus, if γ_t is a properly chosen stepsize, (5.38) is a gradient descent algorithm that converges to a critical point of the function $l: \mathcal{R}^{d \times d} \rightarrow \mathcal{R}$, where l is given by

$$l(\mathbf{W}) = -\sum_{i=1}^{d}\sum_{j=1}^{d} c_{ij} w_{ij} + 0.5 \sum_{i=1}^{d}\sum_{j=1}^{d} \lambda w_{ij}^2.$$

The learning objective function l has two terms. The left-hand term obtains a minimum value when $\mathbf{W}$ and $\mathbf{C}$ are very similar as measured by a dot product similarity measure. The similarity measure in the left-hand term obtains its minimum value when the ijth element of $\mathbf{W}$, w_{ij}, is a positive scalar multiple of c_{ij}. The right-hand term obtains a minimum value when all weights in the network are set equal to zero. The right-hand term is called the "complexity term" because it is a measure of the complexity of the neural network, while the left-hand term is called the "performance term" because it measures the performance of the neural network.

A learning algorithm that simultaneously optimizes both performance and complexity terms is essentially a learning rule searching for the most parsimonious solution to the performance problem. Moreover, because the Hessian of l is simply the identity matrix multiplied by λ, the convergence rate of this gradient descent algorithm is approximately superlinear and independent of both c_{ij} and λ if the stepsize is optimally chosen. Also note that because the eigenvalues of the Hessian of l are strictly positive, this implies that l is a strictly convex function. Thus any critical point of l will be the unique strict global minimum of l. And because the critical point of the learning objective function occurs when $w_{ij} = c_{ij}/\lambda$, all trajectories converge to a matrix whose ijth element is c_{ij}/λ.

Convergence Analysis of Besag's (1986) Iterated Conditional Modes (ICM) Algorithm

Problem.   The Hopfield (1982) algorithm may be viewed as a special case of the Boltzmann machine (Ackley, Hinton, and Sejnowski 1985) when the temperature parameter is sufficiently close to zero. Similarly, Besag's ICM algorithm (1986) may be viewed as a special case of the Gibbs sampler algorithm when the temperature parameter of the Gibbs sampler algorithm is sufficiently close to zero.

Let $\mathbf{x}(t) = [x_1(t),\ldots, x_d(t)] \in \{1,\ldots, m\}^d$ be a d-dimensional vector whose ith element is the activation level of the ith unit at iteration t in an ICM ANN classification dynamical system. Each unit can take on one of m possible values. Let $V: \{1,\ldots, m\}^d \rightarrow \mathcal{R}$ be the potential function for the ICM ANN system. Let $x_i(t)$ be the activation level of the ith unit chosen at iteration t of the algorithm. It is assumed that $x_i(t)$ can take on only the values: 1, 2,..., m. Let

$$\mathbf{n}_i(t) = [x_1(t),\ldots, x_{i-1}(t), x_{i+1}(t),\ldots x_d(t)]$$

be the set of activation levels of the neighbors of the ith unit at iteration t of the algorithm ($i = 1\ldots d$, $t = 0$, 1, 2,...). Finally, define probability mass function $p: S \rightarrow (0, 1)$ (where $S = \{1,\ldots, m\}^d$) such that for all $\mathbf{x} \in S$: $p(\mathbf{x}) = Z^{-1} \exp[-V(\mathbf{x})]$ where $Z = \sum_{\mathbf{x} \in S} \exp[-V(\mathbf{x})]$.

The ICM algorithm generates a sequence of d-dimensional real vectors $\mathbf{x}(0)$, $\mathbf{x}(1)$, $\mathbf{x}(2)$,... according to the following algorithm.

- Step 1: Choose one of d units at random.

- Step 2: Update activation level of chosen unit. Define $q_{it}(l)$ such that

$q_{it}(l) = V[x_1(t), \ldots, x_{i-1}(t), x_i(t) = l, x_{i+1}(t), \ldots x_d(t)].$

Compute

$$p(x_i(t) = k \mid \mathbf{n}_i(t)) = \frac{p(x_i(t) = k, \mathbf{n}_i(t))}{p(\mathbf{n}_i(t))} = \frac{\exp\left[-q_{it}(k)\right]}{\sum_{j=1}^{m} \exp\left[-q_{it}(j)\right]}$$

Let $x_i(t + 1) = K^*$ where K^* is chosen such that:

$$p(x_i(t) = K^* \mid \mathbf{n}_i(t)) \geq p(x_i(t) = k \mid \mathbf{n}_i(t))$$

for $k = 1 \ldots m$. Let $t = t + 1$.

• Step 3: Go to step 1 until algorithm converges.

The ICM algorithm can be expressed abstractly as a discrete-time, dynamical system of the form $\mathbf{x}(t + 1) = \mathbf{f}_t(\mathbf{x}(t))$, where $\mathbf{f}_t: \mathcal{R}^d \rightarrow \mathcal{R}^d$ is a noncontinuous function whose functional form is dependent upon the potential function V.

Explain why convergence to a global minimum is *not guaranteed* by the ICM algorithm. Give one advantage to using the ICM algorithm over the Gibbs sampler algorithm. Let

$$\mathcal{H} = \{\mathbf{x} \in \{1, \ldots, m\}^d : V(\mathbf{f}_t(\mathbf{x})) = V(\mathbf{x})\}.$$

Prove that $\mathbf{x}(t) \rightarrow \mathcal{H}$ as $t \rightarrow \infty$. Also show that for $t = 0, 1, 2, \ldots$: $V(\mathbf{x}(t + 1)) \leq V(\mathbf{x}(t))$.

Solution. First, convergence to a global minimum is not guaranteed for the ICM algorithm because, like the Hopfield (1982) algorithm, the ICM algorithm is a deterministic algorithm that can be caught in local minima. Second, for some problems, the ICM algorithm may converge much more rapidly than the Gibbs sampler to the same solution (Besag 1986). To prove the ICM convergence theorem, note that

$$p(\mathbf{x}(t + 1)) = p(x_i(t + 1) \mid \mathbf{n}_i(t)) p(\mathbf{n}_i(t))$$

where

$$\mathbf{n}_i(t) = [x_1(t), \ldots, x_{i-1}(t), x_{i+1}(t), \ldots x_d(t)]$$

because the activation of only one unit (in this case, the ith unit) is updated at each iteration (in this case, iteration t). By definition of the ICM algorithm,

$$p(x_i = K^* \mid \mathbf{n}_i(t)) \geq p(x_i = k \mid \mathbf{n}_i(t))$$

for $k = 1 \ldots m$. This implies that

$$\begin{aligned} p(\mathbf{x}(t + 1)) &= p(x_i = K^* \mid \mathbf{n}_i(t)) p(\mathbf{n}_i(t)) \\ &\geq p(x_i = x_i(t) \mid \mathbf{n}_i(t)) p(\mathbf{n}_i(t)) = p(\mathbf{x}(t)). \end{aligned}$$

for $k = 1 \ldots m$. Since $p(\mathbf{x}(t + 1)) \geq p(\mathbf{x}(t))$ and p is a monotonically decreasing function of the potential function V, it follows that $V(\mathbf{x}(t + 1)) \leq V(\mathbf{x}(t))$.

At each iteration of the ICM algorithm, either

(i) $V(\mathbf{x}(t + 1)) < V(\mathbf{x}(t))$,

or

(ii) $V(\mathbf{x}(t + 1)) = V(\mathbf{x}(t))$.

If the ICM algorithm generates a sequence of states $\mathbf{x}(t)$, $\mathbf{x}(t + 1)$,... such that

$$V(\mathbf{x}(t)) = V(\mathbf{x}(t + 1)) = V(\mathbf{x}(t + 2)) = \ldots,$$

then the convergence theorem is proved. If $V(\mathbf{x}(t + 1)) < V(\mathbf{x}(t))$, then the ICM algorithm can never generate the state $\mathbf{x}(t)$ again because the constraint $V(\mathbf{x}(t + 1)) \leq V(\mathbf{x}(t))$ would be violated. Because the state space consists of only a finite number (in particular m^d) states, the maximum number of times that the event $V(\mathbf{x}(t + 1)) < V(\mathbf{x}(t))$ can occur is bounded by m^d. Thus eventually, $\mathbf{x}(t) \to \mathscr{H}$ as $t \to \infty$.

5.6   Chapter Summary

Basic concepts from the field of nonlinear optimization theory relevant to ANN system analysis and design were reviewed. The beginning of the chapter introduced the concepts of a critical point, local minimum, local maximum, global minimum, and global maximum in order to precisely state the computational goal of a nonlinear optimization algorithm.

Applying the Descent Algorithm Convergence Theorem

The steps for applying the Descent Algorithm Convergence Theorem are as follows.

• Step 1: Express algorithm in standard descent algorithm format. The form of a descent algorithm is given by

$$\mathbf{x}(t + 1) = \mathbf{x}(t) + \gamma_t \mathbf{f}(t),$$

where $\gamma_t \in [0, \infty)$ is the stepsize, $\mathbf{f} \colon \mathscr{R} \to \mathscr{R}^d$ is a function of the time index t, and $\mathbf{x}(0) \in \mathscr{R}^d$ is a known initial condition.

• Step 2: Check if algorithm is descent algorithm. Let $V \colon \mathscr{R}^d \to \mathscr{R}$ be a function such that the Hessian of V is continuous on $\mathscr{R}^d$. Let $\mathbf{g} \colon \mathscr{R}^d \to \mathscr{R}^d$ be the gradient V. Let $\mathbf{g}_t$ be the gradient of V evaluated at $\mathbf{x}(t)$. Check if for $t = 0, 1, 2, \ldots$ either:

(i) $\mathbf{g}_t^T \mathbf{f}(t) < 0$,

or

(ii) $|\mathbf{g}_t| = |\mathbf{f}_t| = 0$.

• Step 3: Check if stepsize is properly chosen. Let a and β be positive real numbers such that $0 < a < \beta < 1$. For each $t = 0, 1, 2,\ldots$ where $|\mathbf{f}(t)| \neq 0$, check if γ_t satisfies the following two inequalities:

$$V(\mathbf{x}(t) + \gamma_t \mathbf{f}(t)) \leq V(\mathbf{x}(t)) + a\gamma_t \mathbf{g}(\mathbf{x}(t))^T \mathbf{f}(t)$$

and

$$\mathbf{g}(\mathbf{x}(t) + \gamma_t \mathbf{f}(t))^T \mathbf{f}(t) \geq \beta \mathbf{g}(\mathbf{x}(t))^T \mathbf{f}(t).$$

• Step 4: Check if V has lower bound.

• Step 5: If appropriate, conclude that as $t \to \infty$, (i) $\mathbf{x}(t)$ converges to set of critical points of V, (ii) angle between $\mathbf{f}(t)$ and $\mathbf{g}_t$ converges to 90 degrees, or (iii) $\{\mathbf{x}(t)\}$ is not bounded.

It is very important to note that the stepsize γ_t does *not* have to be an optimal stepsize. The theorem is still valid even for suboptimal stepsizes provided the stepsize is properly chosen. This flexibility in stepsize selection means that the Descent Algorithm Convergence Theorem can be applied to the analysis and design of a large class of interesting time-variant, discrete-time dynamical ANN systems. From a computational perspective, this flexibility is also useful because ANN optimization problems tend to be high-dimensional optimization problems, where calculating the *exact* optimal stepsize at each algorithm iteration is computationally expensive.

Gibbs Sampler Convergence Theorem

The important Gibbs Sampler Convergence Theorem, which provides a unified framework for analyzing a very large class of Boltzmann machine–like ANN classification dynamical systems, was also reviewed. Such ANN classification dynamical systems consist of d computing units where each unit can take on a finite number of possible activation levels. The analysis is a generalization of the Boltzmann machine in the sense that (1) the activation level of a unit may take on more than two values (but only a finite number of values), and (2) the probabilistic rule for updating a unit is chosen by the user in order to minimize almost any desired objective function of interest. The Gibbs Sampler Convergence Theorem may be used to prove convergence to the set of *global minima* of the objective function of interest. The disadvantage of the Gibbs sampler approach is that the convergence time tends to be too long for some practical applications. A heuristic solution to this latter problem is Besag's (1986) deterministic ICM algorithm (see section 5.5.2).

Modified Newton Convergence Theorem

The important class of modified Newton algorithms, a special case of the general class of descent algorithms considered by the Descent Algorithm Convergence Theorem, was introduced. In particular, a modified Newton algorithm is defined by the descent algorithm

$$\mathbf{x}(t + 1) = \mathbf{x}(t) - \gamma_t \mathbf{Q}(t)\mathbf{g}(\mathbf{x}(t)),$$

where $\mathbf{g}$ is the gradient of some objective measure $V \colon \mathcal{R}^d \to \mathcal{R}$, $\mathbf{x}(0) \in \mathcal{R}^d$, $\gamma_t \in (0, \infty)$ is a properly chosen stepsize, and $\mathbf{Q}(t)$ is a positive definite matrix. Given some additional assumptions, $\mathbf{x}(t)$ converges to the set of critical points of V as $t \to \infty$.

The modified Newton algorithm provides a unified perspective for viewing a large class of popular dynamical system nonlinear optimization algorithms which have been used as ANN classification and ANN learning dynamical systems in the literature. In particular, the steepest descent, Newton, Levenberg-Marquardt, and Shanno algorithms, as well as the generic conjugate gradient algorithm (which includes the Polak-Ribière and Fletcher-Reeves algorithms as special cases) are important special cases of the modified Newton algorithm, which in turn is a special type of descent algorithm.

5.7   Elementary Problems

5.1-1. Let

$$f(x_1, x_2) = [x_1 + x_2]^2 + x_1 x_2 + x_1,$$

where $\mathbf{x} = [x_1, x_2]$. Compute the gradient of f.

5.1-2. Show that any eigenvalue λ of a symmetric 2×2 matrix, $\mathbf{w}$, whose ijth element is denoted by w_{ij} is a solution to the quadratic equation

$$(w_{11} - \lambda)(w_{22} - \lambda) - w_{12}^2 = 0.$$

Use the quadratic formula, which states that a solution to the equation

$$ax^2 + bx + c = 0$$

for the variable x (a, b, and c are constants) is given by

$$x = -b/2a \pm \left[\sqrt{b^2 - 4ac}\right]/2a,$$

to derive a formula for computing the eigenvalues of a 2×2 symmetric matrix.

5.1-3. Compute the Hessian of f, where f is defined as in problem 5.1-1.

5.1-4. Let f be defined according to

$$f(x_1, x_2) = \log (x_1^2 + x_2^2) + (2x_1 x_2 - x_1)^4.$$

Identify all critical points of the function f, classifying them as (1) strict local minima, (2) nonstrict local minima, (3) strict global minima, or (4) saddle points. HINT: You can compute the eigenvalues of the two-dimensional Hessian of f using a computer program or using the results of problem 5.1-2.

5.1-5. Identify all critical points of the function f defined in problem 5.1-1, classifying them as (1) strict local minima, (2) nonstrict local minima, (3) strict global minima, or (4) saddle points. HINT: You can compute the eigenvalues of the two-dimensional Hessian of f using a computer program or using the results of problem 5.1-2.

5.2-1. Suggest a batch version of the Widrow-Hoff learning rule guaranteed to converge to a critical point of a specific quadratic objective function. Explicitly define that objective function and all conditions required to prove convergence of the learning rule. Assume a finite number of stimuli in the training set.

5.2-2. Suggest a batch version of the Widrow-Hoff learning rule *with weight decay* (see section 4.3.2) that is guaranteed to converge to a critical point of a specific quadratic objective function. Explicitly define that objective function and all conditions required to prove convergence of the learning rule. Assume a finite number of stimuli in the training set.

5.2-3. What constraints must hold on the stimuli in the training set so that the algorithm in problem 5.2-1 converges to the unique strict global minimum of the quadratic objective function?

5.2-4. What constraints must hold on the stimuli in the training set so that the algorithm in problem 5.2-2 converges to the unique strict global minimum of the quadratic objective function?

5.3-1. Repeat problem 5.2-1 but propose an on-line version of the Widrow-Hoff learning rule where the stepsize is decreased at each iteration that generates a stochastic sequence of weight vectors $\tilde{\mathbf{w}}(1)$, $\tilde{\mathbf{w}}(2)$,.... Identify sufficient conditions for this stochastic sequence to converge with probability one to the global minimum of a specific quadratic objective function if it is assumed that $\{\tilde{\mathbf{w}}(t)\}$ is a bounded stochastic process.

5.3-2. Repeat problem 5.2-1 but propose an on-line version of the Widrow-Hoff learning rule *with weight decay* where the stepsize is decreased at each iteration that generates a stochastic sequence of weight vectors $\tilde{\mathbf{w}}(1)$, $\tilde{\mathbf{w}}(2)$,.... Identify sufficient conditions for this stochastic sequence to converge with probability one to a critical point of a specific quadratic objective function if it is assumed that $\{\tilde{\mathbf{w}}(t)\}$ is a bounded stochastic process.

5.3-3. Consider a Gibbs sampler algorithm for which the global joint probability mass function $p: \{0, 1\}^d \rightarrow (0, 1)$ is defined such that for all $\mathbf{x} \in \{0, 1\}^d$

$$p(\mathbf{x}) = Z^{-1} \exp[Q(\mathbf{x})],$$

where

$$Q(\mathbf{x}) = \sum_{i=1}^{d} x_i b_i + \sum_{i=3}^{d} \sum_{j=2}^{i-1} \sum_{k=1}^{j-1} x_i x_j x_k b_{ijk}$$

and Z is a normalization constant guaranteeing that $\sum_{\mathbf{x} \in \{0, 1\}^d} p(\mathbf{x}) = 1$. Obtain an explicit formula for $p(x_i(t+1) = 1 \mid \mathbf{n}_i(t))$.

5.3-4. Redo problem 5.3-3 using the Q function defined by

$$Q(\mathbf{x}) = \sum_{i=2}^{d} \sum_{j=1}^{i-1} x_i x_j w_{ij}.$$

5.4-1. Let $\mathbf{H}$ be the Hessian of the objective function in problem 5.2-1 and let $\mathbf{G}$ be the Hessian of the objective function in problem 5.2-2. Show that the ith eigenvalue of $\mathbf{G}$, g_i, can be expressed as some constant plus h_i where h_i is the ith eigenvalue of $\mathbf{H}$. Explicitly derive an expression for that constant. (See problem 5.4-2 to find out why this result is useful.)

5.4-2. Use the results of problem 5.4-1 to compare the convergence ratio of the algorithm in problem 5.2-1 with the convergence ratio of the algorithm in problem 5.2-2. Explicitly identify all assumptions underlying the comparison.

5.5-1. Derive an explicit algorithm for a batch version of the Widrow-Hoff learning rule based upon the Shanno algorithm.

5.5-2. Derive an explicit algorithm for a batch version of the Hebbian learning rule with weight decay based upon the Shanno algorithm.

5.8 Problems

5-1.   Consider an alternative derivation of the classical batch backpropagation learning algorithm based upon the work of Le Cun (1988). (This derivation is useful for deriving learning algorithms for complex backpropagation networks such as recurrent backpropagation learning algorithms.) Let the training set consist of the M training stimuli

$$(\mathbf{s}^1, \mathbf{o}^1), (\mathbf{s}^2, \mathbf{o}^2),\ldots, (\mathbf{s}^M, \mathbf{o}^M),$$

where $\mathbf{s}^k$ is the kth input vector and $\mathbf{o}^k$ is the kth target vector. Let the function $\underline{\mathcal{S}}: \mathcal{R}^d \rightarrow (0, 1)^d$ be defined as

$$\underline{\mathcal{S}}(\cdot) = [\mathcal{S}_1(\cdot),\ldots, \mathcal{S}_d(\cdot)],$$

where $\mathcal{S}_i(x) = 1/(1 + \exp[-x])$ for all $x \in \mathcal{R}, i = 1\ldots d$.
   Now, following Le Cun (1988), derive the backpropagation learning algorithm by considering the problem of searching for a critical point of l, where

$$
l(\mathbf{W}, \mathbf{V}, \mathbf{b}, \mathbf{d}, \lambda_1,\ldots\lambda_M, \delta_1,\ldots\delta_M, \mathbf{r}^1,\ldots, \mathbf{r}^M, \mathbf{h}^1,\ldots\mathbf{h}^M) = \\
(1/2)\sum_{k=1}^{M} |\mathbf{o}^k - \mathbf{r}^k|^2 + \sum_{k=1}^{M} \lambda_k^T[\mathbf{r}^k - \underline{\mathcal{S}}(\mathbf{W}\mathbf{h}^k + \mathbf{b})] + \sum_{k=1}^{M} \delta_k^T[\mathbf{h}^k - \underline{\mathcal{S}}(\mathbf{V}\mathbf{s}^k + \mathbf{d})].
$$

(5.39)

HINT: Search for $\mathbf{W}$, $\mathbf{V}$, $\mathbf{b}$, and $\mathbf{d}$ using an iterative gradient descent algorithm. Set the gradient of l with respect to the remaining variables equal to zero, and then explicitly solve for

$$\lambda_1,\ldots\lambda_M, \delta_1,\ldots\delta_M, \mathbf{r}^1,\ldots, \mathbf{r}^M, \mathbf{h}^1,\ldots, \mathbf{h}^M$$

in terms of $\mathbf{W}$, $\mathbf{V}$, $\mathbf{b}$, and $\mathbf{d}$.

5-2.   Repeat problem 5-1 using the cross-entropy learning objective function, l, which is defined such that

$$l = -\sum_{k=1}^{M} \sum_{i=1}^{d} \left[o_i^k \log\left[r_i^k\right] + \left(1 - o_i^k\right) \log\left[1 - r_i^k\right]\right],$$

where the ith element of $\mathbf{o}^k$, o_i^k, is either 0 or 1, and the ith element of $\mathbf{r}^k$ is r_i^k ($i = 1\ldots d$). HINT: Note that $r_i^k \in (0, 1)$.

5-3.   Consider the following one-layer connectionist network model. Let r_i^k be the activation of the ith output unit ($i = 1\ldots m$) given the kth input stimulus activation pattern. Let o_i^k be the desired (or target) activation of the ith output unit ($i = 1\ldots m$), given the kth input stimulus activation pattern. Let s_j^k be the activation of the jth input unit ($j = 1\ldots h$), given the kth input activation pattern. Let l be the learning objective function that the network is designed to minimize. Now define

$$l = -(1/n)\sum_{k=1}^{n} \sum_{i=1}^{m} \left[o_i^k \log\left(r_i^k\right) + \left(1 - o_i^k\right) \log\left(1 - r_i^k\right)\right],$$

where

$$r_i^k = \mathcal{S}\left[\sum_{j=1}^{h} w_{ij} s_j^k\right],$$

$$\mathcal{S}[x] = 1/[1 + \exp[-x]],$$

and $o_i^k \in \{0, 1\}$.

Derive a gradient descent learning algorithm that finds weights w_{ij} such that l is minimized. Derive a Newton learning algorithm that finds weights w_{ij} such that l is minimized. HINT: Compute the gradient and Hessian of the learning objective function with respect to the weight subvector associated with each individual output unit. Use the results of this computation to construct the gradient and Hessian of the learning objective function with respect to the entire weight vector.

5-4. Repeat problem 5-1 but assume that the output units and the hidden units are linear, so that $\mathcal{S}$ is defined such that for all $x \in \mathcal{R}$: $\mathcal{S}_k(x) = x$ for $k = 1 \ldots d$.

5-5. Using the Hessian of the learning objective function computed in problem 5-3, provide explicit conditions guaranteeing that the learning objective function will have a unique strict global minimum. Or in other words, prove conditions for the learned weights w_{ij} to be unique regardless of which learning algorithm or which initial conditions are used!

5-6. Compute the Hessian of the learning objective function in problem 5-3. Then discuss heuristically (in a few sentences) how the convergence ratio of the gradient descent algorithm varies as a function of the linear dependence relationships among the stimuli and additional nonlinear factors. That is, consider two cases. Case 1: Each output unit works like a digital feature detector for every pattern and decides whether a feature is present or absent. Case 2: Each output unit operates in its linear range, so that $\mathcal{S}(x)$ is approximately equal to x. HINT: Assume that the eigenvalues of a particular matrix for case 2 are known.

5-7. Consider a special type of Elman-style, recurrent, three-layer backpropagation network that learns sequences of events by *only* receiving a response feedback signal for the *last* event in each event sequence. Let

$$\mathbf{x}^k = \{\mathbf{s}^k(1), \mathbf{s}^k(2), \mathbf{s}^k(3), \ldots, (\mathbf{s}^k(M_k), \mathbf{o}^k(M_k))\},$$

where $\mathbf{x}^k$ is the kth sequence of training stimuli, $\mathbf{s}^k(t)$ is the tth input stimulus presented in the kth sequence of training stimuli, and $\mathbf{o}^k(t)$ is the tth desired response of the ANN system given $\mathbf{s}^k(t)$, $t = 1 \ldots M_k, k = 1 \ldots n$. Define the learning objective function

$$\hat{l}_n = (1/n)\sum_{k=1}^{n} |\mathbf{o}^k(M_k) - \mathbf{r}^k(M_k)|^2,$$

where for $t = 1 \ldots M_k$:

$$\mathbf{r}^k(t) = \mathcal{S}(\mathbf{W}\mathbf{h}^k(t))$$

is an m-dimensional vector, and $\mathbf{h}^k(t)$ is an a-dimensional column vector defined by

$$\mathbf{h}^k(t) = \mathcal{S}(\mathbf{V}\mathbf{s}^k(t) + \mathbf{R}\mathbf{h}^k(t-1)).$$

Sketch a diagram of this recurrent Elman-style ANN (see chapter 2), and describe how the network integrates incoming sequences.

Use the method of problem 5-1 to derive (a) a gradient descent learning algorithm that minimizes the proposed learning objective function, (b) a conjugate gradient descent learning algorithm that minimizes the proposed learning objective function, and (c) a Shanno (1978) algorithm that minimizes the proposed learning objective function. In practice, these algorithms will not work properly unless bias vectors for the hidden and output sigmoidal units are estimated as well. Explain how to modify your algorithms in order to achieve this goal.

HINT/WARNING: Remember that $\mathbf{h}^k(t)$ is functionally dependent upon $\mathbf{h}^k(t-1), \ldots, \mathbf{h}^k(0)$!

5-8. Consider a one-layer neural network whose ith output unit ($i = 1 \ldots p$) has activation value r_i^l when a d-dimensional input activation pattern $\mathbf{s}^l$ is presented. The activation value r_i^l is given explicitly by the formula

$$r_i^l = \mathbf{w}_i^T \mathbf{s}^l,$$

where $\mathbf{w}_i$ is the ith "weight vector."

Let the "performance error," l_p, be defined as

$$l_p = (1/2n)\sum_{l=1}^{n} |\mathbf{o}^l - \mathbf{r}^l|^2,$$

where the ith element of $\mathbf{r}^l$ is r^l_i and $\mathbf{o}^l$ is the "target" activation pattern (i.e., desired activation pattern over the output units), given input pattern $\mathbf{x}^l$.

Now define a "network complexity measure," l_c, such that

$$l_c = \sum_{j=1}^{d} \log\left[1 + \sum_{i=1}^{p} w_{ij}^2\right],$$

where w_{ij} is the jth element of weight vector $\mathbf{w}_i$.

Let the learning objective function l be defined as

$$l = l_p + \lambda l_c,$$

where λ is a positive number indicating the trade-off between the performance error and network complexity penalty factors.

Write two or three concise sentences that explain what the proposed network complexity measure is designed to accomplish, and how the measure accomplishes this task. Derive a gradient descent algorithm that minimizes the learning objective function l with respect to the weight matrix $\mathbf{W}$, where the ith row of $\mathbf{W}$ is the row vector $\mathbf{w}_i^T$. Suppose that the gradient descent algorithm is to be used to find a strict local minimum of the learning objective function l. Derive an explicit system of nonlinear equations such that, if satisfied by a matrix $\mathbf{W}^*$, then $\mathbf{W}^*$ will be a strict local minimum. This system of equations can then be used to decide when to "stop" the gradient descent algorithm.

5-9. Show that the Hopfield (1982) algorithm is a special case of Besag's (1986) ICM algorithm.

5-10. Show that the Boltzmann machine algorithm described in chapter 2 is a special case of the Gibbs sampler algorithm described in chapter 5. Then conclude that the Gibbs Sampler Convergence Theorem is relevant to the Boltzmann machine algorithm.

5-11. Consider a modified Newton algorithm with an optimally chosen stepsize where $\mathbf{Q}(t)$ is some fixed, symmetric, positive definite, time-invariant matrix, $\mathbf{Q}^*$, for all nonnegative t. Using the geometric interpretation of steepest descent, provide a geometric interpretation of (a) the descent direction, and (b) the convergence rate analysis of this algorithm.

5-12. Show that the Shanno algorithm and the Shanno (inefficient form) algorithm presented in chapter 5 are formally equivalent.

5-13. In the "ANN Applications" section of chapter 5, the problem of stepsize selection for the batch backpropagation algorithm was considered. A five-step procedure was provided for monitoring the behavior of a batch backpropagation learning algorithm in order to facilitate convergence to a critical point of the learning objective function l. Propose an algorithm based upon this five-step procedure that *automatically* adjusts the stepsize of the learning algorithm if the stepsize is found not to satisfy the properly chosen stepsize criteria. The algorithm should decrease the stepsize by some fixed amount if the stepsize is too large, and increase the stepsize by some fixed amount if the stepsize is too small.

5-14. Let $V: \mathcal{R}^d \to \mathcal{R}$. Let $\mathbf{x}(t-1) \in \mathcal{R}^d$, $\mathbf{x}(t) \in \mathcal{R}^d$, and $\mathbf{f}(t-1) \in \mathcal{R}^d$. Let $\mathbf{g}_t$ be the gradient of V evaluated at $\mathbf{x}(t)$. Let γ_{max} be a positive real number. Let

$$V_\gamma: (0, \gamma_{max}) \to \mathcal{R}$$

be defined such that for all $\gamma \in (0, \gamma_{max})$:

$$V_\gamma(\gamma) = V(\mathbf{x}(t-1) + \gamma \mathbf{f}(t-1)).$$

Assume that the second derivative of V_γ is continuous and strictly positive on $(0, \gamma_{max})$, so that there exists a unique strict global minimum of V_γ on $(0, \gamma_{max})$ by the global minimum test. Thus, if γ_t is a critical point of V_γ on $(0, \gamma_{max})$, then γ_t is the unique strict global minimum of V_γ on $(0, \gamma_{max})$.

Use a first-order Taylor expansion to show that γ_t is the unique strict global minimum of V_γ on $(0, \gamma_{max})$, that is, the optimal stepsize on $(0, \gamma_{max})$, if

$$\mathbf{g}_t^T \mathbf{f}(t-1) = 0. \tag{5.40}$$

Use the relation in (5.40) to show that if the stepsize is optimal, then $a_t = 0$ in the Shanno algorithm, and the Shanno algorithm reduces to the generic conjugate gradient algorithm (see Luenberger 1984, 280; Shanno 1978).

Now, again using the relation in (5.40), derive the Polak-Ribière conjugate gradient algorithm from the generic conjugate gradient algorithm.

5-15. Consider a generalization of the Boltzmann machine where the ith unit in the network computes the probability, $p_i(t)$, that it will fire at time t using the formula

$$p_i(t) = \mathscr{G}\left[\sum_{j=2}^{d}\sum_{k=1}^{i} w_{ijk}x_j(t)x_k(t) + \sum_{k=1}^{d} v_{ik}x_k(t) + b_i\right].$$

Show that such a network is a special case of the Gibbs sampler algorithm, where the $V(\mathbf{x})$ has the form

$$V(\mathbf{x}) = -\sum_{i}\sum_{j}\sum_{k} w_{ijk}x_i x_j x_k - \sum_{i}\sum_{k} v_{ik}x_i x_k - \sum_{i} x_i b_i.$$

(See Giles and Maxwell 1987; Besag 1974 for discussions related to this problem.)

5-16. Improve the solution provided in problem 5-13 in two distinct ways. First, after some fixed number of iterations of the stepsize search algorithm, terminate the algorithm and randomly choose a new stepsize in the vicinity of the current stepsize in order to move the search into a new region of the stepsize search space.

Second, approximate V_γ (where V_γ is defined as in problem 5-14) as a quadratic objective function in the vicinity of a strict local minimum. Let $\gamma_{\text{wrong}} \in (0, \gamma_{\text{max}})$ be a stepsize that was initially generated by either decreasing or increasing the default stepsize in order to find a properly chosen stepsize. Thus, at the second iteration of the stepsize search algorithm, one has the following pieces of information: $V_\gamma(0)$, $V_\gamma(\gamma_{\text{wrong}})$, and the derivative of V evaluated at both 0 and γ_{wrong}. If V_γ may be assumed to be a quadratic objective function on $(0, \gamma_{\text{max}})$, derive a formula for *explicitly* computing the strict global minimum of the quadratic approximation to V_γ on $(0, \gamma_{\text{max}})$. Make sure that your algorithm double-checks that the γ estimated from your formula is a properly chosen stepsize with respect to V_γ (the quadratic approximation may not be valid on the interval $(0, \gamma_{\text{max}})$)!

III COMPUTATIONAL LEVEL

Marr's computational level of description (1982) is concerned with justifying and understanding the computational goals of a complex *information-processing* system. Chapters 6, 7, and 8 provide mathematical tools for ANN analysis and design at this level of description (neither nonlinear dynamical systems theory nor nonlinear optimization theory is appropriate for investigating the computational goals of an information-processing system).

Chapter 6 shows how mathematical theories of evidence and rational decision making may be used to formally characterize systems of preferences. It explicitly identifies the conditions under which a particular system of preferences may be represented as an objective function on some set of possible decisions, precisely explaining in what sense ANN systems that minimize an objective function are rational decision-making systems. Chapter 6 also introduces a special type of probability measure known as the "Gibbs probability distribution," which will be exploited in chapter 7 to provide probabilistic objective functions for ANN classification and learning dynamical systems.

Chapter 7 shows how methods from the field of statistical pattern recognition can be applied to characterize and evaluate the rationality of an ANN system's computational goals. Chapter 8 uses results from the field of mathematical statistics as well as the theory developed in chapter 7 to derive (1) bounds on the prediction errors for ANN systems, and (2) methods for selecting the most appropriate ANN system architecture for a given statistical learning environment.

The key, underlying tool for analyzing high-dimensional nonlinear ANN systems that has been continually exploited in this textbook is the concept of an objective function. The objective function concept was used as an organizational tool for classifying ANN systems (chapter 2); Lyapunov-type objective functions were used for investigating asymptotic behavior in deterministic (chapter 3) and stochastic (chapter 4) dynamical systems; and many ANN systems were shown to be optimization algorithms (chapter 5), which seek the global minima of some objective function during either classication or learning processes.

Although such analyses are useful for investigating issues of asymptotic stability and convergence to objective function minima, they cannot justify *why* convergence to an equilibrium point or global minimum corresponds to a reasonable inference. To begin to address this issue, let S be a finite set of situations. Also define the concept of an *event* as some subset of S. The set of all possible subsets of S (when S is finite), $\mathcal{F}$, is called a "sigma field." A *relation* is a set, ω, of ordered pairs $\{(E_1, E_2)\}$ where both members of each ordered pair in the relation are elements of the sigma field $\mathcal{F}$ generated by S. A *relational system* is a triplet $(S, \mathcal{F}, \omega)$. An important type of a relation is a *preference relation, ω,* which is defined with respect to some relational system $(S, \mathcal{F}, \omega)$ such that E_1 is at least as preferable as E_2 (i.e., $(E_1, E_2) \in \omega$).

There is an important connection between the concept of a objective function for an ANN system and the concept of a relational system. To illustrate this relationship, let $V: S \rightarrow \mathcal{R}$ be an objective function for an ANN classification dynamical system, where $S \subseteq \mathcal{R}^d$. Assume the classification dynamical system can be proven to transform an activation pattern at iteration k, $\mathbf{x}(k)$, into an activation pattern at iteration $k + 1$, $\mathbf{x}(k + 1)$ such that $V(\mathbf{x}(k + 1)) \leq V(\mathbf{x}(k))$. Now suppose that a relational system $(S, \mathcal{F}, \omega)$ exists where ω is a preference relation and ω has the property that $(\mathbf{a}, \mathbf{b}) \in \omega$ if and only if $V(\mathbf{a}) \leq V(\mathbf{b})$. Thus, because the ANN system seeks an activation pattern that tends to minimize V,

the ANN classification dynamical system may be formally viewed as a heuristic algorithm designed to *construct an activation pattern that is maximally preferable* with respect to the preference relation, ω, where ω is implicitly defined by the classification objective function V.

Moreover, the inference problem for the ANN system as well as the complete knowledge base of the ANN system has been formally expressed in an algorithm-independent manner! The problem of learning in ANN learning dynamical systems may be viewed in a similar manner. Most ANN learning dynamical systems may be viewed as heuristic algorithms that seek a maximally preferable connection strength parameter vector with respect to some specific relation implicitly defined by the ANN learning system's learning objective function.

It will be shown that only some relational systems can be implicitly identified by an objective function and that such relational systems must satisfy certain axioms of rational decision making. For example, one important classical axiom of rational decision making is the *transitivity axiom,* which states that if event E_1 is at least as preferable as event E_2 and event E_2 is at least as preferable as event E_3, then event E_1 must be at least as preferable as event E_3. From an engineering viewpoint, the identification of such axioms of rational decision making is highly desirable because critical constraints upon the computational goals of the decision-making process are expressed by such axioms. An important goal of chapter 6 is to explicitly characterize the axioms of rational decision making that guide the inference-making behavior of many ANN information-processing systems.

On the other hand, considerable research in the field of human rational decision making (Kahneman and Tversky 1979; Tversky 1969; Wason 1966; Johnson-Laird, Legrenzi, and Legrenzi 1972) has shown that some systems of preference relationships used by humans are not consistent with the transitivity axiom, nor with other classical axioms of rational decision making and logic. Given these experimental findings, the viewpoint that an ANN's relational system should be constrained to be rational may seem misleading to neuroscientists and psychologists. It is important to realize, however, that many ANN systems never achieve their idealized rational computational goals due to their limited computational resources. Thus ANN systems that have been designed from a rational inference-making perspective could still exhibit the classical violations of logic and transitivity observed in human subjects due to intrinsic computational limitations. (Simon 1969 has proposed this explanation of irrationality in human performance.)

This chapter is divided into five major sections. In the first section, the basic theory of modeling relational systems will be formally introduced, the concept of a relational system formally defined, and the equivalence between connected transitive relational systems and objective functions explicitly developed. The second section will focus upon three especially important types of objective functions for relational systems: (1) fuzzy measures, (2) probabilistic fuzzy measures, and (3) expected risk functions. The third section will discuss a specific type of probabilistic fuzzy measure called a "Gibbs probability measure." Such probability measures are important because they may be used to provide computationally tractable probabilistic interpretations for a wide variety of ANN dynamical systems (see chapter 7 for additional details). The fourth section will address the issue of using the knowledge representation theory developed in previous sections to construct *decision rules* for guiding the inference-making behavior of an intelligent agent whose knowledge base can be represented as a relational system with a measure. Finally, in the fifth section, the theory developed in previous sections will be used to introduce a formal theory of generalization and inductive inference.

6.1   Measures for Relational Systems

Suppose that an intelligent agent has knowledge that one out of many possible outcomes could occur but does not know which. Or alternatively, suppose that an intelligent agent has to decide which of several outcomes in the world has already occurred, but the outcome which occurred is unknown to the intelligent agent. The set of all possible outcomes is called a "sample space." An element (outcome) of a sample space is called a "sample point." Typically, intelligent agents are more interested in classes of possible outcomes rather than specific outcomes. For example, an intelligent agent might have knowledge that the lottery ticket that the agent possesses could be the winning lottery ticket. Conceivably, there may be a set of sample points in the sample space that correspond to different situations where the agent has a winning lottery ticket. For example, the agent having a winning lottery ticket on a sunny day might be one such sample point, while another sample point might correspond to the situation where the agent has a winning lottery ticket on a rainy day. The intelligent agent may wish to ignore the weather and focus upon the situation of having a winning lottery ticket. The set of all possible situations where the intelligent agent wins a lottery ticket regardless of the weather is called an "event." Figure 6.1 illustrates these concepts using set notation.

One must be careful, however, in defining the concept of an event for a sample space with an infinite number of outcomes because a small percentage of subsets of an arbitrary infinite sample space have degenerate properties whose discussion lies beyond the scope of this textbook (see Bartle 1966, chap. 2, for further discussion). The following unmotivated definition of the concept of an event, however, will avoid these technical difficulties.

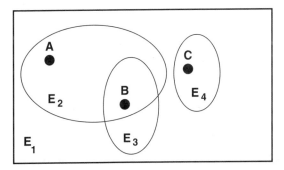

Figure 6.1
Sample points, events, and sample spaces. A sample space consisting of exactly three sample points: A, B, and C. Four of the eight events are shown: $E_1 = \{A, B, C\}$, $E_2 = \{A, B\}$, $E_3 = \{B\}$, and $E_4 = \{C\}$. Note that E_1 defines the sample space and that E_3 and E_4 are elementary events. The sigma field for this sample space is the set of the eight events.

Definition: Sample space and sigma field.   Let a *sample space S* be some set of *sample points* where each sample point corresponds to either a *possible outcome* or *unobservable situation*. The *sigma field*, $\mathcal{F}$, generated from S is the smallest set of all subsets of S that satisfy the following conditions:

1. $\varnothing \in \mathcal{F}$ and $S \in \mathcal{F}$.
2. If $A \in \mathcal{F}$, then the complement of A is in $\mathcal{F}$.
3. Given every sequence $\{A_i\}_{i=1}^{\infty}$ such that $A_i \in \mathcal{F}$, then $\bigcup_{i=1}^{\infty} A_i \in \mathcal{F}$.

Note that if a sample space S consists of a finite number, M, of outcomes, then the sigma field $\mathcal{F}$ consists of the 2^M possible subsets of S.

Definition: Event.   Let $\mathcal{F}$ be a sigma field generated by some sample space, S. An *event* is an element of the sigma field. If $x \in S$, then the event $\{x\}$ is an *elementary event*.

Using the above notation, let us return to the lottery example. Consider a sample space consisting of two sample points: $x_1 = $ *Ralph wins lottery on a sunny day*; $x_2 = $ *Ralph wins lottery on a rainy day*. There are four possible events which can be constructed with respect to this sample space. These four events will be denoted as E_1, E_2, E_3, and E_4.

- Event 1 *(Ralph does not win lottery)*: $E_1 = \{\}$.
- Event 2 *(Ralph wins lottery on a sunny day)*: $E_2 = \{x_1\}$.
- Event 3 *(Ralph wins lottery on a rainy day)*: $E_3 = \{x_2\}$.
- Event 4 *(Ralph wins the lottery)*: $E_4 = \{x_1, x_2\}$.

Now suppose the agent Ralph has a *preference relation* associated with the set of events $\{E_1, E_2, E_3, E_4\}$. In particular, suppose that agent Ralph agrees that events E_2, E_3, and E_4 are equally preferable and that events E_2, E_3, and E_4 are at least as preferable as event E_1. To express the collection of beliefs of agent Ralph formally, let (E_i, E_j) indicate that agent Ralph finds event E_i at least as preferable as event E_j. Then this collection of beliefs of agent Ralph may be formally expressed by the set of ordered pairs:

$$\{(E_2, E_1), (E_3, E_1), (E_4, E_1), (E_2, E_3), (E_3, E_2), (E_2, E_4), (E_4, E_2), (E_3, E_4), (E_4, E_3)\}.$$

A formal definition of the concept of a relation is now provided.

Definition: Relation.   Suppose that x and y are elements of some set $\mathcal{F}$. Let $\omega \subseteq \mathcal{F} \times \mathcal{F}$. If $(x, y) \in \omega$, then x is related to y by the *relation ω* on $\mathcal{F}$. The notation $x\omega y$ means that $(x, y) \in \omega$.

Definition: Relational system.   A *relational system* is a triplet $(S, \mathcal{F}, \omega)$ where $\mathcal{F}$ is a sigma field generated by S and ω is a relation on $\mathcal{F}$.

Definition: Measure for a relational system.   Assume $(S, \mathcal{F}, \omega)$ is a relational system with the property that there exists a function $\mathcal{P}: \mathcal{F} \rightarrow \mathcal{R}$ such that for all $x, y \in \mathcal{F}$: $x\omega y$ if and only if $\mathcal{P}(x) \leq \mathcal{P}(y)$. The function $\mathcal{P}$ is a *measure for the relational system* $(S, \mathcal{F}, \omega)$.

Note that the above definition emphasizes that a measure $\mathcal{P}: \mathcal{F} \rightarrow \mathcal{R}$ may not necessarily exist for every arbitrary relational system $(S, \mathcal{F}, \omega)$. It is also important to realize that a given relational system (e.g., a relational system of preferences) is sufficiently unconstrained that highly "irrational" preference relations may be represented. The following two special types of relations are important because they (1) place some "rational" restrictions on the relation ω, and (2) possess necessary properties of every relation that defines a relational system with a measure.

Definition: Connected relation.   Let $\omega \subseteq \mathcal{F} \times \mathcal{F}$, where $\mathcal{F}$ is a sigma field. Suppose that for every $x \in \mathcal{F}$ and every $y \in \mathcal{F}$: (i) $x\omega y$, (ii) $y\omega x$, or (iii) $x\omega y$ and $y\omega x$. Then ω is a *connected relation* on $\mathcal{F}$.

To illustrate the concept of a connected relation, let ω be a preference relation such that $(x, y) \in \omega$, provided that some intelligent agent A finds choice x at least as preferable as choice y. Then, if ω is a connected relation on some sigma field $\mathcal{F}$, for every pair of events, (x, y), in $\mathcal{F} \times \mathcal{F}$, the agent can make a decision as to whether (1) choice x is at least as preferable as choice y, (2) choice y is at least as preferable as choice x, or (3) choices x and y are equally preferable.

Another important special type of relation is the *transitive relation*.

Definition: Transitive relation.   Let $\omega \subseteq \mathcal{F} \times \mathcal{F}$, where $\mathcal{F}$ is a sigma field. The relation ω is *transitive* if $x\omega y$ and $y\omega z$ implies $x\omega z$ for all (x, y), $(y, z) \in \omega$.

The following example will illustrate the concept of a transitive relation. Let the event *Sandy visits Becky* be denoted as E_1, let the event *Sandy cleans the refrigerator* be denoted as E_2, and let the event *Sandy plays racquetball* be denoted as E_3. As before, let the notation (E_i, E_j) indicate that event E_i is at least as preferable as event E_j with respect to the belief structure of agent Sandy. Given these assumptions, the set

$$\omega_1 = \{(E_1, E_3), (E_3, E_2), (E_1, E_2)\}$$

is a transitive relation since: If Sandy believes event E_1 is at least as preferable as event E_3, and Sandy believes event E_3 is at least as preferable as event E_2, then Sandy believes event E_1 is at least as preferable as event E_2. On the other hand, the set

$$\omega_2 = \{(E_1, E_3), (E_3, E_2)\}$$

is not a transitive relation.

Note that a measure cannot exist for a relational system that is not transitive. To see this, simply note that if $\mathcal{P}$ is a measure for the relational system defined by ω_2, then $\mathcal{P}$ must satisfy the two equations

$$\mathcal{P}(E_1) \leq \mathcal{P}(E_3), \; \mathcal{P}(E_3) \leq \mathcal{P}(E_2),$$

which implies that $\mathcal{P}(E_1) \leq \mathcal{P}(E_2)$. But if $\mathcal{P}(E_1) \leq \mathcal{P}(E_2)$, then ω_2 must contain (E_1, E_2), which leads to a contradiction. In fact, if a relational system has a measure with respect to a finite sample space, then the relation of the relational system must be both transitive and connected (see Olinick 1978, 201).

Theorem: Existence of a Relational System. If $\mathcal{P}: \mathcal{F} \rightarrow \mathcal{R}$ exists, where $\mathcal{F}$ is the sigma field generated by S, then there exists a relational system $(S, \mathcal{F}, \omega)$, where ω is a connected and transitive relation, such that $\mathcal{P}$ is a measure for the relational system $(S, \mathcal{F}, \omega)$.

Proof. For each $x, y \in \mathcal{F}$, define ω such that (i) $(x, y) \in \omega$ if $\mathcal{P}(x) \leq \mathcal{P}(y)$, and (ii) $(x, y) \notin \omega$ if $\mathcal{P}(x) > \mathcal{P}(y)$. Thus the function $\mathcal{P}$ is a measure for the relational system $(S, \mathcal{F}, \omega)$.

Because, for every two numbers $\mathcal{P}(x), \mathcal{P}(y) \in \mathcal{R}$, either $\mathcal{P}(x) \leq \mathcal{P}(y)$ or $\mathcal{P}(y) \leq \mathcal{P}(x)$, it follows from the definition of ω that the relation ω is connected. And because, for every three numbers $\mathcal{P}(x), \mathcal{P}(y), \mathcal{P}(z) \in \mathcal{R}$, if $\mathcal{P}(x) \leq \mathcal{P}(y)$ and $\mathcal{P}(y) \leq \mathcal{P}(z)$, then $\mathcal{P}(x) \leq \mathcal{P}(z)$, it follows from the definition of ω that ω is a transitive relation. ∎

In order to understand the importance of the Existence of a Relational System Theorem, consider the special case where one knows that an ANN system is seeking the global minimum of some classification objective function $V: S \rightarrow \mathcal{R}$, where $S \subseteq \mathcal{R}^d$. A relational system that is consistent with the preferences expressed by the objective function V can be constructed in the following manner. Let $\mathcal{F}$ be the sigma field generated by S. Then define a function $\mathcal{P}: \mathcal{F} \rightarrow \mathcal{R}$ such that: $\mathcal{P}(\{a\}) = V(a)$ for all $a \in S$.

If an ANN system adjusts its activation pattern such that an objective function, V, is minimized, then the ANN system is formally searching for an activation pattern that minimizes the preference measure $\mathcal{P}$ for the connected and transitive relational system $(S, \mathcal{F}, \omega)$. Similarly, if an ANN system adjusts its connection strengths during a learning process such that some learning objective function, l, is minimized, then the ANN system is formally searching for a set of connection strengths that minimizes an appropriately constructed preference measure for a connected and transitive relational system derived from l.

6.2 Special Measures for Relational Systems

6.2.1 Fuzzy Measures

Consider a sigma field $\mathscr{F}$ generated from some sample space. A *belief relation* for some agent on $\mathscr{F}$ is a connected and transitive relation, ω, defined such that $(E_i, E_j) \in \omega$ if the agent believes that event E_i is less likely than event E_j. One approach to representing a belief relation would be to construct an appropriate measure for the belief relation. Still, the construction of such a relation might not fully capture some of the most important properties of beliefs.

For example, consider the following analysis of a simple toss of an unfair coin that is weighted to come up heads more likely than tails. The sample space for this analysis consists of the two sample points $x_1 = $ *Coin comes up heads,* and $x_2 = $ *Coin comes up tails.* The sigma field $\mathscr{F}$ generated from this sample space would then be $\{E_1, E_2, E_3, E_4\}$, where $E_1 = \{\}$, $E_2 = \{x_1\}$, $E_3 = \{x_2\}$, and $E_4 = \{x_1, x_2\}$. Thus the event E_1 corresponds to the situation where the coin does not come up heads or tails, event E_2 corresponds to the situation where the coin comes up heads, event E_3 corresponds to the situation where the coin comes up tails, and event E_4 corresponds to the situation where the coin comes up heads or the coin comes up tails. Note that for a specific coin toss, most agents would be absolutely certain that the coin will come up heads or the coin will come up tails. In addition, most agents would be absolutely certain that the event where the coin does not come up heads and does not come up tails would never occur. Suppose one wants to assign a degree of belief to a specific event, E, in a sigma field $\mathscr{F}$ where the *degree of belief* is defined as the measure evaluated at E for some relational system $(S, \mathscr{F}, \omega)$. It would seem reasonable to attempt to constrain the measure such that the degree of belief assigned to event $E_4 = \{x_1, x_2\}$ would be one (*true*) in order to represent certainty of occurrence. It would also seem reasonable to constrain the measure such that the degree of belief assigned to event $E_1 = \{\}$ would be zero (*false*) to indicate that the situation where the coin comes up either heads or tails could never occur. Another reasonable constraint might be to assume that the belief of $E_2 = \{x_1\}$ or $E_3 = \{x_2\}$ must be less than or equal to $E_4 = \{x_1, x_2\}$. Such constraints on the form of the measure for a relational system designed to measure degrees of belief are the basis for the following definition.

Definition: Fuzzy measure. Let $\mathscr{F}$ be a sigma field generated by S. A *fuzzy measure* (for crisp sets), $\mathscr{B}$, is a measure for a relational system $(S, \mathscr{F}, \omega)$. The notation $\mathscr{B}(E \mid S)$ indicates the value of a fuzzy measure evaluated at an event $E \in \mathscr{F}$. In addition, a fuzzy measure satisfies the following four conditions:

1. *Function condition:* $\mathscr{B}(\cdot \mid S): \mathscr{F} \to \mathscr{R}$.
2. *Boundary condition:* $\mathscr{B}(\varnothing \mid S) = 0$ and $\mathscr{B}(S \mid S) = 1$.

3. *Monotonicity condition:* For every A, $C \in \mathcal{F}$: if $A \subseteq C$, then

$\mathcal{B}(A \mid S) \le \mathcal{B}(C \mid S)$.

4. *Continuity condition:* Let A_1, A_2,... be any sequence of subsets of S. If either $A_1 \subseteq A_2 \subseteq$ ... or $A_1 \supseteq A_2 \supseteq$ ..., then

$$\lim_{i \to \infty} \mathcal{B}(A_i \mid S) = \mathcal{B}\left(\lim_{i \to \infty} A_i \mid S\right).$$

Note that a fuzzy measure is defined with respect to the classical notion of a set (for a review see Rosenlicht 1968, 2–7), referred to as a "crisp set" in the fuzzy set literature (for a review see Klir and Folger 1988, 4–10). A given element of a crisp set either is or is not a member of the set, while a member of a *fuzzy set* can have varying degrees of membership, where the degree of membership is explicitly defined by a set *membership function* (for a review see Klir and Folger 1988, 10–14; Zadeh 1965).

This definition of a fuzzy measure has four important conditions, which will now be discussed in some detail. First, the function condition implies the existence of some belief relation that is connected and transitive. Thus belief relations that are not connected or not transitive cannot be represented by a fuzzy measure (for crisp sets). Second, the boundary condition is used to identify specific limits of belief. In particular, the belief that no event will occur is assigned the value of zero (*false*), while the belief that at least one elementary event will certainly occur is assigned the value of one (*true*).

Third, the monotonicity condition serves two major functions. It constrains the fuzzy measure to assign a greater belief to the occurrence of events relative to special cases of those events. For example, let $A = $ *Ralph wins the lottery on Monday* and $B = $ *Ralph wins the lottery on Tuesday*. The monotonicity condition guarantees that the belief assigned to the union $A \cup B$ (i.e., *Ralph wins the lottery on Monday* OR *Ralph wins the lottery on Tuesday*) must be greater than or equal to the belief A (*Ralph wins the lottery on Monday*). Also note that the monotonicity condition, in conjunction with the boundary condition, constrains the range of the fuzzy measure to lie in the closed interval [0, 1].

And fourth, the continuity condition is always satisfied if the sample space is finite. The situation where the sample space is infinite is now discussed. Let $\mathcal{B}: \mathcal{F} \to [0, 1]$ be a fuzzy measure, where $\mathcal{F}$ is a sigma field generated from the sample space $\mathcal{R}$ defined such that $\mathcal{B}([a, 0)) = 0$ for $a < 0$ and $\mathcal{B}((0, b]) = 1$ for $b > 0$. Note that

$$\mathcal{B}\left(\lim_{a \to 0} [a, 0)\right) = 0$$

for $a < 0$, and

$$\mathcal{B}\left(\lim_{b \to 0} (0, b]\right) = 1$$

for $b > 0$. In this situation, it is unclear how to assign a value of the fuzzy measure to small intervals containing zero in a consistent manner. The fourth condition directly addresses this problem by placing an appropriate restriction on the form of $\mathcal{B}$, so that values of the fuzzy measure are assigned in a consistent manner. If the sample space is $\mathcal{R}^d$, then the continuity condition can be satisfied by requiring the fuzzy measure to be continuous on the sigma field generated by $\mathcal{R}^d$ (Klir and Folger 1988, 109).

6.2.2 Probabilistic Fuzzy Measures

The fuzzy measure is an important tool for representing a large class of rational relational systems with fuzzy measures that satisfy the (1) function (which implies connectivity and transitivity), (2) boundary, (3) monotonicity, and (4) continuity conditions. One very reasonable *additional* set of "rational" constraints is that calculations involving fuzzy measures should be consistent with the Boolean algebra (i.e., deductive logic). The following concept of a *logical fuzzy measure* is based upon the work of R. T. Cox (1946).

Definition: Logical fuzzy measure.   Let $\mathcal{F}$ be the sigma field generated from some sample space $S \subseteq \mathcal{R}^d$. A *logical fuzzy measure* $\mathcal{B}(\cdot \mid S): \mathcal{F} \to \mathcal{R}$ is a fuzzy measure that also satisfies the following two conditions:

1. A continuous function $g: [0, 1] \to [0, 1]$ exists such that for every $A \in \mathcal{F}$:

$$\mathcal{B}(\neg A \mid S) = g[\mathcal{B}(A \mid S)], \tag{6.1}$$

where $g(0) = 1$ and $g(1) = 0$.

2. A function $h: [0, 1] \times [0, 1] \to [0, 1]$ continuous in both arguments exists such that for every $D, E \in \mathcal{F}$ where $D \subset E$:

$$\mathcal{B}(D \cap E \mid S) = h[\mathcal{B}(E \mid S), \mathcal{B}(D \mid E, S)], \tag{6.2}$$

where $h(0, 0) = 0$, $h(0, 1) = 0$, $h(1, 0) = 0$, and $h(1, 1) = 1$.

The assumptions of a logical fuzzy measure essentially select out a particular group of fuzzy measures from the universe of possible fuzzy measures that are consistent with the deductive logic. Which means, in those rare and exceptional circumstances where one knows a particular event definitely will or will not occur, inductive inferences made using the logical fuzzy measure will be consistent with the deductive inferences of Boolean algebra. Hence the name, "*logical* fuzzy measure." The following discussion will help clarify this concept and the interpretation of the definition of a logical fuzzy measure.

Equation (6.1) defines the constraint g that the belief some event A will occur should uniquely determine the belief event A will not occur. In addition, (6.1) introduces boundary constraints on g such that the belief event A definitely will occur (i.e., $\mathcal{B}(A \mid S) = 1$) should automatically imply that event A definitely will not occur (i.e., $\mathcal{B}(\neg A \mid S) = 0$). For example, if the event $A = $ *It will rain today,* then constraint (6.1) means that an agent who has some belief *It will rain today* should be able to uniquely compute the belief *It will NOT rain today.* Moreover according to (6.1), if the agent holds with absolute certainty the belief *It will rain today,* then the agent must hold with absolute certainty the belief *It will NOT rain today.* Although one might think that the constraint in (6.1) should be automatically included in the definition of every fuzzy measure, it is worth noting that the Dempster-Schafer theory of belief does not require it (Klir and Folger 1988, 111).

Equation (6.2) defines the constraint h that the belief the conjunction of two events D and E will occur in context S (i.e., $\mathcal{B}(D \cap E \mid S)$) should be uniquely computable from (1) the belief in event E (i.e., $\mathcal{B}(E \mid S)$), and (2) the belief event D will occur given the occurrence of event E (i.e., $\mathcal{B}(D \mid E, S)$). In addition, (6.2) introduces three boundary constraints on h with respect to sample space context S. The first boundary constraint states that the belief event E definitely will not occur (i.e., $\mathcal{B}(E \mid S) = 0$) implies the belief that both events D AND E definitely will not occur (i.e., $h(0, 0) = 0$ and $h(0, 1) = 0$). The second boundary constraint states that the belief event D will definitely not occur given event E has occurred (i.e., $(\mathcal{B}(D \mid E, S) = 0$) implies the belief that both events D AND E definitely will not occur (i.e., $h(0, 0) = 0$ and $h(1, 0) = 0$). The third boundary constraint states that the belief event D will definitely occur given event E has occurred (i.e., $\mathcal{B}(D \mid E, S) = 1$) and the belief event E will definitely occur (i.e., $\mathcal{B}(E \mid S) = 1$) implies the belief both events D AND E will definitely occur (i.e., $h(1, 1) = 1$).

For example, suppose that event $D = $ *It will rain tomorrow* and event $E = $ *It is raining today.* The constraint in (6.2) states that an agent who can compute (1) the belief *It will rain tomorrow,* given the event *It is raining today,* and (2) the belief *It is raining today* should be able to uniquely compute the belief *It will rain tomorrow* AND *It is raining today.* In addition, (6.2) implies that if the agent does not hold the belief *It is raining today,* then the agent does not hold the belief *It will rain tomorrow* AND *It is raining today* ($h(0, 0) = 0$ and $h(0, 1) = 0$). The constraint $h(1, 1) = 1$ in conjunction with (6.2) implies that if (1) the agent holds with certainty the belief *It is raining today,* and (2) the agent holds with certainty the belief *It will rain tomorrow* given the event *It is raining today,* then the agent should hold with certainty the belief *It will rain tomorrow* AND *It is raining today.*

Notice that the functions g and h in (6.1) and (6.2) are *combining functions* that can be used to calculate and compute beliefs. For purposes of computation, it is worthwhile to try to choose the simplest possible combining functions for a belief calculus. One very important special case of the logical fuzzy measure is a probabilistic fuzzy measure, which is now defined.

Definition: Probabilistic fuzzy measure.   A *probabilistic fuzzy measure p* is a logical fuzzy measure where g in (6.1) is given by the formula

$$g(x) = 1 - x \tag{6.3}$$

for every $x \in [0, 1]$, and h in (6.2) is given by the formula

$$h(x, y) = xy \tag{6.4}$$

for every $x, y \in [0, 1]$.

It is important to note that the combining functions g and h for a probabilistic belief calculus are special cases of the more general definitions of g and h in (6.1) and (6.2). Note that g in (6.3) is continuous and satisfies both $g(0) = 1$ and $g(1) = 0$. Also note that h in (6.4) is continuous and satisfies $h(0, 0) = 0$, $h(0, 1) = 0$, $h(1, 0) = 0$, and $h(1, 1) = 1$.

Many mathematicians and computer scientists (e.g., Cheeseman 1986; Cox 1946; Lindley 1982 1987; Pearl 1988; Savage 1972; Wise 1986) believe, as do I, that the assumptions of a logical (and therefore probabilistic) fuzzy measure are quite natural and appropriate for modeling a variety of interesting rational decision-making problems. On the other hand, an equally large number of mathematicians and computer scientists (e.g., Klir and Folger 1988; Shafer 1987; Zadeh 1986) believe that these assumptions (although appropriate in some very special cases) are too restrictive for most such problems. (McNeill and Freiberger 1993, chap. 9, provides a popular, nonformal review of this controversy; for a formal discussion and a relatively good unbiased perspective, the reader should consult Klir and Folger 1988.)

6.2.3 Probability Mass (Density) Functions

The equivalence between a probabilistic fuzzy measure and the traditional definition of a conditional probability mass (density) function is formally established by the following theorem, which *derives* the axioms of probability theory from the properties of a probabilistic fuzzy measure. The statement and proof of the following theorem is an adaptation and straightforward extension of selected results from the work of Cox (1946).

Definition: Sequence of pairwise disjoint sets.   Let $\mathcal{F}$ be a sigma field. Define $A = \{A_1, A_2, A_3, \ldots\}$ such that for every $A_i \in A$ and every $A_j \in A$: (i) A_i, $A_j \in \mathcal{F}$, and (ii) $A_i \cap A_j = \varnothing$. Then the sequence $A_1, A_2, \ldots$ is a *sequence of pairwise disjoint sets* in $\mathcal{F}$.

Theorem: Fundamental Probabilistic Belief Theorem.   Let $\mathcal{F}$ be a sigma field generated by a sample space S. Given a probabilistic fuzzy measure $\mathcal{B}(\cdot \mid S): \mathcal{F} \to \mathcal{R}$, the following axioms and definition of classical probability theory are satisfied by $\mathcal{B}$ for every $D, E \in \mathcal{F}$:

- Axiom 1: $\mathcal{B}(E \mid S) \geq 0$;
- Axiom 2: $\mathcal{B}(S \mid S) = 1$;

- Axiom 3:

$$\mathcal{B}\left(\bigcup_{i=1}^{\infty} A_i \mid S\right) = \sum_{i=1}^{\infty} \mathcal{B}(A_i \mid S)$$

for every sequence of pairwise disjoint sets, $(A_1, A_2, \ldots)$, in $\mathcal{F}$;

- Definition 1: $\mathcal{B}(D \cap E \mid S) = \mathcal{B}(D \mid E, S)\mathcal{B}(E \mid S)$.

Note that definition 1 is sometimes referred to as the "definition of a conditional probability."

Proof. Axioms 1 and 2 are proved using the fact that a probabilistic fuzzy measure satisfies the function, boundary, and monotonicity conditions of a fuzzy measure. These three conditions imply that $\mathcal{B}(A \mid S) \geq 0$ for all $A \in \mathcal{F}$ and $\mathcal{B}(S \mid S) = 1$. The definition of a conditional probability (definition 1) follows from the specific functional form chosen for the combining function h in (6.2) and (6.4), which was $h(x, y) = xy$. Thus the only remaining problem is to prove axiom 3. Let $b, c \in \mathcal{F}$. Using definition 1,

$$\mathcal{B}(c \cap b \mid S) + \mathcal{B}(\neg c \cap b \mid S) = [\mathcal{B}(c \mid b \cap S) + \mathcal{B}(\neg c \mid b \cap S)]\mathcal{B}(b \mid S). \quad (6.5)$$

Using (6.3),

$$\mathcal{B}(c \mid b \cap S) + \mathcal{B}(\neg c \mid b \cap S) = 1. \quad (6.6)$$

Now substituting (6.6) into (6.5),

$$\mathcal{B}(c \cap b \mid S) + \mathcal{B}(\neg c \cap b \mid S) = \mathcal{B}(b \mid S). \quad (6.7)$$

Using (6.3) and the logical relation (DeMorgan's theorem)

$$c \cup b = \neg[\neg c \cap \neg b],$$

we obtain

$$\mathcal{B}(c \cup b \mid S) = 1 - \mathcal{B}(\neg(c \cup b) \mid S) = 1 - \mathcal{B}(\neg c \cap \neg b \mid S). \quad (6.8)$$

From (6.7) and (6.8),

$$\mathcal{B}(c \cup b \mid S) = 1 - \mathcal{B}(\neg c \cap \neg b \mid S) = 1 - [\mathcal{B}(\neg b \mid S) - \mathcal{B}(c \cap \neg b \mid S)]. \quad (6.9)$$

From (6.3) and (6.9),

$$\mathcal{B}(c \cup b \mid S) = \mathcal{B}(b \mid S) + \mathcal{B}(c \cap \neg b \mid S). \quad (6.10)$$

Using (6.7),

$$\mathcal{B}(b \cap c \mid S) + \mathcal{B}(\neg b \cap c \mid S) = \mathcal{B}(c \mid S). \quad (6.11)$$

Substituting (6.11) into (6.10),

$$\mathcal{B}(c \cup b \mid S) = \mathcal{B}(c \mid S) + \mathcal{B}(b \mid S) - \mathcal{B}(c \cap b \mid S). \tag{6.12}$$

Equation (6.12) is the general rule for combining probabilities used in classical probability theory.

By induction, (6.12) implies that for $n = 1, 2, 3,\ldots$:

$$\mathcal{B}\left(\bigcup_{i=1}^{n} A_i \mid S\right) = \sum_{i=1}^{n} \mathcal{B}(A_i \mid S) \tag{6.13}$$

for every sequence of pairwise disjoint sets $\{A_i\}_{i=1}^{n}$ in $\mathcal{F}$. Thus axiom 3 has been derived where S is a finite set. The case where S is an infinite set is now considered.

To complete the proof, it is thus only necessary to show that

$$\mathcal{B}\left(\bigcup_{i=1}^{\infty} A_i \mid S\right) = \sum_{i=1}^{\infty} \mathcal{B}(A_i \mid S)$$

for every sequence of pairwise disjoint sets $\{A_i\}_{i=1}^{\infty}$ in $\mathcal{F}$.

Note that there exists an element $y \in \mathcal{F}$ such that

$$y = \bigcup_{i=1}^{\infty} A_i$$

because $\mathcal{F}$ is a sigma field. Note also that $\mathcal{B}$ maps the elements of $\mathcal{F}$ into the range $[0, 1]$ because $\mathcal{B}$ is a fuzzy measure. Thus, since

$$0 \leq \mathcal{B}\left(\bigcup_{i=1}^{\infty} A_i \mid S\right) \leq 1,$$

it follows that $\left| \mathcal{B}(\bigcup_{i=1}^{\infty} A_i \mid S) \right| < \infty$.

For notational convenience, assume for the remainder of the proof that A_1, $A_2,\ldots$ is an arbitrary sequence of pairwise disjoint sets in $\mathcal{F}$. Now for every positive integer n from (6.13):

$$\mathcal{B}\left(\bigcup_{i=1}^{n} A_i \mid S\right) = \sum_{i=1}^{n} \mathcal{B}(A_i \mid S) \leq \sum_{i=1}^{\infty} \mathcal{B}(A_i \mid S) \tag{6.14}$$

because $\mathcal{B}(\cdot \mid S)$ is nonnegative. Also from

$$\bigcup_{i=1}^{n} A_i \subseteq \bigcup_{i=1}^{n+1} A_i$$

and condition 3 of the definition of a fuzzy measure, it follows that

$$\mathscr{B}\left(\bigcup_{i=1}^{n} A_i \mid S\right), \ \mathscr{B}\left(\bigcup_{i=1}^{n+1} A_i \mid S\right), \ \mathscr{B}\left(\bigcup_{i=1}^{n+2} A_i \mid S\right), \ldots \tag{6.15}$$

is a nondecreasing series with a finite upper bound because $\left|\mathscr{B}\left(\bigcup_{i=1}^{\infty} A_i \mid S\right)\right|$ is finite. Thus (6.15) converges to $\mathscr{B}\left(\bigcup_{i=1}^{\infty} A_i \mid S\right)$. Using this observation with (6.14) gives

$$\mathscr{B}\left(\bigcup_{i=1}^{\infty} A_i \mid S\right) \leq \sum_{i=1}^{\infty} \mathscr{B}(A_i \mid S). \tag{6.16}$$

Also for every positive integer n:

$$\mathscr{B}\left(\bigcup_{i=1}^{\infty} A_i \mid S\right) \geq \mathscr{B}\left(\bigcup_{i=1}^{n} A_i \mid S\right) = \sum_{i=1}^{n} \mathscr{B}(A_i \mid S) \tag{6.17}$$

from $\bigcup_{i=1}^{n} A_i \subseteq \bigcup_{i=1}^{\infty} A_i$ and condition 3 of the definition of a fuzzy measure. Note that

$$\sum_{i=1}^{n} \mathscr{B}(A_i \mid S), \ \sum_{i=1}^{n+1} \mathscr{B}(A_i \mid S), \ldots$$

is a nondecreasing sequence with a finite upper bound by (6.17) since $0 \leq \mathscr{B}\left(\bigcup_{i=1}^{\infty} A_i \mid S\right) \leq 1$. Thus

$$\mathscr{B}\left(\bigcup_{i=1}^{\infty} A_i \mid S\right) \geq \sum_{i=1}^{\infty} \mathscr{B}(A_i \mid S). \tag{6.18}$$

But (6.16) and (6.18) cannot both be true unless

$$\mathscr{B}\left(\bigcup_{i=1}^{\infty} A_i \mid S\right) = \sum_{i=1}^{\infty} \mathscr{B}(A_i \mid S). \quad \blacksquare$$

Note that a probabilistic fuzzy measure is defined in a manner totally independent of the relative frequency of events in the environment. Thus it is sometimes referred to as a type of "subjective probability measure" because the agent assigns a degree of belief to a given event that is essentially arbitrary. An important advantage of subjective probability measures is that they are flexible enough to model a great variety of alternative agent belief structures. The relationship between probabilistic fuzzy measures and the classical concepts of subjective and objective probability measures should be clarified by the following definitions.

Definition: Subjective probability mass (density).   Let $\mathscr{B}$ be a probabilistic fuzzy measure such that $\mathscr{B}: \mathscr{F} \to \mathscr{R}$, with $\mathscr{F}$ generated by sample space S, where

$S \subseteq \mathcal{R}^d$. A *subjective probability mass (density) function*, $p: S \rightarrow [0, \infty)$ for $\mathcal{B}$, has the property that

$$\mathcal{B}(U) = \sum_{\mathbf{x} \in U} p(\mathbf{x})$$

for each $U \in \mathcal{F}$ if S is finite or countably infinite, and

$$\mathcal{B}(U) = \int_{\mathbf{x} \in U} p(\mathbf{x}) d\mathbf{x}.$$

for each $U \in \mathcal{F}$ if S is an infinite set that is not countably infinite.

Definition: Environmental probability mass (density). Consider an *environment, e,* defined by a stochastic sequence of independent and identically distributed random vectors $\tilde{\mathbf{x}}(0), \tilde{\mathbf{x}}(1),\ldots$ with common probability mass (density) function $p_e: S \rightarrow [0, \infty)$, where $S \subseteq \mathcal{R}^d$. The probability mass (density) function p_e is the *environmental probability mass (density) function* for e.

Definition: Probability model. A *probability model, F_W,* is a set of probability mass (density) functions defined with respect to sample space S, where the elements of F_W are indexed by a real-valued parameter vector $\mathbf{w} \in W$, so that

$$F_W = \{(p(\cdot \mid \mathbf{w}): S \rightarrow [0, \infty)): \mathbf{w} \in W\}.$$

In most applications involving probabilistic fuzzy measures, a learning machine begins with some probability model and attempts to identify an element that is the environmental probability mass (density) function (i.e., the actual data-generating process). Of course, it is quite possible the probability model that represents an agent's beliefs does not contain the environmental probability mass (density) function!

Definition: Misspecified probability model. A probability model, F_W, is *misspecified* with respect to a given environmental probability mass (density) function, p_e, if p_e is not a member of F_W.

6.2.4 Expected Risk Functions

A relational system designed to solve the following type of problem will be developed in this section. Suppose that a coin is weighted so that, when flipped, it will come up *heads* 60 percent of the time and *tails* 40 percent of the time. Also suppose that an agent A is asked to decide if the coin will come up *heads* or *tails*. In addition, suppose that the agent receives $5 if the guess is correct, but loses $1,000 if the guess is incorrect.

The information specifying this simple coin-flipping problem may be conveniently represented as an ordered pair consisting of the probabilities [0.6, 0.4] and the respective outcomes [*heads, tails*]. Such an ordered pair is referred to as a "gamble."

One way to approach the problem of constructing a relational system with a measure on a set of gambles is simply to define a fuzzy measure on the set of gambles, where the fuzzy measure value assigned to a particular gamble G represents the agent's degree of belief that gamble G is the preferred gamble. Thus, from this perspective, the problem of representation of risk is simply a special case of the problem of representation of belief. Or in other words, a probabilistic fuzzy measure can be used to represent the agent's preferences.

A second method of representing an agent's preferences differentiates between the agent's subjective belief in the occurrence of a particular event and the agent's subjective loss associated with that event. Let a probabilistic fuzzy measure on $\mathscr{F}$ be a measure of an agent's belief that a particular event in $\mathscr{F}$ is *likely to occur*. For example, consider an ANN that has to decide whether poison is present or absent in a given food sample. The ANN system may estimate the belief poison is present to be relatively low and the belief poison is absent to be relatively high. However, this does not mean the ANN system should eat the food sample simply because the belief poison is present is relatively low. If the poison is deadly, the loss associated with deciding poison is absent from the food sample when in fact the food sample is actually poisoned is quite different from the loss associated with correctly deciding poison is absent from the food sample. Thus such representations of loss must somehow be integrated with the ANN system's representation of uncertainty in order to generate rational decisions that simultaneously consider both the likelihood and value of expected environmental events.

Von Neumann and Morgenstern in 1944 (see von Neumann and Morgenstern 1953 for the revised edition of their 1944 book) were among the earliest researchers to address the problem of combining representations of uncertainty with representations of loss. In particular, they proved a theorem justifying the use of a special objective function for rational decision making that combines losses and uncertainties in an additive manner. This objective function is commonly known as the "expected risk function" in the field of statistical pattern recognition. Although their theorem is also valid for subjective probabilities, von Neumann and Morgenstern tended to view their probability distributions as objective probability mass/density functions.

While the von Neumann and Morgenstern (1944, 26–27) axioms have been considerably improved and refined over the years (see Luce and Suppes 1965 for an excellent review of later extensions of the original theorem; also see Savage 1972 and DeGroot 1970 for related approaches), those of the original theorem are relatively straightforward to interpret and state. Let the notation $([x_1, x_2], [p, 1 - p])$ refer to a gamble consisting of two alternative outcomes x_1, x_2 with respective subjective probabilities $p, 1 - p$. The notation $(x, 1)$ will be used to refer to a gamble where the outcome x occurs with certainty (i.e., $(x, 1) = ([x, x_2], [p, 1 - p])$, where $p = 1$).

Von Neumann and Morgenstern made the following assumptions:

• *Existence, connectivity, and transitivity.* Assume the existence of a connected and transitive preference relation for comparing elements within a set of gambles.

• *Stability of preferences when probabilities are perturbed.* Assume that if gamble $(x, 1)$ is preferred to gamble $(y, 1)$, then for every $p \in (0, 1)$: Gamble $(x, 1)$ is preferable to gamble $([x, y], [p, 1 - p])$. Also assume that if gamble $(x, 1)$ is preferred to gamble $(y, 1)$ and gamble $(y, 1)$ is preferred to gamble $(z, 1)$, then there exists a $p \in (0, 1)$ such that gamble $(y, 1)$ is preferable to gamble $([x, z], [p, 1 - p])$.

• *Irrelevant naming of gambles.* Assume that for every $p \in (0, 1)$: the gamble $([x, y], [p, 1 - p])$ and the gamble $([y, x], [1 - p, p])$ are equally preferable.

• *Equivalence of sequential composite gambles.* Assume that for every p_1, $p_2 \in (0, 1)$: the gamble $([[(x, y), (p_1, 1 - p_1)], y], [p_2, 1 - p_2])$ and the gamble $([x, y], [p_1 p_2, 1 - p_1 p_2])$ are equally preferable.

Granted these assumptions, von Neumann and Morgenstern proved there exists a real-valued function, l, that maps gambles into numbers as follows. First, $l[([x, y], [p, 1 - p])]$ is uniquely determined by the formula

$$l[([x, y], [p, 1 - p])] = k_1[pl((x, 1)) + (1 - p)l((y, 1))] + k_2,$$

where k_1 is an arbitrary positive number and k_2 is an arbitrary number. Second, if gamble G_1 is preferred to gamble G_2, $l(G_1) < l(G_2)$ for all $k_2 \in \mathcal{R}$ and for all $k_1 \in (0, \infty)$. Thus, without any loss in generality, one usually sets $k_1 = 1$ and $k_2 = 0$. The function l is referred to as an "expected Bayes risk function."

The important expected Bayes risk function concept will now be formally defined. In the following discussion, a *decision* is simply a vector of real numbers indicating the particular choice, action, or decision selected by the decision maker. A *situation* is also a vector of real numbers indicating the specific context in which a given decision is made.

Definition: Loss function.   Let $D \subseteq \mathcal{R}^d$ be a set of decisions. Let $Q \subseteq \mathcal{R}^q$ be a set of situations. A *loss function*,

$c(\cdot \mid \cdot): D \times Q \rightarrow \mathcal{R},$

for an agent A is defined such that $c(\mathbf{x} \mid \mathbf{y})$ is the subjective loss incurred by agent A for choosing decision $\mathbf{x} \in D$ in situation $\mathbf{y} \in Q$.

Definition: Subjective Bayes risk function.   Let $D \subseteq \mathcal{R}^d$ be a set of decisions. Let $Q \subseteq \mathcal{R}^q$ be a set of situations. Let $c(\cdot \mid \cdot): D \times Q \rightarrow \mathcal{R}$ be a loss function for some agent A. Let $p: Q \to [0, \infty)$ be a subjective probability mass (density) function for the random vector $\tilde{\mathbf{y}}$ with respect to agent A. The function $l: D \to \mathcal{R}$ is a *subjective Bayes risk function* with respect to loss function c and subjective probability mass (density) p if

$$l(\mathbf{x}) = E_{\tilde{\mathbf{y}}}[c(\mathbf{x} \mid \tilde{\mathbf{y}})]$$

is finite for each $\mathbf{x} \in D$.

Definition: Objective Bayes risk function. Let $D \subseteq \mathcal{R}^d$ be a set of decisions. Let $l: D \to \mathcal{R}$ be a subjective Bayes risk measure with respect to a subjective probability mass (density) function p and loss function c. If p is an environmental probability mass (density) function, then l is an *objective Bayes risk function* with respect to p and c.

6.3   Gibbs Probability Measures (Markov Random Fields)

Most decision spaces for ANN systems are extremely high dimensional. For example, consider the analysis of the Boltzmann machine in section 5.3 using the Gibbs sampler algorithm (the reader may want to reread the analysis of section 5.3 at this point). In this example, a probability mass is assigned to each d-dimensional activation pattern vector in a sample space with 2^d activation pattern vectors, where d is the number of units in the ANN classification dynamical system (see equation 5.26). For d large (e.g., $d = 100$), this is a very high dimensional sample space.

The stochastic environment of a Boltzmann machine may be modeled as a collection of d random variables: $\tilde{\mathbf{x}} = [\tilde{x}_1,\ldots, \tilde{x}_d]$ such that $\tilde{x}_i$ can take on only the values of zero or one. An activation pattern vector is an observed value of the d-dimensional random vector $\tilde{\mathbf{x}}$. The *global joint probability mass function* p_τ may be interpreted as a probabilistic fuzzy measure that assigns a degree of preference to each of the possible 2^d activation pattern vectors. The computational goal of the Boltzmann machine is to find a global maximum of p_τ (i.e., a most probable or most preferred point in the sample space with respect to p_τ).

Because it would be computationally intractable to directly search the domain of p_τ: $\{0, 1\}^d \to (0, 1)$ for large d, the Gibbs sampler algorithm was used to search for a global maximum of p_τ (see section 5.3). The Gibbs sampler algorithm requires that one compute the *local conditional probability mass function* (see equation 5.27) given by

$$p_\tau(x_i = 1 \mid x_1,\ldots, x_{i-1}, x_{i+1},\ldots, x_d) = \mathcal{S}\left[\frac{\sum_{j=1, j\neq i}^{d} w_{ij} x_j}{\tau}\right],$$

which defines the conditional probability mass function for the ith random variable $\tilde{x}_i$, given the observed values of the other random variables in the Boltzmann machine. This example provides a nice illustration of how the factorization of a global joint probability distribution defined on some high-dimensional sample space can result in an analysis that is computationally more tractable as well as more easily interpretable.

This section explores these issues in both greater depth and greater generality. First, the concepts of a local conditional probability distribution and a global joint probability distribution are introduced within the relatively familiar context of Markov chains. Second, the concept of a Markov random field is introduced as a generalization of the Markov chain concept. And third, the Fundamental Markov Random Field Theorem is stated and proved. The theorem provides a methodology for defining an appropriate global joint probability distribution in terms of the functional form of a set of local conditional probability distributions; it shows how a given global joint probability distribution can be factored into the product of a set of local conditional probability distributions. (The content and organization of the following discussion of Markov random fields is based primarily upon Besag 1974; also see Marroquin 1985 for a helpful introduction.)

6.3.1   Markov Chains

The concept of a Markov chain provides an important foundation for introducing the more general concept of a Markov random field.

Let $\tilde{x}_i$ be the identity of the ith random variable in a set of random variables. It will also be convenient to assume that the probability of every realization of the Markov chain is strictly positive. This assumption will be referred to as the "positivity assumption." Given the above assumptions, consider a finite set of M random variables $\{\tilde{x}_1,\ldots, \tilde{x}_i,\ldots, \tilde{x}_M\}$ such that the probability distribution of $\tilde{x}_i$ is functionally dependent only upon $\tilde{x}_1,\ldots, \tilde{x}_{i-1}$. For example, typically the index i refers to a time-index, so that the probability distribution of a given state is only functionally dependent upon the past history of states.

Let $y_1,\ldots, y_M$ be a particular realization (i.e., sample value) of $\tilde{x}_1,\ldots, \tilde{x}_M$. Also assume for the purposes of this discussion that for every realization $y_1,\ldots, y_M$: $p(y_1,\ldots, y_M) > 0$. Then by the definition of a conditional probability, it follows that

$$p(y_2 \mid y_1) = \frac{p(y_2, y_1)}{p(y_1)}.$$

The joint probability $p(y_1,\ldots, y_M)$ can then be factored as follows:

$$p(y_1,\ldots, y_M) = p(y_1)\prod_{i=2}^{M} p(y_i \mid y_{i-1}, y_{i-2},\ldots, y_1) \qquad (6.19)$$

The chain of M random variables, however, is not a Markov chain unless additional independence assumptions are introduced. For a first-order Markov chain, these assumptions would be expressed as

$$p(y_i \mid y_{i-1}, y_{i-2}, \ldots, y_1) = p(y_i \mid y_{i-1}) \tag{6.20}$$

for $i = 2 \ldots M$. More generally, for a kth-order Markov chain, these assumptions would be expressed as

$$p(y_i \mid y_{i-1}, \ldots, y_1) = p(y_i \mid y_{i-1}, \ldots, y_{i-k})$$

for each i, $k = 2 \ldots M$ such that $i > k$.

Substituting (6.20) into (6.19), the joint probability $p(y_1, \ldots, y_M)$ can be factored into the following form:

$$p(y_1, \ldots, y_M) = p(y_1) \prod_{i=2}^{M} p(y_i \mid y_{i-1}). \tag{6.21}$$

Equation (6.21) expresses the essence of the meaning of a first-order Markov chain, demonstrating that the *global* probability distribution $p(y_1, \ldots, y_M)$ can be expressed as the product of *local* probability distributions of the form $p(y_i \mid y_{i-1})$ and the marginal distribution $p(y_1)$. Notice that the selection of an appropriate parametric form of $p(y_1, \ldots, y_M)$ is quite difficult if M is large. On the other hand, selection of an appropriate parametric form for $p(y_i \mid y_{i-1})$ is relatively straightforward and independent of the number of random variables in the Markov chain.

A slightly more general class of Markov chain probability distributions is now considered. In particular, let the notation $p(x_i \mid \mathcal{N}_i(\mathbf{x}))$ indicate the probability mass (density) function of the random variable $\tilde{x}_i$, given the values of the *neighbors* of random variable $\tilde{x}_i$. The neighbors of random variable $\tilde{x}_i$ are the elements of the set $\mathcal{N}_i \subseteq \{\tilde{x}_1, \ldots, \tilde{x}_{i-1}\}$. The set $\mathcal{N} = \{\mathcal{N}_1, \ldots, \mathcal{N}_d\}$ is called the "neighborhood system" for $\{\tilde{x}_1, \ldots, \tilde{x}_d\}$. A particular set of values of the neighbors of $\tilde{x}_i$ when $\tilde{\mathbf{x}}$ takes on the value $\mathbf{x}$ will be denoted as $\mathcal{N}_i(\mathbf{x})$. Then

$$p(x_1, \ldots, x_d) = p(x_1) \prod_{i=2}^{d} p(x_i \mid \mathcal{N}_i(\mathbf{x})). \tag{6.22}$$

This more general case of a Markov chain, which subsumes (6.21) as a special case, will be introduced by considering a simple example involving a set of four random variables, $\tilde{x}_1$, $\tilde{x}_2$, $\tilde{x}_3$, and $\tilde{x}_4$, each of which is associated with a proposition. The value of the ith random variable indicates whether the ith proposition should be classified as *true* or *false*. In particular, if $\tilde{x}_i$ takes on the value of one, then the ith proposition is classified as *true*. If $\tilde{x}_i$ takes on the value of zero, then the ith proposition is classified as *false*.

To fix ideas, suppose the following four propositions are associated with $\tilde{x}_1$, $\tilde{x}_2, \tilde{x}_3, \tilde{x}_4$ as follows:

1. $\tilde{x}_1$: *KG wants to buy some clothes.*
2. $\tilde{x}_2$: *KG went to the clothing store.*
3. $\tilde{x}_3$: *KG bought clothes at the store.*
4. $\tilde{x}_4$: *KG wore new clothes to work.*

Let a realization (sample point) of the four random variables be indicated by the four-dimensional vector $\mathbf{x} = [x_1, x_2, x_3, x_4]$, where $x_i \in \{0, 1\}$ for $i = 1\ldots 4$. It is not obvious how to construct a joint probability mass function, p, such that $p(\mathbf{x})$ assigns a probability mass to each sample point $\mathbf{x}$ and the resulting probability mass function p is a semantically meaningful measure for a relational system on the sigma field generated by the 2^4 element sample space. On the other hand, rather than generate the global probability mass function p directly it is usually possible to generate semantically meaningful local conditional probability mass functions in a relatively direct manner.

For example, one might make the assumption that the local conditional probability distribution of $\tilde{x}_2$ (*KG went to the clothing store*) is functionally dependent upon the realization $\tilde{x}_1$ (*KG wants to buy some clothes*). In such a situation, the random variable $\tilde{x}_1$ is a *neighbor* of the random variable $\tilde{x}_2$. This relation can be graphically expressed by drawing an arrow from a node labeled $\tilde{x}_1$ to a node labeled $\tilde{x}_2$ on some graph, as shown in figure 6.2, where the local conditional probability distribution of $\tilde{x}_3$ (*KG bought clothes at the store*) is

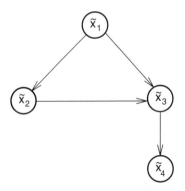

Figure 6.2
Neighborhood system for four random variables. Each node is associated with a random variable in the Markov chain. The probability distribution of the random variable associated with a particular node is functionally dependent *only* on the values of the random variables having arrows into that node. Thus, for example, the probability distribution of $\tilde{x}_3$ is functionally dependent only on the values taken on by random variables $\tilde{x}_1$ and $\tilde{x}_2$. The joint probability distribution of $\{\tilde{x}_1, \tilde{x}_2, \tilde{x}_3, \tilde{x}_4\}$ defined with respect to the neighborhood system in this figure may be factored using Markov chain factorization methods.

functionally dependent upon the value of the random variable $\tilde{x}_1$ (*KG wants to buy some clothes*) and random variable $\tilde{x}_2$ (*KG went to the clothing store*).

In this case, the functional form of such local conditional probability distributions can be specified almost by inspection. For example, note that the likelihood of $\tilde{x}_2$ should be high when $\tilde{x}_1$ takes on the value of one and the likelihood of $\tilde{x}_2$ should be low when $\tilde{x}_1$ takes on the value of zero. Thus one possible functional form of the local conditional probability distribution relating these two random variables would be to define

$$p(x_2 = 1 \mid x_1) = \mathcal{S}(x_1),$$

where for all $u \in \mathcal{R}$:

$$\mathcal{S}(u) = 1/[1 + \exp(-u)].$$

Although the local conditional probability distributions are relatively straightforward to specify, the unique global probability mass (density) $p(x_1, x_2, x_3, x_4)$ is required to make inferences. Suppose one wants to compute a MAP estimate, x_2^*, of the random variable $\tilde{x}_2$, given observed values of the random variables $\tilde{x}_1$, $\tilde{x}_3$, and $\tilde{x}_4$. The MAP estimate x_2^* is the global maximum of the local conditional probability mass (density) function $p_{\tilde{x}_2}(\cdot \mid x_1, x_3, x_4)$. The local conditional probability mass (density) function may be derived from the global probability mass (density) function using the definition of a conditional probability:

$$p(x_2 \mid x_1, x_3, x_4) = \frac{p(x_1, x_2, x_3, x_4)}{p(x_1, x_3, x_4)}.$$

In addition, the global probability mass (density) function $p(x_1, x_2, x_3, x_4)$ may be expressed as a product of local conditional probability mass (density) functions:

$$p(x_1, x_2, x_3, x_4) = p(x_4 \mid x_3, x_2, x_1) \, p(x_3 \mid x_2, x_1) \, p(x_2 \mid x_1) \, p(x_1).$$

Now making use of the conditional independence assumptions in figure 6.2 we then have

$$p(x_1, x_2, x_3, x_4) = p(x_4 \mid x_3) \, p(x_3 \mid x_2, x_1) \, p(x_2 \mid x_1) \, p(x_1).$$

Note that in order for the Markov chain framework to be applicable, it must be possible to express the joint distribution $p(x_1, x_2, x_3, x_4)$ as a simple product of local conditional probability distributions. The Markov chain framework is not applicable since an appropriate ordering of random variables is not always possible. Figure 6.3 provides an example of a graph of neighborhood relations among a set of four random variables which can not be modeled in a straightforward manner using the Markov chain framework. The critical difference between figure 6.2 and figure 6.3 is the addition of just one new link from the node associated with random variable $\tilde{x}_4$ (*KG wore new clothes to work*) to the

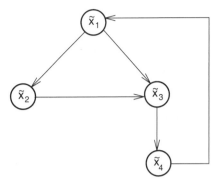

Figure 6.3
Neighborhood system for distribution that cannot be analyzed as Markov chain in straightforward manner. The joint probability distribution of $\{\tilde{x}_1, \tilde{x}_2, \tilde{x}_3, \tilde{x}_4\}$ defined with respect to the neighborhood system in this figure cannot be factored in a straightforward manner using the Markov chain methods of section 6.3.1 because an appropriate "causal" ordering of these four random variables is not obvious.

random variable $\tilde{x}_1$ (*KG wants to buy some clothes*). This new link implies that the random variable $\tilde{x}_4$ is a neighbor of the random variable $\tilde{x}_1$.

6.3.2   The Multiple Factorization Problem

A Markov random field is essentially a generalization of the concept of a Markov chain. Unlike Markov chains, Markov random fields are not restricted to a set of random variables that can be causally ordered. This flexibility turns out to be very important in ANN system analysis and design applications because most ANN systems consist of large numbers of units that are sparsely connected but not necessarily causally ordered.

An important goal of the following sections is to introduce a theorem analogous to (6.21) and (6.22) for Markov random fields that (1) establishes an equivalence relationship between the local and global probability distributions in the field, and (2) develops a straightforward method for specifying and constructing the global probability distribution in terms of its local components. Before addressing these issues, however, it will be helpful to explain in some detail why the more general case of Markov random fields is considerably less straightforward than the Markov chain situation (the following explanation of this issue is based upon the insightful discussion in Besag 1974).

Let $p: S \rightarrow [0, \infty)$ be a probability mass (density) function. Let $\mathbf{x} = [x_1,\ldots, x_d]$ and $\mathbf{y} = [y_1,\ldots, y_d]$ be two sample realizations of the set of d random variables defined with respect to p such that $p(\mathbf{x}) > 0$ and $p(\mathbf{y}) > 0$ for all $\mathbf{x}, \mathbf{y} \in S$. Then, by the definition of a conditional probability (i.e., Bayes rule), for $k = 1\ldots d$:

$$p(\mathbf{x}) = p(x_k \mid x_1,\ldots, x_{k-1}, x_{k+1},\ldots, x_d)\, p(x_1,\ldots, x_{k-1}, x_{k+1},\ldots, x_d). \qquad (6.23)$$

Using (6.23), we have

$$p(x_1,\ldots, x_{d-1}) = \frac{p(x_1,\ldots, x_{d-1}, y_d)}{p(y_d \mid x_1,\ldots, x_{d-1})} \tag{6.24}$$

and

$$p(\mathbf{x}) = p(x_d \mid x_1,\ldots, x_{d-1})\, p(x_1,\ldots, x_{d-1}). \tag{6.25}$$

Substituting (6.24) into (6.25), we have

$$p(\mathbf{x}) = \left[\frac{p(x_d \mid x_1,\ldots, x_{d-1})}{p(y_d \mid x_1,\ldots, x_{d-1})}\right] p(x_1,\ldots, x_{d-1}, y_d). \tag{6.26}$$

Expanding $p(x_1, x_2,\ldots, x_{d-1}, y_d)$ in a manner similar to (6.26), we obtain

$$p(x_1,\ldots, x_{d-1}, y_d) = \left[\frac{p(x_{d-1} \mid x_1, \ldots, x_{d-2}, y_d)}{p(y_{d-1} \mid x_1,\ldots, x_{d-2}, y_d)}\right]$$
$$p(x_1,\ldots, x_{d-2}, y_{d-1}, y_d). \tag{6.27}$$

Substitution of (6.27) into (6.26) then yields

$$p(\mathbf{x}) = \left[\frac{p(x_d \mid x_1,\ldots, x_{d-1})}{p(y_d \mid x_1,\ldots, x_{d-1})}\right]\left[\frac{p(x_{d-1} \mid x_1,\ldots, x_{d-2}, y_d)}{p(y_{d-1} \mid x_1, \ldots, x_{d-2}, y_d)}\right]$$
$$p(x_1,\ldots, x_{d-2}, y_{d-1}, y_d).$$

Continuing in this manner, the following factorization of $\frac{p(\mathbf{x})}{p(\mathbf{y})}$, analogous to (6.19) and (6.22), is obtained:

$$p(\mathbf{x}) = p(\mathbf{y})\prod_{i=1}^{d}\frac{p(x_i \mid x_1,\ldots, x_{i-1}, y_{i+1},\ldots, y_d)}{p(y_i \mid x_1,\ldots, x_{i-1}, y_{i+1},\ldots, y_d)}. \tag{6.28}$$

Besag (1974) has noted that the above derivation makes three important points. First, (6.28) can be interpreted as assigning a global probability, $p(\mathbf{x})$, to realization $\mathbf{x}$ of the field, given that the local probability structure is known and evaluated at $\mathbf{x}$, and given some other realization of the field, $\mathbf{y}$ (typically $\mathbf{y}$ is chosen to be a vector of zeros), whose strictly positive global probability $p(\mathbf{y})$ is already known. Second, like the Markov chain analysis, the relevance of the positivity condition for factoring the joint distribution $p(\mathbf{x})$ is sufficient to guarantee the construction of appropriate local marginal and conditional distributions.

Besag's third point is a little more subtle, essentially stating that the introduction of arbitrary constraints on the functional form of the local conditional probability distributions could result in logical inconsistencies. To illustrate this point, assume that $\mathbf{x} = [x_1, x_2, x_3]$ and $\mathbf{y} = [y_1, y_2, y_3]$, where $\mathbf{x}$ and $\mathbf{y}$ are two realizations of a set of three binary-valued random variables. Now, using (6.28), we obtain

$$p(\mathbf{x}) = p(\mathbf{y}) \frac{p(x_1 \mid y_2, y_3)}{p(y_1 \mid y_2, y_3)} \frac{p(x_2 \mid x_1, y_3)}{p(y_2 \mid x_1, y_3)} \frac{p(x_3 \mid x_1, x_2)}{p(y_3 \mid x_1, x_2)}. \tag{6.29}$$

On the other hand, because the indexing of the random variables is irrelevant, we also have (switching the index labels for the random variables originally labeled x_1 and x_2) from (6.28)

$$p(\mathbf{x}) = p(\mathbf{y}) \frac{p(x_2 \mid y_1, y_3)}{p(y_2 \mid y_1, y_3)} \frac{p(x_1 \mid x_2, y_3)}{p(y_1 \mid x_2, y_3)} \frac{p(x_3 \mid x_2, x_1)}{p(y_3 \mid x_2, x_1)}. \tag{6.30}$$

If the joint distribution is unique, after equating (6.29) and (6.30) and canceling the common factors $p(x_3 \mid x_2, x_1)/p(y_3 \mid x_2, x_1)$ and $p(\mathbf{y})$, we obtain

$$\left[\frac{p(x_2 \mid y_1, y_3)}{p(y_2 \mid y_1, y_3)} \right] \left[\frac{p(x_1 \mid x_2, y_3)}{p(y_1 \mid x_2, y_3)} \right] = \left[\frac{p(x_1 \mid y_2, y_3)}{p(y_1 \mid y_2, y_3)} \right] \left[\frac{p(x_2 \mid x_1, y_3)}{p(y_2 \mid x_1, y_3)} \right]. \tag{6.31}$$

It is not obvious that relationships of the form expressed in (6.31) will always be satisfied when the local conditional probability distribution functions are arbitrarily chosen. Thus a method for constructing a unique and consistent global probability distribution, given a collection of appropriately constrained local probability distributions, is desirable. The theory of Markov random fields developed in the following section will provide a powerful tool for achieving this goal.

6.3.3   Introduction to Markov Random Fields

Consider the graph of the neighborhood relations among the random variables in figure 6.2. The analogous graph for the Markov random field associated with the neighborhood relations in figure 6.2 is shown in figure 6.4. Notice that figure 6.2 and figure 6.4 are identical except that the arrows in figure 6.2 have been replaced with line segments in figure 6.4. The line segment representation is used to indicate that the neighborhood relations in a Markov random field are bidirectional (i.e., "noncausal"). That is, if random variable $\tilde{x}_2$ is a neighbor of random variable $\tilde{x}_1$, then random variable $\tilde{x}_1$ must be a neighbor of random variable $\tilde{x}_2$.

With this introduction, the general concept of a Markov random field is now defined. The first step is to formally define the idea of a neighborhood system, which was informally introduced with reference to figure 6.4 as a graph of a set of symmetric paired relationships among the random variables in the field.

Definition: Symmetric relation.   Let ω be a relation on a set S with $(x, y) \in \omega$. The relation ω is *symmetric* if and only if $x\omega y$ implies $y\omega x$ for all $(x, y) \in \omega$.

For example, the symmetric relation depicted in figure 6.4 is the set of eight ordered pairs of random variables:

$$\{(\tilde{x}_1, \tilde{x}_2), (\tilde{x}_2, \tilde{x}_1), (\tilde{x}_1, \tilde{x}_3), (\tilde{x}_3, \tilde{x}_1), (\tilde{x}_2, \tilde{x}_3), (\tilde{x}_3, \tilde{x}_2), (\tilde{x}_3, \tilde{x}_4), (\tilde{x}_4, \tilde{x}_3)\}$$

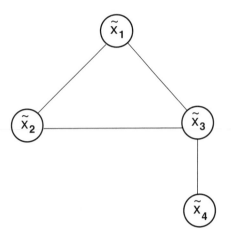

Figure 6.4
Neighborhood system for Markov field. Each node is associated with a random variable. If two nodes are connected, then the probability distribution of one of the two random variables associated with either of the two nodes is functionally dependent on the random variable associated with the other node in the pair. Thus in this figure the probability distribution of $\tilde{x}_1$ is functionally dependent upon the values of the random variables $\tilde{x}_2$ and $\tilde{x}_3$, and the probability distribution of the random variable $\tilde{x}_2$ is functionally dependent upon the random variables $\tilde{x}_1$ and $\tilde{x}_3$. Note that the neighborhood system in this figure is formally equivalent to the neighborhood system in figure 6.2. The Markov random field approach allows one to factor the joint distribution of a given set of random variables with essentially no restrictions (except for the positivity assumption described in the text) on the form of the joint probability distribution for arbitrary neighborhood systems.

Definition: Neighborhood system on a symmetric relation. Let $\tilde{\mathbf{x}} = [\tilde{x}_1,\ldots, \tilde{x}_d]$ be a set of d random variables. Let $\omega \subseteq \tilde{\mathbf{x}} \times \tilde{\mathbf{x}}$ be a symmetric relation on $\tilde{\mathbf{x}}$. Let the *neighborhood* of $\tilde{x}_i$ be defined as a subset, $\mathcal{N}_i$, of $\tilde{\mathbf{x}}$ such that for $j = 1\ldots d$: $\tilde{x}_j \in \mathcal{N}_i$ if both (i) $j \neq i$, and (ii) $(\tilde{x}_i, \tilde{x}_j) \in \omega$. An element $\tilde{x}_j \in \mathcal{N}_i$ is a *neighbor* of $\tilde{x}_i$, and the set

$$\mathcal{N} = [\mathcal{N}_1,\ldots, \mathcal{N}_d]$$

is a *neighborhood system* on ω. Let $\mathcal{N}_i(\mathbf{x})$ be the set of values of the neighbors of $\tilde{x}_i$ when $\tilde{\mathbf{x}} = \mathbf{x}$.

Definition: Markov random field. Let $S \subseteq \mathcal{R}^d$. Let $p: S \to [0, \infty)$ be the joint probability mass (density) function of a set, $\tilde{\mathbf{x}} = [\tilde{x}_1,\ldots, \tilde{x}_d]$, of d random variables with respect to some sample space S. Let ω be a symmetric relation on $\tilde{\mathbf{x}}$. Let $\mathcal{N} = [\mathcal{N}_1,\ldots, \mathcal{N}_d]$ be a neighborhood system on ω. The d-dimensional random vector $\tilde{\mathbf{x}}$ is a *Markov random field* with respect to $\mathcal{N}$ if for every $\mathbf{x} = [x_1,\ldots, x_d] \in S$:

1. $p(x_i \,|\, x_1,\ldots, x_{i-1}, x_{i+1},\ldots, x_d) = p(x_i \,|\, \mathcal{N}_i(\mathbf{x}))$ for $i = 1\ldots d$, and

2. $p(\mathbf{x}) > 0$ (*positivity condition*).

Note that condition 1 in the definition of a Markov random field essentially states that the probability distribution of random variable $\tilde{x}_i$ should only be functionally dependent upon the neighbors of $\tilde{x}_i$, where those neighbors are defined by some specific neighborhood system. Thus condition 1 captures the essence of the concept of a Markov random field. Condition 2, which states that all realizations of the field should occur with a nonzero probability, is relatively more restrictive. This second condition is often referred to as the "positivity condition" and essentially restricts the range of a local conditional probability mass (density) function like $p(\cdot \mid x_1, x_2, x_3)$ to the open interval $(0, 1)$. Thus a probabilistic statement such as

IF $\tilde{x}_1 = x_1$, $\tilde{x}_2 = x_2$ and $\tilde{x}_3 = x_3$, THEN $p(\tilde{x}_4 = x_4) = 1$

cannot be represented as a local conditional probability mass function if $(\tilde{x}_1, \tilde{x}_2, \tilde{x}_3, \tilde{x}_4)$ is a Markov random field. On the other hand, because the positivity condition does not rule out probabilistic statements such as

IF $\tilde{x}_1 = x_1$, $\tilde{x}_2 = x_2$ and $\tilde{x}_3 = x_3$, THEN $p(\tilde{x}_4 = x_4) = 0.999$,

it is not typically a serious restriction on the parametric form of the joint distribution of the Markov random field.

6.3.4 Solving the Multiple Factorization Problem

Although the concept of a Markov random field was formally defined in the previous section, the solution to the multiple factorization problem was not addressed. The purpose of this section is to state and prove the Fundamental Markov Random Field Theorem (i.e., the Hammersley-Clifford theorem), which demonstrates the equivalence between any Markov random field and a specific parametric probability distribution known as the "Gibbs distribution." An elegant solution to this problem was originally proposed by Hammersley and Clifford in 1971 in an unpublished manuscript cited and later popularized by Besag (1974). (Geman and Geman 1984 attributes the origins of Markov random field research to Dobruschin 1968 and Spitzer 1971. As in the previous section, the development presented here is adapted from the approach of Besag 1974.)

The Hammersley-Clifford (1971) theorem explicitly states conditions for the existence and uniqueness of the global distribution of a Markov random field in terms of constraints placed upon the local conditional distributions of the field. Moreover, the theorem provides a computationally tractable constructive procedure for choosing an appropriate and unique global joint probability distribution. Before stating and proving the theorem, however, the concept of a clique must be introduced.

Definition: Clique.   Let $\tilde{\mathbf{x}} = [\tilde{x}_1, \ldots, \tilde{x}_d]$ be a finite set of d random variables. Let $\mathcal{N} = [\mathcal{N}_1, \ldots, \mathcal{N}_d]$ be a neighborhood system on a symmetric relation $\omega \subset \tilde{\mathbf{x}} \times \tilde{\mathbf{x}}$, so that the elements of $\mathcal{N}_i$ are the neighbors of $\tilde{x}_i$ for $i = 1 \ldots d$. A subset of $\tilde{\mathbf{x}}$, κ, is a *clique* with respect to $\mathcal{N}$ if either

1. $\kappa = \{\tilde{x}_i\}$ for some $\tilde{x}_i \in \tilde{\mathbf{x}}$, or

2. for every $(\tilde{x}_i, \tilde{x}_j) \in \kappa \times \kappa$: $\tilde{x}_i \in \mathcal{N}_j$ and $\tilde{x}_j \in \mathcal{N}_i$.

Less formally, a clique is a subset of the random variables defining a Markov random field that is either (1) any set containing exactly one random variable of the field, or (2) every set of two or more random variables of the field such that *all* random variables in the set are neighbors of each other. Figure 6.5 illustrates graphically the identification of all of the nine cliques of random variables for the neighborhood system depicted in figure 6.5. Ellipsoids have been drawn around all sets of random variables which form cliques in Figure 6.5.

For example, since the three random variables $\tilde{x}_1$, $\tilde{x}_2$, and $\tilde{x}_3$ are neighbors of one another, these three random variables form the clique $\{\tilde{x}_1, \tilde{x}_2, \tilde{x}_3\}$ which in turn implies the existence of the six other cliques: $\{\tilde{x}_1\}$, $\{\tilde{x}_2\}$, $\{\tilde{x}_3\}$, $\{\tilde{x}_1, \tilde{x}_2\}$, $\{\tilde{x}_1, \tilde{x}_3\}$, and $\{\tilde{x}_2, \tilde{x}_3\}$. Thus, every subset of a clique (with the exception of the empty set) is also a clique. On the other hand, since the three random variables $\tilde{x}_1$, $\tilde{x}_2$, and $\tilde{x}_4$ are not neighbors of one another (e.g., $\tilde{x}_4$ and $\tilde{x}_1$ are not neighbors), the set of random variables $\{\tilde{x}_1, \tilde{x}_2, \tilde{x}_4\}$ is not a clique.

In addition, the notation $V^{(i)}$ will indicate that $V^{(i)}$ is an arbitrary function subject to the constraint that $V^{(i)}$ is functionally dependent only upon the possible realizations of the random variables which are members of the ith clique with respect to some neighborhood system. For example, suppose that the fourth clique in some neighborhood system is defined by the set of random variables $\{\tilde{x}_3, \tilde{x}_6\}$. Let $s \subseteq \mathcal{R}$. Then $V^{(4)}$: $s \times s \rightarrow \mathcal{R}$ is an arbitrary function of both x_3 and x_6. Thus, $V^{(4)}$ could be defined such that $V^{(4)}(x_3, x_6) = (x_3 + x_6)^2$ or

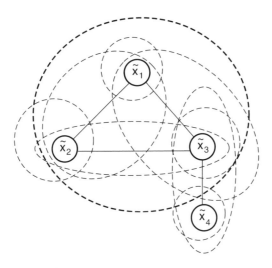

Figure 6.5
Cliques for neighborhood system. Each clique is surrounded by a dashed ellipsoid; all nine cliques for the neighborhood system associated with the graph in figure 6.4 are shown.

$V^{(4)}(x_3, x_6) = x_3 x_6 - 17$ but $V^{(4)}$ could not be defined as a function such as $V^{(4)}(x_3, x_6) = x_3$ or $V^{(4)}(x_3, x_6) = x_1 + x_3 + x_6$. The Fundamental Markov Random Field Theorem (Hammersley-Clifford Theorem) is now stated and proved following the method of proof presented by Besag (1974).

Theorem: Fundamental Markov Random Field Theorem. Let $s \subseteq \mathcal{R}$. Let $\tilde{x} = [\tilde{x}_1, \ldots, \tilde{x}_d]$ be a finite set of d random variables with joint probability mass (density) function $p: s^d \to [0, \infty)$. Let $\mathcal{N} = [\mathcal{N}_1, \ldots, \mathcal{N}_d]$ be a neighborhood system on a symmetric relation $\omega \subset \tilde{x} \times \tilde{x}$ that consists of C cliques. Let n_i be the number of random variables in the ith clique ($i = 1 \ldots C$). Let the notation $V^{(i)}$ denote a function

$$V^{(i)}: s \times s \times \ldots s \to \mathcal{R}$$

with n_i arguments ($i = 1 \ldots C$). Let $V: \mathcal{R}^d \to \mathcal{R}$. The random vector $\tilde{x}$ is a Markov random field with respect to $\mathcal{N}$ and p if and only if

$$p(\cdot) = \frac{\exp[-V(\cdot)]}{Z}, \qquad (6.32)$$

where Z is a unique finite positive real number and $V(\cdot) = \sum_{i=1}^{C} V^{(i)}(\cdot)$.

Proof. See section 6.3.5. ∎

Note that in order for p in (6.32) to be a valid probability density function, it is necessary that the normalization constant

$$Z = \int_{\mathbf{y} \in S} \exp[-V(\mathbf{y})] d\mathbf{y}$$

exist. For arbitrary V functions, Z may not exist. Similarly, for probability mass functions defined with respect to finite (or countably infinite) sample spaces, it is necessary that the normalization constant

$$Z = \sum_{\mathbf{y} \in S} \exp[-V(\mathbf{y})]$$

exist. If the sample space S consists of a finite number of vectors with finite magnitudes and V is continuous on S, then the normalization constant Z will always exist.

Typically, the probability mass (density) function in (6.32) is referred to as a *Gibbs distribution* and the function V is referred to as the *energy* or *potential function* for the Markov random field. The function $V^{(i)}$ is called the *local potential* or *clique function* for the ith clique ($i = 1 \ldots C$).

To illustrate the main idea of the Fundamental Markov Random Field Theorem, consider the random field and its neighborhood system in figure 6.5. Also assume that each random variable can take on only a finite number of values.

Let the notation $V_{i,j,k,l}$ indicate that the function $V_{i,j,k,l}\colon s \times s \times s \times s \longrightarrow \mathfrak{R}$ is functionally dependent *only* upon the values of the random variables $\tilde{x}_i$, $\tilde{x}_j$, $\tilde{x}_k$, and $\tilde{x}_l$. Using the Fundamental Markov Random Field Theorem, the most general form of a probability mass function satisfying the positivity condition and which has the neighborhood system depicted graphically in figure 6.5 is given by

$$p(\mathbf{x}) = \frac{\exp\left[-V(\mathbf{x})\right]}{\displaystyle\sum_{\mathbf{y}\in S} \exp\left[-V(\mathbf{y})\right]}$$

where S is the sample space for p and V is the potential function

$$V(\mathbf{x}) = \sum_{i=1}^{4} V_i(x_i) + \sum_{i=2}^{3}\sum_{j=1}^{i-1} V_{i,j}(x_i, x_j) + V_{3,4}(x_3, x_4) + V_{1,2,3}(x_1, x_2, x_3).$$

Thus the Fundamental Markov Random Field Theorem provides a straightforward approach to constructing the most general global joint probability distribution whose local conditional probability distributions have the desired functional dependencies.

The theorem is also useful because joint probability distributions of the form of (6.32) can be used to easily compute local conditional distributions in terms of the field's global joint distribution. Let $x_1,\ldots, x_d$ and $y_1,\ldots, y_d$ be two realizations of a Markov random field with potential function V. Also let the notation $\mathcal{N}_i(\mathbf{x})$ indicate the values of the neighbors of the random variable $\tilde{x}_i$ when $\tilde{\mathbf{x}}$ takes on the value of $\mathbf{x}$.

By the definition of a conditional probability, we have

$$\frac{p\left(x_i \mid \mathcal{N}_i(\mathbf{x})\right)}{p\left(y_i \mid \mathcal{N}_i(\mathbf{x})\right)} = \frac{p(\mathbf{x})/p(\mathcal{N}_i(\mathbf{x}))}{p(x_1, x_2,\ldots, x_{i-1}, y_i, x_{i+1},\ldots, x_d)/p(\mathcal{N}_i(\mathbf{x}))},$$

$$\frac{p\left(x_i \mid \mathcal{N}_i(\mathbf{x})\right)}{p\left(y_i \mid \mathcal{N}_i(\mathbf{x})\right)} = \frac{p(\mathbf{x})}{p(x_1,\ldots, x_{i-1}, y_i, x_{i+1},\ldots, x_d)},$$

$$p\left(x_i \mid \mathcal{N}_i(\mathbf{x})\right) = \frac{p\left(y_i \mid \mathcal{N}_i(\mathbf{x})\right) p(\mathbf{x})}{p(x_1, x_2,\ldots, x_{i-1}, y_i, x_{i+1},\ldots, x_d)} = p\left(y_i \mid \mathcal{N}_i(\mathbf{x})\right)\exp\left[-U_i(\mathbf{x})\right],$$

where the notation $U_i(\mathbf{x})$ is defined such that

$$U_i(\mathbf{x}) = V(\mathbf{x}) - V(x_1, x_2,\ldots, x_{i-1}, y_i, x_{i+1},\ldots, x_d).$$

Note that because $p\left(y_i \mid \mathcal{N}_i(\mathbf{x})\right)$ is not functionally dependent upon x_i, the probability mass (density) function of x_i given $\mathcal{N}_i(\mathbf{x})$ is obtained using the formula

$$p\left(x_i \mid \mathcal{N}_i(\mathbf{x})\right) = \frac{\exp\left[-U_i(\mathbf{x})\right]}{Z_i}, \tag{6.33}$$

where Z_i is a normalization constant guaranteeing that

$$\sum_{x_i \in S} p(x_i \mid \mathcal{N}_i(\mathbf{x})) = 1$$

if p is a probability mass function and

$$\int_{x_i \in S} p(x_i \mid \mathcal{N}_i(\mathbf{x})) dx_i = 1$$

if p is a probability density function. The quantity $U_i(\mathbf{x})$ may be interpreted as the degree of evidence supporting the hypothesis that the ith random variable, $\tilde{x}_i$, takes on the value x_i, given that the values of the neighbors of the random variable $\tilde{x}_i$ are known.

To summarize, the global probability mass (density) function p nor its global potential function V is intuitively easy to specify for most modeling problems involving high-dimensional random fields. And, although local conditional probability functions such as $p(\cdot \mid x_1, x_2, x_3)$ are much easier to use to build models, they often cannot be directly specified because of the multiple factorization problem. On the other hand, the local potential functions $V^{(1)}$, $V^{(2)}$, ..., $V^{(C)}$ are simply monotonically decreasing functions of their respective local conditional probability functions and are relatively unconstrained. Thus the mathematical modeler has considerable amount of flexibility in specifying the probabilistic structure of the random field in terms of the local potential functions.

6.3.5.   Proof of the Fundamental Markov Random Field Theorem

The proof of the Fundamental Markov Random Field Theorem is now provided (closely following the very readable presentation in Besag 1974.)

Proof.   Assume that a set of d random variables is a Markov random field with joint probability mass (density) function, p, on sample space $S \subseteq \mathcal{R}^d$. Let $\mathbf{x} = [x_1, \ldots, x_d]$ and $\mathbf{y} = [y_1, \ldots, y_d]$ be any two realizations of the field. Thus, by the positivity condition, $p(\mathbf{x}) > 0$ and $p(\mathbf{y}) > 0$, where p is the joint probability mass (density) function.

Now define the $Q: \mathcal{R}^d \to \mathcal{R}$ function such that for every $\mathbf{x}, \mathbf{y} \in S$:

$$Q(\mathbf{x}) = \ln\left[p(\mathbf{x})/p(\mathbf{y})\right]. \tag{6.34}$$

Since $Q(\mathbf{x})$ is functionally dependent upon $p(\mathbf{x})$ by the definition in (6.34), every $p(\mathbf{x})$ specifies a unique $Q(\mathbf{x})$. Also note that the log transformation in (6.34) is invertible so any $Q(\mathbf{x})$ specifies a unique $p(\mathbf{x})$ as well provided that the normalization constant Z exists.

Define $s \subseteq \mathcal{R}$ so that $s^d = S \subseteq \mathcal{R}^d$. Now consider the following particular functional form for a Q function defined with respect to nonzero probability realization of the field $\mathbf{y}$ and evaluated at $\mathbf{x}$:

$$Q(\mathbf{x}) = \sum_{i=1}^{d} (x_i - y_i) G_i(x_i) + \sum_{i=2}^{d} \sum_{j=1}^{i-1} (x_i - y_i)(x_j - y_j) G_{i,j}(x_i, x_j)$$
$$\ldots + (x_1 - y_1)(x_2 - y_2) \ldots (x_d - y_d) G_{1,2,\ldots,d}(x_1,\ldots, x_d), \qquad (6.35)$$

where $G_i: s \to \mathcal{R}$, $G_{i,j}: s \times s \to \mathcal{R}$, $G_{i,j,k}: s \times s \times s \to \mathcal{R}$, and so on, until we have $G_{1,2,\ldots,d}: s \times s \times \ldots s \to \mathcal{R}$ where $G_{1,2,\ldots,d}$ has d arguments.

It will now be shown that every arbitrary p can be represented using the finite expansion in (6.35). Substitute

$$\mathbf{y} = [y_1, y_2,\ldots, y_d]$$

into a $Q(\cdot)$ function defined with respect to some p and $\mathbf{y}$ that satisfies $p(\mathbf{y}) > 0$. Then all terms in (6.35) will vanish, leaving $Q(\mathbf{y}) = 0$. Now consider $\mathbf{x}^i$, defined such that

$$\mathbf{x}^i = [y_1, y_2,\ldots, y_{i-1}, x_i, y_{i+1},\ldots, y_d].$$

Substituting $\mathbf{x}^i$ into the same Q function it follows that

$$Q(\mathbf{x}^i) = G_i(x_i)(x_i - y_i) \qquad (6.36)$$

because all terms but one in (6.35) will vanish. Solving (6.36) for G_i, it follows that

$$G_i(x_i) = Q(\mathbf{x}^i)/(x_i - y_i).$$

Thus formulas for all of the G_i functions have been explicitly obtained.

A similar approach will now be used to obtain formulas for the $G_{i,j}$ functions. Consider $\mathbf{x}^{i,j}$, defined such that

$$\mathbf{x}^{i,j} = [y_1, y_2,\ldots, y_{i-1}, x_i, y_{i+1},\ldots, y_{j-1}, x_j, y_{j+1},\ldots y_d],$$

where without loss of generality it is assumed $j > i$.

Substituting $\mathbf{x}^{i,j}$ into the Q function, it follows that

$$Q(\mathbf{x}^{i,j}) = (x_i - y_i) G_i(x_i) + (x_j - y_j) G_j(x_j)$$
$$+ (x_i - y_i)(x_j - y_j) G_{i,j}(x_i, x_j), \qquad (6.37)$$

and because $G_{i,j}: s \times s \to \mathcal{R}$ is arbitrary, every Q function dependent upon both x_i and x_j can be represented. Equation (6.37) can then be solved for G_{ij} to obtain

$$G_{i,j}(x_i, x_j) = \frac{Q(\mathbf{x}^{i,j}) - \sum_{i=1}^{d} (x_i - y_i) G_i(x_i)}{(x_i - y_i)(x_j - y_j)}.$$

Such an analysis can be continued for the cases $\mathbf{x}^{i,j,k},\ldots, \mathbf{x}^{1,2,\ldots,d}$ to solve for the remaining G functions. Thus, without any loss in generality, any p satisfying the positivity condition can be represented by using (6.34) and the expansion in (6.35). Let

$$\mathbf{y}_i = [x_1, \ldots, x_{i-1}, y_i, x_{i+1}, \ldots x_d].$$

Note that

$$\frac{p(x_i \mid \mathcal{N}_i(\mathbf{x}))}{p(y_i \mid \mathcal{N}_i(\mathbf{x}))} = \frac{p(\mathbf{x})/p(x_1, \ldots, x_{i-1}, x_{i+1}, \ldots, x_d)}{p(\mathbf{y}_i)/p(x_1, \ldots, x_{i-1}, x_{i+1}, \ldots, x_d)},$$

and so

$$p(x_i \mid \mathcal{N}_i(\mathbf{x})) = p(y_i \mid \mathcal{N}_i(\mathbf{x})) \exp[Q(\mathbf{x}) - Q(\mathbf{y}_i)], \qquad (6.38)$$

where

$$Q(\mathbf{x}) - Q(\mathbf{y}_i) = (x_i - y_i)[G_i(x_i) + \sum_{j \neq i} (x_j - y_j)G_{i,j}(x_i, x_j) + \ldots$$

$$+ \sum_{j \neq i} \sum_{k=1}^{j-1} (x_j - y_j)(x_k - y_k)G_{i,j,k}(x_i, x_j, x_k) + \ldots \qquad (6.39)$$

The proof consists of two parts. First it will be proved that if a set of random variables in a Markov random field does not form a clique, then the potential function for that clique must be constant. Suppose $\tilde{x}_l \notin \mathcal{N}_i$. Thus $Q(\mathbf{x}) - Q(\mathbf{y}_i)$ must be independent of x_l by (6.38) and (6.39) for all $\mathbf{x} \in S$. Inspection of (6.38) shows that all potential functions on cliques containing both $\tilde{x}_i$ and $\tilde{x}_l$ must be constant (otherwise, $Q(\mathbf{x}) - Q(\mathbf{y}_i)$ would be functionally dependent on x_l) which would contradict (6.38) and (6.39). Second, it will be proved that given a probability mass (density) function p defined with respect to a Q function as in (6.35), that the set of random variables associated with p is a Markov random field. By (6.38), if the potential function for a set of random variables forming a clique is constant, then $p(x_i \mid \mathcal{N}_i(\mathbf{x}))$ is functionally dependent only upon the neighbors of random variable $\tilde{x}_i$ which are members of cliques with non-constant potential functions. This is the first condition a Markov random field on the neighborhood system $\mathcal{N}$ must satisfy. The positivity condition is satisfied because any probability mass (density) function p defined using (6.35) and (6.34) must satisfy $p(\mathbf{x}) > 0$ for every realization $\mathbf{x}$ of the field. ∎

6.4 Decision Rules

The previous sections of this chapter have been concerned with issues of knowledge representation. Techniques for using these representational schemes to make explicit decisions are now developed.

Definition: Optimal decision.   Let $\mathcal{F}$ be a set of decisions and let $\mathcal{U} \subseteq \mathcal{F}$. Let $(S, \mathcal{F}, \omega)$ be a relational system with measure $\mathcal{P}: \mathcal{F} \to \mathcal{R}$. An *optimal decision* with respect to $(S, \mathcal{F}, \omega)$ and $\mathcal{U}$ is a global minimum of $\mathcal{P}$ on $\mathcal{U}$.

Notice that a decision maker who makes optimal decisions is only making those optimal decisions with respect to a fairly unconstrained relational system. In order to develop a theory of an *intelligent* optimal decision maker, some constraints upon the decision maker's measure and relational system should be introduced. Some very important types of optimal decisions are now defined.

Definition: Fuzzy measure optimal decision.   Let $\mathcal{F}$ be a set of decisions and let $\mathcal{U} \subseteq \mathcal{F}$. Let $(S, \mathcal{F}, \omega)$ be a relational system with respect to fuzzy measure $\mathcal{B}: \mathcal{F} \to [0, 1]$. A *fuzzy measure optimal decision* with respect to $(S, \mathcal{F}, \omega)$ and $\mathcal{U}$ is a global maximum of $\mathcal{B}$ on $\mathcal{U}$.

An important special case of the fuzzy measure optimal decision is the maximum a posteriori (MAP) estimate.

Definition: Maximum a posteriori (MAP) estimate.   Let $S \subseteq \mathcal{R}^d$ be a set of decisions. Let $p: S \to [0, \infty)$ be a subjective probability mass (density) function. A *maximum a posteriori (MAP) estimate* with respect to p is a global maximum of p on S.

An agent who selects an event that is a MAP estimate is selecting a *most probable* element of the sample space S. Equivalently, a MAP estimate with respect to a subjective probability mass (density) function p is a *minimum probability of error* decision, where the probability of error is computed using p.

Definition: Bayes risk decision.   Let $D \subseteq \mathcal{R}^d$ be a set of decisions. Let $Q \subseteq \mathcal{R}^q$ be a set of situations. Let $c: D \times Q \to \mathcal{R}$ be a loss function. Let $p: Q \to [0, \infty)$ be a subjective probability mass (density) function. Let $l: D \to \mathcal{R}$ be a Bayes risk function with respect to c and p. A *Bayes risk decision* with respect to l is a global minimum of l on D.

It is important to note that a MAP estimate decision maker is actually a special case of a subjective Bayesian risk decision maker. To see this, let D be a set of decisions, and let Q be a set of situations. Assume for expository reasons that Q is a finite set, but the following discussion is easily extended to the general case where this restriction on Q does not hold. For $\mathbf{x} \in D$ and $\mathbf{y} \in Q$: suppose that $c(\mathbf{x} \mid \mathbf{y}) = 1$ if the decision $\mathbf{x}$ is incorrect, given situation $\mathbf{y}$, and $c(\mathbf{x} \mid \mathbf{y}) = 0$ if the decision $\mathbf{x}$ is correct, given situation $\mathbf{y}$. Let l be a Bayes risk function with respect to loss function $c: D \times Q \to \mathcal{R}$ and some subjective probability mass function $p: Q \to [0, 1]$. Now suppose that an *error* occurs if situation $\mathbf{y} \in Q$ is a member of the set of situations Ω_x, where the contents of Ω_x are determined by the choice of decision $\mathbf{x} \in D$.

Given the above assumptions, the expression for the Bayes risk function, l, is given by the formula

$$l(\mathbf{x}) = E_{\tilde{\mathbf{y}}}[c(\mathbf{x} \mid \tilde{\mathbf{y}})] = \sum_{\mathbf{y} \in Q} c(\mathbf{x} \mid \mathbf{y}) p(\mathbf{y}) = \sum_{\mathbf{y} \in \Omega_x} p(\mathbf{y}).$$

Inspection of the quantity $\sum_{\mathbf{y} \in \Omega_x} p(\mathbf{y})$ shows that l is now a formula for the probability of error, where probability of error is defined with respect to the subjective probability distribution p. Thus minimizing the Bayes risk function in this very special case is formally equivalent to minimizing the probability of error (i.e., computing a MAP estimate). Thus MAP estimation is a special case of the Bayes risk decision rule.

Note that the MAP estimation decision rule penalizes all errors by an equal amount. Such a strategy is usually quite effective when (1) all errors are approximately equally costly, and (2) the number of possible alternative decisions is relatively small. It is easy, however, to imagine situations where such a decision rule is not especially desirable. For example, consider an intelligent system that is trying to infer the values of 100,000,000 pixels in a large image. An agent using a MAP estimation decision rule would consider the penalty cost for estimating 99,999,999 pixel values correctly with just one mistake to be exactly the same as incorrectly estimating 99,999,999 pixel values with just one correct inference! Or in other words, the MAP estimation decision rule does not give partial credit for reasonably acceptable solutions.

6.5 The Generalization Problem

Suppose that an ANN is trained with a representative sample of stimuli from a given statistical environment. Even if the ANN perfectly learns (i.e., memorizes) the training stimuli, it may not make "correct decisions" (i.e., correct generalizations) when presented with a novel stimulus. This problem of teaching an ANN system to correctly classify stimuli that have never been presented to it is referred to as the "generalization problem."

Now consider the following sequence of numbers:

1, 2, 4, 8, 16, 32, 64, 128, __?__ .

The generalization problem in this simple example is to infer the missing value of the last element in the above sequence. Most people would assume that the last element in the sequence is $2^8 = 256$, but they would be wrong. It is 99. Most people assume the last element is 256 based on the incoming information (prior elements in the sequence) and their past experience in making inductive inferences. Inductive inferences are neither correct or incorrect. The environment always has the final word regarding the correctness of a particular inductive inference.

In this section, a theory of generalization is proposed and the important classical Bayes risk theory of generalization introduced. The relevance of network approximation theorems for understanding the generalization problem is also briefly discussed.

6.5.1 Definition of the Generalization Problem

Definition: Appropriate generalization. An *appropriate generalization* with respect to $(S, \mathcal{F}, \omega)$ and $\mathcal{U}$ is an optimal decision with respect to $(S, \mathcal{F}, \omega)$ and $\mathcal{U}$.

A similar definition can be introduced for Bayes risk functions.

Definition: Appropriate Bayes risk generalization. An *appropriate Bayes risk generalization* with respect to the function $l: D \rightarrow \mathcal{R}$ is a Bayes risk decision with respect to the Bayes risk function l.

Note that the motivation for the above definition of Bayesian generalization is based upon the von Neumann and Morgenstern rational decision-making theorem reviewed in section 6.2.4. The concept of an appropriate Bayes risk generalization is a classical statistical conception of generalization.

A special case of the appropriate Bayes risk generalization concept that occurs frequently in the ANN system literature is now briefly discussed. Define a stochastic process consisting of independent and identically distributed ordered pairs of random vectors such that

$$(\tilde{\mathbf{s}}(1), \tilde{\mathbf{o}}(1)),\ (\tilde{\mathbf{s}}(2), \tilde{\mathbf{o}}(2)),\ldots,$$

where the first element of each ordered pair is a random k-dimensional input stimulus vector and the second element of each ordered pair is a u-dimensional desired response vector. In addition, assume that there exists some (deterministic) function $\mathbf{f}: \mathcal{R}^k \rightarrow \mathcal{R}^u$ such that $\tilde{\mathbf{o}}(t) = \mathbf{f}(\tilde{\mathbf{s}}(t))$ for $t = 1, 2, 3,\ldots$. The learning problem of interest in this special situation is to determine the function $\mathbf{f}$, given a sample path $(\mathbf{s}(1), \mathbf{o}(1)),\ldots,\ (\mathbf{s}(n), \mathbf{o}(n))$ of the stochastic process

$$(\tilde{\mathbf{s}}(1), \tilde{\mathbf{o}}(1)),\ldots,\ (\tilde{\mathbf{s}}(n), \tilde{\mathbf{o}}(n)).$$

This problem of identifying the deterministic function $\mathbf{f}$ is an important type of generalization problem and has been discussed frequently in the mathematical learning theory literature (e.g., Baum and Haussler 1989; Denker et al. 1987; Vapnik 1992).

The deterministic function identification definition of generalization is a special case of the more general notion of an appropriate Bayesian generalization introduced in this section. To see this relationship, consider a probability model such that a particular element of the model has the form of the conditional probability $p(\mathbf{r} \mid \mathbf{s})$, where

$p(\mathbf{r} \mid \mathbf{s}) = 1$ if $\mathbf{r} = \mathbf{f}(\mathbf{s})$

and

$p(\mathbf{r} \mid \mathbf{s}) = 0$ if $\mathbf{r} \neq \mathbf{f}(\mathbf{s})$.

Thus every desired deterministic mapping from stimulus $\mathbf{s}$ to response $\mathbf{r}$ can be modeled by choosing $\mathbf{f}$ in an appropriate manner. Because the global maximum of $p(\cdot \mid \mathbf{s})$ is equal to $\mathbf{r} = \mathbf{f}(\mathbf{s})$, it follows that learning some unknown deterministic functional relationship is a very special case of MAP estimation, which in turn (as previously noted) is a special case of solving a Bayes risk decision problem.

6.5.2   Relevance of Network Approximation Theorems

This section discusses the relevance of key results showing the universal approximation capabilities of backpropagation networks with one layer of hidden units (such as the classical backpropagation algorithm) for learning arbitrary functions. Hornik, Stinchcombe, and White (1989; also see Cybenko 1989; Funahashi 1989; Hecht-Nielsen 1989) have shown that a backpropagation network with one layer of sufficiently many (e.g., possibly billions) hidden units could represent almost every arbitrary function (i.e., stimulus to response mapping) where the hidden units are sigmoidal (i.e., nondecreasing) functions with finite upper and lower bounds. The important Poggio-Girosi (1990) representation theorem considers the case where the hidden units are radial basis functions (also see problem 7–2). Stinchcombe and White (1989; Poggio and Girosi 1990) have proved a similar result for backpropagation networks with one layer of hidden units where the hidden units are radial basis functions. These results are important from the perspective of the definition of generalization just provided because they can be used to provide insights into the class of probability distributions a given backpropagation network can adequately model.

The following points about network representation theorems should be noted. First, such theorems do not imply that a learning algorithm exists that can find the required mapping. Second, they do not imply that the mapping will not require an extraordinary large number of hidden units. And third, they can be used to obtain important insights into the class of probabilistic environments a given network architecture can potentially learn.

6.6   Historical Perspective on Decision Making

In 1713 Bernoulli was one of the earlist theorists to consider a probability as a "degree of confidence" rather than some objective relative frequency of an event (Raiffa 1970). Modern derivations of the concept of a subjective probability from fundamental axioms of rational decision making have been greatly influenced by the prior work of Keynes (1962), Ramsey (see Ramsey 1988 for a review), Cox (1946), and Savage (1972). Von Neumann and Morgenstern (1953) and Savage (1972) considered the relationship between minimizing expected risk and obeying rational decision making axioms. (Olinick 1978 provides a good introductory review of this literature.)

The term *logical fuzzy measure,* peculiar to this textbook, was introduced as an expository device in order to discuss the work of Cox (1946). The more general concept of a fuzzy measure is due to Sugeno (1977). A specific type of a fuzzy measure that is more general than a logical fuzzy measure forms the basis of the modern Dempster-Schafer mathematical theory of evidence (Shafer 1976). Other more general methods for representing and combining knowledge of losses and uncertainties have been investigated (by Kahneman and Tversky, (1979) and by Wakker 1989). (Klir and Folger 1988 provides an exceptionally clear and relatively unbiased discussion of fuzzy measure theory and its relationship to classical probabilistic measures of inductive inference. McNeill and Freiberger 1993, a popular and entertaining review of the fuzzy logic literature, provides an insightful, although nonformal and nonmathematical, discussion of many of the central controversial issues.)

6.7   Chapter Summary

Existence of a Relational System Theorem

To help readers understand how searching for the minimum value of some objective function is formally equivalent to solving certain types of rational inductive inference problems, a statement and proof of the Existence of a Relational System Theorem were presented (see section 6.1). The theorem formally defines the concept of a relational system of preferences and shows that a relational system with a measure can be constructed, given some objective function.

Measures, Fuzzy Measures, and the Bayes Risk Function

Three special types of measures for relational systems were introduced: *fuzzy measure,* which assigns a degree of belief to each event in the sample space; *logical fuzzy measure,* which is a fuzzy measure consistent with the laws of deductive logic; and *probabilistic fuzzy measure,* a logical fuzzy measure chosen for its mathematical tractability.

Also discussed were the concepts of a *probability model,* a set of probability mass (density) functions, and an *environmental* probability mass (density) function, (which generates the observed data). If the environmental probability mass (density) function is not a member of a particular probability model, then the probability model is *misspecified* with respect to the environmental proba-bility mass (density) function.

The key concept of a *Bayes risk function* was introduced. This special type of function, $l: D \rightarrow \mathfrak{R}$, combines in an additive manner the environmental prob-ability mass (density) function, $p_e: Q \rightarrow [0, \infty)$, which generates the observed data, and the *loss* function $c: D \times Q \rightarrow \mathfrak{R}$. The quantity $c(\mathbf{x} \mid \mathbf{y})$ is a measure of the subjective loss incurred by a particular agent A for choosing decision $\mathbf{x} \in D$, given situation $\mathbf{y} \in Q$. In particular,

$$l(\mathbf{x}) = E_{\tilde{\mathbf{y}}}\left[c(\mathbf{x} \mid \tilde{\mathbf{y}})\right]$$

for each decision $\mathbf{x} \in D$ (assuming l exists), where p_e is the probability mass (density) function for the random vector $\tilde{\mathbf{y}}$.

Gibbs Distributions and Markov Random Fields

The Fundamental Markov Random Field Theorem for constructing the most general form of the probability distribution (a Gibbs probability distribution) for a given Markov random field was also described. Briefly, one identifies the cliques associated with the neighborhood system on the Markov random field. The clique structure of the random field allows one to define the most general joint probability distribution for the Markov random field such that the under-lying assumptions regarding the neighborhood system of the Markov field are satisfied. The Fundamental Markov Random Field Theorem was shown to be useful for constructing the neighborhood system for a given joint Gibbs proba-bility mass (density) function.

In addition, the Markov random field approach was seen to encourage the factorization of the joint probability distribution in terms of a large number of computationally tractable local conditional probability distributions and thus to serve as an important tool for handling a large class of probability distributions defined with respect to high-dimensional sample spaces.

Making Decisions with Rational Inference Measures

Finally, a classical statistical concept of generalization was introduced. An *ap-propriate generalization* was defined as a global minimum of $\mathcal{P}$ on a subset of $\mathcal{F}$, where $\mathcal{P}$ is a measure for some relational system of preferences $(S, \mathcal{F}, \omega)$. Given a system of preferences, one can evaluate whether or not the intelligent system is achieving its internal goals. In addition, the "rationality" of the system of preferences can be evaluated using the concepts introduced in this chapter.

An important special case of this definition of generalization was shown to involve computing the global minimum of a Bayes risk function where all cor-rect decisions are not penalized and all errors are equally penalized. This re-sults in a MAP estimate that is a minimum probability of error decision; such a decision may be viewed as a natural generalization of the special definition of generalization, where the learning machine is required to identify an unknown deterministic mapping between its inputs and outputs.

6.8   Elementary Problems

6.1-1. An ANN system has two units. Each unit corresponds to an assertion as follows:

- Unit 1: *Red object is present.*
- Unit 2: *Round object is present.*

The activation level of each unit is restricted to take on only one of two values: one (assertion *true*) or zero (assertion *false*). An activation pattern over these two units consists of a list of two activation levels. Consider a sample space where each point in the sample space is a two-dimensional activation pattern vector. Explicitly define the sample space S and the sigma field $\mathcal{F}$ generated by S. The ANN system exists in a world that consists of only four types of objects: red balls, red cubes, green balls, green cubes. Suppose that the ANN system believes that the event

Red ball is present or *Red cube is present*

is strictly more preferable than every other event where a red ball is present. Define a relation ω_{ANN} that represents the beliefs of the ANN system.

6.1-2. Repeat problem 6.1-1 but now suppose that the ANN system believes every event where a *Red ball is present* to be at least as preferable as the event

Red ball is present or *Red cube is present.*

6.1-3. Is it possible to construct a measure for the relational system in problem 6.1-1? If so, construct such a measure. If not, explain why not.

6.1-4. Is it possible to construct a measure for the relational system in problem 6.1-2? If so, construct such a measure. If not, explain why not.

6.1-5. Is it possible to construct a fuzzy measure for the relational system in problem 6.1-1? If so, construct such a fuzzy measure. If not, explain why not.

6.1-6. Is it possible to construct a fuzzy measure for the relational system in problem 6.1-2? If so, construct such a fuzzy measure. If not, explain why not.

6.1-7. Is it possible to construct a fuzzy logical measure for the relational system in problem 6.1-1? If so, construct such a fuzzy logical measure. If not, explain why not.

6.1-8. Is it possible to construct a fuzzy logical measure for the relational system in problem 6.1-2? If so, construct such a fuzzy logical measure. If not, explain why not.

6.1-9. Is it possible to construct a fuzzy probabilistic measure for the relational system in problem 6.1-1? If so, construct such a fuzzy probabilistic measure. If not, explain why not.

6.1-10. Is it possible to construct a fuzzy probabilistic measure for the relational system in problem 6.1-2? If so, construct such a fuzzy probabilistic measure. If not, explain why not.

6.2-1. Explain how a fuzzy measure can be used to implicitly represent for some rational agent a preference for some decision in terms of (a) the likelihood some event will occur, and (b) the subjective value of the event.

6.3-1. Let

$$\tilde{y}_{t+1} = \tilde{y}_t + \tilde{n}$$

for $t = 1 \ldots M - 1$, where $\tilde{n}$ is a Gaussian random variable with mean zero and variable σ^2 and $\tilde{y}_1$ is a Gaussian random variable with mean zero and variance σ^2. Give an explicit formula for the joint probability density function $p(y_1, \ldots, y_M)$.

6.3-2. A joint probability distribution, $p(x_1, x_2, x_3, x_4, x_5, x_6)$, of six random variables, $\tilde{x}_1, \tilde{x}_2, \tilde{x}_3, \tilde{x}_4, \tilde{x}_5, \tilde{x}_6$, can be factored into the following product of six local conditional probability distributions:

$$p(x_6)p(x_1 | x_2, x_3) p(x_2 | x_4)p(x_4 | x_5) p(x_3 | x_4) p(x_5 | x_6).$$

Graph the model's independence assumptions as in figure 6.2.

6.3-3. Consider a Gibbs distribution representation of a probability mass function, $p: \{0,1\}^d \rightarrow (0, 1)$, which can be expressed in terms of the Q-expansion in (6.35). Show that for this special case all G functions in (6.35) may be replaced with constants without any loss in generality.

6.3-4. Define the five assertions:

1. $a_1 =$ *Martini spills on computer.*
2. $a_2 =$ *Computer is not waterproof.*
3. $a_3 =$ *Martini is precariously balanced near computer.*
4. $a_4 =$ *Computer owner wants a Martini.*
5. $a_5 =$ *Computer must be replaced.*

Also define a group of five random variables, $\tilde{x}_1, \tilde{x}_2, \tilde{x}_3, \tilde{x}_4, \tilde{x}_5$ where $\tilde{x}_i = 1$ indicates assertion a_i is *true* and $\tilde{x}_i = 0$ indicates assertion a_i is *false*. Suppose an intelligent agent S has a belief structure that consists of the following three causal relationships.:

1. If a_4 is true and a_3 is true, then a_1 is likely to occur.
2. If a_1 is true and a_2 is true, then a_5 is likely to occur.
3. If a_5 is true, then a_4 is likely to occur.

Explain why these three causal relationships for this belief structure have been modeled as the relation:

$$\omega = \{(\tilde{x}_1, \tilde{x}_3), (\tilde{x}_1, \tilde{x}_4), (\tilde{x}_1, \tilde{x}_5), (\tilde{x}_2, \tilde{x}_5), (\tilde{x}_4, \tilde{x}_5), (\tilde{x}_3, \tilde{x}_1), (\tilde{x}_4, \tilde{x}_1), (\tilde{x}_5, \tilde{x}_1), (\tilde{x}_5, \tilde{x}_2), (\tilde{x}_5, \tilde{x}_4)\}.$$

Construct and graph ω as in figure 6.4.

6.3-5. Construct the most general form of the joint probability mass function

$$p(x_1, x_2, x_3, x_4, x_5)$$

Using the relation ω described in problem 6.3-4 and the result of problem 6.3-3. Now choose the functional form of the general probability mass function so that

$$p(x_1 = 1 | x_2 = 1, x_3 = 1, x_4 = 1, x_5 = 1) > 0.5,$$

$$p(x_5 = 1 | x_1 = 1, x_2 = 1, x_3 = 1, x_4 = 1) > 0.5,$$

and

$$p(x_4 = 1 | x_1 = 1, x_2 = 1, x_3 = 1, x_5 = 1) > 0.5.$$

Also suppose that

$$p(x_1 = 1 | x_2 = 0, x_3 = 0, x_4 = 0, x_5 = 0) < 0.5,$$

$$p(x_5 = 1 | x_1 = 0, x_2 = 0, x_3 = 0, x_4 = 0) < 0.5,$$

and

$$p(x_4 = 1 | x_1 = 0, x_2 = 0, x_3 = 0, x_5 = 0) < 0.5.$$

These inequalities are designed to model the three causal knowledge assertions described in problem 6.3-4. Suppose that assertion a_1 was true, so that $\tilde{x}_1 = 1$. Explain how the Gibbs sampler algorithm could be used to estimate the most probable assignment of values (zero or one) to the remaining four random variables, $\tilde{x}_2, \tilde{x}_3, \tilde{x}_4$, and $\tilde{x}_5$. Explain how the derived Gibbs sampler algorithm is related to the Boltzmann machine algorithm (Ackley, Hinton, and Sejnowski 1985) described in chapter 2.

6.3-6. Define the set of four assertions a_1, a_2, a_3, a_4 as follows:

1. $a_1 =$ *An ant was drowning in a river,*
2. $a_2 =$ *A dove dropped a leaf in the river,*
3. $a_3 =$ *The ant climbed on a leaf,*
4, $a_4 =$ *The dove wanted to save the ant.*

Also define a group of four binary-valued random variables, $\tilde{x}_1, \tilde{x}_2, \tilde{x}_3,$ and $\tilde{x}_4$, where $\tilde{x}_i = 1$ if assertion a_i is *true* and $\tilde{x}_i = 0$ if assertion a_i is *false*. Suppose an intelligent agent, JG, has a belief structure that consists of the following two causal relationships:

1. If a_4 is true and a_1 is true, then a_2 is likely to occur.
2. If a_2 is true and a_1 is true, then a_3 is likely to occur.

Construct and graph a symmetric relation consistent with the belief structure of agent JG. Then construct the most general form of the joint probability mass function $p(x_1, x_2, x_3, x_4)$, using the result of problem 6.3-3, consistent with the functional dependencies embedded within the belief structure of agent JG. Now choose the functional form of the general probability mass function so that

1. $p(x_3 = 1 \mid x_1 = 1, x_2 = 1) > 0.9,$
2. $p(x_3 = 1 \mid x_1 = 0, x_2 = 0) < 0.1,$
3. $p(x_2 = 1 \mid x_1 = 1, x_3 = 1, x_4 = 1) > 0.9,$
4. $p(x_2 = 1 \mid x_1 = 0, x_3 = 0, x_4 = 0) < 0.1.$

Explain how these four inequalities are designed to model the two causal knowledge assertions described above. Suppose that assertion a_1 is true, so that $\tilde{x}_1 = 1$. Explain how the Gibbs sampler algorithm could be used to estimate the most probable assignment of values (zero or one) to the remaining three random variables, $\tilde{x}_2, \tilde{x}_3,$ and $\tilde{x}_4$.

6.4-1. Construct a Bayesian decision rule that attempts to make the *maximum* number of errors.

6.4-2. Suppose an ANN system can be shown to be searching for an activation pattern that is the global minimum of some classification objective function $V: \mathcal{R}^2 \to \mathcal{R}$, defined such that for all $\mathbf{x} = [x_1, x_2] \in \mathcal{R}^2$:

$$V(\mathbf{x}) = V(x_1, x_2) = -(x_1 - 0.5)(x_2 - 0.5).$$

Provide an explicit formula relating V to some probabilistic fuzzy measure $\mathcal{B}$ such that for all $\mathbf{x}$ in the sample space: the belief of an elementary event $\{\mathbf{x}\}$ is some monotonically nonincreasing function of $V(\mathbf{x})$. Explain why your formula, however easy to construct, may be used to provide important insights into the generalization behavior of the ANN system.

6.5-1. Suppose a researcher proves that an ANN system is an optimization algorithm that always succeeds in finding a global minimum of some real-valued performance function $l: \mathcal{R}^q \to \mathcal{R}$. Define an appropriate preference relational system such that the ANN system always makes appropriate generalizations.

Expected Risk Classification and Learning Theory

As noted in the previous chapter, an ANN searching for the minimum of some objective function $V: \mathcal{R}^d \to \mathcal{R}$ on $\Omega \subseteq \mathcal{R}^d$ may be viewed as an information-processing system seeking an appropriate generalization (or equivalently, an optimal decision) with respect to a particular relational system of preferences. By precisely and explicitly defining how computing a global minimum and a rational decision are formally equivalent, chapter 6 provided the missing link between the objective function optimization algorithm analyses described in chapters 3, 4, and 5 and the problem of understanding ANN systems as rational inference machines.

For example, consider a brain-state-in-a-box (BSB) neural model (see chapter 2 for a review) whose system state for the classification (activation updating) dynamics is a state vector $\mathbf{x} \in \mathcal{R}^d$. Let the ith element of $\mathbf{x}$ be the activation level of the ith unit in the ANN system. Let $\mathbf{W}$ be a d-dimensional symmetric real matrix whose ijth element is the connection strength w_{ij} from unit j to unit i. Let $V: [-1, 1]^d \times \mathcal{R}^{d \times d} \to \mathcal{R}$. The BSB model seeks (usually unsuccessfully) an activation pattern $\mathbf{x}^* \in [-1, 1]^d$ that is a global minimum of some function $V(\cdot; \mathbf{W}): [-1, 1]^d \to \mathcal{R}$, where $V(\cdot; \mathbf{W})$ is defined such that for all $\mathbf{x} \in [-1, 1]^d$:

$$V(\mathbf{x}; \mathbf{W}) = -(1/2)\mathbf{x}^T \mathbf{W} \mathbf{x}. \tag{7.1}$$

Using the theoretical framework developed in chapter 6, let $\mathcal{U}$ be the set of elementary events that are members of some sigma field $\mathcal{F}$ generated from the sample space $S = [-1, 1]^d$. Let $\mathcal{P}: \mathcal{F} \times W \to \mathcal{R}$, where $W \subseteq \mathcal{R}^{d \times d}$. Define a measure $\mathcal{P}(\cdot; \mathbf{W}): \mathcal{F} \to \mathcal{R}$ such that $\mathcal{P}(\{\mathbf{x}\}; \mathbf{W}) = V(\mathbf{x}; \mathbf{W})$, where V is defined in (7.1), $\mathbf{x} \in S$, and $\{\mathbf{x}\} \in \mathcal{U}$. The Existence of a Relational System Theorem then implies the existence of some relational system, $(S, \mathcal{F}, \omega_{\mathbf{W}})$, where $\omega_{\mathbf{W}}$ is connected and transitive such that $\mathcal{P}$ is a measure for the relational system $(S, \mathcal{F}, \omega_{\mathbf{W}})$. The relation $\omega_{\mathbf{W}}$ may be interpreted as a preference relation, which changes as a function of $\mathbf{W}$, that is, different patterns of connection strengths index different preference relational systems. Given this assumption, the BSB model's classification dynamics may be interpreted as seeking the elementary event $\{\mathbf{x}^*\}$ that is the most preferred event in $\mathcal{U}$ with respect to the preference relational system $(S, \mathcal{F}, \omega_{\mathbf{W}})$.

Suppose that the sample space S contains only the 2^d vertices of the d-dimensional hypercube associated with the BSB model. This assumption implies that the *informational property* of an activation pattern is derived by simply classifying the activation level of each unit as *active* or *inactive*. Thus, $S = \{-1, 1\}^d$, so that S consists of the vertices of a d-dimensional hypercube. This latter definition would simply result in a different relational system. The power of the theoretical framework developed in chapter 6 is that such a framework forces one to semantically define the relevant informational characteristics of quantities such as activation patterns and connection strengths.

Now let us turn to the problem of learning. For a given connection strength parameter matrix $\mathbf{W} \in W$, consider an uncoupled ANN dynamical system whose classification dynamical system uses the measure $\mathcal{P}(\cdot; \mathbf{W})$: $\mathscr{F} \to \mathscr{R}$ for the preference relational system $(S, \mathscr{F}, \omega_{\mathbf{W}})$ to make a decision during the classification process. The learning problem may be generally defined as choosing a particular connection strength parameter matrix $\mathbf{W}^* \in W$ such that the preference relations for the ANN dynamical system will be appropriate in some sense.

Because such a general formulation provides the ANN learning dynamical system little guidance in selecting an appropriate connection strength parameter matrix $\mathbf{W}^*$, it is helpful to break up the relational measure $\mathcal{P}$ into two components: a representation of the relative frequency of occurrence of events in the environment and a representation of subjective loss for making a particular decision in the context of a particular environmental event. The relative frequency of events in the ANN learning dynamical system's environment are usually directly observable. A classical version of this approach uses a Bayes expected risk function, as described in chapter 6. Now the learning machine simply needs to acquire a representation of the relative frequency of events in its environment and combine that information with its representation of subjective loss using the Bayes expected risk function to make optimal decisions with respect to its implicit relational system of preferences.

Assume the classification dynamical system of the BSB model is a maximum a posteriori (MAP) estimation algorithm with respect to the subjective probability model, F_W, where F_W is defined such that

$$F_W = \{p(\cdot \mid \mathbf{W}): \mathbf{W} \subseteq W\},$$

and $p(\cdot \mid \mathbf{W})$: $\{-1, 1\}^d \to (0, 1)$ is a subjective probability mass function for every $\mathbf{W} \in W$ such that

$$p(\mathbf{x} \mid \mathbf{W}) = (1/Z)\exp[-V(\mathbf{x}; \mathbf{W})], \tag{7.2}$$

where $V(\cdot; \mathbf{W})$ is defined as in (7.1) and

$$Z = \sum_{\mathbf{y} \in \{-1, 1\}^d} \exp[-V(\mathbf{y}; \mathbf{W})].$$

Inspection of (7.2) shows that the BSB model classification dynamical system is seeking a global maximum of $p(\cdot \mid \mathbf{W})$ for a given $\mathbf{W}$, and thus the BSB model classification dynamical system is a MAP estimation algorithm with respect to $p(\cdot \mid \mathbf{W})$. Note that both $V(\cdot \mid \mathbf{W})$ and $-p(\cdot \mid \mathbf{W})$ are classification objective functions for the ANN classification dynamical system.

Suppose that it is known that the classification (activation updating) dynamics of a given ANN system is seeking a global maximum of every explicit subjective probability measure $p \in F_W$. That is, the ANN classification dynamical system is a MAP estimation algorithm with respect to all $p \in F_W$. Then one immediately has a theory of the class of statistical environments (i.e., the complement of the set F_W) the ANN system will *never* be able to properly represent! For example, if the subjective probability model for an ANN system is the set of uniform probability density functions and the environmental probability density function is a univariate Gaussian probability density function with zero mean and unit variance, then the ANN system will never be able to obtain absolute knowledge of its statistical environment. Such insights can be extremely valuable for deciding which of several ANN system architectures is most appropriate for a given statistical environment (see chapter 8 for additional details).

Now consider an ANN system such that each possible pattern of connection strengths identifies a specific subjective probability mass (density) function in some subjective probability model F_W. Also assume that the classification dynamics of the ANN system is a MAP estimation algorithm with respect to all members of F_W. The goal of learning in the ANN system is to find the member of F_W that is "closest" in some sense to the environmental probability mass (density) function, p_e. Thus knowledge of the subjective probability model F_W can be used as an aid in learning algorithm analysis and design. The ANN system design engineer can select a learning algorithm that minimizes the distance between the subjective probability model F_W and the environmental distribution p_e. Or, for analysis applications, the ANN system engineer can evaluate a given learning algorithm to determine whether the learning algorithm is minimizing the distance between F_W and p_e.

In addition, after the learning process has been completed, there will always be an intrinsic sampling error in the parameter estimates, that is, the ANN system will make less effective inferences because the size of the training data set is finite. Methods can also be developed for estimating the magnitude of this sampling error (see chapter 8 for additional details).

This chapter is organized in two parts. First, it will describe a heuristic method for *constructing* a subjective probability model for a given ANN system such that the ANN classification dynamical system is a MAP estimation algorithm with respect to each member of the ANN's subjective probability model. Second, it will present a method for *deriving* what risk function an ANN system should minimize during the learning process, given the assumptions that both the ANN classification and learning dynamical systems are MAP estimation algorithms. This optimal risk function may be used to derive optimal learning algorithms or evaluate the rationality of existing learning algorithms.

7.1   The Optimal Classification Assumption

Classical statistical pattern recognition assumes a particular probability model of the environment and then derives a MAP estimation algorithm that seeks a mode of that distribution. In many ANN system analysis and design problems, however, the classification and learning algorithms are provided without a statistical modeling interpretation of their computational goals. The ANN engineer in this latter case must solve a *reverse* engineering problem and propose a statistical model that justifies the computational goals of a given ANN system.

A number of researchers have suggested solutions to the ANN reverse engineering problem in the context of statistical modeling (for example, Ackley, Hinton, and Sejnowski 1985; Amari 1967; Amari and Murata 1993; Barron and Barron 1989; Baum and Wilczek 1988; Bridle 1990; Cheng and Titterington 1994; Golden 1988a,b,c; Jaakkola, Jordan, and Singh 1994; Kohonen 1984; MacKay 1992; Marroquin 1985; Ripley 1994; Rumelhart et al 1995; Smolensky 1986; Specht 1967, 1988, 1990; Tishby, Levin, and Solla 1989; Levin, Tishby, and Solla 1990; Van Hulle and Orban 1991; and White 1989a,b). This chapter will focus upon an extension of the theoretical framework described by Golden (1988a,b,c).

Referring to figure 7.1, the classical statistical pattern recognition approach begins by assuming some probabilistic model of the environment. The probabilistic model is then used to derive classification and learning algorithms. The

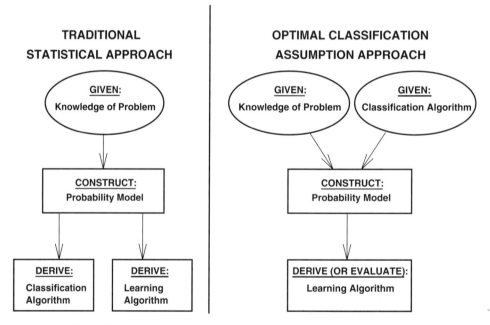

Figure 7.1
Comparison of traditional statistical and optimal classification methods. In the classical approach to statistical pattern recognition, one assumes the existence of a probability model and then proceeds to derive algorithms for classification and learning. Typically in ANN system analysis and design, the classification and possibly even the learning algorithms are provided without a probability model. Thus the optimal classification assumption approach involves *constructing* a probability model, F_W, that is consistent with the hypothesis that the ANN classification dynamical system is a MAP estimation algorithm with respect to each probability mass (density) function in F_W. The constructed probability model may be used to derive new learning algorithms or evaluate existing learning algorithms.

optimal classification assumption method, however, assumes that the ANN classification dynamical system is a MAP estimation algorithm with respect to some subjective probability model. It is assumed that a particular element of the ANN's subjective probability model is a probability mass (density) function, $p(\cdot \mid \mathbf{w})$, for some particular pattern of connection strengths $\mathbf{w}$.

The quantity $p(\mathbf{x} \mid \mathbf{w})$ is interpreted as the ANN system's *expectation* (or belief) that the activation pattern $\mathbf{x}$ is present in the environment, given a particular belief system indexed by the connection strength parameter vector $\mathbf{w}$. The quantity $p(\mathbf{x} \mid \mathbf{w})$ *does not mean* that the ANN system *produces* response activation pattern $\mathbf{x}$ with probability $p(\mathbf{x} \mid \mathbf{w})$, given connection strength parameter vector $\mathbf{w}$.

The essential difficulty concerning the application of the optimal classification assumption approach in practice is the methodology needed to construct an appropriate subjective probability model for a given ANN dynamical system. The following theorem (a streamlined version of the approach suggested by Golden 1988a,b,c) provides a useful tool for constructing a probability model for a given ANN classification dynamical system, so that the ANN classification dynamical system may be formally viewed as a type of MAP estimation algorithm.

Before presenting the theorem, however, it will be useful to introduce the general concept of an *objective-optimal deterministic ANN classification dynamical system*, which seeks (in a precise sense described below) to compute an *optimal decision* (as defined in chapter 6) with respect to a specific relational system.

Definition: Objective-optimal deterministic ANN classification dynamical system.   Let $T = \{0, 1, 2,...\}$ or $T = [0, \infty)$. Let $\Omega \subseteq \mathcal{R}^d$ be a set of output response activation patterns. Let $W \subseteq \mathcal{R}^q$, $\Omega^* \subseteq \Omega$, and $T^* \subseteq T$. Let $V: \Omega \times W \to \mathcal{R}$ define an objective function $V(\cdot; \mathbf{w})$ for every $\mathbf{w} \in W$. Let

$$\Psi_C: \Omega \times T \times T \times E \times W \to \Omega$$

be an ANN classification dynamical system. If for every initial state $\mathbf{x}_0 \in \Omega^*$, every initial time $t_0 \in T^*$, every event history function $\eta \in E$, and every $\mathbf{w} \in W$:

$$\mathbf{x}(t) = \Psi_C(\mathbf{x}_0, t_0, t, \eta, \mathbf{w}) \to \mathcal{H}$$

as $t \to \infty$, where $\mathcal{H}$ is the set of global minima of the *classification objective function* $V(\cdot; \mathbf{w})$ on Ω^*, then Ψ_C is an *objective-optimal deterministic ANN classification dynamical system* with respect to V, T^*, W, and Ω^*.

Note that the above definition applies to classification dynamical systems that generate a sequence of states converging to a strict local minimum. In such cases, the set Ω^* is chosen to be a sufficiently small δ-neighborhood of the strict local minimum of interest.

Informally, an objective-optimal deterministic ANN classification dynamical system (discrete-time or continuous-time) is a deterministic algorithm that seeks some global minimum of a classification objective function. A similar definition is now developed for discrete-time ANN classification dynamical systems that are stochastic algorithms. (Continuous-time ANN classification dynamical systems that can be expressed as stochastic algorithms are not considered.)

Note that the notation $\tilde{\mathbf{x}}(t) \to \mathcal{H}$ in distribution as $t \to \infty$ means that

$$\inf\{|\tilde{\mathbf{x}}(t) - \mathbf{y}| : \mathbf{y} \in \mathcal{H}\} \to 0$$

in distribution as $t \to \infty$.

Definition: Objective-optimal stochastic ANN classification dynamical system. Let $T = \{0, 1, 2,...\}$. Let $\Omega \subseteq \mathcal{R}^d$ be the set of output response activation patterns. Let $W \subseteq \mathcal{R}^q$. Let $V: \Omega \times W \to \mathcal{R}$ define an objective function $V(\cdot; \mathbf{w})$ for every $\mathbf{w} \in W$. For every $t_o \in T$ and every $t \in T$ such that $t > t_0$: let $\tilde{\mathbf{n}}(t_0),..., \tilde{\mathbf{n}}(t-1)$ be a stochastic sequence of m-dimensional random vectors. Let

$$\mathbf{\Psi}_C: \Omega \times T \times T \times E \times W \to \Omega$$

be an ANN classification dynamical system. Let $\tilde{\mathbf{x}}_0$ be a random vector with probability mass (density) function $p_0: \Omega^* \to [0, \infty)$, where $\Omega^* \subseteq \Omega$. If for every $t_0 \in T^* \subseteq T$, and for every $\mathbf{w} \in W$:

$$\tilde{\mathbf{x}}(t) = \mathbf{\Psi}_C(\tilde{\mathbf{x}}_0, t_0, t, \{\tilde{\mathbf{n}}(t_0),..., \tilde{\mathbf{n}}(t-1)\}, \mathbf{w}) \to \mathcal{H}$$

in distribution as $t \to \infty$, where $\mathcal{H}$ is the set of global minima of the *classification objective function* $V(\cdot; \mathbf{w})$ on Ω^*, then $\mathbf{\Psi}_C$ is an *objective-optimal stochastic ANN classification dynamical system* with respect to V, T^*, W, and Ω^*.

Note that an objective-optimal (deterministic or stochastic) ANN classification dynamical system is not an ANN temporal memory dynamical system, which is much more difficult to analyze directly and rigorously (see Kuan, Hornik, and White 1994 for some example analyses). On the other hand, the above definitions apply to a surprisingly large class of discrete-time ANN temporal memory dynamical systems, provided that the system state space, Ω, is defined in an appropriate manner. Consider a discrete-time ANN temporal memory dynamical system that observes the following set of n *temporal learning sequences*:

$$[\mathbf{x}_{1,1},..., \mathbf{x}_{1,M_1}],..., [\mathbf{x}_{n,1},..., \mathbf{x}_{n,M_n}], \tag{7.3}$$

where the finite positive integer M_i is the number of training stimuli or *length* of the ith temporal sequence, and $\mathbf{x}_{i,j} \in \mathcal{R}^d$ is the jth ($j = 1... M_i$) training stimulus in the ith temporal sequence ($i = 1... n$). For example, consider an ANN system whose goal is to balance a pole. The ANN system must learn to make small adjustments to the pole's state within a particular statistical environment. The end of each temporal sequence is identified when the pole falls. After training the ANN learning system with many examples of how to balance the pole (each example is a temporal learning sequence), the ANN learning system may learn to balance the pole by itself.

The objective-optimal ANN classification dynamical system definition applies if one defines a *temporal sequence training stimulus* $\mathbf{x}(k) = [\mathbf{x}_{k,1},\ldots, \mathbf{x}_{k,M_k}]$. The set of *n temporal sequence training stimuli* in (7.3) may then be interpreted as a sample path of the stochastic process $\tilde{\mathbf{x}}(1),\ldots, \tilde{\mathbf{x}}(n)$ whose elements are independent and identically distributed temporal sequence training stimuli with common probability mass function $p_e: \Omega \rightarrow [0, 1]$, where the finite set Ω is the set of possible temporal sequence training stimuli. An objective-optimal ANN classification dynamical system in this case has an implicit relational system designed to decide which of two temporal sequence training stimuli is preferable. (Problems 4-7, 5-7, and 7-3 provide some specific examples of this type of modeling approach.)

Definition: ANN system probability model.   Let $S \subseteq \Omega \subseteq \mathcal{R}^d$ be a set of output response activation patterns. Assume that for every $\mathbf{w} \in W \subseteq \mathcal{R}^q$: $\mathbf{\Psi}_c(\cdot, \cdot, \cdot, \cdot, \mathbf{w})$, where

$$\mathbf{\Psi}_c: \Omega \times T \times T \times E \times W \rightarrow \Omega,$$

is an objective-optimal (deterministic or stochastic) ANN classification dynamical system with respect to $T^* \subseteq T, \Omega^* \subseteq \Omega$, and probability mass (density) function $-p(\cdot \mid \mathbf{w}): S \rightarrow [0, \infty)$. The *ANN system probability model* for the *MAP-optimal ANN classification dynamical system* $\mathbf{\Psi}_c$ is the set

$$F_W = \{p(\cdot \mid \mathbf{w}): \mathbf{w} \in W\}.$$

Theorem: MAP-Optimal Classification Dynamics.   Let $S \subseteq \Omega \subseteq \mathcal{R}^d$ be a set of output response activation patterns. Let $W \subseteq \mathcal{R}^q$. Let $V: \Omega \times W \rightarrow \mathcal{R}$. Let $p: S \times W \rightarrow [0, \infty)$. Let

$$\mathbf{\Psi}_C: \Omega \times T \times T \times E \times W \rightarrow \Omega$$

be an objective-optimal (stochastic or deterministic) ANN classification dynamical system with respect to classification objective function V. Suppose that for every $\mathbf{w} \in W$: there exists a finite strictly positive real number $Z_{\mathbf{w}}$ such that

$$p(\cdot \mid \mathbf{w}) = (1/Z_{\mathbf{w}}) \exp [-V(\cdot; \mathbf{w})] \qquad (7.4)$$

is a probability mass (density) function. Then

$$F_W = \{p(\cdot \mid \mathbf{w}): \mathbf{w} \in W\}$$

is a ANN system probability model for $\mathbf{\Psi}_C$.

Proof.   Let $\mathbf{w} \in W$. If $Z_{\mathbf{w}}$ exists, then

$$0 < p(\mathbf{x} \mid \mathbf{w}) = (1/Z_{\mathbf{w}}) \exp\left[-V(\mathbf{x}; \mathbf{w})\right] < 1$$

for all $\mathbf{w} \in W$ and $\mathbf{x} \in S$. Note $Z_{\mathbf{w}}$ is chosen so that

$$\sum_{\mathbf{x} \in S} p(\cdot \mid \mathbf{w}) = 1$$

for all $\mathbf{w} \in W$ if p is a probability mass function. Note $Z_{\mathbf{w}}$ is chosen so that

$$\int_{\mathbf{x} \in S} p(\cdot \mid \mathbf{w}) d\mathbf{w} = 1$$

for all $\mathbf{w} \in W$ if p is a probability density function. Thus $p(\cdot \mid \mathbf{w})$ is a probability mass (density) function for every $\mathbf{w} \in W$.

Let $\mathbf{x}^*$ be a global minimum of $V(\cdot; \mathbf{w})$ on Ω^*:

$$V(\mathbf{x}; \mathbf{w}) \geq V(\mathbf{x}^*; \mathbf{w}) \tag{7.5}$$

for all $\mathbf{x} \in \Omega^*$. Because the exponential function $\exp: \mathcal{R} \to [0, \infty)$ has the property that $\exp[V_1] \geq \exp[V_2]$ if and only if $V_1 \geq V_2$, it immediately follows from (7.5) that

$$\exp\left[-V(\mathbf{x}; \mathbf{w})\right] \leq \exp\left[-V(\mathbf{x}^*; \mathbf{w})\right] \tag{7.6}$$

for all $\mathbf{x} \in \Omega^*$. Dividing both sides of (7.6) by the strictly positive constant $Z_{\mathbf{w}}$ implies that $\mathbf{x}^*$ is a global maximum of $p(\cdot \mid \mathbf{w})$ on Ω^*.   ∎

The MAP-Optimal Classification Dynamics Theorem states that if one can find an objective function $V: S \to \mathcal{R}$ that is minimized by an ANN classification dynamical system, then one may construct a probability mass (density) function $p(\cdot; \mathbf{w}): S \to (0, \infty)$ that is maximized by the ANN classification dynamical system. The ANN system is thus a MAP estimation algorithm with respect to $p(\cdot; \mathbf{w})$. The set of probability distributions indexed by $\mathbf{w}$ and specifically defined by

$$F_W = \{p(\cdot; \mathbf{w}): \mathbf{w} \in W\}$$

is called the "ANN system's probability model."

A (nonunique) formula for computing $p(\cdot; \mathbf{w})$ is also provided. Choose $p(\cdot; \mathbf{w})$ such that

$$p(\mathbf{x} \mid \mathbf{w}) = Z_{\mathbf{w}}^{-1} \exp\left[-V(\mathbf{x}; \mathbf{w})\right]$$

for all $\mathbf{x} \in S$, where S is the sample space. Note that $Z_{\mathbf{w}}$ may be a function of $\mathbf{w}$ but is not a function of $\mathbf{x}$. Thus p increases as $V(\cdot; \mathbf{w}): S \to \mathcal{R}$ decreases because $\exp[-V]$ is a monotonically decreasing function of V. Also the exponential function maps any possible value of V (the range of V is the real numbers) into the interval $(0, \infty)$. The *normalization constant* $Z_\mathbf{w}$ is uniquely determined and chosen (when it exists) such that the integral of

$$\int_{\mathbf{x} \in S} p(\mathbf{x} \mid \mathbf{w}) d\mathbf{x} = 1$$

if $p(\cdot \mid \mathbf{w})$ is a probability density function, and

$$\sum_{\mathbf{x} \in S} p(\mathbf{x} \mid \mathbf{w}) = 1$$

if $p(\cdot \mid \mathbf{w})$ is a probability mass function.

The selection of an appropriate sample space S requires careful and thoughtful consideration. Different choices of S will result in quite different subjective probability models for a MAP-optimal ANN classification dynamical system. A rich source of constraints on the sample space S may be obtained by examining the structure of the training stimuli. For example, if the training stimulus is always a d-dimensional vector $\mathbf{x}$ whose elements are always either equal to zero or one, then it is reasonable to select $S = \{0, 1\}^d$. Generalization performance for the ANN system should improve if S is appropriately chosen because when S is correctly chosen, the subjective probability model for the ANN system will not be misspecified with respect to the environmental probability distribution. The choice of S is also important from the perspective of computational efficiency. If S can be chosen so that the normalization constant $Z_\mathbf{w}$ in the MAP-optimal classification dynamical systems theorem is not functionally dependent upon the connection strength parameter vector $\mathbf{w}$, then the design of computationally efficient MAP estimation learning algorithms will be greatly facilitated (see section 7.2).

It is also important to note that the classification objective function V for an objective-optimal ANN classification dynamical system or a MAP-optimal ANN classification dynamical system is more than a mere mechanism for investigating the long-term behavior of the classification dynamical system. Rather, the classification objective function V in conjunction with the sample space S implies a very specific theory of (1) how knowledge is represented in the ANN system, (2) what aspects of the classification dynamics are relevant and irrelevant for information processing, and (3) how the explicit relational system used by the network to make decisions is characterized. If V is not unique, then the ANN system engineer must decide which of several alternative classification objective functions best captures the relevant relational system. In some cases, different classification objective functions for the same ANN system may be required to analyze different modes of the system's performance.

In summary, the Map-Optimal Classification Dynamics Theorem is a useful tool for providing ANN classification dynamical systems with a probabilistic interpretation. The theorem shows how to explicitly construct a subjective probability model for a given ANN classification dynamical system that is known to be minimizing some particular objective function. Once constructed, the probability model F_W can provide important insights into the class of statistical environments that the ANN dynamical system can *never* absolutely learn as well as insights into methods for designing and evaluating ANN learning dynamical systems. (These topics will be considered in section 7.2, as well as in chapter 8; section 7.3 and the problems at the end of the chapter will apply the MAP-optimal classification dynamics theorem to a variety of ANN classification dynamical systems.)

7.2   Rational ANN Learning Goals

7.2.1   General Theory

Chapter 6 provided arguments supporting the proposal that an appropriate computational goal for learning in ANN systems is to compute the global minimum of the objective Bayes expected risk function. In particular, the ANN learning dynamical system should choose a connection strength parameter vector, **w**, that minimizes the ANN system's expected risk. This chapter will first introduce the concept of a stochastic environment for learning, then formulate the computational goal of learning, given the unrealistic assumption that the ANN system has absolute knowledge of its stochastic environment, and finally consider an appropriate goal for learning when absolute knowledge of the stochastic environment is not available.

Stochastic Environment for Learning

In order to study the learning process, the stochastic environment within which learning takes place must be carefully defined. Let the *training stimuli*

$$\mathbf{x}(1), \mathbf{x}(2),\dots$$

be a sample path of the stochastic sequence of independent and identically distributed random vectors

$$\tilde{\mathbf{x}}(1), \tilde{\mathbf{x}}(2),\dots$$

that have the common environmental probability mass (density) function p_e: $S \to [0, \infty)$, where $S \subseteq \mathcal{R}^d$. The set of training stimuli may be an infinite set (as in the analysis of learning for on-line backpropagation ANN learning systems; see chapter 4) or, alternatively, a finite set, in which case the number of training stimuli will be denoted by the positive integer n.

In a supervised learning paradigm, the training stimulus $\mathbf{x}(k)$ may be partitioned into two subvectors, so that $\mathbf{x}(k) = [\mathbf{s}(k) \ \mathbf{o}(k)]$, where $\mathbf{s}(k)$ is the stimulus activation pattern and $\mathbf{o}(k)$ is the desired response activation pattern. In an unsupervised learning paradigm, the training stimulus $\mathbf{x}(k) = \mathbf{s}(k)$. That is, there is no component of $\mathbf{x}(k)$ that is a response feedback signal. In a scalar reinforcement learning paradigm, the training stimulus may be partitioned into a stimulus activation pattern $\mathbf{s}(k)$ and scalar reinforcement signal $o(k)$, so that $\mathbf{x}(k) = [\mathbf{s}(k)\ o(k)]$. Finally, for the case of temporal ANN learning systems, one may choose the *temporal sequence training stimulus* $\mathbf{x}(k)$ to be a temporally ordered sequence of subvectors such that

$$\mathbf{x}(k) = [\mathbf{x}_{k,1}, \ldots, \mathbf{x}_{k,M_k}],$$

where $\mathbf{x}_{k,j}$ is the jth observed *training stimulus* in the kth observed temporal sequence $\mathbf{x}(k)$ for $k = 1 \ldots n$ (where n is possibly infinite) and $j = 1 \ldots M_k$.

Thus the framework for learning considered here is sufficiently general to handle a variety of ANN learning paradigms, including supervised, unsupervised, reinforcement, and temporal learning paradigms.

General Risk Functions for Learning in ANN Systems

Let the set of connection strength parameter vectors, W, be a subset of $\mathcal{R}^q$. In the following discussion, the alternative terminology *true risk function* will be used to refer to an objective Bayes risk function (see chapter 6), $l\colon W \to \mathcal{R}$, defined with respect to some environmental probability mass (density) function p_e and loss function c. The global minimum of l on W may be interpreted as a Bayes risk decision (or appropriate Bayes risk generalization) which has been made with respect to some implicit relational system $(S, \mathcal{F}, \omega)$ and some subset of $\mathcal{F}$ (see chapter 6). Thus, a desirable computational goal for the learning dynamics of an ANN system is to find a global minimum, $\mathbf{w}^*$, of the true risk function l. Unfortunately, however, the true risk function l is usually not observable because knowledge of the environmental probability mass (density) function p_e is usually not available to the ANN learning system. For this reason, it is useful to introduce the concept of a sample risk function, which is an estimate of the true risk function based upon the observable data.

Definition: Sample risk function. Let $S \subseteq \Omega \subseteq \mathcal{R}^d$ and $W \subseteq \mathcal{R}^q$. Let l be a true risk function with respect to the environmental probability mass (density) function $p_e\colon S \to [0, \infty)$ and the loss function $c\colon W \times \Omega \to \mathcal{R}$. Let $\mathbf{x}(1), \ldots, \mathbf{x}(n)$ be a sample path of $\tilde{\mathbf{x}}(1), \ldots, \tilde{\mathbf{x}}(n)$ that is a stochastic sequence of independent and identically distributed random vectors with the common environmental probability mass (density) function p_e. Let $\hat{l}_n\colon W \times S^n \to \mathcal{R}$. A *sample risk function* for l, $\hat{l}_n(\cdot; \{\mathbf{x}(1), \ldots, \mathbf{x}(n)\})\colon W \to \mathcal{R}$, is defined such that for all $\mathbf{w} \in W$:

$$\hat{l}_n(\mathbf{w}; \{\mathbf{x}(1), \ldots, \mathbf{x}(n)\}) = (1/n) \sum_{i=1}^{n} c(\mathbf{w} \mid \mathbf{x}(i)).$$

Relationships between the Sample Risk and True Risk Functions

In this section, some close relationships between the sample risk function and the true risk function will be identified. In order to discuss these relationships, however, it will be helpful first to introduce the concept of *dominated by an integrable function*.

Definition: Dominated by an integrable function.   Let $S \subseteq \Omega \subseteq \mathcal{R}^d$, and let $W \subseteq \mathcal{R}^q$ be a closed and bounded set. Let $p_{\tilde{\mathbf{x}}}: S \rightarrow [0, \infty)$ be a probability mass (density) function. Let $c(\cdot \mid \cdot): W \times \Omega \rightarrow \mathcal{R}$ be defined such that $c(\cdot \mid \mathbf{x})$ is continuous on W for all $\mathbf{x} \in S$. Assume $c(\mathbf{w} \mid \cdot)$ is continuous on Ω for all $\mathbf{w} \in W$. If there exists a function $h: \Omega \rightarrow \mathcal{R}$ such that (i) $\left| c(\mathbf{w} \mid \mathbf{x}) \right| \leq h(\mathbf{x})$ for all $\mathbf{x} \in \Omega$ and for all $\mathbf{w} \in W$, and (ii) $E_{\tilde{\mathbf{x}}}[h(\tilde{\mathbf{x}})]$ is finite, then c is *dominated by an integrable function* on W with respect to $p_{\tilde{\mathbf{x}}}$.

For example, suppose that $\tilde{\mathbf{x}}$ is a random vector such that there exists some finite constant K where $\left| \tilde{\mathbf{x}} \right| < K$ and assume the function $c(\cdot \mid \cdot): W \times \Omega \rightarrow \mathcal{R}$ is continuous in both arguments. In this case, c is dominated by the integrable function K on W with respect to $p_{\tilde{\mathbf{x}}}$.

Theorem: Sample Risk Function Convergence Theorem.   Let W be a closed and bounded subset of $\mathcal{R}^q$. Let $S \subseteq \Omega \subseteq \mathcal{R}^d$. Let $\tilde{\mathbf{x}}(1), \tilde{\mathbf{x}}(2),\dots$ be a sequence of independent and identically distributed random vectors with the common probability mass (density) function $p_{\tilde{\mathbf{x}}}: S \rightarrow [0, \infty)$. Let $c(\cdot \mid \cdot): W \times \Omega \rightarrow \mathcal{R}$ be dominated by an integrable function on W with respect to $p_{\tilde{\mathbf{x}}}$. Then for every $\mathbf{w} \in W$: as $n \rightarrow \infty$,

$$(1/n)\sum_{i=1}^{n} c(\mathbf{w} \mid \tilde{\mathbf{x}}(i)) \rightarrow E_{\tilde{\mathbf{x}}}[c(\mathbf{w} \mid \tilde{\mathbf{x}})]$$

with probability one.

Proof.   Because c is dominated on the closed and bounded set W by an integrable function with respect to $p_{\tilde{\mathbf{x}}}$: there exists a function $h: S \rightarrow \mathcal{R}$ such that

$$E[\left| c(\cdot \mid \tilde{\mathbf{x}}) \right|] \leq E[\left| h(\tilde{\mathbf{x}}) \right|] < \infty.$$

Thus, by Kolmogorov's Strong Law of Large Numbers (see chapter 4), as $n \rightarrow \infty$,

$$(1/n)\sum_{i=1}^{n} c(\mathbf{w} \mid \tilde{\mathbf{x}}(i)) \rightarrow E_{\tilde{\mathbf{x}}}[c(\mathbf{w} \mid \tilde{\mathbf{x}}(i))]$$

with probability one for all $\mathbf{w} \in W$.   ∎

It will now be convenient to define the concept of a *regular* loss function (which will be used throughout chapter 8).

Definition: Regular loss function.   Let $W \subseteq \mathcal{R}^q$ and $\Omega \subseteq \mathcal{R}^d$. Let $c(\cdot \mid \cdot)$: $W \times \Omega \rightarrow [0, \infty)$ be a loss function defined with respect to the probability mass (density) function $p_{\tilde{\mathbf{x}}}$: $S \rightarrow [0, \infty)$, where $S \subseteq \Omega$. Assume $c(\cdot \mid \mathbf{x})$ has continuous third partial derivatives on W for every $\mathbf{x} \in \Omega$. Let ∇c: $W \times \Omega \rightarrow W$ be defined such that $\nabla c(\cdot \mid \mathbf{x})$ is the gradient of $c(\cdot \mid \mathbf{x})$ for all $\mathbf{x} \in S$. Let $\nabla^2 c$: $W \times \Omega \rightarrow \mathcal{R}^{q \times q}$ be defined such that $\nabla^2 c(\cdot \mid \mathbf{x})$ is the Hessian of $c(\cdot \mid \mathbf{x})$ for all $\mathbf{x} \in S$. Assume c, ∇c, $\nabla^2 c$, are dominated by integrable functions on W with respect to $p_{\tilde{\mathbf{x}}}$. Assume $l(\cdot)$ which is defined as $E[c(\cdot \mid \tilde{\mathbf{x}})]$ exists and is a continuous function on W. Assume that both $\nabla l = E[\nabla c(\cdot \mid \tilde{\mathbf{x}})]$ and $\nabla^2 l = E[\nabla^2 c(\cdot \mid \tilde{\mathbf{x}})]$ exist and are continuous on W. Then the loss function c is a *regular loss function* with respect to $p_{\tilde{\mathbf{x}}}$.

A slightly stronger version of the following sample risk local minimum convergence theorem is stated and proved by White (1989a); related results are reviewed in Serfling 1980 and Manoukian 1986 in the context of M-estimation. The theorem provides a very useful tool for investigating the relationship between the strict local (and global) minima of the sample risk function and the strict local (and global) minima of the true risk function.

Theorem: Sample Risk Local Minimum Convergence Theorem.   Let W be a closed and bounded subset of $\mathcal{R}^q$. Let $S \subseteq \Omega \subseteq \mathcal{R}^d$. Let $\tilde{\mathbf{x}}(1)$, $\tilde{\mathbf{x}}(2)$,... be a sequence of independent and identically distributed random vectors with common probability mass (density) function p_e: $S \rightarrow [0, \infty)$. Let $c(\cdot \mid \cdot)$: $W \times \Omega \rightarrow \mathcal{R}$ be a regular loss function with respect to p_e. Let l: $W \rightarrow \mathcal{R}$ be the true risk function defined with respect to p_e and c. Let $\hat{l}_n$: $W \times S^n \rightarrow \mathcal{R}$ define the sample risk function for l. Then for every $n = 1, 2, 3,...$ there exists a global minimum, $\tilde{\mathbf{w}}_n$, of $\hat{l}_n(\cdot, \{\tilde{\mathbf{x}}(1),..., \tilde{\mathbf{x}}(n)\})$ on W. In addition, $\tilde{\mathbf{w}}_n$ converges with probability one to the set of global minima of l on W as $n \rightarrow \infty$.

Proof.   See White (1989a, Theorem 1, 457).   ∎

In practice, the above theorem is usually applied by considering some small closed and bounded neighborhood, W, of a strict local minimum, $\hat{\mathbf{w}}_n$, of the sample risk function, $\hat{l}_n$, and assuming that the interior of W contains exactly one strict local minimum, $\mathbf{w}^*$, of l. Given these assumptions, the Sample Risk Local Minimum Convergence Theorem implies that if $\tilde{\mathbf{w}}_n$ is sufficiently close to $\mathbf{w}^*$ (a strict global minimum of l on W) for n sufficiently large, then $\tilde{\mathbf{w}}_n \rightarrow \mathbf{w}^*$ with probability one as $n \rightarrow \infty$.

In summary, a rational goal for an ANN learning dynamical system is to search for a global minimum of the true risk function. Because the true risk function is typically not available, the ANN learning dynamical system's realistic goal is to search for a global minimum of the *sample* risk function. The Sample Risk Local Minimum Convergence Theorem provides some justification for this latter strategy. The theorem explicitly identifies conditions such that if one chooses W to be some sufficiently small neighborhood of $\mathbf{w}^*$, a particular strict local (or global) minimum of the true risk function, then the global minimum of the sample risk function on W exists for every sample size and will eventually converge with probability one to $\mathbf{w}^*$. (These ideas are illustrated in figure 7.2.)

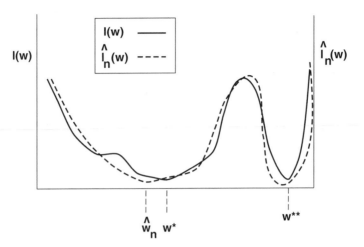

Figure 7.2
Convergence of sample risk function to true risk function. The solid line in the figure is a plot of the true risk function, l, which has a strict local minimum at $\mathbf{w}^*$. The dashed line in the figure is a plot of the sample risk function, $\hat{l}_n$, which has a strict local minimum at $\hat{\mathbf{w}}_n$. As $n \to \infty$, the sample risk function converges to the true risk function under fairly general conditions by the strong law of large numbers. The point $\mathbf{w}^{**}$ is a second strict local minimum of the true risk function.

7.2.2   Log Likelihood Risk Functions

Before defining the concept of a negative log likelihood risk function, it will be helpful to introduce some definitions. Let Ψ_C be a MAP-optimal ANN classification dynamical system with respect to probability model

$$F_W = \{[p(\cdot \mid \mathbf{w}): S \to [0, \infty)]: \mathbf{w} \in W\},$$

where $S \subseteq \mathcal{R}^d$ and $W \subseteq \mathcal{R}^q$. Let the set of n *training stimulus activation patterns* $\mathbf{x}(1),\ldots, \mathbf{x}(n)$ be a sample path of the stochastic process $\tilde{\mathbf{x}}(1),\ldots, \tilde{\mathbf{x}}(n)$, which consists of independent and identically distributed random vectors with the common environmental probability mass (density) function $p_e: S \to [0, \infty)$.

A sample risk function that maps a given connection strength parameter vector $\mathbf{w}$ into the likelihood of the observed training data $\mathbf{x}(1),\ldots, \mathbf{x}(n)$ will now be constructed, where the likelihood of the observed data is computed with respect to the probability model F_W. A sample risk function of this type is said to be a "negative log likelihood risk function."

Such a risk function is a highly desirable objective function for an ANN learning dynamical system because an ANN system minimizing the negative likelihood of the observed training data is seeking a connection strength parameter vector $\mathbf{w}$ that makes the observed data most likely (where the likelihood of the observed training data is computed using F_W). Note that if $p_e \notin F_W$, then the MAP-optimal ANN classification dynamical system can never acquire absolute knowledge of p_e. In practice, because this situation occurs frequently, the assumption that $p_e \in F_W$ will not be made.

Note that, with respect to the probability model F_W, the likelihood of a single training stimulus $\mathbf{x}(1)$ for a particular connection strength parameter vector $\mathbf{w}$ is given by the formula

$$p(\mathbf{x}(1) \mid \mathbf{w}).$$

The likelihood of two training stimuli given $\mathbf{w}$ is given by the formula

$$p(\mathbf{x}(1), \mathbf{x}(2) \mid \mathbf{w}) = p(\mathbf{x}(1) \mid \mathbf{w})p(\mathbf{x}(2) \mid \mathbf{w})$$

because both the stochastic environment and the probability model F_W assume the training stimuli are observations of a stochastic process consisting of independent and identically distributed random vectors.

In general, the likelihood of the observed data $\mathbf{x}(1), \ldots, \mathbf{x}(n)$, given $\mathbf{w}$, may be expressed as

$$p(\mathbf{x}(1), \ldots, \mathbf{x}(n) \mid \mathbf{w}) = \prod_{i=1}^{n} p(\mathbf{x}(i) \mid \mathbf{w}). \tag{7.7}$$

Now define $\hat{l}_n \colon \mathcal{R}^q \times S^n \to [0, \infty)$ such that

$$\hat{l}_n(\mathbf{w}; \{\mathbf{x}(1), \ldots, \mathbf{x}(n)\}) = -(1/n) \log \left[p(\mathbf{x}(1), \ldots, \mathbf{x}(n) \mid \mathbf{w}) \right]. \tag{7.8}$$

Substituting (7.7) into (7.8) results in the expression

$$\hat{l}_n(\mathbf{w}; \{\mathbf{x}(1), \ldots \mathbf{x}(n)\}) = -(1/n) \sum_{i=1}^{n} \log[p(\mathbf{x}(i) \mid \mathbf{w})], \tag{7.9}$$

which is recognized as a type of sample risk function. The sample risk function in (7.9) is called the "negative log likelihood function" because it is a measure of the likelihood of the data $\mathbf{x}(1), \ldots, \mathbf{x}(n)$, given the parameter vector $\mathbf{w}$.

The formula in (7.9) is a key formula because it allows one to derive a learning objective function,

$$\hat{l}_n(\cdot; \{\mathbf{x}(1), \ldots, \mathbf{x}(n)\}) \colon W \to [0, \infty),$$

from the probability model F_W such that a global minimum of

$$\hat{l}_n(\cdot; \{\mathbf{x}(1), \ldots, \mathbf{x}(n)\})$$

is a connection strength parameter vector, which makes the observed data (i.e., the training stimulus set) $\mathbf{x}(1), \ldots, \mathbf{x}(n)$ most likely with respect to the ANN system's probability model F_W.

Definition: Negative log likelihood function. Let $W \subseteq \mathcal{R}^q$. Let $S \subseteq \mathcal{R}^d$. Let F_W be a probability model defined such that

$$F_W = \{(p(\cdot \mid \mathbf{w}) \colon S \to [0, \infty)) \colon \mathbf{w} \in W\},$$

where $p(\cdot \mid \mathbf{w})$ is a probability mass (density) function for every $\mathbf{w} \in W$. Let $\tilde{\mathbf{x}}(1),\ldots, \tilde{\mathbf{x}}(n)$ be a sequence of independent and identically distributed random vectors with the common probability mass (density) function $p_e\colon S \rightarrow [0, \infty)$. Let $\mathbf{x}(1),\ldots, \mathbf{x}(n)$ be a sample path of $\tilde{\mathbf{x}}(1),\ldots, \tilde{\mathbf{x}}(n)$. Let $c\colon W \times S \rightarrow [0, \infty)$ be a regular loss function such that for all $\mathbf{x} \in S$ and for all $\mathbf{w} \in W$: $c(\mathbf{w} \mid \mathbf{x}) =$ $-\log [p(\mathbf{x} \mid \mathbf{w})]$. Let $\hat{l}_n\colon W \times S^n \rightarrow [0, \infty)$. The *negative log likelihood* function $\hat{l}_n(\cdot; \{\mathbf{x}(1),\ldots, \mathbf{x}(n)\})\colon W \rightarrow [0, \infty)$ is a sample risk function defined with respect to c and $\{\mathbf{x}(1),\ldots, \mathbf{x}(n)\}$. A global minimum, $\hat{\mathbf{w}}_n$, of $\hat{l}_n(\cdot; \{\mathbf{x}(1),\ldots, \mathbf{x}(n)\})$ on W is called a *quasi-maximum likelihood estimate* on W with respect to F_W and $\{\mathbf{x}(1),\ldots, \mathbf{x}(n)\}$. If in addition $p_e \in F_W$, then $\hat{\mathbf{w}}_n$ is called a *maximum likelihood estimate* on W with respect to F_W and $\{\mathbf{x}(1),\ldots, \mathbf{x}(n)\}$.

By the Sample Risk Function Convergence Theorem, it is known that the negative log likelihood function will converge with probability one (under fairly general conditions) to some deterministic risk function, $l\colon W \rightarrow [0, \infty)$ of the parameter weight vector $\mathbf{w}$ with respect to the environmental probability mass (density) function, $p_e\colon S \rightarrow [0, \infty)$, which generated the stochastic training sequence. This function l will be referred to as the *Kullback-Leibler information criterion (KLIC)* risk function, defined such that for all $\mathbf{w} \in W$:

$$l(\mathbf{w}) = -\sum_{\mathbf{x} \in S} p_e(\mathbf{x}) \log [p(\mathbf{x} \mid \mathbf{w})]$$

if p_e is a probability mass function (i.e., S is finite or countably infinite), and defined such that for all $\mathbf{w} \in W$:

$$l(\mathbf{w}) = -\int_{\mathbf{x} \in S} p_e(\mathbf{x}) \log [p(\mathbf{x} \mid \mathbf{w})] d\mathbf{x}$$

if p_e is a probability density function (i.e., S is infinite and not countably infinite). In subsequent discussions, the negative log likelihood function will sometimes be referred to as the *KLIC sample risk function* to emphasize its relationship to the KLIC risk function, l.

It is worth noting that the addition of an appropriate constant to the KLIC function yields what is commonly known as the "cross-entropy," "divergence," or "information gain" between $p(\cdot \mid \mathbf{w})$ and $p_e(\cdot)$. Kullback and Leibler (1951) showed that the minimum value of the KLIC risk function is obtained if and only if the probability mass (density) functions $p_e(\cdot)$ and $p(\cdot \mid \mathbf{w})$ are identical on a given sample space S. For this reason, the KLIC risk function may be viewed as a type of nonsymmetric "distance" between the environmental distribution, $p_e(\cdot)$, and a particular member, $p(\cdot \mid \mathbf{w})$, of the probability model F_W. Given this interpretation of the KLIC risk function, an ANN learning dynamical system that is searching for a global minimum of the negative log likelihood risk function may be viewed as searching for a probability distribution in F_W that "best matches" the environmental distribution p_e.

7.2.3 MAP Risk Functions

Given a specific set of training data, the quasi-maximum likelihood estimate is a particular set of weights, $\hat{\mathbf{w}}_n^*$, that makes the observed data most probable with respect to the ANN system's subjective probability model F_W. This computational goal does not seem as intuitively desirable as computing a set of weights, $\hat{\mathbf{w}}_n^{**}$, that is most probable, given the observed training data. The connection strength parameter vector $\hat{\mathbf{w}}_n^{**}$ is referred to as a "maximum a posteriori (MAP) estimate" with respect to a given set of training data, and is defined as a global minimum of a special objective function known as the "MAP risk function."

Let $\mathbf{\Psi}_C$ be a MAP-optimal ANN classification dynamical system with respect to the known probability model

$$F_W = \{(p(\cdot \mid \mathbf{w}): S \rightarrow [0, \infty)): \mathbf{w} \in W \subseteq \mathcal{R}^q\},$$

where $S \subseteq \mathcal{R}^d$. Let the training stimulus set $\mathbf{x}(1), \ldots, \mathbf{x}(n)$ be a sample path of the stochastic process $\tilde{\mathbf{x}}(1), \ldots, \tilde{\mathbf{x}}(n)$ whose elements are independent and identically distributed with the common environmental probability mass (density) function $p_e: S \rightarrow [0, \infty)$. Define the function $\hat{l}_n: W \times S^n \rightarrow [0, \infty)$. The goal of the following analysis is to express the MAP risk function

$$\hat{l}_n(\cdot; \{\mathbf{x}(1), \ldots, \mathbf{x}(n)\}): W \rightarrow [0, \infty),$$

defined by the expression

$$\hat{l}_n(\mathbf{w}; \{\mathbf{x}(1), \ldots, \mathbf{x}(n)\}) = -(1/n) \log \left[p(\mathbf{w} \mid \mathbf{x}(1), \ldots, \mathbf{x}(n)) \right],$$

in terms of the probability model F_W.

In order to achieve the goal of expressing the MAP risk function in terms of the probability model F_W, it is necessary to define an additional *prior* (marginal) probability mass (density) function, $p_o: W \rightarrow [0, \infty)$. The probability mass (density) function, p_o, is defined such that $p_o(\mathbf{w})$ is the ANN learning system's *preference* for connection strength parameter vector $\mathbf{w}$ *before* any training data has been observed by the ANN system! Thus, if p_o has the property that $p_o(\mathbf{w}_1) > p_o(\mathbf{w}_2)$ for $\mathbf{w}_1, \mathbf{w}_2 \in W$, then this inequality means that the ANN learning system prefers weight vector $\mathbf{w}_1$ to weight vector $\mathbf{w}_2$, given that the ANN learning system has not had the opportunity to observe any training data.

Let

$$p(\mathbf{w} \mid \mathbf{x}(1), \ldots, \mathbf{x}(n)) = \frac{p(\mathbf{x}(1), \ldots, \mathbf{x}(n) \mid \mathbf{w}) p_o(\mathbf{w})}{p(\mathbf{x}(1), \ldots, \mathbf{x}(n))}, \tag{7.10}$$

where $p(\mathbf{x}(1),\ldots,\mathbf{x}(n))$ is not functionally dependent upon $\mathbf{w}$. Define K_n such that

$$K_n = [p(\mathbf{x}(1),\ldots,\mathbf{x}(n))]^{-1}.$$

Using the definition of K_n and (7.10), it follows that

$$p(\mathbf{w}\mid\mathbf{x}(1),\ldots,\mathbf{x}(n)) = K_n p_o(\mathbf{w})\prod_{i=1}^{n} p(\mathbf{x}(i)\mid\mathbf{w}).$$

The MAP risk function is defined as proportional to the negative logarithm of $p(\cdot\mid\mathbf{x}(1),\ldots,\mathbf{x}(n))$ on W. In particular,

$$\hat{l}_n(\mathbf{w};\{\mathbf{x}(k)\}) = -(1/n)\log\left[p(\mathbf{w}\mid\mathbf{x}(1),\ldots,\mathbf{x}(n))\right],$$

$$\hat{l}_n(\mathbf{w};\{\mathbf{x}(k)\}) = -(1/n)\log\left[K_n p_o(\mathbf{w})\prod_{i=1}^{n} p(\mathbf{x}(i)\mid\mathbf{w})\right],$$

$$\hat{l}_n(\mathbf{w};\{\mathbf{x}(k)\}) = -(1/n)\log[K_n] - (1/n)\log[p_o(\mathbf{w})]$$
$$- (1/n)\sum_{i=1}^{n}\log[p(\mathbf{x}(i)\mid\mathbf{w})].$$

Because the global maximum of $\hat{l}_n(\cdot;\{\mathbf{x}(1),\ldots,\mathbf{x}(n)\})$ does not change as a function of the value of K_n, it is convenient to introduce the following definition of a MAP risk function.

Definition: MAP risk function.   Let $W \subseteq \mathcal{R}^q$. Let $S \subseteq \mathcal{R}^d$. Let F_W be a probability model defined such that

$$F_W = \{(p(\cdot\mid\mathbf{w})\colon S\to[0,\infty))\colon \mathbf{w}\in W\}.$$

Let $\tilde{\mathbf{x}}(1),\ldots,\tilde{\mathbf{x}}(n)$ be a sequence of independent and identically distributed random vectors with the common probability mass (density) function $p_e\colon S\to[0,\infty)$. Let $\mathbf{x}(1),\ldots,\mathbf{x}(n)$ be a sample path of $\tilde{\mathbf{x}}(1),\ldots,\tilde{\mathbf{x}}(n)$. Let $\hat{l}_n\colon W\times S^n\to[0,\infty)$. Let $p_o\colon W\to[0,\infty)$ be the *prior* probability mass (density) function. The *MAP risk function* for F_W is a function

$$\hat{l}_n(\cdot;\{\mathbf{x}(1),\ldots,\mathbf{x}(n)\})\colon W\to[0,\infty),$$

defined for all $\mathbf{w}\in W$ such that

$$\hat{l}_n(\mathbf{w};\{\mathbf{x}(1),\ldots,\mathbf{x}(n)\}) = -(1/n)\log[p_o(\mathbf{w})]$$
$$- (1/n)\sum_{i=1}^{n}\log[p(\mathbf{x}(i)\mid\mathbf{w})]. \tag{7.11}$$

A global minimum of $\hat{l}_n(\cdot;\{\mathbf{x}(1),\ldots,\mathbf{x}(n)\})$ is a *MAP estimate* with respect to the prior p_o, probability model F_W, and $\{\mathbf{x}(1),\ldots,\mathbf{x}(n)\}$.

The first term on the right-hand side of (7.11) corresponds to the ANN learning system's *prior knowledge* and *expectations* before observing any training data. The second term on the right-hand side of (7.11) corresponds to the ANN learning system's *experiences* with the training data. Thus (7.11) indicates how to optimally combine prior knowledge with experience in order to obtain a connection strength parameter vector that is most likely, given the observed data, where the likelihood of a parameter vector is defined with respect to the probability model F_W and prior knowledge distribution p_o. Note that if $n = 2$, then the effects of prior knowledge are quite strong, while if n is large (e.g., 10,000,000) then the effects of prior knowledge are quite weak.

To better understand the effects of the prior knowledge term, suppose the ANN learning system has *only* prior knowledge that $\mathbf{w} \in W$, where W is a closed and bounded subset of $\mathcal{R}^q$. In such a case, the a priori ignorance of the learning system may be modeled by defining $p_o(\mathbf{w})$ to be a uniform probability mass (density) function on W. In this special case, because the $\log[p_o(\mathbf{w})]$ term in the definition of the loss function for a MAP risk function is not functionally dependent upon $\mathbf{w}$, it may be ignored; the MAP risk function is therefore *identical* to the negative log likelihood function (aside from an irrelevant additive constant) for all $n = 1, 2, \dots$. It immediately follows that, as $n \to \infty$, the MAP risk function converges to the KLIC function with probability one (provided appropriate regularity conditions hold).

Now consider the following, relatively weak restriction on $p_o(\mathbf{w})$, namely, that $\log[p_o(\mathbf{w})]$ is finite for all $\mathbf{w} \in W$. This assumption is satisfied, for example, if there exists some strictly positive small number, ε, such that $p_o(\mathbf{w}) > \varepsilon$ for all $\mathbf{w} \in W$. In this special case, there exists some finite constant K such that $\left|\log[p_o(\mathbf{w})]\right| < K < \infty$, and thus, as $n \to \infty$, the MAP risk function converges to the KLIC function with probability one.

These special cases provide important insights into the MAP risk function and its relationship to the negative log likelihood (sample KLIC) function. In particular, the MAP risk function may be viewed as a formula for "weighting" prior knowledge (i.e., the distribution p_o) of the connection strength parameter vector $\tilde{\mathbf{w}}$ relative to knowledge obtained through environmental observations (i.e., the negative log likelihood function term in the MAP risk function). As the sample size, n, becomes large, the prior knowledge becomes less and less important under fairly general conditions. Thus, for small sample sizes where one has some prior expectations regarding the prior probability distribution on the parameter vector, $\tilde{\mathbf{w}}$, the MAP risk function is the correct formula to use for selecting the *most probable* parameter vector. On the other hand, if the sample size is large or knowledge regarding the prior probability distribution of the parameter vector $\tilde{\mathbf{w}}$ is not available, then the global minima of the sample KLIC function will correspond to the global minima of the MAP risk function under fairly general conditions.

7.3   ANN Applications

7.3.1   Hopfield (1982) and Boltzmann ANN Systems

Problem.   Let the classification objective function $V: \Re^d \to \Re$ be defined such that $V(\mathbf{x}) = -(1/2)\mathbf{x}^T\mathbf{W}\mathbf{x} - \mathbf{x}^T\mathbf{b}$, where $\mathbf{W} \in \Re^{d \times d}$ is a symmetric matrix of connection strengths and $\mathbf{b} \in \Re^d$ is a vector of unit biases. The Hopfield (1982) and Boltzmann machine (Ackley, Hinton, and Sejnowski 1985) are ANN classification dynamical systems that seek a global minimum of V. Note that the Hopfield (1982) model is an objective-optimal *deterministic* ANN classification dynamical system, while the Boltzmann machine is an objective-optimal *stochastic* ANN classification dynamical system.

Also assume that for both the Hopfield (1982) model and the Boltzmann machine that the only relevant informational state of a unit is the unit's activation. That is, if the activation level of the unit is above some threshold, then this indicates that some abstract feature has been detected. (Otherwise, it is assumed that the unit has not detected the abstract feature.)

Construct a probability model, F_W, which is a subjective probability model for both the deterministic Hopfield (1982) and the stochastic Boltzmann machine ANN classification dynamical systems. Use the constructed probability model F_W to derive a learning objective function to train these ANN dynamical systems. The learning objective function, $\hat{l}_n$, should have the property that every global minimum of $\hat{l}_n$ is a quasi-maximum likelihood estimate with respect to the constructed subjective probability model.

Solution.   First, in order to construct the subjective probability model F_W, use

$$V(\mathbf{x}) = -(1/2)\mathbf{x}^T\mathbf{W}\mathbf{x} - \mathbf{x}^T\mathbf{b}$$

to define the relevant classification objective function.

Second, the sample space S for the probability model F_W must be chosen. Note that the state space of the Hopfield (1982) and Boltzmann machine is $\{0, 1\}^d$ (see chapter 2). That is, the Hopfield (1982) and Boltzmann machine units have activation levels that are either *on* or *off*. In addition, the problem statement makes the assumption that the relevant *informational* characteristics of a unit are that the unit is either *active* or *inactive*. These assumptions suggest that a reasonable choice for the structure of the sample space S would be $S = \{0, 1\}^d$.

Third, the probability model F_W is constructed. Substitute V and S into (7.4) to obtain

$$p(\mathbf{x} \mid \mathbf{W}, \mathbf{b}) = \frac{\exp\left[(1/2)\mathbf{x}^T\mathbf{W}\mathbf{x} + \mathbf{x}^T\mathbf{b}\right]}{Z_{\mathbf{W}}}, \tag{7.12}$$

where the normalization constant $Z_{\mathbf{W}}$ is given by

$$Z_{\mathbf{W}} = \sum_{\mathbf{y} \in S} \exp[(1/2)\mathbf{y}^T \mathbf{W} \mathbf{y} + \mathbf{y}^T \mathbf{b}].$$

Thus the probability model

$$F_W = \{ p(\cdot \mid \mathbf{W}, \mathbf{b}) \colon \mathbf{W} \in \mathcal{R}^{d \times d}, \mathbf{b} \in \mathcal{R}^d \}$$

is obtained, where $p(\cdot \mid \mathbf{W}, \mathbf{b})$ is defined as in (7.12).

Fourth, an appropriate learning objective function is constructed using F_W. Substitute the probability mass function in (7.12) into the formula for the sample KLIC risk function to obtain

$$\hat{l}_n([\mathbf{W}, \mathbf{b}]) = -(1/n) \sum_{i=1}^{n} \log[p(\mathbf{x}(i) \mid \mathbf{W}, \mathbf{b})],$$

$$\hat{l}_n([\mathbf{W}, \mathbf{b}]) = -(1/n) \sum_{i=1}^{n} [(1/2)\mathbf{x}(i)^T \mathbf{W} \mathbf{x}(i) + \mathbf{x}(i)^T \mathbf{b}] + \log[Z_{\mathbf{W}}]. \qquad (7.13)$$

7.3.2 Continuous-Target Backpropagation

Problem. Consider a backpropagation ANN system with multiple layers of hidden units, where the only restriction on the functional form of the hidden unit transfer functions is that they be differentiable. Such a network can be represented by a nonlinear function $\mathbf{f} \colon \mathcal{R}^k \times \mathcal{R}^q \to \mathcal{R}^u$ such that

$$\mathbf{r} = \mathbf{f}(\mathbf{s}, \mathbf{w}),$$

with k-dimensional input vector $\mathbf{s}$, u-dimensional output vector $\mathbf{r}$, and weights and biases arranged in the q-dimensional vector $\mathbf{w}$. Assume the target activation patterns generated by the statistical environment during the learning process for the model are real-valued. Construct a subjective probability model F_W for the backpropagation ANN classification dynamical system. Then use the constructed probability model to derive a negative log likelihood objective function for the backpropagation network's ANN learning dynamical system.

Solution. First, find a function V such that when the classification dynamics of the network are complete, $V(\cdot; \mathbf{s}, \mathbf{w})$ will obtain a global minimum at the point $\mathbf{r} = \mathbf{f}(\mathbf{s}, \mathbf{w})$. One possible choice for V is

$$V(\mathbf{o}; \mathbf{s}, \mathbf{w}) = |\mathbf{o} - \mathbf{f}(\mathbf{s}, \mathbf{w})|^2$$

because the unique global minimum, $\mathbf{r}$, of $V(\cdot; \mathbf{s}, \mathbf{w})$ occurs at the point where $\mathbf{r} = \mathbf{o}$ and $\mathbf{r} = \mathbf{f}(\mathbf{s}, \mathbf{w})$.

Second, because the u-dimensional target vectors are real-valued and the k-dimensional input vectors are known, assume the sample space is $S = \mathcal{R}^u$.

Third, substitute V and the sample space $\mathcal{R}^u$ into (7.4) to obtain

$$p(\mathbf{o} \mid \mathbf{s}, \mathbf{w}) = (1/Z) \exp[-|\mathbf{o} - \mathbf{f}(\mathbf{s}, \mathbf{w})|^2], \qquad (7.14)$$

where Z is given by

$$Z = \int_{\mathbf{x} \in \mathscr{R}^u} \exp\left[-|\mathbf{x} - \mathbf{f}(\mathbf{s}, \mathbf{w})|^2\right] d\mathbf{x} = \pi^{u/2}.$$

Thus p is a conditional multivariate Gaussian density function with mean vector $\mathbf{f}(\mathbf{s}, \mathbf{w})$ and covariance matrix $\mathbf{I}/2$, where $\mathbf{I}$ is the identity matrix. Note that the normalization constant Z is *not* functionally dependent upon $\mathbf{w}$. This particular subjective probability mass (density) function is therefore relatively tractable computationally. The resulting probability model, F_W, is given using (7.14) by

$$F_W = \{ p(\cdot \mid \cdot, \mathbf{w}): \mathbf{w} \in W \subseteq \mathscr{R}^q \}.$$

A learning objective function whose global minima are quasi-maximum likelihood estimates of $\mathbf{w}$ with respect to F_W is now derived using (7.14). In particular, the following KLIC sample risk (i.e., negative log likelihood) function is obtained:

$$\hat{l}_n(\mathbf{w}) = -(1/n) \sum_{i=1}^{n} \log\left[p(\mathbf{o}(i) \mid \mathbf{s}(i), \mathbf{w}) \right],$$

$$\hat{l}_n(\mathbf{w}) = K + (1/n) \sum_{i=1}^{n} |\mathbf{o}(i) - \mathbf{f}(\mathbf{s}(i), \mathbf{w})|^2,$$

where K is a constant which is not functionally dependent upon $\mathbf{w}$.

7.3.3   Binary-Target Backpropagation

Problem.   Consider a backpropagation ANN system with multiple layers of hidden units, where the only restriction on the functional form of the hidden unit transfer functions is that they be differentiable. Such a network can be represented by a nonlinear function $\mathbf{f}: \mathscr{R}^k \times \mathscr{R}^q \rightarrow \mathscr{R}^u$ such that

$\mathbf{r} = \mathbf{f}(\mathbf{s}, \mathbf{w})$,

with k-dimensional input vector $\mathbf{s}$, u-dimensional output vector $\mathbf{r}$, and weights and biases arranged in the q-dimensional vector $\mathbf{w}$. Assume the target activation patterns generated by the statistical environment during the learning process for the model are *binary-valued,* so that a training stimulus has the form $(\mathbf{s}(i), \mathbf{o}(i))$, where the jth element of $\mathbf{o}(i)$ is either zero or one. Also assume that the ith element of $\mathbf{f}$ is a function $f_i: \mathscr{R}^k \times \mathscr{R}^q \rightarrow (0, 1)$. Thus all elements of $\mathbf{r}$ have values in the open interval $(0, 1)$. Construct a subjective probability model F_W for the backpropagation classification dynamical system in this problem. Construct a learning objective function for the backpropagation network with respect to F_W, so that the global minima of the learning objective function will be quasi-maximum likelihood estimates.

Solution.   Following the suggested heuristic procedure of section 7.2, choose the same V as in continuous backpropagation:

$$V(\mathbf{o};\mathbf{s},\mathbf{w}) = |\mathbf{o} - \mathbf{f}(\mathbf{s},\mathbf{w})|^2.$$

Using the Map-Optimal Classification Dynamics Theorem and finite sample space $S = \{0, 1\}^u$,

$$p(\mathbf{o}\mid\mathbf{s},\mathbf{w}) = (1/Z)\exp[-V(\mathbf{o};\mathbf{s},\mathbf{w})],$$

$$p(\mathbf{o}\mid\mathbf{s},\mathbf{w}) = (1/Z)\exp\left[-|\mathbf{o} - \mathbf{f}(\mathbf{s},\mathbf{w})|^2\right],$$

and

$$Z = \sum_{\mathbf{y}\in\{0,1\}^u}\exp\left[-|\mathbf{y} - \mathbf{f}(\mathbf{s},\mathbf{w})|^2\right],$$

where the summation has 2^u terms and Z is functionally dependent upon $\mathbf{w}$. Thus $p(\mathbf{o}\mid\mathbf{s},\mathbf{w})$ is computationally intractable when the dimension of $\mathbf{o}$ is large.

Now consider an alternative choice for V. Let o_j be the jth element of the u-dimensional vector $\mathbf{o}$. Then

$$V(\mathbf{o};\mathbf{s},\mathbf{w}) = -\sum_{j=1}^{u}\left[o_j\log[f_j(\mathbf{s},\mathbf{w})] + (1-o_j)\log[1-f_j(\mathbf{s},\mathbf{w})]\right],$$

which obtains a global minimum of V at the point

$$o_j = 1 \quad\text{if}\quad f_j(\mathbf{s},\mathbf{w}) > 0.5$$

and

$$o_j = 0 \quad\text{if}\quad f_j(\mathbf{s},\mathbf{w}) \leq 0.5.$$

Now use V, the sample space $\{0,1\}^u$, and the Map-Optimal Classification Dynamics Theorem to obtain

$$p(\mathbf{o}\mid\mathbf{s},\mathbf{w}) = \left(\frac{1}{Z}\right)\exp\left[\sum_{j=1}^{u}\left[o_j\log[f_j(\mathbf{s},\mathbf{w})] + (1-o_j)\log[1-f_j(\mathbf{s},\mathbf{w})]\right]\right],$$

with

$$Z = \sum_{\mathbf{y}\in\{0,1\}^u}\exp\left[\sum_{j=1}^{u}\left[y_j\log[f_j(\mathbf{s},\mathbf{w})] + (1-y_j)\log[1-f_j(\mathbf{s},\mathbf{w})]\right]\right].$$

Although this expression seems mathematically untractable, note that,

$$\exp\left[\sum_{j=1}^{u}y_j\log[f_j(\mathbf{s},\mathbf{w})]\right] = \prod_{j=1}^{u}f_j(\mathbf{s},\mathbf{w})^{y_j}$$

This relationship implies that

$$p(\mathbf{o} \mid \mathbf{s}, \mathbf{w}) = (1/Z) \prod_{j=1}^{u} f_j(\mathbf{s}, \mathbf{w})^{o_j} (1 - f_j(\mathbf{s}, \mathbf{w}))^{1-o_j}, \tag{7.15}$$

with

$$Z = \sum_{\mathbf{y} \in \{0, 1\}^u} \prod_{j=1}^{u} f_j(\mathbf{s}, \mathbf{w})^{y_j} (1 - f_j(\mathbf{s}, \mathbf{w}))^{1-y_j} = 1.$$

Thus Z is a constant which is not functionally dependent upon $\mathbf{w}$. This choice of V yields a more computationally tractable normalization constant Z for the subjective probability distribution when the sample space of the output unit activation patterns is $\{0, 1\}^u$. Thus, (7.15) is used to define

$$F_W = \{p(\cdot \mid \cdot, \mathbf{w}) : \mathbf{w} \in W \subseteq \mathfrak{R}^q\}.$$

A learning objective function is now derived by substituting $p(\mathbf{o} \mid \mathbf{s}, \mathbf{w})$ in (7.15) into the general formula for the KLIC sample risk function to obtain

$$\hat{l}_n(\mathbf{w}) = -(1/n) \sum_{i=1}^{n} \log[p(\mathbf{o}(i) \mid \mathbf{s}(i), \mathbf{w})],$$

$$\hat{l}_n(\mathbf{w}) = -(1/n) \sum_{i=1}^{n} \sum_{j=1}^{u} \Big[o_j(i) \log[f_j(\mathbf{s}, \mathbf{w})] + (1 - o_j(i)) \log[1 - f_j(\mathbf{s}, \mathbf{w})] \Big].$$

7.4   Chapter Summary

Constructing an ANN System Probability Model

Various tools were presented to arrive at probabilistic interpretations of the computational goals for the classification dynamics of ANN systems. For cases where the ANN system classification (activation updating) algorithm and possibly even the learning algorithm are given in the absence of a probabilistic interpretation, a method for constructing an ANN system probability model was also provided. Let $\mathbf{x}$ be an activation pattern for a particular ANN system and $\mathbf{w}$ be the weight vector for the ANN system. Let $V : \mathfrak{R}^d \times \mathfrak{R}^q \to \mathfrak{R}$. The basic idea of constructing an ANN system probability model is to find a classification objective function $V(\cdot; \mathbf{w}) : \mathfrak{R}^d \to \mathfrak{R}$ that is minimized by the classification dynamics of the ANN system with connection strength parameter vector $\mathbf{w}$ for every $\mathbf{w} \in W \subseteq \mathfrak{R}^q$. Assume there exists a set of finite real numbers $\{Z_{\mathbf{w}}\}$ such that

$$F_W = \left\{ \left(p(\cdot \mid \mathbf{w}) = \frac{\exp[-V(\cdot; \mathbf{w})]}{Z_{\mathbf{w}}} \right) : \mathbf{w} \in W \subseteq \mathfrak{R}^q \right\}$$

is a set of probability mass (density) functions, then F_W is the subjective probability model for the ANN classification dynamical system. This simply means that for all $\mathbf{w} \in W$: The ANN system may be viewed as a MAP estimation algorithm seeking a global maximum of each probability mass (density) function $p(\cdot; \mathbf{w})$ in F_W on some selected subset Ω^* of $\mathcal{R}^d$ because the system seeks a minimum of every objective function $V(\cdot; \mathbf{w})$ on Ω^*.

Deriving and Evaluating an ANN Learning Objective Function

The constructed probability model for a given ANN system was seen to have several important uses. First, the model provides an implicit summary of the knowledge base of the ANN system and what aspects of the classification dynamics are relevant for information processing. Thus the model is a theory of the ANN system's knowledge structures. Second, the model can be used as a guide to determine whether the ANN system can acquire absolute knowledge of a given environmental probability distribution. Third, the model can be used to either evaluate an existing learning algorithm for the ANN system or derive new learning algorithms for the ANN system. For example, the basic formula for the negative log likelihood ANN learning objective function $\hat{l}_n(\cdot; \{\mathbf{x}(1),\ldots, \mathbf{x}(n)\})$: $W \to \mathcal{R}$ given by:

$$\hat{l}_n(\mathbf{w}; \{\mathbf{x}(1),\ldots, \mathbf{x}(n)\}) = -(1/n)\sum_{i=1}^{n} \log[p(\mathbf{x}(i) \mid \mathbf{w})],$$

where $p(\cdot \mid \mathbf{w})$ $(\mathbf{w} \in W)$ is an element of the ANN system's subjective probability model and $\mathbf{x}(1),\ldots, \mathbf{x}(n)$ are the n training stimuli observed by the ANN learning dynamical system during the learning process.

7.5   Elementary Problems

7.1-1. Consider the family of differential equations

$$D_W = \left\{\frac{dx}{dt} = 4(x - 2w): w \in \mathcal{R}\right\}.$$

Construct a probability model F_W such that every differential equation in D_W is a MAP estimation algorithm with respect to some probability mass (density) function in F_W. HINT: View the above set of differential equations as a set of continuous-time gradient descent algorithms.

7.1-2. Consider an ANN system with one output unit and three input units. The activation level of the output unit is denoted as r. The activation levels of the three input units are denoted as s_1, s_2, s_3. Let $\mathcal{S}: \mathcal{R} \to (0, 1)$ be a sigmoidal logistic function defined such that $\mathcal{S}(x) = 1/(1 + \exp[-x])$. The ANN system computes the activation of the output unit, r, according to the classification dynamics formula

$$r = \mathcal{S}\left[\sum_{i=1}^{3} w_i s_i + b\right],$$

where the weights of the network are w_1, w_2, w_3 and the network bias parameter is b. Thus the *desired response* or *target response* of the network can be expressed as a random variable $\tilde{o}$ where

$\bar{o} \in \{0, 1\}$. Assume a subjective probability mass function $p(o \,|\, s_1, s_2, s_3)$ defined such that $p(\bar{o} = 1 \,|\, s_1, s_2, s_3) = r$. Give an explicit formula for $p(o \,|\, s_1, s_2, s_3)$. Derive the *unique* decision rule that allows one to interpret the ANN classification dynamical system with respect to this subjective probability mass function as a MAP estimation algorithm.

7.1-3. The brain-state-in-a-box (BSB) model (see chapter 2 for a review) is an ANN classification dynamical system on a state space defined by the exterior and interior of an origin-centered unit hypercube. In particular, a system state (activation pattern) in the BSB model is a d-dimensional vector $\mathbf{x}$ such that $\mathbf{x} \in [-1, 1]^d$. In some applications, it makes sense to view each element of $\mathbf{x}$ as the activation level of a particular abstract unit which detects the presence or absence of a feature. It can be shown that the BSB model is an algorithm that seeks a minimum value of the classification objective function $V: [-1, 1]^d \to \mathscr{R}$ which is defined such that for all $\mathbf{x} \in [-1, 1]^d$:

$$V(\mathbf{x}) = -\mathbf{x}^T \mathbf{W} \mathbf{x},$$

where $\mathbf{W}$ is a d-dimensional symmetric real square matrix whose ijth element is the connection strength from the jth unit to the ith unit. Propose (a) a reasonable sample space for this ANN classification dynamical system, and (b) an explicit expression for this ANN classification dynamical system's probability model using the sample space you have proposed. In one or two sentences justify your choice of a sample space for this modeling problem.

7.2-1. Derive a learning algorithm for estimating the parameter w of the ANN system in problem 7.1-1. Assume that the training stimuli for the ANN system consist of the n one-dimensional activation patterns (i.e., real numbers) $x^1, \ldots, x^n$. Design a learning algorithm that seeks the w that makes the observed set of training data most probable with respect to the ANN system's subjective probability model.

7.2-2. Derive a learning algorithm for estimating the parameter w of the ANN system in problem 7.1-2. Assume that the training stimuli for the ANN system consist of the n four-dimensional activation patterns $(\mathbf{s}^1, o^1), (\mathbf{s}^2, o^2), \ldots, (\mathbf{s}^n, o^n)$, where $\mathbf{s}^i = [s_1^i, s_2^i, s_3^i]$ is the ith training stimulus $i = 1 \ldots n$. Design a learning algorithm that seeks the b, w_1, w_2, w_3 that makes the observed set of training data most probable with respect to the ANN system's subjective probability model.

7.2-3. Let $S \subseteq \mathscr{R}^d$. Let $p_e: S \to [0, \infty)$ be an environmental probability mass function. Let F_W be a probability model for a particular ANN classification dynamical system. Assume $\hat{l}_n: \mathscr{R}^q \times S^n \to [0, \infty)$ defines the negative log likelihood function with respect to p_e and F_W. Let $\hat{G}_n: \mathscr{R}^q \times S^n \to [0, \infty)$ define a sample risk function with respect to p_e and some loss function. Assume $\hat{l}_n$ and $\hat{G}_n$ are different functions. Let $\{\mathbf{x}(i)\} \in S^n$. Assume $\hat{l}_n(\cdot; \{\mathbf{x}(i)\})$ and $\hat{G}_n(\cdot; \{\mathbf{x}(i)\})$ have exactly the same global minima on $\mathscr{R}^q$. Is a global minimum of $\hat{G}_n(\cdot, \{\mathbf{x}(i)\})$ a quasi-maximum likelihood estimate with respect to the probability model F_W and a particular data set $\{\mathbf{x}(i)\}$? What would be the advantage of using $\hat{l}_n(\cdot, \{\mathbf{x}(i)\})$ as the ANN learning dynamical system's learning objective function instead of $\hat{G}_n(\cdot, \{\mathbf{x}(i)\})$?

7.2-4. Consider the analysis of batch Hebbian learning with weight decay in the ANN system applications section of chapter 5. Show how the learning objective function can be interpreted as a MAP risk function if one assumes a Gaussian prior on the ANN system weights.

7.2-5. Identify *all* relationships between (1) Bayes decision theory risk function, (2) Kullback-Leibler information criterion (KLIC) risk function, (3) maximum a posteriori (MAP) estimation, and (4) maximum likelihood (ML) estimation.

7.6   Problems

7-1. Consider the on-line backpropagation learning algorithm discussed in chapter 2, where the network architecture function that maps $\mathbf{s}(t)$ into $\mathbf{r}(t)$ is specified as follows. Define $\underline{\mathscr{S}}$ to be a vector-valued sigmoidal function as in *classical* backpropagation. Also suppose that

$$\mathbf{h}(t) = \underline{\mathscr{S}}(\mathbf{V}\mathbf{s}(t) + \mathbf{q}),$$

where $\mathbf{V}$ and $\mathbf{q}$ are free parameters (i.e., input unit to hidden unit layer weights and biases) that must be estimated. Also suppose that

$\mathbf{u}(t) = \mathbf{W}\mathbf{h}(t) + \mathbf{b},$

where $\mathbf{W}$ and $\mathbf{b}$ are free parameters that must be estimated. Let the activation level of the ith output unit, $r_i(t)$, be defined such that

$$r_i(t) = \frac{\exp[u_i(t)]}{\sum_{j=1}^{M} \exp[u_j(t)]},$$

where $r_i(t)$ is the ith element of the M-dimensional vector $\mathbf{r}(t)$ and $u_i(t)$ is the ith element of $\mathbf{u}(t)$.

Draw a figure of this backpropagation network with one layer of input units (the s-unit layer), two layers of hidden units (the h-unit layer and the u-unit layer), and one layer of output units (the r-unit layer). Show that

$0 < r_i(t) < 1$

and that

$$\sum_{i=1}^{M} r_i(t) = 1.$$

Thus interpret the activation of the ith output unit as the probability of one out of M mutually exclusive outcomes (Bridle 1990). Compare and contrast the statistical environment this network is best suited for with the statistical environments of backpropagation networks with continuous targets (section 7.3.2) and binary targets (section 7.3.3). Construct a learning objective function for this ANN dynamical system such that every strict global minimum of the objective function is a maximum likelihood (ML) estimate of the network's parameters. Then explicitly derive backpropagation equations (either scalar or matrix form) for minimizing the learning objective function you proposed.

7-2. Consider the on-line backpropagation learning algorithm discussed in chapter 2 where the network architecture function maps $\mathbf{s}(t)$ into $\mathbf{r}(t)$ as follows. Let the jth hidden unit in the network have activation level denoted as $h_j(t)$ at iteration t of the algorithm. Also define $\mathbf{w}_j(t)$ to be the weight vector associated with the jth hidden unit in the network at iteration t of the algorithm. Let

$$h_j(t) = \frac{\exp[-|\mathbf{s}(t) - \mathbf{w}_j(t)|^2/(2\sigma)^2]}{\sigma\sqrt{2\pi}},$$

where σ is a known positive constant. Let

$\mathbf{r}(t) = \mathbf{V}(t)\mathbf{h}(t) + \mathbf{b}(t),$

where $\mathbf{V}(t)$ and $\mathbf{b}(t)$ are free parameters of the network and $\mathbf{h}(t) = [h_1(t),\ldots, h_k(t)]$. Note that the hidden units in the above network are often referred to as "Gaussian" or "*radial basis function* hidden units" (Poggio and Girosi 1990). This network architecture is also well known in the engineering literature as a "Gaussian mixture model" (e.g., Duda and Hart 1973; Patrick 1972).

Construct a subjective probability model for this ANN dynamical system, with a learning objective function such that every strict global minimum is a maximum likelihood (ML) estimate of the network's parameters with respect to the constructed model. Then explicitly derive backpropagation equations (either scalar or matrix-form) for minimizing the learning objective function you have proposed.

7-3. Construct a negative log likelihood risk function for the ANN temporal reinforcement learning dynamical system described in problem 4-7. How would you extend your construction in order to develop a negative log likelihood risk function for the ANN temporal reinforcement learning dynamical system described in problem 4-9? HINT: You may want to do problem 7-5 before you do this problem.

7-4. Consider an on-line backpropagation network, as described in chapter 2, whose network architecture is described by the following formulas. Suppose that

$\mathbf{h}(t) = \mathcal{S}(\mathbf{V}\mathbf{s}(t) + \mathbf{q}),$

where the vector-valued sigmoidal function, $\mathcal{S}$, is defined as in classical backpropagation, and $\mathbf{V}$ and $\mathbf{q}$ are free parameters (i.e., input unit to hidden unit layer weights and biases respectively). Let

$$\mathbf{r}(t) = \mathbf{U}\mathbf{h}(t) + \mathbf{b},$$

where $\mathbf{U}$ is the connection strength parameter matrix whose ijth element indicates the connection strength weight from the jth hidden unit to the ith output unit, and the ith element of $\mathbf{b}$ is the bias parameter for the ith output unit. Consider a backpropagation network that searches for the parameters $\mathbf{V}$, $\mathbf{q}$, $\mathbf{U}$, and $\mathbf{b}$. For convenience, let $\mathbf{w}$ be a d-dimensional vector whose elements are the elements of the matrices $\mathbf{V}$ and $\mathbf{U}$, and vectors $\mathbf{q}$ and $\mathbf{b}$. Now define the sample risk function, $\hat{l}_n(\mathbf{w})$, such that

$$\hat{l}_n(\mathbf{w}) = (1/n)\sum_{i=1}^{n} |\mathbf{o}(t) - \mathbf{r}(t)|^2 + \lambda \sum_{j=1}^{d} \frac{(w_j/w^0)^2}{1 + (w_j/w^0)^2}, \tag{7.16}$$

where w^0 and λ are positive constants and w_j is the jth element of $\mathbf{w}$. (Note that the second term on the right-hand side of equation (7.16) was suggested by Weigend, Rumelhart, and Huberman 1991.)

Let $\beta = w/w^0$. Plot the function

$$q(\beta) = \frac{\beta^2}{1 + \beta^2}$$

as a function of β. By inspecting the plot you have made, consider the effects of large positive or negative β versus very small β on the value of $q(\beta)$. Explain why it may be difficult to interpret the second term on the right-hand side of (7.16) as the logarithm of an appropriate prior probability density function.

Now consider the following revised MAP risk function

$$\hat{l}_n(\mathbf{V}, \mathbf{q}, \mathbf{U}, \mathbf{b}) = (1/n)\sum_{i=1}^{n} |\mathbf{o}(t) - \mathbf{r}(t)|^2 + \lambda \sum_{j=1}^{d} \left[\frac{(w_j/w^0)^2}{1 + (w_j/w^0)^2} - \frac{(w_j/w^0)^2}{\tau_0} \right], \tag{7.17}$$

where τ_0, w^0 and λ are positive constants and w_j is the jth element of $\mathbf{w}$. Let $\beta = w/w^0$. Plot the function

$$q(\beta) = \left[\frac{\beta^2}{1 + \beta^2} \right] - \beta^2/\tau_0$$

as a function of β for $\tau_0 = 1.9$.

Use the definite integral (Gradshteyn and Ryzhik 1965, 307)

$$\int_0^{\infty} \exp[-x^\mu]\,dx = (1/\mu)\Gamma(1/\mu),$$

where μ is a strictly positive real number and $\Gamma[\cdot]$ is the *gamma function* (see the definition of a chi-square distribution in chapter 4) to show that

$$\int_{-\infty}^{\infty} \exp\left[\frac{\beta^2}{1 + \beta^2} - \beta^2/\tau_0 \right] d\beta < K < \infty, \tag{7.18}$$

where K is a finite positive real number and τ_0 is a real number that satisfies $0 < \tau_0 < 2$.

Use the result in (7.18) to demonstrate that the second term on the right-hand side of (7.17) may be interpreted as the logarithm of an appropriate prior probability density function on the network weights. Construct a probability model for the ANN classification dynamical system corresponding to this ANN learning dynamical system such that both the ANN classification dynamical system and ANN learning dynamical system are both MAP estimation algorithms with respect to the ANN system's probability model.

7-5. Construct a probability model for a classical feedforward backpropagation network using the Chauvin penalty term (chapter 2) such that the learning objective function may be interpreted as a negative log likelihood risk function. Explain why, unlike problem 7-4, the Chauvin penalty term *cannot* be easily viewed as a prior probability distribution on the network weights. HINT: In this case, the data set and network architecture are sufficiently ill conditioned so that it is reasonable to represent the ANN system's probability model by a probability density function where the hidden unit activation vector is treated as an additional response whose desired target vector is a vector of zeros.

7-6. Construct a probabilistic interpretation of the nonlinear autoencoder backpropagation model described in chapter 2, so that the ANN classification dynamical system for this model is a MAP estimation algorithm, and the ANN learning dynamical system is also a MAP estimation algorithm.

7-7. Provide the Hopfield (1982) network with a probabilistic interpretation in the usual manner, so that a probability mass $p(\mathbf{x})$ is assigned to a given activation pattern $\mathbf{x}$. Let $\mathbf{x}$ be partitioned into a known part, $\mathbf{x}_k$, and an unknown part, $\mathbf{x}_u$, such that $\mathbf{x} = (\mathbf{x}_k, \mathbf{x}_u)$. Also define $p(\mathbf{x}_u \mid \mathbf{x}_k)$ as the conditional probability derived from $p(\mathbf{x})$, that is, from the definition of a conditional probability, $p(\mathbf{x}_u \mid \mathbf{x}_k) = p(\mathbf{x})/p(\mathbf{x}_k)$. Show the Hopfield (1982) network is searching for an $\mathbf{x}_u$ that maximizes $p(\mathbf{x}_u \mid \mathbf{x}_k)$ when the activation pattern $\mathbf{x}_k$ is clamped (i.e., the activations of the units that are known are not updated by the algorithm). Thus, the Hopfield (1982) network is searching for the *most probable* value of the unknown activation pattern, given the known activation pattern where probabilities are assigned according to $p(\mathbf{x})$.

7-8. Propose a subjective probability mass (density) function such that the ANN classification dynamical system for adaptive resonance theory (ART) is a MAP estimation algorithm (see chapter 2 for a review of the ART algorithm). NOTE: This is an interesting research question, which still has me thinking!

7-9. Consider the expression for the learning objective function derived in equation (7.13). Note that $Z_{\mathbf{W}}$ in (7.13) is functionally dependent upon $\mathbf{W}$ and involves the computation of 2^d terms where d is the dimensionality of $\mathbf{x}$. Thus, in the typical case where d is large, this expression for the Kullback-Leibler information criterion (KLIC) sample risk function is not tractable computationally. This problem proposes an alternative version of the KLIC sample risk function, called the "pseudolikelihood function," that is considerably more tractable computationally.

Let $\mathbf{x}^i$ be the ith training stimulus which is a d-dimensional vector. Using a Markov random field argument, show how to derive the local conditional probabilities for $p(\mathbf{x}^i \mid \mathbf{W})$, defined by the formula

$$p(x_j^i \mid x_1^i, \ldots, x_{j-1}^i, x_{j+1}^i, \ldots x_d^i) = x_j p_j^i + (1 - x_j)(1 - p_j^i),$$

where

$$p_j^i = p(x_j^i = 1 \mid x_1^i, \ldots, x_{j-1}^i, x_{j+1}^i, \ldots, x_d^i) = \mathscr{S}\left(\sum_{k=1}^d w_{jk} x_k^i + b_j\right),$$

b_j is the jth element of $\mathbf{b}$, w_{jk} as the jkth element of the real symmetric matrix $\mathbf{W}$, and $\mathscr{S}(x) = 1/[1 + \exp(-x)]$. The probability p_j^i is the probability that the jth element of the ith d-dimensional training stimulus vector takes on the value of one, given the observed values of the remaining $(d-1)$ elements of the ith training stimulus.

Now consider the alternative *pseudolikelihood* (Besag 1986) risk function

$$\hat{l}_n(\mathbf{w}) = -(1/dn)\sum_{j=1}^d \sum_{i=1}^n \log\left[x_j^i p_j^i + (1 - x_j^i)(1 - p_j^i)\right],$$

which, since $x_j^i \in \{0, 1\}$, can be simplified to obtain:

$$\hat{l}_n(\mathbf{w}) = -(1/dn)\sum_{j=1}^d \sum_{i=1}^n \left(x_j^i \log[p_j^i] + (1 - x_j^i)\log[1 - p_j^i]\right). \tag{7.19}$$

Explain why the risk function in (7.19) is called a "pseudolikelihood risk function" and is not strictly a true negative log likelihood risk function.

7-10. Consider a learning algorithm for the learning objective function derived in equation (7.13), following the Boltzmann machine learning algorithm (Ackley, Hinton, and Sejnowski 1985; also see Smolensky 1986).

Let $p(\cdot \mid \mathbf{W})$ be an element of the Hopfield (1982) ANN dynamical system. Geman and Geman (1984) demonstrated that the Gibbs sampler algorithm can be used to sample from p for a given $\mathbf{W}$

in a computationally tractable way. The procedure works by using the Gibbs sampler algorithm (but *not* decreasing the temperature) and setting the temperature parameter τ to be equal to one. In this case, representative samples of $p(\cdot \mid \mathbf{W})$ are generated for fixed $\mathbf{W}$ as the number of iterations of the Gibbs sampler algorithm becomes large. Explain why the following learning algorithm works.

- Step 1: Train the network once with Hebbian learning on entire set of training stimuli.
- Step 2: Fix $\mathbf{W}$ and generate samples of $\tilde{\mathbf{x}}$ using $p(\cdot \mid \mathbf{W})$.
- Step 3: Train network once with training data created in step 2 using "anti-Hebbian" learning rule (i.e., Hebbian learning with negative learning rate).
- Step 4: Return to step 1 until stopping criterion is satisfied.

7-11. Problem 7-10 showed how to derive a learning rule for the Boltzmann machine and Hopfield (1982) ANN systems that minimizes the learning objective function defined by (7.13). The result of problem 7-9, however, may be used to derive a very simple deterministic gradient descent algorithm that seeks a minimum of the learning objective function defined by (7.19).

Show that gradient descent on (7.19) leads to a deterministic batch learning rule. Also derive a stochastic on-line learning rule such that (7.19) is a stochastic Lyapunov function for the new learning rule. Compare both learning rules to the classical Widrow-Hoff learning rule, which minimizes a sum-squared error measure.

A typical approach for evaluating the *generalization performance* of an ANN learning system is to divide a given set of data into two parts: a *training set* and a *test set*. The parameters of the ANN learning system are estimated (i.e., learned) using the training set data only; the performance of the system is then evaluated using both training set and test set data. Performance on the test data set provides important information regarding the ANN system's generalization performance.

There are two difficulties, however, with the above approach. First, because in many cases one wishes to use *all* of the data, it is a waste of valuable resources to train an ANN learning system on only half of the available data. Second, the above evaluation process is still based upon only two samples of the stochastic process that generated the observed data: if the training and test data samples coincidentally are very similar or very different, then it will be difficult to evaluate the system's generalization performance from these samples alone.

In this chapter, mathematical methods from the field of asymptotic statistical inference will be used to characterize the reliability of observed parameter estimates and various functions of the parameter estimates. In addition, explicit expressions for estimating specific types of reliability measures and how such reliability measures vary as a function of sample size will be obtained. Moreover, all of the analyses in this chapter require only a single set of training data and do not also require a test data set. More specifically, the following two important problems in ANN learning system analysis and design are discussed:

• Problem 1: Sampling error. Estimate error bounds (confidence intervals) on the predictions of a given ANN system in a given statistical environment.

• Problem 2: Model selection. Decide which of two ANN systems will perform more effectively in a given statistical environment.

Noting that statistical inference methods could be used to evaluate what an ANN system has learned, White (1989a,b) specifically showed how statistical tests could be constructed for deciding which of two ANN systems best fits a given statistical environment. However, most researchers in the field of ANN systems have tended to approach the model selection problem in a more heuristic manner, through the use of *saliency measures.*

Saliency measures are often used in deciding which connections in a back-propagation network architecture can be eliminated as either redundant or irrelevant (Gorodkin et al. 1993; Hassibi and Stork 1993; Hassibi et al. 1994; Le Cun, Denker, and Solla 1990; Levin, Leen, and Moody 1994; Moody and Utans 1992; Moody 1994; Mozer and Smolensky 1988; Svarer, Hansen, and Larsen 1993; Svarer et al. 1993; White, 1989a,b). The parameters of the reduced network are then reestimated. Sometimes a saliency measure is computed both before and after the connections are eliminated. The change in the saliency measure's value is then used to measure the importance of the deleted parameters. In the ANN system literature, such procedures are often referred to as "network pruning" or "optimal brain damage."

A similar strategy involving saliency measures has also been developed and effectively used for *growing* new connections in an existing backpropagation network (Moody 1994; Moody and Utans 1992; Wynne-Jones 1992). Moody (1994) refers to these strategies as "inverse network-pruning" strategies and proposes a useful "sequential network construction" (SNC) scheme for implementing inverse network-pruning strategies.

Under certain conditions, Moody notes, many popular pruning and inverse pruning strategies involving saliency measures can be naturally interpreted within a classical mathematical statistics framework. One important goal of this chapter is to understand in detail the underlying assumptions behind such a framework, and thus also the power and limitations of pruning and inverse pruning methods for ANN system analysis and design. Another important benefit of this strategy will be that statistical tests (as opposed to uninterpretable saliency measures) will be derived for making decisions about growing and pruning ANN system parameters. (The mathematical development in this chapter is most closely related to the methods reviewed by Golden 1988a,b,c; Moody 1994; Amari and Murata 1993; Paas 1993; and especially White 1989a,b.)

An overview of the general strategy for characterizing the generalization performance of an ANN learning system using a classical statistical methodology is now described. Suppose an ANN learning system has been trained with a set of n training stimuli $\mathbf{x}(1),\ldots,\mathbf{x}(n)$, where $\mathbf{x}(t) \in \mathcal{R}^d$ for $t = 1 \ldots n$, that are representative in some sense of the ANN learning system's statistical environment. Suppose also that the learning algorithm generates an "acceptable solution" $\hat{\mathbf{w}}_n \in \mathcal{R}^q$ (i.e., a connection strength parameter vector sufficiently close to a strict local minimum of some sample risk function). It is important to emphasize that the solution $\hat{\mathbf{w}}_n$ is a strict local minimum of the sample risk function (i.e., a function of the observed data) and not the true risk function (i.e., a function of the unobservable environmental distribution).

The connection strength parameter vector $\hat{\mathbf{w}}_n$ may be expressed as some deterministic function Γ_n of the n observed training stimuli $\mathbf{x}(1),\ldots,\mathbf{x}(n)$ by the formula

$$\hat{\mathbf{w}}_n = \Gamma_n(\mathbf{x}(1),\ldots,\mathbf{x}(n)).$$

Thus the random vector $\tilde{\mathbf{w}}_n$ may be defined by the formula

$$\tilde{\mathbf{w}}_n = \Gamma_n(\tilde{\mathbf{x}}(1),\ldots,\tilde{\mathbf{x}}(n)),$$

where $\mathbf{x}(1),\ldots,\mathbf{x}(n)$ is a sample path of the stochastic process $\tilde{\mathbf{x}}(1),\ldots,\tilde{\mathbf{x}}(n)$. The probability distribution of $\tilde{\mathbf{w}}_n$ is a quantity of great interest because the random vector $\tilde{\mathbf{w}}_n$ implicitly contains information regarding how the parameter estimates vary as a function of the training data for training samples of some fixed size n.

Inference errors made by an ANN classification dynamical system using $\hat{\mathbf{w}}_n$ (which arise solely because the observed data provides only partial information about the unobservable environmental distribution), can thus be investigated by examining the probability distribution of $\tilde{\mathbf{w}}_n$ and various functions of $\tilde{\mathbf{w}}_n$. For example, any prediction of the ANN classification dynamical system is functionally dependent upon $\hat{\mathbf{w}}_n$ (or equivalently $\tilde{\mathbf{w}}_n$). Thus it is also of great interest to develop methods of characterizing the probability distribution of arbitrary functions of $\tilde{\mathbf{w}}_n$.

This chapter is organized in two parts. First, it will introduce two powerful methods that are extremely useful for characterizing the probability distribution of $\tilde{\mathbf{w}}_n$, and then apply this characterization to constructing error bounds on the predictions of an ANN system. Second, after a brief review of the principles of hypothesis testing, it will discuss the problem of developing statistical tests to decide which of several ANN systems "best fits" a given statistical environment.

8.1   Asymptotic Distribution of Sampling Error

8.1.1   Asymptotic Formulas

Asymptotic Distribution of Parameter Estimates

Let the training sample $\mathbf{x}(1),\ldots,\mathbf{x}(n)$ be a sample path of a stochastic process $\tilde{\mathbf{x}}(1),\ldots,\tilde{\mathbf{x}}(n)$ consisting of independent and identically distributed random vectors with the common environmental probability mass (density) function p_e: $S \rightarrow [0, \infty), S \subseteq \mathcal{R}^d$.

Let $\hat{l}_n: W \times S^n \rightarrow [0, \infty)$, where $W \subseteq \mathcal{R}^q$. During the learning process, the ANN system then seeks a strict local minimum, $\hat{\mathbf{w}}_n^*$, of the sample risk function, $\hat{l}_n(\cdot; \{\mathbf{x}(1),\ldots,\mathbf{x}(n)\}): W \rightarrow [0, \infty)$. The estimate $\hat{\mathbf{w}}_n$ is an observed value of the random vector $\tilde{\mathbf{w}}_n$, a strict local minimum of $\hat{l}_n(\cdot; \{\tilde{\mathbf{x}}(1),\ldots,\tilde{\mathbf{x}}(n)\})$ with probability one for n sufficiently large. Let $\mathbf{w}^*$ be a strict local minimum of the true risk function $l: W \rightarrow [0, \infty)$, defined with respect to the loss function for $\hat{l}_n$ and p_e. Assume that $\tilde{\mathbf{w}}_n \rightarrow \mathbf{w}^*$ with probability one as $n \rightarrow \infty$ (explicit conditions justifying this assertion can be obtained using theorems such as the Sample Risk Local Minimum Convergence Theorem in chapter 7).

Under fairly general conditions, it will be shown that for n sufficiently large, the probability distribution of $\tilde{\mathbf{w}}_n$ is approximately Gaussian with mean $\mathbf{w}^*$ and covariance matrix $n^{-1}\mathbf{C}^*$, where the population covariance matrix $\mathbf{C}^*$ can be estimated using a simple formula involving the first and second partial derivatives of l. This important and practical result allows one to precisely characterize the *sampling error distribution* (i.e., $\tilde{\mathbf{w}}_n - \mathbf{w}^*$), and thus determine how the effects of sample size influence the generalization performance of an ANN system.

Before proceeding, however, some useful concepts will be introduced. The first concept is called "bounded in probability" and may be viewed as a "weaker" version of the bounded stochastic process concept introduced in chapter 4.

Definition: Bounded in probability. Let $S \subseteq \mathcal{R}^d$. Let $\tilde{\mathbf{x}}(1), \tilde{\mathbf{x}}(2),\dots$ be a stochastic sequence of random vectors with respective probability mass (density) functions $p_1, p_2,\dots$ where $p_n: S \to [0, \infty)$ for $n = 1, 2, 3,\dots$. The stochastic sequence $\tilde{\mathbf{x}}(1), \tilde{\mathbf{x}}(2),\dots$ is *bounded in probability* if, for every strictly positive real number ε, there exists a finite real number M_ε and there exists a finite integer N_ε such that

$$p_n\big(\,\big|\tilde{\mathbf{x}}(n)\big| \leq M_\varepsilon\big) > 1 - \varepsilon$$

for all $n > N_\varepsilon$. The notation $\tilde{x}(n) = O_p(1)$ indicates that $\{\tilde{x}(n)\}$ is bounded in probability. The notation $\tilde{x}(n) = o_p(1)$ indicates that $\tilde{x}(n) \to 0$ in probability as $n \to \infty$.

For a given sample of size n, $\mathbf{x}(1),\dots, \mathbf{x}(n)$, a strict local minimum, $\hat{\mathbf{w}}_n$, of the sample risk function $\hat{l}_n(\cdot; \{\mathbf{x}(1),\dots, \mathbf{x}(n)\})$ is the *solution* to the learning problem, given the sample of size n. A sequence of samples defined such that n is continually increasing thus generates the sequence $\hat{\mathbf{w}}_1, \hat{\mathbf{w}}_2,\dots$, which may be interpreted as a sample path of the *stochastic solution sequence* $\tilde{\mathbf{w}}_1, \tilde{\mathbf{w}}_2,\dots$. The following concept identifies certain assumed properties of the stochastic solution sequence that are especially useful.

Definition: Stochastic solution sequence. Let W be a closed and bounded subset of $\mathcal{R}^q$. Let $S \subseteq \Omega \subseteq \mathcal{R}^d$. Let $\tilde{\mathbf{x}}(1), \tilde{\mathbf{x}}(2),\dots$ be a sequence of independent and identically distributed random vectors with the common probability mass (density) function $p_e: S \to [0, \infty)$. Let $c(\cdot \mid \cdot): W \times \Omega \to \mathcal{R}$ be a regular loss function with respect to p_e. Let l be the true risk function, defined with respect to c and p_e. A *stochastic solution sequence* with respect to c and p_e is a stochastic process $\tilde{\mathbf{w}}_1, \tilde{\mathbf{w}}_2,\dots$ such that

1. $\tilde{\mathbf{w}}_n$ converges with probability one to a strict local minimum in the interior of W, $\mathbf{w}^*$, of l as $n \to \infty$,

2. the stochastic sequence $\{\sqrt{n}(\tilde{\mathbf{w}}_n - \mathbf{w}^*)\}$ is bounded in probability, and

3. with probability one, $\tilde{\mathbf{w}}_n$ is a strict local minimum of

$$\hat{l}_n(\cdot; \{\tilde{\mathbf{x}}(1),\dots, \tilde{\mathbf{x}}(n)\}) = (1/n)\sum_{i=1}^{n} c(\cdot \mid \tilde{\mathbf{x}}(i))$$

for n sufficiently large.

Note that condition (1) of the definition of a stochastic solution sequence means that as the sample size n increases, the stochastic solution sequence converges with probability one to a unique solution. The Strict Local Minimum

Convergence Theorem (chapter 7) is helpful for understanding when condition (1) is satisfied. Condition (2) of the definition of a stochastic solution sequence implies that the rate at which $\tilde{\mathbf{w}}_n$ converges to $\mathbf{w}^*$ must be sufficiently fast. Serfling (1980, 8) notes that a sufficient condition for $\{\sqrt{n}(\tilde{\mathbf{w}}_n - \mathbf{w}^*)\}$ to be bounded in probability is for $\sqrt{n}(\tilde{\mathbf{w}}_n - \mathbf{w}^*)$ to converge in distribution to some random vector as $n \to \infty$. Condition (3) is a "weaker" version of the assumption that $\hat{\mathbf{w}}_n$ must always be a strict local minimum of $\hat{l}_n(\cdot; \{\mathbf{x}(1),..., \mathbf{x}(n)\})$. In particular, the assumption that $\hat{\mathbf{w}}_n$ is a strict local minimum of $\hat{l}_n(\cdot; \{\mathbf{x}(1),..., \mathbf{x}(n)\})$ for $n = 0, 1, 2,...$ will satisfy condition (3).

The Asymptotic Sampling Error Theorem is now presented and proved, following the approach of White (1981, 1982, 1989a,b, 1994) and Serfling (1980, Theorem B of section 7.2.2); White 1989a,b, 1994 state and prove a more general version of the theorem; Serfling 1980, 250–251 notes that such theorems are a variant of the approach taken in Huber 1964. In the statistics literature, theorems such as the Asymptotic Sampling Error Theorem are concerned with characterizing the asymptotic distribution of strict local minima of a sample risk function. Such strict local minima are usually referred to as "M-estimators" (Manoukian 1986; Serfling 1980, chap. 7; for related research concerned with characterizing the asymptotic distribution of M-estimators, see Huber 1964; Jennrich 1969; Manoukian 1986; Serfling 1980; and White 1981, 1982.)

Theorem: Asymptotic sampling error. Let W be a convex, closed and bounded subset of $\mathcal{R}^q$. Let $S \subseteq \Omega \subseteq \mathcal{R}^d$. Let $\tilde{\mathbf{x}}(1), \tilde{\mathbf{x}}(2),...$ be a sequence of independent and identically distributed random vectors with the common probability mass (density) function $p_e: S \to [0, \infty)$. Let $c(\cdot | \cdot): W \times \Omega \to \mathcal{R}$ be a regular loss function with respect to p_e. Let $\mathbf{g}: W \times \Omega \to W$ be defined such that $\mathbf{g}(\cdot | \mathbf{x})$ is the gradient of $c(\cdot | \mathbf{x})$ for all $\mathbf{x} \in S$. Let $\mathbf{H}: W \times \Omega \to \mathcal{R}^{q \times q}$ be defined such that $\mathbf{H}(\cdot | \mathbf{x})$ is the Hessian of $c(\cdot | \mathbf{x})$ for all $\mathbf{x} \in S$. Let $\tilde{\mathbf{w}}_1, \tilde{\mathbf{w}}_2,...$ be a stochastic solution sequence with respect to c and p_e that converges to $\mathbf{w}^*$ with probability one. Assume that

$\mathbf{A}^* = E[\mathbf{H}(\mathbf{w}^* | \tilde{\mathbf{x}})]$, and $\mathbf{B}^* = E[\mathbf{g}(\mathbf{w}^* | \tilde{\mathbf{x}})\mathbf{g}(\mathbf{w}^* | \tilde{\mathbf{x}})^T]$

exist and are nonsingular. Then as $n \to \infty$, $\sqrt{n}(\tilde{\mathbf{w}}_n - \mathbf{w}^*)$ converges in distribution to a random Gaussian vector with mean $\mathbf{0}_q$ and covariance matrix

$$\mathbf{C}^* = [\mathbf{A}^*]^{-1}[\mathbf{B}^*][\mathbf{A}^*]^{-1}. \tag{8.1}$$

Proof. Because c is regular, the sample risk convergence theorem implies that as $n \to \infty$:

$$\tilde{\mathbf{A}}_n^* = (1/n)\sum_{i=1}^{n} \mathbf{H}(\mathbf{w}^* | \tilde{\mathbf{x}}(i)) \to \mathbf{A}^*$$

with probability one. Thus $\tilde{\mathbf{A}}_n^* = \mathbf{A}^* + o_p(1)$.

Because $\mathbf{w}^*$ is a strict local minimum of l, the gradient of l is equal to $\mathbf{0}_q$, the Hessian of l is positive definite (by the Weak Local Minimum Test of chapter 5). Thus, $\mathbf{A}^*$ is positive definite. And because c is regular,

$$\nabla_{\mathbf{w}^*} l = E_{\tilde{\mathbf{x}}}[\mathbf{g}(\mathbf{w}^* \mid \tilde{\mathbf{x}})] = \mathbf{0}_q.$$

Let $\tilde{\mathbf{g}}_i^* = \mathbf{g}(\mathbf{w}^* \mid \tilde{\mathbf{x}}(i))$. Because c is a regular loss function, $\nabla \hat{l}_n$, may be expanded about $\mathbf{w}^*$ and evaluated at $\tilde{\mathbf{w}}_n$ and $\tilde{\mathbf{x}}(1),\ldots, \tilde{\mathbf{x}}(n)$ as follows:

$$\nabla \hat{l}_n\big(\tilde{\mathbf{w}}_n; \{\tilde{\mathbf{x}}(1),\ldots, \tilde{\mathbf{x}}(n)\}\big) = (1/n)\sum_{i=1}^{n} \mathbf{g}\big(\tilde{\mathbf{w}}_n \mid \tilde{\mathbf{x}}(i)\big)$$

$$= (1/n)\sum_{i=1}^{n} \tilde{\mathbf{g}}_i^* + \tilde{\mathbf{A}}_n^*[\tilde{\mathbf{w}}_n - \mathbf{w}^*] + \mathbf{1}_q O(|\tilde{\mathbf{w}}_n - \mathbf{w}^*|^2). \tag{8.2}$$

Note that $[\mathbf{A}^*]^{-1}$ exists because $\mathbf{A}^*$ is positive definite. Substitute $\tilde{\mathbf{A}}_n^* = \mathbf{A}^* + o_p(1)$ into (8.2) and multiply by $\sqrt{n}[\mathbf{A}^*]^{-1}$. By the definition of $\tilde{\mathbf{w}}_n$,

$$(1/n)\sum_{i=1}^{n} \mathbf{g}(\tilde{\mathbf{w}}_n \mid \tilde{\mathbf{x}}(i))$$

in (8.2) is equal to a vector of zeros for sufficiently large n with probability one. Therefore, (8.2) becomes, with probability one for n sufficiently large,

$$\mathbf{0}_q = \sqrt{n}[\mathbf{A}^*]^{-1}(1/n)\sum_{i=1}^{n} \tilde{\mathbf{g}}_i^* + \sqrt{n}[\tilde{\mathbf{w}}_n - \mathbf{w}^*] + \tilde{R}_n, \tag{8.3}$$

where

$$\tilde{R}_n = \sqrt{n}[\tilde{\mathbf{w}}_n - \mathbf{w}^*] o_p(1) + \mathbf{1}_q O(\sqrt{n}|\tilde{\mathbf{w}}_n - \mathbf{w}^*|^2)$$

and

$$\sqrt{n}[\tilde{\mathbf{w}}_n - \mathbf{w}^*] = -[\tilde{\mathbf{A}}_n^*]^{-1}(1/\sqrt{n})\sum_{i=1}^{n} \tilde{\mathbf{g}}_i^* + \tilde{R}_n. \tag{8.4}$$

The random vector

$$\tilde{\mathbf{y}}_n = (1/\sqrt{n})\sum_{i=1}^{n} \tilde{\mathbf{g}}_i^*$$

converges in distribution to a Gaussian random vector, $\tilde{\mathbf{y}}^*$, with a mean vector of zeros and covariance matrix $\mathbf{B}^*$, by the Multivariate Central Limit Theorem (chapter 4), the assumption that $\mathbf{B}^*$ is finite and nonsingular, and the observation that $E_{\tilde{\mathbf{x}}}[\mathbf{g}(\mathbf{w}^* \mid \tilde{\mathbf{x}})] = \mathbf{0}_q$.

Note that, by assumption, $\{\sqrt{n}(\tilde{\mathbf{w}}_n - \mathbf{w}^*)\}$ is bounded in probability and since $\tilde{\mathbf{w}}_n - \mathbf{w}^* \to 0$ with probability one as $n \to \infty$, the remainder term $\tilde{R}_n$ in

(8.4) converges to zero in probability by Corollary 2.36 of White (1984, 26). By Slutsky's theorem and the Gaussian Random Vector Linear Transformation Theorem (chapter 4), the right-hand side of (8.4) converges in distribution to a Gaussian random vector with mean zero and covariance matrix $[\mathbf{A}^*]^{-1}\mathbf{B}^*[\mathbf{A}^*]^{-1}$. ∎

In practice, $\mathbf{A}^*$ and $\mathbf{B}^*$ are not observable and must be estimated. Because c is regular and $\{\tilde{\mathbf{w}}_n\}$ is a stochastic solution sequence, the Sample Risk Function Convergence Theorem may be used to show that as $n \to \infty$:

$$\tilde{\mathbf{A}}_n = n^{-1}\sum_{i=1}^{n} \mathbf{H}(\tilde{\mathbf{w}}_n \mid \tilde{\mathbf{x}}(i)) \to \mathbf{A}^* \tag{8.5}$$

with probability one and

$$\tilde{\mathbf{B}}_n = n^{-1}\sum_{i=1}^{n} \mathbf{g}(\tilde{\mathbf{w}}_n \mid \tilde{\mathbf{x}}(i))\mathbf{g}(\tilde{\mathbf{w}}_n \mid \tilde{\mathbf{x}}(i))^T \to \mathbf{B}^* \tag{8.6}$$

with probability one. Thus $\mathbf{A}^*$ and $\mathbf{B}^*$ may be estimated (given that appropriate assumptions hold) by $\hat{\mathbf{A}}_n$ and $\hat{\mathbf{B}}_n$, which are observed values of the random matrices $\tilde{\mathbf{A}}_n$ and $\tilde{\mathbf{B}}_n$, respectively.

Also note that because $\mathbf{A}^*$ is real symmetric positive definite, as $n \to \infty$:

$$\tilde{\mathbf{C}}_n = [\tilde{\mathbf{A}}_n]^{-1}\tilde{\mathbf{B}}_n[\tilde{\mathbf{A}}_n]^{-1} \tag{8.7}$$

converges with probability one to $\mathbf{C}^*$ (see problem 8-10 for a proof), suggesting that $\mathbf{C}^*$ may be estimated by

$$\hat{\mathbf{C}}_n = [\hat{\mathbf{A}}_n]^{-1}\hat{\mathbf{B}}_n[\hat{\mathbf{A}}_n]^{-1}.$$

An important special case of White's (1982, 1989a,b, 1994) theorem is the classical theory of the asymptotic distribution of maximum likelihood estimates, which may be derived from the asymptotic sampling error theorem, given the following two assumptions. First, the sample risk function is assumed to be the KLIC sample risk function with respect to some probability model

$$F_W = \{(q_f(\cdot \mid \mathbf{w}): S \to [0, \infty)): \mathbf{w} \in W \subseteq \mathcal{R}^q\}$$

and some environmental probability mass (density) function $p_e: S \to [0, \infty)$. Second, it is assumed that F_W is *correctly specified* with respect to p_e, so that there exists a $\mathbf{w}^* \in W$ such that $p_e(\cdot) = q_f(\cdot \mid \mathbf{w}^*)$ on the sample space S. In the case of correct probability model specification it can be shown that under certain regularity conditions (see problem 8-5) the *Fisher information matrix equality* (White 1982, 1994, chap. 6), given by $\mathbf{A}^* = \mathbf{B}^*$, is satisfied. Thus the formula in (8.1) reduces to

$$\mathbf{C}^* = [\mathbf{A}^*]^{-1}\mathbf{B}^*[\mathbf{A}^*]^{-1} = [\mathbf{B}^*]^{-1}\mathbf{B}^*[\mathbf{B}^*]^{-1} = [\mathbf{B}^*]^{-1}$$

or to

$$\mathbf{C}^* = [\mathbf{A}^*]^{-1}\mathbf{B}^*[\mathbf{A}^*]^{-1} = [\mathbf{A}^*]^{-1}\mathbf{A}^*[\mathbf{A}^*]^{-1} = [\mathbf{A}^*]^{-1}.$$

The formula $[\mathbf{B}^*]^{-1} = [\mathbf{A}^*]^{-1}$ is well known as the "asymptotic covariance matrix of maximum likelihood estimates" (Riefer and Batchelder 1988; Manoukian 1986; Serfling 1980; Wilks 1962).

Asymptotic Distribution of a Function of the Parameter Estimates

The response of a feedforward ANN classification dynamical system (e.g., a typical backpropagation ANN system) can usually be expressed as a function $\boldsymbol{\Phi}: \mathcal{R}^d \times \mathcal{R}^q \to \mathcal{R}^m$, with continuous second partial derivatives such that $\hat{\mathbf{r}}_n = \boldsymbol{\Phi}(\mathbf{s}, \hat{\mathbf{w}}_n)$, where $\mathbf{s}$ is a stimulus activation pattern vector, $\hat{\mathbf{w}}_n$ is a connection strength parameter vector estimated from a training sample consisting of n training stimuli, and the response of the ANN system $\hat{\mathbf{r}}_n$ is the activation pattern vector indicating the response of the ANN system given a stimulus $\mathbf{s}$ and connection strength pattern vector $\hat{\mathbf{w}}_n$. Notice that $\hat{\mathbf{w}}_n$ is actually an observed value of the random vector $\tilde{\mathbf{w}}_n$ whose asymptotic probability distribution has just been characterized. The following theorem provides a simple formula for characterizing the asymptotic distribution of $\tilde{\mathbf{r}}_n = \boldsymbol{\Phi}(\mathbf{s}, \tilde{\mathbf{w}}_n)$ in terms of the asymptotic distribution of $\tilde{\mathbf{w}}_n$.

Theorem: Asymptotic Function of Sampling Error. Let W be a convex, closed, and bounded subset of $\mathcal{R}^q$. Let $\mathbf{w}^*$ be in the interior of W. Let $U \subseteq \mathcal{R}^d$. Let $\tilde{\mathbf{w}}_1, \tilde{\mathbf{w}}_2, \ldots$ be a stochastic process that converges with probability one to $\mathbf{w}^*$. Assume that as $n \to \infty$: $\sqrt{n}(\tilde{\mathbf{w}}_n - \mathbf{w}^*)$ converges in distribution to a random vector that has a multivariate Gaussian distribution with zero mean and covariance matrix $\mathbf{C}^*$. Let $\boldsymbol{\Phi}: U \times W \to \mathcal{R}^m$. Assume the Hessian of $\boldsymbol{\Phi}(\mathbf{s}, \cdot)$ exists and is continuous on W for all $\mathbf{s} \in U$. Let the stochastic process $\tilde{\mathbf{r}}_1(\mathbf{s}), \tilde{\mathbf{r}}_2(\mathbf{s}), \ldots$ for all $\mathbf{s} \in U$ be defined such that $\tilde{\mathbf{r}}_n(\mathbf{s}) = \boldsymbol{\Phi}(\mathbf{s}, \tilde{\mathbf{w}}_n)$. Let $\mathbf{F}: W \times U \to \mathcal{R}^{m \times q}$ be defined such that for all $\mathbf{w} \in W$ and for all $\mathbf{s} \in U$:

$$\mathbf{F}(\mathbf{w}, \mathbf{s}) = \frac{d\boldsymbol{\Phi}(\mathbf{s}, \mathbf{w})}{d\mathbf{w}}.$$

Assume $\mathbf{F}(\mathbf{w}^*, \mathbf{s})$ has rank m ($m \leq q$) for all $\mathbf{s} \in U$. Then as $n \to \infty$: $\sqrt{n}(\tilde{\mathbf{r}}_n[\mathbf{s}] - \mathbf{r}^*[\mathbf{s}])$ converges in distribution to a random vector that has a multivariate Gaussian distribution with zero mean and covariance matrix $\mathbf{F}(\mathbf{w}^*, \mathbf{s})\,\mathbf{C}^*\mathbf{F}(\mathbf{w}^*, \mathbf{s})^T$ for all $\mathbf{s} \in U$, where $\mathbf{r}^*[\mathbf{s}] = \boldsymbol{\Phi}(\mathbf{s}, \mathbf{w}^*)$.

Proof.   Because the Hessian of $\boldsymbol{\Phi}(\mathbf{s}, \cdot)$ is continuous on W by assumption, $\boldsymbol{\Phi}(\mathbf{s}, \cdot)$ may be expanded in a Taylor expansion about $\mathbf{w}^*$ and evaluated at $\tilde{\mathbf{w}}_n$ to obtain for all $\mathbf{s} \in U$,

$$\boldsymbol{\Phi}(\mathbf{s}, \tilde{\mathbf{w}}_n) = \boldsymbol{\Phi}(\mathbf{s}, \mathbf{w}^*) + \mathbf{F}(\mathbf{w}^*, \mathbf{s})[\tilde{\mathbf{w}}_n - \mathbf{w}^*] + \mathbf{1}_q O\big(|\tilde{\mathbf{w}}_n - \mathbf{w}^*|^2\big),$$

$$\sqrt{n}\,\tilde{\mathbf{r}}_n[\mathbf{s}] = \sqrt{n}\,\mathbf{r}^*[\mathbf{s}] + \sqrt{n}\,\mathbf{F}(\mathbf{w}^*, \mathbf{s})[\tilde{\mathbf{w}}_n - \mathbf{w}^*] + \mathbf{1}_q O\big(\sqrt{n}|\tilde{\mathbf{w}}_n - \mathbf{w}^*|^2\big). \tag{8.8}$$

Note $\{\sqrt{n}[\tilde{\mathbf{w}}_n - \mathbf{w}^*]\}$ is bounded in probability because $\sqrt{n}[\tilde{\mathbf{w}}_n - \mathbf{w}^*]$ converges in distribution as $n \to \infty$ (Serfling 1980, 8) and that $\tilde{\mathbf{w}}_n - \mathbf{w}^* \to 0$ with probability one as $n \to \infty$. Thus, the third term on the right-hand side of (8.8) converges in probability to zero as $n \to \infty$ by Corollary 2.36 of White (1984, 26). The assumption that $\sqrt{n}(\tilde{\mathbf{w}}_n - \mathbf{w}^*)$ converges in distribution to a Gaussian random vector with mean zero and covariance matrix $\mathbf{C}^*$ as $n \to \infty$ also implies (Gaussian Random Vector Linear Transformation Theorem; chapter 4) that

$$\sqrt{n}\,\mathbf{r}^*[\mathbf{s}] + \sqrt{n}\,\mathbf{F}(\mathbf{w}^*, \mathbf{s})[\tilde{\mathbf{w}}_n - \mathbf{w}^*]$$

converges in distribution to a Gaussian random vector with mean $\sqrt{n}\,\mathbf{r}^*[\mathbf{s}]$ and covariance matrix $\mathbf{F}(\mathbf{w}^*, \mathbf{s})\mathbf{C}^*[\mathbf{F}(\mathbf{w}^*, \mathbf{s})]^T$ as $n \to \infty$. Therefore, by Slutsky's Theorem, the right-hand side of (8.8) converges in distribution to a Gaussian random vector with mean $\sqrt{n}\,\mathbf{r}^*[\mathbf{s}]$ and covariance matrix $\mathbf{F}(\mathbf{w}^*, \mathbf{s})\mathbf{C}^*[\mathbf{F}(\mathbf{w}^*, \mathbf{s})]^T$ as $n \to \infty$. ∎

The Asymptotic Function of the Sampling Error Theorem and the Sample Risk Function Convergence Theorem suggest the following formula for computing approximate error bounds (i.e., confidence intervals) on the predictions of feedforward ANN systems. For a given stimulus $\mathbf{s}$ and for sufficiently large n, the response of the ANN system is approximately a Gaussian random vector $\tilde{\mathbf{r}}_n[\mathbf{s}] = \mathbf{\Phi}(\mathbf{s}, \tilde{\mathbf{w}}_n)$ with mean $\mathbf{r}^*[\mathbf{s}] = \mathbf{\Phi}(\mathbf{s}, \mathbf{w}^*)$ and covariance matrix

$$n^{-1}\mathbf{C}_{\mathbf{r}}^*[\mathbf{s}] = n^{-1}\mathbf{F}(\mathbf{w}^*, \mathbf{s})\mathbf{C}^*[\mathbf{F}(\mathbf{w}^*, \mathbf{s})]^T.$$

Thus, for sufficiently large n, the ith element of $\tilde{\mathbf{r}}_n[\mathbf{s}]$, $\tilde{r}_{n,i}$, has an approximately Gaussian probability distribution with mean $r_{n,i}^*$ and variance $c_{r_i^*}/n$ where $c_{r_i^*}$ is the ith on-diagonal element of $\mathbf{C}_{\mathbf{r}^*}[\mathbf{s}]$.

Thus also

$$p\left(\left| [\tilde{r}_{n,i} - r_{n,i}^*][c_{r_i^*}/n]^{-1/2} \right| < Z_a \right) = 1 - a \tag{8.9}$$

where Z_a is defined such that

$$\int_{-Z_a}^{+Z_a} (1/\sqrt{2\pi}) \exp\left[-x^2/2\right] dx = 1 - a. \tag{8.10}$$

Equation (8.9) may be interpreted as stating that the probability is approximately $1 - a$ that $\tilde{r}_{n,i}$ is greater than $r_{n,i}^* - [c_{r_i^*}/n]^{1/2}Z_a$ and less than $r_{n,i}^* + [c_{r_i^*}/n]^{1/2}Z_a$.

Finally note that the integral in (8.10) may be explicitly evaluated by using commonly available computer software (e.g., Press et al. 1986) or using tables for selected values of Z_a (e.g., Mendenhall, Scheaffer, and Wackerley 1981; Walpole and Myers 1978). It is convenient to note that $Z_{0.05} = 1.96$, and that $\chi_a^2(1) = Z_a^2$. (A more conservative confidence interval may be constructed using the Markov Inequality introduced in chapter 4.)

8.1.2   Bootstrap Approach

An alternative to the Asymptotic Sampling Error Theorem, the bootstrap approach proposed by Efron (1982) can also be used to characterize the sampling distribution of the parameter estimates for an extremely large class of highly nonlinear risk functions as well as arbitrary functions of those estimates. The only major disadvantages of the bootstrap approach are that it requires considerable computational resources and (like the Asymptotic Sampling Error Theorem) is only valid for sufficiently large sample sizes.

A number of researchers have used the bootstrap approach successfully to estimate the prediction error of classification rules. In particular, Paas (1993) has provided some empirical studies supporting the applicability of the bootstrap approach to characterizing the probability distribution of the sampling error for feedforward backpropagation ANN systems. Golden (1995) has used the bootstrap approach to check the assumptions of the Asymptotic Sampling Error Theorem with respect to a specific ANN application. Baxt and White (1995) have used the bootstrap approach for understanding the relative effects of different input variables upon an outcome measure generated by a backpropagation network.

To keep the analysis simple, it is assumed that the sample space S is finite. Efron (1982, 35) notes that the bootstrap approach can be shown to be valid under conditions where the sample space is not necessarily finite, but that such analyses are considerably complex. In practice, most environmental probability density functions can be approximated effectively by probability mass functions on extremely high-dimensional finite sample spaces.

Let the *original sample* (e.g., the training data) be a sample path of the stochastic process $\tilde{\mathbf{x}}(1),\ldots,\tilde{\mathbf{x}}(n)$ that consists of independent and identically distributed random vectors with common environmental probability mass function $p_e\colon S \to [0, 1]$, $S \subseteq \mathcal{R}^d$. The goal of an ANN learning system is to compute a local (or preferably, a global) minimum, $\mathbf{w}^*$, of the expected risk function l, defined with respect to some loss function c and distribution p_e. Thus $\mathbf{w}^*$ is some complicated function of p_e. However, because only a sample path, $\mathbf{x}(1),\ldots,\mathbf{x}(n)$, of $\tilde{\mathbf{x}}(1),\ldots,\tilde{\mathbf{x}}(n)$ is directly observable, the ANN learning system must compute an estimate, $\hat{\mathbf{w}}_n$, of $\mathbf{w}^*$. The process of computing $\hat{\mathbf{w}}_n$ may be expressed in terms of a function $\mathbf{e}_n$ that maps $\mathbf{x}(1),\ldots,\mathbf{x}(n)$ into $\hat{\mathbf{w}}_n$ as follows:

$$\hat{\mathbf{w}}_n = \mathbf{e}_n(\mathbf{x}(1),\ldots,\mathbf{x}(n)),$$

which is an observed value of the random vector

$$\tilde{\mathbf{w}}_n = \mathbf{e}_n(\tilde{\mathbf{x}}(1),\ldots,\tilde{\mathbf{x}}(n)).$$

The probability distribution of $\tilde{\mathbf{w}}_n$ is important for estimating the sampling error of $\hat{\mathbf{w}}_n$.

Another typical goal of an ANN learning system is to compute some function $\mathbf{\Phi}: \mathcal{R}^d \times \mathcal{R}^q \to \mathcal{R}^m$. For example, the response $\mathbf{r} \in \mathcal{R}^m$, of an ANN feedforward classification dynamical system may be expressed as $\mathbf{r} = \mathbf{\Phi}(\mathbf{s}, \mathbf{w}^*)$, where $\mathbf{s} \in \mathcal{R}^d$ is an input stimulus activation pattern vector. Because $\mathbf{w}^*$ is usually estimated by the vector $\hat{\mathbf{w}}_n$ for a finite sample of size n, the probability distribution of

$$\tilde{\mathbf{r}}_n = \mathbf{\Phi}(\mathbf{s}, \tilde{\mathbf{w}}_n),$$

given $\mathbf{s}$, is an important quantity of interest for characterizing the ANN system's prediction error. Thus the random vector $\tilde{\mathbf{r}}_n$ is a deterministic function evaluated at $\tilde{\mathbf{w}}_n$ which, in turn, is a deterministic function evaluated at $\tilde{\mathbf{x}}(1),\ldots, \tilde{\mathbf{x}}(n)$.

Both of the above important cases as well as other situations can be handled by investigating the probability distribution of an arbitrary function, $\mathbf{\Gamma}_n$, evaluated at $\tilde{\mathbf{x}}(1),\ldots, \tilde{\mathbf{x}}(n)$. In particular, define $\mathbf{\Gamma}_n: S^n \to \mathcal{R}^u$ such that

$$\tilde{\mathbf{\Gamma}}_n = \mathbf{\Gamma}_n(\tilde{\mathbf{x}}(1),\ldots, \tilde{\mathbf{x}}(n)).$$

The goal of the bootstrap algorithm is to characterize the probability distribution of the random vector $\tilde{\mathbf{\Gamma}}_n$.

The following sampling procedure may be used to directly characterize the asymptotic probability distribution of $\tilde{\mathbf{\Gamma}}_n$ for a *fixed sample size n* if an essentially infinite amount of training data is available. First, collect K sets of training data, where the ith training data set ($i = 1\ldots K$) is a sample of n vectors $\mathbf{x}^i(1),\ldots, \mathbf{x}^i(n)$, which in turn is a sample path of the stochastic process $\tilde{\mathbf{x}}^i(1), \ldots, \tilde{\mathbf{x}}^i(n)$, whose elements are independently and identically distributed according to p_e. Second, for each of the K sets of training data of size n, compute $\hat{\mathbf{\Gamma}}_n^i = \mathbf{\Gamma}_n(\mathbf{x}^i(1),\ldots, \mathbf{x}^i(n))$ for $i = 1\ldots K$. As K becomes large, the relative frequency of an observed value $\hat{\mathbf{\Gamma}}_n^i$ will converge to the probability of that value. Thus the sampling distribution of $\tilde{\mathbf{\Gamma}}_n$ can be directly estimated in this case.

The bootstrap approach exploits the above computationally intensive approach but makes the assumption that a sufficiently large amount of training data is *not* available. Because only one set of training data of size n is available in practice, the environmental probability mass function p_e is estimated using the *empirical* environmental probability mass function $\hat{p}_e$, which in turn uses the relative frequency of an observation in the sample to estimate the probability of that observation in the population. Once $\hat{p}_e$ is computed, K sets of training data are generated by sampling with replacement from the empirical environmental probability mass function $\hat{p}_e$. These K *bootstrap data sets* are then used to compute K estimates of $\tilde{\mathbf{\Gamma}}_n$, so that the sampling distribution of $\tilde{\mathbf{\Gamma}}_n$ may be characterized. The notation $\mathbf{x}(1)^{*i},\ldots, \mathbf{x}(n)^{*i}$ will be used to denote the ith bootstrap data set ($i = 1\ldots K$).

One is usually interested in the mean of $\tilde{\Gamma}_n$, $\overline{\Gamma}_n$, and the covariance matrix of $\tilde{\Gamma}_n$, $\mathbf{C}_n$. This information may be used to construct statistical tests for hypothesis testing as well as confidence intervals on the ANN system's predictions. The bootstrap estimates of $\overline{\Gamma}_n$ and $\mathbf{C}_n$ are now computed. Define

$$\hat{\Gamma}_n^{*\,i} = \Gamma_n(\mathbf{x}(1)^{*i}, \ldots, \mathbf{x}(n)^{*i}).$$

Then $\overline{\Gamma}_n$ and $\mathbf{C}_n$ may be estimated by $\hat{\overline{\Gamma}}_n^*$ and $\hat{\mathbf{C}}_n^*$, respectively, where

$$\hat{\overline{\Gamma}}_n^{*i} = (1/K)\sum_{i=1}^{K} \hat{\Gamma}_n^{*i}$$

and

$$\hat{\mathbf{C}}_n^* = (1/K)\sum_{i=1}^{K} [\hat{\Gamma}_n^{*i} - \hat{\overline{\Gamma}}_n^*][\hat{\Gamma}_n^{*i} - \hat{\overline{\Gamma}}_n^*]^T.$$

The number of bootstrap data sets K is chosen to be sufficiently large so that the estimates of $\overline{\Gamma}_n$ and $\mathbf{C}_n$ converge to values sufficiently close to $\overline{\Gamma}_n$ and $\mathbf{C}_n$ according to some criterion.

It is useful at this point to define the concept *symmetric in its arguments*.

Definition: Symmetric in its arguments. Let $G_n: A \times A \times \ldots A \to B$ be a function with n arguments. The function G_n is *symmetric in its arguments* if it has the property that for all $x_1, x_2, \ldots, x_n \in A$:

$$G_n(x_1, x_2, \ldots, x_n) = G_n(x_{i_1}, x_{i_2}, \ldots, x_{i_n}),$$

where the sequence $i_1, i_2, \ldots, i_n$ is any permutation of the sequence $1, 2, \ldots, n$.

The *bootstrap algorithm* is now formally presented (the motivation for this version is discussed in problem 8-1).

Algorithm: Bootstrap algorithm. Let $\mathbf{x}(1), \ldots, \mathbf{x}(n)$ be the *original sample of size n* a particular sample path of the stochastic process $\tilde{\mathbf{x}}(1), \ldots \tilde{\mathbf{x}}(n)$ that consists of n, independent and identically distributed random vectors with the common environmental probability mass function $p_e: S \to [0, 1]$, where S is a finite set of d-dimensional real vectors. Let F be the set of all probability mass functions on S. Let the *estimation procedure function* $\Gamma_n: S \times S \times S \ldots S \to \mathcal{R}^q$ be symmetric in its n arguments. Define the random vector $\tilde{\Gamma}_n$ according to the formula

$$\tilde{\Gamma}_n = \Gamma(\tilde{\mathbf{x}}(1), \ldots, \tilde{\mathbf{x}}(n)).$$

The goal of the bootstrap algorithm is to estimate the probability distribution of $\tilde{\Gamma}_n$ for a given sample size n.

• Step 1: Compute empirical distribution. Compute the maximum likelihood estimate, $\hat{p}_n: S \to [0, 1]$, for the probability model F with respect to the original data sample $\mathbf{x}(1),\ldots,\mathbf{x}(n)$. It can be shown (see problem 8-1) that this maximum likelihood estimate is unique and determined, for $t = 1\ldots n$, by the formulas

$$\hat{p}_n(\tilde{\mathbf{x}}(t) = \mathbf{x}(t)) = 1/n$$

and

$$\hat{p}_n(\tilde{\mathbf{x}}(t) = \mathbf{y}) = 0$$

for all $\mathbf{y} \in \{\mathbf{x} \in S: \mathbf{x} \notin \{\mathbf{x}(1),\ldots,\mathbf{x}(n)\}\}$. Set loop index $i = 1$.

• Step 2: Sample empirical distribution. The ith bootstrap sample is a sequence of vectors, $\mathbf{x}(1)^{*i},\ldots, \mathbf{x}(n)^{*i}$, that is the ith sample path of $\tilde{\mathbf{x}}(1)^*, \ldots, \tilde{\mathbf{x}}(n)^*$ whose elements are independently and identically distributed with the common probability mass function $\hat{p}_n$.

• Step 3: Compute desired bootstrap estimate from bootstrap sample. Compute

$$\hat{\Gamma}_n^{*i} = \Gamma_n(\mathbf{x}(1)^{*i},\ldots, \mathbf{x}(n)^{*i}).$$

• Step 4: Record computed bootstrap estimate and continue generating bootstrap estimates until enough have been generated. Record bootstrap estimate $\hat{\Gamma}_n^{*i}$, let $i = i + 1$, and then terminate bootstrap algorithm if the empirical distribution of bootstrap estimates has converged to some empirical distribution according to some desired criterion. Otherwise, go to step 2.

8.2   Model Selection

Hypothesis-testing methods can provide a valuable methodology for developing practical and reliable methods for addressing the problem of evaluating the effectiveness of an ANN system within a given statistical environment (Moody 1994; White 1989a,b). For example, consider two distinct ANN systems which have each been trained on exactly the same set of training data. The ANN engineer wishes to decide which of the two ANN learning systems is a most appropriate model of the environmental distribution which generated the training data. In this case, the engineer must decide which of the two ANN learning systems provides a better fit to the data or whether the two ANN systems provide equally effective fits to the data.

8.2.1   Hypothesis Testing

This section reviews elements of hypothesis testing relevant to ANN learning systems using the methods of White (1982, 1994) and Vuong (1989).

Frequently in the evaluation of ANN system learning models, it is necessary to construct statistical tests when (1) the probability model of the ANN system is not correctly specified with respect to the data generating process, (2) the objective function for the ANN learning system is not a negative log likelihood function, or (3) the solution to the ANN learning problem is a strict local minimum (and not necessarily a strict global minimum). The following definition of a null (alternative) hypothesis (see DeGroot 1970 and White 1994 for similar definitions), while considerably more general than the concept of hypothesis testing in a classical statistical framework (e.g., Manoukian 1986), is required to address these issues.

Definition: Null and alternative hypotheses.   Let $S \subseteq \mathcal{R}^d$. Let

$$F_W = \{(p(\cdot \mid \mathbf{w}): S \rightarrow [0, \infty)): \mathbf{w} \in W \subseteq \mathcal{R}^q\}$$

be a probability model consisting of a set of probability mass (density) functions on S. Let f_W be a subset of F_W. Let $p^* = p(\cdot \mid \mathbf{w}^*) \in F_W$ be defined such that $\mathbf{w}^*$ is a strict local minimum of an expected risk function $l: \mathcal{R}^q \rightarrow \mathcal{R}$, defined with respect to loss function $c: W \times S \rightarrow \mathcal{R}$, and an environmental probability mass (density) function $p_e: S \rightarrow [0, \infty)$. A *null hypothesis*, $H_0: p^* \in f_W$, defined with respect to c, F_W, and p_e, is an assertion that $p^* \in f_W$ is a true statement. The *alternative hypothesis*, $H_A: p^* \notin f_W$ is an assertion that $H_0: p^* \in f_W$ is not a true statement.

The following example is helpful for understanding the above definition. Let $p_e: \mathcal{R} \rightarrow [0, \infty)$ be an environmental probability density function. Let F_W be the set of all possible univariate Gaussian probability density functions with common variance equal to one so that

$$F_W = \{p(\cdot \mid \mu): \mu \in \mathcal{R}\},$$

where $p(\cdot \mid \cdot): \mathcal{R} \times \mathcal{R} \rightarrow (0, \infty)$ is defined such that for every $x, \mu \in \mathcal{R}$:

$$p(x \mid \mu) = [\sqrt{2\pi}]^{-1} \exp\left[-(x - \mu)^2/2\right]. \tag{8.11}$$

Let the risk function $l: \mathcal{R} \rightarrow [0, \infty)$ be defined such that for every $\mu \in \mathcal{R}$:

$$l(\mu) = -\int_{x \in \mathcal{R}} p_e(x) \log\left[p(x \mid \mu)\right] dx,$$

where $p(x \mid \mu)$ is defined as in (8.11). The unique strict global minimum, μ^*, of l happens to be given by the formula (show this!)

$$\mu^* = \int_{x \in \mathcal{R}} x p_e(x) \, dx.$$

Let

$$f_W = \{p(\cdot \mid \mu): \mu > 2\},$$

where $p(\cdot \mid \mu)$ is defined as in (8.11). That is, f_W is the set of univariate Gaussian probability density functions whose population mean parameter is strictly greater than two, with variance equal to one. The null hypothesis in this example is then given by the assertion

H_0: $p(\cdot \mid \mu^*) \in f_W$,

which is typically expressed as

H_0: $\mu^* > 2$.

Definition: Statistic.   Let $S \subseteq \mathcal{R}^d$. Let $\tilde{\mathbf{x}}(1),\dots, \tilde{\mathbf{x}}(n)$ be a stochastic process consisting of independent and identically distributed random vectors with the common environmental probability mass (density) function p_e: $S \to [0, \infty)$. Let φ_n: $S \times S \times S \times \dots S \to \mathcal{R}$ be a function with n arguments. Then the random variable

$$\tilde{\varphi}_n = \varphi_n(\tilde{\mathbf{x}}(1),\dots, \tilde{\mathbf{x}}(n))$$

is a *statistic*.

Definition: Statistical test.   Let $S \subseteq \mathcal{R}^d$. Let $\mathbf{x}(1),\dots, \mathbf{x}(n)$ be a sample path of a stochastic process of independent and identically distributed random vectors with the common environmental probability mass (density) function p_e: $S \to [0, \infty)$. A (nonrandomized) *statistical test* is a function φ_n: $S \times S \times \dots S \to \{0, 1\}$ with n arguments defined with respect to a null hypothesis H_0 such that

1. If $\varphi_n(\mathbf{x}(1),\dots, \mathbf{x}(n)) = 1$, then H_0 is *rejected* (i.e., decide H_0 is *false*),

2. If $\varphi_n(\mathbf{x}(1),\dots, \mathbf{x}(n)) = 0$, then H_0 is *accepted* (i.e., decide H_0 is *true*).

Definition: Type I and type II errors.   Let $S \subseteq \mathcal{R}^d$. Let F_W be a set of probability mass (density) functions on sample space S. Let $f_W \subset F_W$. Let $\mathbf{x}(1),\dots, \mathbf{x}(n)$ be a sample path of a stochastic process consisting of independent and identically distributed random variables, $\tilde{\mathbf{x}}(1),\dots, \tilde{\mathbf{x}}(n)$, with common probability mass (density) function p_e: $S \to [0, \infty)$. Let the null hypothesis H_0: $p^* \in f_W$ be defined with respect to the probability model F_W, loss function c, and environmental probability mass (density) function p_e. Let

$$\varphi_n\colon S \times S \times \dots S \to \{0, 1\}$$

be a statistical test with respect to the null hypothesis H_0: $p^* \in f_W$. If

$$\varphi_n(\mathbf{x}(1),\dots, \mathbf{x}(n)) = 1$$

(i.e., H_0 is rejected) and $p^* \in f_W$ (i.e., H_0 is true), then a *type I error* has occurred. If

$$\varphi_n(\mathbf{x}(1),\dots, \mathbf{x}(n)) = 0$$

(i.e., H_0 is accepted) and $p^* \notin f_W$ (i.e., H_0 is false), then a *type II error* has occurred.

Table 8.1 provides an illustration of the definition of a type I error and a type II error. A type I error occurs when the decision maker decides to reject the null hypothesis when in fact it is true. A type II error occurs when the decision maker decides to accept the null hypothesis when in fact it is false. The concept of a consistent statistical test is now introduced.

Definition: Consistent statistical test.   Let $S \subseteq \mathcal{R}^d$. Let F_W be a set of probability mass (density) functions on sample space S. Let $f_W \subseteq F_W$. Let $\mathbf{x}(1),\ldots,$ $\mathbf{x}(n)$ be a sample path of a stochastic process consisting of independent and identically distributed random variables, $\tilde{\mathbf{x}}(1),\ldots, \tilde{\mathbf{x}}(n)$, with the common environmental probability mass (density) function $p_e: S \rightarrow [0, \infty)$. Let the null hypothesis $H_0: p^* \in f_W$ be defined with respect to the probability model F_W, a loss function c, and p_e. The statistical test

$$\varphi_n: S \times S \times \ldots S \rightarrow \{0, 1\}$$

is a *consistent statistical test* if both

1. $p^* \notin f_W$, and
2. $p[\varphi_n(\tilde{\mathbf{x}}(1),\ldots, \tilde{\mathbf{x}}(n)) = 1] \rightarrow 1$ as $n \rightarrow \infty$.   (8.12)

Note that $p^* \notin f_W$ indicates that the null hypothesis is actually false and should be rejected, while $p[\varphi_n(\tilde{\mathbf{x}}(1),\ldots, \tilde{\mathbf{x}}(n)) = 1]$ in (8.12) is the probability of rejecting the null hypothesis. Thus a statistical test is consistent if the probability of a type II error can be made as small as desired given a sufficiently large set of observed data.

The typical structure of most (nonrandomized) statistical tests and all statistical tests considered in this textbook is based upon the following procedure. First, one computes the probability of a type I error with respect to some null hypothesis H_0 using the observed data. Second, one rejects the null hypothesis H_0 if the probability of a type I error is less than some critical threshold known as the *significance level*, a, of the statistical test.

This procedure thus guarantees that the probability of a type I error will always be less than the significance level a. Typically, a is chosen to be equal to

Table 8.1
Type I and Type II errors.

	REALITY: H_0 is true	**REALITY:** H_0 is false
DECISION: Accept H_0	Correct decision	Type II error
DECISION: Reject H_0	Type I error	Correct decision

0.05 or 0.01; or if K statistical tests are done on the same data set, then a is sometimes chosen to be $0.05/K$ or $0.01/K$. Given that the type I error is bounded in this manner, the only other decision error that could be made is a type II error. If the statistical test is consistent, then the probability of a type II error will be minimized automatically, provided the sample size, n, is sufficiently large. Because a detailed analysis of the type II error probability is often difficult, experimenters design their hypothesis-testing experiments so that (1) if the null hypothesis is rejected, one concludes that it is false, and (2) if the null hypothesis is accepted, one concludes that additional data and/or experiments are required to determine its veridity.

8.2.2   Generalized Likelihood Ratio Test (GLRT)

The first statistical test for model selection is the popular Wilks (1938; also see Vuong 1989, and Serfling 1980, 151–160) generalized likelihood ratio test (GLRT). The goal of the GLRT is to decide whether a probability model, F_W, that is a subset of a probability model, G_Y, is sufficient for modeling the environmental distribution p_e that generated the data. It is assumed that the environmental probability mass (density) function, p_e, is a member of G_Y.

In particular, let $p(\cdot \mid \cdot): S \times Y \to [0, \infty)$, where $S \subseteq \mathcal{R}^d$ and $Y \subseteq \mathcal{R}^q$. Define the *full probability model*

$$G_Y = \{p(\cdot \mid \mathbf{y}): \mathbf{y} \in Y\}, \tag{8.13}$$

where each element of G_Y is a probability mass (density) function. Let $\hat{l}_n: Y \times S^n \to [0, \infty)$ define the Kullback-Leibler information criterion (KLIC, or negative log likelihood) sample risk function with respect to G_Y and $p_e = p(\cdot \mid \mathbf{y}^*) \in G_Y$. Let $\mathbf{x}(1),\dots, \mathbf{x}(n)$ be a sample path of the stochastic process $\tilde{\mathbf{x}}(1),\dots, \tilde{\mathbf{x}}(n)$ which consists of independent and identically distributed random vectors with common probability mass (density) function p_e.

Assume $\tilde{\mathbf{y}}_n$ is a strict local minimum of the KLIC sample risk function (i.e., the likelihood function) $\hat{l}_n(\cdot; \{\tilde{\mathbf{x}}(1),\dots, \tilde{\mathbf{x}}(n)\})$ on Y with probability one for n sufficiently large. Let an observed value of $\tilde{\mathbf{y}}_n, \hat{\mathbf{y}}_n$, be a maximum likelihood estimate of G_Y with respect to environmental distribution p_e. Also assume that $\tilde{\mathbf{y}}_n \to \mathbf{y}^*$ with probability one as $n \to \infty$, and that $\tilde{\mathbf{y}}_n$ has an asymptotic Gaussian distribution (see section 8.1).

The purpose of the GLRT is to test the null hypothesis that some subset of r elements of $\mathbf{y}^*$ is equal to a set of r known constants. For example, if one interprets a classical feedforward backpropagation network learning algorithm as computing a set of maximum likelihood estimates, one might be interested in testing the null hypothesis that all of the connection strengths connecting a particular input unit to the rest of the network would converge to zero as the sample size n (i.e., amount of training data) increases (see section 8.3 for additional details).

The null hypothesis for the GLRT is formally expressed as

H_0: $\mathbf{y}^{(1*)} = \mathbf{w}^*$,

where $\mathbf{w}^* \in \mathcal{R}^r$, and the r-dimensional vector $\mathbf{y}^{(1*)}$ is defined such that

$$\mathbf{y}^* = [\mathbf{y}^{(1*)} \, \mathbf{y}^{(2*)}] \in Y \subseteq \mathcal{R}^q,$$

where $\mathbf{y}^{(2*)} \in \mathcal{R}^{q-r}$. F_W, the subset of G_Y that is consistent with the null hypothesis H_0: $\mathbf{y}^{(1*)} = \mathbf{w}^*$, is called the "reduced model" and is defined by

$$F_W = \{ p(\cdot \mid [\mathbf{w}^* \, \mathbf{y}^{(2)}]) \colon \mathbf{y}^{(2)} \in \mathcal{R}^{q-r} \},$$

where $\mathbf{w}^* \in \mathcal{R}^r$, while $p(\cdot \mid \cdot)$ is defined as in (8.13). The relationship between F_W and G_Y is usually referred to as a "nesting relationship," where F_W is "nested" within G_Y.

Define the r-dimensional random vector $\tilde{\mathbf{y}}_n^{(1)}$ and $(q - r)$-dimensional random vector $\tilde{\mathbf{y}}_n^{(2)}$ such that $[\tilde{\mathbf{y}}_n^{(1)} \, \tilde{\mathbf{y}}_n^{(2)}] = \tilde{\mathbf{y}}_n$. The basic strategy underlying the GLRT is to compute the *log likelihood ratio* test statistic

$$\hat{\delta}_n = -2n[\hat{l}_n(\hat{\mathbf{y}}_n; \{\mathbf{x}(1),\dots,\mathbf{x}(n)\}) - \hat{l}_n([\mathbf{w}^* \, \hat{\mathbf{y}}_n^{(2)}]; \{\mathbf{x}(1),\dots,\mathbf{x}(n)\})].$$

Note that $\hat{\delta}_n$ is larger if the likelihood of the observed data given G_Y is greater than the likelihood of the observed data given F_W. The Generalized Likelihood Ratio Test (GLRT) Theorem interprets $\hat{\delta}_n$ as the observed value of a random variable, $\tilde{\delta}_n$, and then shows that $\tilde{\delta}_n$ has a chi-square distribution with r degrees of freedom, given that H_0 is true and that $\tilde{\delta}_n \to \infty$ with probability one as $n \to \infty$ if H_0 is false. Thus $\tilde{\delta}_n$ may be used to construct a consistent statistical test to decide if the probability model G_Y fits the observed data more effectively than the probability model F_W.

Theorem: Generalized Likelihood Ratio Test (GLRT).   Let Y be a convex, closed and bounded subset of $\mathcal{R}^q$. Let $S \subseteq \Omega \subseteq \mathcal{R}^d$. Let $G_Y = \{ p(\cdot \mid \mathbf{y}) \colon \mathbf{y} \in Y \}$ be a probability model. Let $\tilde{\mathbf{x}}(1)$, $\tilde{\mathbf{x}}(2),\dots$ be a sequence of independent and identically distributed random vectors with the common probability mass (density) function $p_e \colon S \to [0, \infty)$. Let $c(\cdot \mid \cdot) \colon Y \times \Omega \to \mathcal{R}$ be a regular loss function with respect to p_e, defined such that $c(\mathbf{y} \mid \mathbf{x}) = -\log[p(\mathbf{x} \mid \mathbf{y})]$ for all $\mathbf{y} \in Y$ and for all $\mathbf{x} \in S$. Assume $l \colon Y \to \mathcal{R}$ and $\hat{l}_n \colon Y \times S^n \to \mathcal{R}$ define the true and sample risk functions respectively with respect to c and p_e. Assume that $p_e(\cdot) = p(\cdot \mid \mathbf{y}^*)$ on S, where $\mathbf{y}^*$ is the unique strict global minimum on Y. Let $\tilde{\mathbf{y}}_1$, $\tilde{\mathbf{y}}_2,\dots$ be a stochastic solution sequence with respect to c and p_e that converges to $\mathbf{y}^*$ such that as $n \to \infty$: $\sqrt{n}(\tilde{\mathbf{y}}_n - \mathbf{y}^*)$ converges in distribution to a Gaussian random vector with mean $\mathbf{0}_q$ and covariance matrix $[\nabla^2 l(\mathbf{y}^*)]^{-1}$. Let $[\tilde{\mathbf{y}}_n^{(1)} \, \tilde{\mathbf{y}}_n^{(2)}] = \tilde{\mathbf{y}}_n$ and let $[\mathbf{y}^{(1*)} \, \mathbf{y}^{(2*)}] = \mathbf{y}^*$ such that $\tilde{\mathbf{y}}_n^{(1)} \to \mathbf{y}^{(1*)}$ with probability one and $\tilde{\mathbf{y}}_n^{(2)} \to \mathbf{y}^{(2*)}$ with probability one as $n \to \infty$. Let $\mathbf{w}^* \in \mathcal{R}^r$ such that $[\mathbf{w}^* \, \mathbf{y}^{(2*)}] \in Y$.

If H_0: $\mathbf{y}^{(1*)} = \mathbf{w}^*$ is true, then

$$\tilde{\delta}_n = -2n[\hat{l}_n(\tilde{\mathbf{y}}_n; \{\tilde{\mathbf{x}}(1),\dots, \tilde{\mathbf{x}}(n)\}) - \hat{l}_n([\mathbf{w}^* \;\; \tilde{\mathbf{y}}_n^{(2)}]; \{\tilde{\mathbf{x}}(1),\dots, \tilde{\mathbf{x}}(n)\})]$$

converges in distribution to a chi-square random variable with r degrees of freedom as $n \to \infty$. If H_0 is false, then $\tilde{\delta}_n \to \infty$ with probability one as $n \to \infty$.

Proof. By assumption, $\log[p(\mathbf{x} \mid \cdot)]$ is a regular loss function and $\{\tilde{\mathbf{y}}_n\}$ is a stochastic solution sequence. The Sample Risk Convergence Theorem therefore implies that

$$\hat{l}_n(\cdot, \{\tilde{\mathbf{x}}(1),\dots, \tilde{\mathbf{x}}(n)\}),$$

and

$$\nabla^2 \hat{l}_n(\cdot, \{\tilde{\mathbf{x}}(1),\dots, \tilde{\mathbf{x}}(n)\})$$

converge with probability one to l and $\nabla^2 l$, respectively, on Y as $n \to \infty$.

Let $\tilde{\mathbf{y}}_n$ be a strict local minimum of $\hat{l}_n(\cdot; \{\tilde{\mathbf{x}}(1),\dots, \tilde{\mathbf{x}}(n)\})$ in the interior of Y with probability one for n sufficiently large. Let $\tilde{\mathbf{X}}_n = \{\tilde{\mathbf{x}}(1),\dots, \tilde{\mathbf{x}}(n)\}$. Expand $\hat{l}_n(\cdot; \tilde{\mathbf{X}}_n)$ in a second-order Taylor expansion about $\tilde{\mathbf{y}}_n$ and evaluate at $[\mathbf{w}^* \;\; \tilde{\mathbf{y}}_n^{(2)}]$ to obtain

$$\hat{l}_n([\mathbf{w}^* \;\; \tilde{\mathbf{y}}_n^{(2)}]; \tilde{\mathbf{X}}_n) = \hat{l}_n(\tilde{\mathbf{y}}_n; \tilde{\mathbf{X}}_n) + [\nabla_{\tilde{\mathbf{y}}_n} \hat{l}_n(\tilde{\mathbf{y}}_n; \tilde{\mathbf{X}}_n)]^T \left[[\mathbf{w}^* \;\; \tilde{\mathbf{y}}_n^{(2)}] - \tilde{\mathbf{y}}_n \right]$$
$$+ (1/2)\left[[\mathbf{w}^* \;\; \tilde{\mathbf{y}}_n^{(2)}] - \tilde{\mathbf{y}}_n \right]^T [\nabla_{\tilde{\mathbf{y}}_n}^2 \hat{l}_n(\tilde{\mathbf{y}}_n; \tilde{\mathbf{X}}_n)] \left[[\mathbf{w}^* \;\; \tilde{\mathbf{y}}_n^{(2)}] - \tilde{\mathbf{y}}_n \right] \qquad (8.14)$$
$$+ O\left(|[\mathbf{w}^* \;\; \tilde{\mathbf{y}}_n^{(2)}] - \tilde{\mathbf{y}}_n|^3 \right)$$

because $\hat{l}_n$ has continuous third partial derivatives on the closed and bounded set Y. And because the Hessian of $\hat{l}_n$ is continuous on Y, $\tilde{\mathbf{y}}_n \to \mathbf{y}^*$ with probability one as $n \to \infty$, and $\nabla^2 \hat{l}_n \to \nabla^2 l$ with probability one as $n \to \infty$:

$$\nabla_{\tilde{\mathbf{y}}_n}^2 \hat{l}_n(\tilde{\mathbf{y}}_n; \tilde{\mathbf{X}}_n) = \mathbf{H}^* + o_p(1), \qquad (8.15)$$

where $\mathbf{H}^* \in \mathscr{R}^{q \times q}$ is defined as the Hessian of l evaluated at $\mathbf{y}^*$.

Because $\tilde{\mathbf{y}}_n$ is a strict global minimum of $\hat{l}_n(\cdot; \tilde{\mathbf{x}}(1),\dots, \tilde{\mathbf{x}}(n))$ on Y with probability one for sufficiently large n, the gradient term in (8.14) vanishes with probability one for n sufficiently large. Also $\mathbf{H}^*$ is positive definite (by the Strict Local Minimum Test of chapter 5). Thus, substituting (8.15) into (8.14), multiplying by $2n$, and using the definition of $\tilde{\delta}_n$,

$$\tilde{\delta}_n = n[[\mathbf{w}^* \;\; \tilde{\mathbf{y}}_n^{(2)}] - \tilde{\mathbf{y}}_n]^T \mathbf{H}^* [[\mathbf{w}^* \;\; \tilde{\mathbf{y}}_n^{(2)}] - \tilde{\mathbf{y}}_n] + \tilde{R}_n, \qquad (8.16)$$

where the remainder term, $\tilde{R}_n$, is given by

$$\tilde{R}_n = o_p(1)O(n|[\mathbf{w}^* \;\; \tilde{\mathbf{y}}_n^{(2)}] - \tilde{\mathbf{y}}_n|^2) + O(n|[\mathbf{w}^* \;\; \tilde{\mathbf{y}}_n^{(2)}] - \tilde{\mathbf{y}}_n|^3). \qquad (8.17)$$

Case 1: Assume H_0: $\mathbf{y}^{(1*)} = \mathbf{w}^*$ is *true*. Because $\sqrt{n}(\tilde{\mathbf{y}}_n - \mathbf{y}^*)$ converges in distribution as $n \to \infty$ by assumption, this implies that $O(\sqrt{n}|[\mathbf{w}^* \;\; \tilde{\mathbf{y}}_n^{(2)}] - \tilde{\mathbf{y}}_n|)$ is bounded in probability (Serfling, 1980, 8). Using corollary 2.36 of White

(1984, 26), this observation in conjunction with the observation that $\tilde{\mathbf{y}}_n \to \mathbf{y}^*$ with probability one as $n \to \infty$ implies that the remainder term $\tilde{R}_n$ in (8.16) converges in probability to zero as $n \to \infty$. Using $\tilde{R}_n = o_p(1)$ and the definition

$$[[\mathbf{w}^* \; \tilde{\mathbf{y}}_n^{(2)}] - \tilde{\mathbf{y}}_n] = [[\mathbf{w}^* - \tilde{\mathbf{y}}_n^{(1)}] \quad \mathbf{0}_{q-r}],$$

(8.16) reduces to

$$\tilde{\delta}_n = n[\mathbf{y}^{(1*)} - \tilde{\mathbf{y}}_n^{(1)}]^T \mathbf{H}^{(1,1)*}[\mathbf{y}^{(1*)} - \tilde{\mathbf{y}}_n^{(1)}] + o_p(1), \tag{8.18}$$

where the ijth element of the r-dimensional matrix $\mathbf{H}^{(1,1)*}$ ($i, j = 1 \ldots r$), is defined as the element in the ith row and jth column of $\mathbf{H}^*$.

Note that $\mathbf{H}^{(1,1)*}$ is a symmetric positive definite matrix because $\mathbf{H}^*$ is a symmetric positive definite matrix. Note that the first term on the right-hand side of (8.18) converges in distribution as $n \to \infty$ to a random vector that is the sum of the squares of r Gaussian random variables each with mean zero and variance equal to one (Chi-Square/Normal Distribution Theorem, chapter 4). By Slutsky's Theorem, the right-hand side of (8.18) converges in distribution to a chi-square random variable with r degrees of freedom.

Case 2: Assume H_0 is false. From the definition of $\tilde{\delta}_n$,

$$\frac{\tilde{\delta}_n}{n} = -2\left[\hat{l}_n(\tilde{\mathbf{y}}_n; \{\tilde{\mathbf{x}}(1),\ldots,\tilde{\mathbf{x}}(n)\}) - \hat{l}_n\left([\mathbf{w}^* \; \tilde{\mathbf{y}}_n^{(2)}]; \{\tilde{\mathbf{x}}(1),\ldots,\tilde{\mathbf{x}}(n)\}\right)\right]. \tag{8.19}$$

By assumption, $\tilde{\mathbf{y}}_n^{(2)}$ converges with probability one to $\mathbf{y}^{(2*)}$ as $n \to \infty$. The right-hand side of (8.19) converges with probability one to a nonzero real number as $n \to \infty$ because (i) $\hat{l}_n(\cdot; \{\tilde{\mathbf{x}}(1),\ldots,\tilde{\mathbf{x}}(n)\})$ converges to $l(\cdot)$ on Y with probability one as $n \to \infty$, and (ii) $l(\mathbf{y}^*) < l([\mathbf{w}^* \; \mathbf{y}^{(2*)}])$ ($\mathbf{y}^*$ being the unique strict global minimum of l on Y). Therefore, $\tilde{\delta}_n \to \infty$ with probability one as $n \to \infty$ if H_0 is false. ∎

Using the Generalized Likelihood Ratio Test (GLRT)

The key steps required for using the GLRT are as follows:

- Step 1: Check that loss function, $-\log[p(\cdot \mid \cdot)]$, is regular.
- Step 2: Compute maximum likelihood estimate $\hat{\mathbf{y}}_n \in \mathscr{R}^q$ for full model.
- Step 3: Check that $\hat{l}_n$ provides good fit to observed data and that $\hat{\mathbf{y}}_n$ is strict local minimum.
- Step 4: Compute maximum likelihood estimate $\hat{\mathbf{y}}_n^{(2)} \in \mathscr{R}^{q-r}$ for reduced model such that r-dimensional vector $\mathbf{y}^{(1*)} = \mathbf{w}^*$.
- Step 5: Use standard cumulative chi-square distribution table or computer program to compute critical value $\chi_a^2(r)$ such that chi-square random variable with r degrees of freedom will exceed $\chi_a^2(r)$ with probability (significance level) a.

- Step 6: Reject the null hypothesis that $\mathbf{y}^{(1*)} = \mathbf{w}^*$ if $\hat{\delta}_n > \chi_a^2(r)$, where $\hat{\delta}_n$ is observed value of $\tilde{\delta}_n$.

Note that two of the critical assumptions of the GLRT are that (1) the reduced model is nested in the full model, and (2) the full model is correctly specified with respect to the environmental probability mass (density) function. Vuong (1989; see Golden 1995 for a review; see also problem 8-3) has developed an important generalization of the GLRT that can be used to compare probability models that are not necessarily fully nested, and which does not require that either probability model contain the environmental probability distribution p_e.

8.2.3 Wald Test

Wald (1943) proposed another useful hypothesis-testing technique that White (1989a,b) has noted is helpful for evaluating what an ANN system has learned. The Wald test examines hypotheses that certain subsets (or linear combinations) of connection strengths or weights in a *particular* ANN learning system are equal to zero. Thus, unlike the GLRT approach, only a single network needs to be trained.

To begin our discussion of the Wald test, let the q-dimensional vector $\mathbf{w}^*$ be a strict local minimum of a true risk function l. The null hypothesis H_0 for one version of the Wald test may be defined as H_0: $\mathbf{R}\mathbf{w}^* = \mathbf{r}$, where $\mathbf{R}$ is an $m \times q$ matrix ($m \leq q$) of rank m called the *selection matrix,* and $\mathbf{r}$ is an m-dimensional column vector called the *selection vector.* Different choices of $\mathbf{R}$ and $\mathbf{r}$ result in different null hypotheses. For example, let $\mathbf{r}$ be a one-dimensional vector (scalar) consisting of the number zero. Let $\mathbf{R}$ be a $1 \times q$ selection matrix which contains the number one in position j and zeros in all remaining $(q - 1)$ elements in the selection matrix. The null hypothesis, H_0: $\mathbf{R}\mathbf{w}^* = \mathbf{r}$, then reduces to H_0: $w_j^* = 0$, where w_j^* is the jth element of $\mathbf{w}^*$. The key theorem for the Wald test, typically used in conjunction with the Asymptotic Sampling Error Theorem, is now presented.

Theorem: Wald Test.   Let W be a convex, closed, and bounded subset of $\mathcal{R}^q$. Let $\mathbf{w}^*$ be in the interior of W. Let $\tilde{\mathbf{w}}_1, \tilde{\mathbf{w}}_2, \ldots$ be a stochastic sequence converging to $\mathbf{w}^*$ such that as $n \to \infty$, $\sqrt{n}(\tilde{\mathbf{w}}_n - \mathbf{w}^*)$ converges in distribution to a Gaussian random vector with mean zero and real symmetric positive definite covariance matrix $\mathbf{C}^*$. Define the null hypothesis

H_0: $\mathbf{R}\mathbf{w}^* = \mathbf{r}$,

where $\mathbf{R}$ is an $m \times q$ matrix of rank m and let $\mathbf{r}$ be an m-dimensional column vector. Let

$$\tilde{\mathcal{W}}_n = n[\mathbf{R}\tilde{\mathbf{w}}_n - \mathbf{r}]^T[\mathbf{R}\mathbf{C}^*\mathbf{R}^T]^{-1}[\mathbf{R}\tilde{\mathbf{w}}_n - \mathbf{r}]. \tag{8.20}$$

If the null hypothesis H_0 is true, then as $n \to \infty$: $\tilde{\mathcal{W}}_n$ converges in distribution to a chi-square random variable with m degrees of freedom. If the null hypothesis H_0 is false, then $\tilde{\mathcal{W}}_n \to \infty$ with probability one as $n \to \infty$.

Proof.   Consider the following two cases.

Case 1. Assume H_0: $\mathbf{Rw}^* = \mathbf{r}$ is *true*. Define

$$\tilde{\mathbf{z}}_n = \sqrt{n}[\mathbf{RC}^*\mathbf{R}^T]^{-1/2}[\mathbf{R}\tilde{\mathbf{w}}_n - \mathbf{r}].$$

Note that, as $n \to \infty$, $\tilde{\mathbf{z}}_n$ converges in distribution to a Gaussian random vector with mean zero and covariance matrix equal to an identity matrix of dimension m because $\tilde{\mathbf{z}}_n$ is a continuous linear function of $\tilde{\mathbf{w}}_n$ (see Linear Transformation of a Gaussian Random Vector Theorem in chapter 4). Thus $|\tilde{\mathbf{z}}_n|^2$ converges in distribution to a sum of the squares of m independent normal Gaussian random variables with zero mean and unit variance as $n \to \infty$, which has a chi-square distribution with m degrees of freedom (Chi-Square/Normal Distribution Theorem, chapter 4). Thus, if H_0 is true, $\tilde{\mathcal{W}}_n$ converges in distribution to a chi-square random variable with m degrees of freedom as $n \to \infty$.

Case 2. Assume H_0 is *false*. Given that $\tilde{\mathbf{w}}_n \to \mathbf{w}^*$ with probability one as $n \to \infty$ and $\mathbf{Rw}^* \neq \mathbf{r}$,

$$\frac{\tilde{\mathcal{W}}_n}{n} \to K$$

with probability one as $n \to \infty$, where K is a finite positive real number because $\mathbf{RC}^*\mathbf{R}^T$ is positive definite. Therefore, $\tilde{\mathcal{W}}_n \to \infty$ with probability one as $n \to \infty$.   ∎

Using the Wald Test

Typically, the Wald test theorem is used in conjunction with the Convergence of Strict Local Minimum Theorem (chapter 7) and the Asymptotic Sampling Error Theorem to characterize the probability distribution of $\tilde{\mathbf{w}}_n$ for n sufficiently large. The mechanics of using the Wald test are straightforward:

• Step 1: Check to make sure that stochastic sequence of q-dimensional random vectors $\sqrt{n}(\tilde{\mathbf{w}}_n - \mathbf{w}^*)$ converges in distribution to a Gaussian random vector with mean zero and covariance matrix $\mathbf{C}^*$.

• Step 2: Estimate Wald statistic, $\tilde{\mathcal{W}}_n$ in (8.20), given particular sample path $\mathbf{x}(1),\dots,\mathbf{x}(n)$, to obtain number $\hat{\mathcal{W}}_n$ with respect to a given null hypothesis, H_0: $\mathbf{Rw}^* = \mathbf{r}$, where $\mathbf{R}$ is an $m \times q$ matrix of rank m.

• Step 3: Decide H_0 is true if $\hat{\mathcal{W}}_n > \chi_a^2(m)$. Otherwise, reject H_0 at the a significance level.

One typical application of the Wald test in ANN system applications is to identify which subsets of connection strengths of the ANN system may be set equal to zero without a loss in generalization performance. These connection strengths can then be set equal to zero in order to obtain a reduced model. The original ANN learning system (i.e., the full model) can then be compared with the reduced model, using the GLRT.

Another typical application of the Wald test in ANN learning system applications is to identify redundant patterns of connection strengths. For example, the null hypothesis that the mapping from the input units to hidden unit 1 is identical to the mapping from the input units to hidden unit 2 in an ANN system may be tested (see problem 8.2-5).

8.3   ANN Applications

8.3.1   Prediction Error Bounds

Problem.   Let W be a closed, bounded, and convex subset of $\mathcal{R}^q$. Let U be a closed, bounded, and convex subset of $\mathcal{R}^d$. A multilayer feedforward backpropagation network may be expressed as a function $\mathbf{\Phi}\colon U \times W \to \mathcal{R}^m$ with continuous third partial derivatives on W such that $\mathbf{r} = \mathbf{\Phi}(\mathbf{s}, \mathbf{w})$, where $\mathbf{w} \in W$ is the connection strength parameter vector, $\mathbf{s} \in U$ is the input stimulus vector, and $\mathbf{r} \in \mathcal{R}^m$ is the output response vector. Let

$$\tilde{\mathbf{X}}_n = \{(\tilde{\mathbf{s}}^1, \tilde{\mathbf{o}}^1),\ldots(\tilde{\mathbf{s}}^n, \tilde{\mathbf{o}}^n)\}$$

be a sequence of independently and identically distributed random vectors such that an observed value, $\mathbf{X}_n$, of $\tilde{\mathbf{X}}_n$ is defined as

$$\mathbf{X}_n = \{(\mathbf{s}^1, \mathbf{o}^1),\ldots(\mathbf{s}^n, \mathbf{o}^n)\},$$

where $\mathbf{s}^k \in U$ and $\mathbf{o}^k \in \mathcal{R}^m$ for $k = 1 \ldots n$. Let $Y = W \times (0, \infty)$.

Assume that the learning algorithm seeks a strict local (but preferably strict global) minimum of the sample risk function, $\hat{l}_n(\cdot\,; \mathbf{X}_n)\colon Y \to [0, \infty)$, defined such that for all $\mathbf{w} \in W$ and for all $\sigma^2 \in (0, \infty)$:

$$\hat{l}_n\big([\mathbf{w}, \sigma^2]; \mathbf{X}_n\big) = (1/[2n\sigma^2]) \sum_{i=1}^{n} \big|\mathbf{o}^i - \mathbf{\Phi}(\mathbf{s}^i, \mathbf{w})\big|^2.$$

Assume the backpropagation network provides a reasonable fit to the data. That is, assume there exists a q-dimensional real vector $\mathbf{w}^*$ and real number σ^2 such that

$$\tilde{\mathbf{o}}^i = \mathbf{\Phi}(\tilde{\mathbf{s}}^i, \mathbf{w}^*) + \tilde{\mathbf{n}},$$

where $\tilde{\mathbf{n}}$ is an m-dimensional Gaussian random vector with mean vector zero and covariance matrix $\sigma^2 \mathbf{I}$. Assume $0 < \sigma^2 < \infty$.

Show that the function $\hat{l}_n$ is a negative log likelihood function plus some constant. Note there are $(q + 1)$ free parameters: the q-dimensional real vector

w and the real scalar variable σ^2. Write down an explicit expression for the Gaussian density function. Show that the classification dynamics of the ANN system defines a MAP estimation algorithm with respect to an appropriate probability model.

Derive a simple closed form expression for a maximum likelihood estimate of σ^2, $\hat{\sigma}_n^2$, given the maximum likelihood estimate, $\hat{\mathbf{w}}_n$, of $\mathbf{w}^*$. Show how $\hat{\sigma}_n$ may be used to derive a confidence interval on the predictions of the backpropagation network *without* using either the Asymptotic Sampling Error Theorem or the bootstrap algorithm if $|\tilde{\mathbf{w}}_n - \mathbf{w}^*| \ll \sigma^2$.

Solution. Because the data-generating process is assumed to be a good fit to the network architecture, the probability model for the network is defined by the formula

$$p(\mathbf{r}|\mathbf{s}, \mathbf{w}, \sigma^2) = [\sigma^2 \pi]^{-m/2} \exp\left[-(|\mathbf{r} - \mathbf{\Phi}(\mathbf{s}, \mathbf{w})|^2)/(2\sigma^2)\right],$$

where the parameters of the distribution function are $\mathbf{w}$ and σ^2.

The log likelihood risk function, l_{ml}, is defined as

$$l_{ml}([\mathbf{w}, \sigma^2]) = -(1/n)\sum_{i=1}^{n} \log[p(\mathbf{r}^i | \mathbf{s}^i, \mathbf{w}, \sigma^2)],$$

$$l_{ml}([\mathbf{w}, \sigma^2]) = \left[(1/(2n\sigma^2))\sum_{i=1}^{n} |\mathbf{r}^i - \mathbf{\Phi}(\mathbf{s}^i, \mathbf{w})|^2\right] + (m/2) \log[\pi\sigma^2].$$

The maximum likelihood estimates, $\hat{\mathbf{w}}_n$ and $\hat{\sigma}_n^2$, are obtained by taking partial derivatives of l_{ml} with respect to $\mathbf{w}$ and σ^2, evaluating the resulting partial derivatives at $\hat{\mathbf{w}}_n$ and $\hat{\sigma}_n^2$, and then setting the entire expression equal to a vector of zeros. Note that

$$\frac{dl_{ml}}{d[\sigma^2]} = -(1/(2n\sigma^4))\sum_{i=1}^{n} |\mathbf{r}^i - \mathbf{\Phi}(\mathbf{s}^i, \hat{\mathbf{w}}_n)|^2 + (m/2\sigma^2). \tag{8.21}$$

The maximum likelihood estimate, $\hat{\sigma}_n^2$, is computed by evaluating (8.21) at the point $(\hat{\mathbf{w}}_n, \hat{\sigma}_n^2)$, setting (8.21) equal to zero, and solving for $\hat{\sigma}_n^2$ to obtain

$$(1/(2n\hat{\sigma}_n^4))\sum_{i=1}^{n} |\mathbf{r}^i - \mathbf{\Phi}(\mathbf{s}^i, \hat{\mathbf{w}}_n)|^2 - (m/2\hat{\sigma}_n^2) = 0,$$

$$\hat{\sigma}_n^2 = (mn)^{-1}\sum_{i=1}^{n} |\mathbf{r}^i - \mathbf{\Phi}(\mathbf{s}^i, \hat{\mathbf{w}}_n)|^2.$$

Thus, the maximum likelihood estimate $\hat{\sigma}_n^2$ has been expressed as a simple function of $\hat{\mathbf{w}}_n$.

The maximum likelihood estimate $\hat{\mathbf{w}}_n$ given any positive σ^2 is obtained by setting the gradient of l_{ml} evaluated at $\hat{\mathbf{w}}_n$ equal to a vector of zeros so that

$$\nabla_{\hat{\mathbf{w}}_n} l_{ml} = \nabla_{\hat{\mathbf{w}}_n} (1/(2\sigma^2))(1/n) \sum_{i=1}^{n} |\mathbf{r}^i - \mathbf{\Phi}(\mathbf{s}^i, \hat{\mathbf{w}}_n)|^2 = \mathbf{0}_q. \tag{8.22}$$

Note that the solution $\hat{\mathbf{w}}_n$ obtained by a batch backpropagation algorithm is a strict local minimum of $\hat{l}_n$ for all positive σ^2, and thus satisfies (8.22). Once $\hat{\mathbf{w}}_n$ has been computed, the formula previously derived for $\hat{\sigma}_n^2$ may be used to estimate σ^2.

Approximate confidence intervals on the ANN system's predictions, using the above estimates, are now derived. In particular, let $\hat{r}_{n,i}$ be the ith element of $\mathbf{\Phi}(\mathbf{s}, \hat{\mathbf{w}}_n)$ (i.e., the activation level of the ith output unit in a multilayer feedforward backpropagation network). Assuming a $(1 - a)100$ percent confidence interval, it follows that the probability is approximately $(1 - a)$ that $\tilde{r}_{n,i}$ (the unobservable "correct" prediction) is greater than $\hat{r}_{n,i} - \hat{\sigma}_n Z_a$ and less than $\hat{r}_{n,i} + \hat{\sigma}_n Z_a$. For example, suppose that $\hat{\sigma}_n = 0.01$ and that $\hat{r}_{n,i} = 0.8$. Assume that a 95 percent confidence interval is desired so that $a = 0.05$ and $Z_{0.05} = 1.96$. Then the probability is approximately 95 percent that $\tilde{r}_{n,i}$ lies in the interval $[0.8 - 0.01(1.96), 0.8 + 0.01(1.96)]$.

8.3.2 Wald Test Analysis of Hidden Unit Representations

Problem. A classical backpropagation network is proposed to predict alternative diagnoses of some medical condition given a set of symptoms. Thus the medical database consists of n records of the form

$$\mathbf{X}_n = \{[\mathbf{s}(1), \mathbf{o}(1)], [\mathbf{s}(2), \mathbf{o}(2)], \ldots, [\mathbf{s}(n), \mathbf{o}(n)]\},$$

where $[\mathbf{s}(i), \mathbf{o}(i)]$ is the ith record in the database and $\mathbf{s}(i)$ is the d-dimensional input symptom vector and $\mathbf{o}(i)$ is the m-dimensional output diagnosis vector. It is assumed that the n data records are a sample path of a stochastic process

$$\tilde{\mathbf{X}}_n = \{[\tilde{\mathbf{s}}(1), \tilde{\mathbf{o}}(1)], [\tilde{\mathbf{s}}(2), \tilde{\mathbf{o}}(2)], \ldots [\tilde{\mathbf{s}}(n), \tilde{\mathbf{o}}(n)]\},$$

consisting of n independent and identically distributed $(d + m)$-dimensional random vectors according to some finite environmental probability mass function on some finite sample space that is a subset of $\mathcal{R}^{d+m}$.

It will be assumed that the researcher has used the backpropagation algorithm to construct a reasonable input to hidden unit mapping and now wants to decide which hidden units are relevant. The researcher's strategy is to use the results of backpropagation learning to define a function $\mathbf{\Phi}$: $\mathcal{R}^d \rightarrow \mathcal{R}^h$ that maps a given input unit activation pattern $\mathbf{s}(i)$ into a hidden unit activation pattern $\mathbf{h}(i)$ according to the rule $\mathbf{h}(i) = \mathbf{\Phi}(\mathbf{s}(i))$. In order to evaluate the characteristics of the input to hidden unit mapping, $\mathbf{\Phi}$, the researcher then retrains the network to reestimate $\mathbf{W}$ and $\mathbf{b}$, using the originally estimated parameters for the hidden to output unit mapping as initial guesses for the learning algorithm, but does *not* reestimate $\mathbf{\Phi}$. The kth element of $\mathbf{r}(i)$, $r_k(i)$, is interpreted as the network's probability that the patient has disease k, given the set of symptoms, $\mathbf{s}(i)$. That is, $r_k(i) = p(\tilde{o}_k = 1 \mid \mathbf{s}(i))$ where $\tilde{o}_k \in \{0, 1\}$, $k = 1,\ldots, m$.

The architecture of the network is specified by

$$\mathbf{r}(i) = \underline{\mathscr{S}}(\mathbf{W}\mathbf{h}(i) + \mathbf{b}),$$

where $\underline{\mathscr{S}}: \mathscr{R}^m \to (0, 1)^m$ is defined such that the ith element of $\underline{\mathscr{S}}$ is the function $\mathscr{S}: \mathscr{R} \to (0, 1)$, which in turn is defined such that for all $x \in \mathscr{R}$:

$$\underline{\mathscr{S}}(x) = \frac{1}{1 + \exp(-x)}.$$

Quasi-maximum likelihood estimates of the connection strengths, $(\hat{\mathbf{W}}_n, \hat{\mathbf{b}}_n)$ are then computed, where $\hat{\mathbf{W}}_n \in \mathscr{R}^{m \times h}$ and $\hat{\mathbf{b}}_n \in \mathscr{R}^m$. It can be shown (problem 8-4) that these quasi-maximum likelihood estimates are unique.

The following notation will be useful here. Let the operator .* indicate element by element multiplication, so that if $\mathbf{a}$ and $\mathbf{b}$ are m-dimensional vectors, then $\mathbf{a}$.* $\mathbf{b}$ is an m-dimensional vector whose kth element ($k = 1\ldots m$) is $a_k b_k$, where a_k is the kth element of $\mathbf{a}$ and b_k is the kth element of $\mathbf{b}$. The notation $\mathbf{log}[\mathbf{x}]$ means that $\mathbf{log}[\mathbf{x}]$ is a real vector of the same dimension as $\mathbf{x} = [x_1,\ldots, x_d]$, where the ith element of $\mathbf{log}[\mathbf{x}]$ is equal to $\log[x_i]$.

Now assume $(\hat{\mathbf{W}}_n, \hat{\mathbf{b}}_n)$ is a strict local minimum of the sample KLIC risk function $\hat{l}_n$ defined such that

$$\hat{l}_n([\mathbf{W}, \mathbf{b}]) = -(1/n)\sum_{i=1}^{n} \mathbf{log}[\mathbf{o}(i) \text{ .* } \mathbf{r}(i) + (\mathbf{1}_m - \mathbf{o}(i)) \text{ .* } (\mathbf{1}_m - \mathbf{r}(i))],$$

which can be equivalently expressed as

$$\hat{l}_n([\mathbf{W}, \mathbf{b}]) = -(1/n)\sum_{i=1}^{n} [\mathbf{o}(i) \text{ .* } \mathbf{log}[\mathbf{r}(i)] + (\mathbf{1}_m - \mathbf{o}(i)) \text{ .* } \mathbf{log}[\mathbf{1}_m - \mathbf{r}(i)]]$$

because the kth element of $\mathbf{o}(i)$, $o_k(i)$, is defined such that $o_k(i) \in \{0, 1\}$ for $k = 1\ldots m$ and $i = 1\ldots n$.

Derive a Wald test in order to decide whether the jth hidden unit in the ANN system is relevant for the prediction task. Allow for the presence of model misspecification by *not* making the assumption that the ANN system probability model is correctly specified with respect to the environmental probability mass function.

Solution.   For convenience, let $\mathbf{Y} = [\mathbf{W} \ \mathbf{b}]$ and define the $(h + 1)$-dimensional column vector $\mathbf{u}(i) = [\mathbf{h}(i) \ 1]$, $i = 1\ldots n$. Let $\mathbf{y}_k$ be the kth row of $\mathbf{Y}$ for $k = 1\ldots m$. Then

$$\nabla_{\mathbf{y}_k} \hat{l}_n = -(1/n)\sum_{i=1}^{n} [o_k(i) - r_k(i)][\mathbf{u}(i)]^T$$

and

$$\hat{\mathbf{A}}_n^k = \nabla_{\mathbf{y}_k}^2 \hat{l}_n = (1/n)\sum_{i=1}^{n} r_k(i)[1 - r_k(i)]\mathbf{u}(i)[\mathbf{u}(i)]^T.$$

Also, the gradient of

$$-[o_k(i)\log\,[r_k(i)] + (1 - o_k(i))\log\,[1 - r_k(i)]]$$

is given by

$$\mathbf{g}_i^k = -[o_k(i) - r_k(i)][\mathbf{u}(i)]^T.$$

Then

$$\hat{\mathbf{B}}_n^k = (1/n)\sum_{i=1}^{n} \mathbf{g}_i \mathbf{g}_i^T = (1/n)\sum_{i=1}^{n} [o_k(i) - r_k(i)]^2 \mathbf{u}(i)[\mathbf{u}(i)]^T.$$

Define a vector $\mathbf{y}$ which is $(h + 1)$ m-dimensional whose first $(h + 1)$ elements are the first row of $\mathbf{Y}$, whose second $(h + 1)$ elements are the second row $\mathbf{Y}$, and so on. Let $\hat{\mathbf{A}}_n$ be the Hessian of $\hat{l}_n$ with respect to $\mathbf{y} \in \mathcal{R}^{m(h+1)}$. Let $\hat{\mathbf{B}}_n$ be the gradient of $\hat{l}_n$ with respect to $\mathbf{y} \in \mathcal{R}^{m(h+1)}$. Now note that $\hat{\mathbf{A}}_n$ is a $(h + 1)$ m-dimensional matrix with m submatrices on its main diagonal, where the kth submatrix is the $(h + 1)$-dimensional submatrix $\hat{\mathbf{A}}_n^k$, and whose remaining $(m^2 - m)$ off-diagonal submatrices contain only zeros.

Note that $\hat{\mathbf{B}}_n$ is a $(h + 1)$ m-dimensional matrix with m submatrices on its main diagonal, where the jkth submatrix is the $(h + 1)$-dimensional submatrix $\hat{\mathbf{B}}_n^{j,k}$, which is given by the formula

$$\hat{\mathbf{B}}_n^{j,k} = (1/n)\sum_{i=1}^{n} [o_j(i) - r_j(i)][o_k(i) - r_k(i)]\mathbf{u}(i)\mathbf{u}(i)^T.$$

Substituting the formulas for $\hat{\mathbf{A}}_n$ and $\hat{\mathbf{B}}_n$ (estimates of $\mathbf{A}^*$ and $\mathbf{B}^*$, respectively) into (8.1),

$$\hat{\mathbf{C}}_n = [\hat{\mathbf{A}}_n]^{-1}\hat{\mathbf{B}}_n[\hat{\mathbf{A}}_n]^{-1}.$$

Let $\hat{\mathbf{y}}_n \in \mathcal{R}^{m(h+1)}$ be the quasi-maximum likelihood estimate of $\mathbf{y}^* \in \mathcal{R}^{m(h+1)}$, which is the strict local minimum of the risk function associated with this hypothesis-testing problem. Let the solution $\mathbf{Y}^*$ be a matrix with m rows and $(h + 1)$ columns such that the kth row of $\mathbf{Y}^*$, $\mathbf{y}_k^*$, is defined by the $[(k - 1)(h + 1) + 1]$th through $k(h + 1)$th elements of $\mathbf{y}^*$. Let $\mathbf{W}^*$ and $\mathbf{b}^*$ be defined such that $\mathbf{Y}^* = [\mathbf{W}^* \ \mathbf{b}^*]$.

To test the null hypothesis H_0 that the set of connection strengths from hidden unit j to the m output units is equal to zero, choose a selection matrix $\mathbf{R}_j$ such that $\mathbf{R}_j\mathbf{y}^*$ is equal to the jth column of $\mathbf{W}^*$. Thus the null hypothesis is formally expressed as

H_0: $\mathbf{R}_j \mathbf{y}^* = \mathbf{0}_m$

and is tested by computing the Wald statistic

$$\hat{W}_n = n \hat{\mathbf{y}}_n^T \mathbf{R}_j^T [\mathbf{R}_j \hat{\mathbf{C}}_n \mathbf{R}_j^T]^{-1} \mathbf{R}_j \hat{\mathbf{y}}_n.$$

The null hypothesis H_0 is rejected (i.e., conclude that the jth hidden unit in the ANN system is relevant for the prediction task) if $\hat{W}_n > \chi_a^2(m)$. If $\hat{W}_n \leq \chi_a^2(m)$, then conclude that the jth hidden unit may be eliminated without a loss in generalization performance.

8.3.3   Comparing Different ANN Systems with the GLRT

Problem.   Let U be a closed, bounded, and convex subset of $\mathcal{R}^d$. Let Y be a closed, bounded, and convex subset of $\mathcal{R}^q$. Let $\varphi\colon U \times Y \to (0, 1)$ define a backpropagation network architecture such that the activation level of the network's output unit, $r = \varphi(\mathbf{s}, \mathbf{y})$, where $\mathbf{s} \in U$ is an input unit activation pattern and $\mathbf{y} \in Y$ is a connection strength parameter vector. Assume $-\log[\varphi(\mathbf{s}, \cdot)]$: $Y \to (0, 1)$ has continuous third partial derivatives on Y for all $\mathbf{s} \in U$. Since $r \in (0, 1)$, assume that r is the ANN system's estimate of the conditional probability that a given response feedback signal of the ANN system, $\tilde{o}$, will take on the value of one, given $\mathbf{s}$ and $\mathbf{y}$. That is, assume $r = p(\tilde{o} = 1 \mid \mathbf{s}, \mathbf{y})$ defines the ANN system's subjective probability mass function for a given $\mathbf{s}$ and $\mathbf{y}$ where $\tilde{o} \in \{0, 1\}$.

The parameters of the network are estimated by searching for a strict local minimum of the Kullback-Leibler information criterion (KLIC) sample risk function, $\hat{l}_n$, given the training data defined by the formula

$$\hat{l}_n(\mathbf{y}; \{(\mathbf{s}(i), \mathbf{o}(i))\}) = -(1/n) \sum_{i=1}^{n} \log[o(i)r(i) + (1 - o(i))(1 - r(i))],$$

where $o(i) \in \{0, 1\}$,

$r(i) = \underline{\mathcal{S}}(\mathbf{q}^T \mathbf{h}(i) + b)$,

and

$\mathbf{h}(i) = \underline{\mathcal{S}}(\mathbf{V}\mathbf{s}(i) + \mathbf{f})$,

where in turn $\mathbf{V}$ is a $N_h \times N_d$ matrix, $\mathbf{f}$ is an N_h-dimensional column vector, b is a scalar, $\mathbf{q}$ is a N_h-dimensional column vector, and $\mathbf{y}$ is a vector containing the elements of $\mathbf{V}$, $\mathbf{f}$, $\mathbf{q}$, and b. The function $\underline{\mathcal{S}}\colon \mathcal{R}^m \to (0, 1)^m$ is a vector-valued function that maps the kth ($k = 1 \ldots m$) element, x_k, of an m-dimensional real vector into $1/(1 + \exp[-x_k])$. A backpropagation network with a log likelihood error function is trained by systematically varying the number of input units (i.e., varying the column dimension of $\mathbf{V}$ that is N_d).

The backpropagation network is originally trained with 3 input units and 10 hidden units. The learning process in this case converged to a critical point (i.e., the gradient of the error function vanished). Moreover, numerical simulations where values of the error function were computed in the vicinity of the critical point suggest that the critical point is a strict local minimum; for this reason, it is assumed to be so. In addition, the conditional probabilities of response category given stimulus in the network seem to reflect fairly accurately those observed in the environment; for this reason, the probability model is assumed to be correctly specified.

Now note that, with 3 input units, 10 hidden units, and 1 output unit, the network has 10 bias parameters for the 10 hidden units, 1 bias parameter for the output unit, 30 weight parameters for the input to hidden unit connection strengths, and 10 weight parameters for the hidden unit to output unit connection strengths. Thus the number of free parameters of this correctly specified "full model" is equal to 51. Note that a necessary but not a sufficient condition for a strict local minimum of the KLIC sample risk function to exist is that the number of elements in the training set must be greater than or equal to the number of free parameters in the model, here 51 (see problem 8-6). Let $\hat{\mathbf{w}}_0$ denote the identity of this strict local minimum.

The estimated Kullback-Leibler cross-entropy error, $\hat{l}_n$, is recorded for the correctly specified 51-parameter full model. The number of "effective" input units was then changed by constraining a subset of the weights in the correctly specified full model to be equal to zero. The resulting constrained architecture will be called the "reduced model." Using the same set of training stimuli and the weight vector $\hat{\mathbf{w}}_0$ as the "initial guess" for the weights in the reduced model, a new strict local minimum in the vicinity of $\hat{\mathbf{w}}_0$ is obtained through additional learning trials.

The following set of simulation data was then collected using the procedure described above. There were 450 training stimuli in the training set. Note that if N_h is the number of hidden units and N_d is the number of input units, then the total number of parameters in a backpropagation network with 1 output unit, N_h hidden units, and N_d input units is equal to $(1 + N_h) + (N_h + N_h N_d)$ because there are $(1 + N_h)$ bias parameters and $(N_h + N_h N_d)$ pairwise connection weights.

Table 8.2 shows some "made-up" simulation data designed to illustrate the application of the GLRT to ANN system evaluation. (For an actual application of these techniques to a real-world application, see Niederberger, Pursell, and Golden 1996.) The full model is estimated in simulation 1 and found to provide a good fit to the data, indicating that the ANN system's probability model is correctly specified in this situation. The parameter estimates are found to be a strict local minimum. The third input unit is then removed and the parameters of the full model are reestimated in simulation 2 using as initial weights the

Table 8.2
Simulation data (GLRT problem).

Simulation number	Number of hidden units	Number of input units	Number of weights	$\hat{l}_n$
1	10	3	51	0.0210
2	10	2	41	0.0450

weights estimated in simulation 1. It is observed that the algorithm in simulation 2 has converged to a strict local minimum close to the strict local minimum obtained from simulation 1.

Use the Generalized Likelihood Ratio Test (GLRT) to decide whether the third input unit should be included or excluded from the model with 10 hidden units.

Solution. First, check the GLRT assumptions for the relevant probability model and stochastic environment (do this!). The test statistic for deciding whether the third input unit should be included or excluded from the model with 10 hidden units is constructed using the data obtained from simulations 1 and 2 in table 8.2. Let $\mathbf{X}_n = \{\mathbf{x}(1),\ldots, \mathbf{x}(n)\}$. Compute the GLRT statistic

$$\hat{\delta}_n = -2n\left[\hat{l}_n(\hat{\mathbf{y}}_n; \mathbf{X}_n) - \hat{l}_n\left([\mathbf{w}^* \ \hat{\mathbf{y}}_n^{(2)}]; \mathbf{X}_n\right)\right].$$

And since $n = 450$, $\hat{l}_n(\hat{\mathbf{y}}_n; \mathbf{X}_n) = 0.021$, $\hat{l}_n([\mathbf{w}^* \ \hat{\mathbf{y}}_n^{(2)}]; \mathbf{X}_n) = 0.045$, it follows that

$$\hat{\delta}_n = -2(450)(0.021 - 0.045) = 21.6.$$

The critical value,

$$\chi_a^2(r) = \chi_{0.05}^2(51 - 41) = 18.31,$$

is obtained by numerical integration or referring to appropriate chi-square distribution tables (refer to chapter 4 for additional details). Therefore, because 21.6 is greater than 18.31, the null hypothesis that the two models are equivalent is rejected. The implication of this conclusion is that the third input unit is playing a relevant role in the prediction solution acquired by the ANN system.

8.4   Chapter Summary

Asymptotic Sampling Error Theorem

In the first section, methods for characterizing the sampling error distribution for ANN learning systems were described, and the Asymptotic Sampling Error Theorem used to establish explicit conditions when the asymptotic distribution of the parameter estimates is Gaussian. Formulas for estimating the mean and covariance matrix of the asymptotic Gaussian distribution of the parameter estimates were also provided.

Let $\mathbf{x}(1),\ldots, \mathbf{x}(n)$ be a sample path (set of training stimuli) of a sequence of independent and identically distributed random vectors with the common environmental probability mass (density) function p_e. For each training stimulus $\mathbf{x}(i)$ in the set of training data, let $\mathbf{g}(\cdot \mid \mathbf{x}(i))$ and $\mathbf{H}(\cdot \mid \mathbf{x}(i))$ be the gradient and Hessian of the regular loss function $c(\cdot \mid \mathbf{x}(i))$, respectively, evaluated at $\mathbf{w}$ and $\{\mathbf{x}(1),\ldots, \mathbf{x}(n)\}$. Let $\tilde{\mathbf{w}}_n$ be a strict local minimum of

$$\hat{l}_n(\cdot; \tilde{\mathbf{x}}(1),\ldots, \tilde{\mathbf{x}}(n)) = (1/n)\sum_{i=1}^{n} c(\cdot \mid \tilde{\mathbf{x}}(i))$$

with probability one for n sufficiently large. Assume $\hat{\mathbf{w}}_n$ is an observed value of the random vector $\tilde{\mathbf{w}}_n$ where $\{\tilde{\mathbf{w}}_n\}$ is a stochastic solution sequence converging to a strict local minimum of the true risk function defined with respect to c and p_e.

A key result of this chapter was that under fairly general conditions for n sufficiently large, the probability distribution of $\tilde{\mathbf{w}}_n$ is approximately a Gaussian distribution whose mean may be estimated by $\hat{\mathbf{w}}_n$ and whose covariance matrix, $n^{-1}\hat{\mathbf{C}}_n$, may be estimated using the formula

$$n^{-1}\hat{\mathbf{C}}_n = n^{-1}[\hat{\mathbf{A}}_n]^{-1}[\hat{\mathbf{B}}_n][\hat{\mathbf{A}}_n]^{-1},$$

where

$$\hat{\mathbf{A}}_n = (1/n)\sum_{i=1}^{n} \mathbf{H}(\hat{\mathbf{w}}_n \mid \mathbf{x}(i))$$

and

$$\hat{\mathbf{B}}_n = (1/n)\sum_{i=1}^{n} \mathbf{g}(\hat{\mathbf{w}}_n \mid \mathbf{x}(i))\mathbf{g}(\hat{\mathbf{w}}_n \mid \mathbf{x}(i))^{T}.$$

In addition, if $\hat{\mathbf{w}}_n$ is a maximum likelihood estimate (i.e., F_W is correctly specified with respect to p_e and c is a log likelihood loss function), then $\hat{\mathbf{A}}_n = \hat{\mathbf{B}}_n$ by the Fisher-Information matrix equality (see problem 8-5). In this special case, it immediately follows that $n^{-1}\hat{\mathbf{C}}_n = n^{-1}[\hat{\mathbf{B}}_n]^{-1}$, which is considerably more tractable computationally than the general case because only first derivative information is required.

Function of Asymptotic Sampling Error Theorem

The Asymptotic Function of the Sampling Error Theorem was shown to be useful in characterizing the prediction error for the response of an ANN system. The response, $\mathbf{r}$, of some ANN systems may be expressed as a function $\mathbf{\Phi}$: $U \times W \to \mathscr{R}^m$ of the estimated connection strength parameter vector $\hat{\mathbf{w}}_n \in W$

and the input stimulus $\mathbf{s} \in U$. In particular, for n sufficiently large and under some additional fairly general conditions, the estimated prediction error,

$$\tilde{\mathbf{r}}_n[\mathbf{s}; \tilde{\mathbf{w}}_n] - \hat{\mathbf{r}}_n[\mathbf{s}; \hat{\mathbf{w}}_n],$$

has approximately a Gaussian probability distribution with mean zero and co-variance matrix $n^{-1}\hat{\mathbf{C}}_{\mathbf{r}}$, where

$$n^{-1}\hat{\mathbf{C}}_{\mathbf{r}} = n^{-1}\left[\frac{d\Phi(\mathbf{s}, \hat{\mathbf{w}}_n)}{d\mathbf{w}}\right]\hat{\mathbf{C}}_n\left[\frac{d\Phi(\mathbf{s}, \hat{\mathbf{w}}_n)}{d\mathbf{w}}\right]^T.$$

Bootstrap Algorithm

The bootstrap sampling algorithm, which estimates the environmental probability mass function by using the relative frequency of an observed random variable's value in a data set, was seen to provide an alternative computationally intensive methodology for characterizing the sampling error probability distribution. K samples of size n (n is assumed to be the size of the original data sample) are generated by sampling with replacement from the estimated environmental probability mass function. The parameters of the ANN system are then estimated for each of the K synthetically generated bootstrap data samples. Thus K distinct sets of connection strength parameter vectors are obtained. The mean and covariance of these K vectors are estimates of the mean and covariance matrix of $\tilde{\mathbf{w}}_n$. The bootstrap algorithm can be extended in a straightforward manner to the more general case where one is interested in characterizing the large sample distribution of an arbitrary deterministic function of $\tilde{\mathbf{w}}_n$.

Generalized Likelihood Ratio Test

In the second section, a general framework for hypothesis testing was introduced, the important Generalized Likelihood Ratio Test (GLRT) was discussed. This statistical test was shown to be useful for deciding which of several ANN system architectures is most appropriate for a given statistical environment. The GLRT is relatively easy to compute but requires that the two ANN system architectures be nested and that the *full model* provides a good fit to the observed data. Let $\hat{l}_n^{\text{ful}}$ be the estimated negative log likelihood error for the *full* ANN system, which provides a good fit to the observed data in a sample of size n. Assume the full model has q free parameters such that $\hat{l}_n^{\text{ful}}$: $\mathcal{R}^q \times S^n \rightarrow [0, \infty)$, where $S \subseteq \mathcal{R}^d$.

Now set r parameters in the ANN system (i.e., the probability model for the ANN system) equal to zero to obtain a *reduced* model. Reestimate the parameters of the reduced model using the estimated parameters of the full model as initial conditions for the learning process. Let $\hat{l}_n^{\text{red}}$ be the estimated negative log likelihood error for the reduced model. The reduced model has $q - r$ free parameters so that $\hat{l}_n^{\text{red}}$: $\mathcal{R}^{q-r} \times S^n \rightarrow [0, \infty)$.

For n sufficiently large with some additional assumptions (see GLRT Theorem), the GLRT states that if the quantity (evaluated at the estimated parameters and the observed data)

$$\hat{\delta}_n = -2n(\hat{l}_n^{\text{ful}} - \hat{l}_n^{\text{red}})$$

is greater than $\chi_a^2(r)$ (see chapter 4 for the definition of this quantity), then conclude that the full model provides a better fit to the data than the reduced model at the a significance level.

Wald Test

Finally, the Wald test was discussed. Consider the hypothesis that certain subsets (or linear combinations) of connection strengths (i.e., a linear combination of the subset of elements of a vector $\mathbf{w}^* \in \mathcal{R}^q$) in an ANN system are equal to zero, given an estimate of the connection strength parameter vector derived from observing a set of n training stimuli. In particular, define the quantity

$$\hat{\mathcal{W}}_n = n[\mathbf{R}\hat{\mathbf{w}}_n - \mathbf{r}]^T[\mathbf{R}\hat{\mathbf{C}}_n\mathbf{R}]^{-1}[\mathbf{R}\hat{\mathbf{w}}_n - \mathbf{r}].$$

In the Wald test, the null hypothesis

$$H_o: \mathbf{R}\mathbf{w}^* = \mathbf{r}$$

is rejected at the a significance level if $\hat{\mathcal{W}}_n$ is greater than $\chi_a^2(m)$, where m is the number of rows of the $m \times q$ ($m \leq q$) selection matrix $\mathbf{R}$ and it is assumed that the rank of $\mathbf{R}$ is equal to m.

8.5   Elementary Problems

8.1-1. Let $x^1,\ldots,x^n$ be a sample path of a stochastic process $\tilde{x}^1,\ldots,\tilde{x}^n$ that consists of n independent and identically distributed random variables with the common probability density function $p: \mathcal{R} \to (0, \infty)$. Let F_W be a probability model whose elements are all univariate Gaussian probability density functions with the variance parameter $\sigma^2 = 2$. In particular, define F_W such that

$$F_W = \{[p(\cdot|\mu): \mathcal{R} \to (0, \infty)]: \mu \in \mathcal{R}\},$$

where

$$p(x|\mu) = \frac{\exp[-(1/4)(x-\mu)^2]}{\sqrt{2}\sqrt{2\pi}}.$$

A quasi-maximum likelihood estimate of μ, $\hat{\mu}_n$, is computed using observations $x^1, x^2,\ldots, x^n$ and F_W. Note that $\hat{\mu}_n$ is an observed value of the random variable $\tilde{\mu}_n$.
    Let the estimated variance of $\tilde{\mu}_n$, using (8.5), be defined as $n^{-1}[\hat{A}_n]^{-1}$. Let the estimated variance of $\tilde{\mu}_n$, using (8.6), be defined as $n^{-1}[\hat{B}_n]^{-1}$. Let the estimated variance of $\tilde{\mu}_n$, using (8.7), be defined as $n^{-1}[\hat{C}_n]^{-1}$. Show how to compute $\hat{\mu}_n, \hat{A}_n, \hat{B}_n$, and $\hat{C}_n$. What assumptions must be satisfied in order for all three formulas to be valid? What assumptions must be satisfied in order for the formula for $\hat{C}_n$ to be valid? What is the origin of the "randomness" of $\tilde{\mu}_n$? List two reasons why a formula for the asymptotic variance of the parameter estimates is useful.

8.1-2. Repeat problem 8.1-1, but now assume that *both* of the parameters σ and μ must be estimated from the data. Thus the matrices $\hat{\mathbf{A}}_n$, $\hat{\mathbf{B}}_n$, and $\hat{\mathbf{C}}_n$ will be two-dimensional.

8.1-3. If the probability model is correctly specified with respect to the environmental distribution, then the Fisher-Information matrix equality holds, and it follows that the asymptotic covariance matrix of the parameter estimates can be estimated using either $[\hat{\mathbf{A}}_n]^{-1}$ or $[\hat{\mathbf{B}}_n]^{-1}$ instead of $\hat{\mathbf{C}}_n$. Using the results of problem 8.1-1, comment on the robustness of the derived formulas.

8.1-4. Repeat problem 8.1-3 using the probability model in problem 8.1-2.

8.1-5. Suppose that $\tilde{\mathbf{r}}[\mathbf{s}]$ is an observed random response activation pattern of a given ANN system when stimulus $\mathbf{s}$ is presented to the network. Using either the bootstrap methodology or asymptotic formulas, a researcher has estimated the conditional expected value of $\tilde{\mathbf{r}}[\mathbf{s}]$ given by $E[\tilde{\mathbf{r}}[\mathbf{s}]]$ and the conditional covariance matrix $\mathbf{C}^*[\mathbf{s}]$ of $\tilde{\mathbf{r}}[\mathbf{s}]$ conditioned on $\mathbf{s}$. The researcher wants to compute prediction error bounds (confidence intervals on the ANN system's predictions) that do not require the assumption $\tilde{\mathbf{r}}[\mathbf{s}]$ is a Gaussian random vector. Use the Markov Inequality to derive formulas for a_a and b_a in order to obtain prediction error bounds given by the expression

$$p(a_a < \tilde{\mathbf{r}}[\mathbf{s}] - E[\tilde{\mathbf{r}}[\mathbf{s}]] < b_a) > 1 - a,$$

where a_a and b_a are real numbers functionally dependent upon the chosen confidence level a.

8.1-6. Write a short computer program that generates bootstrap data samples from an original data sample. Explain how you would use this computer program to implement the bootstrap algorithm.

8.1-7. Let 1, 2, 2, 1, 1, 2, 1, 1, 1 be a sample path of some sequence of nine independent and identically distributed random variables with a common probability mass function and common mean μ. Using a random number generator (e.g., tossing a coin), generate four bootstrap samples from the original sample. Then compute an estimate of the bootstrap estimate of μ from the four bootstrap samples.

8.1-8. Let $a^*, b^* \in \mathcal{R}$. Prove that if $\tilde{a}_n = a^* + o_p(1)$ and $\tilde{b}_n = b^* + o_p(1)$, then

$$\tilde{a}_n + \tilde{b}_n = a^* + b^* + o_p(1).$$

8.1-9. Let $a^* \in \mathcal{R}$. Prove that if $\tilde{a}_n \to a^*$ with probability one as $n \to \infty$, then

$$\tilde{a}_n = a^* + o_p(1).$$

8.2-1. Two experimenters each train up the same backpropagation network using the same deterministic learning algorithm with exactly the same (batch backpropagation learning) data set. The two experimenters, however, each use different initial weights for their respective backpropagation networks. Experimenter 1 does a statistical test and rejects the null hypothesis that all of the weights connecting input unit 1 to the rest of the network are equal to zero. Experimenter 2 does a statistical test and accepts the null hypothesis that all of the weights connecting input unit 1 to the rest of the network are equal to zero. Explain why the conclusions of each researcher are (1) valid, and (2) consistent with one another.

8.2-2. Suppose a null hypothesis for the Wald test is given by

H_0: $\mathbf{R}\mathbf{w}^* = \mathbf{r}$,

where m is the rank of $\mathbf{R}$. An experimenter collects and analyzes a data set using the Wald test but is unable to reject H_0. The experimenter suspects that H_0 is false but the sample size n is too small. Show how to derive the formula

$$\hat{n}' > n[\chi_a^2(r)/\hat{\mathcal{W}}_n],$$

which estimates the required sample size, $\hat{n}'$, for obtaining a Wald statistic $\hat{\mathcal{W}}_n$ whose value exceeds the desired threshold $\chi_a^2(m)$. Explain how the experimenter can use the information obtained from an experiment where the null hypothesis was not rejected to estimate how much data should be collected in order to reject the null hypothesis (if it is in fact false) in a second experiment.

8.2-3. Let (reduced) probability model 1 be a univariate Gaussian density function with known mean μ_0 and unknown variance σ^2. Let (full) probability model 2 be a univariate Gaussian density function with unknown mean μ and unknown variance σ^2. Test the null hypothesis that $H_0: \mu = \mu_0$ by using the Generalized Likelihood Ratio Test (GLRT).

8.2-4. Explain how the Generalized Likelihood Ratio Test can be used to analyze hidden unit representations in a classical backpropagation network by fixing the mapping from the input to hidden units after training the network, and then retraining only the weights representing the hidden to output unit mapping. List a major advantage and a major disadvantage of assuming a fixed input to hidden unit mapping for evaluating what a classical backpropagation network has learned.

8.2-5. Let $\hat{\mathbf{W}}_n$ be a 3×2 matrix such that the ijth element of $\hat{\mathbf{W}}_n$, $\hat{w}_n(i,j)$, indicates the connection strength from the jth input unit to the ith hidden unit ($i = 1\ldots 3, j = 1, 2$). It is assumed that $\hat{\mathbf{W}}_n$ is a unique quasi-maximum likelihood estimate with respect to some convex, closed, and bounded subset of $\mathcal{R}^{3\times 2}$, and that $\bar{w}_n(i,j) \to w^*(i,j)$ with probability one as $n \to \infty$. A researcher wants to test the null hypothesis that hidden unit number 1 and hidden unit number 3 are picking up redundant information. That is, the researcher wants to construct a statistical test in order to decide whether any observed differences between $\hat{w}_n(1,k)$ and $\hat{w}_n(3,k)$ for $k = 1, 2$ are due to sampling error. It is assumed that the covariance matrix $\mathbf{C}^*$ has been estimated. Explain how the Wald test may be used to test the null hypothesis of interest. Explicitly define the selection matrix and selection vector for the Wald test. Show that a strict local minimum of the true risk function cannot exist if the null hypothesis is true for a *classical* backpropagation ANN, and so this analysis is not applicable in such situations.

8.6 Problems

8-1. Suppose that the environmental probability mass function has the form

$$p_e(x^i) = p_i,$$

where

$$\sum_{i=1}^{M} p_i = 1,$$

and x^i is the ith value of the random variable $\tilde{x}$. The parameters $p_1,\ldots, p_M$ will be estimated using quasi-maximum likelihood estimation. Let n_i indicate that x^i occurs n_i times in the data sample. Then the log likelihood function is given by

$$-\sum_{i=1}^{M} (n_i/n) \log[p_i].$$

Show that maximizing the log likelihood function, subject to the constraints that

$$0 \leq p_i \leq 1$$

and

$$\sum_{i=1}^{M} p_i = 1,$$

results in the intuitively plausible conclusion that the relative frequency of an observation is the unique quasi-maximum likelihood estimate of the probability mass attached to that observation. Discuss how this conclusion justifies the bootstrap approach when the parameters of a probability mass function are estimated.

8-2. Consider a backpropagation network with h radial basis function hidden units as in problem 7-2, where, however, the weight vectors $\mathbf{w}_1, \mathbf{w}_2,\ldots, \mathbf{w}_h$ are assumed to be known. Typically, these weight vectors are chosen to be representative examples of categories of stimuli typically encountered by the network (e.g., Poggio and Girosi 1990; Specht 1988). Thus the only free parameters of the network are the matrix $\mathbf{V}$ and the bias vector $\mathbf{b}$. Find (1) the quasi-maximum likelihood estimates, and (2) the asymptotic covariance matrix of the estimates. Investigate when the quasi-maximum likelihood estimates will be unique. Finally, show how a Wald test could be used to decide which radial basis function hidden units can be eliminated from the network. HINT: Do the analysis in such a general manner that it can be applied to any arbitrary multilayer backpropagation network where the hidden unit activation pattern to output unit activation pattern mapping is linear. (See section 8.3.2 for additional help.)

Repeat this problem, assuming that $\mathbf{V}$ and $\mathbf{b}$ are known, and $\mathbf{w}_1,\ldots, \mathbf{w}_h$ are the only free parameters.

8-3. The generalized likelihood ratio test (GLRT) requires that the two probability models of interest satisfy a particular nesting relationship. Vuong (1989) has provided a generalization of the GLRT (see Golden 1995 for a review). An important special case of his theory is the case of *strictly nonnested* models, where one has two probability models,

$$F_W = \{(p^f(\cdot \mid \mathbf{w}): S \rightarrow [0, \infty)): \mathbf{w} \in W\}$$

and

$$G_Y = \{(p^g(\cdot \mid \mathbf{y}): S \rightarrow [0, \infty)): \mathbf{y} \in Y\},$$

such that $F_W \cap G_Y = \varnothing$. State and prove a theorem analogous to the Generalized Likelihood Ratio Test that can be applied to strictly nonnested models.

In particular, let $-\log[p^f(\cdot \mid \cdot)]: S \times W \rightarrow [0, \infty)$ and $-\log[p^g(\cdot \mid \cdot)]: S \times W \rightarrow [0, \infty)$ be regular loss functions. Let $\mathbf{w}^*$ and $\mathbf{y}^*$ be strict local minima of $l^f(\cdot) = -E[\log[p^f(\tilde{\mathbf{x}} \mid \cdot)]]$ and $l^g(\cdot) = -E[\log[p^g(\tilde{\mathbf{x}} \mid \cdot)]]$ respectively. Let $\mathbf{x}(1),\ldots, \mathbf{x}(n)$, be a sample path of $\tilde{\mathbf{x}}(1),\ldots, \tilde{\mathbf{x}}(n)$, and let $\hat{\sigma}^2_{v_n}$ be an observed value of:

$$\tilde{\sigma}^2_{v_n} = (1/n)\sum_{i=1}^{n} \left(\log\left[p^f(\tilde{\mathbf{x}}(i) \mid \tilde{\mathbf{w}}_n)\right] - \log\left[p^g(\tilde{\mathbf{x}}(i) \mid \tilde{\mathbf{y}}_n)\right]\right)^2 - (\hat{l}^f_n - \hat{l}^g_n)^2 \tag{8.23}$$

where the stochastic solution sequences $\{\tilde{\mathbf{w}}_n\}$ and $\{\tilde{\mathbf{y}}_n\}$ are assumed to converge with probability one to $\mathbf{w}^*$ and $\mathbf{y}^*$ respectively as $n \rightarrow \infty$.

Show that given the null hypothesis that $l^f(\mathbf{w}^*) = l^g(\mathbf{y}^*)$ is true:

$$\tilde{V}_n = \frac{\hat{l}^f_n(\tilde{\mathbf{w}}_n; \tilde{\mathbf{x}}(1),\ldots, \tilde{\mathbf{x}}(n)) - \hat{l}^g_n(\tilde{\mathbf{y}}_n; \tilde{\mathbf{x}}(1),\ldots, \tilde{\mathbf{x}}(n))}{\tilde{\sigma}_{v_n}/n^{1/2}} \tag{8.24}$$

converges in distribution to a normally distributed random variable with mean zero and variance one as $n \rightarrow \infty$. Also show that given the alternative hypothesis $l^f(\mathbf{w}^*) \neq l^g(\mathbf{y}^*)$ is true that $|\tilde{V}_n| \rightarrow \infty$ with probability one as $n \rightarrow \infty$.

8-4. Consider a one-layer backpropagation network, as in section 8.3.2, whose response unit activation pattern $\mathbf{r}$ is computed from a given input vector $\mathbf{h}$ given the formula

$$\mathbf{r} = \mathcal{S}[\mathbf{Wh} + \mathbf{b}],$$

where $\mathcal{S}: \mathcal{R}^d \rightarrow (0, 1)^d$ is a sigmoidal logistic function defined such that the ith element of $\mathcal{S}(\mathbf{x})$, is equal to $1/(1 + \exp[-x_i])$, where x_i is the ith element of $\mathbf{x}$. The $d \times q$ matrix $\mathbf{W}$ is the connection strength matrix and the d-dimensional column vector $\mathbf{b}$ is the bias vector. Using the Strict Global Minimum Test (chapter 5), identify a set of explicit conditions guaranteeing that any quasi-maximum likelihood estimate of $\mathbf{W}$ and $\mathbf{b}$ for this network is unique. Derive explicit formulas for estimating the asymptotic covariance matrix of the sampling distribution for the quasi-maximum likelihood estimates of $\mathbf{W}$ and $\mathbf{b}$.

8-5. Prove the Fisher information matrix equality. Let p_e be an environmental probability mass (density) function associated with random variable $\tilde{\mathbf{x}}$. Let $q_f(\cdot, \mathbf{w}): S \rightarrow [0, \infty)$ be a probability mass (density) function for all $\mathbf{w} \in \mathcal{R}^q$. Assume that q_f has continuous second partial derivatives of $\mathbf{w}$ on $\mathcal{R}^q$. Let $\mathbf{w}^*$ be a strict local minimum of l, defined such that for all $\mathbf{w} \in \mathcal{R}^q$:

$$l(\mathbf{w}) = -E_{\tilde{\mathbf{x}}}[\log[q_f(\tilde{\mathbf{x}}, \mathbf{w})]],$$

where the expectation is taken with respect to p_e. Define

$$\mathbf{g}(\mathbf{x}, \mathbf{w}) = -\nabla_{\mathbf{w}}\log[q_f(\mathbf{x}, \mathbf{w})]$$

and

$$H(\mathbf{x}, \mathbf{w}) = -\nabla_{\mathbf{w}}^2 \log[q_f(\mathbf{x}, \mathbf{w})].$$

Let

$$\mathbf{A}^* = E_{\tilde{\mathbf{x}}}[\mathbf{H}(\tilde{\mathbf{x}})]$$

and

$$\mathbf{B}^* = E_{\tilde{\mathbf{x}}}[\mathbf{g}(\tilde{\mathbf{x}}, \mathbf{w})\mathbf{g}(\tilde{\mathbf{x}}, \mathbf{w})^T].$$

Show that if the probability model $\{q_f(\cdot; \mathbf{w})\}$ is correctly specified with respect to p_e, then $\mathbf{A}^* = \mathbf{B}^*$.
HINT: Start with

$$\int_{\mathbf{x} \in S} q_f(\mathbf{x} \mid \mathbf{w}) \, d\mathbf{x} = 1 \qquad (8.25)$$

and take the gradient and Hessian of (8.25) to obtain two useful identities.

8-6. Prove the following theorem. A necessary condition for a critical point of the log likelihood function to be a strict local minimum is that the number of free parameters be less than or equal to the training sample size n. Explicitly identify all assumptions of your theorem.

8-7. A backpropagation network is proposed to predict alternative diagnoses of some medical condition, given a set of symptoms. In particular, let the jth stimulus vector $\mathbf{s}^j$ be a d-dimensional binary-valued vector whose kth element, s_k^j, indicates the presence or absence of the kth symptom. If $s_k^j = 1$, then symptom k is present for the jth set of symptoms. If $s_k^j = 0$, then symptom k is absent for the jth set of symptoms. Let $\mathbf{o}^j$ be an m-dimensional vector whose elements indicate the presence or absence of the kth symptom out of m possible diagnoses, given symptom vector $\mathbf{s}^j$. A medical database, consisting of n records of the form

$$[\mathbf{s}^1, \mathbf{o}^1], [\mathbf{s}^2, \mathbf{o}^2], \ldots, [\mathbf{s}^n, \mathbf{o}^n], \quad \text{where} \quad \mathbf{s}^j \in \{0, 1\}^d \quad \text{and} \quad \mathbf{o}^j \in \{0, 1\}^m,$$

is used to train the network. The architecture of the backpropagation network is specified by

$$\mathbf{r}^j = \underline{\mathscr{S}}(\mathbf{W}\mathbf{h}^j + \mathbf{b})$$

and

$$\mathbf{h}^j = \underline{\mathscr{S}}(\mathbf{V}\mathbf{s}^j + \mathbf{q}),$$

where $\underline{\mathscr{S}}$ is a vector-valued function whose kth element, $\mathscr{S}_k$, is a scalar-valued function of the form

$$\mathscr{S}_k(x) = \frac{1}{1 + \exp(-x)}.$$

The kth element of $\mathbf{r}^j$, r_k^j, is interpreted as the network's belief (probability) that the patient has diagnosis k, given the set of symptoms $\mathbf{s}^j$. The sample risk function, $\hat{l}_n$, for the network is the negative log likelihood function, so that the estimated parameters, $\hat{\mathbf{W}}_n, \hat{\mathbf{V}}_n, \hat{\mathbf{b}}_n$, and $\hat{\mathbf{q}}_n$, are quasi-maximum likelihood estimates. Thus the backpropagation learning algorithm seeks a strict local minimum, $(\hat{\mathbf{W}}_n, \hat{\mathbf{V}}_n, \hat{\mathbf{b}}_n, \hat{\mathbf{q}}_n)$, of

$$\hat{l}_n(\mathbf{W}, \mathbf{V}, \mathbf{b}, \mathbf{q}) = -(1/n)\sum_{j=1}^n \hat{l}_n^j,$$

where

$$\hat{l}_n^j = (1/n)\sum_{j=1}^n \left[\sum_{k=1}^m o_k^j \log[r_k^j] + (1 - o_k^j) \log[1 - r_k^j] \right].$$

Derive a Wald test in order to decide whether the ith symptom (i.e., ith element in $\mathbf{s}^j$) in the ANN system is relevant for the prediction task. Explicitly identify all assumptions that are required for the Wald test to be valid, and suggest some practical methods for checking the validity of those assumptions.

8-8. Consider the exponential probability density function defined by

$$p(x) = a\exp[-ax] \text{ for } x > 0, a > 0$$

and

$$p(x) = 0 \text{ for } x \leq 0.$$

Explicitly derive a simple formula for the quasi-maximum likelihood estimate of a. Let $\mathcal{S}: \mathcal{R} \rightarrow \{0, 1\}$ be defined such that $\mathcal{S}(x) = 1$ if $x \geq 0$ and $\mathcal{S}(x) = 0$ if $x < 0$. Explain why the univariate Gaussian probability model

$$F = \{p(x; \mu) = [\sqrt{\pi}]^{-1} \exp[-(x-\mu)^2]: \mu \in \mathcal{R}\}$$

and the exponential probability model

$$G = \{p(x; a) = a\exp[-ax]\mathcal{S}(x): a \in (0, \infty)\}$$

are strictly nonnested models. Now use the strictly nonnested models test from problem 8-3 to derive a formula for deciding which of the two probability models makes the observed data most probable. Give two reasons why the Generalized Likelihood Ratio Test could not be used to solve this problem if the probability models F and G are strictly nonnested and either or both probability models are misspecified.

8-9. Derive a goodness-of-fit test using Wilks's Generalized Likelihood Ratio Test (1938). Let S be a finite subset of $\mathcal{R}^d$. Let $\mathbf{x}(1),\ldots, \mathbf{x}(n)$ be a sample path of the stochastic process $\tilde{\mathbf{x}}(1),\ldots, \tilde{\mathbf{x}}(n)$ that consists of a set of n d-dimensional real training stimulus vectors with the common probability mass function $p_e: S \rightarrow [0, 1]$. Let F_W be a subjective probability model for some ANN system defined such that $p_s(\cdot \mid \mathbf{w}): S \rightarrow [0, 1]$ is an element of F_W for all $\mathbf{w} \in W$, where W is some closed and bounded subset of $\mathcal{R}^q$. Assume $-\log[p_s(\cdot \mid \cdot)]: S \times W \rightarrow [0, \infty)$ is a regular loss function on W. Let $\mathbf{w}^*$ be a strict local minimum of $-E[\log[p_s(\tilde{\mathbf{x}} \mid \cdot)]]$ on W. Assume $\{\tilde{\mathbf{w}}_n\}$ is a stochastic solution sequence which converges with probability one to $\mathbf{w}^*$. Develop a statistical test to decide if the subjective probability mass function $p_s(\cdot \mid \mathbf{w}^*)$ is identical to p_e on sample space S.

8-10. State explicit conditions such that $\tilde{\mathbf{C}}_n \rightarrow \mathbf{C}^*$ with probability one as $n \rightarrow \infty$, where $\tilde{\mathbf{C}}_n$ and $\mathbf{C}^*$ are defined as in (8.1) and (8.7) with respect to some stochastic solution sequence $\{\tilde{\mathbf{w}}_n\}$ converging to $\mathbf{w}^*$, regular loss function c, and risk function $l: W \rightarrow \mathcal{R}$. Then provide a formal proof showing how those explicit conditions give the desired result.

HINT: The key problem here is to show that $[\tilde{\mathbf{A}}_n]^{-1}$ (see equation 8.5) exists for n sufficiently large with probability one, and that $[\tilde{\mathbf{A}}_n]^{-1}$ converges with probability one as $n \rightarrow \infty$ to the inverse of the Hessian of l, $[\mathbf{A}^*]^{-1}$, evaluated at $\mathbf{w}^*$. If $\mathbf{w}^*$ is a strict local minimum of l, then the inverse of the Hessian of l evaluated at $\mathbf{w}^*$ will exist. Use the fact that the eigenvalues of $[\mathbf{A}^*]^{-1}$ are continuously dependent upon $\mathbf{w}^*$ because $\mathbf{A}^*$ is a real positive definite matrix (Franklin 1968, 191).

Epilogue

A Brief Review

The organization of this book was based upon Marr's theory of complex information-processing systems (1982). Marr suggested that a complete description of a complex information-processing system requires understanding the system on at least three distinct levels: the implementational, the algorithmic, and the computational.

Implementational Level

In chapters 3 and 4 dynamical systems theory was shown to be useful for characterizing the *behavior* of an ANN system independently of issues concerned with the efficiency of the system's algorithms or the "rationality" of its inferences. Dynamical systems theory is relevant for understanding the implementational level description of an ANN information-processing system.

Algorithmic Level

In chapter 5 optimization theory was shown to be useful for comparing and contrasting methods to achieve specific computational goals. Given the computational goal of finding the minimum of some objective function, methods for designing algorithms (or equivalently, for evaluating existing algorithms) were described to achieve this computational goal. The relative efficiency of various algorithms designed to achieve the same computational goal was also briefly discussed. Thus optimization theory is relevant for understanding the algorithmic level description of an ANN information-processing system.

Computational Level

In chapter 6 the mathematical theories of evidence and rational decision making were shown to be useful for understanding in what sense computing the minimum value of an expected risk function is a *rational* decision that yields appropriate generalizations. Chapter 6 directly identified the computational goal of an ANN information-processing system, and explained in what sense that computational goal is unique.

In chapter 7 the classical theory of MAP estimation for classification and learning from the field of statistical pattern recognition was shown to provide important insights into how the analyses of ANN systems in chapters 3, 4, and 5 could be practically related to the theory of rational decision making developed in chapter 6. Thus chapter 7 provided mathematical methods for the construction and evaluation of ANN classification and learning objective functions.

In chapter 8, based upon classical and well-known approaches from the field of asymptotic statistical inference, mathematical methods were introduced that describe how the generalization performance of an ANN system varies as a direct function of the sample size. Thus chapters 7 and 8 were concerned with understanding the computational goals of an ANN system, and evaluating the degree to which those goals are achieved.

A Final Word

My goal in writing this book was to provide a solid, concise mathematical foundation for advanced study in the area of ANN system analysis and design. Toward this end, I have attempted to emphasize well-established theoretical concepts and principles from engineering science that have already stood the test of time, yet are particularly relevant to understanding current research in the field of ANN systems. With a solid grounding in these classical theoretical concepts and principles, the reader will be well prepared to evaluate more recent theoretical results.

There are many paths to understanding ANN system analysis and design. I have described one path, which I have followed and which makes sense to me. I sincerely hope the reader finds this path both useful and accessible.

Problem Solutions

The following solutions to the odd-numbered problems vary considerably in their attention to detail. The reader should use the solutions to problems in the main text as examples of "complete solutions" and the answers presented in this section primarily as hints.

Chapter 1

Elementary Problems

1.1-1. (a) Implementational level: dynamical system defined by electronic schematic diagrams. (b) Algorithmic level: specific algorithms used by electronic circuitry to receive and transmit sound waves specified in sufficient details so that such algorithms can be simulated on a computer. (c) Computational level: a formal description of the functions (e.g., transmitting electronic signal, receiving electronic signal, converting sound waves to electronic signal, converting electronic signal to sound waves) computed by the algorithms.

1.1-3. Neuroscience is concerned with describing and understanding all aspects of brain functioning, including aspects irrelevant to information-processing tasks. Similarly, dynamical systems theory is concerned with describing and understanding all aspects of a dynamical system model of a physical system without regard to the system's computational goals. Marr's implementational level (1982) is concerned with describing the implementational details of information-processing systems and is thus relevant to both neuroscience and dynamical systems theory.

1.1-5. Engineering is concerned with building systems that work and have some useful function. Statistics is a mathematical theory that allows one to make inductive inferences in a principled manner, and thus can be used to guide the design and analysis of inference systems by characterizing their computational goals. Marr's computational level (1982) is also concerned with justifying and defining computational goals.

1.2-1. (a) ANN system version: Consider two groups of d units. Let each unit have a state called the activation level of that unit. The activation pattern over the first group of units will be represented by the state vector $\mathbf{r}$, while the activation pattern over the second group of units will be represented by the state vector $\mathbf{f}$. Let the activation of the ith unit in the first group be denoted as r_i. Assume that $r_i = \sum_{j=1}^{d} w_{ij} f_j$, where f_j is the activation level of the jth unit in the second group of units and w_{ij} is the connection strength from the jth unit in the second group of units to the ith unit in the first group of units. Let w_{ij} be the ijth element ($i, j = 1 \ldots d$) of the matrix $\mathbf{W}$.

(b) Non-ANN system version: Implement a vector by matrix multiplication using FORTRAN programming code.

1.3-1. The group of scientists are experimental psychologists who have found that the basic behavioral properties of the ANN algorithm are similar to behavioral characteristics observed in human performance. Moreover, the ANN algorithm explains a considerable amount of existing behavioral data (but not neuroscience data) even though the algorithm's overall performance is relatively poor.

1.3-3. (a) Zipser and Andersen 1988: biological system identification. (b) Rescorla and Wagner 1972; Sutton and Barto 1981: behavioral classical conditioning experiments. (c) Kohonen 1990; Waibel et al. 1989: speech processing.

1.3-5. See discussion of Rescorla-Wagner and Widrow-Hoff learning rules in section 1.3.2.

1.3-7. Let $0 < \mu \le 1$ and $0 < \delta < 1$. Let $w_{ii} = \mu$ for $i = 1 \ldots d$. Let $w_{ij} = -\delta$ for $i, j = 1 \ldots d$, $i \ne j$. Assume μ and δ parameters chosen to correctly implement a lateral inhibition network. Case 1: Eventually only unit 5 will be active. Case 2: Eventually only unit 4 will be active. Case 3: Eventually only units 4 and 7 will be active.

1.3-9. See discussion of abstract model of *Tritonia* neural network in section 1.3.1.

1.3-11. Try to construct a set of four-letter word stimuli which can be divided into two groups. Let group 1 be words with substantial visual regularities and let group 2 be words without substantial visual regularities. For every word in group 1 (e.g., *ROAD*) there should be a corresponding word in group 2 (e.g., *RODE*), so that the phonetic structure is held constant. One method of measuring "visual regularities" is to examine the relative frequency that a particular letter appears in a particular position in a four-letter word in the English language. Then do an experiment to decide if the magnitude of the word superiority effect is greater for group 1 stimuli relative to group 2 stimuli. If this is so, the findings would support the hypothesis that structural visual regularities aid letter within word perception when phonetic structure is held constant.

1.3-13. One typical *prediction* configuration attempts to predict an uncorrupted version of the signal given the corrupted version, although this configuration has a tougher learning problem because it does not exploit prior knowledge that the noise is additive or that the probability distribution of the noise at time t can be specified in terms of the observed value of the noise at time $(t-1)$.

Another typical *interference-canceling* configuration (see Widrow and Stearns 1985 for further discussion) attempts to remove interference from a given signal that is assumed to be corrupted by some partially predictable additive noise process. In this situation, the input to the supervised learning backpropagation network is the noise process without the signal, and the backpropagation network attempts to predict the future behavior of the noise. The final prediction is obtained by subtracting the output of the backpropagation network from the noise-corrupted signal in order to yield an approximate reconstruction of the original input signal. The interference-canceling configuration exploits the prior knowledge that the noise is known to be *added* to the signal.

Math Review Problems

1-1. Let

$$h(x) = (x + 10)^2.$$

Then

$$f(x) = e^{h(x)}.$$

And by the chain rule,

$$df/dx = [df/dh][dh/dx].$$

Thus you need only to compute df/dh and dh/dx. Note that

$$df/dh = e^h$$

and

$$dh/dx = 2(x + 10).$$

So the answer is

$$df/dx = [df/dh][dh/dx] = e^{h(x)}[2(x + 10)] = [e^{(x+10)^2}][2(x + 10)].$$

1-3. Note that

$$df/dx = 2(x + 3) + \cos(x)$$

and

$$d^2f/dx^2 = 2 - \sin(x).$$

Thus

$$df/dx_0 = 2(7 + 3) + \cos(7)$$

and

$$d^2f/dx_0^2 = 2 - \sin(7)$$

with $x_0 = 7$.

Plugging into the formula given in the hint,

$$f(x) \approx [(7+3)^2 + \sin(7)] + [2(7+3) + \cos(7)](x-7) + (1/2)(x-7)^2[2 - \sin(7)].$$

Assuming that the arguments to the sin and cos functions are degrees, it follows that $\sin(7) = 0.12$ and $\cos(7) = 0.99$, and thus

$$f(x) \approx 100.12 + 21(x-7) + 0.94(x-7)^2$$

which is a quadratic approximation to the original nonlinear function f in the vicinity of the point $x = 7$.

1-5. Suppose that, for every positive real number ε, there exists a number N such that for all $n > N$, the expression $|x_n - a| < \varepsilon$ is satisfied. Then $x_n \to a$ as $n \to \infty$.

1-7. Since:

$$\partial f / \partial x = 2x + 2,$$

$$\partial f / \partial y = 2y,$$

it follows that

$$\mathbf{g} = [2x + 2 \quad 2y].$$

The Hessian $\mathbf{H}$ is the identity matrix multiplied by 2 (i.e., a two-dimensional matrix where off-diagonal elements are equal to zero and on-diagonal elements are equal to two). To see this, note that

$$\partial^2 f / \partial x^2 = 2,$$

$$\partial^2 f / \partial y^2 = 2,$$

and

$$\partial^2 f / \partial x \partial y = \partial^2 f / \partial y \partial x = 0.$$

1-9. The notation defines a function $\mathbf{G}$ that has three arguments and that returns a real $d \times l$ matrix. The first argument to the matrix-valued function $\mathbf{G}$ is a q-dimensional real vector, the second argument to $\mathbf{G}$ is a real number, and the third argument is a member of the set Q.

1-11. Note that $[1 \quad 0 \quad 1] + [0 \quad 0 \quad 1] = [1 \quad 0 \quad 2]$.

1-13. The rank of a matrix is defined as the number of linearly independent row vectors (or column vectors—you get same answer either way) of the matrix. The rank of a matrix is invariant with respect to linear transformations (i.e., pre- and postmatrix multiplies using other matrices of full rank). Thus you can consider mapping this problem into a new vector space where $\mathbf{M}$ is diagonal (i.e., on-diagonal elements are positive eigenvalues). It then immediately follows that because all rows of the diagonalized matrix are orthogonal to one another, the row vectors of the matrix are linearly independent. Thus the answer is d.

1-15.

$$\bar{x} = E[x] = \int_{-\infty}^{+\infty} xp(x)\,dx = \int_2^5 (x/3)\,dx = (5)^2/6 - (2)^2/6 = 21/6.$$

$$VAR[x] = \int_{-\infty}^{+\infty} (x-\bar{x})^2 p(x)\,dx = \int_2^5 ((x-\bar{x})^2/3)\,dx = 3/4.$$

1-17. Let B_i indicate the event *Box i is chosen* for $i = 1 \ldots 3$, and let R indicate the event *Red ball is chosen*. It is known that

$$p(R|B_1) = 2/5,$$

$$p(R|B_2) = 0.5,$$

and

$p(R|B_3) = 1.$

By definition of a conditional probability, we have

$p(B_3|R) = [p(R|B_3)p(B_3)]/p(R),$

and we also know that

$p(R) = p(R|B_1)p(B_1) + p(R|B_2)p(B_2) + p(R|B_3)p(B_3)$

and thus

$p(R) = (2/5)(1/3) + (0.5)(1/3) + (1)(1/3) = 19/30.$

Therefore,

$p(B_3|R) = [p(R|B_3)p(B_3)]/p(R) = (1)(1/3)/(19/30) = 10/19.$

Chapter 2

Problems

2-1. Use algorithms given in text as models for the computer program. Identify activation patterns that are "stable" (i.e., where activation levels of units do not change given additional iterations of the algorithm). Evaluate performance by examining the number of iterations until algorithm converges to a stable activation pattern. To check the "error correction" capabilities of the models, perturb a "stable" activation pattern, using that as an initial condition for the dynamical system, and see if the perturbed pattern is mapped into the original activation pattern.

2-3. This answer will focus only on the brain-state-in-a-box (BSB) model; review section 2.12 for (b), section 2.21 for (c) and (d), and section 2.2.2 for (e). The state vector of the BSB model can be interpreted as an activation pattern (characteristic 1). The BSB model does not learn, although its knowledge base is represented in the weight matrix, which can be interpreted as a matrix of synaptic information transmission coefficients (characteristic 2). The BSB model works well if dimensionality of state vector is large (characteristic 3). Local connectivity in the weight matrix is not required but can easily be built into the BSB model by requiring that most of the connections in the weight matrix take on the value of zero (characteristic 4). The BSB model is a parallel processing algorithm if vector-by-matrix multiplication is implemented in a parallel machine (characteristic 5). The BSB model is robust to brain damage (characteristic 6; see Anderson 1983). The activation updating rule in the BSB model is quasi-linear (characteristic 7). All units in the BSB model update their activation levels according to same rule (characteristic 8). The BSB model is robust in presence of local imprecision (characteristic 9). And the BSB model is an analog machine (characteristic 10).

2-5. Assume that the identity and location of the object are represented as the conjunction of two disjoint activation patterns. That is, the activation pattern over one group of units represents the position of an object, and the activation pattern over another group represents the identity of the object. There seems to be neurophysiological evidence supporting the existence of such coding schemes.

2-7. (a) Design the backpropagation network so that each hidden unit responds to exactly one input stimulus and no two hidden units respond to the same input stimulus. (b) Note that four possible activation patterns [0 0], [1 0], [0 1], and [1 1] can be approximately represented over the hidden units. Set up the network to generate each of the above four patterns when each of the four input vectors is presented.

2-9. See answer for problem 5-7 for some ideas.

2-11. See answer for problem 4-7 and problem 5-7 for some ideas.

2-13. The network initially responds strongly to all possible stimuli and then learns to respond weakly to familiar stimuli. Thus the network learns to be a novelty detector.

Chapter 3

Elementary Problems

3.1-1.

1. $V(x) = 1/x$ is not defined at $x = 0$ and $dV/dx = -1/x^2$ is also not defined at $x = 0$. V does not satisfy a Lipschitz condition on $\mathcal{R}$.

2. $V(x) = |x|^2$ is continuous everywhere and has continuous first partial derivatives everywhere. V does not satisfy a Lipschitz condition on $\mathcal{R}$.

3. $V(x) = \log[x]$ is not defined at $x = 0$, and $dV/dx = 1/x$ is not defined at $x = 0$. V does not satisfy a Lipschitz condition on $\mathcal{R}$.

4. $V(x) = \exp[x]$ is continuous everywhere and has a continuous first derivative. V does not satisfy a Lipschitz condition on $\mathcal{R}$.

5. $V(x) = x$ is continuous everywhere and has a continuous first derivative. V satisfies a Lipschitz condition on $\mathcal{R}$ because the derivative of V is bounded on $\mathcal{R}$.

3.1-3.

$$|df/dx| = |\cos(x)| \leq 1 < \infty,$$

so that f satisfies a Lipschitz condition on $\mathcal{R}$.

3.1-5.

$$\mathbf{x}(k) = \boldsymbol{\Psi}(\mathbf{x}(0), k) = \mathbf{A}^k \mathbf{x}(0).$$

Note that $\boldsymbol{\Psi}$ is continuous in its first argument on $\mathcal{R}^d$.

3.1-7.

1. $G = \{\{x_1, x_2\} \in \mathcal{R}^2 : x_1, x_2 \in [0, 1]\}$ is closed.
2. $G = \{\mathbf{x} \in \mathcal{R}^d : |\mathbf{x}|^2 < 16\}$ is not closed.
3. $G = \{x \in \mathcal{R} : 1/x \leq 16\}$ is closed.

3.2-1. There are 2^d equilibrium points of the form $x_i = 1$ or $x_i = 0$ for $i = 1 \ldots d$.

3.2-3. The set of equilibrium points is the set of eigenvectors having eigenvalues equal to one and a d-dimensional vector of zeros. (a) At least one eigenvalue with absolute value greater than one (unstable). (b) All eigenvalues have magnitudes less than or equal to one but at least one eigenvalue has magnitude equal to one (marginally stable). (c) All eigenvalues have magnitudes strictly less than one (asymptotically stable).

3.3-1. Let $f_i = -\gamma(o - r)s_i$ be the ith element of the generator for the dynamical system in (3.23). Then

$$\frac{\partial f_i}{\partial w_j} = \gamma s_i s_j.$$

Thus $\partial f_i / \partial w_j$ is bounded on $\mathcal{R}^q$. This implies (by the EUC Theorem for Continuous-Time Dynamical Systems) that (1) the generator for (3.23) satisfies a Lipschitz condition and (2) a unique solution exists that is a continuous function of the dynamical system's initial state.

Consider the learning objective function

$$l(\mathbf{w}) = (1/2)(o - r(\mathbf{w}))^2.$$

In the following discussion, notation explicitly showing the functional dependence of r on $\mathbf{w}$ will be suppressed, so that in writing expressions such as

$$l(\mathbf{w}) = (o - r)^2,$$

r is understood to be functionally dependent upon $\mathbf{w}$.

The gradient of l is given by

$$dl/d\mathbf{w} = -(o - r)\mathbf{s}.$$

Using the definition of $d\mathbf{w}/dt$ in (3.23),

$$\dot{l} = (dl/d\mathbf{w})^T (d\mathbf{w}/dt) = -\gamma(o - r)^2 |\mathbf{s}|^2 \leq 0$$

for all $\mathbf{w} \in \mathcal{R}^q$. Because $dl/d\mathbf{w}$ is continuous on $\mathcal{R}^q$ and $\dot{l} \leq 0$ on $\mathcal{R}^q$, l is a Lyapunov function on $\mathcal{R}^q$.

In order to use the Invariant Set Theorem, construct a set Ω_s such that

$$\Omega_s = \{\mathbf{w} \in \mathcal{R}^q : l(\mathbf{w}) = (o - r(\mathbf{w}))^2 \leq s\},$$

where s is any finite positive real number. By the Closed, Bounded, Invariant Set Proposition, it follows that Ω_s is a closed, bounded, and invariant set. Thus the Invariant Set Theorem applies, and every trajectory initiated in Ω_s will converge to the largest invariant set, where $\dot{l} = \gamma(o - r)^2 |\mathbf{s}|^2 = 0$, which is the set of system equilibrium points. Also note that any $\mathbf{w}$ having the property that $r = o$ is a system equilibrium point.

3.3-3. Let

$$r = (1 - x^2 - y^2).$$

Then

$$\partial V/\partial x = -4xr$$

and

$$\partial V/\partial y = -4yr.$$

Thus

$$\dot{V} = (\partial V/\partial x)(dx/dt) + (\partial V/\partial y)(dy/dt)$$
$$\dot{V} = -4xyr - 4x^2r^2 + 4xyr - 4y^2r^2 = -4(1 - r)r^2 \leq 0.$$

3.3-5. Construct the closed set

$$\Omega_s = \{(x, y) \in \mathcal{R} \times \mathcal{R} : V(x, y) \leq s\},$$

where V is defined as in problem 3.3-3. Note that as $x \to \infty$ or $y \to \infty$, it follows that $V(x, y) \to \infty$. Thus Ω_s is a bounded set. It is assumed that any trajectory initiated in Ω_s is a continuous function of its initial condition, and the solution set of trajectories is unique on Ω_s. Because V is a Lyapunov function, Ω_s is also an invariant set. Thus, given any initial condition, construct Ω_s to contain that initial condition. The trajectory generated from the initial condition will be a unique continuous function of the initial condition and will converge to the largest invariant set where $\dot{V} = 0$. This set of points consists of the equilibrium point $(0, 0)$ and a circle of radius 1 centered at $(0, 0)$. Note that the circle of radius 1 is called a "limit cycle."

3.4-1. Because we need only show one example to justify the claim, we will pick a simple example. Let l be defined such that

$$l(w) = (1/2)w^2.$$

Then

$$w(t + 1) = w(t) - \gamma w(t).$$

Thus

$$\dot{l} = l(w(t+1)) - l(w(t)) = (w(t) - \gamma w(t))^2 - w(t)^2$$

$$\dot{l} = -2\gamma w(t)^2 + \gamma^2 w(t)^2 = -\gamma w(t)^2(2 - \gamma).$$

Since

$$\dot{l} = -\gamma w(t)^2(2 - \gamma),$$

simply choose $\gamma > 2$ to show that

$$l(w(t+1)) > l(w(t)).$$

Problems

3-1. Note that the ith eigenvalue, λ_i, of **C** is given by the formula

$$\lambda_i = \mathbf{e}_i^T \mathbf{C} \mathbf{e}_i,$$

where λ_i is a nonnegative real number and also that

$$\mathbf{e}_i^T \mathbf{C} \mathbf{e}_k = 0$$

for $i \neq k$.
   Thus

$$a(i, t+1) = a(i, t) + \gamma(1/n)\mathbf{e}_i^T \left[\sum_{k=1}^n [\mathbf{s}_k - \mathbf{W}(t)\mathbf{s}_k]\mathbf{s}_k^T \right] \mathbf{e}_i$$

$$a(i, t+1) = a(i, t) + \gamma \mathbf{e}_i^T \mathbf{C} \mathbf{e}_i - \gamma \mathbf{e}_i^T \mathbf{W}(t)\mathbf{C}\mathbf{e}_i$$

$$a(i, t+1) = a(i, t) + \gamma\lambda_i - \gamma\lambda_i a(i, t) = a(i, t)(1 - \gamma\lambda_i) + \gamma\lambda_i.$$

The quantity $a(i, t)$ converges to the value 1, provided that $|\gamma\lambda_i| < 1$ and $\lambda_i \neq 0$. The quantity $a(i, t)$ grows at a rate proportional to its corresponding eigenvalue λ_i. Thus the connection strength matrix is learning a linear subspace where familiar stimuli are amplified (i.e., are eigenvectors) and unfamiliar stimuli are orthogonal to the learned subspace.

3-3. If $\mathbf{x}^*$ is an asymptotically stable equilibrium point, then perturbations (i.e., *exemplars* of $\mathbf{x}^*$ will be mapped into $\mathbf{x}^*$) by the BAM dynamical system. Thus forcing $\mathbf{x}^*$ to be an asymptotically stable equilibrium point may be viewed as a goal of the learning process. Let **A** be a matrix of zeros with two on-diagonal submatrices, **W** and **U**, respectively. Let $\mathbf{x}(t)$ be a vector of the form

$$\mathbf{x}(t) = [\mathbf{a}(t), \mathbf{b}(t)],$$

where $\mathbf{a}(t)$ has ith element $a_i(t)$ and $\mathbf{b}(t)$ has ith element $b_i(t)$. Then an activation pattern **x** is an equilibrium point if the jth element of $\mathbf{A}\mathbf{x}$ has the same sign as the jth element of **x** for $j = 1, \ldots, p + d$. To prove all trajectories converge to the largest set of system equilibrium points, simply note that this network is a special case of the Hopfield (1982) network where **A** is the weight matrix and **x** is the system state vector.

3-5. The strategy for solving this problem will be to try to use the Invariant Set Theorem to prove that every trajectory approaches the largest invariant set where the change in the Lyapunov function's value is zero. Then try to show that the largest invariant set is in fact exactly the set of system equilibrium points. Define $\mathbf{x}_k = [x_k(1), \ldots, x_k(d)]$ as the d-dimensional real vector at the kth iteration of the algorithm.
   The discrete-time dynamical system generates $\mathbf{x}_{k+1}$ as a continuous function of $\mathbf{x}_k$ which means a given initial condition specifies a unique trajectory that is a continuous function of the system's initial condition. Also note, all trajectories are confined to a d-dimensional hypercube that is a closed, bounded, invariant set, and the candidate Lyapunov function is a continuous function of the system state $\mathbf{x}_k$. The only thing you need to show is that

$$V(\mathbf{x}_{k+1}) \leq V(\mathbf{x}_k).$$

Actually, if you can prove a slightly stronger condition on $V(\mathbf{x})$, this will help you show that the largest invariant set is exactly the set of system equilibrium points. This slightly stronger condition is

$$V(\mathbf{x}_{k+1}) < V(\mathbf{x}_k)$$

if and only if

$$\mathbf{x}_{k+1} \neq \mathbf{x}_k.$$

If you can prove this, it means that the set where

$$V(\mathbf{x}_{k+1}) = V(\mathbf{x}_k)$$

is in fact the set of system equilibrium points!

It will also be helpful to use the "hint" provided in the problem. According to the "hint," an $a(i, k) \geq 0$ can be always chosen for the BSB dynamical system such that

$$x_{k+1}(i) = x_k(i) + \gamma a(i,k) \sum_{j=1}^{d} a_{ij} x_k(j). \tag{8.26}$$

To prove this, simply note that the piecewise-linear sigmoidal nonlinearity in the BSB model preserves the "sign" of the expression

$$x_k(i) + \gamma \sum_{j=1}^{d} a_{ij} x_k(j)$$

and thus must be nonnegative. For example, if

$$x_k(j) = 1$$

and the net input to unit j is increased, then

$$x_{k+1}(j) = 1$$

and

$$a(i,k) = 0.$$

On the other hand, choose

$$a(i,k) = 1$$

if the BSB dynamical system is operating in the linear range. The variable $a(i, k)$ can take on other positive values if the "linear response" of the unit is truncated.

Returning to $V(\mathbf{x})$, note that

$$\Delta = V(\mathbf{x}_{k+1}) - V(\mathbf{x}_k) = -(1/2)[\mathbf{x}_{k+1}^T \mathbf{A} \mathbf{x}_{k+1} - \mathbf{x}_k^T \mathbf{A} \mathbf{x}_k].$$

Here it will be convenient to define $\mathbf{g}_k = \mathbf{A} \mathbf{x}_k$ and to define $\mathbf{\alpha}_k$ as a d-dimensional square diagonal matrix whose ith on-diagonal element is $a(i, k)$. Using (8.26) as an expression for $\mathbf{x}_{k+1}$,

$$\Delta = -(1/2)[(\mathbf{x}_k + \gamma \mathbf{\alpha}_k \mathbf{g}_k)^T \mathbf{A}(\mathbf{x}_k + \gamma \mathbf{\alpha}_k \mathbf{g}_k) - \mathbf{x}_k^T \mathbf{A} \mathbf{x}_k],$$

and because $\mathbf{A}$ is symmetric,

$$\Delta = -(1/2)[2\gamma \mathbf{g}_k^T \mathbf{\alpha}_k \mathbf{A} \mathbf{x}_k + \gamma^2 \mathbf{g}_k^T \mathbf{\alpha}_k \mathbf{A} \mathbf{\alpha}_k \mathbf{g}_k].$$

The second term in the above expression must be nonnegative because $\mathbf{A}$ is positive semidefinite. Thus to show that when

$$\mathbf{x}_{k+1} \neq \mathbf{x}_k,$$

that

$$V(\mathbf{x}_{k+1}) < V(\mathbf{x}_k),$$

you simply need to show that

$$\mathbf{g}_k^T \boldsymbol{a}_k \mathbf{A} \mathbf{x}_k > 0.$$

Now define

$$\mathbf{y}_k = \sqrt{\boldsymbol{a}_k} \mathbf{A} \mathbf{x}_k = \sqrt{\boldsymbol{a}_k} \, \mathbf{g}_k,$$

where $\sqrt{\boldsymbol{a}_k} \sqrt{\boldsymbol{a}_k} = \boldsymbol{a}_k$. Then

$$\mathbf{g}_k^T \boldsymbol{a}_k \mathbf{A} \mathbf{x}_k = \mathbf{x}_k^T \mathbf{A} \boldsymbol{a}_k \mathbf{A} \mathbf{x}_k = \mathbf{y}_k^T \mathbf{y}_k \geq 0.$$

Now suppose that for some iteration k that $\mathbf{x}_k$ is an equilibrium point, which means that, for all $i = 1 \ldots d$, either $a(i, k) = 0$ or $g_k(i) = 0$. Thus, if $\mathbf{x}_{k+1} \neq \mathbf{x}_k$ from (8.26), an $i \in \{1, \ldots, d\}$ must exist such that

$$a(i, k) \neq 0 \quad AND \quad g_k(i) \neq 0$$

or equivalently, $y_k(i) \neq 0$. This condition implies that (8.27) must be strictly greater than zero if $\mathbf{x}_{k+1} \neq \mathbf{x}_k$ because $\mathbf{y}_k$ cannot be a vector of zeros.

3-7. Let $\mathbf{q}$ be sufficiently close to $\mathbf{c}$, where the ith element of $\mathbf{q}$ is given by

$$q_i(\varepsilon_i) = c_i(1 - \varepsilon_i),$$

c_i is the ith element of $\mathbf{c}$, and $0 \leq \varepsilon_i \leq 1$. Let $\boldsymbol{\varepsilon}$ be a vector whose ith element is ε_i.

Thus you need to show that $V(\mathbf{q}(\boldsymbol{\varepsilon})) > V(\mathbf{c})$ for ε_i sufficiently small for $i = 1 \ldots d$ subject to the constraint that $\boldsymbol{\varepsilon}$ is not a vector of zeros (because then $\mathbf{q}(\boldsymbol{\varepsilon}) = \mathbf{c}$). The notation $\mathbf{q}$ instead of $\mathbf{q}(\boldsymbol{\varepsilon})$ and q_i instead of $q_i(\varepsilon_i)$ will be used in the following discussion to keep the notation simple.

Now note that:

$$V(\mathbf{q}) - V(\mathbf{c}) = -(1/2) \sum_i \sum_j [a_{ij} q_i q_j - a_{ij} c_i c_j].$$

And using (8.28),

$$V(\mathbf{q}) - V(\mathbf{c}) = -(1/2) \sum_i \sum_j [a_{ij} c_i c_j (1 - \varepsilon_i)(1 - \varepsilon_j) - a_{ij} c_i c_j].$$

$$V(\mathbf{q}) - V(\mathbf{c}) = -(1/2) \sum_i \sum_j [-(\varepsilon_i + \varepsilon_j) a_{ij} c_i c_j + O((\varepsilon_i \varepsilon_j))].$$

Now because $\sum_j a_{ij} c_j$ has the same sign as c_i (i.e., $\mathbf{Ac}$ remains in the same hypercube quadrant as $\mathbf{c}$) and $\mathbf{q} \neq \mathbf{c}$, the double summation on the right hand side is strictly positive. Thus, for the magnitude of $\boldsymbol{\varepsilon}$ sufficiently small and $\mathbf{q} \neq \mathbf{c}$,

$$V(\mathbf{q}) > V(\mathbf{c}).$$

By a variation of the Lyapunov Stability Theorem described in problem 3-11 and the observation that if the stepsize of the BSB algorithm is chosen to be sufficiently small to prevent the system state from "jumping" too far from $\mathbf{c}$, the problem may be completed.

This problem is relevant because the "classification problem" can be defined as a mapping problem that maps some set of vectors into a single category. Represent that category as an asymptotically stable equilibrium point. Then the members or "exemplars" of that category are initial states of the dynamical system that initiate trajectories approaching the asymptotically stable equilibrium point. Taking this one step further, if you want to design a learning algorithm to teach the BSB dynamical system a particular "category" (i.e., asymptotically stable equilibrium point) vertex $\mathbf{c}$, then you might try to prove that the learning algorithm forces the matrix $\mathbf{A}$ to have the property that $\mathbf{Ac}$ has the same sign as hypercube vertex $\mathbf{c}$.

3-9. The generator function for this dynamical system is defined by $\mathbf{f}(\mathbf{x}) = \mathbf{W}\mathbf{x}$ for all $\mathbf{x} \in \mathfrak{R}^d$. Thus, $\nabla \mathbf{f} = \mathbf{W}$ which is a finite constant and thus bounded. This implies that the generator function satisfies a global Lipschitz condition.

Now note that

$$\dot{V} = V(\mathbf{x}(t+1)) - V(\mathbf{x}(t)) = |\mathbf{x}(t+1)|^2 - |\mathbf{x}(t)|^2$$

$$\dot{V} = \mathbf{x}(t)^T \mathbf{W}^T \mathbf{W} \mathbf{x}(t) - \mathbf{x}(t)^T \mathbf{I} \mathbf{x}(t),$$

where $\mathbf{I}$ is the identity matrix. Thus, $\dot{V}$ is strictly less than zero provided that the real symmetric matrix $\mathbf{WW} - \mathbf{I}$ is a matrix with strictly negative eigenvalues. If the magnitudes of all of the eigenvalues of $\mathbf{W}$ are strictly less than one, then $\mathbf{WW} - \mathbf{I}$ will have strictly negative eigenvalues. Also note that V and $\dot{V}$ are continuous on $\mathcal{R}^d$.

Let

$$\Omega_s = \{\mathbf{x} \in \mathcal{R}^d : V(\mathbf{x}) = |\mathbf{x}|^2 \le K\},$$

where K is a positive finite real number. Because V is a Lyapunov function when $\mathbf{W}$ has eigenvalues whose magnitudes are strictly less than one, it follows from the Closed, Bounded, Invariant Set Proposition that Ω_s is a closed, bounded, and invariant set. Thus all trajectories initiated in Ω_s converge to the largest invariant set where $V(\mathbf{x}) = 0$, which is the set $\{\mathbf{0}_d\}$. Note that $\mathbf{0}_d$ is an equilibrium point by the following argument. If $\mathbf{x}^*$ is an equilibrium point, then $\mathbf{x}^* = \mathbf{W}\mathbf{x}^*$. Thus because $\mathbf{W}$ has full rank, the unique equilibrium point is $\mathbf{x}^* = \mathbf{0}_d$, and $\mathbf{0}_d$ is a globally asymptotically stable equilibrium point.

3-11. The proof of the theorem follows immediately from the Invariant Set Theorem and the definition of an asymptotically stable equilibrium point.

An example where Ω_δ is not an invariant set would arise in the case where the Lyapunov function V is defined such that for all $x \in \mathcal{R}$:

$$V(x) = (x-1)^2 + (x-2)^2$$

and the dynamics of the discrete-time dynamical system $\boldsymbol{\Psi}$ are such that all trajectories converge to $\{1, 2\}$ without converging to either the set $\{1\}$ or the set $\{2\}$. That is, the system state "jumps" back and forth between the two elements of $\{1, 2\}$. Let $\Omega_\delta = \{x \in \mathcal{R} : |x-1| \le \delta\}$ where the finite positive real number δ is chosen such that $\Omega_\delta \cap \{2\}$ is an empty set. In this case, Ω_δ is closed and bounded but Ω_δ is not an invariant set since a trajectory of the dynamical system $\boldsymbol{\Psi}$ could leave Ω_δ.

Chapter 4

Elementary Problems

4.1-1. Note that because, for some finite K, $|\tilde{\mathbf{x}}(i)| < K$, and because V is continuous: $E[|V(\tilde{\mathbf{x}}(i))|] < K < \infty$. Let $C = \sum_{j=1}^M p(\mathbf{x}^j) V(\mathbf{x}^j)$. Also $E[\tilde{V}_t] = (1/t)\sum_{i=1}^t C = C$, and by the Strong Law of Large Numbers, the sequence of scalar random variables $\tilde{V}_1, \tilde{V}_2, \tilde{V}_3, \ldots$ converges with probability one to C.

4.1-3. Simply follow the procedure of the Mean Square Convergence Implies Convergence In Probability Theorem. Also see answer to problem 4.1-1.

4.2-1. Only the case where $\eta_t = 1/(200 + t)$ for $t > 500$ needs to be considered. Use the integral test (e.g., Rosenlicht 1968, 161), which states that if

$$f: \{x \in \mathcal{R} : x \ge 1\} \to \mathcal{R}$$

is a decreasing positive-valued function, then $\sum_{t=1}^\infty f(t)$ converges if and only if $\int_1^\infty f(t)\,dt$ exists. First note that $1/(200 + t)$ is a nonincreasing function on $[1, \infty)$ whose range is positive for $1 \le t < \infty$. Then note that since

$$\int_1^M \left(1/(200 + t)\right) dt = \log[200 + M] - \log[200 + 1],$$

$\lim_{M \to \infty} \int_1^M \left(1/(200 + t)\right) dt = \infty$. Thus, by the integral test,

$$\lim_{M\to\infty}\sum_{t=1}^{M}(1/(200+t))=\infty.$$

And finally note that since

$$\int_{1}^{M}(1/(200+t)^2)\,dt=-(1/(200+M))+(1/(200+1)),$$

it follows that $\lim_{M\to\infty}\int_{1}^{M}(1/(200+t)^2)\,dt=1/(200+1)$ is finite. Therefore, the sequence of positive real numbers $\eta_1,\eta_2,\ldots$ satisfies (4.1) and (4.2).

4.2-3. Let $a=t/\tau$. Note that as $t\to\infty$, $a\to\infty$. Using an argument similar to solution of problem 4.2-1, since

$$\sum_{1}^{\infty}\left|\frac{1}{a}\right|=\infty$$

and

$$\left|\frac{1}{a}\right|<\left|\frac{a+1}{a^2+1}\right|=\left|\frac{1}{a}+\frac{1-(1/a)}{1+a^2}\right|$$

for $a=2,3,\ldots$ by the divergence form of the comparison test (Goldberg 1964, 81, theorem 3.6D), it follows that

$$\sum_{1}^{\infty}\frac{a+1}{a^2+1}=\infty.$$

Now note that for $a>1$:

$$\left|\frac{(a+1)^2}{(a^2+1)^2}\right|\le\left|\frac{(a+1)^2}{a^4}\right|\le\frac{(2a)^2}{a^4}=\frac{4}{a^2}.$$

Thus since

$$\sum_{1}^{\infty}(1/a^2)<\infty,$$

it follows from the comparison test (Rosenlicht 1968, 144) that

$$\sum_{1}^{\infty}\frac{(a+1)^2}{(a^2+1)^2}<\infty.$$

4.3-1. First, $\tilde{n}(t)$ is a bounded stochastic sequence of independent and identically distributed random variables. Second, η_t satisfies (4.1) and (4.2) using the methods of problem 4.2-1. Third, $\tilde{x}(0)$ is a constant and thus finite. Fourth, the function $f:\mathscr{R}\times\mathscr{R}\to\mathscr{R}$, defined for all $x\in\mathscr{R}$ and for all $n\in\mathscr{R}$ by

$$f(x,n)=-[(x-1)^3+(x-14)^7]+n,$$

is continuous in both arguments. And, fifth, $\bar{f}(\cdot)=E[f(\cdot,\tilde{n})]$ exists and is given by

$$\bar{f}(x)=-[(x-1)^3+(x-14)^7]$$

for all $x\in\mathscr{R}$.

Try to find a stochastic Lyapunov function V by integrating $\bar{f}$ with respect to x. This strategy yields a stochastic Lyapunov function $V:\mathscr{R}\to(0,\infty)$ defined such that for all $x\in\mathscr{R}$:

$$V(x)=(1/4)(x-1)^4+(1/8)(x-14)^8.$$

Note that V has a continuous Hessian, given by

$3(x-1)^2 + 7(x-14)^6$.

Because, in addition, for all $x \in \mathcal{R}$,

$U(x) = (dV/dx)\bar{f}(x) = -[\bar{f}(x)]^2 \leq 0$,

either the stochastic process $\tilde{x}(0), \tilde{x}(1), \ldots$ is not bounded or it converges with probability one to the set $\mathcal{H}$ defined by

$\mathcal{H} = \{x \in \mathcal{R}: (x-1)^3 + (x-14)^7 = 0\}$.

4.3-3. First, note that $|\tilde{w}_{ijk}(0)| < K$ for some finite K. Second, show that $\eta_0, \eta_1, \eta_2, \ldots$ satisfy (4.1) and (4.2). This condition is verified using the integral test as in problem 4.2-1. Third, note that

$f_{ijk}(w_{ijk}, [\tilde{x}_i \ \tilde{x}_j \ \tilde{x}_k]) = -\lambda w_{ijk} + \tilde{x}_i \tilde{x}_j \tilde{x}_k$.

The expected value of $f_{ijk}(w_{ijk}, [\tilde{x}_i \ \tilde{x}_j \ \tilde{x}_k])$ is given by

$\bar{f}_{ijk}(w_{ijk}) = -\lambda w_{ijk} + c_{ijk}$,

where

$$c_{ijk} = \sum_{l=1}^{M} p_l x_i^l x_j^l x_k^l$$

is finite because M is finite, where $|x_i^l|$ is finite for all $i = 1 \ldots d$, and where $l = 1 \ldots M$ by assumption. Fourth, note that $\bar{f}_{ijk}$ is a continuous function of w_{ijk}. Fifth, try to find a stochastic Lyapunov function by integrating $\bar{f}_{ijk}$ with respect to w_{ijk}. Define V_{ijk} such that

$$V_{ijk}(w_{ijk}) = -\int [-\lambda w_{ijk} + c_{ijk}] dw_{ijk} = (\lambda/2) w_{ijk}^2 - c_{ijk} w_{ijk} + K_{ijk}.$$

Choose $K_{ijk} = c_{ijk}^2/(2\lambda)$ so that

$V_{ijk}(w_{ijk}) = (\lambda/2)(w_{ijk} - [c_{ijk}/\lambda])^2$.

Now define

$$V(\mathbf{W}) = \sum_{i=1}^{d} \sum_{j=1}^{d} \sum_{k=1}^{d} V_{ijk}(w_{ijk}).$$

And sixth, note that V has a continuous Hessian. Since

$dV_{ijk}/dw_{ijk} = \lambda w_{ijk} - c_{ijk}$,

$$U(\mathbf{W}) = \sum_{i=1}^{d} \sum_{j=1}^{d} \sum_{k=1}^{d} \left(dV_{ijk}/dw_{ijk} \right) \bar{f}_{ijk} \leq 0.$$

The second derivative of V_{ijk} is positive everywhere since

$d^2 V_{ijk}/dw_{ijk}^2 = \lambda > 0$,

provided that $\lambda > 0$. Thus the point where $dV/dw_{ijk} = 0$ is unique. Thus, for $i = 1 \ldots d, j = 1 \ldots d$, and $k = 1 \ldots d$, either the stochastic process $\tilde{w}_{ijk}(0), \tilde{w}_{ijk}(1), \ldots$ converges with probability one to the set $\mathcal{H}$ defined by

$\mathcal{H} = \{w_{ijk} \in \mathcal{R}: w_{ijk} = c_{ijk}/\lambda\}$,

or $\tilde{w}_{ijk}(0), \tilde{w}_{ijk}(1), \ldots$ is not bounded. At $\lambda = 0$, $\mathcal{H}$ contains a point at ∞.

4.4-1. If $E[\,|U(\tilde{\mathbf{x}}(t))|\,] \to 0$ as $t \to \infty$, this implies that $U(\tilde{\mathbf{x}}(t))$ converges in probability to zero by the definition of convergence in probability and the Markov inequality.

Problems

4-1. First, note that $(\tilde{\mathbf{s}}(t), \tilde{\mathbf{o}}(t))$ is a bounded stochastic process consisting of independent and identically distributed random variables for $t = 0, 1, 2, \ldots$. Second, choose $\gamma_0, \gamma_1, \gamma_2, \ldots$ to satisfy (4.1) and (4.2). Third, note that

$$\mathbf{F}(\mathbf{W}, (\tilde{\mathbf{s}}, \tilde{\mathbf{o}})) = [\tilde{\mathbf{o}}(t) - \mathbf{W}\tilde{\mathbf{s}}(t)]\tilde{\mathbf{s}}(t)^T,$$

so that the expected value of $\mathbf{F}(\mathbf{W}, (\tilde{\mathbf{s}}, \tilde{\mathbf{o}}))$ with respect to $(\tilde{\mathbf{s}}, \tilde{\mathbf{o}})$, $\mathbf{F}$, exists because

$$\mathbf{F}(\mathbf{W}) = \mathbf{B} - \mathbf{W}\mathbf{C},$$

where $\mathbf{B} = E[\tilde{\mathbf{o}}\tilde{\mathbf{s}}^T] < \infty$ and $\mathbf{C} = E[\tilde{\mathbf{s}}\tilde{\mathbf{s}}^T] < \infty$. The constant matrices $\mathbf{B}$ and $\mathbf{C}$ are finite because the probability distribution is a probability mass function on a finite sample space whose elements are vectors with finite magnitudes. Fourth, note that $\mathbf{F}$ is a continuous function of $\mathbf{W}$. Fifth, try to show that $l(\mathbf{W}) = E[\,|\tilde{\mathbf{o}} - \mathbf{W}\tilde{\mathbf{s}}|^2]$ is a stochastic Lyapunov function. To test this hypothesis, note that

$$l(\mathbf{W}) = E[\,|\tilde{\mathbf{o}} - \mathbf{W}\tilde{\mathbf{s}}|^2] = \sum_{k=1}^{M} p_k |\mathbf{o}^k - \mathbf{W}\mathbf{s}^k|^2,$$

so that

$$dl(\mathbf{W})/d\mathbf{W} = \sum_{k=1}^{M} p_k (d/d\mathbf{W}) |\mathbf{o}^k - \mathbf{W}\mathbf{s}^k|^2 = -2 \sum_{k=1}^{M} p_k [\mathbf{o}^k - \mathbf{W}\mathbf{s}^k][\mathbf{s}^k]^T$$

$$dl(\mathbf{W})/d\mathbf{W} = -2\mathbf{B} + 2\mathbf{W}\mathbf{C}.$$

Thus the element by element matrix dot product of $dl(\mathbf{W})/d\mathbf{W}$ and $\mathbf{F}(\mathbf{W})$ is:

$$U(\mathbf{W}) = -2|\mathbf{B} - \mathbf{W}\mathbf{C}|^2 \le 0,$$

where $|\mathbf{B} - \mathbf{W}\mathbf{C}|^2$ is defined as the sum of the squares of the elements of $\mathbf{B} - \mathbf{W}\mathbf{C}$.

Now compute the gradient of $\nabla_{\mathbf{W}} l$ with respect to $\mathbf{W}$ in order to obtain the Hessian of l, and show that the Hessian of l is $\mathbf{C}$, which is continuous. Thus the stochastic process $\tilde{\mathbf{W}}(0), \tilde{\mathbf{W}}(1), \ldots$ either is not bounded or converges with probability one to the set $\mathcal{H}$ defined by

$$\mathcal{H} = \{\mathbf{W} \in \mathcal{R}^{o \times s}: \mathbf{B} - \mathbf{W}\mathbf{C} = \mathbf{O}_{o \times s}\},$$

where $\mathbf{O}_{o \times s}$ is an $o \times s$ matrix of zeros. Note that if $\mathbf{C}$ has full rank, then $\mathcal{H}$ consists of the single point $\mathbf{W} = \mathbf{B}\mathbf{C}^{-1}$.

4-3. This algorithm is a special case of the on-line version of backpropagation analyzed in section 4.3.1. Note that the Hessian of l is continuous. Also note that the sequence of positive stepsizes $\gamma_1, \gamma_2, \ldots$ satisfies (4.1) and (4.2), and that the stochastic process $\{(\tilde{\mathbf{s}}, \tilde{\mathbf{o}})\}$ is bounded and consists of independent and identically distributed random variables.

It is necessary to show that

$$\tilde{w}_{kj}(t+1) = \tilde{w}_{kj}(t) - \gamma_t dl/d\tilde{w}_{kj}(t),$$

$$\tilde{v}_{ji}(t+1) = \tilde{v}_{ji}(t) - \gamma_t dl/d\tilde{v}_{ji}(t),$$

$$\tilde{b}_k(t+1) = \tilde{b}_k(t) - \gamma_t dl/d\tilde{b}_k(t),$$

and

$$\tilde{q}_j(t+1) = \tilde{q}_j(t) - \gamma_t dl/d\tilde{q}_j(t),$$

where the notation $dl/d\tilde{w}_{kj}(t)$ refers to the partial derivative of l with respect to w_{kj} and evaluated at $\tilde{w}_{kj}(t)$.

Let

$$\bar{\delta}_{r_k} = \sum_{n=1}^{M} p_n(o_n^k - r_n^k) = -dl/dr_k.$$

Note that

$$dl/dw_{kj} = [dl/dr_k][dr_k/d\varphi_k][d\varphi_k/dw_{kj}] = -\bar{\delta}_{r_k}[r_k(1 - r_k)][h_j],$$

$$dl/db_k = [dl/dr_k]\left[dr_k/d\varphi_k\right]\left[d\varphi_k/db_k\right] = -\bar{\delta}_{r_k}[r_k(1 - r_k)].$$

$$dl/dv_{ji} = \left[\sum_{k=1}^{p} (dl/dr_k)\left(dr_k/d\varphi_k\right)\left(d\varphi_k/dh_j\right)\right]\left[dh_j/d\psi_j\right]\left[d\psi_j/dv_{ji}\right]$$

$$dl/dv_{ji} = \bar{\delta}_{h_j}[h_j(1 - h_j)]s_i,$$

where

$$\bar{\delta}_{h_j} = -\sum_{k=1}^{p} w_{kj}[r_k(1 - r_k)]\bar{\delta}_{r_k}$$

and

$$dl/dq_j = \left[\sum_{k=1}^{p} (dl/dr_k)(dr_k/d\varphi_k)(d\varphi_k/dh_j)\right]\left[dh_j/d\psi_j\right]\left[d\psi_j/dv_{ji}\right]$$

$$dl/dq_j = \bar{\delta}_{h_j}[h_j(1 - h_j)].$$

4-5. The approach to this problem is similar to the solution of problem 4-3. Verify this problem is a special case of on-line backpropagation as described in section 4.3.1 by computing the gradient of equation (2.12) and explicitly showing the relationship between this problem and the on-line backpropagation algorithm discussed in chapter 2.

4-7. The purpose of the $\mathbf{D}^k(t)$ matrix is used to indicate which subset of elements of $\mathbf{o}^k(t)$ is observable for the tth training stimulus in the kth sequence. The purpose of the $\left| \mathbf{r}^k(t) - \mathbf{r}^k(t-1) \right|^2$ term is to introduce a "smoothness" constraint as suggested by Jordan (1992), so that the response of the ANN system to the tth stimulus in the kth sequence will be similar to the response of the ANN system to the $(t-1)$th stimulus and the $(t+1)$th stimulus in the kth sequence. Given that the response feedback signal from the environment is not observable, a reasonable strategy is to control the automobile at time t_0 in a way similar to how you controlled the automobile at time $(t_0 - 1)$ and how you *plan* to control the automobile at time $(t_0 + 1)$.

Also note that for $t = 2 \ldots M_k$:

$$dl^k/d\mathbf{r}^k(t) = -2\mathbf{D}^k(t)[\mathbf{o}^k(t) - \mathbf{r}^k(t)] - 2\lambda[\mathbf{r}^k(t+1) - \mathbf{r}^k(t)] + 2\lambda[\mathbf{r}^k(t) - \mathbf{r}^k(t-1)],$$

and $dl^k/d\mathbf{W}$ is given by the formula

$$dl^k/d\mathbf{W} = [dl^k/d\mathbf{r}^k(t)][\mathbf{s}^k(t-1)]^T,$$

where $dl^k/d\mathbf{r}^k(t)$ and $\mathbf{s}^k(t-1)$ are column vectors. Complete the problem by applying the Stochastic Approximation Theorem, using the above hints. Note that you need to write down some type of explicit formula for $dl/d\mathbf{W}$ and then to show that l is an almost stochastic Lyapunov function. You will also need to exploit the assumption that the sample space of a random training stimulus $\tilde{\mathbf{x}}(k)$ is a bounded set in $\mathcal{R}^d$.

4-9. As in problems 4-3 and 4-7, verify that you have a special case of on-line backpropagation as described in section 4.3 by computing the necessary first derivatives and by showing the necessary correspondences between this problem and on-line backpropagation.

Chapter 5

Elementary Problems

5.1-1.

$$\nabla f = [2(x_1 + x_2) + x_2 + 1 \qquad 2(x_1 + x_2) + x_1].$$

5.1-3. The Hessian of f is a two-dimensional matrix whose ijth element is w_{ij} $(i, j = 1, 2)$, where $w_{11} = 2$, $w_{12} = 3$, $w_{21} = 3$, and $w_{22} = 2$.

5.1-5. The set of critical points is the set of points (x_1, x_2) that satisfies: $2(x_1 + x_2) + x_2 + 1 = 0$ and $2(x_1 + x_2) + x_1 = 0$. Thus $x_1 = 2/5$ and $x_2 = -3/5$ is the unique solution, that is, there is only one critical point. The eigenvalues of the Hessian of f evaluated at this point are -1 and 5, indicating that this critical point is a saddle point (i.e., not a local minimum and is not a local maximum).

5.2-1. Let $(\mathbf{s}_1, \mathbf{o}_1), \ldots, (\mathbf{s}_M, \mathbf{o}_M)$ be a set of M training stimuli, where $(\mathbf{s}_i, \mathbf{o}_i)$ is the ith training stimulus consisting of a d-dimensional real input vector $\mathbf{s}_i$ and a d-dimensional real desired response vector $\mathbf{o}_i$. A batch version of the Widrow-Hoff learning rule may be defined by

$$\mathbf{W}(k+1) = \mathbf{W}(k) + \gamma_k (1/M) \sum_{i=1}^{M} [\mathbf{o}_i - \mathbf{r}_i(k)] \mathbf{s}_i^T,$$

where $\mathbf{r}_i(k) = \mathbf{W}(k)\mathbf{s}_i$. Note that $\mathbf{r}_i(k)$ is the response of the ANN system with weight matrix $\mathbf{W}(k)$ to stimulus $\mathbf{s}_i$, and that $\mathbf{o}_i$ is the desired or target response of the ANN system to stimulus $\mathbf{s}_i$.

This algorithm can be shown to be a special case of the gradient descent algorithm

$$\mathbf{W}(k+1) = \mathbf{W}(k) + \gamma_k \mathbf{F}(k)$$

by defining the learning objective function $l: \mathcal{R}^{d \times d} \rightarrow \mathcal{R}$ such that for all $\mathbf{W} \in \mathcal{R}^{d \times d}$:

$$l(\mathbf{W}) = (1/2)(1/M) \sum_{i=1}^{M} |\mathbf{o}_i - \mathbf{W}\mathbf{s}_i|^2,$$

and then noting that

$$\mathbf{F}(k) = -\nabla_{\mathbf{W}(k)} l = -(1/M) \sum_{i=1}^{M} [\mathbf{o}_i - \mathbf{r}_i(k)] \mathbf{s}_i^T.$$

Let $\mathbf{w}_j$ refer to the jth row of $\mathbf{W}$. Let $\mathbf{w} = [\mathbf{w}_1, \ldots, \mathbf{w}_d]$. Thus the Hessian of l, $\nabla_{\mathbf{w}}^2 l$, is a d^2-dimensional square matrix whose on-diagonal d-dimensional square matrices are given by the formula

$$\nabla_{\mathbf{w}_j} \nabla_{\mathbf{w}_j} l = (1/M) \sum_{i=1}^{M} \mathbf{s}_i \mathbf{s}_i^T$$

and whose off-diagonal d-dimensional square matrices are given by the formula

$$\nabla_{\mathbf{w}_j} \nabla_{\mathbf{w}_k} l = \mathbf{0}_{d \times d}$$

for $j \neq k$.

Also note that because $\nabla_{\mathbf{w}}^2 l$ is a constant symmetric real matrix which is not functionally dependent upon $\mathbf{W}$, it follows that the Hessian of l is bounded on $\mathbf{W}(0), \mathbf{W}(1), \ldots$. This algorithm thus generates a sequence of matrices $\mathbf{W}(0), \mathbf{W}(1), \ldots$ that converges to the critical points of l if γ_k is a *properly chosen stepsize* at each iteration of the algorithm.

5.2-3. Referring to the solution to problem 5.2-1, note that $\nabla_{\mathbf{w}}^2 l$ is positive definite if $\mathbf{s}_1, \ldots, \mathbf{s}_M$ span the d-dimensional space. By the solution to problem 5.2-1, $\mathbf{W}(0), \mathbf{W}(1), \ldots$ converge to the critical points of l, and l has continuous third partial derivatives. Thus any critical point is a strict local minimum by the Strict Local Minimum Test. Because the Hessian of l is positive definite everywhere in this case, by the Strict Global Minimum Test, any strict local minimum is the unique global minimum in this case.

5.3-1. This solution is similar to the solution to problem 4-1. Explicitly identify the objective function and its global minimum.

5.3-3. The solution of this problem requires computation of the formula given in step 2 of the Gibbs sampler algorithm. Let

$$q_{it}(j) = Q(x_1(t),\ldots, x_{i-1}(t), x_i(t+1) = j, x_{i+1}(t),\ldots, x_d(t)).$$

Then

$$p\big(x_i(t+1) = 1 \mid \mathbf{n}_i(t)\big) = \frac{(1/Z)\exp[q_{it}(1)]}{(1/Z)\exp[q_{it}(0)] + (1/Z)\exp[q_{it}(1)]},$$

which implies that

$$p\big(x_i(t+1) = 1 \mid \mathbf{n}_i(t)\big) = \mathcal{S}(q_{it}(1) - q_{it}(0)),$$

where the sigmoidal logistic function $\mathcal{S}: \mathcal{R} \to (0, 1)$ is defined such that for all $x \in \mathcal{R}$: $\mathcal{S}(x) = 1/(1 + \exp[-x])$. Substituting for the form of Q provided in the problem, it follows that

$$q_{it}(1) - q_{it}(0) = b_i + \sum_{j=2}^{d}\sum_{k=1}^{j-1} x_j x_k b_{ijk}.$$

5.4-1. Let λ be a positive real number. Let l be the learning objective function for problem 5.2-1, and note that

$$l' = l + (1/2)\lambda |\mathbf{W}|^2$$

is the learning objective function for problem 5.2-2 where $|\mathbf{W}|^2$ is the sum of the squares of the elements of $\mathbf{W}$ (see chapter 1 for a review of weight decay). If h_i is the ith eigenvalue of the Hessian of l, then pre- and postmultiply l' by the eigenvectors of the Hessian of l to obtain the eigenvalues of the Hessian l'. Remember that the eigenvectors of a symmetric real matrix are real and orthogonal to one another. From this analysis it follows that $h_i + \lambda$ is the ith eigenvalue of the Hessian of l', and that the eigenvectors of the Hessian of l' are the same as the eigenvectors of the Hessian of l.

5.5-1. From the solution to problem 5.2-1, the gradient of the risk function l is given by

$$\mathbf{g}(k) = -(1/M)\sum_{i=1}^{M} [\mathbf{o}_i - \mathbf{r}_i(k)]\mathbf{s}_i^T,$$

where $\mathbf{r}_i(k) = \mathbf{W}(k)\mathbf{s}_i$. Substitute this formula for the gradient of the learning objective function into the Shanno algorithm, and simplify the resulting expressions to obtain the final answer.

Problems

5-1. First set $\nabla_{\lambda_k} l$ and $\nabla_{\delta_k} l$ equal to zero in order to obtain

$$\mathbf{r}^k = \underline{\mathcal{S}}(\mathbf{W}\mathbf{h}^k + \mathbf{b})$$

and

$$\mathbf{h}^k = \underline{\mathcal{S}}(\mathbf{V}\mathbf{s}^k + \mathbf{d}).$$

From these derived formulas for $\mathbf{r}^k$ and $\mathbf{h}^k$ and the fact that $\nabla_{\mathbf{r}^k} l$ and $\nabla_{\mathbf{h}^k} l$ must vanish at a critical point,

$$\nabla_{\mathbf{r}^k} l = -[\mathbf{o}^k - \mathbf{r}^k] + \lambda_k^T$$

and

$$\nabla_{\mathbf{h}^k} l = -\lambda_k^T \mathbf{D_{r}}_k \mathbf{W} + \delta_k^T,$$

which are set equal to row vectors of zeros. Use the notation $\mathbf{D_{r}}_k$ to denote a diagonal matrix whose ith on-diagonal element is the ith element of $\mathbf{r}_k$ multiplied by the quantity: one minus the ith element of $\mathbf{r}_k$. Thus the error signal for the kth stimulus for the output units

$$\lambda_k^T = [\mathbf{o}^k - \mathbf{r}^k]$$

and the error signal for the kth stimulus for the hidden units

$$\delta_k^T = \lambda_k^T \mathbf{D_{r}}_k \mathbf{W}$$

are obtained. Note that δ_k results from a backward propagation of the error signal at the output units in response to the kth stimulus.

The gradient descent update equation for $\mathbf{V}$ (for example) is given by

$$\mathbf{V}(t+1) = \mathbf{V}(t) - \gamma \nabla_{\mathbf{V}(t)} l,$$

where $\nabla_{\mathbf{V}(t)} l$ is the gradient of l with respect to $\mathbf{V}$ evaluated at $\mathbf{V}(t)$. Thus also

$$\nabla_{\mathbf{V}(t)} l = -\sum_{k=1}^{M} \delta_k \mathbf{D_{h}}_k \mathbf{s}_k^T$$

and the update equations for $\mathbf{W}$, $\mathbf{b}$, and $\mathbf{d}$ are obtained in a similar manner.

5-3. The notation $\log(\mathbf{x})$, where $\mathbf{x}$ is a real vector, means that $\log(\mathbf{x})$ is a vector whose ith element is $\log(x_i)$, where x_i is the ith element of $\mathbf{x}$. In matrix notation,

$$l = -(1/n) \sum_{k=1}^{n} l^k,$$

where

$$l^k = \mathbf{o}^k .* \log(\mathbf{r}^k) + (\mathbf{1}_m - \mathbf{o}^k) .* \log(\mathbf{1}_m - \mathbf{r}^k),$$

$\mathbf{o}^k$ is kth target activation pattern, $\mathbf{r}^k$ is kth output unit activation pattern, and $\mathbf{1}_m$ is an m-dimensional vector of ones. The operator .* denotes element by element matrix multiplication. Thus

$$\mathbf{r}^k = \underline{\mathcal{S}}[\mathbf{W}\mathbf{s}^k].$$

Let $\mathbf{w}_j^T$ be jth row vector of $\mathbf{W}$. Let r_j^k be the jth element of $\mathbf{r}^k$. Thus also

$$dl^k/d\mathbf{w}_j = (dl^k/d\mathbf{r}^k)^T (d\mathbf{r}^k/d\mathbf{w}_j)$$

where $d\mathbf{r}^k/d\mathbf{w}_j$ is an $m \times h$ matrix whose jth row ($j = 1 \dots m$) is given by the row vector:

$$r_j^k(1 - r_j^k)\mathbf{s}^k$$

and whose remaining $m - 1$ rows are filled with zeros,

$$dl^k/dr_j^k = -[o_j^k - r_j^k]/(r_j^k(1 - r_j^k)),$$

and

$$dl^k/d\mathbf{w}_j = -[\mathbf{o}^k - \mathbf{r}^k]\mathbf{s}^k. \tag{8.29}$$

Also note that $d^2l^k/d\mathbf{w}_j d\mathbf{w}_a$ is an h-dimensional matrix of zeros for $j \neq a$. And finally, take the derivative of (8.29) to obtain

$$d^2l^k/d\mathbf{w}_j d\mathbf{w}_a = r_j^k(1 - r_j^k)\mathbf{s}^k(\mathbf{s}^k)^T$$

for $j = a$.

Gradient descent algorithm:

$$\mathbf{w}_j(t+1) = \mathbf{w}_j(t) - \gamma_t \left[\frac{dl}{d\mathbf{w}_j(t)} \right]$$

Newton algorithm:

$$\mathbf{w}_j(t+1) = \mathbf{w}_j(t) - \gamma_t \left[\frac{d^2l}{d\mathbf{w}_j(t)d\mathbf{w}_k(t)} \right]^{-1} \left[\frac{dl}{d\mathbf{w}_j(t)} \right]$$

5-5. To show the Hessian in problem 5-3 is positive definite when the d-dimensional vectors $\mathbf{s}^1,\ldots, \mathbf{s}^M$ completely span the d-dimensional space, premultiply and postmultiply the Hessian by an arbitrary vector and show the resulting quantity is strictly positive. Then use the Strict Global Minimum Test (chapter 5).

5-7. The Lagrange multiplier approach described in problem 5-1 will be used in this problem. The quantity $\hat{l}_n$ is a function of $\mathbf{W}, \{\mathbf{o}^k(t)\}, \{\mathbf{r}^k(t)\}, \mathbf{V}, \mathbf{R}, \{\mathbf{q}^k(t)\}, \{\lambda^k(t)\}$, and $\{\delta^k(t)\}$.

Let the operator .* indicate element-by-element vector multiplication, so that if $\mathbf{a}$ and $\mathbf{b}$ are d-dimensional vectors, the ith element of $\mathbf{a}$.* $\mathbf{b}$ is $a_i b_i, i = 1\ldots d$.

Solve for critical points of $\hat{l}_n$. For $k = 1\ldots n$:

$$l^k = \left| \mathbf{o}^k(M_k) - \mathbf{r}^k(M_k) \right|^2 + \sum_{t=1}^{M_k} \lambda^k(t)^T \left[\mathbf{r}^k(t) - \mathcal{S}[\mathbf{Wh}^k(t)] \right]$$

$$+ \sum_{t=1}^{M_k} \delta^k(t)^T \left[\mathbf{h}^k(t) - \mathcal{S}[\mathbf{Vs}^k(t) + \mathbf{Rh}^k(t-1)] \right].$$

For $k = 1\ldots n$: set

$$dl^k/d\mathbf{r}^k(M_k) = -2\left[\mathbf{o}^k(M_k) - \mathbf{r}^k(M_k) \right] + \lambda^k(M_k) \tag{8.30}$$

to a vector of zeros.

For $t = 1\ldots(M_k - 1), k = 1\ldots n$: set

$$dl^k/d\mathbf{h}^k(t) = -\lambda^k(t)^T \mathbf{D}_{\mathbf{r}}^k(t)\mathbf{W} + [\delta^k(t)]^T - [\delta^k(t+1)]^T \mathbf{D}_{\mathbf{h}}^k(t)\mathbf{R} \tag{8.31}$$

to a vector of zeros, where $\mathbf{D}_{\mathbf{h}}^k(t)$ is a diagonal matrix whose ith on-diagonal element $i = 1\ldots m$ is the ith element of the vector $\mathbf{h}^k(t)$.* $(1 - \mathbf{h}^k(t))$, and where $\mathbf{D}_{\mathbf{r}}^k(t)$ is a diagonal matrix whose ith on-diagonal element $i = 1\ldots m$ is the ith element of the vector $\mathbf{r}^k(t)$.* $(1 - \mathbf{r}^k(t))$.

For $t = M_k$: set

$$dl^k/d\mathbf{h}^k(t) = -[\lambda^k(t)]^T \mathbf{D}_{\mathbf{r}}^k(t)\mathbf{W} + [\delta^k(t)]^T \tag{8.32}$$

to a vector of zeros.

Update weight matrices. The weight matrices $\mathbf{W}, \mathbf{V}$, and $\mathbf{R}$ are then updated using the steepest descent algorithm. The following relevant partial derivatives are *not* explicitly set equal to zero:

$$dl^k/d\mathbf{W} = -\sum_{t=1}^{M_k} \lambda^k(t)\mathbf{D}_{\mathbf{r}}^k(t)[\mathbf{h}^k(t)]^T, \tag{8.33}$$

$$dl^k/d\mathbf{V} = -\sum_{t=1}^{M_k} \delta^k(t)\mathbf{D}_{\mathbf{h}}^k(t)[\mathbf{s}^k(t)]^T. \tag{8.34}$$

$$dl^k/d\mathbf{R} = -\sum_{t=1}^{M_k} \delta^k(t)\mathbf{D}_{\mathbf{h}}^k(t)[\mathbf{h}^k(t-1)]^T. \tag{8.35}$$

With some minor modifications to its step 3 that require "saving" the gradient computed at each iteration to be used at the next iteration, the gradient (steepest) descent algorithm provided here is very similar to the conjugate gradient algorithm.

Algorithm: Version of Elman recurrent backpropagation

- Step 0: Initialization. Set iteration counter $i = 0$.
- Step 1: Forward pass.

For $k = 1 \ldots n$, $t = 1 \ldots M_k$:

a. Compute response of hidden units. Derived by setting $\nabla_{\delta^k(t)}$ equal to a vector of zeros:

$$\mathbf{h}^k(t) = \mathcal{G}[\mathbf{V}\mathbf{s}^k(t) + \mathbf{R}\mathbf{h}^k(t-1)],$$

b. Compute response of output units. Derived by setting $\nabla_{\lambda^k} l$ equal to a vector of zeros:

$$\mathbf{r}^k(t) = \mathcal{G}[\mathbf{W}\mathbf{h}^k(t)].$$

c. Compute error signal at output units. Derived from (8.30):

$$\lambda^k(M_k) = 2[\mathbf{o}^k(M_k) - \mathbf{r}^k(M_k)].$$

End of t loop. End of k loop.

- Step 2: Backward pass.

For $k = 1 \ldots n$, using (8.32),

$$\delta^k(M_k) = [\lambda^k(t)]^T \mathbf{D}_{\mathbf{r}}^k(t) \mathbf{W}.$$

For $t = M_k - 1, M_k - 2, \ldots, 1$, using (8.31),

$$[\delta^k(t)]^T = [\lambda^k(t)]^T \mathbf{D}_{\mathbf{r}}^k(t) \mathbf{W} + [\delta^k(t+1)]^T \mathbf{D}_{\mathbf{h}}^k(t) \mathbf{R}.$$

End of t loop. End of k loop.

- Step 3: Update weight matrices. Using (8.33),

$$\mathbf{W}^{(i+1)} = \mathbf{W}^{(i)} - \gamma^{(i)}(1/n)\sum_{k=1}^{n} dl^k/d\mathbf{W}^{(i)}.$$

Using (8.34),

$$\mathbf{V}^{(i+1)} = \mathbf{V}^{(i)} - \gamma^{(i)}(1/n)\sum_{k=1}^{n} dl^k/d\mathbf{V}^{(i)}.$$

Using (8.35),

$$\mathbf{R}^{(i+1)} = \mathbf{R}^{(i)} - \gamma^{(i)}(1/n)\sum_{k=1}^{n} dl^k/d\mathbf{R}^{(i)}.$$

Let $i = i + 1$. Go to step 1 until magnitude of gradient is sufficiently small.

5-9. See discussion in section 5.3 just before description of Gibbs sampler theorem and consider case where temperature parameter is very close to zero.

5-11. Let $\mathbf{x}(0)$, $\mathbf{x}(1), \ldots$ be generated by the algorithm

$$\mathbf{x}(t+1) = \mathbf{x}(t) - \gamma_t \mathbf{Q}^* \nabla_{\mathbf{x}(t)} V \tag{8.36}$$

with respect to objective function $V: \mathcal{R}^d \to \mathcal{R}$. Let W be some δ-neighborhood of a strict local minimum, $\mathbf{x}^*$, of V. Suppose there exists an $h: W \to \mathcal{R}$ such that $\nabla h = \mathbf{Q}^* \nabla V$ has continuous partial derivatives on W. Thus, (8.36) is a steepest descent algorithm on h whose geometric convergence rate properties in the vicinity of $\mathbf{x}^*$ are determined by the eigenvalues of the Hessian matrix $\nabla^2 h$ evaluated at $\mathbf{x}^*$ which in turn is given by $\mathbf{Q}^* \nabla^2 V$ evaluated at $\mathbf{x}^*$.

5-13. Let $\mathbf{g}(\mathbf{w}(t))$ denote the gradient of learning objective function $l: \mathcal{R}^q \to [0, \infty)$ evaluated at vector $\mathbf{w}(t)$.

- Step 0: Initialize search algorithm. Let η and ε be real numbers between zero and one. Let δ_{max} be a real number between zero and one. Let $\mathbf{w}(0)$ be a q-dimensional real vector whose elements are observed values of a set of independent and identically distributed random variables. Set flag "Stepsize was changed" to value "inactive."

- Step 1: Check if stepsize is too large. IF

$$l(\mathbf{w}(t) + \gamma_t^i \mathbf{f}(t)) > l(\mathbf{w}(t)) + a\gamma_t^i \mathbf{g}(\mathbf{w}(t))^T \mathbf{f}(t),$$

THEN

PRINT: "Stepsize γ_t^i is too large. Decrease γ_t^i."
ACTION: Let γ_t^{i+1} be defined as $\eta\gamma_t^i$.
ACTION: Set flag "Stepsize was changed" to value "active".

- Step 2: Check if stepsize is too small. IF

$$\mathbf{g}(\mathbf{w}(t) + \gamma_t^i \mathbf{f}(t))^T \mathbf{f}(t) < \beta\mathbf{g}(\mathbf{w}(t))^T \mathbf{f}(t),$$

THEN

PRINT: "Stepsize γ_t^i is too small. Increase γ_t^i."
ACTION: Let γ_t^{i+1} be defined as $(1 + \varepsilon)\gamma_t^i$.
ACTION: Set flag "Stepsize was changed" to value "active".

- Step 3: Check if the magnitude of the weights are too large. IF the absolute value of the largest element in $\mathbf{w}(t)$ is greater than w_{max}, THEN

PRINT: "Estimated weights are out of bounds. Restart algorithm."
ACTION: Go to step 0.

- Step 4: Check that search direction $\mathbf{f}(t)$ is acceptable. IF

$$\left[\frac{\mathbf{f}(t)}{|\mathbf{f}(t)|} \right]^T \left[\frac{\mathbf{g}(\mathbf{w}(t))}{|\mathbf{g}(\mathbf{w}(t))|} \right] < \delta_{max},$$

THEN

PRINT: "Search direction is almost orthogonal to gradient. Pick new $\mathbf{f}(t)$."
ACTION: Pick a new search direction that is not orthogonal to gradient. For example, let $\mathbf{f}(t) = -\mathbf{g}(\mathbf{w}(t))$.

- Step 5: Check if a critical point has been reached. IF

$$|\mathbf{g}(\mathbf{w}(t))| < \varepsilon,$$

THEN

PRINT: "Gradient is sufficiently small. A critical point has been reached."
ACTION: Go to step 7.

ELSE

ACTION: Go to step 6.

- Step 6: Update state vector if stepsize is properly chosen. IF flag "Stepsize was changed" is "inactive," THEN

ACTION: Compute $\mathbf{w}(t + 1)$ from $\mathbf{w}(t)$ and γ_t^i using

$$\mathbf{w}(t + 1) = \mathbf{w}(t) + \gamma_t^i \mathbf{f}(t),$$

where $\mathbf{f}(t) = -g(\mathbf{w}(t))$.

ACTION: Go to step 1.

ELSE

ACTION: Set flag "Stepsize was changed" to value "inactive."
ACTION: Increment i counter using $i = i + 1$, and then go to step 1.

- Step 7: Terminate search.

5-15. See discussion in section 5.3 just before description of Gibbs sampler theorem.

Chapter 6

Elementary Problems

6.1-1. The sample space S is defined by

$S = \{(0, 0), (1, 0), (0, 1), (1, 1)\}$.

Use the notation: $\mathbf{x}_1 = (0, 0)$, $\mathbf{x}_2 = (1, 0)$, $\mathbf{x}_3 = (0, 1)$, and $\mathbf{x}_4 = (1, 1)$ so that S may be equivalently expressed as $S = \{\mathbf{x}_1, \mathbf{x}_2, \mathbf{x}_3, \mathbf{x}_4\}$, where $\mathbf{x}_1 = $ *Green cube is present*, $\mathbf{x}_2 = $ *Red cube is present*, $\mathbf{x}_3 = $ *Green ball is present*, $\mathbf{x}_4 = $ *Red ball is present*.
  The sigma field $\mathcal{F}$ generated from S is then

$\mathcal{F} = [\{\}, \{\mathbf{x}_1\}, \{\mathbf{x}_2\}, \{\mathbf{x}_3\}, \{\mathbf{x}_4\}, \{\mathbf{x}_1, \mathbf{x}_2\}, \{\mathbf{x}_1, \mathbf{x}_3\}, \{\mathbf{x}_1, \mathbf{x}_4\}, \{\mathbf{x}_2, \mathbf{x}_3\}, \{\mathbf{x}_2, \mathbf{x}_4\}, \{\mathbf{x}_3, \mathbf{x}_4\}, \{\mathbf{x}_1, \mathbf{x}_2, \mathbf{x}_3\},$
$\quad \{\mathbf{x}_1, \mathbf{x}_2, \mathbf{x}_4\}, \{\mathbf{x}_1, \mathbf{x}_3, \mathbf{x}_4\}, \{\mathbf{x}_2, \mathbf{x}_3, \mathbf{x}_4\}, \{\mathbf{x}_1, \mathbf{x}_2, \mathbf{x}_3, \mathbf{x}_4\}];$

$\omega_{ANN} = \{[(\{\mathbf{x}_4, \mathbf{x}_2\}, \{\mathbf{x}_4\}), (\{\mathbf{x}_4, \mathbf{x}_2\}, \{\mathbf{x}_1, \mathbf{x}_4\}), (\{\mathbf{x}_4, \mathbf{x}_2\}, \{\mathbf{x}_3, \mathbf{x}_4\}), (\{\mathbf{x}_4, \mathbf{x}_2\}, \{\mathbf{x}_1, \mathbf{x}_2, \mathbf{x}_4\}),$
$\quad (\{\mathbf{x}_4, \mathbf{x}_2\}, \{\mathbf{x}_1, \mathbf{x}_3, \mathbf{x}_4\}), (\{\mathbf{x}_4, \mathbf{x}_2\}, \{\mathbf{x}_2, \mathbf{x}_3, \mathbf{x}_4\}), (\{\mathbf{x}_4, \mathbf{x}_2\}, \{\mathbf{x}_1, \mathbf{x}_2, \mathbf{x}_3, \mathbf{x}_4\})]\}.$

6.1-3. Yes. Define $\mathcal{P}: \mathcal{F} \to \mathcal{R}$ such that $\mathcal{P}(\{\mathbf{x}_4, \mathbf{x}_2\}) = -14$ and $\mathcal{P}(y) = 0$ if $y \in \mathcal{F}$ and $y \neq \{\mathbf{x}_4, \mathbf{x}_2\}$.

6.1-5. No. Because (for example) $\mathcal{P}(\{\mathbf{x}_4\}) > \mathcal{P}(\{\mathbf{x}_4, \mathbf{x}_2\})$ violates the *monotonicity condition*.

6.1-7. No. Because a logical fuzzy measure is a special case of a fuzzy measure and problem 6.1-5 showed that a fuzzy measure cannot be constructed.

6.1-9. No. Because a probabilistic fuzzy measure is a special case of a fuzzy measure and problem 6.1-5 showed that a fuzzy measure cannot be constructed.

6.2-1. See discussion in section 6.2.4.

6.3-1. Note that

$p(y_{t+1} \mid y_t) = (1/(\sigma\sqrt{\pi})) \exp[-(y_{t+1} - y_t)^2/(2\sigma^2)]$

and

$p(y_1) = (1/(\sigma\sqrt{\pi})) \exp[-y_1^2/(2\sigma^2)]$.

The joint probability distribution $p(y_1, \ldots, y_M)$ is given by:

$$p(y_1, \ldots, y_M) = p(y_1) \prod_{t=1}^{M-1} p(y_{t+1} \mid y_t).$$

Thus

$$p(y_1, \ldots, y_M) = (\sigma^2\pi)^{-M/2} \exp\left[-\left(y_1^2 + \sum_{t=1}^{M-1} (y_{t+1} - y_t)^2\right)\Big/(2\sigma^2)\right].$$

6.3-3. Consider the expansion in (6.35). Note that x_i and y_i can only take on the values of zero or one. Choose $y_i = 0$ for all $i = 1 \ldots d$ for convenience. If $x_i = 0$, then the value of $G_i(x_i)$ is irrelevant since $x_i G_i(x_i) = 0$. If $x_i = 1$, then $x_i G_i(x_i) = x_i G_i(1)$. Thus, without any loss in generality, the function $G_i(x_i)$ can be replaced with a coefficient a_i whose value is given by $G_i(1)$. A similar argument may be used for the other terms in the Q function expansion. For example, if $x_i = 0$ or $x_j = 0$, then the value of $G_i(x_i, x_j)$ is irrelevant since $x_i x_j G_{ij}(x_i, x_j) = 0$. If $x_i = x_j = 1$, then replace $G_{ij}(x_i, x_j)$ with a coefficient a_{ij} whose value is given by $G_{ij}(1, 1)$.

6.3-5. The eleven cliques for ω are: $\{\tilde{x}_1\}$, $\{\tilde{x}_2\}$, $\{\tilde{x}_3\}$, $\{\tilde{x}_4\}$, $\{\tilde{x}_5\}$, $\{\tilde{x}_1, \tilde{x}_5\}$, $\{\tilde{x}_1, \tilde{x}_3\}$, $\{\tilde{x}_1, \tilde{x}_4\}$, $\{\tilde{x}_4, \tilde{x}_5\}$, $\{\tilde{x}_5, \tilde{x}_2\}$, $\{\tilde{x}_1, \tilde{x}_4, \tilde{x}_5\}$.

Thus the most general functional form of a probability mass function whose neighborhood system is consistent with agent S's beliefs is given by

$$p(x_1, x_2, x_3, x_4, x_5) = (1/Z) \exp[-V(x_1, x_2, x_3, x_4, x_5)],$$

where

$$V(x_1, x_2, x_3, x_4, x_5) = \sum_{i=1}^{5} a_i x_i + a_{1,3} x_1 x_3 + a_{1,4} x_1 x_4 + a_{2,5} x_2 x_5 + a_{1,5} x_1 x_5 + a_{4,5} x_4 x_5$$

$$+ a_{1,4,5} x_1 x_4 x_5,$$

and $a_1, a_2, a_3, a_4, a_5, a_{4,5}, a_{1,3}, a_{1,4}, a_{2,5}, a_{1,5}, a_{1,4,5}$ are parameters of the probability mass function. Now note that

$$p(x_i | x_1, \ldots, x_{i-1}, x_{i+1}, \ldots, x_5) = (1/Z_i) \exp[-\varphi_i(x_i)],$$

where

$$\varphi_i(x_i) = V(x_1, x_2, x_3, x_4, x_5) - V(x_1, \ldots, x_{i-1}, x_i = 0, x_{i+1}, \ldots, x_5)]$$

and Z_i is not functionally dependent upon x_i. And because x_i can only take on the values of zero or one, it follows that

$$Z_i = \exp[\varphi_i(0)] + \exp[\varphi_i(1)].$$

Thus

$$p(x_i = 1 | x_1, \ldots, x_{i-1}, x_{i+1}, \ldots, x_5) = \frac{\exp[\varphi_i(1)]}{\exp[\varphi_i(0)] + \exp[\varphi_i(1)]},$$

which implies

$$p(x_i = 1 | x_1, \ldots, x_{i-1}, x_{i+1}, \ldots, x_5) = \mathcal{S}(\varphi_i(1) - \varphi_i(0)),$$

where $\mathcal{S}: \mathcal{R} \to \mathcal{R}$ is defined such that $\mathcal{S}(x) = 1/(1 + \exp(-x))$. Applying this formula,

$$p(x_1 = 1 | x_3, x_4, x_5) = \mathcal{S}(\exp[\varphi_1(1) - \varphi_1(0)]),$$

where

$$\varphi_1(1) - \varphi_1(0) = V(x_1 = 1, x_2, x_3, x_4, x_5) - V(x_1 = 0, x_2, x_3, x_4, x_5),$$

$$\varphi_1(1) - \varphi_1(0) = a_1 + a_{1,4} x_4 + a_{1,3} x_3 + a_{1,5} x_5 + a_{1,4,5} x_4 x_5.$$

Similarly,

$$p(x_5 = 1 | x_1, x_2, x_4) = \mathcal{S}(\exp[\varphi_2(1) - \varphi_2(0)]),$$

$$p(x_5 = 1 | x_1, x_2, x_4) = \mathcal{S}(a_5 + a_{2,5} x_2 + a_{1,5} x_1 + a_{4,5} x_4 + a_{1,4,5} x_1 x_4),$$

and

$$p(x_4 = 1 | x_1, x_5) = \mathcal{S}(\exp[\varphi_4(1) - \varphi_4(0)]) = \mathcal{S}(a_4 + a_{1,4} x_1 + a_{4,5} x_5 + a_{1,4,5} x_1 x_5).$$

First, choose a_1 to be strictly negative, so that

$$p(x_1 = 1 | x_3 = 0, x_4 = 0, x_5 = 0) < 0.5.$$

Now one may choose $a_{1,4} + a_{1,3} + a_{1,5} + a_{1,4,5} > a_1$, so that

$$p(x_1 = 1 \mid x_3 = 1, x_4 = 1, x_5 = 1) > 0.5.$$

Similarly, one may choose: $a_{2,5} + a_{1,5} + a_{4,5} + a_{1,4,5} > a_5$, and $a_{1,4} + a_{4,5} + a_{1,4,5} > a_4$ and choose a_4 and a_5 to be strictly negative. The remaining coefficients, a_2 and a_3, may be set equal to zero.

Define a connectionist network with five units where each unit has an activation level x_i that can take on only two values: zero or one. The activation level of unit 1 is defined such that $x_1 = 1$. The activation levels of the other four units are *unclamped*. Also define

$$p_\tau(x_i = 1 \mid x_1, \ldots, x_{i-1}, x_{i+1}, \ldots, x_5) = \mathcal{S}([\varphi_i(1) - \varphi_i(0)]/\tau),$$

where τ is the strictly positive temperature parameter. The following Gibbs sampler algorithm will converge to the most probable activation values of the unclamped units, given the clamped activation of unit 1.

- Step 1: Randomly assign to all unclamped units the number: zero or one. Let $k = 0$. Let τ be some sufficiently large positive number.

- Step 2: Let $x_i(k)$ be the activation level of unit i at iteration k. Pick the ith unclamped unit at random ($i = 2, 3, 4, 5$). At iteration k of the algorithm, with probability

$$p_{i,\tau} = p_\tau(x_i = 1 \mid x_1(k-1), \ldots, x_{i-1}(k-1), x_{i+1}(k-1), \ldots x_5(k-1)),$$

let $x_i(k) = 1$, and with probability $1 - p_{i,\tau}$, let $x_i(k) = 0$.
- Step 3. Let $\tau = 1/(1 + \log[k])$. Let $k = k + 1$. Go to step 2 until algorithm converges.

6.4-1. Let $D \subseteq \mathcal{R}^d$ and $Q \subseteq \mathcal{R}^d$. Let $l: D \to \mathcal{R}$ be a Bayes risk measure with respect to $c: D \times Q \to \mathcal{R}$ and some subjective probability mass function $p: Q \to [0, 1]$. Let $c(\mathbf{x} \mid \mathbf{y}) = 1$ if the decision $\mathbf{x}$ is correct, given situation $\mathbf{y}$. Let $c(\mathbf{x} \mid \mathbf{y}) = 0$ if the decision $\mathbf{x}$ is incorrect, given situation $\mathbf{y}$. Assume that an error occurs if $\mathbf{y} \in \Omega_x \subseteq Q$. Thus

$$l(\mathbf{x}) = \sum_{\mathbf{y} \in Q} c(\mathbf{x} \mid \mathbf{y}) = \sum_{\mathbf{y} \notin \Omega_x} p(\mathbf{y})$$

is the probability of a correct decision, and minimizing l on D is equivalent to selecting the decision in D that maximizes the probability of error!

6.5-1. Reread section 6.5 to work this problem.

Chapter 7

Elementary Problems

7.1-1. Let $f(x) = 4(x - 2w)$ define the set of generator functions for this family of dynamical systems. Since $df/dx = 4$, df/dx is bounded on $\mathcal{R}$. Thus df/dx is Lipschitz on $\mathcal{R}$ for every $w \in \mathcal{R}$.

Let $V(x) = (x - 2w)^2$. Note, V has continuous first partial derivatives and that $V(x) \to +\infty$ as $x \to \infty$. Also note $\dot{V} = -(dx/dt)^2 \leq 0$ and $\dot{V}$ is continuous on $\mathcal{R}$. Let s be a positive real number such that $\Omega_s = \{x \in \mathcal{R}: V(x) \leq s\}$ is a closed, bounded, invariant set with respect to the Lyapunov function V. Because the largest invariant set $\mathcal{H} \subset S$ is the subset of Ω_s, where $V(x) = 0$ for all $x \in \mathcal{R}$, it follows that $\mathcal{H} = \{2w\}$, and that $x(t) \to 2w$ as $t \to \infty$.

Also note that $V(x(t)) \to 0$ as $t \to \infty$. The differential equation may thus be viewed as an algorithm that has been designed to seek the minimum value of V. To construct an ANN probability model, a sample space must be defined so that the probability mass (density) function can assign numbers to subsets of that sample space. Let the sample space S be $\mathcal{R}$. Using the optimal classification dynamics assumption,

$$p(x \mid w) = (1/Z) \exp[-V(x \mid w)] = (1/Z) \exp[-(x - 2w)^2],$$

where

$$Z = \int_{x \in S} \exp[-(x - 2w)^2]\, dx = \sqrt{\pi}.$$

Therefore, $x(t) \rightarrow 2w$ as $t \rightarrow \infty$, and $2w$ is the strict global maximum of the Gaussian density function $p(\cdot \mid w) \in F_W$, where the ANN system's subjective probability model F_W is defined as

$$F_W = \{p(\cdot \mid w) = [\pi]^{-1/2} \exp[-(x - 2w)^2] : w \in \mathcal{R}\}.$$

7.1-3. Re-read the first few pages of chapter 7 to work this problem.

7.2-1. Using the Kullback-Leibler information criterion (KLIC) measure and the ANN probability model derived in problem 7.1-1,

$$\hat{l}_n(w) = -(1/n)\sum_{i=1}^{n} \log[p(x \mid w)] = (1/n)\sum_{i=1}^{n} (x^i - 2w)^2 + (1/2)\log[\pi].$$

Thus a gradient descent learning algorithm is given by

$$w(k + 1) = w(k) - \eta_k d\hat{l}_n(w)/dw$$

$$w(k + 1) = w(k) + \eta_k(4/n)\sum_{i=1}^{n} (x^i - 2w),$$

where η_k is chosen to be a properly chosen stepsize at each iteration of the gradient descent algorithm.

7.2-3. The global minima for both ANN learning objective functions are quasi-maximum likelihood estimates. The learning algorithm with the KLIC measure as a learning objective function has the advantage that each iteration of the algorithm is guaranteed to result in a new estimate, which makes the observed data more probable (with respect to the ANN system's probability model) than the previous estimate.

7.2-5. First, MAP estimation is a special case of minimizing a Bayes risk function. Second, ML estimation is a special case of MAP estimation when one does not have prior knowledge of the probability distribution of the parameter estimates. And third, ML estimation seeks a global minimum of the negative log likelihood function, equivalent to the KLIC sample risk function which converges under fairly general conditions (see Sample Risk Function Convergence Theorem in section 7.2.1) to the KLIC risk function.

Problems

7-1. The quantity $r_i(t)$ is strictly positive because the range of the function $\exp[\cdot]$ is strictly positive. Also:

$$\sum_{i=1}^{M} r_i(t) = \frac{\sum_{i=1}^{M} \exp[u_i(t)]}{\sum_{j=1}^{M} \exp[u_j(t)]} = 1.$$

This network is appropriate for statistical environments consisting of independent and identically distributed random vectors where the output response feedback signal is constrained to take on only one of M possible mutually exclusive values.

Let the observation of outcome j ($j = 1 \ldots M$) at iteration t be represented by an M-dimensional vector $\mathbf{o}(t)$, where $\mathbf{o}(t)$ is an M-dimensional vector with a one in the jth location and zeros in the remaining $(M - 1)$ locations. Thus the subjective probability model for this ANN system may be defined using

$$p(\mathbf{o} \mid \mathbf{s}) = \sum_{i=1}^{M} o_i r_i,$$

where r_i is the activation level of the ith output unit of the ANN system.

Express the ANN system's subjective probability model in terms of the following Gibbs distribution:

$$p(\mathbf{o}\,|\,\mathbf{s}) = \exp\left[\sum_{i=1}^{M} o_i \log\,[r_i]\right],$$

which exploits the assumption that if $o_l = 1$, then $o_i = 0$ for $i = 1\dots, l-1, l+1,\dots M$.

Compute a negative log likelihood risk function for learning using the KLIC formula as follows. Let

$$l(\mathbf{V}, \mathbf{q}, \mathbf{W}, \mathbf{b}) = -(1/n)\sum_{k=1}^{n}\log[p(\mathbf{o}^k\,|\,\mathbf{s}^k)] = -(1/n)\sum_{k=1}^{n}\sum_{i=1}^{M} o_i^k \log\,[r_i^k]$$

where n is the number of training stimuli.

In order to derive the on-line backpropagation equations, compute the gradient of l with respect to $\mathbf{V}, \mathbf{q}, \mathbf{W}$ and $\mathbf{b}$. Suppose that outcome $o_i^k = 1$ and for $j \neq i$: $o_j^k = 0$ given stimulus $\mathbf{s}^k$. Thus

$$\partial l/\partial r_i^k = -p_k o_i^k / r_i^k,$$

$$\partial r_i^k/\partial u_i^k = r_i^k(1 - r_i^k),$$

and

$$\partial r_i^k/\partial u_j^k = -r_i^k r_j^k$$

for $i \neq j$.

If $o_i^k = 1$ and $i = j$, then

$$\partial l/\partial u_j^k = -p_k[\partial l/\partial r_i^k][\partial r_i^k/\partial u_i^k] = -p_k(o_i^k/r_i^k)r_i^k(1 - r_i^k).$$

If $o_i^k = 1$ and $i \neq j$,

$$\partial l/\partial u_j^k = -p_k[\partial l/\partial r_i^k][\partial r_i^k/\partial u_j^k] = -p_k(o_i^k/r_i^k)(-r_i^k r_j^k).$$

Thus

$$\partial l/\partial u_j^k = -p_k(o_j^k - r_j^k)$$

for $o_j^k = 0$ or $o_j^k = 1$.

Let $\boldsymbol{\delta}_u^k$ be a column vector whose jth element is $\partial l/\partial u_j^k$. The remaining derivatives are computed in the usual manner. Let h_j^k be the jth element of $\mathbf{h}^k$. Let the notation $\mathbf{D}_{\mathbf{h}^k}$ denote an on-diagonal matrix whose dimension is equal to the dimension of vector $\mathbf{h}^k$ and whose jth on-diagonal element is $h_j^k(1 - h_j^k)$. Then

$$dl/d\mathbf{W}^k = \boldsymbol{\delta}_u^k(\mathbf{h}^k)^T,$$

$$dl/d\mathbf{b}^k = \boldsymbol{\delta}_u^k,$$

$$dl/d\mathbf{h}^k = \mathbf{W}^T\boldsymbol{\delta}_u^k,$$

$$dl/d\mathbf{V}^k = [dl/d\mathbf{h}^k]\mathbf{D}_{\mathbf{h}^k}[\mathbf{s}^k]^T,$$

$$dl/d\mathbf{q}^k = \mathbf{D}_{\mathbf{h}^k}[dl/d\mathbf{h}^k].$$

The student can use the above derivatives to develop either an on-line or off-line backpropagation algorithm. Note that the resulting backpropagation equations are essentially identical to the classical backpropagation equations with the important exception that the error signal at the output units which is backpropagated through the network has a different functional form.

7-3. Let

$$\mathbf{O}^k = [\mathbf{o}^k(0),\ldots, \mathbf{o}^k(M_k)].$$

Let

$$\mathbf{R}^k = [\mathbf{r}^k(0),\ldots, \mathbf{r}^k(M_k)].$$

Let

$$\mathbf{S}^k = [\mathbf{s}^k(0),\ldots, \mathbf{s}^k(M_k)].$$

The following likelihood function will be maximized in this solution:

$$p^k = p(\mathbf{R}^k, \mathbf{O}^k \mid \mathbf{S}^k, \mathbf{D}^k(0),\ldots, \mathbf{D}^k(M_k), M_k, \mathbf{W})\, p(M_k).$$

Assume that the above expression for p^k may be factored to obtain

$$p^k = p(M_k)\prod_{t=1}^{M_k} p(\mathbf{r}^k(t) \mid \mathbf{r}^k(t-1), \mathbf{W})\prod_{t=1}^{M_k} p(\mathbf{o}^k(t) \mid \mathbf{s}^k(t-1), \mathbf{D}^k(t), \mathbf{W}).$$

Let $p(\mathbf{o}^k(t) \mid \mathbf{s}^k(t-1), \mathbf{D}^k(t), \mathbf{W})$ be defined as a conditional multivariate Gaussian probability density function with mean $\mathbf{r}^k(t) = \mathbf{W}\mathbf{s}^k(t-1)$, so that

$$p(\mathbf{o}^k(t) \mid \mathbf{s}^k(t-1), \mathbf{D}^k(t), \mathbf{W}) = \left[\sqrt{2\pi}\sum_{i=1}^{m} d_{k,i}(t)\right]^{-1} \exp\left[-(1/2)(\mathbf{o}^k(t) - \mathbf{r}^k(t))^T\mathbf{D}^k(t)(\mathbf{o}^k(t) - \mathbf{r}^k(t))\right],$$

where $d_{k,i}(t) \in \{0, 1\}$ is the ith on-diagonal element of $\mathbf{D}^k(t)$, $t = 1\ldots M_k$.

Let $p(\mathbf{r}^k(t) \mid \mathbf{r}^k(t-1), \mathbf{W})$ be defined as a conditional multivariate Gaussian probability density function with mean $\mathbf{r}^k(t-1)$, so that

$$p(\mathbf{r}^k(t) \mid \mathbf{r}^k(t-1), \mathbf{W}) = [\sqrt{\pi/\lambda}]^{-1}\exp\left[-\lambda \mid \mathbf{r}^k(t) - \mathbf{r}^k(t-1)\mid^2\right].$$

With the above definitions, it then follows that

$$\hat{l}_n = C - (1/n)\sum_{k=1}^{n} \log p^k,$$

where C is a constant that is not functionally dependent upon $\mathbf{W}$.

7-5. Let H be the number of hidden units, and then define, for a particular stimulus $\mathbf{s}^i$,

$$p(\mathbf{h}^i \mid \mathbf{s}^i) = (\sigma^2\pi)^{-H/2}\exp\left[-\mid\mathbf{h}^i\mid^2/(2\sigma^2)\right]$$

because

$$\int_{-\infty}^{+\infty} p(\mathbf{h}^i \mid \mathbf{s}^i)d\mathbf{h}^i = 1,$$

and the normalization constant $(\sigma^2\pi)^{-H/2}$ is not functionally dependent upon the connection strength parameter vector. The probability density function $p(\mathbf{h}^i \mid \mathbf{s}^i)$ has the interpretation that, given any $\mathbf{s}^i$ observed in the training data set, the ANN classification dynamical system's probability model has the implicit belief that the activation pattern over the hidden units will have a Gaussian distribution with mean $\mathbf{h}_i$ and covariance matrix $\sigma^2\mathbf{I}$. Assume that σ^2 is a known constant but σ^2 can be estimated by the quantity

$$\hat{\sigma}^2 = (1/Hn)\sum_{i=1}^{n} \mid\mathbf{h}^i\mid^2$$

(show how to do this!).

Now use the conditional Gaussian probability density function:

$$p(\mathbf{o}\,|\,\mathbf{s}) = \pi^{-d/2}\exp\left[-\left|\mathbf{o} - \mathbf{r}\right|^2\right],$$

where d is the number of output units needed to construct a typical element of the ANN system's probability model (as shown in section 7.3.2).

The negative log likelihood risk function is given by

$$\hat{l}_n(\mathbf{V}, \mathbf{q}, \mathbf{U}, \mathbf{b}) = -(1/n)\sum_{i=1}^{n} \log\left[p(\mathbf{o}^i\,|\,\mathbf{s}^i)p(\mathbf{h}^i\,|\,\mathbf{s}^i)\right] = -(1/n)\sum_{i=1}^{n}\left(\log\left[p(\mathbf{o}^i\,|\,\mathbf{s}^i)\right] + \log\left[p(\mathbf{h}^i\,|\,\mathbf{s}^i)\right]\right)$$

$$\hat{l}_n(\mathbf{V}, \mathbf{q}, \mathbf{U}, \mathbf{b}) = (1/n)\sum_{i=1}^{n}\left|\mathbf{o}^i - \mathbf{r}^i\right|^2 + (\lambda/n)\sum_{i=1}^{n}\left|\mathbf{h}^i\right|^2 + K$$

where $\lambda = 1/(2\sigma^2)$.

The probabilistic interpretation of $\hat{l}_n$ is that $\hat{l}_n$ measures the joint likelihood of $\mathbf{o}$ and $\mathbf{h}$ so the algorithm seeks a set of parameters $(\mathbf{V}, \mathbf{q}, \mathbf{U}, \mathbf{b})$ such that the likelihood of $\mathbf{o}^1,\ldots, \mathbf{o}^M, \mathbf{h}^1,\ldots, \mathbf{h}^M$ is as large as possible with respect to the subjective probability mass (density) functions $p(\mathbf{o}\,|\,\mathbf{s})$ and $p(\mathbf{h}\,|\,\mathbf{s})$. The quantity $p(\mathbf{o}^i\,|\,\mathbf{s}^i)$ tends to be larger if $\mathbf{o}^i$ and $\mathbf{r}^i$ are similar in a Euclidean distance sense. The quantity $p(\mathbf{h}^i\,|\,\mathbf{s})$ tends to be larger if $\mathbf{h}^i$ is close to an h-dimensional target vector of zeros.

7-7. For expository reasons, consider a Hopfield (1982) network without bias terms. The solution may be extended to the more general case in a straightforward manner. Let $\mathbf{W}$ be the symmetric weight matrix for the Hopfield (1982) network. Let $\mathbf{W}_{k,k}$, $\mathbf{W}_{k,u}$, $\mathbf{W}_{u,k}$, and $\mathbf{W}_{u,u}$ be submatrices of $\mathbf{W}$ such that the potential function $V(\mathbf{x})$ may be written as

$$V(\mathbf{x}) = -(1/2)\mathbf{x}^T\mathbf{W}\mathbf{x} = V_{k,k} + V_{k,u} + V_{u,k} + V_{u,u},$$

where

$$V_{k,k} = -(1/2)\mathbf{x}_k^T\mathbf{W}_{k,k}\mathbf{x}_k$$

is a constant,

$$V_{k,u} = -(1/2)\mathbf{x}_k^T\mathbf{W}_{k,u}\mathbf{x}_u,$$

$$V_{u,k} = -(1/2)\mathbf{x}_u^T\mathbf{W}_{u,k}\mathbf{x}_k,$$

and

$$V_{u,u} = -(1/2)\mathbf{x}_u^T\mathbf{W}_{u,u}\mathbf{x}_u.$$

Note that $\mathbf{W}_{u,k} = \mathbf{W}_{k,u}$ because $\mathbf{W}$ is symmetric.

Now define

$$\mathbf{b}_k = (1/2)(\mathbf{W}_{k,u}^T + \mathbf{W}_{u,k})\mathbf{x}_k,$$

so that

$$\mathbf{x}_u^T\mathbf{b}_k = (1/2)\mathbf{x}_u^T(\mathbf{W}_{k,u}^T + \mathbf{W}_{u,k})\mathbf{x}_k = -V_{u,k} - V_{k,u},$$

which gives

$$V([\mathbf{x}_k, \mathbf{x}_u]) = -(1/2)\mathbf{x}_u^T\mathbf{W}_{u,u}\mathbf{x}_u - \mathbf{b}_k^T\mathbf{x}_u + V_{k,k}. \tag{8.36}$$

Even though $\mathbf{x}_k$ is clamped, (8.36) is still minimized by the clamped Hopfield (1982) dynamics if $\mathbf{b}_k$ is recognized as a bias on the unclamped units and $V_{k,k}$ as a constant not functionally dependent upon $\mathbf{x}_u$.

7-9. The discussions in sections 5.3 and 6.3 provide good examples for deriving the local conditional probabilities.

The pseudolikelihood risk function (7.19) is not strictly a negative log likelihood risk function because the random variables $\tilde{x}_1^i,\ldots, \tilde{x}_d^i$ are not independent for any $i \in \{1,\ldots, n\}$. Nevertheless, as the product of local likelihoods that might be considered approximately independent, this function is an intuitively satisfying risk function. (Note that it is a perfectly legitimate sample risk function!)

7-11. Note that

$$\partial \hat{l}_n / \partial w_{jk} = -(1/dn) \sum_{i=1}^{n} [x_j^i - p_j^i] x_k^i.$$

The on-line learning algorithm is a type of stochastic gradient descent algorithm using the above derivative (see problem 4-1 and on-line backpropagation learning algorithm in section 2). The off-line learning algorithm is a gradient descent algorithm (related to Elementary Problem 5.2-1 and reviewed in the description of the batch backpropagation learning algorithm in section 2).

Chapter 8

Elementary Problems

8.1-1. The first step is to compute a quasi-maximum likelihood estimate of the free parameter μ. The negative log likelihood function is defined for all $\mu \in \Re$:

$$\hat{l}_n(\mu) = -(1/n) \sum_{i=1}^{n} \log[p(x^i | \mu)] = (1/n)(1/4) \sum_{i=1}^{n} (x^i - \mu)^2 + \log[\sqrt{4\pi}].$$

The constant $\hat{\mu}_n$ that minimizes $\hat{l}_n$ is the maximum likelihood estimate. Because $\hat{l}_n$ is differentiable everywhere, $\hat{\mu}_n$ must be a critical point of $\hat{l}_n$ that can be computed by setting $d\hat{l}_n / d\mu = 0$, evaluating the expression at $\hat{\mu}_n$, and then solving for $\hat{\mu}_n$. Now set

$$dl/d\hat{\mu}_n = -2(1/n)(1/4) \sum_{i=1}^{n} (x^i - \hat{\mu}_n) = 0.$$

Solving for $\hat{\mu}_n$ it follows that

$$\hat{\mu}_n = (1/n) \sum_{i=1}^{n} x^i,$$

which is an intuitively satisfying formula for the maximum likelihood estimate of μ!
  Note that the Hessian, $\hat{A}_n$, (a scalar in this case) is positive definite because:

$$\hat{A}_n = d^2 \hat{l}_n / d\hat{\mu}^2 = 1/2$$

is strictly positive everywhere on $\Re$, which implies that the critical point is indeed a strict global minimum (see Strict Global Minimum Test in chapter 5). Also

$$\hat{B}_n = (1/n)(-1/2)^2 \sum_{i=1}^{n} (x^i - \hat{\mu})^2.$$

Thus

$$\hat{C}_n = \left([\hat{B}_n]/[\hat{A}_n]^2\right) = (1/n) \sum_{i=1}^{n} (x^i - \hat{\mu})^2,$$

which is another intuitively satisfying formula for the estimate of the asymptotic variance of $\hat{\mu}$!
  Just four of the assumptions will be mentioned here. One assumption required in this problem is that σ^2 must be strictly positive and finite. Another is that the stochastic process that generated the data must consist of independent and identically distributed random variables with probability density function $p: \Re \rightarrow [0, \infty)$. A third assumption is that c is a regular loss function (verify this!). And a fourth is that A^* and B^* (expected values of $\hat{B}_n$ and $\hat{A}_n$) exist and are both nonsingular.

The asymptotic variance is useful for confidence intervals on location of μ and model selection. The randomness is due to the fact that the parameter estimate is a deterministic function of the training data, which are observed values of a set of random variables.

8.1-3. If the model is not correctly specified, then

$$\hat{C}_n = (1/n)\sum_{i=1}^{n} (x^i - \hat{\mu})^2$$

is the correct estimate of the variance. On the other hand, $[\hat{B}_n]^{-1}$ and $[\hat{A}_n]^{-1}$ are not correct estimates. If model is correctly specified, note that

$$[\hat{B}_n]^{-1} \approx [\hat{A}_n]^{-1} \approx \hat{C}_n \approx 2.$$

8.1-5. This answer follows from direct application of the Markov Inequality (Section 4.1).

8.1-7. Let b_i indicate the ith bootstrap sample. Here are four "representative" bootstrap samples:

$$b_1 = \{1, 2, 2, 1, 2, 2, 1, 1, 1\}$$

$$b_2 = \{1, 1, 2, 1, 1, 2, 1, 1, 1\}$$

$$b_3 = \{1, 1, 1, 1, 1, 1, 2, 2, 2\}$$

$$b_4 = \{1, 1, 1, 1, 1, 1, 1, 1, 1\}$$

Note that $\mu_1 \approx [5(1) + 4(2)]/9 = 1.4$, $\mu_2 \approx [7(1) + 2(2)]/9 = 1.2$, $\mu_3 \approx [6(1) + 3(2)]/9 = 1.3$, and $\mu_4 \approx [9(1) + 0(2)]/9 = 1.0$. Thus the estimate of the bootstrap estimate is $(1.4 + 1.2 + 1.3 + 1.0)/4 = 1.225$. which improves as the number of bootstrap samples becomes sufficiently large.

8.1-9. Let $\tilde{\varepsilon}_n = \tilde{a}_n - a^*$. Then it follows that

$$\tilde{a}_n = a^* + \tilde{\varepsilon}_n.$$

As $n \to \infty$, $\tilde{\varepsilon}_n \to 0$ with probability one. And because convergence with probability one implies convergence in probability,

$$\tilde{\varepsilon}_n = o_p(1).$$

8.2-1. Each experimenter is testing the same null hypothesis with respect to a different strict local minimum.

8.2-3. Define $p: \Re \times \Re \times \Re \to (0, \infty)$ such that

$$p(x | \mu, \sigma^2) = [\sigma\sqrt{2\pi}]^{-1}\exp[-(x-\mu)^2/2\sigma^2].$$

Let $x^1, \ldots, x^n$ be a sample path of the stochastic process $\tilde{x}^1, \ldots, \tilde{x}^n$ consisting of n independent and identically distributed random variables with common Gaussian probability density function whose mean μ and variance σ^2 are unknown. The negative log likelihood function is then expressed as

$$\hat{l}_n = -(1/n)\sum_{i=1}^{n} \log[p(x^i | \hat{\mu}, \hat{\sigma}^2)]$$

$$\hat{l}_n = (1/n)\sum_{i=1}^{n} [(x^i - \hat{\mu})^2]/(2\hat{\sigma}^2) + (1/2)\log[\hat{\sigma}^2 2\pi],$$

where $[\hat{\mu}, \hat{\sigma}]$ is a strict local minimum of $\hat{l}_n$.
    Note that $\partial \hat{l}_n / \partial \hat{\mu}$ is given by:

$$\partial \hat{l}_n / \partial \hat{\mu} = (1/[n\hat{\sigma}^2])\sum_{i=1}^{n} (x^i - \hat{\mu}),$$

which vanishes only if

$$\hat{\mu} = (1/n)\sum_{i=1}^{n} x^i,$$

and that $\partial \hat{l}_n / \partial \hat{\sigma}^2$ is given by

$$\partial \hat{l}_n / \partial \hat{\sigma}^2 = (1/2)[\hat{\sigma}^2]^{-1} - (1/n)\sum_{i=1}^{n} [(x^i - \hat{\mu})^2]/(2\hat{\sigma}^4),$$

which vanishes only if

$$\hat{\sigma}^2 = (1/n)\sum_{i=1}^{n} (x^i - \hat{\mu})^2.$$

It is also necessary to show that the Hessian of $\hat{l}_n$ is a positive definite matrix on $\mathcal{R} \times \mathcal{R}$ (do this!). Thus $\hat{\sigma}^2$ and $\hat{\mu}$ are the *unique* maximum likelihood estimates (by the Strict Global Minimum Test in chapter 5).

The log likelihood ratio test statistic

$$\hat{\delta}_n = -2n\left[\hat{l}_n([\hat{\mu} \ \hat{\sigma}^2]) - \hat{l}_n([\mu_0 \ \hat{\sigma}_0^2])\right]$$

then reduces to

$$\hat{\delta}_n = 2n\left[(1/n)\sum_{i=1}^{n} \log[p(x^i|\hat{\mu}, \hat{\sigma}^2)] - (1/n)\sum_{i=1}^{n} \log[p(x^i|\mu_0, \hat{\sigma}_0^2)]\right],$$

which in turn reduces to:

$$\hat{\delta}_n = 2\sum_{i=1}^{n} (x^i - \mu_0)^2/(2\hat{\sigma}_0^2) - 2\sum_{i=1}^{n} (x^i - \hat{\mu})^2/(2\hat{\sigma}^2) + n\log[\hat{\sigma}_0^2] - n\log[\hat{\sigma}^2],$$

$$\hat{\delta}_n = n - n + n\log[\hat{\sigma}_0^2] - n\log[\hat{\sigma}^2] = n\log[\hat{\sigma}_0^2/\hat{\sigma}^2].$$

8.2-5. Define the six-dimensional column vector $\mathbf{w}$ such that $\mathbf{w}^T = [\mathbf{w}_1^T, \mathbf{w}_2^T, \mathbf{w}_3^T]$, where $\mathbf{w}_k^T$ is the kth row of $\hat{\mathbf{W}}_n$. Test the null hypothesis that $H_0: \mathbf{w}_1 = \mathbf{w}_3$. The corresponding estimate of the co-variance matrix is a six-dimensional square symmetric matrix $\hat{\mathbf{C}}_n$, and the selection vector is a two-dimensional column vector of zeros. Let the selection matrix be a 2×6 matrix whose first row is defined by the row vector $[1, 0, 0, 0, -1, 0]$ and whose second row is defined by the row vector $[0, 1, 0, 0, 0, -1]$. Plug all resulting quantities into the Wald test formula (after checking all required assumptions of the Wald test).

Problems

8-1. Let $\mathbf{x}_j$ refer to the jth element of the finite sample space. Let n_j refer to the number of times that $\mathbf{x}_j$ occurs in the training stimulus set. Use the notation

$$\mathbf{p} = [p_1, \dots, p_M],$$

where

$$p_j = p_e(\mathbf{x}_j)$$

for $j = 1 \dots M$ defines the environmental probability mass function.

Note that

$$0 \le p_j \le 1 \text{ for } j = 1 \dots M,$$

$$\sum_{j=1}^{M} p_j = 1,$$

and

$$\sum_{j=1}^{M} n_j = n.$$

Finally, define

$$f_j = n_j/n.$$

The first step is to compute maximum likelihood estimates of the parameters. Suppose p_e is defined with respect to a finite sample space consisting of M elements. Then the Kullback-Leibler information criterion (KLIC) sample risk function, $\hat{l}_n^g$, whose global minima are maximum likelihood estimates, is defined such that

$$\hat{l}_n^g(\mathbf{p}) = -\sum_{j=1}^{M} f_j \log[p_j],$$

subject to the constraints that $0 \le p_j \le 1$ for $j = 1 \ldots M$ and

$$\sum_{j=1}^{M} p_j = 1.$$

Introduce the constraint

$$\sum_{j=1}^{M} p_j = 1$$

as an auxillary function using the Lagrange multiplier method to obtain the function

$$e(\mathbf{p}) = -\sum_{j=1}^{M} f_j \log[p_j] + \lambda \left[\sum_{j=1}^{M} p_j - 1 \right].$$

A critical point of e, $\hat{\mathbf{p}}$, must satisfy the relation

$$de/dp_k = -\frac{f_k}{\hat{p}_k} + \lambda = 0$$

for $k = 1 \ldots M$, where $\hat{p}_k$ is the kth element of the critical point $\hat{\mathbf{p}}$. Or equivalently,

$$f_k = \lambda \hat{p}_k. \tag{8.37}$$

Summing both sides of (8.37) over the elements of S,

$$\sum_{k=1}^{M} f_k = \lambda \sum_{k=1}^{M} \hat{p}_k = \lambda.$$

Now rearrange (8.37), using

$$\lambda = \sum_{k=1}^{M} f_k$$

to obtain:

$$\hat{p}_k = \frac{f_k}{\sum_{k=1}^{M} f_k}.$$

Also note that since

$$de^2/dp_k^2 = \frac{f_k}{[\hat{p}_k]^2} > 0,$$

the critical point $\hat{\mathbf{p}}$ is a strict global minimum. Therefore, the bootstrap approach is based upon computing maximum likelihood estimates of a nonparametric probability mass function.

8-3. Let

$$\tilde{\mathbf{X}}_n = [\tilde{\mathbf{x}}(1),\dots,\tilde{\mathbf{x}}(n)].$$

Begin by expanding $\hat{l}_n^f$ and $\hat{l}_n^g$ as first-order Taylor expansions:

$$\hat{l}_n^f(\tilde{\mathbf{w}}_n; \tilde{\mathbf{X}}_n) = \hat{l}_n^f(\mathbf{w}^*; \tilde{\mathbf{X}}_n) + O(|\tilde{\mathbf{w}}_n - \mathbf{w}^*|^2),$$

$$\hat{l}_n^g(\tilde{\mathbf{y}}_n; \tilde{\mathbf{X}}_n) = \hat{l}_n^g(\mathbf{y}^*; \tilde{\mathbf{X}}_n) + O(|\tilde{\mathbf{y}}_n - \mathbf{y}^*|^2)$$

because the gradient terms vanish with probability one for n sufficiently large by definition. Show that

$$\tilde{R}_n = O(\sqrt{n}|\tilde{\mathbf{w}}_n - \mathbf{w}^*|^2) + O(\sqrt{n}|\tilde{\mathbf{y}}_n - \mathbf{y}^*|^2) = o_p(1).$$

Then note:

$$\tilde{\sigma}_{v_n}\tilde{V}_n = -\sqrt{n}[\hat{l}_n^g(\mathbf{y}^*; \tilde{\mathbf{X}}_n) - \hat{l}_n^f(\mathbf{w}^*; \tilde{\mathbf{X}}_n)] + \tilde{R}_n,$$

$$\tilde{\sigma}_{v_n}\tilde{V}_n = (1/\sqrt{n})\sum_{i=1}^{n}\Big(\log[p^g(\tilde{\mathbf{x}}(i)|\mathbf{y}^*)] - \log[p^f(\tilde{\mathbf{x}}(i)|\mathbf{w}^*)]\Big) + \tilde{R}_n.$$

Apply the Central Limit Theorem and Slutsky's Theorem to obtain the desired result if the null hypothesis is true. Show that $|\tilde{V}_n| \rightarrow +\infty$ with probability one as $n \rightarrow \infty$ if the null hypothesis is false.

8-5. By proving the case where q_f is a probability density function on S, the proof for the case where q_f is a probability *mass* function on S will become clear.

The fact that

$$\int_{\mathbf{x}\in S} q_f(\mathbf{x}, \mathbf{w})d\mathbf{x} = 1$$

and the assumption that q_f has continuous second partial derivatives allow the integral and differential operators to be interchanged (Rosenlicht 1968, 159). Thus

$$\int_{\mathbf{x}\in S} \nabla_{\mathbf{w}} q_f(\mathbf{x}|\mathbf{w})d\mathbf{x} = \mathbf{0}_q \tag{8.38}$$

and

$$\int_{\mathbf{x}\in S} \nabla_{\mathbf{w}}^2 q_f(\mathbf{x}|\mathbf{w})d\mathbf{x} = \mathbf{0}_{q\times q}, \tag{8.39}$$

where $\mathbf{0}_{q\times q}$ is a q-dimensional matrix of zeros. Now, take the gradient of l with respect to $\mathbf{w}$ to obtain

$$\nabla_{\mathbf{w}} l = -\int_{\mathbf{x}\in S} \frac{\nabla_{\mathbf{w}} q_f(\mathbf{x}|\mathbf{w})p_e(\mathbf{x})}{q_f(\mathbf{w}|\mathbf{x})}d\mathbf{x} \tag{8.40}$$

and

$$\nabla_{\mathbf{w}}^2 l = \int_{\mathbf{x}\in S} \frac{p_e(\mathbf{x})[\nabla_{\mathbf{w}} q_f][\nabla_{\mathbf{w}} q_f]^T}{[q_f(\mathbf{x}, \mathbf{w})]^2}d\mathbf{x} - \int_{\mathbf{x}\in S} \frac{p_e(\mathbf{x})\nabla_{\mathbf{w}}^2 q_f}{q_f(\mathbf{x}, \mathbf{w})}d\mathbf{x}. \tag{8.41}$$

Substituting the identity

$$\nabla_{\mathbf{w}}[\log q_f(\mathbf{x}\mid\mathbf{w})]=\frac{\nabla_{\mathbf{w}}q_f}{q_f(\mathbf{x},\ \mathbf{w})},$$

into the first term on the right-hand side of (8.41) and using the definitions of $\mathbf{A}^*$ and $\mathbf{B}^*$,

$$\mathbf{A}^*=\mathbf{B}^*-\int_{\mathbf{x}\in S}\frac{p_e(\mathbf{x})\nabla_{\mathbf{w}}^2 q_f}{q_f(\mathbf{x}\mid\mathbf{w})}\,d\mathbf{x}. \qquad (8.42)$$

Note that if $q_f(\cdot,\ \mathbf{w}^*)$ is identical to p_e on sample space S, the integral term on the right-hand side of (8.42) is equal to zero by (8.39). Therefore, $\mathbf{A}^*=\mathbf{B}^*$.

8-7. Use the backpropagation learning algorithm to obtain a critical point of $\hat{l}$, $(\hat{\mathbf{W}}_n,\ \hat{\mathbf{V}}_n,\ \hat{\mathbf{b}}_n,\ \hat{\mathbf{d}}_n)$, that satisfies the following two constraints. First, the critical point must be a strict local minimum. One way to check the assumption that the learning process has converged to a strict local minimum is to compute the Hessian of $\hat{l}_n$ and evaluate the Hessian at the critical point. If the eigenvalues of the resulting matrix are strictly positive, then a strict local minimum of $\hat{l}_n$ has been reached (by the Strict Local Minimum Test in chapter 5). If the computation of the Hessian is too difficult, then a heuristic check of the strict local minimum condition can be accomplished by perturbing the critical point with a very small amount of random noise and evaluating the value of $\hat{l}_n$ and the gradient of $\hat{l}_n$ at the points in the vicinity of the critical point. The number of generated perturbations is recommended to be of the same order of magnitude as the number of free parameters in the network. Second, the critical point must result in estimated conditional probabilities that agree closely with the observed conditional probabilities in the medical database. This is essentially a check that the backpropagation network "fits the data" (i.e., successfully passes a goodness-of-fit test).

Let $\hat{\mathbf{v}}_n^i$ be the ith column of the matrix $\hat{\mathbf{V}}_n$. That is, $\hat{\mathbf{v}}_n^i$ is the estimated set of weights connecting the ith input unit to the hidden units in the network. Similarly, let $\hat{\mathbf{w}}_n^i$ be the ith column of the matrix $\hat{\mathbf{W}}_n$. Then define the column vector $\hat{\boldsymbol{\rho}}_n$ such that

$$\hat{\boldsymbol{\rho}}_n=[\hat{\mathbf{w}}_n^1,\dots,\ \hat{\mathbf{w}}_n^h,\ \hat{\mathbf{b}}_n,\ \hat{\mathbf{v}}_n^1,\dots,\ \hat{\mathbf{v}}_n^d,\ \hat{\mathbf{q}}_n],$$

where h is the number of hidden units and d is the number of input units. The vector $\hat{\boldsymbol{\rho}}_n$ is a maximum likelihood estimate from the choice of error function and the fact the model fits the data.

Let $\mathbf{g}_j$ be the gradient of $\hat{l}_j$ evaluated at the strict local minimum, $\hat{\boldsymbol{\rho}}_n$. For sufficiently large sample size, n, the maximum likelihood estimates have a Gaussian distribution with mean $\boldsymbol{\rho}^*$ (a strict local minimum of the true risk function) with covariance matrix $\hat{\mathbf{C}}_n/n$ where $\hat{\mathbf{C}}_n$ is equal to $\hat{\mathbf{B}}_n^{-1}$ by the Fisher information matrix equality because it is assumed the model is correctly specified. The quantity $\hat{\mathbf{B}}_n^{-1}$, in turn, is computed using the formula

$$\hat{\mathbf{B}}_n=(1/n)\sum_{j=1}^n\mathbf{g}_j\mathbf{g}_j^T.$$

Note that the quantity $\mathbf{g}_j$ is sometimes referred to as the "gradient of the error function" for a particular training stimulus pattern. This gradient is automatically computed by the backpropagation learning algorithm.

Let $\mathbf{v}^{i^*}$ be the components of $\boldsymbol{\rho}^*$ corresponding to the weights connecting input unit i to the hidden units. Also define $\tilde{\mathbf{v}}_n^i$ such that $\tilde{\mathbf{v}}_n^i\to\mathbf{v}^{i^*}$ as $n\to\infty$ with probability one, where $\hat{\mathbf{v}}_n^i$ is an observed value of $\tilde{\mathbf{v}}_n^i$. In order to decide whether or not to reject the null hypothesis, H_0, defined such that

$$H_0:\ \mathbf{v}^{i^*}=\mathbf{0}_h,$$

it is necessary to construct a suitable selection matrix $\mathbf{S}$.

Let $\mathbf{I}_{h,h}$ denote an h-dimensional identity matrix and $\mathbf{0}_{a,b}$ denote an $a\times b$ matrix of zeros. The $h\times(m+mh+hd+h)$ selection matrix $\mathbf{S}$, defined by

$$\mathbf{S}=[\mathbf{0}_{h,m+mh},\ \mathbf{0}_{h,h(i-1)},\ \mathbf{I}_{h,h},\ \mathbf{0}_{h,h(d-i)},\ \mathbf{0}_{h,h}]$$

for $1<i<d$ gives rise to the null hypothesis:

$$H_0:\ \mathbf{S}\boldsymbol{\rho}^*=\mathbf{v}^{i^*}=\mathbf{0}_h.$$

(If this is not clear, you should write out the intermediate steps in order to understand the construction of the selection matrix $\mathbf{S}$.)

A statistical test designed to test the null hypothesis that H_0: $\mathbf{v}^{i*} = \mathbf{0}_h$ can then be constructed as follows:

$$\mathcal{W}_n = n\hat{\boldsymbol{\rho}}_n^T [\mathbf{S}\hat{\mathbf{C}}_n \mathbf{S}^T]^{-1} \mathbf{S}\hat{\boldsymbol{\rho}}_n.$$

The null hypothesis that H_0: $\mathbf{v}^{i*} = \mathbf{0}_h$ can be rejected at the a significance level if

$$\mathcal{W}_n > \chi_a^2(h).$$

Note that if $\mathcal{W}_n$ is less than or equal to $\chi_a^2(h)$, it follows that there is not sufficient evidence available to reject the null hypothesis.

8-9. Define the full (nonparametric) probability model G_Y consisting of a set of probability mass functions such that

$$G_Y = \{p: \{\mathbf{x}^1, \dots, \mathbf{x}^M\} \rightarrow [0, 1]\}.$$

Let $\tilde{f}_i^n$ be the relative frequency of the event that $\tilde{\mathbf{x}}(k) = \mathbf{x}^i$ ($i = 1 \dots M$) in sample of size n. Assume $\{\tilde{f}_i^n\}$ is a stochastic solution sequence converging to $p(\mathbf{x}^i)$ as $n \rightarrow \infty$.

Note that the full model has $M - 1$ free parameters, while the reduced subjective probability model p_s has q (where $q < M - 1$) free parameters. Thus, it immediately follows from the GLRT that the quantity

$$\tilde{\delta}_n = 2n\left[\sum_{i=1}^{M} \tilde{f}_i^n \log(\tilde{f}_i^n) - \sum_{i=1}^{M} \tilde{f}_i^n \log[p_s(\mathbf{x}^i | \tilde{\mathbf{w}}_n)] \right]$$

has a chi-square distribution with $(M - 1 - q)$ degrees of freedom if the null hypothesis is true. If the null hypothesis is false, then the GLRT implies that $\tilde{\delta}_n \rightarrow \infty$ with probability one as $n \rightarrow \infty$.

References

Ackley, D. H., Hinton, G. E., and Sejnowski, T. J. (1985). A learning algorithm for Boltzmann machines. *Cognitive Science* 9: 147–169.

Adams, M. J. (1979). Models of word recognition. *Cognitive Psychology* 11: 133–176.

Ahalt, S. C., Chen, P., and Krishnamurthy, A. K. (1989). Performance analysis of two image vector quantization techniques. In *IJCNN International Joint Conference on Neural Networks,* vol. 1, pp. 169–175. San Diego, CA: IEEE TAB Neural Network Committee.

Alexander, S. T. (1986). *Adaptive signal processing: Theory and applications.* New York: Springer.

Amari, S. (1967). Theory of adaptive pattern classifiers. *IEEE Transactions on Electronic Computers* 16: 299–307.

Amari, S. (1972). Characteristics of random nets of analog neuron-like elements. *IEEE Transactions on Systems, Man, and Cybernetics* 2: 643–657.

Amari, S. (1977). Neural theory of association and concept-formation. *Biological Cybernetics* 26: 175–185.

Amari, S. and Murata, N. (1993). Statistical theory of learning curves under entropic loss criterion. *Neural Computation* 5: 140–153.

Andersen, P., Gross, G. N., Lomo, T., and Sveen, O. (1969). Participation of inhibitory and excitatory interneurons in the control of hippocampal cortical output. In M. Brazier (Ed.), *The interneuron,* 415–465. Los Angeles: University of California Press.

Andersen, R. A., Essick, G. K., and Siegel, R. M. (1985). Encoding of spatial location by posterior parietal neurons. *Science* 230: 456–458.

Anderson, B., and Moore, J. B. (1979). *Optimal filtering.* Englewood Cliffs, NJ: Prentice-Hall.

Anderson, J. A. (1968). A memory storage model utilizing spatial correlation functions. *Kybernetik* 5: 113–119.

Anderson, J. A. (1972). A simple neural network generating an interactive memory. *Mathematical Biosciences* 14: 197–220.

Anderson, J. A. (1995). *An introduction to neural networks.* Cambridge, MA: MIT Press.

Anderson, J. A., and Mozer, M. C. (1981). Categorization and selective neurons. In G. Hinton and J. A. Anderson (Eds.), *Parallel models of associative memory,* 213–236. Hillsdale, NJ: Erlbaum.

Anderson, J. A., Pellionisz, A., and Rosenfeld, E. (Eds., 1990). *Neurocomputing 2: Directions for research.* Cambridge, MA: MIT Press.

Anderson, J. A., and Rosenfeld, E. (Eds., 1988). *Neurocomputing: Foundations of research.* Cambridge, MA: MIT Press.

Anderson, J. A., Silverstein, J. W., Ritz, S. A., and Jones, R. S. (1977). Distinctive features, categorical perception, and probability learning: Some applications of a neural model. *Psychological Review* 84: 413–451.

Armijo, L. (1966). Minimization of functions having Lipschitz continuous first partial derivatives. *Pacific Journal of Mathematics* 16: 1–3.

Baldi, P., and Hornik, K. (1989). Neural networks and principal component analysis: Learning from examples without local minimum. *Neural Networks* 1: 53–58.

Barron, A. R., and Barron, R. L. (1989). Statistical learning networks: A unifying view. In E. J. Wegman, D. I. Gantz, and J. J. Miller (Eds.), *Proceedings of the Twentieth Symposium on the Interface: Statistics and Computer Science,* 192–202.

Bartle, R. G. (1966). *The elements of integration.* New York: Wiley.

Barto, A. G. (1990). Connectionist learning for control: An overview. In T. Miller, R. S. Sutton, and P. J. Werbos (Eds.), *Neural networks for control.* Cambridge, MA: MIT Press.

Baruah, A. B., and Holden, A. D. (1991). Adaptive resonance theory and the classical leader algorithm; similarities and additions. In C. H. Dagli, S. R. Kumara, and Y. C. Shin (Eds.), *Intelligent engineering systems through artificial neural networks,* 321–326. New York: ASME Press.

Bas, C. F., and Marks, R. J. (1991). Layered perceptron versus Neyman-Pearson optimal detection. In *1991 IEEE International Joint Conference on Neural Networks,* vol. 2, pp. 1486–1489. Piscataway, NJ: IEEE Press.

Bates, D. M., and Watts, D. G. (1988). *Nonlinear regression analysis and its applications.* New York: Wiley.

Battiti, R. (1989). Accelerated back-propagation learning: Two optimization methods. *Complex Systems* 3: 331–342.

Battiti, R. (1992). First- and second-order methods for learning: Between steepest descent and Newton's method. *Neural Computation* 4: 141–166.

Baum, E. B., and Haussler, D. (1989). What size net gives valid generalization? *Neural Computation* 1: 151–160.

Baum, E. B., and Wilczek, F. (1988). Supervised learning of probability distributions by neural networks. In D. Anderson (Ed.), *Neural information-processing systems,* 52–61. New York: American Institute of Physics.

Baxt, W. G., and White, H. (1995). Bootstrapping confidence intervals for clinical input variable effects in a network trained to identify the presence of acute myocardial infarction. *Neural Computation* 7: 624–638.

Bellman, R. (1971). *Introduction to the mathematical theory of control processes.* New York: Academic Press.

Bellman, R., and Kalaba, R. (1965). *Dynamic programming and modern control theory.* Englewood Cliffs, NJ: Prentice Hall.

Besag, J. (1974). Spatial interaction and the statistical analysis of lattice systems. *Journal of the Royal Statistical Society* B36: 192–236.

Besag, J. (1986). On the statistical analysis of dirty pictures. *Journal of the Royal Statistical Society* B48: 259–302.

Bitmead, R. R. (1983). Convergence in distribution of LMS-type adaptive parameter estimates. *IEEE Transactions on Automatic Control* 28: 54–60.

Blakemore, C., and Cooper, G. F. (1970). Development of the brain depends on the visual environment. *Nature* 228: 477–478.

Blakemore, C., and Mitchell, D. E. (1973). Environmental modification of the visual cortex and the neural basis of learning and memory. *Nature* 241: 467–468.

Blazis, D. E., Desmond, J. E., Moore, J. W., and Berthier, N. E. (1986). Simulation of the classically conditioned nictitating membrane response by a neuron-like adaptive element: A real-time variant of the Sutton-Barto model. In *Proceedings of the Eighth Annual Conference of the Cognitive Science Society,* 176–186. Hillsdale, NJ: Erlbaum.

Block, H. D. (1962). The perceptron: A model for brain functioning I. *Reviews of Modern Physics* 34: 123–135.

Blum, J. (1954). Multivariate stochastic approximation methods. *Annals of Mathematical Statistics* 25: 737–744.

Bourlard, H. A., and Kamp, Y. (1988). Auto-association by multilayer perceptrons and singular value decomposition. *Biological Cybernetics* 59: 291–294.

Bridle, J. S. (1990). Probabilistic interpretation of feedforward classification network outputs, with relationships to statistical pattern recognition. In F. Fougelman-Soulie and J. Herault (Eds.), *Neuro-Computing: Algorithms, architectures, and applications,* 227–236. New York: Springer.

Brown, T. H., Chapman, P. F., Kairiss, E. W., and Keenan, C. L. (1988). Long-term synaptic potentiation. *Science* 242: 724–728.

Brown, T. H., Kairiss, E. W., and Keenan, C. L. (1990). Hebbian synapses: Biophysical mechanisms and algorithms. *Annual Review of Neuroscience* 13: 475–511.

Bucy, R. S. (1965). Stability and positive supermartingales. *Journal of Differential Equations* 1: 151–155.

Burr, D. J. (1988). An improved elastic net method for the travelling salesman problem. In *IEEE International Joint Conference on Neural Networks,* vol. 1, pp. 69–76. Piscataway, NJ: IEEE Press.

Caianiello, E. R. (1961). Outline of a theory of thought-processes and thinking machines. *Journal of Theoretical Biology* 2: 204–235.

Carew, T. J. (1981a). Descending control of spinal circuits. In E. R. Kandel and J. H. Schwartz (Eds.), *Principles of neural science,* 312–321. New York: Elsevier/North-Holland.

Carew, T. J. (1981b). Spinal cord I: Muscles and muscle receptors. In E. R. Kandel and J. H. Schwartz (Eds.), *Principles of neural science,* 284–292. New York: Elsevier/North-Holland.

Carew, T. J. (1981c). Spinal cord II: Reflex action. In E. R. Kandel and J. H. Schwartz (Eds.), *Principles of neural science,* 293–304. New York: Elsevier/North-Holland.

Carpenter, G. A., Grossberg, S., Markuzon, N., Reynolds, J. H., and Rosen, D. B. (1992). Fuzzy artmap: A neural network architecture for incremental supervised learning of analog multidimensional maps. *IEEE Transactions on Neural Networks* 3: 698–713.

Carpenter, G. A., Grossberg, S., and Rosen, D. B. (1991). Fuzzy ART: Fast stable learning and categorization of analog patterns by an adaptive resonance system. *Neural Networks* 4: 759–771.

Chauvin, Y. (1989). A back-propagation algorithm with optimal use of hidden units. In D. S. Touretzky (Ed.), *Neural information-processing systems 1,* 519–526. San Mateo, CA: Morgan Kaufmann.

Chauvin, Y., and Rumelhart, D. E. (1995). *Backpropagation: Theory, architectures, and applications.* Hillsdale, NJ: Erlbaum.

Chellappa, R., and Jain, A. (1993). *Markov random fields: Theory and applications.* New York: Academic Press.

Cheng, B., and Titterington, D. M. (1994). Neural networks: A review from a statistical perspective. *Statistical Science* 9: 2–54.

Cheeseman, P. (1986). Probabilistic versus fuzzy reasoning. In L. N. Kanal and J. F. Lemmer (Eds.), *Uncertainty in artificial intelligence,* 85–102. New York: Elsevier/North-Holland.

Chou, P. B., Cooper, P. R., Swain, M. J., Brown, C. M., and Wixson, L. E. (1993). Probabilistic network inference for cooperative high- and low-level vision. In R. Chellappa and A. Jain (Eds.), *Markov random fields: Theory and applications,* 211–243. New York: Academic Press.

Clifford, S. P., and Nasrabadi, N. M. (1988). Integration of stereo vision and optical flow using Markov random fields. In *IEEE International Conference on Neural Networks,* vol. 1, pp. 577–584. San Diego, CA: IEEE San Diego Section and IEEE TAB Neural Network Committee.

Cohen, F. S., and Cooper, D. B. (1987). Simple parallel hierarchical and relaxation algorithms for segmenting noncausal Markov random fields. *IEEE Transactions on Pattern Analysis and Machine Intelligence,* 9: 195–219.

Cohen, M., and Grossberg, S. (1983). Absolute stability of global pattern formation and parallel memory storage by competitive neural networks. *IEEE Transactions on Systems on Man and Cybernetics,* 13: 815–826.

Côté, L. (1981). Basal ganglia, the extrapyramidal motor system, and diseases of transmitter metabolism. In E. R. Kandel and J. H. Schwartz (Eds.), *Principles of neural science,* 347–356. New York: Elsevier/North-Holland.

Cottrell, G. W., Munro, P., and Zipser, D. (1987). Learning internal representations from grayscale images: An example of extensional programming. In *Ninth Annual Conference of the Cognitive Science Society* (Seattle, 1987), 461–473. Hillsdale, NJ: Erlbaum.

Cowey, A. (1981). Why are there so many visual areas? In F. O. Schmitt, F. G. Worden, G. Adelman, and S. G. Dennis (Eds.), *The organization of the cerebral cortex,* 395–413. Cambridge, MA: MIT Press.

Cox, R. T. (1946). Probability, frequency, and reasonable expectation. *American Journal of Physics* 14: 1–13.

Crick, F., and Asanuma, C. (1986). Certain aspects of the anatomy and physiology of the cerebral cortex. In J. L. McClelland, D. E. Rumelhart, and the PDP Research Group (Eds.), *Parallel distributed processing.* Vol. 2, *Psychological and biological models,* 333–371. Cambridge, MA: MIT Press.

Cybenko, G. (1989). Approximation by superpositions of a sigmoidal function. *Mathematics of control, signals, and systems* 2: 303–314.

Daniell, T. P. (1970). Adaptive estimation with mutually correlated training sequences. *IEEE Transactions on Systems Science Cybernetics* 6: 12–19.

Darken, C., and Moody, J. (1990). Note on learning rate schedules for stochastic optimization. In D. Touretzky and R. Lippman (Eds.), *Advances in neural information-processing systems 3,* 832–838. San Mateo, CA: Morgan Kaufmann.

Darken, C., and Moody, J. (1991). Towards faster stochastic gradient search. In J. E. Moody, S. J. Hanson, and R. P. Lippman (Eds.), *Advances in Neural Information-Processing Systems 4*, 1009–1016. San Mateo, CA: Morgan Kaufmann.

DeGroot, M. H. (1970). *Optimal statistical decisions.* New York: McGraw-Hill.

DeGroot, M. H. (1975). *Probability and statistics.* Reading, MA: Addison-Wesley.

Denker, J., Schwartz, D., Wittner, B., Solla, S., Howard, R., and Jackel, L. (1987). Large automatic learning, rule extraction, and generalization. *Complex Systems* 1: 877–922.

Dennis, J. E., and Schnabel, R. B. (1983). *Numerical methods for unconstrained optimization and nonlinear equations.* Englewood Cliffs, NJ: Prentice-Hall.

Devaney, R. L. (1992). *A first course in chaotic dynamical systems: Theory and experiment.* New York: Addison-Wesley.

Dhawan, A. P., and Arata, L. (1993). Segmentation of medical images through competitive learning. In *Proceedings of the International Joint Conference on Neural Networks,* vol. 3, pp. 1277–1282. New York: IEEE Press.

Dobruschin, P. L. (1968). The description of a random field by means of conditional probabilities and conditions of its regularity. *Theory of Probability and Its Applications* 13: 197–224.

Duda, R. O., and Hart, P. E. (1973). *Pattern classification and scene analysis.* New York: Wiley.

Durbin, R., Szeliski, R., and Yuille, A. (1989). An analysis of the elastic net approach to the traveling salesman problem. *Neural Computation* 1: 348–358.

Durbin, R., and Willshaw, D. (1987). An analogue approach to the travelling salesman problem using an elastic net method. *Nature* 326: 689–691.

Eccles, J. C., Ito, M., and Szentagothai, J. (1967). *The cerebellum as a neuronal machine.* New York: Springer.

Efron, B. (1982). *The jackknife, the bootstrap, and other resampling plans.* Philadelphia: Society for Industrial and Applied Mathematics.

Elman, J. L. (1990). Finding structure in time. *Cognitive Science* 14: 179–212.

Elsley, R. K. (1990). Adaptive control of prosthetic limbs using neural networks. In *IEEE International Joint Conference on Neural Networks,* vol. 2, pp. 771–776. Ann Arbor, MI: IEEE Neural Networks Conference.

Errington, P. A., and Graham, J. (1993). Classification of chromosomes using a combination of neural networks. In *IEEE International Conference on Neural Networks,* vol. 3, pp. 1236–1241. Piscataway, NJ: IEEE Neural Networks Conference.

Estes, W. K. (1972). An associative basis for coding and organization in memory. In A. W. Melton and E. Martin (Eds.), *Coding processes in human memory,* 161–190. Washington, DC: Winston.

Fabian, V. (1994). Comment on White (1989). *Journal of the American Statistical Association* 89: 1571.

Feldman, J. A., and Ballard, D. H. (1982). Connectionist models and their properties. *Cognitive Science* 6: 205–254.

Finnoff, W. (1994). Diffusion approximations for the constant learning rate back-propagation algorithm and resistance to local minima. *Neural Computation* 6: 285–295.

Fletcher, R., and Reeves, C. M. (1964). Function minimization by conjugate gradients. *Computer Journal* 7: 149–154.

Franklin, J. H. (1968). *Matrix theory.* Englewood Cliffs, NJ: Prentice Hall.

Fukushima, K. (1980). Neocognitron: A self-organizing neural network model for a mechanism of pattern recognition unaffected by shift in position. *Biological Cybernetics* 36: 193–202.

Funahashi, K. (1989). On the approximate realization of continuous mappings by neural networks. *Neural Networks* 2: 183–192.

Gallant, S. (1994). *Neural network learning and expert systems.* Cambridge, MA: MIT Press.

Geman, S. (1979). Some averaging and stability results for random differential equations. *SIAM Journal on Applied Mathematics, 36,* 86–105.

Geman, S., and Geman, D. (1984). Stochastic relaxation, Gibbs distributions, and the Bayesian restoration of images. *IEEE Transactions on Pattern Analysis and Machine Intelligence* 6: 721–741.

Getting, P. A. (1983). Mechanisms of pattern generation underlying swimming in *Tritonia:* 2. Network reconstruction. *Journal of Neurophysiology* 49: 1017–1035.

Getting, P. A., Lennard, P. R., and Hume, R. I. (1980). Central pattern generator mediating swimming in *Tritonia:* 1. Identification and synaptic interactions. *Journal of Neurophysiology* 44: 151–164.

Ghez, C. (1981a). Cortical control of voluntary movement. In E. R. Kandel and J. H. Schwartz (Eds.), *Principles of neural science,* 323–333. New York: Elsevier/North-Holland.

Ghez, C. (1981b). Motor systems of the brain: Reflex and voluntary control of movement. In E. R. Kandel and J. H. Schwartz (Eds.), *Principles of neural science,* 271–283. New York: Elsevier/North-Holland.

Ghez, C., and Fahn, S. (1981). The cerebellum. In E. R. Kandel and J. H. Schwartz (Eds.), *Principles of neural science,* 334–346. New York: Elsevier/North-Holland.

Giles, C. L., and Maxwell, T. (1987). Learning, invariance, and generalization in high-order neural networks. *Applied Optics,* 26, 4972–4978.

Gillund, G., and Shiffrin, R. M. (1984). A retrieval model for both recognition and recall. *Psychological Review* 19: 1–65.

Goldberg, R. R. (1964). *Methods of real analysis.* Lexington, MA: Xerox College Publishing.

Goldstein, A. A. (1966). Minimizing functionals on normed-linear spaces. *Journal of SIAM Control* 4: 81–89.

Golden, R. M. (1986a). The brain-state-in-a-box neural model is a gradient descent algorithm. *Journal of Mathematical Psychology* 30: 73–80.

Golden, R. M. (1986b). A developmental neural model of visual word perception. *Cognitive Science* 10: 241–276.

Golden, R. M. (1988a). Probabilistic characterization of neural model computations. In D. Z. Anderson (Ed.), *Neural networks and information processing,* 310–316. New York: American Institute of Physics.

Golden, R. M. (1988b). Relating neural networks to traditional engineering approaches. In *Proceedings of the Artificial Intelligence and Advanced Computer Technology Conference,* Glen Ellyn, IL: Tower Conference Management. 255–260.

Golden, R. M. (1988c). A unified framework for connectionist systems. *Biological Cybernetics* 59: 109–120.

Golden, R. M. (1993). Stability and optimization analyses of the generalized brain-state-in-a-box neural network model. *Journal of Mathematical Psychology* 37: 282–298.

Golden, R. M. (1995). Making correct statistical inferences using a wrong probability model. *Journal of Mathematical Psychology* 38: 3–20.

Gorodkin, J., Hansen, L. K., Krogh, A., Svarer, C., and Winther, O. (1993). A quantitative study of pruning by optimal brain damage. *International Journal of Neural Systems* 4: 159–169.

Gradshteyn, I. S., and Ryzhik, I. M. (1965). *Table of integrals, series, and products.* New York: Academic Press.

Grajski, K. A., and Merzenich, M. M. (1990). Neural network simulation of somatosensory representational plasticity. In D. S. Touretzky (Ed.), *Advances in neural information processing systems,* vol. 2, pp. 52–59. San Mateo, CA: Morgan Kaufmann.

Grimshaw, R. (1990). *Nonlinear ordinary differential equations.* Oxford: Blackwell Scientific.

Grossberg, S. (1988). Nonlinear neural networks: Principles, mechanisms, and architectures. *Neural Networks* 1: 17–61.

Grossberg, S. (1972). Pattern learning by functional-differential neural networks with arbitrary path weights. In K. Schmitt (Ed.), *Delay and functional differential equations and their applications,* 121–160. New York: Academic Press.

Grossberg, S. (1973). Contour enhancement, short term memory, and constancies in reverberating neural networks. *Studies in Applied Mathematics* 52: 213–257.

Grossberg, S. (1974). Classical and instrumental learning by neural networks. *Progress in Theoretical Biology* 3: 51–141.

Grossberg, S. (1976). Adaptive pattern classification and universal recoding: 1. Parallel development and coding of neural feature detectors. *Biological Cybernetics* 23: 121–134.

Grossberg, S. (1980). How does a brain build a cognitive code? *Psychological Review* 85: 592–596.

Grossberg, S., and Levine, D. S. (1987). Neural dynamics of attentionally modulated Pavlovian conditioning: Blocking, inter-stimulus interval, and secondary reinforcement. *Applied Optics* 26: 5015–5030.

Grossberg, S., and Stone, G. (1986). Neural dynamics of attention switching and temporal order information in short-term memory. *Memory and Cognition* 14: 451–468.

Hagan, M. T., and Menhaj, M. B. (1994). Training feedforward networks with the Marquardt algorithm. *IEEE Transactions on Neural Networks* 5: 989–993.

Hainsworth, T. J., and Mardia, K. V. (1993). A Markov random field restoration of image sequences. In R. Chellappa and A. Jain (Eds.), *Markov random fields: Theory and application,* 409–445. New York: Academic Press.

Hammersley, J. M., and Clifford, P. (1971). *Markov fields on finite graphs and lattices.* Unpublished manuscript.

Hanson, S. J., and Pratt, L. Y. (1989). Comparing biases for minimal network construction with back-propagation. In D. S. Touretzky (Ed.), *Advances in Neural Information-Processing Systems 1.* San Mateo, CA: Morgan Kaufmann.

Hartline, H. K., and Ratliff, F. (1957). Inhibitory interactions of receptor units in the eye of *Limulus. Journal of General Physiology* 40: 351–376.

Hartline, H. K., and Ratliff, F. (1972). Inhibitory interaction in the retina of *Limulus.* In M. Fuortes (Ed.), *Handbook of Sensory Physiology. Volume 2. Physiology of Photoreceptor Organs,* vol. 40, pp. 381–447. New York: Springer Verlag.

Hassibi, B., and Stork, D. G. (1993). Second-order derivatives for network pruning: Optimal brain surgeon. In S. J. Hanson, J. D. Cowan, and C. L. Giles (Eds.), *Advances in Neural Information Processing Systems 5,* 164–171. San Mateo, CA: Morgan Kaufmann.

Hassibi, B., Stork, D. G., Wolff, G., and Watanabe, T. (1994). Optimal brain surgeon: Extensions and performance comparisons. In J. D. Cowan, G. Tesauro, and J. Alspector (Eds.), *Advances in neural information processing systems 6,* 263–270. San Francisco: Morgan Kaufmann.

Hassoun, M. H. (1995). *Fundamentals of artificial neural networks.* Cambridge, MA: MIT Press.

Haykin, S. (1994). *Neural networks: A comprehensive foundation.* New York: Macmillan.

Hebb, D. O. (1949). *The organization of behavior.* New York: Wiley.

Hecht-Nielson, R. (1989). Theory of the back-propagation neural network. In *Proceedings of the International Joint Conference on Neural Networks,* vol. 1, pp. 593–606. New York: IEEE Press.

Hergert, F., Finnoff, W., and Zimmerman, H. G. (1992). A comparison of weight elimination methods for reducing complexity in neural networks. In *International Joint Conference on Neural Networks,* vol. 3, pp. 980–987. Piscataway, NJ: IEEE Press.

Hertz, J., Krogh, A., and Palmer, R. G. (1991). *Introduction to the theory of neural computation.* Reading, MA: Addison-Wesley.

Hilgard, E. R., and Bower, G. H. (1966). *Theories of learning.* New York: Meredith.

Hillner, K. P. (1979). *Conditioning in contemporary perspective.* New York: Springer.

Hinton, G. E. (1989). Connectionist learning procedures. *Artificial Intelligence* 40: 185–234.

Hirsch, H., and Spinelli, D. N. (1970). Visual experience modifies distribution of horizontally and vertically oriented receptive fields in cats. *Science* 168: 869–871.

Hirsch, M. W. (1989). Convergent activation dynamics in continuous time networks. *Neural Networks* 2: 331–349.

Hopfield, J. J. (1982). Neural networks and physical systems with emergent collective computational abilities. *Proceedings of the National Academy of Sciences* 79: 2554–2558.

Hopfield, J. J. (1984). Neurons with graded response have collective computational properties like those of two-state neurons. *Proceedings of the National Academy of Sciences* 81: 3088–3092.

Hornik, K., Stinchcombe, M., and White, H. (1989). Multilayer feedforward networks are universal approximators. *Neural Networks* 2: 359–366.

Hu, Y. H., Tompkins, W. J., and Xue, Q. (1992). Artificial neural network for ECG arrhythmia monitoring. In *International Joint Conference on Neural Networks,* vol. 2, pp. 987–991. Piscataway, NJ: IEEE Press.

Hubel, D. H., and Wiesel, T. N. (1963). Receptive fields of cells in striate cortex of very young, visually experienced kittens. *Journal of Neurophysiology* 26: 994–1002.

Hubel, D. H., and Wiesel, T. N. (1968). Receptive fields and functional architecture of monkey striate cortex. *Journal of Physiology* 195: 215–243.

Huber, P. (1964). Robust estimation of a location parameter. *Annals of Mathematical Statistics, 35,* 73–101.

Hui, S., and Zak, S. H. (1992). Dynamical analysis of the brain-state-in-a-box (BSB) neural models. *IEEE Transactions on Neural Networks* 3: 86–94.

Hwang, J., and Tseng, Y. (1993). 3D motion estimation using single perspective sparse range data via surface reconstruction neural networks. In *Proceedings of the International Joint Conference on Neural Networks,* vol. 3, pp. 1696–1701. New York: IEEE Press.

Jaakkola, T., Jordan, M. I., and Singh, S. P. (1994). Convergence of stochastic iterative dynamic programming algorithms. In J. D. Cowan, G. Tesauro, and J. Alspector (Eds.), *Advances in Neural Information Processing Systems 6* (Vols. 703–710). San Francisco, CA: Morgan Kaufmann.

Jain, A. K., and Nadabar, S. G. (1993). Range image segmentation using MRF models. In R. Chellappa and A. Jain (Eds.), *Markov random fields: Theory and applications.* New York: Academic Press.

James, W. (1948). *Psychology* 1892. Reprint, Cleveland: World.

Jamison, T., and Schalkoff, R. (1988). Image labelling: A neural network approach. *Image and Vision Computing* 6: 203–214.

Jenkins, W. M., and Merzenich, M. M. (1987). Reorganization of neocortical representations after brain injury. In F. J. Seil, E. Herbert, B. Carlson (Eds.), *Neural regeneration: Progress in brain research,* 71, 249–266. New York: Elsevier Press.

Jenkins, W. M., Merzenich, M. M., Ochs, M. T., Allard, T., and Guic-Robles, E. (1990). Functional reorganization of primary somatosensory cortex in adult owl monkeys after behaviorally controlled tactile stimulation. *Journal of Neurophysiology* 90: 82–104.

Jennrich, R. I. (1969). Asymptotic properties of nonlinear least squares estimators. *Annals of Mathematical Statistics* 40: 633–643.

Johansson, E. M., Dowla, F. U., and Goodman, D. M. (1992). Backpropagation learning for multilayer feed-forward neural networks using the conjugate gradient method. *International Journal of Neural Systems* 2: 291–301.

Johnson-Laird, P. N., Legrenzi, P., and Legrenzi, M. (1972). Reasoning and a sense of reality. *British Journal of Psychology* 63: 395–400.

Johnston, J. C. (1978). A test of the sophisticated guessing theory of word perception. *Cognitive Psychology* 10: 123–154.

Jones, K. L., Lustig, I. J., and Kornhauser, A. L. (1990). Optimization techniques applied to neural networks: Line search implementation for back propagation. In *IEEE International Joint Conference on Neural Networks,* vol. 3, pp. 933–939. Ann Arbor, MI: IEEE Neural Networks Conference.

Jordan, M. I. (1986). An introduction to linear algebra in parallel distributed processing. In D. E. Rumelhart, J. L. McClelland, and the PDP Group (Eds.), *Parallel distributed processing.* Vol. 1, *Foundations,* 365–422. Cambridge, MA: MIT Press.

Jordan, M. I. (1992). Constrained supervised learning. *Journal of Mathematical Psychology* 36: 396–425.

Jordan, M. I., and Rumelhart, D. E. (1992). Forward models: Supervised learning with a distal teacher. *Cognitive Science* 16: 307–354.

Kahneman, D., and Tversky, A. (1979). Prospect theory: An analysis of decision under risk. *Econometrica* 47: 263–291.

Kalman, R. E., Falb, P. L., and Arbib, M. A. (1969). *Topics in mathematical systems theory.* New York: McGraw-Hill.

Kamin, L. J. (1969). Predictability, surprise, attention, and conditioning. In B. A. Campbell and R. M. Church (Eds.), *Punishment and aversive behavior,* 279–296. New York: Appleton Century Crofts.

Kandel, E. R. (1981a). Brain and behavior. In E. R. Kandel and J. H. Schwartz (Eds.), *Principles of neural science,* 3–13. New York: Elsevier/North-Holland.

Kandel, E. R. (1981b). Nerve cells and behavior. In E. R. Kandel and J. H. Schwartz (Eds.), *Principles of neural science,* 14–23. New York: Elsevier/North-Holland.

Kandel, E. R. (1981c). Somatic sensory system III: Central representation of touch. In E. R. Kandel and J. H. Schwartz (Eds.), *Principles of neural science,* 184–198. New York: Elsevier/North-Holland.

Kandel, E. R. (1981d). Visual system III: Physiology of the central visual pathways. In E. R. Kandel and J. H. Schwartz (Eds.), *Principles of neural science,* 236–247. New York: Elsevier/North-Holland.

Kandel, E. R., and Schwartz, J. H. (1981). *Principles of neural science.* New York: Elsevier/North-Holland.

Karlin, S., and Taylor, H. M. (1975). *A first course in stochastic processes.* New York: Academic Press.

Karr. (1993). *Probability.* New York: Springer.

Kelly, D. D. (1981a). Somatic sensory system IV: Central representations of pain and analgesia. In E. R. Kandel and J. H. Schwartz (Eds.), *Principles of neural science,* 199–211. New York: Elsevier/North-Holland.

Kelly, J. P. (1981b). Auditory system. In E. R. Kandel and J. H. Schwartz (Eds.), *Principles of neural science,* 258–268. New York: Elsevier/North-Holland.

Kelly, J. P. (1981c). Visual system II: Anatomy of the central visual pathways. In E. R. Kandel and J. H. Schwartz (Eds.), *Principles of neural science,* 199–211. New York: Elsevier/North-Holland.

Keynes, J. M. (1962). *A treatise on probability.* New York: Harper and Row.

Kirkpatrick, S., Gelatt, C. D., and Vecchi, M. P. (1983). Optimization by simulated annealing. *Science* 220: 671–680.

Kleinfeld, D., and Sompolinsky, H. (1988). Associative neural network model for the generation of temporal patterns. *Biophysical Journal* 54: 1039–1051.

Klir, G. J., and Folger, T. A. (1988). *Fuzzy sets, uncertainty, and information.* Englewood Cliffs, NJ: Prentice Hall.

Knapp, A. G., and Anderson, J. A. (1984). Theory of categorization based on distributed memory storage. *Journal of Experimental Psychology: Learning, Memory, and Cognition* 10: 616–637.

Knopp, K. (1956). *Infinite sequences and series.* New York: Dover.

Kohonen, T. (1972). Correlation matrix memories. *IEEE Transactions on Computers* 21: 353–359.

Kohonen, T. (1982). Self-organized formation of topologically correct feature maps. *Biological Cybernetics* 43: 59–69.

Kohonen, T. (1984). *Self-organization and associative memory.* New York: Springer.

Kohonen, T. (1989). *Self-organization and associative memory.* 3d ed. Berlin, Germany: Springer.

Kohonen, T. (1990). The self-organizing map. *Proceedings of the IEEE* 78: 1464–1480.

Kosko, B. (1988). Bidirectional associative memories. *IEEE Transactions on Systems, Man, and Cybernetics* 18: 49–60.

Kosko, B. (1992). *Neural networks and fuzzy systems.* Englewood Cliffs, NJ: Prentice Hall.

Kramer, A. H., and Sangiovanni-Vincentelli, A. (1989). Efficient parallel learning algorithms for neural networks. In D. S. Touretzky (Ed.), *Neural information-processing systems 1,* 40–48. San Mateo, CA: Morgan Kaufmann.

Kristan, W., Lockery, S., Wittenberg, G., and Cottrell, G. (1989). Behavioral choice—in theory and in practice. In R. Durbin, C. Miall, and G. Mitchison (Eds.), *The computing neuron,* 180–204. New York: Addison Wesley.

Krogh, A., Thorbergsson, G. I., and Hertz, J. A. (1990). A cost function for internal representations. In D. S. Touretzky (Ed.), *Advances in neural information-processing systems 2,* 733–740. San Mateo, CA: Morgan Kaufmann.

Kuan, C., Hornik, K., and White, H. (1994). A convergence result for learning in recurrent neural networks. *Neural Computation* 6: 420–440.

Kullback, S., and Leibler, R. A. (1951). On information and sufficiency. *Annals of Mathematical Statistics* 22: 79–86.

Kung, S. Y. (1993). *Digital neural networks.* Englewood Cliffs, NJ: Prentice Hall.

Kushner, H. J. (1965). On the stability of stochastic dynamical systems. *Proceedings of the National Academy of Sciences* 53: 8–12.

Kushner, H. J. (1966). On the construction of stochastic Lyapunov functions. *IEEE Transactions on Automatic Control,* 11: 477–478.

Kushner, H. J. (1967). *Stochastic stability and control.* New York: Academic Press.

Kushner, H. J. (1984). *Approximation and weak convergence methods for random processes, with applications to stochastic systems theory.* Cambridge, MA: MIT Press.

Kushner, H. J., and Clark, D. S. (1978). *Stochastic approximation methods for constrained and unconstrained systems.* New York: Springer.

Larson, H. J., and Shubert, B. O. (1979). *Probabilistic models in engineering sciences.* Vol. 1, *Random variables and stochastic processes.* New York: Wiley.

LaSalle, J. P. (1960). Some extensions of Liapunov's second method. *IRE Transactions on Circuit Theory* 7: 520–527.

LaSalle, J. P. (1976). *The stability of dynamical systems.* Bristol: Society for Industrial and Applied Mathematics and J. W. Arrowsmith.

Lashley, K. S. (1950). In search of the engram. *Symposia of the Study of Experimental Biology* 4: 454–482.

Le Cun, Y. (1985). Une procédure d'apprentissage pour réseau à seuil asymétrique. *Proceedings of Cognitiva* 85: 599–604.

Le Cun, Y. (1988). A theoretical framework for back-propagation. In D. Touretzky, G. Hinton, and T. Sejnowski (Eds.), *Proceedings of the 1988 Connectionist Models Summer School,* 21–28. San Mateo: CA: Morgan Kaufmann.

Le Cun, Y., Boser, B., Denker, J. S., Henderson, D., Howard, R. E., Hubbard, W., and Jackel, L. D. (1990a). Handwritten digit recognition with a back-propagation network. In D. Touretzky (Ed.), *Advances in neural information-processing systems 2,* 396–404. San Mateo, CA: Morgan Kaufmann.

Le Cun, Y., Boser, B., Denker, J. S., Henderson, D., Howard, R. E., Hubbard, W., and Jackel, L. D. (1990b). Back-propagation applied to handwritten zip code recognition. *Neural Computation* 1: 541–551.

Le Cun, Y., Denker, J. S., and Solla, S. A. (1990). Optimal brain damage. In D. S. Touretzky (Ed.), *Advances in neural information-processing systems 2,* 598–605. San Mateo, CA: Morgan Kaufmann.

Leighton, W. (1976). *An introduction to the theory of ordinary differential equations.* Belmont, CA: Wadsworth.

Levin, A. U., Leen, T. K., and Moody, J. E. (1994). Fast pruning using principal components. In J. D. Cowan, G. Tesauro, and J. Alspector (Eds.), *Advances in neural information-processing systems 6,* 35–42. San Francisco, CA: Morgan Kaufmann.

Levin, E., Tishby, N., and Solla, S. A. (1990). A statistical approach to learning and generalization in layered neural networks. *Proceedings of the IEEE* 78: 1568–1574.

Levine, D. S. (1991). *Introduction to neural and cognitive modeling.* Hillsdale, NJ: Erlbaum.

Lewandowsky, S., and Murdock, B. B. (1989). Memory for serial order. *Psychological Review* 96: 25–57.

Liapunov, A. M. (1907). Problème général de la stabilité du mouvement. *Annales, Faculté de Sciences de Mathématiques Toulouse:* 9: 203–474. French translation of original 1893 mémoire.

Lindley, D. V. (1982). Scoring rules and the inevitability of probability. *International Statistical Review* 50: 1–26.

Lindley, D. V. (1987). The probability approach to the treatment of uncertainty in artificial intelligence and statistics. *Statistical Science* 2: 17–24.

Lisa, F., Carrabina, J., Avellana, N., and Valderrama, E. (1993). Two-bit weights are enough to solve the vehicle license recognition problem. In *Proceedings of the International Joint Conference on Neural Networks,* vol. 3, pp. 1242–1246. New York: IEEE Press.

Little, W. A. (1974). The existence of persistent states in the brain. *Mathematical Biosciences* 19: 101–120.

Ljung, L. (1977). Analysis of recursive stochastic algorithms. *IEEE Transactions on Automatic Control* 22: 551–575.

Ljung, L., Pflug, G., and Walk, H. (1992). *Stochastic approximation and optimization of random systems*. Boston: Birkhauser.

Lo, N. W., and Hafez, H. M. (1992). Neural network channel equalization. In *International Joint Conference on Neural Networks*, vol. 2, pp. 981–986. Piscataway, NJ: IEEE Press.

Lu, Y., and Thomborson, C. D. (1991). Gate array global routing using a neural network. In C. H. Dagli, S. R. Kumara, and Y. C. Shin (Eds.), *Intelligent engineering systems through artificial neural networks*, 895–900. New York: ASME Press.

Luce, R. D., and Suppes, P. (1965). Preference, utility, and subjective probability. In R. D. Luce, R. R. Bush, and E. Galanter (Eds.), *Handbook of mathematical psychology*, 249–410. New York: Wiley.

Luenberger, D. G. (1979). *Introduction to dynamic systems: Theory, models, and applications.* New York: Wiley.

Luenberger, D. G. (1984). *Linear and nonlinear programming*. Reading, MA: Addison-Wesley.

Lukacs, E. (1975). *Stochastic convergence*. New York: Academic Press.

Macchi, O., and Eweda, E. (1983). Second-order convergence analysis of stochastic adaptive linear filtering. *IEEE Transactions on Automatic Control* 28: 76–85.

MacKay, D. (1992). A practical Bayesian framework for backpropagation networks. *Neural Computation* 4: 448–472.

Manikopoulos, C., Antoniou, G., and Metzelopoulou, S. (1990). LVQ of image sequence source and ANS classification of finite state machine for high-compression coding. In *International Joint Conference on Neural Networks*, vol. 1, pp. 481–486. Ann Arbor, MI: IEEE Neural Networks Council.

Mano, M. M. (1986). *Digital design*. Englewood Cliffs, NJ: Prentice Hall.

Manoukian, E. B. (1986). *Modern concepts and theorems of mathematical statistics*. New York: Springer.

Marcus, C. M., and Westervelt, R. M. (1989). Dynamics of iterated-map neural networks. *Physical Review* A40: 501–504.

Marlow, W. H. (1978 [republished in 1993]). *Mathematics for operations research*. Meniola, N.Y.: Dover.

Marr, D. (1982). *Vision*. San Francisco: Freeman.

Marroquin, J. L. (1985). *Probabilistic solution of inverse problems*. (A.I. memo no. 860). Cambridge, MA: MIT Artificial Intelligence Lab.

Marsden, J. E., and Tromba, A. J. (1981). *Vector calculus*. New York: Freeman.

Martin, J. H. (1981a). Somatic sensory system I: Receptor physiology and submodality coding. In E. R. Kandel and J. H. Schwartz (Eds.), *Principles of neural science*, 157–168. New York: Elsevier/North-Holland.

Martin, J. H. (1981b). Somatic sensory system II: Anatomical substrates for somatic sensation. In E. R. Kandel and J. H. Schwartz (Eds.), *Principles of neural science*, 170–183. New York: Elsevier/North-Holland.

Mason, M. (1975). Reading ability and letter search time: Effects of orthographic structure defined by single-letter positional frequency. *Journal of Experimental Psychology: General* 104: 146–166.

McClelland, J. L. (1976). Preliminary letter identification in the perception of words and nonwords. *Journal of Experimental Psychology: Human Perception and Performance* 1: 80–91.

McClelland, J. L., and Johnston, J. C. (1977). The role of familiar units in perception of words and nonwords. *Perception and Psychophysics* 22: 249–261.

McClelland, J. L., and Rumelhart, D. E. (1981). An interactive activation model of context effects in letter perception: 1. An account of basic findings. *Psychological Review* 88: 375–497.

McClelland, J. L., Rumelhart, D. E., and the PDP Research Group. (1986). *Parallel distributed processing*. Vol. 2, *Psychological and biological models*. Cambridge, MA: MIT Press.

McCormick, G. P., and Ritter, K. (1972). Methods of conjugate gradients versus quasi-Newton methods. *Mathematical Programming* 3: 101–111.

McCulloch, W. S., and Pitts, W. (1943). A logical calculus of the ideas immanent in nervous activity. *Bulletin of Mathematical Biophysics* 5: 115–133.

McNeill, D., and Freiberger, P. (1993). *Fuzzy logic.* New York: Simon and Schuster.

Medin, D. L. and Schaffer, M. M. (1978). Context theory of classification learning. *Psychological Review* 85: 207–238.

Mendenhall, W., Scheaffer, R. L., and Wackerly, D. D. (1981). *Mathematical statistics with applications.* Boston: Duxbury.

Menon, M. M., and Wells, W. (1990). Massively parallel image restoration. In *International Joint Conference on Neural Networks,* vol. 1, pp. 511–516. Ann Arbor, MI: IEEE Neural Networks Council.

Minsky, M. L. (1967). *Computation: Finite and infinite machines.* Englewood Cliffs, NJ: Prentice Hall.

Minsky, M. L., and Papert, S. A. (1969). *Perceptrons.* Cambridge: MIT Press.

Mitra, U., and Poor, H. V. (1993). Neural network techniques for multi-user demodulation. In *Proceedings of the International Joint Conference on Neural Networks,* vol. 3, pp. 1539–1543. New York: IEEE Press.

Møller, M. F. (1990). *A scaled conjugate gradient algorithm for fast supervised learning.* Aarhus, Denmark: Technical Report PB-339 Aarhus University Computer Science Department.

Montgomery, D. C., and Peck, E. A. (1982). *Introduction to linear regression analysis.* New York: Wiley.

Moody, J. (1994). Prediction risk and architecture selection for neural networks. In V. Cherkassky, J. H. Friedman, and H. Wechsler (Eds.), *From statistics to neural networks: Theory and pattern recognition applications,* (147–165) New York: Springer.

Moody, J. E., and Utans, J. (1992). Principled architecture selection for neural networks: Application to corporate bond rating prediction. In J. E. Moody, S. J. Hanson, and R. P. Lippmann (Eds.), *Advances in neural information-processing systems 4* (pp. 683–690). San Mateo, CA: Morgan Kaufmann.

Mozer, M. (1993). Neural network architectures for temporal pattern processing. In A. S. Weigend and N. A. Gershenfeld (Eds.), *Time series prediction: Forecasting the future and understanding the past. Sante Fe Institute Studies in the Sciences of Complexity, Proceedings,* Vol. 17, 243–264. Redwood City, CA: Addison-Wesley.

Mozer, M. C., and Smolensky, P. (1990). Skeletonization: A technique for trimming the fat from a network via relevance assessment. In D. S. Touretzky (Ed.), *Advances in neural information-processing systems 1,* 107–115. San Mateo, CA: Morgan Kaufmann.

Munro, P. W. (1987). A dual back-propagation scheme for scalar reinforcement learning. In *Proceedings of the Ninth Annual Conference of the Cognitive Science Society,* vol. 9, pp. 165–176. Hillsdale, NJ: Erlbaum.

Murdock, B. B. (1982). A theory for the storage and retrieval of item and associative information. *Psychological Review* 89: 609–626.

Murdock, B. B. (1983). A distributed memory model for serial-order information. *Psychological Review* 90: 316–338.

Nakano, K. (1972). Associatron: A model of associative memory. *IEEE Transactions on Systems, Man, and Cybernetics* 2: 380–388.

Niederberger, C. S., Pursell, S., and Golden, R. M. (1996). A neural network to predict lifespan and new metastases in patients with renal cell cancer. In E. Fiesler, R. Beale, G. L. Murphy, C. Niederberger, K. Torkkola, and C. Wellekens (Eds.), *Handbook of neural computation.* New York: Oxford University Press and Bristol: Institute of Physics.

Nilsson, N. J. (1965). *Learning machines.* New York: McGraw-Hill.

Olinick, M. (1978). *An introduction to mathematical models in the social and life sciences.* Menlo Park, CA: Addison-Wesley.

O'Toole, A. J., Abdi, H., Deffenbacher, K. A., and Valentin, D. (1993). Low-dimensional representation of faces in higher dimensions of the face space. *Optical Society of America* 10: 405–411.

Paas, G. (1993). Assessing and improving neural network predictions by the bootstrap algorithm. In S. J. Hanson, J. D. Cowan, and C. L. Giles (Eds.), *Advances in neural information-processing systems 5,* 196–203. San Mateo, CA: Morgan Kaufmann.

Parker, D. B. (1985). *Learning-logic (TR-47).* Cambridge, MA: MIT, Center for Computational Research in Economics and Management Science.

Patrick, E. A. (1972). *Fundamentals of pattern recognition.* Englewood Cliffs, NJ: Prentice Hall.

Pavlov, I. P. (1927). *Conditioned reflexes.* London: Oxford University Press.

Pearl, J. (1988). *Probabilistic reasoning in intelligent systems: Networks of plausible inference.* San Mateo, CA: Morgan Kaufmann.

Perkel, D. H., Mulloney, B., and Budelli, R. W. (1981). Quantitative methods predicting neuronal behavior. *Neuroscience* 6: 823–837.

Piaget, J. (1954). *The construction of reality in the child.* Translated by M. Cook. New York: Basic Books.

Platt, J. C., and Barr, A. H. (1987). Constrained differential optimization. In D. Z. Anderson (Ed.), *Neural information-processing systems,* 612–621. New York: American Institute of Physics.

Plumer, E. S. (1993). Time-optimal terminal control using neural networks. In *Proceedings of the International Joint Conference on Neural Networks,* vol. 3, pp. 1926–1931. New York: IEEE Press.

Poggio, T., and Girosi, F. (1990). Networks for approximation and learning. *Proceedings of the IEEE* 78: 1481–1497.

Poggio, G. F., and Viernstein, L. J. (1964). Time series analysis of impulse sequences of thalamic somatic sensory neurons. *Journal of Neurophysiology* 27: 518–545.

Polak, E., and Ribière, G. (1969). Note sur la convergence de méthodes de directions conjurées. *Revue Française d'Informatique et de Recherche Opérationnelle* 16: 35–43.

Poliac, M. O., Lee, E. B., Slagle, J. R., and Wick, M. R. (1987). A crew scheduling problem. In *Proceedings of the International Joint Conference on Neural Networks,* vol. 4, pp. 779–786. New York: IEEE Press.

Pollatsek, A., Well, A. D., and Schindler, R. M. (1975). Familiarity affects visual processing of words. *Journal of Experimental Psychology: Human Perception and Performance* 1: 328–338.

Posner, M. I., and Keele, S. W. (1968). On the genesis of abstract ideas. *Journal of Experimental Psychology* 77: 353–363.

Press, W. H., Flannery, B. P., Teukolsky, S. A., and Vetterling, W. T. (1986). *Numerical recipes: The art of scientific computing.* New York: Cambridge University Press.

Qian, N., and Sejnowski, T. J. (1988). Predicting the secondary structure of globular proteins using neural network models. *Journal of Molecular Biology* 202: 865–884.

Quinlan, P. (1991). *Connectionism and psychology.* Chicago: University of Chicago Press.

Raiffa, H. (1970). *Decision analysis: Introductory lectures on choices under uncertainty.* Menlo Park, CA: Addison-Wesley.

Ramamurthy, A. C., and Uriquidi-Macdonald, M. (1993). Stone impact damage to automotive paint finishes: A neural net analysis of electrochemical impedance data. In *Proceedings of the International Joint Conference on Neural Networks,* vol. 3, pp. 1708–1712. New York: IEEE Press.

Ramsey, F. P. (1988). Truth and probability. In P. Gardenfors and N. Sahlin (Eds.), *Decision, probability, and utility: Selected readings,* 19–47. Cambridge: Cambridge University Press.

Rangarajan, A., and Chellappa, R. (1993). A continuation method for image estimation using the adiabatic approximation. In R. Chellappa and A. Jain (Eds.), *Markov random fields,* 69–91. New York: Academic Press, Inc.

Rashevsky, N. (1960). *Mathematical biophysics,* Vol. 2. New York: Dover.

Refenes, A. N., Azema-Barac, M., and Zapranis, A. D. (1993). Stock ranking: Neural networks vs. multiple linear regression. In *Proceedings of the International Joint Conference on Neural Networks,* vol. 3, pp. 1419–1426. New York: IEEE Press.

Reicher, G. (1969). Perceptual recognition as a function of meaningfulness of stimulus material. *Journal of Experimental Psychology* 81: 275–280.

Rescorla, R. A., and Wagner, A. R. (1972). A theory of Pavlovian conditioning: Variations in the effectiveness of reinforcement and nonreinforcement. In R. A. Black and W. F. Prokasy (Eds.), *Classical conditioning II: Current research and theory.* New York: Appleton Century Crofts.

Ridgway, W. C. (1962). *An adaptive logic system with generalizing properties. Technical report 1556-1.* Stanford, CA: Stanford University, Stanford Electronics Laboratories.

Riefer, D. M., and Batchelder, W. H. (1988). Multinomial modeling and the measurement of cognitive processes. *Psychological Review* 95: 318–339.

Ripley, B. D. (1994). Neural networks and related methods for classification. *Journal of the Royal Statistical Society* B56: 409–456.

Robbins, H., and Monro, S. (1951). A stochastic approximation method. *Annals of Mathematical Statistics* 22: 400–407.

Rosenblatt, F. (1958). The perceptron: A probabilistic model for information storage and organization in the brain. *Psychological Review* 65: 386–408.

Rosenblatt, F. (1962). *Principles of neurodynamics: Perceptrons and the theory of brain mechanisms.* Washington DC: Spartan.

Rosenlicht, M. (1968). *Introduction to analysis.* New York: Dover. Reprinted in 1986.

Rowland, L. P. (1981). Spinal cord III: Clinical syndromes. In E. R. Kandel and J. H. Schwartz (Eds.), *Principles of neural science,* 155–169. New York: Elsevier/North-Holland.

Rumelhart, D. E., Durbin, R., Golden, R. M., and Chauvin, Y. (1995). Backpropagation: The basic theory. In Y. Chauvin and D. E. Rumelhart (Eds.), *Backpropagation: Theory, architectures, and applications,* 1–34. Hillsdale, NJ: Erlbaum.

Rumelhart, D. E., Hinton, G. E., and Williams, R. J. (1986). Learning internal representations by error propagation. In D. E. Rumelhart, J. L. McClelland, and the PDP Group (Eds.), *Parallel distributed processing.* Vol. 1, *Foundations,* 318–362. Cambridge, MA: MIT Press.

Rumelhart, D. E., and McClelland, J. L. (1982). An interactive activation model of context effects in letter perception: Part 1. The contextual enhancement effect and some tests and extensions of the model. *Psychological Review* 89: 60–94.

Rumelhart, D. E., and McClelland, J. L. (1986). PDP models and general issues in cognitive science. In D. E. Rumelhart, J. L. McClelland, and the PDP Research Group (Eds.), *Parallel distributed processing.* Vol. 1: *Foundations,* 110–146. Cambridge, MA: MIT Press.

Rumelhart, D. E., McClelland, J. L., and the PDP Research Group. (Eds., 1986). *Parallel distributed processing.* Vol. 1, *Foundations.* Cambridge, MA: MIT Press.

Rumelhart, D. E., Smolensky, P., McClelland, J. L., and Hinton, G. E. (1986). Schemata and sequential thought processes in PDP models. In J. L. McClelland and D. E. Rumelhart (Eds.), *Parallel distributed processing.* Vol. 2: *Psychological and biological models,* 7–57. Cambridge, MA: MIT Press.

Savage, L. J. (1972). *The foundations of statistics.* New York: Dover.

Schley, C., Chauvin, Y., Henkle, V., and Golden, R. (1991). Neural networks structured for control application to aircraft landing. In D. Touretzky and R. Lippman (Eds.), *Advances in neural information-processing systems 3.* San Mateo, CA: Morgan Kaufmann.

Selfridge, O. G. (1958). Pandemonium: A paradigm for learning. In *Mechanisation of Thought Processes: Proceedings of a Symposium Held at the National Physical Laboratory,* 513–526. London: HMSO.

Selverston, A., and Mazzoni, P. (1989). Flexibility of computational units in invertebrate CPGs. In R. Durbin, C. Miall, and G. Mitchison (Eds.), *The computing neuron,* 205–228. New York: Addison-Wesley.

Selverston, A. I., and Moulins, M. (1985). Oscillatory neural networks. *Annual Review of Physiology* 47: 29–48.

Serfling, R. J. (1980). *Approximation theorems of mathematical statistics.* New York: Wiley.

Shafer, G. (1976). *A mathematical theory of evidence.* Princeton, NJ: Princeton University Press.

Shafer, G. (1987). Probability judgment in artificial intelligence and expert systems. *Statistical Science* 2: 3–16.

Shanno, D. F. (1978). Conjugate gradient methods with inexact line searches. *Mathematics of Operations Research* 3: 244–256.

Sibul, L. H. (1987). *Adaptive signal processing.* New York: IEEE Press.

Simon, H. A. (1969). *The sciences of the artificial.* Cambridge, MA: MIT Press.

Sivilotti, M. A., Mahowald, M. A., and Mead, C. A. (1987). Real-time visual computations using analog CMOS processing arrays. In P. Losleben (Ed.), *Advanced Research in VLSI: Proceedings of the 1987 Stanford Conference,* 295–312. Cambridge, MA: MIT Press.

Smolensky, P. (1986). Information processing in dynamical systems: Foundations of harmony theory. In D. E. Rumelhart, J. L. McClelland, and the PDP Group (Eds.), *Parallel distributed processing.* Vol. 1, *Foundations,* 194–281. Cambridge, MA: MIT Press.

Specht, D. F. (1967). Generation of polynomial discriminant functions for pattern recognition. *IEEE Transactions on Electronic Computers* 16: 308–319.

Specht, D. F. (1988). Probabilistic neural networks for classification, mapping, or associative memory. In *IEEE International Conference on Neural Networks,* vol. 1, pp. 525–532. San Diego, CA: IEEE San Diego Section and IEEE TAB Neural Network Committee.

Specht, D. F. (1990). Probabilistic neural networks. *Neural Networks* 3: 109–118.

Spitzer, F. (1971). Markov random fields and Gibbs ensembles. *American Mathematical Monthly* 78: 142–154.

Stefanis, C. (1969). Interneuronal mechanisms in the cortex. In M. Brazier (Ed.), *The interneuron,* 497–526. Los Angeles: University of California Press.

Steinbuch, K., and Schmitt, E. (1967). Adaptive systems using learning matrices. In H. L. Oestricher and D. R. Moore (Eds.), *Cybernetic problems in bionics,* 751–768. New York: Gordon and Breach.

Stinchcombe, M., and White, H. (1989). Universal approximation using feedforward networks with non-sigmoid hidden layer activation functions. In *Proceedings of the International Joint Conference on Neural Networks,* vol. 1, pp. 593–606. New York: IEEE Press.

Stork, D. (1989). Is back-propagation biologically plausible? *International Joint Conference on Neural Networks* 2: 241–246.

Sugeno, M. (1977). Fuzzy measures and fuzzy integrals: A survey. In M. M. Gupta, G. N. Saridis, and G. R. Gaines (Eds.), *Fuzzy automata and decision processes,* 89–102. New York: North-Holland.

Sutton, R. S. (1988). Learning to predict by the methods of temporal differences. *Machine Learning* 3: 9–44.

Sutton, R. S., and Barto, A. G. (1981). Toward a modern theory of adaptive networks: Expectation and prediction. *Psychological Review* 88: 135–170.

Svarer, C., Hansen, L. K., and Larsen, J. (1993). On design and evaluation of tapped-delay neural network architectures. In H. R. Berenji (Ed.), *International Conference on Neural Networks,* vol. 1, pp. 46–51. Piscataway, NJ: IEEE.

Svarer, C., Hansen, L. K., Larsen, J., and Rasmussen, C. E. (1993). Designer networks for time series processing. In C. A. Kamm (Ed.), *Neural networks for signal processing,* vol. 3, pp. 78–87. Piscataway, NJ: IEEE.

Szentagothai, J. (1967). The "module-concept" in cerebral cortex architecture. *Brain Research* 95: 475–496.

Tansel, I. N., Mekdeci, C., Ozdamar, O., and Lopez, C. N. (1991). Classification of phonocardiograms with unsupervised neural networks. In C. H. Dagli, S. R. Kumara, and Y. C. Shin (Eds.), *Intelligent engineering systems through artificial neural networks,* 345–350. New York: ASME Press.

Taylor, G. A., Miller, T., and Juola, J. F. (1977). Isolating visual units in the perception of words and nonwords. *Perception and Psychophysics* 21: 377–386.

Tazaki, K., and Cooke, I. M. (1983). Neuronal mechanisms underlying rhythmic bursts in crustacean cardiac ganglia. In A. Roberts and B. L. Roberts (Eds.), *Neural origin of rhythmic movements,* 129–157. Cambridge: Cambridge University Press.

Tesauro, G. (1990). Neurogammon: A neural-network backgammon program. In *IJCNN International Joint Conference on Neural Networks,* vol. 3, pp. 33–39. Ann Arbor, MI: IEEE Neural Networks Council.

Thacore, S., Pang, V., Palaniswami, M., and Bairaktaris, D. (1991). Image data compression using a self-organizing neural network with adaptive thresholds. In *1991 International Joint Conference on Neural Networks,* vol. 1, pp. 646–652. Piscataway, NJ: IEEE.

Tishby, N., Levin, E., and Solla, S. (1989). Consistent inference of probabilities in layered networks: Predictions and generalization. In *Proceedings of the International Joint Conference on Neural Networks,* vol. 2, pp. 403–409. New York: IEEE Press.

Tversky, A. (1969). Intransitivity of preferences. *Psychological Review* 76: 31–48.

Van Hulle, M. M., and Orban, G. A. (1991). Representation and processing in a stochastic neural network: An integrated approach. *Neural Networks* 4: 643–655.

Vapnik, V. N. (1992). Principles of risk minimization for learning theory. In J. E. Moody, S. J. Hanson, and R. P. Lippmann (Eds.), *Advances in neural information-processing systems 4,* 831–838. San Mateo, CA: Morgan Kaufmann.

Vidyasagar, M. (1978). *Nonlinear systems analysis.* Englewood Cliffs, NJ: Prentice-Hall.

von der Malsburg, C. (1973). Self-organization of orientation sensitive cells in the striata cortex. *Kybernetik* 14: 85–100.

von Neumann, J. (1958). *The computer and the brain.* New Haven: Yale University Press.

von Neumann, J., and Morgenstern, O. (1953). *Theory of games and economic behavior.* Princeton, NJ: Princeton University Press. Original edition published in 1944.

Vuong, Q. H. (1989). Likelihood ratio tests for model selection and non-nested hypotheses. *Econometrica* 57: 307–333.

Waibel, A. (1989). Consonant recognition by modular construction of large phonemic time-delay neural networks. In D. Touretzky (Ed.), *Advances in neural information-processing systems 1,* 215–223. San Mateo, CA: Morgan Kaufmann.

Waibel, A., Hanazawa, T., Hinton, G., Shikano, K., and Lang, K. J. (1989). Phoneme recognition using time-delay neural networks. *IEEE Transactions on Acoustics, Speech, and Signal Processing* 37: 328–339.

Waibel, A., Sawai, H., and Shikano, K. (1989). Modularity and scaling in large phonemic neural networks. *IEEE Transactions on Acoustics, Speech, and Signal Processing* 37: 1888–1899.

Wakker, P. P. (1989). *Additive representations of preferences.* Boston: Kluwer.

Wald, A. (1943). Tests of statistical hypotheses concerning several parameters when the number of observations is large. *Transactions of the American Mathematical Society* 54: 426–482.

Walk, H. (1992). Foundations of stochastic approximation. In *Stochastic approximation and optimization of random systems,* 1–51. Boston: Birkhauser.

Walpole, R. E., and Myers, R. H. (1978). *Probability and statistics for engineers and scientists.* New York: Macmillan.

Wasan, M. T. (1969). *Stochastic approximation.* Cambridge: Cambridge University Press.

Wason, P. C. (1966). Reasoning. In B. Foss (Ed.), *New horizons in psychology,* 135–151. Harmondsworth, England: Penguin.

Watkins, C., and Dayan, P. (1992). Q-learning. *Machine Learning* 8: 279–292.

Watrous, R. L. (1987). Learning algorithms for connectionist networks: Applied gradient methods for nonlinear optimization. In M. Caudill and C. Butler (Eds.), *IEEE First International Conference on Neural Networks,* vol. 1, pp. 619–628. Piscataway, NJ: IEEE Press.

Weigend, A. S., Rumelhart, D. E., and Huberman, B. A. (1991). Generalization by weight-elimination with application to forecasting. In R. P. Lippmann, J. E. Moody, and D. S. Touretzky (Eds.), *Advances in neural information-processing systems 3* (pp. 875–882). San Mateo, CA: Morgan Kaufmann.

Werbos, P. J. (1974). *Beyond regression: New tools for prediction and analysis in the behavioral sciences.* Ph.D. diss., Harvard University.

Werbos, P. J. (1990). Back-propagation through time: What it does and how to do it. *Proceedings of the IEEE* 78: 1550–1560.

White, H. (1981). Consequences and detection of misspecified nonlinear regression models. *Journal of the American Statistical Association* 76: 419–433.

White, H. (1982). Maximum likelihood estimation of misspecified models. *Econometrica* 50: 1–25.

White, H. (1984). *Asymptotic theory for econometricians.* New York: Academic Press, Inc.

White, H. (1989a). Learning in artificial neural networks: A statistical perspective. *Neural Computation* 1: 425–464.

White, H. (1989b). Some asymptotic results for learning in single hidden-layer feedforward network models. *Journal of the American Statistical Association* 84: 1003–1013.

White, H. (1992). Some asymptotic results for learning in single hidden-layer feedforward network models (correction). *Journal of the American Statistical Association* 87: 1252.

White, H. (1994). *Estimation, inference, and specification analysis.* New York: Cambridge University Press.

Widrow, B., Glover, J. R., McCool, J. M., Kaunitz, J., Williams, C. S., Hearn, R. H., Zeidler, J. R., Dong, E., and Goodlin, R. C. (1975). Adaptive noise cancelling: Principles and applications. *Proceedings of the IEEE* 63: 1692–1716.

Widrow, B., and Hoff, M. E. (1960). Adaptive switching circuits. In *1960 IRE WESCON Convention Records,* 96–104.

Widrow, B., and Lehr, M. A. (1990). Thirty years of adaptive neural networks: Perceptron, madaline, and backpropagation. *Proceedings of the IEEE* 78: 1415–1442.

Widrow, B., and Stearns, S. D. (1985). *Adaptive signal processing.* Englewood Cliffs, NJ: Prentice Hall.

Wilks, S. S. (1938). The large sample distribution of the likelihood ratio for testing composite hypotheses. *Annals of Mathematical Statistics* 9: 60–62.

Wilks, S. S. (1962). *Mathematical statistics.* New York: Wiley.

Williams, D. (1991). *Probability with martingales.* Cambridge: Cambridge University Press.

Williams, R. J. (1988). On the use of back-propagation in associative reinforcement learning. In *IEEE International Conference on Neural Networks,* vol. 1, pp. 263–270. New York: IEEE Press.

Williams, R. J. (1992). Simple statistical gradient-following algorithms for connectionist reinforcement learning. *Machine Learning* 8: 229–256.

Williams, R. J., and Zipser, D. (1989a). A learning algorithm for continually running fully recurrent neural networks. *Neural Computation* 1: 270–280.

Williams, R. J., and Zipser, D. (1989b). Experimental analysis of the real-time recurrent learning algorithm. *Connection Science* 1: 87–111.

Williams, R. J., and Zipser, D. (1995). Gradient-based learning algorithms for recurrent networks and their computational complexity. In Y. Chauvin and D. E. Rumelhart (Eds.), *Backpropagation: Theory, architectures, and applications,* 433–486. Hillsdale, NJ: Erlbaum.

Willows, A. (1967). Behavioral acts elicited by stimulation of single identifiable brain cells. *Science* 157: 570–574.

Willshaw, D. J. and von der Malsburg, C. (1976). Q-learning. *Proceedings of the Royal Society of London,* B194: 431–445.

Wilson, H. R., and Cowan, J. D. (1972). Excitatory and inhibitory interactions in localized populations of model neurons. *Biophysical Journal* 12: 1–24.

Wilson, H. R., and Cowan, J. D. (1973). A mathematical theory of the functional dynamics of cortical and thalamic nervous tissue. *Kybernetik* 13: 55–80.

Wise, B. P. (1986). An experimental comparison of uncertain inference systems. Ph.D. diss. The Robotics Institute, Pittsburgh.

Wolfe, P. (1969). Convergence conditions for ascent methods. *SIAM Review* 11: 226–235.

Wolfe, P. (1971). Convergence conditions for ascent methods II: Some corrections. *SIAM Review* 13: 185–188.

Wynne-Jones, M. (1992). Node splitting: A constructive algorithm for feedforward neural networks. In J. E. Moody, S. J. Hanson, and R. P. Lippmann (Eds.), *Advances in neural information-processing systems 4,* 1072–1079. San Mateo, CA: Morgan Kaufmann.

Yuhas, B. P., Goldstein, M. H., Sejnowski, T. J., and Jenkins, R. E. (1990). Networks for approximation and learning. *Proceedings of the IEEE* 78: 1658–1668.

Zadeh, L. A. (1965). Fuzzy sets. *Information and Control* 8: 338–353.

Zadeh, L. A. (1986). Is probability theory sufficient for dealing with uncertainty in AI: A negative view. In L. N. Kanal and J. F. Lemmer (Eds.), *Uncertainty in artificial intelligence,* 103–116. New York: Elsevier/North-Holland.

Zipser, D., and Andersen, R. A. (1988). A back-propagation programmed network that simulates response properties of a subset of posterior parietal neurons. *Nature* 331: 679–684.

Author Index

Subject Index